CONTEMPORARY SOCIAL WORK

An Introduction
to Social Work
and Social Welfare

CONTEMPORARY SOCIAL WORK

An Introduction to Social Work and Social Welfare

Second Edition

DONALD BRIELAND
University of Illinois

LELA B. COSTIN
University of Illinois

CHARLES R. ATHERTON
University of Alabama

And Contributors

McGraw-Hill Book Company
New York   St. Louis   San Francisco   Auckland   Bogotá   Hamburg   Johannesburg
London   Madrid   Mexico   Montreal   New Delhi   Panama   Paris   São Paulo
Singapore   Sydney   Tokyo   Toronto

CONTEMPORARY SOCIAL WORK
An Introduction to Social Work and Social Welfare

234567890DODO 83210

This book was set in Caledonia by Black Dot, Inc. (ECU). The editors were Nelson W. Black, Eric M. Munson, and David Dunham; the design was done by Caliber Design Planning; the production supervisor was Charles Hess. The chapter-opening illustrations were done by Caliber Design Planning; the drawings were done by J & R Services, Inc.
R. R. Donnelley & Sons Company was printer and binder.

Library of Congress Cataloging in Publication Date

Brieland, Donald, date
    Contemporary social work.

    Includes bibliographical references and index.
    1. Social service—United States—Addresses,
essays, lectures. I. Costin, Lela B., joint
author. II. Atherton, Charles R., joint author.
III. Title.
HV91.B69 1980   361'.973   79-20078
ISBN 0-07-007767-3

Contents

PART FOUR
Social Issues

PART FIVE
Evaluation and Career Planning

List of Contributors

Unless otherwise indicated, the contributors are members of the faculty of the School of Social Work at the University of Illinois, Urbana-Champaign.

Donald Brieland is Dean of the University of Illinois School of Social Work and author of the text *Social Work and the Law*. His interests include public administration, family law, and social work education.

Lela B. Costin is a specialist in school social work and child welfare and author of *Child Welfare: Policies and Problems*.

Charles R. Atherton is Professor at the University of Alabama and coauthor of *Social Welfare Policy Analysis and Formulation*. He teaches courses in research and program evaluation.

Ruppert Downing is Director of field instruction and is especially interested in working with elderly members of minority groups.

Gerald L. Euster is Professor at the University of South Carolina. He is especially interested in group work in hospital settings and in research of aging.

Marilyn Flynn is involved in teaching and research of aging, social planning, income maintenance, and workforce projects.

Ketayun H. Gould teaches courses and conducts research on population and sex-based discrimination.

Charles H. Henderson teaches courses in community work and minorities and directs a training project for public agency workers.

Frank Itzin serves as Associate Dean and teaches social work practice courses.

Bok-Lim Kim conducts research and seminars on Asian-American problems.

Arnold Panitch is a specialist in community work and continuing education at Boise State University, Idaho.

Gary Shaffer developed the field instruction program for the B.S.W. program curriculum and is especially interested in the workforce. He directs a regional child welfare training center.

Ione Dugger Vargus is Dean at Temple University.

Anthony J. Vattano specializes in mental health, family therapy, and special uses of groups.

John C. Watkins, Jr., is a Professor at the University of Alabama. He teaches courses in criminal justice.

Shirley H. Wattenberg teaches social treatment and social work in the health professions.

Nancy Weinberg specializes in vocational rehabilitation and health care.

About This Book

Contemporary Social Work provides a comprehensive introduction to the field. Major topics include social work and basic rights, the way agencies are financed and operated, the methods of social work, the major problem areas that make social work necessary, the people it serves, and its personnel and educational systems.

The book is written by a group of specialists expressly for social work students and edited to a common style for continuity and coherence. In the original development of the book, the authors conducted class sessions in which their material was used. Over 1000 undergraduates provided comments and suggestions for the second edition. We gratefully acknowledge the ideas contributed.

Individual chapters are also used in a variety of graduate courses. Doctoral candidates find the book useful as a basis for review for comprehensive examinations, and agencies use it for staff development and volunteer training.

Contemporary Social Work has a practice focus, a problem focus, and a management focus. It provides comprehensive content for a semester course meeting three or four hours per week. With additional assignments and use of the suggested projects it can serve for a full year's course. For one quarter courses, topics can be used selectively. Instructors will find the material easy to use regardless of the topical order they choose to follow.

The second edition adds two new chapters—"Sexism" and "Planning for a Social Work Career"—and omits several topics on the basis of users' reactions to the first edition. All chapters are fully revised by the authors except Chapter 16 which was updated by the editors.

The Instructor's Manual is comprehensive. It summarizes the class-testing experience on each topic and provides extensive suggestions for each chapter for the teacher who is new to social work education.

We acknowledge the fine cooperation of our colleagues who contributed chapters; the McGraw-Hill Book Company; and the secretarial staff at the University of Illinois School of Social Work, which produced various materials. Special appreciation should go to Juanita Graven, who coordinated the preparation of the manuscript. We are also grateful for the help and patience of our families in this complex project.

DONALD BRIELAND
LELA B. COSTIN
CHARLES R. ATHERTON

PART ONE
An Introduction to the Social Services

Have you decided to become a social worker? Is the introductory course a foundation for your further study?

Are you considering several careers, with social work as one possibility? Do you hope an introductory course will help you make a decision?

Or are you interested in learning how the social services function so you can participate more intelligently as an informed citizen?

This book will be helpful in achieving all of these goals.

Part One deals with basic rights of increasing concern to both social workers and the people they serve. Chapter 1 traces the history of attitudes toward the poor and toward other groups that require special help. The discussion demonstrates how individual rights have increased and identifies issues that require continuing attention.

The first chapter also identifies the political barriers to the provision of social services and concludes that strong concerns about taxation may make us less responsive to human needs. We may be moving to an increased emphasis on self-sufficiency, but our economic system may not be able to provide the opportunities needed for such an approach.

The second chapter gives a description of the maze of social service organizations—their activities and operations. While informal charity is highly desirable, the magnitude of human problems requires us to rely on a variety of specialized governmental and voluntary agencies. The text demonstrates how these two types of organizations are linked together through purchases of care and service.

1

CHAPTER 1
Social Work:
Basic Rights

(Queen Elizabeth I)   (Jane Addams)   (Franklin D. Roosevelt)
Reflections on social welfare.

Social problems must be solved afresh by almost every generation; and the one chance of progress depends upon both an invincible loyalty to a constructive social ideal and upon a correct understanding by the new generation of the actual experience of its predecessors.

—Herbert Croly*

What are social welfare and social work? Where did we get our historic emphasis on work, residency, and institutionalization? What are basic human rights, and how do they extend to special groups—the poor, minorities, children, youthful offenders, families, and institutionalized persons? How are employment opportunities, health, housing, and transportation related to social welfare? Finally, why is a formal social welfare network necessary?

SOCIAL WELFARE AND SOCIAL WORK

Social welfare refers to formally organized and socially sponsored institutions, agencies, and programs to maintain or improve the economic conditions, health, or personal competence of some parts or all of a population. The goals and objectives of such organizations constitute social policy.[1]

Social work is the profession of a group of people who have specified training and skills and engage in providing welfare services.[2] The purposes of social work, according to Pincus and Minahan,[3] are (1) to enhance the problem-solving and coping capacities of people; (2) to link people with systems that provide them with resources, services, and opportunities; (3) to promote the effective and humane operation of these systems; and (4) to contribute to the development and improvement of social policy.

The philosophical foundation for practice developed by the social work profession stresses several propositions:

1. The individual is the primary concern of this society.
2. There is interdependence between individuals in this society.
3. They have social responsibility for one another.
4. There are human needs common to each person, yet each person is essentially unique and different from others.
5. An essential attribute of a democratic society is the realization of the full potential of each individual and the assumption of his social responsibilities through active participation in society.
6. Society has a responsibility to provide ways in which obstacles to this self-realization (i.e., disequilibrium between the individual and his environment) can be overcome or prevented.[4]

*Herbert Croly, *The Promise of American Life*, 1909, quoted in Blanche D. Coll, *Perspectives in Public Welfare: A History*, U.S. Government Printing Office. Washington, D.C., 1969.

THE ORIGINS OF AMERICAN TRADITIONS

The current concern about human rights is relatively new. The basic governmental system of aid to the poor came from England. It began as the feudal system gave way to mercantilism and the growth of cities. Starting in 1349, able-bodied people in England were expected to accept employment and could not legally beg for alms. The poor were prohibited from leaving their own parish to seek better benefits. The able-bodied poor came to be termed "sturdy beggars." Later, the almshouse developed as the cheapest way to meet the needs of the "worthy poor" for food and shelter and to regulate their activities.

The main framework was provided in the English poor laws.

English Poor Law Precedent

During the medieval period in Europe, poor relief was a church responsibility. The poor were respected and given alms without question when resources were available. Churches today still care for persons in need, but the main responsibility has shifted to government. This shift began around the mid-fourteenth century. Civil governments made their first significant attempts to legislate on the growing social problems of aid for the destitute, repression of vagrancy, and treatment of the migrant, able-bodied worker. This collection of civil codes has commonly been referred to as the "poor laws."

No European country failed to adopt poor laws of some sort, but the English example is usually selected for special scrutiny. The Elizabethan Poor Law of 1601, the Settlement and Removal Acts beginning in 1662, and the Poor Law of 1834 were particularly important in terms of impact on the United States. These laws were often adopted word for word by local governments in this country.

The famous Elizabethan Poor Law of 1601 was really a clarification and modification of several earlier statutes. Three separate programs were set up for the destitute, depending upon age and ability to work.

"Rogues, vagabonds, or sturdy beggars" were to be whipped and imprisoned or sent back to their birthplace upon refusal to work. This penalty applied to any common laborer who would not work "for such reasonable wages . . . as is commonly given in such parts as such persons . . . happen to dwell." Any worker who was unemployed but willing to work could be placed in a workhouse or given raw materials upon which to work at home.

Different provisions were made for the "impotent" poor. These persons were helpless because of severe disability, old age, or blindness. No work could be expected of them. A local magistrate was to decide the weekly amount necessary to meet the needs of these dependents and set a tax rate accordingly, the latter to be levied on citizens of the locality with "visible property." The Overseer of the Poor was made responsible for collecting the "poor's rates," making disbursements, and setting the able-bodied to work. Paupers' children between the ages of five and fourteen for whom the parents could not provide were to be bound out as apprentices.

The Poor Law of 1601 established the principle of categorical relief by distinguishing between the able-bodied and "impotent" poor. Eligibility was no longer universal. The able-bodied sturdy beggar was treated as undeserving and subjected to a work test, while the aged or disabled—the impotent poor—were viewed as deserving and exempted from work requirements. Financing of public relief was a local responsibility, based on property taxes, and administered by a local government appointee. National government took no direct hand in caring for the poor, other than authorizing local governments to do so at their own option. In fact, local communities moved very sluggishly in offering relief out of tax funds. Most governmental units were too small, and the tax base was too fragmented. Benefits were therefore very uneven and often absent altogether. This seems to be an inevitable consequence of local control over income maintenance programs.[5]

Eligibility   The only other major addition to the 1601 Poor Law was made in 1662, when the first Law of Settlement was passed. This law provided that destitute persons should be given relief only by the community where they were born. (In both England and the United States, any individual automatically had "settlement" by virtue of birth into a community.) Parish officers were allowed to "remove" any poor person who might become dependent on the "poor's rates," sending the luckless paupers back to their birthplaces. This measure was a way to eliminate vagrants from the parish register. At the same time, wealthier parishes would be protected from raids on their resources by the paupers from other districts. Wealthier states today have similar fears.

Settlement laws in this country gradually gave way to "residency requirements," which stated that persons were entitled to relief only in the community where they legally had their home. Settlement and residency requirements have never been fully enforced, because people are highly inventive in finding ways around the law. The laws have, moreover, been very costly, resulting in protracted squabbles between localities, and were finally outlawed by the Supreme Court.[6]

The Poor Law of 1834 was enacted as a means of reducing the relief rolls, which grew very rapidly in England with the onset of the Industrial Revolution and the Napoleonic Wars. Use of the workhouse for the able-bodied was required, and the "principle of less eligibility" was formulated.

This principle says that paupers dependent on relief should be supported at a level less than the lowest going wage rate for productive workers. This was an effort to preserve work incentive, and it originally applied only to the able-bodied poor. However, in administrative practice, this principle defined the benefit standard for all recipients. It meant that public relief benefits were pegged at below-subsistence levels. This idea was implemented in the United States.

American Concerns about Poverty

After the Poor Law of 1834, a controversy raged in both England and the United States between advocates of the workhouse and supporters of "outdoor relief"—assistance to persons in their own homes. Many Americans feared that politicians were too corrupt to handle public monies for relief purposes. The example of Tammany Hall in New York City was not reassuring. Other people worried about fraud. Early social workers believed that cash handouts might destroy moral fiber. On the other hand, almshouses were generally overcrowded and unsanitary, and contrary to their purpose they offered no activity for the able-bodied. The urban almshouses along the Atlantic seaboard were a major exception; these institutions grew into great teaching hospitals, serving the medically indigent.[7] The issue was finally resolved in America by the Social Security Act of 1935. According to this act, states wishing to receive matching federal funds for certain categories of public aid were required to give "unrestricted cash grants" to recipients. The era of the workhouse was over.

The English system's stress on work is our approach as well. Residency requirements have given way to the question of how much of the expenditure for aiding the poor should be paid by the state or local authorities and how much by the federal establishment. The workhouse is gone, but institutionalization for children and the elderly still generates controversy.

Traditions of charity also developed in Europe. St. Vincent de Paul founded the Sisters of Charity in 1633 after establishing a program for volunteers some years earlier. An account of helping individuals comes from France in 1833, when a group of students led by Frederick Ozanam joined together in the service of God to help the poor:

> The poor were to be visited at their own dwellings, in hospitals and prisons, and to be assisted by every means within their power. A portion of the very greatest misery of the poor often proceeds from their not knowing how to help themselves out of a difficulty once they have gotten into it; they fall into distress through accidental circumstances, arising from their own fault or other people's and they are too ignorant to see their way out of it. The law frequently has a remedy ready for them, but they don't know this, and there is no one to tell them. Their one idea when they fall into distress is to hold out their hand for an alm, a system which generally proves as ineffectual as it is demoralizing. Ozanam's young friends responded to the suggestion that they should try to remedy this lamentable state of things by placing their education, their intelligence, their special knowledge of law or science, and their general knowledge of life, at the disposal of the poor; that instead of only taking them some little material relief, they should strive to win their confidence, learn all about their affairs, and then see how they could best help them to help themselves.[8]

The Charity Organization Society movement (COS) during the 1800s was the first major attempt in the United States to achieve rational order out of the chaos of emerging health and welfare services. With an economic depression in 1873, severe changes led to new demands for voluntary assistance. Rapid unbanization had begun to occur as rural people moved to create urban industrial work forces. Industrialization was also accompanied by massive immigration.

Patterned after the London Society for Organizing Charitable Relief and Repressing Mendicity, the society was to provide a solution for the chaos of indiscriminate giving, fraud, duplication, and other evils of benevolent charity.[9] In its early attempts to bring voluntary social agencies together, the COS assumed that financial assistance had to be closely supervised and coordinated. If not, the poor would exploit the available resources and further undermine their already questionable moral character. "Pauperism" was more of a concern to communities than the bitter wretchedness of the poverty being endured. The COS movement caught on, since the philosophy at that time viewed economic deprivation largely as a result of moral failure and depended on moral uplift and proper education for the assimilation of the poor. Obviously, this explanation for poverty is still widely accepted.

The societies worked personally with individuals caught in poverty. These early caseworkers stressed moral reform of the individual. The poor were divided into two groups—the worthy poor, who were capable of moral reforms, and the unworthy poor, who were not. The former were provided with food, clothing, and further service. The latter were considered ineligible. Investigations were made for "furnishing guidance and knowledge for a long course of 'treatment' by which weak wills might be strengthened, bad habits cured, and independence developed."[10]

Octavia Hill, one of the founders of the Charity Organization Society, commented:

> By knowledge of character more is meant than whether a man is a drunkard or a woman is dishonest; it means knowledge of the passions, hopes, and history of people; where the temptation will touch them, what is the little scheme they have made of their lives, or would make, if they had encouragement; what training long past phases of their lives may have afforded; how to move, touch, teach them. Our memories and our hopes are more truly factors of our lives than we often remember.[11]

The settlement house movement, typified by Hull House in Chicago, was especially important in the United States beginning in the 1880s. The settlements helped immigrants meet the demands of urban life through self-help, community resource development, democratic citizenship, social reform, and social action. They offered cultural, education, and recreation programs that continue today. Jane Addams, the founder of Hull House, insisted that her staff members live in the Hull House community to participate in its political life.

In 1909 newer principles for dealing with the poor, which recognized curative treatment and rehabilitation but still emphasized the need for restraint of vagrants and separation of the mentally ill from the rest of society, were affirmed in English law. Children could be removed from their parents and were required to attend school. Child labor was controlled.

The 1930s saw the passage of the Social Security Act in the United States under President Franklin Roosevelt to cope with a depression in which millions of people suddenly found themselves among the worthy poor. Social insurance had begun in Germany under Bismarck, but it took an economic crisis to bring

Hull House, Chicago. (Photo courtesy of Hull House.)

it to the United States. The depression also made it clear that the federal government must assist private and local public agencies in the financing of social welfare programs.

Meanwhile, social casework was also seen as a means to cope with personal problems and needs. While Jane Addams was dealing with social injustices at a wholesale or societal level, social work at the retail level was developing a set of skills for use with individuals. These themes will be expanded in later chapters.

BASIC RIGHTS

Since the 1950s, basic rights have become a major concern. The users of social services have a right to be served by competent personnel and to confidentiality. They also should have the right to accept or refuse services. In some cases, however, services are imposed to protect the individual or society. Services should be imposed only after due process of law when the service is in the client's best interest.

Social workers have the duty to set forth the terms on which service is offered, including eligibility provisions, goals, and costs, if any. If the client does not have full freedom of choice regarding a social service, the limits on such freedom should be discussed and clarified. The client and social worker should come to a clear agreement. Often a written contract is desirable to assure mutual understanding.

The Rights of the Poor

In our society, being poor means being at risk. Poverty is especially difficult when you have to live from transfer payments—the tax dollars of other citizens. Unfortunately, in the poor law tradition the dependent poor have been seen by a segment of the public as lazy, dishonest, and immoral while the formal standards of society imply the right to an adequate income.

Poor people are the special concern of social work. People come to public agencies when they need money for food, clothing, or housing. Except for short-term emergencies, the agency has to be certain that the person is eligible to receive help. One who already has adequate financial means cannot receive continuing monetary aid. A *means test* must be applied to each applicant. An agency staff member is expected to determine eligibility and to focus attention on employability.

Trying to assist people in poverty may involve constant conflict about the eligiblity requirements and the relationships between public assistance and work. Since most of the people in poverty who apply for help are aged, crippled, blind, or single parents of young children, the goal of employability is often unrealistic.

The social work student must be aware of the rights of the poor as well as their responsibilities. Often these rights have been the subject of legal action. Not only did the Supreme Court determine that financial help does not depend upon a certain period of residence in a state or community, but eligibility for financial support for the family does not require approved sexual conduct of a parent.[12] Yet a poor person receiving assistance has to permit a social worker to visit the home[13] and must cooperate with local authorities to help find fathers who may be able to contribute to the support of the family.

In work with the poor, the social agency may have considerable discretion in the amount of aid granted. Public welfare is a prerogative of the states. Some states provide more generous social supports than others. In October 1978 three jurisdictions paid less than $100 per family for AFDC benefits— Mississippi, South Carolina, and Puerto Rico; eight paid over $300 per family—California, Connecticut, Hawaii, Massachusetts, Michigan, Minnesota, and Wisconsin.[14]

The Rights of Minorities

The struggle for civil rights for minorities was intense during the 1950s and 1960s, when the issues of fair housing, fair employment, voting rights, and school desegregation loomed large.

Racial and ethnic groups advanced their cause through social action. Basic reforms came both in law and in the attitudes of society. The struggle continues, but it has recently involved fewer demonstrations and dramatic confrontations. Some people feel that it has lost its vitality and that we have slipped back into discrimination. Meanwhile, questions of reverse discrimination recently confronted the Supreme Court.[15]

Civil rights efforts extended in the 1970s to other groups—particularly to women and the handicapped, who became "protected classes" under the law. Employment opportunities expanded for women, but their economic status, as measured by wage and salary rates, actually declined slightly. The handicapped advanced their demands by the familiar mechanism of a White House Conference.

Minority demands from social work are advanced by welfare-rights groups organized by public assistance clients. Social workers representing the various minorities organized special membership groups to help clients, develop their own rights as employees, and affect social policy. Social workers who assisted groups of clients were also seen by some of them as a target since social workers had to enforce regulations that welfare-rights groups considered unfair.

The Rights of Children

The state takes a special responsibility for children because they cannot usually represent their own best interests. Children's rights are limited because of their age. They are expected to obey their parents and conform to special rules that do not apply to adults. They must attend school. They must be home at a certain hour if the community has a curfew. A runaway child is returned to the parents if they want the child back. A parent may demand to receive the earnings of a minor child for whom support is being provided. Emancipation is achieved if a child under eighteen moves out with parental permission, gets married or becomes a parent, is abandoned, or joins the armed forces. Social workers play a key role in family conflicts with youth. They are especially likely to serve children whose parents neglect or abuse them or youngsters who break the law.

A Bill of Rights   The National Association of Social Workers drafted a bill of rights for children that includes twelve basic propositions. It emphasizes many of the central values of the social work profession, yet it is only a position statement. It has no official status. The complete preface, the major propositions, and the section on advocacy are reproduced here.

Bill of Rights for Children and Youth
National Association of Social Workers

Preface
Historically, children have been considered as property with laws governing the relationship between parent and child relegating the child to little more than chattel. Nineteenth century reformers challenged this philosophy and initiated legislation to protect children from undue hardship and provide for more basic developmental needs. Despite the advances made on behalf of children, children too often remain second class citizens.

It is essential that public social policy recognize the child as an individual with rights, including the right to be a part of a family. The well-being of the child is most frequently advanced by public social policy which supports the well-being of the family. Children's needs as dependent persons requiring nurture must be reconciled with the protection of children's basic human rights and civil liberties.

The guarantee of such protection should not deny children greater participation in society. In the past, basic rights extended for adults have not applied to children. This has resulted in circumstances of gross injustice and isolation. Rather than keeping youth "infants until sudden adulthood," emancipation from dependency should be a gradual process from greater protection to greater participation and responsibility at key stages of maturity.

I. The Right to Sound Preparation for Life

II. The Right to Individuality

III. The Right to a Positive Social Identity

IV. The Right to a Good Parenting Experience

V. The Right to a Healthy Environment

VI. The Right to Health

VII. The Right to a Relevant Education

VIII. The Right to Participatory Citizenship

IX. The Right to Representation

X. The Right to Legal Status, Legal Protection, and Legal Rules

XI. The Right to Service

XII. The Right to Advocacy

The professional social worker must advocate for all clients, especially those who cannot advocate for themselves. Therefore, we as a professional association, must reaffirm our professional responsibility of advocating for children to insure that the rights of children herein defined become a reality. Children must have the right to advocacy services to provide assurance that they will be guaranteed full benefit of the legal rights established by our society for the protection and well-being of all citizens.[16]

The United Nations developed a Declaration of the Rights of the Child in 1959 that was given reemphasis as part of the observance of the International Year of the Child in 1979. It includes:

The right to affection, love, and understanding.
The right to adequate nutrition and medical care.
The right to free education.
The right to full opportunity for play and recreation.
The right to a name and nationality.
The right to special care, if handicapped.
The right to be among the first to receive relief in times of disaster.
The right to be a useful member of society and to develop individual abilities.

The right to be brought up in a spirit of peace and universal brotherhood.
The right to enjoy these rights, regardless of race, color, sex, religion, national or
social origin. [17]

Children who have to be removed from their family homes are particularly at risk. A foster home is designed as a temporary arrangement, but removal is
often permanent. The child may live in a series of foster homes, gaining little
sense of security or self-worth.

In one family that came to the attention of a federal district court, four
children were in a total of fifteen separate foster home placements and eight
juvenile home placements from 1969 to 1974. [18]

Youth in Conflict with the Law   Young social workers often have a special
interest in youth in trouble with the law and demonstrate success in making
community plans for them. Paradoxically, the rights of the juvenile offender are
better defined than those of persons with less serious behavior problems. Since
the Gault decision of the U.S. Supreme Court a decade ago, [19] a teenager may
not be kept in a correctional program longer than an adult who commits the
same offense. The youth is entitled to most of the rights of the accused adult,
except for trial by jury. [20] Although the juvenile judge is no longer seen as a
benign parental figure, a determined effort is still made by most juvenile courts
to keep the young person out of correctional institutions.

While the state stands in the role of parent, it needs to consider the
wishes and aspirations of the children for whom it is responsible. Society often
accords the social worker the role of child- and youth-advocate but is especially
unresponsive to the needs of the youthful offender.

Rights of Families
Society has been quite specific in its standards for family formation and
behavior. Recently, because of reliable methods of contraception, sexual
conduct appears to have undergone a profound change. Women have also
demanded greater autonomy and have redefined traditional roles. Longer life
expectancy has led to greater reluctance to tolerate family life characterized by
conflict. These changes often put family members at risk.

Social work has the mandate for much of the family counseling related to
cohabitation, marriage, divorce, child custody, and remarriage. To be successful, counseling must bring individual and group goals together in a compromise.

The right to pluralism in family formation and functioning is fundamental,
but permissiveness is extended more willingly to those who are self-sufficient
than to people who become dependent. The social worker's own values and
behaviors may also be barriers to an effective helping role.

When must the state intervene in family life? The state is compelled to act
when there is a valid complaint that children are abused or neglected and are in
need of supervision that the parents are unable to provide. Some judges would

like to see children in divorce proceedings represented by counsel for their protection. Some states also provide for intervention in family life when older persons are abused by their relatives. The state also can intervene on behalf of battered wives or husbands. The state only involves itself in family matters when a complaint is based on evidence of harm. No agency or institutional network is charged with the mission of supervising family life. The state may inspect a home for violations of the fire code and it may patrol the highways looking for violations of the laws regulating automobiles, but it may not oversee the day-to-day interactions of family life without a legally valid reason.

Rights of Institutionalized Persons

In our society, the hospitalized mental patient and the nursing home resident may suffer some curtailment of rights and freedoms.

The courts have affirmed the principle that one should not be hospitalized against his or her will without due process of law. States may require a jury trial or a hearing before a judge before a person can be hospitalized for mental health treatment on a nonvoluntary basis. Following the precedent of *Wyatt v. Stickney*,[21] a person who is found to be in need of mental treatment has a right to receive appropriate treatment in the least restrictive atmosphere consistent with the safety of both the patient and the public. In practice this principle is often disregarded. In some states a mental patient still may lose the right to vote, to sign contracts, and to carry on normal business. Because of a lack of funds, many state hospitals are also unable to deliver the promises of the new directions in the law.

Further, to follow the principle that a person should be released from treatment as soon as he or she has received maximum benefit, some states have discharged patients prematurely. They often end up living in dilapidated hotels in slum areas or drifting about the community.

The nursing home resident also has an uncertain status. Some states have high standards of care and exercise close supervision of nursing home operations. Consequently, some nursing homes offer high-quality care. However, the quality of nursing homes in the United States is uneven. In many, the patient has little freedom and less privacy. There may be little for the patient to do, and a minimal level of care.

The social worker can be an important influence on behalf of the rights of individuals who live in institutions. Many institutionalized people have no advocate and can easily be forgotten because of their relatively powerless position. The humanizing of institutional services is an important social work task.

A RESPONSIVE SOCIETY

More than any other "helping professional," the social worker is expected to understand the influence of the environment—both the broad societal context and the more immediate environment as they contribute to individual situations. Job opportunities, health care, housing, transportation, and schools may be both resources and problems in themselves. The immediate home environment is of special concern for those for whom poverty or child neglect is a problem. When social work interviews are held solely in the office, the understanding provided by direct observations of the home is lost.

One of the special tasks of the social worker is to help make society responsive to the needs of clients. Sometimes responsiveness is limited, even in the social agency. Staff members may increase the client's negative evaluation of self. The right to dignity should be preserved in the transactions of the agency.

We will now look at some of the major societal elements with which social workers are concerned.

EMPLOYMENT AND SELF-SUFFICIENCY

Employment is a major environmental element in creating opportunities in a society. Not only is an income necessary to meet basic needs, but work is fundamental to identity. People usually identify themselves first by what they do. Social workers can help people get jobs when there is a demand for labor, but when the demand is lacking, even the highly motivated applicant may be unsuccessful. The agencies especially concerned with employment are the state employment services and the U.S. Department of Labor.

Unemployment Rates

As Figure 1-1 indicates, the unemployment rate, based on those working and those seeking work, fluctuates from time to time but has increased in the last few years. What really constitutes full employment is difficult to determine. Some people will always be in the process of moving from job to job, and others will be unemployable. Unexpected events like the energy crisis or a major strike may have a depressing effect on employment. Paradoxically, a substantial improvement in the labor market often results in a temporary increase in unemployment, because more people begin to seek work at that time.

The national unemployment average can be multiplied several times for urban adolescents from minority groups and female heads of households who have had no previous work experience.

Skilled workers also face unemployment when a large industry has major contracts canceled and its plants close. Relocation of industries from the center city to the suburbs works to the disadvantage of employees who cannot move with the industry. They may lose employee pension benefits along with their jobs.

Economic conditions which produce more jobs are the primary remedy for unemployment. Unless we develop more jobs in the private sector, full employment will be achieved only by making the government the employer of last resort. This is a question of primary interest to social workers who work with the poor. Can we afford such a policy? Can we not afford it?

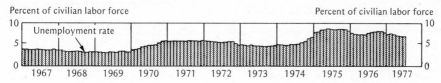

Percent of civilian labor force

Figure 1.1 Trends in unemployment. (SOURCE: U.S. Bureau of the Census, Data from U.S. Bureau of Labor Statistics, *Statistical Abstract of the United States 1977*, p. 386.)

Job Satisfaction

The social worker is also interested in job satisfaction. To get accurate data on this question requires careful research. Strauss[22] has observed that statements of job satisfaction cannot always be taken at face value. When a worker claims to have a pretty good job and the interviewer asks what makes it a "good" job, the employee may reply, "Don't get me wrong. I didn't say it is a good job. It's an OK job—about as good a job as someone like me might expect. The boss leaves me alone and it pays well. But I would never call it a good job. It doesn't amount to much, but it's not bad."

Social workers also soon find that many people, especially those who are not members of any profession, expect little satisfaction from their jobs. We like to talk about the importance of promotions, but for many people the only realistic advancement is more pay for the same kind of work.

OPPORTUNITIES FOR HEALTH

Several questions about health trouble our citizens: Why is the world's wealthiest nation not the healthiest? Why does health take a bigger and bigger bite out of our gross national product? Why is the American public not getting anything like adequate health care for the $120 billion it spends each year? Why are both the mother's and the baby's chances for survival worse in the United States than in many other countries?

Maternal and Child Health

Maternal mortality, miscarriages, stillbirths, and deaths in early infancy are far too common. Regardless of one's views on population control, family planning, and abortion, crises attendant to birth have no defenders. These problems involve not only medical management techniques during pregnancy and childbirth but antecedent health and nutritional status. The correlation of maternal and child health problems with poverty is well known.

One of the major roles for social workers has been the facilitation of services for pregnant women—especially those who are younger and unmarried and characterized by high risk. Family-income levels sufficient to assure adequate living standards before and during pregnancy and medical care throughout pregnancy are required. Educational programs on human reproduction are essential to reduce the number of unwanted pregnancies and to assure that women seek medical care after they become pregnant.

Health Care Needs of the Aged

For the aged, economic and psychological status needs are interwoven with the need for medical services. A sense of worth is closely related to a sense of health and well-being. To add years to life is easier than to add life to the years. It is tragic when some elderly people have to choose between food and medicine. It is more tragic when relatively healthy older people get the message from society that they really have nothing to live for.

Access and Cost

Social workers have two special concerns about health services—getting the patient to the care, and finding the means to meet the cost. Urban and rural areas have parallel problems concerning accessibility of service. When doctors leave the ghettos, family care is given through hospital emergency rooms—the least efficient and most expensive way. In rural areas, people may have to drive fifty miles to a doctor who will not live in a small town—especially if it has no hospital.

High costs and lack of an adequate delivery system deter medical care for rural and city people alike and discourage both the poor and the middle-class groups from seeking the care they need. We will return to the issues of health care in Chapter 10 and population and family planning in Chapter 15.

SOUND HOUSING IN A SAFE NEIGHBORHOOD

Living in a certain neighborhood includes a series of conditions that may expand opportunities or constrict them. Aaron illustrates the pervasive effect of location on the resident.

> When a homeowner or renter chooses a house or apartment, he purchases not only housing services, but also a wide range of goods and services—public schools, stores, parks, public transportation, neighbors, and other amenities. Though they cost him nothing beyond the price of housing and attendant property taxes, his satisfaction—indeed his welfare—depends on these conditions as much as on his housing. He does not express in the marketplace his demand for housing but for the entire package. Statistics on housing expenditures really measure the value placed by residents on housing and residential services.
>
> The residents of poor neighborhoods are victims of high prices, inferior merchandise, high interest rates, and aggressive and deceptive sales practices. They pay for the cost of doing business where pilferage and default risks are above average. Costs are averaged over all customers so that reliable households suffer from living where high cost customers are particularly numerous. Such extra costs of living are among costs of residential services that affect the price people will pay for housing services. Another social cost that varies by neighborhood is the probability of crime. The major market response the individual can make to differences in crime rates is to alter the price he is willing to pay for housing.[23]

Poverty restricts options, especially for housing. The poor are often effectively prevented from owning their own homes. The choice of paying more to get into a better neighborhood, as identified by Aaron, is not realistic for the poor.

Common Housing Problems

We are familiar with the problems of older structures—poor sanitation, faulty wiring, rats, inadequate provisions for garbage, and lead paint that threatens children's lives. Housing problems are perceived as urban, but we find the same conditions in rural slums. They do not seem so bad because they are more scattered and, therefore, less obvious. Varying definitions of substandard housing make it difficult to determine national progress on housing programs. For purposes of classification, type of plumbing has been more important than the general condition of the house.

The economics of slum ownership cannot be ignored. Converting large units to smaller ones to get more rent, spending as little as possible for maintenance and repairs, and finally abandoning the building when the property reaches an advanced stage of disrepair are a familiar story. When the property is abandoned, residents may try to stay there without heat or light until fire or thieves turn them into the street.

Violations of housing regulations often involve long legal battles followed by token fines. Inspectors may also accept payoffs from owners. Tenants cannot complain too much or they will face eviction. The next place may be even worse. It is little wonder that dramatic presentations about poverty often begin with housing conditions.

A Mother Speaks from Experience

During the early years of raising my family I lived with my mother, but it was too crowded and I finally had to find a place of my own. The only place I could find was a four room apartment across the street. With ten children we were cramped, but that was not the worst problem. The water pipes were always breaking, and this meant no water, and leaks. The floor round the commode was rotted from the water, it leaked so often. One time I had just gotten up when the ceiling plaster fell down all over the bed. Another time the mantelpiece fell over into the front room, all in one piece. If my baby had been there it most likely would have killed her. That is when I began to feel that I just had to move. I had asked the rent lady to fix these things, all along. She always said she would, if I gave her the rent, but she never did.

Finally, I told her I was not going to pay the rent any more. She threatened to call the High Constable. So, we both went down to the agency [social service bureau] to complain about each other. My social worker talked to the landlady first, then to me. My social worker said I should pay the rent, but she would try to find a better place for me and my family. She must have called the health department because an inspector came out and condemned the house. This meant I had to move in 30 days.

I got a lot of help looking for a place, both from my social worker and from the Neighborhood Center. But people just do not like to rent to families with a lot of kids. Even if the houses are big—6 or 7 rooms—they don't want large families.

Finally, I found the house I'm in now. It's a whole house. I told the landlord that I had only six children and he rented it to me.

He wanted two months' rent in advance, and a security deposit—$140 all together. That was the biggest problem. I borrowed $100 from my mother, and the agency gave me the rest. I paid them back out of my next check.

I moved last December and have not had too many problems since then. One or two things have gone wrong, but the landlord fixed them. My biggest problems now are utilities and furniture. But, at least I have a house, and as long as I pay my rent I guess I won't have any problems now. If I do, my social worker is ready to help me with them.

I have been asked—what would those on welfare like to see done to help them with housing problems? The main ones are:

1. For the city to enforce the minimum code for good housing.
2. Require that landlords keep houses fixed up—the repairs.
3. Owners should inspect their property more often than once a year, and should inspect inside as well as outside.
4. The welfare department should help with the security deposit in emergencies and allow us over the maximum for rent and utilities.

All of these things would help us in having a decent place to live and in which to raise our children.[24]

U.S. Government Printing Office, *A Right to a Decent Home*

Roles of Social Workers in Housing

Social workers have not played a large role in housing policy. Social workers have helped organize tenant unions. They have sometimes been able to get the help of legal aid to enforce fair housing laws. They have assisted in resettlement of residents while new housing was being built, but the original residents seldom moved back. They could not afford to. In some public housing projects, social workers offer a range of services including job counseling and day care, but they have had too little involvement as policy-makers.

Public Housing: A Disappointing Solution

Public housing was supposed to be the ideal answer for urban society. Slums would be replaced by new dwelling units that would be clean and safe. With public funding, housing could be made available at low cost. First, massive slum clearance was tried, then spot renewal, in which sound structures were not replaced. Unfortunately the solutions have not been simple or successful. There has not been enough public housing, and it has not been cheap to build. In order to safeguard the property, management philosophies in successful projects have been conservative. No one wants people destroying property. Income ceilings forced people to move when they began to improve their earning power. Also, public housing has been largely racially segregated, in fact if not by policy. With these constraints, as one could have predicted, public housing has worked better for the aged than for families with children.

High-rise projects in the largest cities have developed large concentrations of multiproblem families characterized by fear and isolation resulting from high rates of crime and vandalism. Some of these projects, which promised potential progress, have been virtually deserted and are being torn down.

The Federal Housing Authority has served middle-class home buyers, and programs for subsidies to rent or purchase dwelling units have been very limited.

Urban Crime

When you choose a neighborhood, you choose conditions that may be associated with the crime rate. While the stress has been on crime in the streets, stealing and other crimes against property are much more frequent. Strangers avoid the slums because of fear of violence. Most crimes there are perpetrated by residents against residents. As a result, urban life involves increasing uneasiness. Calls for more street lighting and added police protection may go unanswered. Better locks and other individual security measures require the means to meet the added expense and the confidence that they will be effective.

In many cities possible physical danger affects the practice of social work. Whereas regular home visits used to be standard procedure, workers no longer visit clients in some neighborhoods because of crime or harassment.

TRANSPORTATION AND MOBILITY

People have become increasingly mobile. Management personnel expect frequent transfers in order to advance. Members of the armed forces have tours of duty. Most people move several times for better jobs or better living conditions. Their quest often takes them across the country. Such states as California, Arizona, Florida, and Texas have been especially popular.

Mobility and the Social Services

The jurisdiction of state and county agencies depends on geographic boundaries. Private agencies also operate under geographic limitations. United Fund contributions usually have to be spent where the monies are raised. If the agency is to help "outsiders," it must do so with other funds.

Only one social agency has problems associated with travel as its specialized concern. The Travelers Aid Society provides a range of short-term emergency services to newcomers and to those who are stranded before they reach their destinations. It receives the help of such agencies as the Salvation Army to meet needs for food and lodging.

Mobility is a special problem for migrant farm and food-processing workers. This group includes some of the most deprived members of our society. Their transiency gives them little opportunity to exercise their claim to services.

Transportation Increases Opportunities

Efficient transportation enlarges a person's lifespace. The family car has become the symbol of mobility and prestige. Boulding considers the attachment to the automobile and its relation to the energy crisis:

> The automobile, especially, is remarkably addictive. I have described it as a suit of armor with 200 horses inside, big enough to make love in. It is not surprising that

it is popular. It turns its driver into a knight with the mobility of the aristocrat and perhaps some of his other vices. The pedestrian and the person who rides public transportation are, by comparison, peasants looking up with almost inevitable envy at the knights riding by in their mechanical steeds. Once having tasted the delights of a society in which almost everyone can be a knight, it is hard to go back to being peasants. I suspect, therefore, that there will be very strong technological pressures to preserve the automobile in some form, even if we have to go to nuclear fusion for the ultimate source of power and to liquid hydrogen for the gasoline substitute. The alternative would seem to be a society of contented peasants, each cultivating his own little garden and riding to work on the bus, or even on an electric streetcar. Somehow this outcome seems less plausible than a desperate attempt to find new sources of energy to sustain our knightly mobility.[25]

Many people who have poor housing used to make up for it with their car. In crowded cities, however, the family car is too expensive and inefficient for use to get to work. Gasoline shortages and high prices are new problems that discourage driving; also, many young people cannot afford a car, and many old people have vision and hearing problems so they cannot drive. Unrestricted bus routes above and below the traffic are needed for efficiency. Metropolitan transit systems are affected by rising costs and inadequate subsidies, resulting in higher fares. Fare increases mean fewer riders, and fares go still higher. Fortunately some cities now offer very low fares to older people for transportation in non-rush hours.

The relocation of plants and offices to the suburbs and the outskirts of our cities creates new needs. Rush-hour schedules are still directed toward the central city. People who do not want to move or cannot do so may be forced to seek a new job downtown, where opportunities are decreasing.

Transportation and the Social Services

Local transportation is important to the delivery of social services. Services such as day care must be accessible to make it possible for a mother to work. Ideally, decentralized neighborhood offices are established for basic services, but use of specialized resources still requires considerable travel. In many cities, the Red Cross provides a motor pool to offer transportation for some types of services.

Efficient transit services are important for employment and for educational and leisure-time programs, and especially for those served by social agencies. Government subsidies have been helpful to some mass transit districts, but public transportation in the United States still needs improvement.

REPONSIVE GOVERNMENTAL STRUCTURES

The way social agencies are organized and the way they treat people may make them unresponsive. Unresponsiveness is a special problem for governmental agencies. Governmental agencies usually play the key roles in providing human services. They are responsible for voter registration, land-use and housing codes, police and fire protection, schools, parks, libraries, water supply, street lighting, garbage and sewage disposal, air and water pollution control, mosquito abatement, public health and control of contagious diseases, operation of passenger trains and airports, jails and prisons, ambulance service, and dozens of other services. On the other hand, basic services that are publicly operated in other countries are privately managed here—telephone and electrical service, and more recently the mails.

Political Structures: Overlap and Confusion

With federal, state, county, city, and district, borough, or township programs, plus dozens of special agencies, such as regional planning bodies, school, sewage, and fire districts, that cross political boundaries, even the intelligent long-term resident often does not know where to go for help. In New York City, for example, many agencies are responsible for various problems related to housing. Problems with water involve at least five different agencies, according to Purcell and Specht.[26] If there is no water, one calls the Health Department. If the supply is inadequate, the call goes to the Department of Water Supply. Small leaks are reported to the Buildings Department, but large leaks to the Department of Water Supply. "No hot water" is the responsibility of the Buildings Department. If water overflows from an apartment above, call the Police Department; but water coming up through a sewer inlet is a problem for the Sanitation Department.

Information and Referral Services   Short of governmental reorganization, several means are used to reduce confusion. Some cities have a municipal information service to direct people to the appropriate service. A few have ombudsmen who will also act as advocates to represent citizens to further their requests or complaints. Antipoverty programs developed many neighborhood information services and also provided community agents to represent residents of a neighborhood. Welfare councils often sponsor community referral services. Most services are available during business hours and do not provide around-the-clock coverage. With all these sources of information, however, social workers in direct service roles still must learn the maze of agencies and services to help guide people through it.

Consolidation   A more fundamental approach to overlapping political bodies and boards is the development of metropolitan government, in which cities and suburbs are combined into a single governmental unit. Both Dade County (Miami), Florida, and Toronto moved in this direction, but fear of high taxes is a serious deterrent to consolidation.

Attitudes of Staff   Finally, responsiveness depends upon the attitudes and motivations of staff members and the bureaucratic rules under which they operate. Even when people find the right agency, employees may express little interest in their complaints or requests. Some agencies make people register only at certain times and then wait for hours. With the demands for accountability, the multiple forms required by social agencies make them seem quite unresponsive. An application for service or registering a complaint may take too much time to make it seem worthwhile.

NEED FOR A SOCIAL WELFARE SYSTEM

Almost everyone has a stake in social welfare. You probably have been a recipient of some form of social welfare service. Millions of college students have low-interest government loans. Other young men and women get educational benefits because of military service. Over 5 million war veterans receive hospital care and pension benefits. Eight million blue-collar, white-collar, and professional workers collect benefits because they are out of work. Thirty million people receive social security checks, and virtually all who are employed pay social security taxes. Thirty-three million people get care through Medicare or Medicaid. About 25 million children eat a low-cost or free school lunch, and more than 18 million people use food stamps.

Who Uses Social Work?

Although most people participate in the social welfare system at some point, they do not ordinarily see a social worker. One can grow up eating federally supported school lunches, attend a publicly or privately supported college, receive unemployment benefits, be compensated for on-the-job accidents, and retire to receive the benefits of social security and Medicare without ever consulting a social worker.

For many people who are unable to cope with crucial problems, social work is needed. The child who requires protection because of parental neglect, the adult with no work skills or no money, the delinquent who sees crime as the alternative to boredom, the sick or mentally ill person, the elderly person with little meaning in his or her life, the powerless neighborhood—all are central concerns of social work.

Informal Charity Is Not Enough

Many people would like to see their fellow citizens get the help they need, but informally. If Sally Brown needs money, her parents send her a check and advise her to be more careful with her cash in the future—she gets help. When Dick Jones has a run of hard luck, the local druggist who forgets about his medicine bill is helping informally. Civic club members volunteer their time to work with groups of "underprivileged" kids. Betty Smith, a lawyer, gives time to a neighborhood council to negotiate grievances with City Hall. The informal social service network involves family, relatives, friends, and others who offer assistance when they can.

Personal ties are important for informal service. In a highly mobile and urban society, such personalized bonds are looser and less dependable. Also, the group that is enthusiastic about working with delinquents may turn next year to recycling glass and paper. Professional people cannot donate enough time consistently to community self-help organizations. Ongoing basic services cannot be wholly entrusted to the spontaneous goodwill of well-intentioned busy people. The informal helper can only do so much, since he or she has a living to make and other duties to perform. Needs are so great that adequate, effective volunteer effort is simply not available. Nor can all services be provided through private contributions, because in hard times contributions shrink just when they are most needed. The informal social welfare process is also obscure and inaccessible. Although numerous informal social services exist, their total impact remains small, fragmented, and highly variable.

The Formal Social Welfare Network

Social work is found in organizations with a specific charge from the community for a designated function. Community schools are mandated to educate children; the Lions Club is not, although it may choose to participate. Public assistance programs must provide support in some form for the poor; friends of the impoverished family need not. Eligibility requirements for services or assistance are spelled out by law or regulations subject to community review.

The demands on social agencies run the range of human problems. People need money, jobs, better skills as parents, emotional support, group services, and neighborhood and community action to solve common problems. Sometimes people need simple advice; more often it is social or psychological treatment. Sometimes they need help to organize to achieve group and community goals.

People may seek services from the formal network on their own initiative or may be referred by someone else. Patients, probationers, or truants may be required by some public authority to deal with the social worker.

The formal network in which social work is offered is complex and often frustrating, but it is the major source of help because it has the financial capability. Throughout the country, the formal social welfare network recruits and employes a quarter of a million people in social work tasks. Our next chapter concerns social agencies—the components of the formal network.

Tax Reforms and Support for Social Services

The passage of Proposition 13 in California to reduce real estate taxes has put both state and federal governments under strong pressure to curtail spending. Since people who pay the major share of taxes are infrequent users of social services, welfare programs and other services are being curtailed. We cannot predict how extensive the cuts will be. The problem is especially difficult because the same inflationary pressures that operate on taxpayers raise the cost of living for the poor and increase the cost of special services for people who fall below the poverty line when they are faced with an emergency.

SUMMARY AND APPLICATION

This chapter has provided a preview of *Contemporary Social Work*. It traced the history of social welfare, emphasizing those attitudes that have persisted since the passage of the English poor laws. It discussed the rights of several special groups that are likely to use social services. It looked at the environment and the political structures that contribute to the quality of life. Finally, the chapter illustrated the importance and the shortcomings of informal charity and the problems that may result from strong tax-reform movements.

—Donald Brieland

Charles R. Atherton

KEY TERMS

social work
social welfare
English poor laws
settlement laws
settlement house
Social Security Act
means test

protected classes
Gault decision
Travelers Aid Society
informal charity
Proposition 13
Charity Organization Society

REFERENCES AND NOTES

1. Harold L. Wilensky and Charles N. Lebaux, *Industrial Society and Social Welfare*, Free Press, New York, 1965, p. 17.
2. Ibid.
3. Allen Pincus and Anne Minahan, *Social Work Practice: Model and Method*, Peacock, Itasca, Ill., 1973, p. 9.
4. William E. Gordon, "A Critique of the Working Definition," *Social Work*, vol. 7, October 1962, pp. 3–13.
5. C. J. Ribton-Turner, *A History of Vagrants and Vagrancy and Beggars and Begging*, Chapman & Hall, London, 1887, pp. 161–182; Blanche Coll, *Perspectives in Public Welfare*, U.S. Government Printing Office, Washington, D.C., 1969, p. 6; E. M. Hampson, *The Treatment of Poverty in Cambridgeshire, 1597–1834*, Cambridge University Press, England, 1934, pp. 31–37; see Report from *His Majesty's Commissioners for Inquiring into the Administration and Practical Operation of the Poor Laws*, Fellowes, London, 1834.
6. *Shapiro v. Thompson*, 394 U.S. 618 (1969).
7. Coll, op. cit., pp. 17–18.
8. Kathleen O'Meara, *Frederick Ozanam: His Life and Works*, Catholic Publication Society, New York, 1878, pp. 61–62.
9. Ralph M. Kramer and Harry Specht, *Readings in Community Organization Practice*, Prentice-Hall, Englewood Cliffs, N.J., 1964, p. 13.
10. Mary E. Richmond, *Social Diagnosis*, Russell Sage, New York, 1917, p. 31.
11. C. Edmund Maurice, *Life of Octavia Hill*, Macmillan, London, 1913, p. 258.
12. *King v. Smith*, 392 U.S. 309 (1968).
13. *Wyman v. James*, 200 U.S. 309 (1971).
14. *Social Security Bulletin*, vol. 421, April 1979, p. 72.
15. *Regents of the University of California v. Allan Bakke*, U.S. 57, L Ed. 2d 750, 98 S Ct; *United Steel Workers of America, A.F.L.-C.I.O.-C.L.C., v. Bryan F. Weber et al.* 47L,W,4851(1979).

16. *National Association of Social Workers News*, vol. 20, no. 7, 1975, pp. 27–28.
17. United Nations, *Official Records of the General Assembly*, Fourteenth Session Supplement #16, 1960.
18. *Alsager v. District Court of Polk County, Iowa*, 384 F. Supp. 643 (1974).
19. *Application of Gault*, 387 U.S. 1 (1967).
20. *McKeiver v. Pennsylvania*, 403 U.S. 528 (1971).
21. *Wyatt v. Stickney*, 344 F. Supp. 373 (1972).
22. *Work in America: Report of a Special Task Force to the Secretary of Health, Education, and Welfare*, M.I.T. Press, Cambridge, n.d., pp. 14–15.
23. Henry J. Aaron, *Shelter and Subsidies: Who Benefits from Federal Housing Policies?*, Brookings, Washington, D.C., 1972, p. 5.
24. *A Right to a Decent Home*, U.S. Government Printing Office, Washington, D.C., 1970, pp. 17–18.
25. Kenneth E. Boulding, "The Social System and the Energy Crisis," *Science*, vol. 184, April 1974, pp. 255–259.
26. Francis P. Purcell and Harry Specht, "The House on Sixth Street," *Social Work*, vol. 10, October 1965, p. 72.

FOR FURTHER STUDY

John E. Bebout and Harry C. Bradmeier, "American Cities as Social Systems," *Journal of the American Institute of Planners*, vol. 29, 1963, pp. 64–76.

Blanche D. Coll, *Perspectives in Public Welfare: A History*, U.S. Government Printing Office, Washington D.C., 1969.

Donald E. Gatch, "Malnutrition and Federal Food Service Programs," in Paul E. Weinberger, *Perspectives on Social Welfare*, Macmillan, New York, 1974, pp. 967–971.

Michael Kindred et al. (eds.), *The Mentally Retarded Citizen and the Law*, Free Press, New York, 1976.

David Macarov, *The Design of Social Welfare*, Holt, Rinehart, & Winston, New York, 1978.

National Commission for the Observance of International Women's Year, *To Form a More Perfect Union: Justice for American Women*, U.S. Government Printing Office, Washington, D.C., 1976.

Wilfred Owen, *The Metropolitan Transportation Problem*, Brookings, Washington, D.C., 1966.

David M. Smith, *The Geography of Social Well-Being in the United States*, McGraw-Hill, New York, 1973.

Kenneth R. Wing, *The Law and the Public's Health*, Mosby, St. Louis, 1976.

The American Civil Liberties Union publishes a series of inexpensive handbooks on human rights, including mental patients, the poor, prisoners, students, teachers, women, hospital patients, gay people, mentally retarded persons, aliens, and young people. They are published by Avon Books, 250 West 55th Street, New York, N.Y. 10019.

FOR DISCUSSION

1. Differentiate between social work and social welfare.
2. What are some of the barriers in our society to the full realization of each individual's potential?

3. What was a "sturdy beggar"?
4. Under the English poor laws, what was the residency requirement?
5. To what modern issue is the almshouse related?
6. What is a means test? Why is it said that "you pass a means test by failing it"?
7. What two groups have recently obtained recognition as minorities?
8. What are some laws that apply only to children?
9. How can bills of rights for children be useful?
10. How does the state act as parent?
11. Does any governmental agency supervise family life? Explain.
12. If a mental patient is institutionalized, to what is he or she entitled?
13. What agencies are concerned especially with employment?
14. What two major problems make it difficult to obtain adequate health services?
15. What other choices does the selection of housing tend to influence?
16. What major environmental need has received special attention because of the energy crisis?
17. How could "metropolitan" government make social services more efficient?
18. What are some self-help groups that illustrate informal charity? Why can't they be depended on fully?

PROJECTS

1. Using the references in this chapter, make a report on conditions under the English poor laws.
2. Evaluate the strong movement toward deinstitutionalization in the United States. How has it affected services for children, the mentally ill, legal offenders, and the elderly?
3. Demonstrate the differences in public assistance benefits by gathering data on current grants in your state and in all adjoining states. The *Social Security Bulletin* published by the U.S. Department of Health, Education and Welfare will provide the data.
4. Visit the local housing authority. Find out what governmental counseling and financial services are available to aid people in purchasing or renting housing. Make a chart of the programs and their eligibility requirements.
5. Get a map of your metropolitan area showing public transportation provisions. Locate the offices of the major social services. Report on their accessibility. What improvements would you suggest?
6. Choose several practical environmental problems, such as inadequate heat or possible danger of lead poisoning. Play the role of a tenant. Use the telephone to seek information from governmental agencies. Record the responses and evaluate the interest and adequacy of the service provided.
7. Choose a major issue of public social welfare policy before your state legislature. Find out what efforts social work groups are making to influence opinions. Include major public agencies, the National Association of Social Workers, the state welfare association, the local welfare council, and similar organizations. Summarize your findings.
8. Trace the development of tax-reduction efforts in your state since 1978. How have they affected social services?

CHAPTER 2
Public and Voluntary Agencies

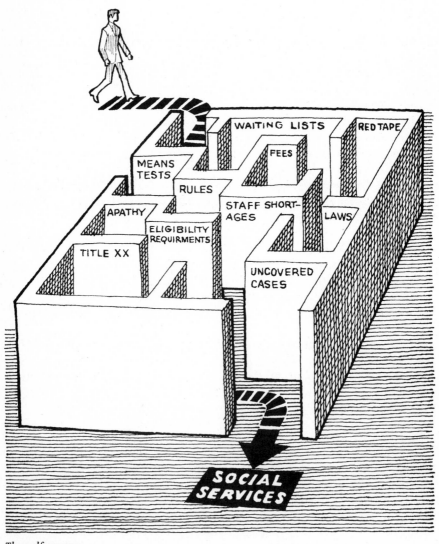

The welfare maze.

The feds have the money; the states have the power; and the locals have the problems.

—Neal R. Peirce*

Because the social service system in the United States involves complex relationships between federal, state, and local governments, it is no wonder that most people find the structure and financing of social services confusing. Each state provides mental health and child welfare programs, health and rehabilitation services, as well as public assistance and corrections. In addition, an estimated 37,000 social welfare organizations are classified as private nonprofit groups.

This chapter will discuss the various types of social service organizations. (1) *Public agencies*, authorized by statute and supported primarily by taxes, account for about two-thirds of the annual national expenditure of $250 billion for health and welfare services. (2) *Voluntary agencies*, chartered by the states as nonprofit corporations, are governed by a board of directors, and are traditionally financed from gifts, bequests, and foundation grants. (3) *Proprietary agencies*, organized to make a profit, typically provide day care and nursing home care; their services are frequently purchased by governmental bodies, and some hospitals and mental health institutions are also proprietary.

PUBLIC AGENCIES

Some critics visualize public agencies as composed of employees tied to their chairs by red tape. This view, however, obscures the scope and power of public programs. These programs carry the major responsibility for social welfare, produce the most significant volume of services, and are expected to be the most accountable.

A study of public agencies gives insight into an important segment of American values and political processes. Adequacy, accessibility, and cost of services have become major themes. The public agency is the target for pressure from many quarters, including taxpapers' groups, the National Association of Social Workers, and recipients of financial services who are members of the National Welfare Rights Organization. In many parts of the country, due to the uneven distribution of private services, public agencies constitute the only resources for special needs. Though they vary both quantitatively and qualitatively, all public services have a clear legal responsibility to provide programs. Taxpayers have come to demand services, and now they often back up their demands with legal action. Parents of the mentally retarded have scored impressive successes in their campaigns for the right to

*Neal R. Peirce, "Power and (Dis)trust," *Public Welfare*, vol. 36, Summer 1978, p. 15.

education and treatment and constitute a clear example of the effective use of social action.

What Is a Public Agency?

Public agencies are authorized by law, operated by governmental units, and supported from tax revenues. While most of them are financed, administered, and operated by the state, some are run by counties or by larger towns or cities. Some townships also administer general assistance payments for persons who are not able to qualify for a federally aided program.

Purposes Most public agencies were established to provide services to individuals rather than groups. However, programs for children and adults also include recreation and skill activities on a group basis. Out-patient and residential mental health facilities have found group services effective. Correctional programs also use groups for self-goverance and program activities.

In addition to helping people, public social agencies have the function of protecting society through mental health services, corrections, and child welfare programs.

Public Agencies as Bureaucracies

Elaborate bureaucratic structures are characteristic of our society. Bureaucracies are not automatically bad. They reflect the high degree of specialization found in business, industry, and government. They try to keep differentiated functions efficient and productive.

We usually characterize governmental agencies as having many rules to maintain control. These organizations are created by a legal authority that defines their character and specifies their jurisdiction. Their administration is intended to be objective and formal, subject to clear rules and regulations. A bureaucracy is a hierarchy; therefore, it reminds one of a pyramid. Except for the top executives, personnel are selected for their positions according to merit and consider themselves permanent. Each job requires specialization and expertise. If complex activities are to be carried on effectively, bureaucratic organizations are indispensable. As a movement grows, it will proclaim a specialization, evolve a structure, and hire permanent employees; then it has the major characteristics of a bureaucracy. Even antiestablishment organizations become bureaucratic.

Criticisms of Bureaucracies

While bureaucracies are necessary to modern life, most people emphasize their shortcomings. Clients of social welfare bureaucracies, for example, protest that huge, impersonal organizations are inflexible and unresponsive. Controls seem to be imposed over more and more aspects of personal life, so that people become only numbers or cases. Not only can the large bureaucracy usurp rights and choices that belong to the individual, but the individual may lose awareness of the possibility of choice.

One consequence of bureaucratic monopoly is the alienation of individuals from social institutions. When people feel powerless to influence their surroundings, a sense of estrangement sets in. Life may seem meaningless. Individuals may surrender their own values and purposes. Therefore, making social welfare bureaucracies humane is one of the major challenges for social workers.

Peter Blau believes that bureaucracies have the capacity to change.

> Bureaucracies are not such rigid structures as is popularly assumed. Their organization does not remain fixed according to the formal blueprint, but always evolves into new forms. Conditions change, problems arise, and, in the course of coping with them, the members of the organization establish new procedures and often transfer their social relationship, thereby modifying the structure.[1]

Blau emphasizes that the organization's operations must further the attainment of its objectives. The administrative problem is how to bring this about without sacrificing human rights.

Authority of Public Agencies

Most federal participation in social welfare programs stems from the authority of four words in the Constitution: *promote the general welfare.* The federal government does not force a state to provide programs, but federal grants are a major incentive for program development. American public welfare programs, for the most part, require authorization from each state legislature.

The Power of Rule-making   The power and discretion of a public agency are generally more significantly contained in its rule-making and policy-making functions than in legislation. Rule-making power can be used to limit or extend services. Consider one example of the importance of rule-making powers.

Federal guidelines specify that children over eighteen are ineligible for benefits from Aid to Families with Dependent Children (AFDC) unless they remain in school. In its rules, one state department of public welfare held that the term "school" included technical or trade school but not college. As a result, parents of college students receiving AFDC filed suit. In 1971 in *Townsend v. Swank*,[2] the U.S. Supreme Court held the rule to be invalid and ended the discrimination.

Townsend v. Swank was a "class action" suit since it was filed on behalf of all AFDC recipients attending college. A similar case in another state involved a recipient who wanted to enter a professional nursing education program, but training support had been offered only on the condition that she become a licensed practical nurse. Both examples indicate the tendency to stigmatize the poor and place a ceiling on their achievement.

Licensing   Public agencies are given the authority to license programs operated under private auspices. A public agency is expected to meet its own licensing requirements in its service-giving, even though it does not technically license itself. Protection of those served by the facility is the primary purpose of licensing. Standards for fire and safety are more easily developed than enforceable standards for good programs. Rules can specify the level of education of a teacher or a nurse, but they tend to avoid specifying desired personality characteristics or behaviors.

Agencies providing such services as adoption, institutions of all sizes, group homes operated by agencies, and private homes that regularly care for other people's children full-time or part of the day must be licensed. Departments of health license mental health facilities. Public departments approve children's institutions and agencies, adoptive and foster family homes, and day care homes and centers. Out-patient counseling programs usually are not licensed.

Licensing may present major problems. Many day care centers are organized on a profit-making basis with little money for alteration of facilities or expansion of staff. Unrealistic standards may put centers out of business and drive people to use alternatives that are more dangerous. Licensing standards are expected to be equitable. Review and appeal procedures must be provided to ensure fair treatment. Controversy arises especially when licensing requirements increase costs for programs operated for profit.

Although the legal purpose of licensing is to provide protection, public agencies also use the licensing relationship to provide consultation to help facilities improve their programs. The public sees licensing as policing, but social workers often consider opportunities for consultation more important than the granting of the license.

Investigatory Powers   Public agencies also have a variety of investigatory powers. Perhaps the most interesting example concerns alleged child abuse or neglect. Investigatory powers are often shared by the welfare department, the police, and the courts, and may involve a clash of philosophies. The agency may feel that the police are aggressive or punitive. The courts may seem to minimize serious situations by supporting the rights of parents. The agency may be seen as either too permissive or too prone to remove children from their home. In serious situations that require legal action, social workers must become familiar with rules of evidence and prepare testimony so that conclusions follow from facts rather than from vague feelings or impressions.

Social workers who prefer to work with highly motivated people actively seeking help often have difficulty accepting investigatory and authoritative roles such as those involved in the prevention of child abuse. Not only do they have to gain access to families that are reported for neglect or abuse, but they have to find ways to work with them. Hostility is not limited, however, to those people who receive service unwillingly. Persons that seek service also often become critical and uncooperative.

Financing of Public Agencies

While public social agencies are generally financed from tax funds, they may also receive foundation grants and may charge fees for service. Fees are more likely to be charged for continuing residential care than for short-term counseling. Relatives of mental hospital patients and parents of children in foster care may be expected to pay according to their financial ability, but persons who cannot pay are not denied service.

Revenue Sharing   The State and Local Assistance Act was passed by Congress in 1972 and extended for another five years in 1977. The act provides about $6 billion annually to local government units for distribution in eight categories—public safety, environmental protection, public transportation, health, recreation, libraries, social services for the poor and the aged, and fiscal administration. Although public and voluntary social welfare organizations are eligible for the funds, revenue-sharing monies have gone mostly to public safety, education, and transportation. Local governments have stressed tangible capital (building) projects that affect a wide population rather than services to the poor and the aged. Various forms of tax relief have also been popular. Most communities have expended the funds for short-term projects that do not imply any continuing financial commitment. Revenue sharing has had few advantages over federal ear-marked grants.

Title XX   A major reform in the Social Security Act came in 1975 when Title XX incorporated the previous public welfare provisions for social services. To obtain federal funds for 75 percent of the cost of the services, each state submits a plan to meet several broad goals—increasing the economic support and self-sufficiency of their clients, preventing neglect and abuse, reducing inappropriate institutional care, and assuring referral for institutional care when other forms of care are inappropriate. States are encouraged to make use of voluntary agencies in their plans. For every dollar a voluntary agency turns over to the designated public agency, three matching federal dollars can be obtained. The public agency then returns the donated funds and the federal matching funds to the voluntary agency through a contractual agreement. An annual ceiling of $2.9 billion was included to control the total cost, and each state was assigned a maximum amount to be reimbursed.

Public Agency Personnel—Civil Service

Since the Pendleton Act of 1883, civil service has been relied upon for the recruitment, selection, and retention of competent government employees dedicated to the public interest. Most social workers in public agencies work under federal or state civil service. A recent Supreme Court decision curtailed the use of political patronage in allocating government jobs.[3]

For most direct service positions, candidates take examinations that are objectively scored. For higher-level jobs, oral examinations may also be given. Training and experience and veteran status may also contribute to the final score. Selection is limited to the group scoring highest—often the top three applicants who would accept the position. After a probationary period, the employee is permanently certified for the position. The highest policy-making positions are filled by appointments from outside the civil service.

President Carter, in a message to Congress on March 2, 1978, termed the civil service system "a bureaucratic maze which neglects merit, tolerates poor performance, permits abuse of legitimate employee rights, and mires every personnel action in red tape, delay, and confusion."[4] A civil servant has been compared to a defective rocket that doesn't work and can't be fired.

While the President's observations concerned the federal system, his analysis also applies to state personnel systems. Some tend to be inefficient and have become increasingly politicized. To pass the examination for entry-level positions, a social worker often has to study outdated materials. A federal interest in the personnel policies of state programs receiving federal grants-in-aid used to provide pressure to enforce merit principles, but these watchdog efforts have largely disappeared.

The new Civil Service Reform Act (PL95-454) passed in October 1978 contained seven new revisions.

1. Creation of an Office of Personnel Management to replace the Civil Service Commission, which has become "manager, rule maker, prosecutor, and judge," and a Merit Systems Protection Board as the adjudicatory arm of the new personnel system. Prohibited personal practices are enumerated in the law.
2. A senior executive service for 8,000 top managers permitting transfer of executives among senior positions, salary adjustments rather than automatic pay increases, and substantial cash bonuses for superior performance.
3. Merit pay for other federal managers and supervisors with "performance" pay increases and limited cash bonuses.
4. A fairer and speedier disciplinary system to provide more rapid hearings for employees' grievances and more readily permit discharge of nonperforming employees.
5. A Federal Labor Relations Authority to hear complaints about unfair labor practices.
6. Decentralization of personnel decision-making from the single commission to the departments and agencies. Performance agreements would be negotiated between the Office of Personnel Management and the agencies.
7. The right to join unions and bargain collectively without the right to strike or to make payment of union dues mandatory.

A critical issue in state civil service is the reduction of professional standards for many social service positions. In many states, positions formerly open only to professional social workers are now available to people with widely varied education and training.

Structure of State Agencies

Unfortunately the structure and interrelationships of agencies are hardly comparable in any two states, let alone across fifty. For broken families with the father and mother living miles apart, administrative problems are compounded by interstate differences. The federal pattern of health, education, and welfare in a single department is not followed in any state. Because of the historical emphasis on local financing and control of the common schools, education is administered separately.

For some years, most states have attempted to follow a human relations concept by combining some other programs in the same department with those involving public welfare. The resultant organizations however, are not the same for any two states. Of the thirty-six that have some combinations, mental health and retardation are included in twenty-six, public health and adult corrections in ten each, and employment-unemployment compensation in six. Only Oregon offers public welfare and all of the other four in a single agency. A detailed chart is available to show the location of all programs by state.[5]

Centralization versus Decentralization   How many state agencies should there be to provide effective service?

Providing services in a considerable number of independent specialized state agencies has some advantages: a specialist can be selected as executive; program advocacy can be specific and clear-cut; self-help groups can be enlisted for support; budgets appear smaller and cannot be reduced as easily by across-the-board cuts; small specific programs may reduce waste, accountability may be stricter, and the span of control may be smaller. The staff may also have easier direct access to the governor. Disadvantages are also evident: families with multiproblems have more difficulty obtaining the variety of services needed; interagency planning is made harder, and agencies may spend too much time in competition for support; management costs may be higher because of duplication in such supportive services as data processing and accounting.

Consolidation of agencies is often preferred by management consultants so as to develop better control systems and greater efficiency. Salaries for top management can be higher in order to recruit more outstanding leaders; planning efforts involving several programs can be more successfully mandated; budgeting can be more responsive to the program goals of an administration in power. On the other side are the dangers of concentration of power and of competition among program divisions as much as among separate departments.

Most states tend to be dissatisfied with their current organizational patterns. When there are many public agencies, strong pressure builds up for consolidation. After consolidation, moves are made to break empires into smaller units. The trend is illustrated by the diamond-shaped diagram in Figure 2-1. Too often reorganization becomes a smokescreen used to delay innovations. The development of information systems and effective cooperative relationships is more important for the improvement of direct services.

A Student Proposal   A group of students reviewed the organization of public agencies across the country. They found the familiar problems—gaps, overlap, little assurance that persons with a range of needs would get help quickly and effectively.[6] As a result they developed a model organization plan for state

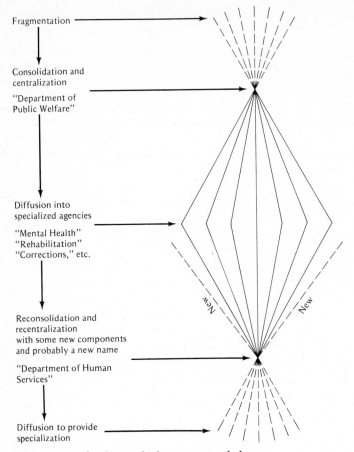

Fragmentation

Consolidation and
centralization

"Department of
Public Welfare"

Diffusion into
specialized agencies

"Mental Health"
"Rehabilitation"
"Corrections," etc.

Reconsolidation and
recentralization
with some new components
and probably a new name

"Department of Human
Services"

Diffusion to provide
specialization

Figure 2.1   The diamond of organizational change.

services (see Figure 2-2). The major innovation is the Division of Client
Advocacy intended to ensure that people obtain the services they need. Note
also that community corrections are part of the Division of Rehabilitation.

Major Public Agency Programs

A wide variety of public agency programs employ social services
personnel. Each type of program has somewhat different standards for selecting
staff members and requires special knowledge. Most programs provide specific
training on the job, but previous experience in a given field of practice provides
an advantage in initial hiring. A discussion of several of the major programs is
useful to indicate the range of possibilities.

Income Maintenance   "Welfare" programs designed primarily to give money
to the poor are the most familiar social service function. Many people are

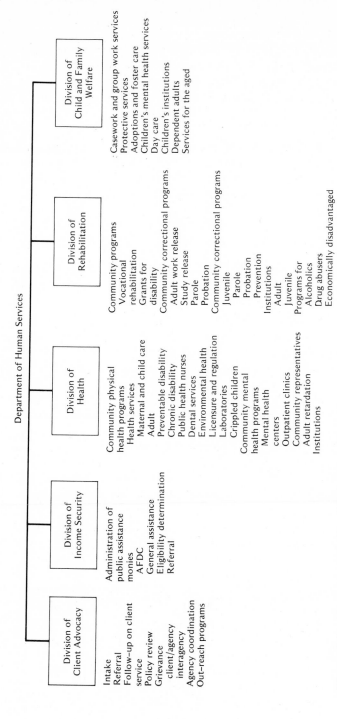

Department of Human Services

Division of Client Advocacy

Intake
Referral
Follow-up on client service
Policy review
Grievance client/agency interagency
Agency coordination
Out-reach programs

Division of Income Security

Administration of public assistance monies
AFDC
General assistance
Eligibility determination
Referral

Division of Health

Community physical health programs
Health services
Maternal and child care
Adult
Preventable disability
Chronic disability
Public health nurses
Dental services
Environmental health
Licensure and regulation
Laboratories
Crippled children
Community mental health programs
Mental health centers
Outpatient clinics
Community representatives
Adult retardation
Institutions

Division of Rehabilitation

Community programs
Vocational rehabilitation
Grants for disability
Community correctional programs
Adult work release
Study release
Parole
Probation
Community correctional programs
Juvenile
Parole
Probation
Prevention
Institutions
Adult
Juvenile
Programs for Alcoholics
Drug abusers
Economically disadvantaged

Division of Child and Family Welfare

Casework and group work services
Protective services
Adoptions and foster care
Children's mental health services
Day care
Children's institutions
Dependent adults
Services for the aged

Figure 2.2   An organizational model for states' services.

employed to take applications, determine eligibility, and offer various social services. Professional social workers usually supervise the direct-service personnel. The major stated goal of these programs is to help clients cope with their problems of daily living. However, in practice it frequently turns out that the program's real goal is limited to finding jobs for recipients and getting them off the rolls. This discrepancy of goals is disagreeable to many trained social workers and may explain, in part, the high turnover in professional staff in many public agencies.

Families and Children   Public agencies provide a range of protective services for children, including foster care and adoption. They may also offer institutional services. They work with the courts to deal with neglected children and with those having serious behavior problems, including delinquency. Public agencies counsel parents and provide homemaker service and day care directly or by purchase from other agencies.

Mental Health   In-patient services for the mentally ill are most often operated directly by public agencies. Some private hospitals also have mental health units, but they are very costly for extended treatment. Out-patient programs are more likely to be operated by private agencies. Many community-based mental health centers are privately organized but receive a major proportion of their budgets from public funds in return for services to returned mental patients and services that keep people out of the state mental hospitals.

Developmental Disabilities   Public services for the mentally handicapped are often operated by the department of mental health, but advocates for this clientele prefer services under an independent administrative unit. Recent legislation has also favored the development of community-based programs under both voluntary and proprietary auspices.

Corrections   The costs of correctional programs for adults are borne by the states and local governments. Federal grants are available for special purposes from the Law Enforcement Assistance Administration. Local and state funds are sometimes used for the purchase of rehabilitative services for juvenile offenders who require special programs.

Neighborhood Agencies   The antipoverty and model cities programs established in the 1960s resulted in public agencies taking more active roles in neighborhood development. Board members of model cities programs were elected from the communities. Electors often included all residents over the age of sixteen. Publicly sponsored community organization programs have often been hampered by a major problem: the political establishment has operated the social institutions most in need of social change. Even lead poisoning and rat control programs have been played down because they implied possible criticism of the establishment in power.

The next issue concerns attitudes toward the various programs.

RELATIVE STATUS OF CLIENTELES

Some Are More Equal than Others

Understanding of the delivery systems for public services also requires recognition of special status and privileges accorded to the many self-help groups; for instance, parents' organizations on behalf of the mentally retarded, federations of the blind, and veterans' groups.

The Retarded   Parents of the mentally retarded were mentioned earlier as being effective in extending and improving care and services for their children. Institutional programs have been improved—some of them dramatically. Many children are also now served in the community rather than in custodial facilities miles away. Such parents' groups usually have demanded neither administrative control nor staff positions in programs for retarded children.

The Blind   As a group, the blind have successfully obtained special consideration. The group includes the visually handicapped (who have difficulty reading print) as well as those who are totally blind. The blind get talking books and record players mailed postage-free from the Library of Congress, and they receive an extra exemption on their federal income tax. Services for the blind are in a separate category in public assistance; they are usually offered in a separate bureau or in a different department from the rest of rehabilitation. This maintains high priority and guarantees jobs for blind persons at both professional and clerical levels. The deaf, whom most professionals consider to have a more serious handicap, have had no comparable success, probably because their handicap is less evident.

War Veterans   Veterans get preference on civil service examinations and in public employment agencies. They also staff the 20,000 positions of the Veterans Administration. Special benefits also include federal pensions for veterans and their dependents, a separate federal hospital system that treats illnesses both related and unrelated to their military service, and free burial and tombstones.

A HIERARCHY OF PUBLIC AGENCIES

Public Acceptance and Support

Some public agency programs obviously have greater public acceptance than others. This section presents a speculative ordering intended to reflect American values. See whether you agree.

Vocational Rehabilitation Services for Crippled Children and the Retarded
These services are not widely known because of their specialized clientele and rather small volume of service, but the public has been supportive of efforts for the disabled and of the major medical services these agencies offer. Americans

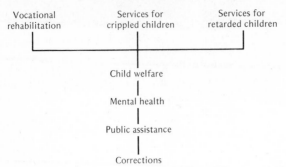

Figure 2.3 Public acceptance of public services—A hierarchy.

identify with an agency that tries to put people to work—the major goal of vocational rehabilitation. Budgets for services for the disabled are rarely controversial. Legislators sometimes say they support such programs in thankfulness for their own freedom from handicaps. Similar support has been generated for services for developmental disabilities—the current term for the mentally handicapped.

Child Welfare   Children have been one of the major concerns of society, with our tradition of the state as parent with a clear interest in the welfare of the child. Both crippled children and those receiving child welfare services receive favorable interest—especially previous to adolescence. Child welfare services have generated goodwill through the publicity efforts of voluntary agencies that have offered adoption and foster care services. This goodwill has rubbed off on public child welfare programs, although foster care is generally misperceived as a service for orphans. Actually the vast majority of children in foster care are from broken homes. Adoption has had a particular appeal. Perhaps it captures the imagination of the American public because they see adoption as long-term altruism.

Mental Health   The image of mental health services has improved. Short-term hospitalization and community-based services, along with successful use of drugs, have been helpful in maintaining the interest and responsibility of the patient's family. Many communities have conducted successful referendums to provide local tax funds for their own mental health clinics, indicating local support.

Public Assistance   "Welfare" has suffered from a widespread image of fraud and the fear that people will not want to work if they get used to being "on relief." People refuse to accept research indicating that most recipients of public assistance would prefer to work. The lack of available opportunities, rather than the attitude of the poor toward work, is the basic problem. That AFDC recipients rarely remain on the rolls permanently is also not understood.

Racism has also played a significant part in determining attitudes toward public assistance. Since blacks make up a large proportion of the urban poor, it has been difficult to separate attitudes toward poverty from racism. This is apparent in discussions of illegitimacy. As an example of a double standard, sterilization is sometimes advocated to reduce public assistance costs, but it is considered undesirable for members of the middle class.

The Aid to Families with Dependent Children program generates opposition because recipients in many instances are still of child-bearing age and are perceived as employable. Providing AFDC benefits to intact families with unemployed fathers has also resulted in opposition. These benefits are available in only about half the states. Welfare reform proposals suggest that negative feelings toward AFDC might be reduced if payments were made through a general program such as social security.

The attitudes of recipients toward public assistance are now also becoming more evident through welfare rights organizations. The size of grants, need of special funds for seasonal items, such as winter clothing, and condescending treatment by staff members are examples of common problems. The great discretion of assistance staff in giving special allowances has resulted in proposals for flat grants that could be administered more easily and fairly.

Correctional Services   Programs for offenders are at the bottom of the hierarchy. English and American criminal law tends to be punitive. Comparatively long sentences are standard procedure. Prisons tend to be both outmoded and overcrowded. Job discrimination against ex-convicts is commonplace and persists for years after release. Recently problems with "crime in the streets," riots in prisons, and exposes in the press have led to public support for improvements in the correctional system, but people are also increasingly afraid. Among juveniles, crimes like armed robbery—not car thefts for joyrides—are becoming more typical. The public is particularly unsympathetic to growing crime and delinquency of suburban youth—"young people who have had every advantage."

If services are to be strongly supported, a better understanding of each one is essential. That college students are taking a greater interest in the development of an effective system of public assistance and reforms in corrections in a hopeful sign.

Means of Coordination

Coordination of services involves effective relationships between the units that constitute the service delivery system. People often need more than one service. A confusing web of differing jurisdictions, requirements, and operating policies makes it easy to get lost in the system. Also, personnel from several agencies may advocate very different solutions to the same problem. The key to coordination is often found in the referral process. A social worker must know the related services in the community and be able to get other agencies to respond to requests for help.

Establishment of uniform areas, regions, or districts and the provision of basic services in the same building, however the agencies are organized, may achieve better service. A multiservice center can reduce the confusion created by differing geographical concepts and lead to the use of generalists who may represent several agencies. Agency autonomy and the need to be familiar with a variety of complicated and sometimes conflicting policies, however, impede cooperation. An ombudsman to receive and act on requests and complaints from any citizen may reduce inefficiency and buck-passing, but considering the passivity of many users of services, those that most need an ombudsman may be the last to find one.

The idea of advocacy is especially attractive. Social workers serving individuals can also provide better coordination by acting as advocates for their clients to obtain needed resources from whatever source and to develop new services that are needed. Public agencies have been too timid about giving their workers sanction for such roles. Client organizations and self-help groups have often been able to apply pressures without social work help, but systems are often too formidable and impenetrable for their efforts to succeed. Agencies are increasingly aware of the need for coordination of services, and some have demonstrated considerable success. As the chapter on evaluating social services will indicate, emphasis on both efficiency and effectiveness may produce both better service and greater coordination.

Public Agency Budgeting

Preparing a budget differs somewhat from agency to agency and state to state, but usually past expenditures and existing programs are taken into account to establish baselines. Agencies have generally expected to get the same amount next year as they do in the current year. Proposed new programs have been put in supplementary budgets or given other special justification. Too much emphasis on the status quo can lead to the continuance of outmoded programs. This has led to interest in zero-based budgeting,* in which each program—old or new—is considered as a "decision package." Established services compete with new ones for approval.

Especially in public assistance programs, costs have sometimes been routinely underestimated, with the realization that a deficiency bill will have to be introduced in the legislature before the end of the fiscal period. This provides the illusion of lower costs. Increased personnel are often the most controversial item in the budget because legislators associate personnel with needless expansion. Consequently most social agencies in the public sector have inadequate numbers of staff.

Budgeting by gross *line items*—e.g., salaries, food, and transportation—is gradually giving way to *program* budgeting in which costs are presented by major activities, rather than objects. Thus an agency must request one amount for out-patient clinic services, another for adoption, and another for recreation-

*In zero-based budgeting, the entire program of an agency is evaluated and priorities established among the subunits. No priority is given to established programs simply because they have been operated for some years.

al programs aimed at delinquency prevention. A program budget provides a way to show the true cost of a specific activity and is essential for zero-based budgeting.

Many agencies ask regional or district directors to determine the projected costs of their particular units. These proposals are used to determine the total budget request. An agency usually presents an optimum budget to be reviewed (and often reduced) by the administration and finally made a part of its fiscal package. The budget may also be studied by a special legislative budgetary control unit. Then an appropriation bill is drafted, testimony is presented at hearings before appropriations committees of both houses, and the bill is ultimately passed and signed by the governor. Obviously this process provides several opportunities for budgets to be cut. An administrator tries to revise the total budget at each stage and wherever possible seeks the discretion to apply any required cuts where they will be least harmful. Whether attempts are to be made to restore proposed cuts is often a decision of the administration rather than the prerogative of the agency executive.

Even with the signing of the appropriation bill, the agency is not home free. If revenues do not keep up with estimates, the administration may freeze expenditures to provide cost control—especially in the personnel category.

The "Profit Motive" in Public Agencies

Business operations are relatively easy to understand because a firm must already have or must create a market for its product and must ultimately make a profit which justifies continuing in business; on the other hand, public agencies have a larger market for their services than they can generally supply, and they are nonprofit by definition. What replaces the profit motive for them?

With the large market for their services, saving money is not the primary aim of the agency. Their goal, akin to the profit motive, is the establishment of public confidence that leads to a mandate to offer more and better service programs and to serve more people. For the agency that considers itself vital to a better society, these motivators are just as strong as profit.

Public Services and the Social Security Act

The depression of the 1930's provided the stimulus for public services as we know them today. Following the emergency relief programs of the early thirties, the Social Security Act was passed in 1935. Federal participation in welfare programs has grown rapidly since 1937, when the old-age insurance provisions of the act were declared constitutional by the Supreme Court.

Modified by frequent amendments, the act has provided the framework for federal-state cooperation for major public services except mental health and corrections. The power has come largely from the federal government's authority to set standards as a condition to receive federal funds.

Social Insurance and Financial Assistance   The original legislation created a social insurance system involving a payroll tax from employers and employees, provided unemployment compensation for a specified time while a worker looked for a new job, and established three categories of persons entitled to financial assistance—the needy aged, the needy blind, and dependent children. In 1950 aid to the needy disabled was added. In 1960 AFDC benefits were broadened so states could choose to include families in which the father was unemployed, and in 1960 and 1965 provisions provided payments for medical services to the aged and then for medically indigent people. In 1974 assistance programs for the aged, the blind, and the disabled, as we have seen, were transferred from the states to the federal government in the Supplemental Security Income Program (SSI).

Some needy persons are not covered for welfare payments under the provisions of the Social Security Act. Single individuals who are not aged, blind, or disabled, married couples without children, and families that are underemployed must depend on general assistance. Support, standards, and practices vary widely since these programs do not receive federal funds. In some places general assistance brings to mind the ancient English system of poor relief, with a political figure serving as overseer of the poor.

Grants to the States   The Social Security Act made grants available to the states for maternal and child health, child welfare, vocational rehabilitation, and crippled children's services. Formulas to determine the size of grants are complicated, involving the population and wealth of the state and its rural or urban character. Grants were made to extend services to rural areas and, later, to urban ghettos, to improve staff competence, and to promote services that had a high priority. Agencies and individuals may also apply for federal research-and-demonstration grants for special projects to develop and test innovations.

Job Opportunities in Public Agencies

Improved public attitudes are essential to provide support for better public social service programs. Understanding the issues involved in public services affects your behavior as a citizen-taxpayer-voter. You may want to volunteer to help provide direct services or to interpret the program of the agency to the community. Perhaps you will be invited to serve on a public agency board to influence agency policy and to be an advocate for the program.

Public agencies may include several unique elements. A social worker can expect to give services without the protection of a waiting list and in most programs to deal with people who have economic as well as social problems. A worker may well have to represent authority to reluctant clients. Civil service rules will require a probationary period and convey tenure. Vacation and other fringe benefits may be somewhat less generous than in a voluntary agency, especially for new employees. Professional social workers in a public agency are likely to work with other personnel who have a wide range of education, including indigenous workers who have first-hand knowledge of the people being served. Since many public agencies are large, service workers may find it difficult to communicate through channels to top administrative personnel. The public agencies have the crucial problems and the major resources making employment both important and rewarding.

Human Rights and Public Social Services

Many social workers and agency clients have been concerned about the entitlement to social services as well as the right to considerate and humane treatment by agencies. Denial of service without adequate cause may be formally appealed. Most public agencies provide administrative "fair hearings" in which a client may claim his or her rights. The right to be represented by a lawyer is also recognized. Such hearings have resulted in an increasing recognition of clients' rights, yet they usually settle such disputes without resorting to the courts. The right of public assistance recipients to hearings was recognized by the Supreme Court in 1970 in *Goldberg v. Kelley*.[7] Recipients were specifically accorded the right to confront and cross-examine witnesses, but such a guarantee is often meaningless unless they are helped to secure legal services. Clients are unfamiliar with legal procedures and fearful of losing their benefits. Advocacy by social workers and by legal aid programs can help disadvantaged clients overcome some of the barriers to social services. The family of Malcolm X needed an advocate but had no one to represent them.

Malcolm X and the Welfare Department

. . . the state Welfare people kept after my mother. By now, she didn't make it any secret that she hated them, and didn't want them in her house. But they exerted their right to come, and I have many, many times reflected upon how, talking to us children, they began to plant the seeds of division in our minds. They would ask such things as who was smarter than the other. And they would ask me why I was "so different."

I think they felt that getting children into foster homes was a legitimate part of their function, and the result would be less troublesome, however they went about it.

And when my mother fought them, they went after her—first through me. I was the first target. I stole; that implied that I wasn't being taken care of by my mother.

All of us were mischievous at some time or another, I more so than any of the rest. Philbert and I kept a battle going. And this was just one of the dozen things that kept building up the pressure on my mother.

I'm not sure just how or when the idea was first dropped by the Welfare workers that our mother was losing her mind.

But I can distinctly remember hearing "crazy" applied to her by them when they learned that the Negro farmer who was in the next house down the road from us had offered to give us some butchered pork—a whole pig, maybe even two of them—and she had refused. We all heard them call my mother "crazy" to her face for refusing good meat. It meant nothing to them even when she explained that we had never eaten pork, that it was against her religion as a Seventh Day Adventist.

They were as vicious as vultures. They had no feelings, understanding, compassion, or respect for my mother. They told us, "She's crazy for refusing food." Right then was when our home, our unity, began to disintegrate. We were having a hard time, and I wasn't helping. But we could have made it, we could have stayed together. As bad as I was, as much trouble and worry as I caused my mother, I loved her.

The state people, we found out, had interviewed the Gohannas family, and the Gohannas' had said that they would take me into their home. My mother threw a fit, though, when she heard that—and the home wreckers took cover for a while.[8]

Malcolm X, *Autobiography*.

While formal hearings are relatively easily obtained, courtesy and empathy in dealing with users of service is often more difficult. Both staff training and pressure from welfare rights groups has been directed toward increasing helpfulness to the client. Simplified procedures for determining eligibility also help because they show more respect for privacy.

Public agencies also have systems of protection for employees through civil service. Certified employees are entitled to the same administrative fair hearings as recipients of service. Employees of public agencies also join unions to gain bargaining power and secure job protection.

PURCHASE OF CARE AND SERVICE

In the next section we will consider voluntary agencies. The bridge between public and voluntary agencies is provided by purchase agreements. Public funds play an increasingly large part in agency budgets. Ninety percent of the funds of some private agencies come from governmental sources, but there are still a few agencies that will accept no governmental funds at all.

The purchase arrangement operates on a free market basis. The voluntary agency need not offer its services for pay, and the public agency may choose not to buy. The process gets a little more complicated, however, when a voluntary agency begins to serve a child and then expects the public agency to assume responsibility for payment, even though public agency personnel have never seen the child. Such arrangements are common in some states but are impossible in others.

Certain costs are excluded from purchase-of-care agreements. Physical plant and depreciation often are not covered. In sectarian agencies, religious instruction and training costs are excluded. Parental payments, of course, are deducted. After determining the items to be excluded, the public agency may pay the full remaining cost or only a portion thereof. Purchase-of-care agreements set the rates. If care alone is provided, the cost may be low. If both casework and care are covered, costs will be higher. If intensive treatment is included, rates will be further increased. Purchase makes sense in many ways. Specialized care and service are made available to the public agency at less cost than providing it directly. Existing facilities are used and duplication discour-

Purchase of care links public and voluntary agencies together.

aged. At least traditionally, voluntary treatment services have been of higher quality than those offered by public programs. Monetary advantages to the payees are obvious. Payments provide basic budget support that would be impossible to obtain through contributions alone. Agencies can use their facilities and staff members more efficiently because the volume of activities is increased.

Disadvantages of Purchase Purchase of care may retard development of a public agency's specialized services, so that if a private resource is full or unresponsive, a needed program may be unavailable. The paying agency also may get strong pressure from payees to use services that may be inappropriate or ineffective. The cost of some services may be well beyond the reach of many public agencies. Residential treatment at an annual per capita cost of $20,000 or more may be impossible to finance.

Disadvantages to the voluntary agency include the tendency to become dependent upon public agency referrals. Policies and programs may be dictated by the public agency. The agency that becomes a contractor for traditional services may avoid needed innovations.

Cost Accounting As public agencies have had to respond to demands for increased accountability, purchase agreements have placed greater emphasis on the use of uniform systems for calculating costs. In the past many agencies with several types of programs had no idea of specific costs. Their total expenditures were divided by the number of people served or the number of days of care given in order to get averages, but their bookkeeping systems were not designed for budgeting by programs. Uniform agency accounting standards related to purchase of care have been a stimulus for better business management.

These data have often led to conclusions about the relative *efficiency* of agencies. *Effectiveness*—improvement in the condition of persons served—is a more difficult area to measure. An indicator of efficiency would be the proportion of total time spent directly with clients. An indicator of effectiveness would be the degree of change in behavior resulting from services.

Problems of Change   Purchase agreements have other problems. Costs go up every year. Agencies consider that their rates, based on past experience, are already out of date. Also, they may value their own services at a higher figure than does the agency controlling the purse strings. Sometimes agencies tool up for new programs but find that public agency needs or policies have changed. Then new services are not purchased, and the agency is worse off financially. Public agencies are also fickle. At times there is a strong emphasis on foster care. After a number of children flunk out of foster homes, institutional placement is rediscovered, but institutions are impersonal and costly. Then the agency may decide to remove the children and put them back in foster homes. Agencies also complain at times that personal dislike of a program by key public agency staff members may isolate the agency and cause it to "starve."

Other Frustrations   The public agency may find that the eligibility standards are not clear. One child is accepted—the next one with similar characteristics is not. The situation may be the result of lack of beds or of highly subjective criteria for admission. Delays often come in decision-making because the voluntary agency insists on repeating the study and diagnostic process. This leads public agency staff to develop concerns about inferiority. The receiving agency may also summarily return the person to the public department for inadequate reasons. In short, purchase of care has elements of uneasiness for all participants; nevertheless, we are likely to see more of it.

The need for a partnership between governmental and voluntary agencies was clearly stated by Arthur H. Kruse, former director of the Crusade of Mercy of Chicago.

> Let none of us who believe in the voluntary system delude ourselves. The mass thrust to move the poor from economic dependency to economic opportunity must be financed by government. The voluntary human care program is a major partner with government in our total objective to improve human performance in all walks of life and particularly for those who are most disadvantaged. As government and voluntary agencies work together, let us beware of easy solutions. We can legislate civil rights but not the elimination of prejudice. We can legislate law enforcement to protect us from irresponsible behavior but not the building of character. We can legislate the opportunity for economic achievement but not the incentive or the self discipline to grasp it. We may even try to legislate a great society, but we cannot legislate a great people. Only a great

people can create a great society. Our voluntary welfare program should be judged in the future by its contribution to the creation of a society of great people.[9]

VOLUNTARY SOCIAL SERVICES

The voluntary or private nonprofit agency is authorized to raise funds by a charter issued by the state. The charter includes a statement of purpose and the names of the officers and board members of the corporation. The charter can be revoked for cause, but this rarely occurs. Usually the statement of purpose in the charter is very general. The broad goals expressed need to be translated into objectives and the objectives into programs. As a nonprofit corporation, the agency is usually required to issue reports to the Secretary of State. In most states, any agency property used for commercial purposes will be taxed, but the agency is exempt from paying taxes on facilities for program purposes. Nonprofit agencies are also exempt from federal taxes.

No single pattern typifies voluntary agencies. They differ too much in size, type, and program impact. Their variety reflects the free enterprise system in the human service area. Voluntary social service agencies are more likely than public agencies to be managed by professional social workers who have worked up to the post of director. Voluntary agencies rely mainly on professional staff with the master's degree, especially when they provide "treatment." The voluntary agency can regulate the amount of work by using waiting lists or by "closing intake"—not accepting applications. For many of its activities, the public agency does not have this option.

We have been using the term "voluntary" rather than "private" agencies. The general public often uses the term "private," but most social workers prefer "voluntary." Private sounds too exclusive and includes proprietary agencies organized for profit as well as nonprofit organizations. Furthermore, "private" may be confusing, since many voluntary agencies receive public funds either as grants or through purchase of services.

Voluntary Agencies in American History

Voluntary agencies have a distinguished history. Their volunteer programs have given citizens experience in direct service activities. Use of influential people on their boards has provided status for the agencies. Many citizens have also become familiar with agency programs through fund raising. Interest in a voluntary agency has often broadened people's understanding of the total range of human needs and made them advocates of policies favorable toward public human services programs. Public agencies have found that their cause is enhanced when leaders from the voluntary field lobby and testify on their behalf.

Until the nineteenth century, voluntary social welfare agencies were related to the churches or to nationality groups. In 1817 the New York Society for the Prevention of Pauperism was organized without religious or ethnic sponsorship. Many progressive proposals were made on behalf of the poor and were picked up later by other agencies.

The Association for Improving the Condition of the Poor was formed in 1843. It served individuals who could be "morally and physically elevated" and who were not served by other agencies, and it tried to reject all others. It gave relief and also concentrated on the improvement of housing and sanitary provisions. The first report on tenement housing led to the construction of a model tenement in 1855. Programs for mothers and children, vacation schools, and settlement houses were also provided. The association was merged with the New York Charity Organization Society in 1939 to form the Community Services Society. The general pattern set by the association was followed in other cities, but the agencies tended to emphasize relief and to have less success with other objectives. The Community Services Society was responsible for the development of a professional school of social work that is now a part of Columbia University.

Working in a Voluntary Agency

Professional people who like the concept of altruism and prefer services supported by gifts rather than taxes may prefer to work in a voluntary agency. Fewer people may have to be served at a given time because the agency can more easily control the number of people accepted. There may be a greater stress on professionalism and less of an atmosphere of bureaucracy. Personnel policies are used instead of civil service rules, but there is less assurance of tenure unless the agency workers are covered by a union contract. Such coverage is not usual but is becoming more common.

In some agencies, the staff is very conscious of fund-raising efforts and will have close relationships with board members. In large agencies, this is less true.

Rising costs are a threat to voluntary agencies, but fees for service, government grants, and increasing use of purchase of care have strengthened them. At the same time they have become less clearly the embodiment of traditional private charity.

Types of Voluntary Programs

Voluntary agencies have many purposes. They may provide direct services in a city, county, or district. Some are statewide. Many of them were organized to provide assistance to the poor. Later, when public agencies took over financial aid, family counseling became the core service. Marriage counseling, homemaker service, activities for the aged, and family life education are all included in family service.

Programs designed to provide care for orphans have developed into broader child welfare programs offering institutional and family foster care, adoption, protective services, day care, and counseling for children in their own homes. Family agencies often merged with children's agencies or with mental health centers.

Child guidance clinics were established to aid in the prevention and control of delinquency, but now they provide treatment for behavior problems primarily through casework with children and parents. Clinic services are frequently offered in a more comprehensive mental health center. These centers have added a planning function to develop a network of mental health services through public and private agencies.

A range of private institutions for the mentally ill, the retarded, and the disabled provide treatment and training. Many of the programs have vocational emphasis. Some provide transitional "halfway" services from restricted environments to the community.

Nonprofit hospitals and clinics receive some local charitable contributions for serving the poor. They also provide services for which other agencies are billed. They have received federal funds for plant expansion and equipment.

Many settlement houses which were originally developed for immigrants and other new urban residents have become community centers offering programs of socialization, treatment, education, and recreation. Both group work and casework are now principal methods in these agencies. Senior citizens' groups are often operated by settlement houses or by other agencies.

In addition, there are a range of youth-serving agencies—Boy Scouts, Girl Scouts, Campfire Girls, Boys' and Girls' Clubs, YM and YWCAs, YM and YWHAs. Big Brothers and Big Sisters have been oriented especially to the disadvantaged. In contrast, the 4-H program, operated by the extension service of the Department of Agriculture, is the only publicly sponsored national youth program. 4-H has also developed urban activities in ghetto areas.

Alcoholics Anonymous, Parents Without Partners, the Association for the Retarded, and Recovery—an association of former mental patients—illustrate the variety of self-help and parents' groups. These organizations differ in their policies toward the use of professional staff. Some welcome social workers; others prefer volunteer leadership. They ordinarily do not engage in extensive fund raising and may remain remote from other agencies.

Community legal services recently have provided help to residents in consumer fraud cases, in debt counseling and credit reform, and in a host of class actions against state agencies, city departments, and other organizations. While the legal services offices operate with the freedom of a voluntary agency, they are funded through a Legal Services Corporation established by Congress. Controversy has resulted when legal services offices have filed suit against governmental bodies. They have been accused of biting the hand that feeds them.

Church Sponsorship of Agencies

Church wardens played a major role in the provision of care for the poor in England, but in the United States separation of church and state has made the church's efforts distinctly private. Churches developed institutions for orphans and for the aged in their congregations. They also collected alms for the poor and provided food, clothing, and shelter to the needy. Adoption and foster care were added later. Counseling was seen basically as pastoral advice, but clergy often found that problems required other expert help. This led to new counseling programs and to specialized family and children's agencies.

Jewish agencies have provided particularly significant leadership in the development of professional social work services. With the concentration of Jews in certain neighborhoods, in addition to casework and financial assistance, settlement houses and community center services were developed. Aid to displaced persons and immigrants has particular importance. Although the agencies are not typically owned by a congregation, a major emphasis has been on Jewish education and culture. Many of the agencies have opened their services to non-Jews.

Catholic agencies provide social services in the various dioceses. They have advocated services for children that guarantee religious training in a Catholic institution or foster home. Concern about spiritual development led to a variety of institutional services. The agencies have tended to provide few services to non-Catholics.

Protestant welfare services provide a mixed picture over the country. A few communities have Protestant federations. Lutherans have organized their services into a separate federation in some communities. The agencies show the individualism of Protestant denominations and historically have been more willing to extend services outside their own membership group—perhaps because the criteria for membership are less clear-cut.

Lutheran agencies are likely to be church-owned. Other Protestant agencies tend to be church-related. This term generally means that churches are solicited for financial support but are not offered much real control of the program. A few also have social service organizations at the national or state level, but strong authority is not ordinarily exercised.

Management Trends   The most important tie between the churches and their agencies comes in funding. Church leaders also play dominant roles on the boards of the agencies. Funding from church bodies is inadequate to meet the costs of agency operation. Both participation in federated funding and payments for services from public agencies have become characteristic for sectarian agencies. Increasing pressure to serve a wider community beyond their members has resulted in a reduction of church control. Merger of related church bodies has led to merger of sectarian agencies, especially within the Lutheran group.

Agencies are tending to become less sectarian. Their eligibility policies retain priority for their own members, but—especially in the case of Protestant agencies—the majority of persons served are often not members of the group sponsoring the agency. Jewish and Catholic agency eligibility policies differ from agency to agency.

Nonsectarian agencies are organized apart from religious sponsorship, but they often serve members of churches. To guarantee confidentiality, some people would rather be served by a nonsectarian agency, especially if they are very active in their church. With scarce services, such as the provision of infants for adoption, applicants may be involved with both sectarian and nonsectarian agencies—sometimes simultaneously.

In a few states, especially in the South, the separation of church and state is taken so seriously that sectarian institutions have been exempt from licensing. This clearly denies whatever protection licensing provides for sectarian services. Standards should be applied to sectarian and nonsectarian agencies alike.

Racial and Ethnic Agencies

The avowed goal of both public and private agency policy has been to serve people in need without reference to race or ethnic origin. Agencies that receive public funds are covered under the Federal Civil Rights Act. Many states will not purchase services from agencies that have discriminatory practices. This issue has been considered largely in terms of the adverse effects of white racism. But what of the agency that serves only blacks or another minority? Black colleges and some black institutions may have no written policies against accepting whites, but whites just do not go there. In that case, the program may not be discriminatory in a legal sense. The new trend is to organize programs for blacks, Chicanos, or American Indians or to establish separate units for them within a larger agency program. We have such agencies as Afro-American Family Service, Martin Luther King Community Center, and many others. The Iowa Family and Children's Service in Des Moines operates a children's group home that serves only blacks.

The rationale for separatism is clear. The services fill a need that arose because of racism. Proponents feel that it takes members of the group to fully understand the problem of their brothers and sisters. The agencies have a special appeal to minority givers. Some agencies have been able to get exceptions to the rules of the United Ways—concerning both segregation and the length of time required before an agency can qualify for grants.

All other things being equal, blacks prefer black service givers.[10] They want competent service even more, but ideally they want both, simultaneously. No doubt private agency leaders find reverse segregation both troubling and difficult to implement. The only consistency in such instances may be inconsistency.

Public agencies often find that when a person wants to be served by a member of his or her own race, the request must be denied because of civil rights regulations. To grant the request is best, since we cannot relive the years that have led to polarization. At this stage in our development there is a place for special racial and ethnic programs. We may see a parallel with the situation in the traditional Jewish agencies. As conditions have changed, eligibility requirements have been broadened.

Human Rights in a Voluntary Agency

Unlike the public agency, the voluntary agency cannot be forced to provide service to any person. Because of their private character, voluntary agencies can be and are selective. They usually close intake if they cannot keep up with requests for service and use waiting lists to manage their supply-and-demand problems.

Generally speaking, they have the reputation of treating clients more responsibly than public agencies. This may be because they depend on public acceptance for their funds. In many states, voluntary agencies may be penalized for racial discrimination or other civil rights violations. If they receive federal funds, they may have to give up any sectarian preference policies.

Employees of voluntary agencies generally have fewer explicit rights than public employees since there is no civil service protection. Social workers in larger voluntary agencies often form unions to achieve job protection. Grievances may also be filed with the National Association of Social Workers.

Coordination of Agencies

The coordinator for social service agencies in local communities of any size has been a welfare council or council of social agencies that serves as a planning body. It may also be responsible for data gathering for the Community Fund or United Way. Welfare councils should take positions on controversial community issues and develop plans for meeting critical needs. Councils may be satellites of the fund and may represent only a segment of the health and welfare agencies, frequently excluding the public social welfare agencies and public education. Welfare councils often need more innovative plans, more power, and more funds to be effective, with comprehensive planning coalitions beginning at the neighborhood level.

Community councils and similar organizations involve a wide range of coordination, planning, and service objectives. They often assist residents in obtaining housing and employment and in bettering the environment. They may get governmental grants for special projects and often carry on a lobbying function with city councils and other governmental units. The Economic Opportunity Act helped start urban progress centers to provide similar services. Some OEO programs were later incorporated as voluntary agencies but are often quasi-public because of their political ties.

Research and Innovations in Voluntary Agencies

The voluntary agency has important freedoms that should promote the development of research and demonstration projects to advance knowledge and improve services. It can choose its own program objectives freely. The private agency may deny or extend services to applicants without elaborate explanation. It can choose to provide short-term help to large numbers or intensive service to a smaller group. It has the flexibility to experiment with costly methods without strong public criticism. It can drop programs that do not seem effective and replace them with new programs. Also, it may have the prestige to get government grants more easily than the public agency.

One agency, the Community Services Society of New York, has made a sustained effort to produce basic studies concerning social welfare policies and programs. It was responsible for the development of the Hunt-Kogan

Movement Scale to evaluate changes in client functioning as a result of casework service and other important research. That more agencies did not use the scale suggests a common problem—the underutilization of available techniques for evaluation.

Voluntary agencies participate in special projects from time to time, but few carry on continuing research programs. Even successful demonstration projects are not always continued by sponsoring agencies—often because of cost or lack of commitment. So-called research departments often do little more than collect statistics. In spite of greater constraints, the most promising projects have come out of public agencies.

With the responsibility for large-volume services going to the public agencies, private agency leadership must be developed in research and demonstration efforts. Similar opportunities exist for participation in innovative manpower training projects in cooperation with schools of social work and other academic departments.

National agencies like the Child Welfare League of America and the Family Service Association of America involve their member agencies in important research. Large projects have generally been financed by governmental or foundation grants.

Governance—The Board of Trustees

The essence of voluntarism is nonprofit status, private funding, and control and accountability vested in a board of trustees. The board bears the legal responsibility for the program of the agency and for paying its bills. To get a broad slice of community leadership, agency boards tend to be large. Often they meet but a few times a year, with the operation of the agency falling to the executive director. Specific policy responsibility is vested in an executive committee made up of the officers and a few board members. Sometimes people are nominated to agency boards in the hope that they will make large gifts, but such gifts are rare. Board members are likely to be chosen for their status in the community, their time and energy available to the agency as volunteers, or their expert knowledge in such areas as financial management, institutional operation, or adjunctory services. One board includes a leading stockbroker, a general contractor interested in plant maintenance, and the local superintendent of schools. Some board members do not attend many general board meetings but are willing to give time as consultants in their area of expertise. Such people may be of special value even though they seem inactive.

The board acts as a representative of the agency in the community. To gain influence it is desirable to have many advocates; therefore board memberships should be rotated. Former board members are expected to continue their loyalty, and their successors are expected to develop loyalty. Rotation also prevents long-term control by a very small group. For people who give outstanding service, the category of honorary board member is often used.

The relationship between the board and the executive director can be quite different from one agency to another. In some agencies, the director works closely with the board and serves at its pleasure. In others, the board seems to work for the executive director and serves at his or her pleasure. Unfortunately for agency vitality, the board may become a rubber stamp.

Board membership is also the road to other kinds of public service. In some communities there is a hierarchy of agencies. People start on one board and move to another considered to have greater prestige. They may move from local boards to state boards, or to the United Way board, or its allocation committees. For the person interested in social services short of a career involvement, the board member role provides significant participation.

Mergers of Voluntary Agencies

Mergers of agencies of equal strength are not common except as a consequence of the merger of church bodies. Most mergers in recent years have involved combinations of two weak programs or the assimilation of a weak program by a stronger one. The criterion for a merger should be whether the result is an increase in volume or quality of service.

Strong agencies typically have been unwilling to surrender their independence through merger. In some cases United Funds insist on merger to reduce administrative costs and promote efficiency, but the result can be increased costs and no gain in efficiency. Merged agencies include family and children's services, family services and mental health, and child welfare and child protective programs. Mergers are most likely when two agencies have similar functions.

A Plea for Consolidation

I question whether or not the traditional organization and structuring of the voluntary social welfare field has the potential to be efficient and effective. This view grows out of what, I think, are the implications of the average size of the voluntary agency. Recently, in Chicago, we packaged 10 settlement houses with average budgets of $150,000 into one settlement house with a budget of one and one-half million. Instead of having 10 executives that were paid an average of ten to twelve thousand dollars a year, one man was hired and paid thirty. Instead of having 10 executive jobs, which, when you study them from a job study point of view, weren't executive jobs at all, we had one executive. The former had been part time janitors, part time accountants, part time group workers, and part time public relations directors. If you really looked at their jobs, only about 10% was being an executive. Nobody is so bright or able that they can do all those jobs. Furthermore, you can't get talent for that price to do a leadership job that is going to do the things that the manager has to do by way of planning and leading.

We have come to a conclusion, that we need an agency which is large enough to organize a management capability which provides specialization and competence on the management level, so that we have a director whose job is full time management, a program director, a business and finance director, and a research and development person. Otherwise, we are not going to have the kind of leadership that can help hold up the head of the voluntary field in the face of the competition and pressure of government to do the total welfare job.[11]

Arthur H. Kruse, *What the Community Expects of the United Fund.*

Voluntary Priorities

United Way organizations designed to consolidate and coordinate voluntary giving have conducted priority studies to determine who should receive the contributions collected. Several issues are important:

1. Services for the disadvantaged versus services for contributors and their families.
2. Shifts in governmental support. Strong support should not go to agencies that receive large payments from public sources. Hospitals and clinics are major examples.
3. Preventive versus custodial programs, with priority for the former.
4. Greater emphasis on services for minority groups, with control vested in the groups and agencies organized to serve a designated minority exclusively.
5. Charges for services, calculated on the basis of income, to release more contributed funds for services to low-income families.

Recommendations often tend to elicit hostility from existing agencies, and a power struggle leads to restudy. Priority studies have not always assured success in implementing the new priorities.

The Financing of Private Agencies

To supplement the unsolicited gifts they receive, private agencies appeal directly to the donor for unrestricted gifts to cover current expenses through mail appeals, solicitation by neighbors, benefits, and tag days. In addition, agencies receive bequests, income from investments, fees that users pay or another agency remits on their behalf, and less often, foundation or governmental grants. Fund-raising efforts are often reviewed within the state attorney general's office to see whether monies are expended for the purposes for which they were collected. Both failure to use the money for the purpose specified in an organization's charter and very high fund-raising costs can lead to revocation of a license.

Direct Mail Appeals   Fund raising by mail results in less than a 10 percent response. Such mailings may include an agency magazine or newsletter that recounts cases which have been served successfully. One of the more objectionable methods includes sending of unsolicited items for possible purchase. Appeals often attempt to link fund raising to altruistic impulses related to Christmas, Easter, Mother's Day, and other festive times. Direct appeals are considered important to remind the public of the agency and its work.

Sales and Solicitations   Bake sales and rummage thrift shops, for example, are common methods of fund raising. Individuals may spend more time and effort preparing what is sold than the cash receipts justify, but if articles are donated and people contribute their time, the agency gains. Also, contributions in kind are tax deductible. The main by-product is the development of a cohesive corps of volunteers who enjoy working together and who can aid the agency in a variety of other ways.

Tag days, poppy days, and "white cane" days require a large staff of volunteers to cover the main locations where people congregate. At least a minimum gift is expected, and the symbol obtained buys immunity from further solicitation.

Apart from the purpose and program of the agency, ethical questions about funding concern costs and benefits to a target group and to society. Efforts can involve high promotional expense that may border on fraud. Agencies often prefer independent rather than cooperative fund-raising efforts, because they involve minimum control from outside sources and no responsibility to share the proceeds.

Personal friendships are used to get solicitors for "mothers' marches" sponsored by national health agencies. Women often agree to serve in the knowledge that their neighbors will play a similar role in other fund drives. In that way a variety of their favorite causes are supported.

Federated Financing   To overcome a rash of individual fund drives and make possible "one-shot" fund raising, the system of federated financing was started. The system has had at least four different names. The Community Chest, the Community Fund, the United Fund, or now the United Way emphasizes *one* gift for *all*. The agencies submit their asking budgets to be analyzed. The total of approved askings often becomes the goal of the fund drive. Top officials and other employees are expected to contribute to the general goal by meeting the quota for their plan or business. This system includes provision for payroll deduction of gifts and has had the support of organized labor. United Way annual drives now raise over $1 billion for the member agencies.

Fewer solicitations, lower fund-raising costs, and screening and approval of the programs of the agency by a citizen body are all advantages of the plan. Difficulties come in the restrictions placed on member agencies. Their programs are reviewed by the United Way board. Approval must be obtained for new projects, substituting one program for another, or hiring additional staff. The United Way may be conservative about admitting new agencies into the system. More agencies mean more money must be raised, but competing fund drives damage the rationale. Therefore, agencies may constitute themselves as an elite and discourage fund raising by nonmembers.

Although some large United Way organizations provide only a portion of agency budgets and permit their members to have fund drives at other times of the year than during the general campaign, the more typical plan is to take over virtually all solicitation and make up the deficits of its agencies. Except for user payments, payments from public agencies, investment income, and perhaps earmarked gifts, money comes from the United Way. This gives it great fiscal power.

The monopolistic tendencies of some United Way groups have generated special opposition from national health agencies, unions, and agencies designed especially to serve minorities. Since pledges are deducted from earnings, pressure is brought to make the United Way policies less restrictive or employees will refuse to contribute.

The United Way under Fire

Improbable though it seems, America's leading institutional philanthropist the United Way has come under heavy fire in the last few years. The salvos bear more than a superficial resemblance to criticisms regularly directed at big business and any number of public welfare agencies, perhaps indicating that no institution, no matter how noble its stated aim, can expect unreserved public plaudits at a time when institutions are generally held in low esteem.
Fund-raisers for causes less traditional than the Boy Scouts or the YMCA feel frustrated and shortchanged by the United Way's supposed favoritism for the homespun and unobjectionable. United Way's critics feel that the traditional mission of charity—to aid the needy—has been replaced by a preoccupation with middle-class recreation and welfare. Blacks detect racism, not only in the group's choice of beneficiaries, but in its hierarchy. And a wide panoply of charitable groups claims that the United Way's privileged use of payroll deductions in many American corporations empties reservoirs of largesse before the competition can reach them. The stakes in the controversy are huge: In the last few years the United Way has mushroomed into a billion-dollar charity business, with 2,200 local agencies.
. . . the local United Ways had to offer comprehensive packages of charities. For years they trumpeted the slogan, "Give once and give for all." But this federated approach had a grave pitfall: A single unpopular agency could sabotage the whole gift. The fortunes of the Girl Scouts and an abortion clinic became inextricably linked. The result was predictable. UW citizen boards came to favor safe, uncontroversial agencies—crowd-pleasers instead of boat-rockers. Today the Boy Scouts, the Girl Scouts, the Salvation Army, the Red Cross, the YMCA, the YWCA, and seven other national agencies walk off with 40 percent of United Way monies nationwide—a remarkable cluster considering that funds are voted by 2,200 separate campaigns.
Among the causes that have generally failed to awaken the sympathy of the local citizens' boards that channel United Way funds are birth control, abortion, desegregation, and other issues especially pertinent to minorities. Groups unpopular at a certain time and in a certain place have often been left by the UW board to fend for themselves.[12]

Ron Cherhow, "Cornering the Goodness Market: Uncharitable Doings of the United Way."

Bequests and Annuities   Bequests are still an important source of funds. Bequests may be worked out with an agency by a person long before he or she dies, or they may come as a complete surprise. Generally the agency prefers unrestricted bequests because of the strong need for funds for purposes that change from year to year. However, if the local United Way insists that undesignated bequests be used to meet current expenses and reduce its asking budget, an agency may seek restricted bequests.

Large bequests for capital projects are one of the major ways to get new facilities. The interest of surviving family members may result in conflict between standards for a suitable memorial and agency program needs. The top priority may be a counseling program, but the family may insist on giving a residential center for children.

An annuity plan is used by some agencies—for example, the Salvation Army. A donor purchases an annuity and receives monthly payments during his or her lifetime. Upon the donor's death, the principal goes to the charitable organization. This method reduces the uncertainty of bequests because the arrangement is not revocable. Also, some agencies encourage interested persons to buy life insurance and make the agency the beneficiary.

Endowment Funds   Investing large gifts and using the earnings is a preferred method of funding. Business executives on the board, or a professional investment counselor, manage the investment portfolio. Large and long-established agencies often have substantial worth.

If agencies have difficulty in financing ongoing programs, pressure arises to use unrestricted endowment funds to meet current expenses. Unless these funds are replaced by new gifts, the agency may rapidly lose its investment income and must then depend on current contributions.

Foundations   By establishing a foundation, people of wealth have the chance to gain tax advantages and accumulate funds for useful purposes. Grants may be made on application from the agency or sometimes on an unsolicited basis. Foundation gifts may be small or large. They may involve considerable special negotiation. While some foundations are willing to pay the heating bill or to buy diapers, larger ones usually limit their grants to more innovative purposes. Foundation monies are regarded as venture capital for time-limited new projects. Foundation-sponsored programs often face a crisis toward the end of the grant if the program has not been gradually built into the regular budget of the agency. The result is often abandonment of worthwhile projects.

Foundations also have a special interest in research projects and frequently finance evaluations of programs. Voluntary as well as public agencies also seek research grants from federal programs.

Fees for Service

Earlier in this chapter we saw the importance of purchase of care and service from private agencies. Now we will look at fees for service—payments from individuals for the help they receive. Usually the agencies have a sliding fee scale related to net worth and annual income. The United Way may also insist that a fee policy be developed. Voluntary agencies indicate that fees make for a more businesslike procedure. Those who pay fees may also be asked to make gifts once service is terminated. Payments are also thought to increase the value of the service and provide motivation for treatment.

The agency needs to have an accounting system capable of determining the costs of each program. The difficulties in the fees charged are illustrated in the case of adoption. Some agencies seem to base their fees more on the income of the applicants than on documented evidence of full cost. Most voluntary agencies charge fees to adoptive parents, whereas most public agencies do not. The few which purport to cover costs vary from less than $200 to more than $2,000. Fees are reduced or eliminated for lower-income families.

These questions relate to determining costs of adoptions: (1) Are only the costs of social workers included? (2) Are clerical and administrative costs apportioned? (3) Are all or part of the medical care costs for the unmarried mother included? (4) Are the costs of the service to unsuccessful applicants amortized and paid by successful applicants? (5) Are costs adjusted in terms of the service given? Ordinarily the amount of service required when a couple adopts a second child from the same agency will be substantially less. Original data gathering need not be repeated. Investigations of parental capacity are aided by the presence of the first child. Logically, the fee should be lower for such a placement.

Fees for service may discourage low-income families who either are not aware that fees are based on income or do not want to get "charity" after failing the agency's means test.

The reverse principle of fees is seen in both public and voluntary agencies in the new programs for subsidizing adoptions, with monthly payments for varying lengths of time to adoptive parents to cover costs of care. Subsidies are used for special medical costs, for long-term payments to foster parents who wish to adopt a child but cannot afford to do so, and for other low-income families—especially those who adopt children that are hard to place.

Works of Mercy Versus Services for Ourselves

Students can learn a great deal about local social policy by studying the allocation of money. With the vast growth of public agencies and the increase in taxes for health, education, and welfare, citizen-givers tend to show relatively less interest in supporting private services designed for the poor and the disadvantaged and relatively more interest in services that their friends and their children can use, such as the Boy Scouts, Girl Scouts, the YMCA, and the YWCA. While these agencies have outreach programs for the poor, the bulk of their membership is middle-class. The organizations often make demands on the parents to become volunteer leaders—a hard system to institute successfully in many low-income neighborhoods. Also, these programs tend to have the support of very influential business leaders, so they are likely to have prominence in the community pecking order of agencies and in the United Way.

Social work has often been critical of recreation and character-building activities which are considered to have lower priority for public funds than services that concentrate their effort on the poor or provide treatment. The question is: Should the users of group and recreational services pay the full cost whenever they can afford to do so, leaving charitable contributions for use for the disadvantaged? Thus far, the answer of citizen-givers has been to shift the services for the disadvantaged to the public sector and to continue to give a relatively high proportion of contributions to the services for the middle class.

The Voice of the Recipient of Services

The National Welfare Rights Organization was created to represent the recipients of public welfare. Recipient leadership is hard to develop. Self-governance is an important technique to give institutional residents more of a voice in their own programs, but this may be window dressing with very little real power. Alumni groups made up of former patients or convicts have been formed, but the institutional graduate would prefer to forget mental illness and criminal conviction. Services for unmarried mothers or crippled children have the same limitation—the problems do not constitute an appropriate basis for grouping once the need for service has ended.

Use of former and present recipients on a board of directors is one way to get some feedback from users of a service, but the individuals are often highly selected and are such a numerical minority that only tokenism results. Influence of consumers is not likely to grow until people regard services more as rights than privileges, and until recipient groups attract more powerful advocates from community leadership, including both contributors and legislators.

NATIONAL AGENCIES

National agencies are particularly important in the health field. They include the National Foundation (concentrating primarily on birth defects), the Mental Health Association, the American Cancer Society, the American Heart Association, and programs for many other diseases—tuberculosis and respiratory diseases, arthritis and rheumatism, muscular dystrophy, cerebral palsy, multiple sclerosis, and brain damage leading to perceptual handicaps. National associations emphasize research and study of these diseases. They usually operate drives outside the United Way. Some of the most important diseases, in terms of incidence and social importance, have not led to a specialized organization—German measles, responsible for great prenatal damage; gonorrhea, prevalent among young people; and stroke, a serious problem among older adults.

National health organizations do not typically provide local medical services but issue educational materials, carry on research, and lobby for governmental funds. Some of the agencies have been criticized for high fund-raising and overhead costs, while others are efficient.

The Red Cross is a long-established organization with special quasi-governmental status. At the local level it is especially concerned with disaster relief, hospital service programs, and provision of transportation for other agencies. In recent years it has joined the United Way in many communities.

Other broad citizen groups can be involved in coalitions because of their interest in social work issues: the League of Women Voters frequently sponsors studies leading to legislative reform; the National Parent Teachers Association espouses the needs of the school-age child and legislation supporting education; a host of civil rights organizations, as well as the National Urban Coalition and Common Cause, have concerns for social betterment.

Of particular interest to social workers are the national organizations with accreditation and standard-setting functions. The Family Service Association of America, the Child Welfare League of America, and the American Hospital Association study and evaluate agencies as a condition of continuing membership. Membership in the organization is associated with high standards of performance and protection of the public. Standards are higher than those of licensing bodies.

The American Public Welfare Association is made up of departments of welfare and individuals. This group has served as congressional spokesman for the state directors of welfare and for large city and county welfare organizations.

The National Association of Social Workers

In social work the central membership organization has been the National Association of Social Workers, formed in 1956 from a number of more specialized groups. It offers individual memberships but not agency memberships. All professional social workers as well as social work students are eligible to join. It enforces a code of ethics. It sponsors the Academy of Certified Social Workers for persons who pass an examination after a mandatory period of social work practice. The association publishes *Social Work* and several more specialized journals, sponsors symposia and institutes, and cooperates in the National Conference on Social Welfare. NASW also issues a periodic directory of social workers and produces a basic reference, the *Encyclopedia of Social Work*. It is active in lobbying and has its principal office in Washington. The association functions through chapters organized on a statewide basis, regional coalitions, and a national delegate assembly. In 1979 dues for B.S.W. students were $22.

PROPRIETARY AGENCIES

Proprietary agencies get less attention from social workers than public or voluntary agencies, yet these organizations, established to make a profit, play central roles in the health and child welfare fields. The majority of nursing homes and child care centers are established under private ownership and organized as any other business. Licensing by state health or social services departments is the major means to safeguard the health, well-being, and civil rights of users of these services. Proprietary organizations employ few social work staff, but social workers often enforce the state standards of care and service that qualify the facilities to be licensed as resources for clients. Minimums are also set by the federal government in order for a program to be eligible for federal funds.

Both nursing homes and child care centers have existed for many years under the ownership of individual operators. Generally they have made a modest profit as family businesses. With the availability of public funds for the purchase of care and the removal of large numbers of people from mental hospitals, the large demand for nursing home services has led to the development of chains and franchised organizations. Fee-setting policies on a cost-plus basis have encouraged corporate ownership. With the emphasis on maternal employment and job training for women who head families, there has also been an increase in the need for day care facilities and somewhat more public funds to pay the costs. Multiple ownership and franchising have developed in day care as well, but less rapidly.

Nursing Homes

Nursing homes developed after the enactment of the Social Security Act over four decades ago. Federal mortgage guarantees have been available for purchasing and remodeling such facilities. Growth was slow until the passage of Medicare and Medicaid in the mid 1960s. Under Medicare nursing homes could qualify as post-hospital facilities to provide extended care for a specified period. Medicaid payments for the impoverished elderly were made available through the states to provide either skilled nursing care or custodial services. Nursing homes now depend upon public funds for about two-thirds of their income. Fiscal support has led to the development of larger and more costly nursing homes so that the majority of users are served by facilities with over 100 beds.

Women occupy about 70 percent of nursing home beds and the average age at entry is over eighty years. Two-thirds of the elderly placed in nursing homes die within three years. Significantly, less than 5 percent of the occupants are nonwhite. The users transferred from mental hospitals are substantially younger than the elderly patients who come from family homes.[13]

Nursing homes have been the subject of intense criticism from many quarters, including the Ralph Nader group.[14] Since 1971 strong federal efforts have been made to upgrade home care, but there are still many complaints. The National Association of Social Workers has operated training projects to serve social workers who are consultants to nursing homes, but these staff are limited in numbers, and many consultants spend very little time in the nursing home. A few nursing homes have begun to hire social workers to deal with the social aspects of patient care.

Profit or Nonprofit Nursing Homes

The term "nonprofit" does not mean what it would seem to mean: there are plenty of opportunities for profit in a nonprofit operation. All it means is that the home by law does not produce profits for tax purposes: it does not return cash dividends to its owners. A church or a fraternal order or a union or a group of individuals can set up a nonprofit entity to run a nursing home. Once having achieved nonprofit status, the home enjoys some important advantages. It does not pay income taxes, in some states it does not pay the local property tax, and in various places it is exempt from water taxes. It also enjoys official favor. The federal government and foundations prefer nonprofit operations in giving grants for special projects. In some states, health insurers like Blue Cross will only pay for care in nonprofit institutions.

Owners of proprietary homes complain about the favoritism and immunity from criticism accorded to the nonprofits. One category of complaints has to do with the nonprofits' tax advantages. Because they pay less in taxes but collect from government at the same rate, the nonprofits can pay higher salaries to their administrators, a spokesman from the Ohio Nursing Home Association said, adding that the nonprofits were actually concealing, as salary, profits larger than those earned by their proprietary rivals. Another complaint is motivated by the hypocrisy of the nonprofit designation. Like certain accusations about the clergy, it boils down to the thought that the nonprofits are human also. To me this has a faintly comic ring, for given the general level of dishonesty in the industry, what they seem to be saying about the nonprofits is, they steal just as much as we do! When I see notorious swindlers in the industry setting up nonprofit operations, I cannot help agreeing with what the proprietary operators say.[15]

Mary A. Mendelson, *Tender Loving Greed.*

Day Care
Child care facilities have been subject to much less criticism than nursing homes. They do not have the full responsibility for care of the children they serve and do not need to deal with serious health problems. In comparing the proprietary child care facility with those under the auspices of nonprofit agencies, one is struck by the higher per-capita cost of the latter due to the smaller staff-child ratios and the availability of more specialized services. Franchising is criticized as giving inadequate attention to learning activities and too much attention to commercial management issues.[16] However, nationally developed training and staff development programs should have a better potential for success than the isolated proprietary child care center working on its own.

Problems of Proprietary Agencies
One must recognize a general prejudice against proprietary agencies on the part of social workers. They believe that it is impossible to deliver adequate services at a reasonable cost without nonprofit status and supplemental funding from community philanthropy. The dilemma faced in licensing standards comes from the great need for both nursing home beds and day care center facilities. The public is often critical of stringent licensing standards for profit-making social services because they feel that individual freedom may be

curtailed and that standards are often unrealistic. If licensing standards are too high, the facilities go out of business and people have to make even less adequate arrangements. In the child care field about a quarter of a million children are served by family day care homes. This service is especially important for infants. In these proprietary arrangements, a woman expects to get paid for her time spent in child care. While family day care homes are licensed, they are less closely monitored than the group centers. The majority of children of working mothers, however, are cared for through informal arrangements with baby-sitters who come to their homes and are not subject to any licensing standards.

The rights of both clients and employees have the least protection in proprietary facilities. The person who complains about the food or the care in a nursing home is often summarily discharged. The parent who does not like a day care center program is told to take the child elsewhere. Employees generally do not have any tenure rights and are easily dismissed. As a result, nursing home employees in the larger facilities are good candidates for union membership.

SUMMARY AND APPLICATION

This chapter has indicated the different ways in which social service organizations are financed and operated. You have seen some of the problems of bureaucracies and of the smaller voluntary agencies. You also have some understanding of the importance of profit-making programs—especially to serve the elderly. As an aspiring social worker, one of your most important tasks is to learn how to help people select appropriate resources. If your university does not supply a directory of community agencies, your class may have to compile one as a referral resource. The more you can learn about specific agencies, the better.

As you get to know agencies, look at the way they treat applicants. Are they concerned about human rights and dignity? About the legal rights of clients? Are their costs reasonable? Do they extend themselves to provide services? Do they provide good care and service? What are their employment practices? Do they provide incentives for effective performance? How do they reward merit? Do they provide specific ways for you to increase your knowledge and skills?

—*Donald Brieland*

KEY TERMS

public agencies
voluntary agencies
proprietary agencies
welfare rights organization
bureaucracies

AFDC
class action suit
licensing of agencies
revenue sharing
Title XX (Social Security Act)

civil service
income maintenance
advocacy
zero-based budgeting
SSI
purchase of care

not-for-profit charter
nonsectarian agencies
board of trustees
merger of agencies
United Way
nursing homes

REFERENCES AND NOTES

1. Peter M. Blau, *Bureaucracy in Modern Society*, Random House, New York, 1956, p. 57.
2. *Townsend v. Swank*, 404 U.S. 282 (1971).
3. *Elrod v. Burns*, 98 S.CT. 2673 (1976).
4. President Jimmy Carter, "Federal Civil Service Reform," Message to Congress, March 2, 1978, *Presidential Documents*, vol. 14, #9, March 6, 1978, pp. 444–449.
5. Harold Hagan and John E. Hansan, "How the States put the Programs Together," *Public Welfare*, vol. 36, Summer 1978, pp. 44–45.
6. Philip Brown, Joseph Julius, and Judith Voelker, "The Department of Human Services: A New Model," unpublished paper, 1973.
7. *Goldberg v. Kelly*, 397 U.S. 254 (1970).
8. Malcolm X, *Autobiography*, Grove Press, New York, 1965, pp. 17–18.
9. Arthur Kruse, *The Future of Voluntary Welfare Services*, Community Fund, Chicago, 1965, p. 17.
10. Donald Brieland, "Black Identity and the Helping Person," *Children*, vol. 16, 1969, pp. 171–176.
11. Arthur Kruse, *What the Community Expects of the United Fund*, Community Fund, Chicago, 1968, pp. 8–9.
12. Ron Cherhow, "Cornering the Goodness Market: Uncharitable Doings of the United Way," *Saturday Review*, vol. 5, October 28, 1978, pp. 15–16.
13. Robert N. Butler, *Why Survive? Being Old in America*, Harper & Row, New York, 1975, p. 267.
14. See Claire Townsend, *Old Age: The Last Segregation*, Grossman, New York, 1971.
15. Mary A. Mendelson, *Tender Loving Greed*, Knopf, New York, 1974, p. 196.
16. Joseph Featherstone, "Kentucky Fried Children," *New Republic*, vol. 153, September 1967, pp. 12–16.

FOR FURTHER STUDY

Herman Levin, "Voluntary Organizations in Social Welfare," *Encyclopedia of Social Work*, 1977, pp. 1573–1582.
Michael S. March and Edward Newman, "Financing Social Welfare: Government Allocation Procedures," *Encyclopedia of Social Work*, 1977, pp. 457–467.
William L. Morrow, *Public Administration, Politics and the Political System*, Random House, New York, 1975.
Robert M. Rice, "Impact of Governmental Contracts on Voluntary Social Agencies," *Social Casework*, vol. 56, pp. 378–395.
Gabriel O. Rudney, *Scope of the Private Voluntary Charitable Sector, 1974*, Commission on Private Philanthropy and Public Needs, Washington, D.C., 1975.

Mike Suzuki, "The Future of Social Services," *Public Welfare*, vol. 33, Spring 1975, pp. 10–14.

Aaron Wildavsky, *The Politics of the Budgetary Process*, Little, Brown, Boston, 1974.

Michael J. Murphy, "Financing Social Welfare: Voluntary Organizations," *Encyclopedia of Social Work*, 1977, pp. 478–484.

"The Politics and Organization of Services: A Special Issue," *Public Welfare*, vol. 36, Summer 1978.

FOR DISCUSSION

1. What are the three types of social agencies discussed in the chapter? How do they differ?
2. What are the advantages and disadvantages of a bureaucracy?
3. If the public child welfare agency operates a day care center, does it license itself? Explain your answer.
4. Explain Revenue Sharing and the provisions of Title XX of the Social Security Act that affect voluntary agencies.
5. Get a copy of P.L.95-454. What are its main provisions for civil service reform?
6. In the majority of states, what is the organization that provides public social welfare services?
7. Explain and illustrate the diamond of organizational change.
8. Do you agree with the hierarchy of public agencies in the chapter? What criticism do you have?
9. Explain how grants to the states are made under the Social Security Act.
10. Why are administrative hearings an important part of clients' rights?
11. How are public and voluntary agencies brought together in cooperative partnerships?
12. Who legally authorizes a voluntary nonprofit agency to operate?
13. How are legal aid programs for the poor funded?
14. How do sectarian and nonsectarian agencies differ?
15. How are social services coordinated in most larger communities?
16. Explain the purpose of a board of trustees in a voluntary agency?
17. Why do many voluntary social agencies charge fees based on the ability to pay?
18. Explain federated financing in the voluntary field.
19. What is the major controversy in "works of mercy versus services for ourselves"?
20. What have been some of the major criticisms of nursing homes?
21. Explain what is meant by a "day care home."
22. What are some of the human rights in a social agency?

PROJECTS

1. Study an annual report of a public agency. Ask an official of the agency at the policy-making level to respond to questions provided in advance.
2. Identify the changes in organization of social services in your state over the past two decades.
3. Debate the question: "Resolved, that the federal government should operate the AFDC program."
4. If you have foreign students in your class, have them compare public agency programs in their country of origin with those in your state.

5. If you were responsible for a public agency's program, how would you measure the effectiveness of its services?
6. Select several members of the class to analyze the approved plan for Title XX in your state.
7. Choose a member of your class as chairperson. Organize a panel of voluntary agency executives to talk to your group. Choose a major issue and frame several questions to use as the basis for discussion. Possible topics are: meeting rising costs, problems of purchase of care, how boards of trustees function, and to what extent services to the poor should have priority.
8. Compare the financial statements in the annual report of several voluntary agencies to determine the source of funds. What proportion of income is derived from contributions, fees for service, purchase of care, endowments, foundation grants, and new bequests? How much do the agencies differ?
9. Organize a role-play in which the chairperson of the local human relations commission discusses the organization of the board of a specific agency that has involved the same upper- and middle-class white membership for several years. Include a discussion of recruiting former clients as board members and of a rotation system that would result from limiting terms.
10. Find out the requirements for membership in the local United Way. Analyze the provisions in terms of needs for new services.
11. Study the periodicals *Social Work*, *Social Casework*, *Public Welfare*, and *Child Welfare*. Classify and compare the topics discussed in the last year.

PART TWO
Methods of
Social Work

Social work has traditionally emphasized three methods: casework, group work, and community work. The various social work theories, derived from many fields, lead to different views of what kinds of intervention are appropriate and effective.

Casework enjoys the preeminent position because it is the oldest of the social work methods and the technique used by the majority of personnel.

The demand for group work has increased both within and outside of social agencies. New types of groups have created new opportunities and, some feel, new hazards that should be avoided.

Community work has helped to give neighborhoods more control over their own services as well as achieving larger political and social goals. It attracts social workers who are especially interested in advocacy and social action.

After the development of these methods, other innovations provide additional options for the student interested in a social work career. Part Two will summarize the different methods of individuals and philosophies used in helping individuals, the use of group activities in the helping process, efforts to assist in social action, and generalist approaches involving all the social work methods.

CHAPTER 3
Casework

The many faces of casework.

What kind of creature am I? Where did I come from? How do I function? How can I understand and control myself, my own behavior, my life, and my future?

—Naomi J. Brill*

We all face personal problems that we cannot resolve by ourselves. Sometimes family members, friends, or acquaintances can help, but frequently more specialized skill is needed to obtain goods and services, to deal with feelings about ourselves, or to cope with marriage or family relationships. We face problems at school or at work, health concerns, or sudden catastrophes that affect our ability to care for ourselves or for others. Furnishing personal help is what social work is all about. Most social workers spend at least part of their time working with individuals—that is, practicing social casework.

The vast majority of caseworkers are employed by a social agency supported by taxes or by private contributors. Fees may be charged based on the ability of the client to pay. Some social workers, primarily in the area of mental health, offer their services as private practitioners. They see children and adults and receive payment as does a private physician. Most private practitioners have had extensive experience in social agencies.

ACTIVITIES OF CASEWORKERS

This chapter deals first with what caseworkers do—the people they serve, and how they serve them. Several fields of practice will be considered.

Child Welfare

The social worker in a public child welfare agency is faced with serious problems of children and their families. The first task is the assessment of the quality and character of family life. Can the natural family be supported and strengthened through counseling? Are there additional services that would provide what is needed to improve the situation? Social workers help people link up to appropriate community services, Big Brothers, Big Sisters, recreational programs, and a number of group services. The social worker also helps people to use homemaker services, health care, rehabilitation services, and financial aids. In some agencies, training in parental skills is provided.

The child welfare worker may also be needed to assist adolescents who are trying to move out of the family and into independent living. Adolescents may need to be linked to support networks that will enable them to move into adulthood.

If the family cannot be supported well enough to function, the child

*Naomi J. Brill. *Working with People: The Helping Process*, Lippincott, Philadelphia, 1973, p. 1.

welfare worker may need to consider placing some or all of the children in a foster home. This is intended to be a temporary solution that allows the time to help the parent or parents to regain their ability to function.

When cases of child abuse or neglect are reported, the public child welfare worker is legally mandated to investigate in order to ascertain the facts. If there is evidence of abuse or neglect, the social worker will usually try to correct the situation through counseling and the provision of supportive services. If this does not bring about a situation in which the child can grow physically and emotionally, the social worker may have to file a formal legal complaint and testify in court on behalf of the child's rights. Legal action may result in a court order to move the child into a temporary foster home. In drastic situations, the child may be removed from his or her parents' care permanently and placed for adoption.

The social worker in the voluntary agency shares many of the tasks and concerns of his or her counterpart in the public agency. However, as a general rule, the social worker in the voluntary agency is primarily concerned with clients who are motivated to seek help. Some voluntary agencies offer counseling to unmarried parents. Although the present trend is for women who are single mothers to keep their babies, the voluntary agency can also help the mother who wishes to offer her child for adoption. The social worker will assist the mother to arrange for medical and hospital services, regardless of her decision to keep or relinquish her baby. If the mother decides to keep the baby, the social worker will aid in providing housing, financial, and child care services.

The social worker in the family service agency deals with the problems of marital partners and difficulties in relations between parents and children. The caseworker may counsel with family members individually, but in many instances families are seen and worked with as a unit; the behavior of family members as well as communication difficulties must be the focus of attention. Increasingly, social workers engage in financial and budget counseling. They may participate in family-life education and in programs for the elderly. Homemaker services are also often sponsored by a family agency.

The Aged
To provide services to help older persons sustain and enrich independent living and maintain or establish linkages with the community, caseworkers may do many things. They may use a home visit to give information about the older person's rights and the services which are available. Often the initial contact comes in response to a crisis—the death or illness of a spouse, return from hospitalization, or a relative's effort to provide an older person with nursing or shelter care. The social worker may help arrange for a homemaker, meals-on-wheels, or visiting nurse services. The social worker may arrange a membership in an organized group of older persons, or may even help start a group. The social worker may recruit volunteers to provide transportation to group meetings, to visit a clinic, or to go shopping.

The older person may need counseling concerning nursing homes or shelter care and the opportunity for trying out the facilities. The caseworker also frequently helps obtain the material things needed for the older person's well-being. He or she works with relatives' concerns and anxieties and marshals other community resources. Social workers are also often asked to organize and serve with older persons on planning, nursing home, or medical care committees in the community.

The Handicapped

Personnel in a community agency serving the developmentally disabled or physically or emotionally handicapped encourages disabled people to increase and sustain their motivation, helps in the development of interpersonal competence and the other basic skills needed for increasingly independent living, and assists in negotiating a client's interpersonal transactions. The social worker may give information and support to the client's family, and enlist educational, medical, training, vocational, and employment resources on behalf of clients. Frequently social workers help clients to utilize small institutions as well as foster homes and independent living. Community-based facilities with rehabilitation programs have replaced larger custodial institutions; bringing services closer to the consumer.

Health

A social worker as a part of the hospital or health center team helps the patient and family cope with the emotional and social aspects of illness, including fear and anxiety about medical procedures, denial of the implications or consequences of the condition, and facing a terminal illness or death. Illness may result in serious restrictions of activity and earning capacity or changing roles and life-styles. A social worker in a hospital inevitably is involved in discharge planning for patients leaving the hospital. The social worker may help the patient and family locate and use nursing care facilities or visiting nurse and homemaker services. Recently social workers have also become a part of the staff in hospital emergency rooms, helping patients and families deal with accidents and emergency illnesses.

Mental Health

The social worker in a community mental health center, together with other mental health professionals, assists in dealing with emotional problems. He or she may counsel with people to help them explore and clarify their feelings, and develop more satisfying modes of behavior. The mental health worker may assist people to develop meaning and a sense of purpose in their lives when they perceive life as meaningless and barren, or may assist chronically ill persons with crises, and encourage them to participate in community activities. The social worker may work with adults, adolescents, or children and their families. Alcoholism or drug programs, outreach or drop-in centers, and crisis or suicide line programs are examples of mental health services.

The social worker in a residential treatment center, together with other staff members, works with deprived and traumatized children. An individual treatment program for each child must be worked out that includes meeting specialized educational, vocational, and social needs. Treatment may include the use of group and individual methods. The social work staff is involved in the transition of children from the structured group living of an institution to the greater freedom of living in a group home, a foster home, or with their own families. They help the children to deal with how the family will fit into their lives and how they will fit into the family.

Youth Services

The tasks of the social worker in a youth service bureau or youth outreach program are somewhat like those of public child welfare workers, but the focus is on "emancipated" youth. Young people may have a wide range of problems, including being at odds with their families, the police, and other community institutions, and tending to be overlooked by traditional community services. The social worker needs the skills to establish credibility and to develop a relationship with them. At the same time effective relationships with police and courts are essential. Counseling usually is crisis rooted and task focused, and the youth worker is frequently the advocate for the young person in obtaining service. The worker has to be related to school, financial, housing, job, medical, and mental health resources.

The Courts

The social worker in the courts often serves as a probation officer, and is responsible for following the accused person through the court system. The probation officer gathers personal, social, and family data about the accused to be used by the court in making its decisions. Offenders placed on probation receive support from their probation officers. Close liaison with police, enforcement officials, and the court is necessary. The probation officer may also help the probationer use educational, vocational, employment, recreational, mental health, public assistance, and medical resources in the community.

Police Services

In police departments the social worker deals especially with noncriminal activity with which the police inevitably become involved. Crises include family and neighborhood disputes, alcohol or drug abuse, emergency psychiatric problems, including suicide threats or attempts, child abuse or abandonment, assault and rape, stranded transients, runaways, and older persons in crisis. The crisis is usually dealt with by getting the person to a source of help, reducing the crippling anxiety and feelings of helplessness, and supporting the person to muster his or her own personal strengths and resources. The worker in a police social service unit has to be familiar with all resources in the community and be able to use them immediately.

Social Services in Industry

Industry and labor unions provide new and promising settings for social workers. Many serious problems are related to the workplace. Job adjustment, marriage counseling, treatment for alcoholism, and planning for retirement are only a few of the major activities of the industrial social worker. We can expect this specialty to grow as employers become increasingly concerned with the well-being of their employees. They are coming to see that social services are justified as a good business investment.

From these brief examples one can see that caseworkers must have the knowledge and skill to establish meaningful communication with clients, to appraise and assess the client-problem situation, and to plan the process of helping the client. They must have knowledge of a wide range of community resources and services and how they can be used to help individual clients. In brief, caseworkers have to understand how to help individuals mobilize resources to help themselves, how to work with families, and starting with their own agency, how to utilize and mobilize the organizations and systems in the community for the benefit of clients.

CASEWORK TECHNIQUES AND THEORIES

Following the philosophy of the Charity Organization Societies, caseworkers in the early decades of this century amassed long and detailed social evidence from which diagnoses could be inferred and treatment plans developed. Case histories contained facts to objectify inferences and decisions that previously would have been based on moral judgments. The histories increasingly included material related to the economic, moral, social, and hereditary causes of poverty. Even more important, the histories indicated the personal and social resources needed to serve the client.[1]

Influence of Freud

In the 1920s and 1930s the impact of individual psychology affected the direction and emphasis of social casework. Freud was the dominant influence. Others developed and refined his formulations. Sexual and aggressive drives (the *id*)—the instinctual drives seen as the primary forces underlying the behavior of man—constituted the initial emphasis. The *ego*—the rational, reality-oriented part of the person—was important because it mediated between the clamor of the id and the moralism of the *superego*—Freud's term for conscience.

The defense mechanisms were devices employed to channel the basic drives. Repression was seen as the chief mechanism of control to keep basic sexual and aggressive impulses from conscious awareness. A person's early childhood relationships, especially with his or her mother, determined how drives were controlled or channeled and how well adjusted he or she would be as an adult. Relationships and deprivations in early childhood were associated with later emotional and mental illnesses and personality characteristics. Clinical evidence was developed to support these associations.

The Freudian formulation of personality development changed the direction of social casework. It included two assumptions that became basic principles of social casework: human behavior is *purposeful* and *determined*, and some of the determinants of behavior are *unconscious*. Social casework was no longer a method to be used only for the poor. These new psychiatric insights applied to all people. Early childhood experiences and memories, rather than external social forces and events between the recipient of service and the caseworker, became the material for social histories and diagnosis.

A close and accepting relationship was necessary to talk about intimate and personal events and to recall early childhood memories that had been repressed. Conscious recollection of events and how one felt about them aided in the solution of problems. The relationship with the caseworker was used to resolve conflicts. Interviews were held one or two hours a week for a year or longer. The need to safeguard the confidentiality of the content of the client's communication was recognized and incorporated into casework practice.

Psychosocial Treatment

As the concept of the ego and ego psychology gradually developed, the focus of social casework moved more toward the social functioning of the individual. Psychosocial treatment became the dominant school of thought within social casework.

> Casework has always been a psychosocial treatment method. It recognizes the interplay of both internal psychological and external social causes of dysfunctioning and endeavors to enable the individual to meet his needs more fully and to function more adequately in his social relationship.
>
> Clients come for casework treatment because there has been a breakdown in their social adjustment.[2]

Ego psychology is concerned with the adaptive capacities of the individual. How is the individual coping? Are his or her coping mechanisms appropriate to the situation? Are they effective? How realistic are the person's perceptions of himself or herself and of the outside world? How valid are his or her judgments based on these perceptions? What is his or her capacity for control and direction of internal drives and feelings concerning specific elements in the external environment? Further questions also confront the caseworker. What is the nature and extent of the internal stress? What constitutes effective and ineffective coping? How does the person seek and use help?

Increasingly, coping activities have been linked with specific problems or outside pressures. For example, the sudden loss of a spouse or loved one predictably diminishes coping ability. Usually a numbing sense of loss, removal of self from ties with others, physical symptoms, and blaming others or oneself for the loss culminates in reintegration and reinvestment with others. Coping activities have also been linked with the more predictable changes and risks an individual faces. The developmental scheme of Erik Erikson covering birth to old age has affected the practice of many caseworkers, particularly in its stress on basic trust for the infant and identity for the adolescent.

Psychosocial treatment, the most popular conceptual framework, has sharpened the process of individualization and helped to develop insights into human behavior and the helping relationship.

Psychosocial treatment is deterministic. Individuals are governed by their basic drives and by their early life experiences. Psychosocial treatment lends itself best to persons who are intelligent and sophisticated, articulate, and capable of introspection. The focus is on the individual and his or her adaptive capacity. The pressures of environmental change receive less attention. Psychosocial treatment has not lent itself very well to evaluation, that is, to the development of either an empirical base for practice or effective criteria for judging the outcome.

Functional Casework

Although ego psychology within the framework of psychosocial treatment has been dominant, *functional casework,* based partially on the system of psychology of Otto Rank, has also had a continuing influence. The drive to life, health, and fulfillment is seen as basic to human beings. Human beings struggle to grow. The process of growth is the central core of activity in working with individual clients. Human beings use human relationships, including the relationship with the social worker, to find and to strengthen their own purpose and to move to its realization. Casework is "a method of administering some specific social service with such psychological understanding of and skill in the helping process that the agency service has the best chance of being used for individual and social welfare."[3]

Emphasis is placed on giving and receiving help. The offer of service unites the person with the skill of the caseworker and the function and services of the agency. This process includes a definition of the service being offered and whether the client can use it. Time limits are set for the help. Empathy with the client in using the help as well as honesty and openness of worker communication are especially important.[4]

The functional approach has emphasized the individual's use of choices in working on his or her problem. Agency function as well as worker skill are positive elements in helping individuals.

Social Casework as Problem Solving

The problem-solving approach to social casework emerged in the 1950s from the work of Helen Harris Perlman at the University of Chicago. Problem solving involved a branching out from the psychosocial treatment and functional approaches. It also takes into account the individual, the problem, and the agency or institution from which services are received.

> A *person* beset by a *problem* seeks help with that problem from a *place* (either a social agency or some other social institution) and is offered such help by a professional social worker who uses a *process* which simultaneously engages and enhances the person's own problem-solving functions, and supplements the person's problem-solving resources.[5]

Perlman summarizes problem solving:

> On the basis of the assumption of a deficit in problem-solving means—motivation, capacity, and/or opportunity—the problem-solving process consists of actions on the helper's part:
>
> 1. To release, energize, and give direction to the client's *motivation*, that is, to

minimize disabling anxiety and fears and provide the support and safety that encourage a lowering of disabling ego defenses, a heightening of reward expectations, and a freeing of ego energies in the task at hand.

2. To release and then repeatedly exercise the client's mental, emotional and action *capacities* for coping with his problem and/or himself in connection with it; thus to release and then exercise the ego functions of perception, feeling, cognition, comprehension, selection, judgment, choice, and action as they are required by the problem.

3. To find and make accessible to the client the *opportunities* and resources necessary to the solution or mitigation of the problem; thus to aim to make accessible those opportunities in his environment that are essential conditions and instruments for satisfactory role   performance.[6]

The problem-solving approach has received wide acceptance because Perlman clearly specified the guidelines for helping.

Crisis-oriented Short-term Casework

Recently, increasing attention has been given to the vulnerability of individuals in coping with personal crises as well as their capability for using help.

Crisis-oriented short-term casework combines observations about what happens to people in times of personal stress with the increasing evidence that many people can be helped in relatively brief periods of time.

In crisis the individual experiences a high degreee of personal upset and helplessness resulting in anxiety, shame, guilt, hostility, and a lessening of the ability to think. A person's capacity for confidence about resolutions of his or her predicament is diminished.

The primary values of this approach are immediacy in entering into the helping situation and dealing with emotional upset, brevity of the service, and evidence of effectiveness.[7]

Task-centered Casework

Task-centered casework has been developed by Reid and Epstein.[8] This model incorporates some elements of crisis intervention and the problem-solving and functional approaches. It is based in part on studies by Reid and Shyne[9] of short-term casework.

The problems perceived by the client are considered in the initial interview or two. The target problem is agreed upon by client and worker. A task related to the resolution of the target problem is specified, and the activities of both client and worker in accomplishing the task are delineated. The task represents both an immediate goal for the client and a means of achieving a larger goal. The worker and client decide on the time necessary to achieve the task—usually not more than eight to twelve interviews, say, two to four months. More than one task may be worked on simultaneously, although diffusion of efforts on multiple tasks is not seen as desirable. A succession of

I hear you're good at problem solving. (Glenn Hanson.)

target problems or tasks can be worked on through repeating the process. This model provides a basis for evaluation of the service given by both client and worker. The use of defined time limits may well enhance productive activity in problem-solving by both worker and client.

Behavior Modification

During the past few years, learning theory also has been increasingly used to help individuals. All behavior, including social behavior, is considered to be learned. Problematic behavior follows the same laws of learning as nonproblem behavior and is amenable to the careful application of knowledge about learning and modification.[10]

The focus of the helping person is on observable behavior. Behavior generally can be categorized into two classes, operant and respondent behavior.[11]

Operant behavior generally is voluntary. A person emits a response to a situation, and something happens that is contingent upon the response. The modifying techniques used with operant behavior are: positive reinforcement, negative reinforcement, extinction, differential reinforcement, response shaping, and adverse stimuli (punishment).

Respondent behavior is not voluntary but is preceded by a stimulus which elicits the response. The techniques used for respondent behavior are systematic desensitization, operant desensitization, and covert desensitization. Generalized techniques used for both operant and respondent behavior include exchange systems, verbal instructions, behavioral reversal (role-playing), rule making, model presentation, and positive structuring.

Behavior modification has been criticized as an instrument to control the individual and deal with symptoms rather than causes of problems. Neither of these criticisms is well founded. The cooperation of the client is important in helping in the behavioral approach. Conversely, being free from problematic behaviors and learning new adaptive behaviors can give a client more control over his or her destiny. The potential for control, either open or subtle, exists in any system of helping. Behaviorists would answer the second criticism by pointing out that any given symptom implies an underlying causal factor or illness, and that such causes have not been very adequately demonstrated in human behavior.

The behavioral approach directs its focus on behavior as consisting of describable, definable entities. It directs attention to outcome, making evaluation an integral part of helping. It has produced favorable outcomes with a range of problematic behaviors after other approaches have had limited effect.

MAJOR EMPHASES IN CASE WORK

Individualization

The person to be helped is the unit of attention for the activities of the social worker. Carol Meyer has suggested individualization as both the goal and the process for social work practice.[12] Basic to all social work is the belief in human dignity and in the maximum realization of each individual's potential throughout his or her life.[13] Casework is characterized by expressed interest, empathy which is conveyed to clients, honesty on the part of the caseworker, and activity that maximizes the client's participation and safeguards his or her personal integrity and privacy.

Individualization can best be implemented through activity which increases the client's range of choices using his or her capacity for choosing, and by enhancing the right of self-determination. Caseworkers may become anxious about their activity lest it infringe on clients' rights of self-determination. Then resultant worker behavior with clients is characterized by passivity, emotional disengagement or distance, and lack of involvement. Clients interpret these behaviors as indicating lack of concern or interest, thus confirming the client's own feelings of worthlessness or helplessness. These elements in a worker-client relationship impede helping and make the situation worse.

Communication   People who cannot bring themselves to ask for help directly, or clearly explain their predicament, do not know what choices are relevant for them.

Asking for help is difficult. Most of us would be happy if someone would magically understand our need and volunteer the necessary help. Many times we cannot articulate our problems, especially if we blame ourselves or are ashamed. We deny we have a problem or project the responsibility for the problem on someone else.

Taking Help

Most people who are in trouble both want help and are terrified of it. Indeed in most cases the fear of any kind of help that would really induce change or movement is greater at first than the desire for it.

We can understand this fear better, perhaps, if we consider what asking for help demands. The person who asks for the kind of help that will really make a difference to him must, in fact, do four things. He must recognize that something is wrong with him or lacking in his situation which he can do nothing about by himself. He must be willing to tell someone else about his problem. He must accord to this other person at least a limited right to tell him what to do or to do things for him. And finally he must be willing to change in some way himself. This means giving up whatever adjustments he has been able to make to the present situation—adjustments that may have and probably have cost him a great deal to make and have become part of himself and wholly necessary to him—in favor of a new kind of life, which he may have some reason to believe will be more satisfactory but which, at the same time, is an unknown quantity, full of possible dangers.

But the difficulty is greatly increased if up to the time of asking for help a person's experience of permitting another to take some control of his affairs has been that he is taken advantage of; if telling another has meant that his confidence is abused; if his attempts to live a supposedly more productive life have always resulted in defeat. And these have been the experiences of all too many of those who are in need of help.

Yet for the most part this tremendous demand made on the person to be helped has gone unrecognized. People who refuse help are still thought of as ungrateful when all they really are is afraid. Others are thought to be insensitive, not to know there is something wrong or to lack simple common sense, when in fact, they are acutely aware of the wrongness but even more afraid of what it would cost them to put it right. Many are stigmatized as content with unsatisfactory or degrading conditions when all that they are is scared to act on their discontent . . . [14]

Alan Keith-Lucas, *Giving and Taking Help.*

The caseworker needs to recognize a person's difficulty in asking for help, to create a climate which is not threatening and help a client discuss the situation. The feelings expressed must be recognized empathically. The shame, guilt, and anxiety or anger behind the mechanisms of denial, displacement, or projection expressed by the person asking for help must also be recognized. These elements receive special emphasis in psychosocial treatment. Support must be given to the person in helping to focus and clarify his or her thoughts and feelings and the reality of the situation he or she is facing.

Information   Not knowing what choices are available seriously limits self-determination. None of us can exercise options of which we are not aware. In such instances help is needed in clarifying the situation and in defining the dimensions of the problems. The range of choices that are applicable and their potential consequences must be explored. The client then chooses the course of action to be followed. The emphasis may be task-centered. The tasks that need to be accomplished in implementing a course of action are identified. The client and worker together decide the responsibility each will assume in carrying out these tasks in achieving the mutually defined goal.

Effect of Crisis   People in a crisis situation are always seriously incapacitated in their ability to choose or to act, or to perceive choices or courses of action open to them. Lydia Rapoport identified the antecedents of a state of crisis:

> Three interrelated factors produce a state of crisis: (1) one or a series of hazardous events which pose some threat; (2) a threat to current or past instinctual needs which are symbolically linked to earlier threats that result in vulnerability or conflict; and (3) an inability to respond with adequate coping mechanisms. [15]

Frequently the crisis is a loss or a threat of loss of personal relationships, resources, abilities, status, or roles which leaves a person feeling personally incapable, and vulnerable. The person reacts to the crisis with disbelief or an inability or refusal to face the situation. Frequently there is an emotional numbness and confusion or agitation and other behavioral and physiological responses. Often there is angry blaming or deep feelings of guilt. The person's capacity for resolution of the predicament and ability to think and perform are diminished. [15]

Helping a person in a state of crisis is characterized by: (1) access to the person needing help; (2) immediate and direct dealing with the feelings of the individual, while at the same time clarifying the problem and exploring its dimensions; (3) rationally directed and purposefully focused activity on the part of the caseworker while taking an active role in helping resolve the crisis or carrying out the tasks resulting from it; (4) worker activity geared to enlarging the client's sense of autonomy and mastery of the situation. [16]

Anxiety   People may be so caught up by their anxiety that they cannot choose; having to choose or make a decision virtually immobilizes them. Empathic understanding by the caseworker is the beginning step. Emotional support is necessary to help the person feel he or she is not alone either in having the anxiety or in facing it. Systematic desensitization is used increasingly to help clients reduce and control their anxious feelings. [17]

Guilt   Some people may be so guilt-ridden that only self-defeating choices are perceived. Some people are so depressed that no potentially positive outcomes can be envisaged. Generalized depressive feelings are increasingly encountered in both older and younger people who perceive themselves as failures. Help for these clients requires empathy and a great deal of support on the part of the caseworker. Genuine interest, concern, and an ability to inject an element of hope into the situation are most important. The self-defeating consequences of the client's behavior need to be recognized, but even more important, the client should be helped to refocus his or her energies and directions to more rewarding activities and choices. The caseworker can help clients to break up self-defeating behavior patterns and begin to do the things which allow them to feel good about themselves.

Self-concept   The self-concept of some people may be so low that they are unable to perceive themselves as possessing the right, much less the potential capacity, for choosing. These people have been buffeted by life and society. Apathy may best describe their attitude and behavior. Injecting realistic feelings of hope that the person might accomplish something if he or she risks trying; helping the person risk setting some goals, even though they may be modest; and assisting the person to achieve these goals are important steps in helping. Often persons with low self-esteem receive cues or messages from significant persons in their social environment which reinforce their feelings of worthlessness. If these messages come from family members, family-focused helping or family therapy may be indicated. [18] The caseworker's adeptness in identifying, enlarging on, and encouraging the use of skills and abilities possessed by the client frequently is the crucial factor in the outcome.

Purpose   A person who lacks meaning and purpose in life may see choosing as pointless or irrelevent and choices as hollow or empty. Frankl and May refer to this personal emptiness as existential frustration or anxiety. [19] Individuals should be encouraged to face their humanness; that is, that they are responsible and can be helped to develop personal values and a belief in their importance. The focus is on present and future opportunities and demands. Within this framework the person is helped to find concrete meaning for his or her personal existence. The specific nature of the choices is not as important as the fact that they are made.

Escape   Some people engage in running away or other types of escape rather than thinking or facing their feelings. Running away, verbal or physically abusive responses to difficult situations, and chronic antisocial behavior are frequent examples. The habitual use of alcohol or drugs as automatic responses to problems of living also is common. Giving help in these kinds of situations is not easy because usually help is not wanted. The caseworker may be faced with a client who denies that a problem exists or places the blame for the situation on someone else. The caseworker has to confront the client with the reality of his or her behavior while at the same time conveying interest and concern. Confrontation should not be perceived by the client as blaming or accusation or as confirmation of feelings of ineptitude or failure. The client needs to perceive the caseworker's genuine interest and concern in order to face his behavior. The client's situation must be explored and other choices for action identified. When the client makes a decision, the caseworker must provide or arrange for support and use the client's needs and wants to implement the new course of action.

Influence of Environment   The external environment of many persons is so limited or so impoverished, or needed resources are so far beyond their control, that few choices are available for them. Needed support systems and resources for some people do not exist within family, friendship, or neighborhood groups, perhaps not even in the community in which they reside. In this situation, the caseworker may need to approach church or community groups, as well as appropriate public officials, to obtain resources. After serving a number of clients in this predicament, caseworkers often take the initiative within their agencies or communities in a needs assessment which could lead to more adequate services in the future.

Some people may feel that they lack the power to obtain the resources they need for their maintenance or for resolving their problems. The caseworker may act as a broker for the client in negotiating with families, neighborhood resources, or community agencies or institutions. The worker may also act as an advocate for the client. Two potential dangers are inherent in representing the powerless. The caseworker may be so overwhelmed by the injustice of the situation as to act without the client's full permission or knowledge; or the caseworker may tend to use the client as an instrument for changing the system without adequate regard for the client's welfare.

Institutionalization

People in an institution obviously have limitations placed on their activities and choices. But limitations that are not directly related to the individual's purposes and goals are dysfunctional.

Schools, nursing homes, medical hospitals, mental hospitals, residential treatment centers for children and adolescents, centers for developmentally disabled persons, and correctional facilities may restrict rights of choice. For clients who may be singled out unfairly or for whom the restrictions obviously negate the desired institutional goal, the caseworker may take on the role of broker or advocate with the appropriate persons in the organization. If the limitations or restrictions adversely affect a number of persons, the caseworker may begin negotiating to bring about changes in the system.

Previous Learning

Persons who have not learned functional or adaptive behavior and skills, or who have learned maladaptive or dysfunctional behavior, have serious restrictions on the choices they can exercise.

> The working behavior therapist is likely to ask three questions: (a) what behavior is maladaptive; that is, what subject behaviors should be increased or decreased; (b) what environmental contingencies currently support the subject's behavior (either to maintain his undesirable behavior or to reduce the likelihood of his performing a more adaptive response); and (3) what environmental changes, usually reinforcing stimuli, may be manipulated to alter the subject's behavior.[20]

As we have seen earlier in this chapter, behavior modification has been criticized as a device to control individuals. The potential for possible control, either open or subtle, exists in any system of helping. Gambrill suggests involving the client in the behavioral change process to the greatest possible extent. "Such involvement includes designing a clear counselor-client contract that identifies the responsibilities and expectations of each party. It also includes assuring the conditions for informed consent in selecting both change procedures and objectives. This is an ethical stance that also helps clients make decisions for themselves." Gambrill also stresses self-management procedures—"the extent to which the client learns how to create changes in his or her own environment. Self-management can mean learning how to regulate anxiety, learning new social behaviors that allow one to expand his range of social interactions, or learning negotiation skills that allow, for example, a teenager to remain with her parents rather than be removed from home."[21]

Agency Policies

Finally, the great number, complexity, and lack of visibility of agencies and organizations, together with the maze of rules and requirements governing eligibility, make exercising choices difficult. This situation prevails for problems and needs in the following areas: income maintenance and employment benefits, health care, taxes, personal care services such as homemaker or home help, the whole range of scattered and piecemeal personal social services, mental health services, the range of entitlements of older persons, and legal rights, including housing and consumer protection. More effective information and referral services are needed to assist citizens with many of these problems.

To help clients through organizational and bureaucratic labyrinths, caseworkers must (1) start with a sensitive and perceptive understanding of the client's needs and desires; (2) know the resources which are available and the specific conditions governing their use; (3) engage in the activity needed to get the client securely in touch with the source of help; (4) finally, and ideally, monitor the outcome to know what was provided and whether the helping process was successful.

Many situations and personal states limit choices and the ability to choose. Obviously human predicaments in real life do not occur in neat categories. The categories may overlap. More important, the person in real life may find his or her choices limited by several factors.

Steps in Helping

The general pattern of helping activities by caseworkers includes (1) establishing initial communication; (2) exploring and clarifying the problem; (3) assessing the situation with the client; (4) mutually determining the focus and goal to be pursued, the methods to be used, and the tasks involved in attaining the goals; (5) engaging in appropriate activity to help the client; (6) evaluating progress and outcome with the client; (7) and most important, providing the sensitivity, concern, interest, hope, integrity, and support necessary for the client to engage in the previous steps.

Assessing Family Relationships

In the assessment process, ecology is important in understanding influences that affect relationships. Ann Hartman of the University of Michigan has developed the ECO-map technique in which basic relationships may be graphically represented. An example of a five-person household is presented as Figure 3-1.[22]

Elements in Effective Counseling

Skills in interpersonal relationships influence whether or not a person receives help. First, the caseworker must be sensitive to the client's feelings and must have capacity to communicate his or her understanding of them to the client. This means sensitivity to the client's fears, anxieties, guilt, anger, hopes, and aspirations, whether communicated openly or covertly. This capacity is called *accurate empathy*. Second, the caseworker must have the capacity to respect and care for the client as a separate person who is allowed to have his or her own feelings and experiences without being rejected, ridiculed, or diminished. This is called *nonpossessive warmth* or *unconditional positive regard*. Third, the caseworker has to be *genuine* or authentic. The caseworker is not defensive or phony, but open, real, and honest. Studies indicate that positive outcomes in therapy are produced when the client perceives accurate empathy, genuineness, and unconditional positive regard.[23]

Over twenty years ago Biestek listed seven client needs and rights: (1) to be treated as an individual; (2) to express feelings; (3) to get sympathetic responses to problems; (4) to be recognized as a person; (5) not to be judged; (6) to make his or her own choices and decisions; and (7) to keep secrets about him or herself. He translated these into corresponding principles for caseworkers: (1) individualization of the client; (2) purposeful expression of feelings; (3) controlled emotional involvement; (4) acceptance; (5) nonjudgmental attitude; (6) client self-determination; and (7) confidentiality.[24]

Mayer and Timms, in their report of working-class clients' perceptions of casework, conclude that "only workers who are perceived as caring, as being concerned, are in a position to make their supportive efforts felt."[25]

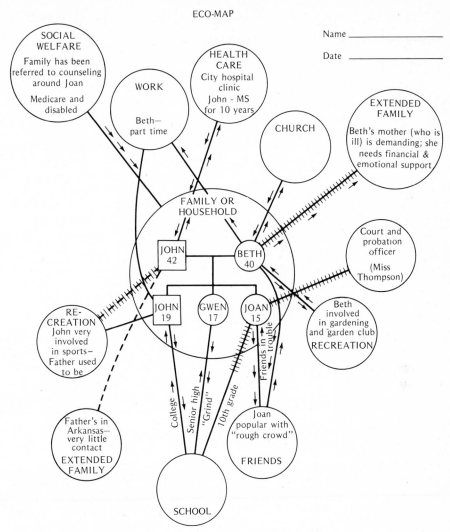

ECO-MAP

Name _____

Date _____

Fill in connections where they exist.
Indicate nature of connections with a descriptive word or by drawing different kinds of lines;
——————— for strong, – – – – – – for tenuous, ++++++ for stressful.
Draw arrows along lines to signify flow of energy, resources, etc. → → →
Identify significant people and fill in empty circles as needed.

Figure 3.1 Diagramatic assessment of family relationships.

Expectations

The skill of the caseworker in conveying realistic confidence and hope for the resolution of the problem is an important factor related to a client's continuing to see the caseworker. As Lilian Ripple reported:

. . . there was a high association (almost complete in the case of clients with external problems) between continuance and "strong encouragement," characterized by warmly positive affect, efforts to relieve discomfort, assurance that the situation could at least be improved, and a plan to begin work on the problem in the next interview. Both strong and intermediate levels of encouragement may be seen to compensate for limitations in the client's own motivation and capacity or deterrent environmental influences. If all or most of the factors in the client's situation are strongly positive, the effect of mere encouragement or even neutrality (non-encouragement) is not so immediate; as these factors become weaker or even negative, however, discontinuance is almost certain unless a compensating factor is introduced through the strength of encouragement.[26]

Increasing evidence during the past decade has suggested that client withdrawal from help and client dissatisfactions with how they had been treated were related to discrepancies between client and caseworker perceptions about the nature of the problem or ambiguity about their mutual expectations. For example, Mayer and Timm's study of client reactions indicated that many clients were both puzzled by and unresponsive to their caseworkers. Clients expected more recognition of their practical problems and help in dealing with them rather than developing insight about their feelings. The authors state: "Viewed from a distance, the worker client interactions have the aura of a Kafka scene: two persons ostensibly playing the same game but actually adhering to rules that are private."[27]

Similar findings were reported by Rhodes in her study of client and caseworker expectations in a medical and psychiatric outpatient facility. "Clients expect workers to offer friendship, concrete advice, and relief and to provide solutions; whereas workers do not plan to do so. . . . Clients tend to wait for social work activity that will never be forthcoming and may eventually become frustrated and dissatisfied, while workers fail to communicate some aspects of their role which relate to their willingness to provide concrete services."[28] Caseworkers frequently have placed too much emphasis on a single method or system of viewing clientele and their problems and how to help. They have sometimes been unable or unwilling to include the client in the system they are using.

Conversely, several elements related to successful outcomes form a structure for helping: (1) identifying the specific aims and goals to be achieved, usually short-term definitive goals; (2) clarifying what the worker and the agency have to offer; (3) structuring the role and what is expected of the client; (4) specifying the tasks needed to be accomplished in reaching the goals (specific planning of task implementation is especially important); (5) using time, usually a specified short period.[29]

To incorporate elements which enhance positive outcomes, caseworkers increasingly use written contracts with clients. Maluccio and Marlowe define a social work contract as *the explicit agreement between the worker and the client concerning target problems, the goals and the strategies of social work intervention, and the roles and tasks of the participants.* Its major features are mutual agreement, differential participation in the intervention process, reciprocal accountability, and explicitness. In practice these features are closely interrelated."[30]

Empathy and the Certainty of Uncertainty

An awareness of individual imperfection and incompleteness draws one to an idea of responsible relations with fellow men. Who knows the extent of his personal vulnerability? Who knows the description of all his deficiencies? Who knows the moment when fortune will be favorable or fickle? Empathy with those afflicted with misfortune and identification with those oppressed by difficulty can involve one in the desire and willingness to join forces with fellow men against these uncertainties. But the fact that the uncertainties are a dead certainty for *everyone* can impel all men toward a common defense against them.

Social work is a profession developed from a commitment to shared experience, from a welcome assumption of social responsibility and a desire to express and implement this responsibility. It rests ultimately on the conviction, common to religious and secular perceptions about the conditions of human existence, that men are involved with each other in the process of existence, whatever its origin and whatever its destiny.[31]

Neva L. Itzin, *Right to Life, Subsistence, and the Social Services.*

SUMMARY AND APPLICATION

The need for individualized services in our increasingly complex, impersonal, and mechanistic society is great. To address the problems of children, families, the elderly, the handicapped, the emotionally upset, and offenders, a wider range of individualized services and the personnel to provide them will be needed. Significantly, among social work personnel the largest demand is for caseworkers involved in direct service to individuals and families.

You are aware of the values involved in the helping process and the basic right of self-determination. The goals of social casework are to help people to seek help effectively and at the same time to preserve and enhance their autonomy.

Frank Itzin

KEY TERMS

family service agency
homemaker services
community mental health center
residential treatment center
probation officer
social services in industry
Freud
psychosocial treatment

ego psychology
functional approach
problem solving
crisis-oriented casework
task-centered casework
behavior modification
individualization
ECO-map

REFERENCES AND NOTES

1. Mary E. Richmond, *Social Diagnosis*, Russell Sage, New York, 1917, pp. 134–203.
2. Florence Hollis, *Casework: A Psychosocial Therapy*, Random House, New York, 1972, p. 9.
3. Ruth E. Smalley, "Social Casework: The Functional Approach," in *Encyclopedia of Social Work*, 1971, p. 1195.
4. The functional approach is explained in Ruth E. Smalley and Tybel Bloom, "Social Casework: The Functional Approach," in *Encyclopedia of Social Work*, 1977, pp. 1280–1290, and in Virginia P. Robinson, *Jessie Taft: Therapist and Social Work Educator*, University of Pennsylvania Press, Philadelphia, 1962, pp. 193–342.
5. Helen H. Perlman, *Social Casework: A Problem Solving Process*, University of Chicago Press, Chicago, 1957.
6. Helen H. Perlman, "Social Casework: The Problem-Solving Approach," in *Encyclopedia of Social Work*, 1977, pp. 1290–1299.
7. Howard J. Parad, "Crisis Intervention," in *Encyclopedia of Social Work*, 1977, pp. 228–237.
8. See William J. Reid and Laura Epstein, *Task-Centered Casework*, Columbia University Press, New York, 1972, and William J. Reid and Laura Epstein (eds.), *Task-Centered Practice*, Columbia University Press, New York, 1977.
9. William J. Reid and Ann W. Shyne, *Brief and Extended Casework*, Columbia University Press, New York, 1969.
10. Richard B. Stuart, "Applications of Behavior Theory to Social Casework," in Edwin J. Thomas (ed.), *The Socio-Behavioral Approach and Applications to Social Work*, Council on Social Work Education, New York, 1967, pp. 19–38.
11. Edwin J. Thomas, "Social Casework and Social Group Work: The Behavioral Modification Approach," in *Encyclopedia of Social Work*, 1977, pp. 1309–1321.
12. Carol H. Meyer, *Social Work Practice: A Response to the Urban Crisis*, Free Press, New York, 1970, pp. 103–185.
13. Harriett M. Bartlett, *The Common Base of Social Work Practice*, National Association of Social Workers, New York, 1970, pp. 65–69.
14. Alan Keith-Lucas, *Giving and Taking Help*, University of North Carolina Press, Chapel Hill, 1972, pp. 20–21.
15. Lydia Rapoport, "Crisis Intervention as a Mode of Brief Treatment," in Robert W. Roberts and Robert H. Nee (eds.), *Theories of Social Casework*, University of Chicago Press, Chicago, p. 277.
16. For further review of crisis intervention, see Naomi Golan, *Treatment in Crisis Situations*, Free Press, New York, 1978; Lydia Rapoport, "The State of Crisis: Some Theoretical Considerations," in Howard J. Parad (ed.), *Crisis Intervention*, Family Service Association, New York, 1965, pp. 22–31.
17. For additional information about systematic desensitization, see Joel Fischer and Harvey L. Gochros, *Planned Behavior Change: Behavior Modification in Social Work*, Free Press, New York, 1975, pp. 214–217; Eileen D. Gambrill, *Behavior Modification: Handbook of Assessment, Intervention and Evaluation*, Jossey-Bass, San Francisco, 1977, pp. 449–528.
18. For additional material on family therapy, see Virginia Satir, *Conjoint Family Therapy*, Science and Behavior Books, Palo Alto, 1967; Salvador Minuchin et al., *Families of the Slums*, Basic Books, New York, 1967; and Salvador Minuchin, *Families and Family Therapy*, Harvard University Press, Cambridge, 1974.

19. Viktor E. Frankl, *Man's Search for Meaning*, Washington Square, New York, 1963, and *The Doctor and the Soul*, Knopf, New York, 1957; Rollo May, *Psychology and the Human Dilemma*, Van Nostrand, Princeton, 1967.

20. Leonard P. Ullman and Leonard Krasner, *Case Studies in Behavior Modification*, Holt, New York, 1965, p. 1.

21. Gambrill, op. cit., p. xii.

22. Ann Hartman, "Diagrammatic Assessment of Family Relationships," *Social Casework*, vol. 59, October 1978, p. 470.

23. The importance of accurate empathy, unconditional positive regard, and genuineness are reported in Charles B. Truax and Kevin Mitchell, "Research in Relation to Process and Outcome," in Allen E. Bergin and Sol L. Garfield (eds.), *Handbook of Psychotherapy and Behavior Change: An Empirical Analysis*, Wiley, New York, 1971, pp. 299–344; Carl R. Rogers (ed.), *The Therapeutic Relationship and Its Impact*, University of Wisconsin Press, Madison, 1967; and D. Corydon Hammond, Dean H. Hepworth, and Veon C. Smith, *Improving Therapeutic Communication*, Jossey-Bass, San Francisco, 1977, pp. 1–27.

24. Felix P. Biestek, *The Casework Relationship*, Loyola University Press, Chicago, 1957, p. 17.

25. John E. Mayer and Noel Timms, *The Client Speaks*, Routledge, London, 1970, p. 93.

26. Lilian Ripple, Ernestina Alexander, and Bernice W. Polemis, *Motivation, Capacity and Opportunity*, University of Chicago, School of Social Service Administration, 1964, p. 203.

27. John E. Mayer and Noel Timms, "Clash in Perspective Between Worker and Client," *Social Casework*, vol. 50, January 1969, p. 37.

28. Sonya L. Rhodes, "Contract Negotiation in the Initial Stage of Casework," *Social Service Review*, vol. 51, March 1977, p. 136.

29. See Joel Fischer, *Effective Casework Practice*, McGraw-Hill, New York, 1978, pp. 137–155; Reid and Epstein, op. cit.; William J. Reid, "A Test of a Task-Centered Approach," *Social Work*, vol. 20, January 1975, pp. 3–9.

30. Anthony N. Maluccio and Wilma D. Marlow, "The Case for the Contract," *Social Work*, vol. 19, January 1974, p. 30.

31. Neva L. Itzin, "Right To Life, Subsistence, and the Social Services," *Social Work*, vol. 3, October 1958, pp. 8–10.

FOR FURTHER STUDY

Beulah R. Compton and Burt Galaway, *Social Work Processes*, Dorsey, Homewood, Ill., 1975.

Joel Fischer, *Effective Casework Practice: An Eclectic Approach*, McGraw-Hill, New York, 1978.

John W. Hanks (ed.), *Social Work Skills: Toward Human Dignity in the Human Services*, National Association of Social Workers, Washington, D.C., 1978.

Andrea Holmes and Joan Marzels, *Social Workers and Volunteers*, Allen & Unwin, London, 1978.

Frank M. Loewenberg, *Fundamentals of Social Intervention*, Columbia University Press, New York, 1977.

Allen Pincus and Anne Minahan, *Social Work Practice: Model and Method*, Peacock, Itasca, Ill., 1973.

Arthur Schwartz et al., *Social Casework: A Behavioral Approach*, Columbia University Press, New York, 1975.

Francis J. Turner (ed.), *Social Work Treatment*, Free Press, New York, 1974.

James K. Whittaker, *Social Treatment*, Aldine, Chicago, 1974.

FOR DISCUSSION

1. Are the majority of social workers engaged to serve individuals, groups, or communities?
2. How does private practice of social work differ from agency practice?
3. In child welfare, what is considered to be the first task of the social worker?
4. What services do caseworkers offer to unmarried parents?
5. Why is discharge planning for hospital patients an especially important social work role?
6. What are the functions of a caseworker who serves as a probation officer?
7. Give some examples of typical problems that would lead an industrial firm to have a caseworker.
8. What are the two basic assumptions in the Freudian formulation of personality development?
9. Why were social histories valuable to staff members of the Charity Organization Societies?
10. What are the two Freudian concepts that became basic principles of social casework?
11. Which approach to treatment has been considered the "dominant" school of thought?
12. Who was most instrumental in providing the psychological system for functional casework?
13. Describe the problem-solving approach in your own words.
14. What criticisms have been made of behavior modification?
15. Why are people afraid to seek help?
16. What are the elements in a state of crisis?
17. How does a caseworker act as a broker?
18. How can a social worker get help from other community agencies for a client and still maintain confidentiality?
19. What kind of attitude do clients expect from caseworkers?
20. How would you draw up a contract with a client?

PROJECTS

1. Study one approach to casework discussed in the chapter and develop a role-play to illustrate its characteristics.
2. Ask a member of a local welfare rights organization to discuss the services the welfare workers provide and the additional services needed.
3. Ask an agency for permission to sit in on one or more of its casework interviews. What agency attitudes are revealed by the response to your request? If the agency is

reluctant, are the reasons well founded? If you are granted permission, report to the class on the elements of the process without revealing the identity of the client.

4. Analyze the major elements in individual casework and those that family treatment would add. Why may family therapy be more successful than individual counseling?

5. One agency has devised the concept of the child welfare agency acting as parent, which is similar to the functional approach. Read Edith Zober and Merlin Taber, "The Child Welfare Agency as Parent," *Child Welfare*, vol. 44, 1965, pp. 387–392, and report on the position, indicating its strengths and weaknesses.

6. Interview two social workers and find out what approaches they find most helpful. Collect several examples from them to report to the class.

7. Using the model in the chapter, prepare an ECO-map to illustrate your own family situation. Indicate whether this helped to increase your insight.

CHAPTER 4
Group Work

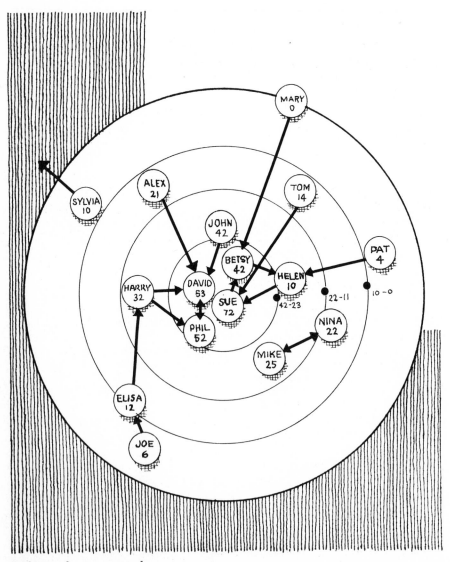

Each group has its core members.

Social group work has burst the too narrow seams of its basketball uniforms and arts-and-crafts smocks; increasingly it appears in the contrasting symbolic garments that bespeak the poles of its present scope—the authority-cool white coats of hospitals and clinical personnel and the play-it-cool windbreaker of the street corner gang worker.

—Helen Harris Perlman*

Group work serves a wide range of people in various agencies, clinical settings, and outreach programs. It may be used in helping schoolchildren, youthful offenders, adolescents living in single-parent families, the physically and educationally handicapped, the mentally ill, residents of slum hotels, and the elderly.

Social work with groups is practiced in institutions for the elderly and infirm, programs for unmarried mothers, adoption agencies, correctional settings, mental hospitals and day hospitals, halfway houses, substance abuse centers, physical rehabilitation centers, public schools, and family service agencies. Group workers are utilized in street gang work, residential and day camping, and child guidance centers, as well as in more traditional settlement houses and community centers. Group work is often used in combination with casework. Social workers in generalist practice roles must have training in group methods to serve clients adequately in our human service systems.

Helen H. Perlman's remarkable description of the changes in group work, presented over a decade ago, suggests the strategic role that social workers may play in serving clients in groups.

> [Group work's] domain has widened . . . to include those agencies and places that are set up to rehabilitate or restore or reform such social functioning as is held to be problematic, impaired, deficient . . . the actual treatment of the individual group member for his particular problems and the relation of such treatment of personal problems to group membership and process—these are in the center of group work concerns today.[2]

Since Perlman's analysis of the changes, much has happened in social group work. Group workers have broadened their mission and stressed a "problem" orientation. Group work has been legitimized through research, conceptualization, and model building.[3] Increasing knowledge from group dynamics, psychology, psychiatry, and other behavioral sciences has provided additional insights for social workers. Many of the conceptual frameworks that are helpful to the application of casework also inform and extend the competence of the group worker.

*Helen H. Perlman, "Social Work Method: A Review of the Past Decade," in *Trends in Social Work Practice and Knowledge*, National Association of Social Workers, New York, 1966, p. 84.

SOCIAL GROUP WORK

Social work with groups is intended to facilitate favorable changes in clients' communications skills, self-awareness, reality assessment, and acquisition of constructive societal values to aid in actualizing chosen life goals. For persons living in institutions, groups are a vehicle for fostering responsibility for group life, accenting cooperative and mutual relationships, arousing the need for creative problem-solving, and moving toward cohesion and a sense of community. Members of groups have the opportunity to exercise social responsibility through mutually agreed upon activities that serve both the individual members and the greater community. Group work is an instrument to facilitate self-governance leading to greater autonomy, dignity, and respect for democratic ideals.

When Should Groups Be Used?

At first thought, groups should be used because there often is not enough time to work with a number of people individually, but this advantage may be an illusion. The arrangements necessary for forming and maintaining a group and the individual conferences that may be required, may mean that groups save little time.

Use of groups is clearly economical when several people have the need for information. Group meetings of prospective adoptive parents are often scheduled to provide information about the agency and give people a chance to ask questions. The pooled questions often give the participants a better understanding of the agency than if each couple were interviewed separately.

Groups are also appropriate when common problems must be solved. Adolescent groups often focus on how to study effectively, dress and use makeup, make friends, or prepare for a specific profession or vocation. People who are already interdependent, as in a dormitory, a group home, or a nursing home, may constitute natural groups. Rule-making and other policy decisions are relevant concerns. From such practical issues, the members of the group can often develop the trust to consider behavior problems and other personal issues.

Groups are useful to share a wide range of experiences from which participants can profit. That other group members have solved similar problems is a source of reassurance and encouragement. In a group with a professional social worker as a leader, the experiences of peers are often more effective influences than the experiences of the leader.

A final obvious value of groups is that they encourage free interchange. The individual group members develop relationships that stimulate discussion. Group sessions may be especially useful for people who have never talked about their problems and are reluctant to do so. They are often encouraged to talk by the model of open expression by others. Group pressures are effective agents for change. A person may independently try to change his or her speech habits, but if the group is agreed that change is necessary, it is often more likely to happen.

In groups concerned with the treatment of personal problems, the leader must be sensitive to those issues that are appropriate for the entire group to discuss and those that should be reserved for individual sessions. Self-disclosure demands a high degree of trust of other group members.

Value of Work with Groups

Social work practice with groups is founded on the premise that people are enriched by interpersonal experiences structured around collectively defined goals, satisfying peer relationships, and shared decision-making pertaining to the content of the group's life. The leader helps individual members to use the group's discussion and activities to negotiate and then to fulfill behavioral and developmental contracts. Continuance and security in group life may further benefit members as expressed and unexpressed needs, problems, and life tasks emerge through the group's process to become the focus of the peer system.

The group worker's role is to assist the group to value its sense of collective purpose as well as to continually reexamine what it may do to modify its goals to meet new and emerging needs arising out of the members' dynamic interactions. The group worker assists the group to achieve socially desirable but highly individualistic growth. Understanding of group processes, aware-ness of members' strengths and limitations, and skills in group facilitation enable the leader to guide the group toward healthier interpersonal relation-ships and group cohesion.

The social worker serving friendship clubs in a community center, or treatment groups in a mental health center, encourages constructive participa-tion to aid members in achieving an optimum level of functioning. To the limit of their capacity, members are encouraged to plan program activities that will enable them to acquire social, creative, and practical skills useful in situations outside the group. Along with discussion, the group may employ sports and games, arts and crafts, dramatics, singing, camping and trips, and parties to aid member-to-member interaction and strengthen group identification.

The leader's knowledge of the members' interests, developmental needs, and physical and psychological functioning provides a basis for choice of program activities for the group. For groups as different as teen-age gangs and aphasic stroke patients, program activities may be a vital tool to promote worker-member involvement until members can achieve sufficient trust to begin to negotiate a collective contract as their basis for meeting together.

Additional values of group work include the opportunity for lonely persons to belong to a purposeful social organization where they can release burdening emotions safely in the presence of others, and where they are reassured by knowing that other persons are also struggling to deal with problems that are obstacles to life satisfaction.

Skill Development

Social group work is a broader societal function predicated upon the belief that people can and should be helped to acquire skills for membership and leadership in neighborhood, labor, professional, business, religious, or civic organizations. As Edward Lindeman said: "If democracy is to be considered as a mode of life, we should be able to describe its basic requirements and hence furnish clearly definable tests for our performances."[4] Thus to Lindeman the chief function of education for democratic values was to help persons expand their range of individual capacities and social relationships. Inherent is the creation of environments in which individuals may discover and experience the sources of dignity through relationships with others and leisure pursuits.[5]

HISTORICAL DEVELOPMENT OF GROUP WORK

Social group work's ideological roots were in the settlements but also in self-help and informal recreational organizations—the YMCA and YWCA, Scouting, Jewish centers, and progressive education. Group-serving agencies emphasized programs for the normal rather than the maladjusted. People came for recreation, informal education, and friendships provided in organized interest groups. Individuals learned to cooperate and get along with others socially; they enriched themselves through new knowledge, skills, and interests, and the overall state of society was bettered through responsible involvement in community problems.[6]

George Williams founded the Young Men's Christian Association in London in 1844 for the purpose of converting young men to Christian ideals. In 1851 YMCAs were founded in Boston and Baltimore. In 1866 the Young Women's Christian Association began in Boston. Other religious and private organizations promoted vacation schools, summer camps, and other youth activities.

Gertrude Wilson analyzes the social reform movement that helped in the founding of social group work.

> Workers engaged in these activities in the early part of the century ferreted out large social problems such as poverty, low wages, long working hours, poor housing, and exploitation by landlords, inadequate sanitation, political corruption, and caste-line treatment of people. They provided direct service to feed the hungry and care for the sick, and created opportunities for cultural and recreational activities. They carried on programs of social action to alleviate or eliminate identified social problems through engaging the privileged and the oppressed in informational activities and by making bridges to local, state, and federal officials to secure social legislation and enforcement.[7]

Social group work has reflected the general purposes of the social work profession. Social group workers, like caseworkers, have sought to enable people to assume greater responsibility in seeking solutions to personal problems and social conditions. Like social casework, social group work aims to assist persons during periods of crisis to reduce environmental pressures and provide more tangible opportunities to experience satisfaction.

The Settlement House—A Solution to Social Problems

The Settlement is an experimental effort to aid in the solution of the social and industrial problems which are engendered by the modern conditions of life in a great city. It insists that these problems are not confined to any one portion of a city. It is an attempt to relieve, at the same time, the overaccumulation at one end of society and the destitution at the other. . . . The one thing to be dreaded in the Settlement is that it lose its flexibility, its power of quick adaptation, its readiness to change its methods as its environment may demand. It must be open to conviction and must have a deep and abiding sense of tolerance. It must be hospitable and ready for experiment. It should demand from its residents a scientific patience in the accumulation of facts and the steady holding of their sympathies as one of the best instruments for that accumulation. It must be grounded in a philosophy whose foundation is on the solidarity of the human race, a philosophy which will not waver when the race happens to be represented by a drunken woman or an idiot boy. Its residents must be emptied of all conceit of opinion and all self-assertion, and ready to arouse and interpret the public opinion of their neighborhood.[8]

Jane Addams, *Twenty Years at Hull House.*

Settlements and Community Centers Today

Many contemporary group work agencies retain some of the earlier emphasis upon self-help, community resource development, democratic participation, and social action. Cultural, educational, and recreational activities have strengthened some agencies, while others have taken on roles as multiservice centers. Day care programs, information and referral services, medical screening and care, and special services for youth and for older adults have been added.

PURPOSES OF GROUPS

The wide range of group work services may be viewed as a hierarchy based upon increasingly difficult goals and the need for increasingly skilled leaders. Groups may be led by nonprofessionals who volunteer to serve as program aides or, at the other end of the spectrum, by highly trained group psychotherapists who have had extensive supervised training and experience in a clinical agency. Groups may be classified by their major purpose, but some members may use the group for different purposes than those that the leader considers dominant.

Recreation Groups

Activities purely for enjoyment, and often practically leaderless, are provided by recreation groups. The agency may offer little more than physical space and the use of some equipment. If such a group is sponsored by a settlement house or community center, the professional staff may seek a resource person or lay leader to engage the members in goal-directed activities. The main responsibility of staff is scheduling a variety of such activities to appeal to a broad range of persons who may enjoy benefit from open-ended activities without the commitment to regular attendance and group structure. An open game room, informal team sports, and spontaneous playground activities are examples.

Recreation-Skill Groups

Instruction and task orientation, but with socialization and enjoyment encouraged, are provided by recreation-skill groups. Newer members of a community, seeking a social outlet, may be advised to register in a swimming, basketball, bridge, exercise, pottery, or French-cooking group where similar newcomers tend to meet. Competitive team sports, bridge tournaments, parties, and art exhibits may be outgrowths of such groups, providing an added dimension by further enhancing social-recreational-learning purposes. Agency administrative personnel must take into account the wide range of members' interests, cultural backgrounds, and current leisure-time trends in structuring activities that will appeal to people.

Education Groups

The learning of more complex skills, often in a more didactic manner, takes place in education groups. Some groups may resemble a class, while others may encourage much more interaction and group planning of the agenda. Groups may be developed for parent effectiveness training, retirement planning, family budgeting, or automobile repair instruction, for example. A family service agency or mental health center may sponsor a group discussion series for couples anticipating marriage; or a community center may conduct a year-long forum on national or local problems and issues. Making new friends is a goal for some participants, while others seek practical help and information.

Leadership requirements include specialized knowledge, the skill to communicate with a diverse group, and the ability to involve participants in constructive discussion. The leader must be capable of focusing the group's agenda, increasing member-to-member involvement, and creating an atmosphere conducive to learning.

Self-Help Groups

Though their members are often antagonistic to professional leadership, since they stress personal involvement in a problem, self-help groups should have a special relevance to social work. Drakeford has identified five criteria stressed by self-help groups—responsibility, standards, confession, lay leadership, and action programs.[9] Typical examples are Alcoholics Anonymous, Weight Watchers, Recovery, Inc. (for former mental patients), Parents Anonymous (involving child abuse), and groups for parents of the mentally retarded. In recent years, women experiencing surgical breast removal, chronic smokers, and widows have also formed self-help organizations. Group meetings of Alcoholics Anonymous and Weight Watchers stress confession and testimony. The meetings of Recovery chapters include lessons from the textbook of its founder, Dr. Abraham Low. Many self-help groups operate community programs and spend much time in fund raising. Parents of the mentally retarded often operate schools, sheltered workshops, and recreation programs when community programs are absent or lacking in services.

While self-help groups often reject professional involvement on principle, social workers and other human service professions are instrumental in promoting the creation of such organizations.

Socialization Groups

Many consider socialization groups as the primary focus of social group work, since their goal is often behavior change and increased social skills of members.

> The major problem focus is inadequate opportunity for role-learning in the social network. The social worker's challenge, therefore, is to provide opportunities for changed role performance and interaction in novel situations. The targets of change are self-concepts, internalized values, and expectations of self and others. The social worker, functioning as an agent of socialization and change, actively teaches, models, invites participation, works for definition of mutual responsibilities, and helps to accelerate learning and competence in social roles.[10]

Elizabeth McBroom proposes that "socialization" has often been associated with informal education and character building, with Scouting, 4-H Clubs, and settlement houses. She strongly suggests the application of socialization theory to treatment groups.[11]

A typical record of group activity is helpful in understanding the group work process. The group known as Pyke's Pack was made up of boys who had had previous experience with delinquency. In the twelfth meeting of the group, the record focuses on Hal—aged sixteen, a tenth-grader who is the second of seven children in a family that was deserted by the father. You will find it worthwhile to read the entire record.

A Record of a Socialization Group

When I entered the building all except Hal were sitting in the lobby chairs. Hal was playing ping-pong. There was an immediate request for a meeting, the first direct request this year. At first there was much talk about the cast on Paul's leg. Everyone was curious about it and asked how long he would have to wear it. This continued until Paul became fed up and said it was the club that we needed to talk about. Harry felt that what happened to the club would depend upon what happened to the boys after the Court hearing. Paul, who was not involved, said there would be a club no matter what happened at the Court, and he felt we should set up rules and decide who could and who could not be members. Paul announced that he would not stay in the club if Tom came back. Hal was quiet during this discussion and didn't register enthusiasm one way or another. . . .

I asked what they wanted to do most at this time. They said they would like to talk about getting jobs and what they might do this summer. Paul was interested in joining the Merchant Marine and wanted help in getting in touch with the office in Philadelphia since he had received no answer to his letters. Harry said that Paul couldn't pass the physical examination. This led to an argument which ended when I suggested that Paul talk it over with his doctor and that, if his doctor thought that he was physically able, I would be glad to be of assistance to him in finding out more about the Merchant Marine. Harry thought that he would like a job as an usher since he was tall enough to qualify. After we had discussed the various theaters, he decided that he would apply at a few of them some day after school. Harold has a permit to be excused from school this week to look for a job. He is sixteen and has to contribute to the support of the family. He now has a part-time job as a soda jerker at a drugstore out of the neighborhood. He wondered if I could help him find a full-time job. He has been to the U.S.E.S. but had found that they don't accept applications from anyone under eighteen. He asked me if I knew of any other employment agencies where he could apply. I told him that I would make inquiry and would have a report ready for him at the next club meeting and that if he didn't want to wait that long he could come and see me any time after tomorrow. The others were interested, too, and so we agreed to discuss this at our next meeting.

After the meeting closed, Hal went to the game room. I went over to talk with him and opened the conversation by saying that I understood why he had not been able to keep the appointment with me yesterday that he had asked for. He said that he guessed that I knew that he had to go down to the Federal Court. I agreed and asked if he wanted to talk with me now. He said that it was no use to talk with me now. I stayed in the game room. Pretty soon Hal came over and said in a low voice that his mother wanted my help to find a lawyer. This I doubted. But I asked Hal if he would like to go up to the office with me to talk about it. We went to the office. Hal said that he had gotten himself into the jam and now it was up to him to get himself out of it. He had talked with no one about it except at the Court and that hadn't helped very much because it had been in terms of what he did and how he had done it. It was not possible for him to talk to his mother because he felt so sad to have caused her so much trouble. He said that I was the only one to whom he could talk. I asked if he thought that I could help. His answer indicated that "help" to him meant getting him out of trouble at the Courts. He didn't think that there was much that I could do. He said that he would never do anything like he had done again if he gets out of this all right. I pointed out that most of us get into trouble of some sort and that we can't get out of the trouble without those who know how to help us. I said that perhaps he did not feel like having someone give him a hand right now but that later on he might. I said that I hoped he would feel that he could come to me for help if he decided that he wanted it. He said that he would think it over and maybe he would come back. I told him that I would be at the agency Monday night.[12]

G. Wilson and G. Ryland, *Social Group Work Practice.*

The group worker, as an agent of socialization, "is a model, a provider of a safe environment, a specifier and developer of settings and situations of the group that are favorable to the socialization process, a leader of purposeful discussions, and an allocator of resources to groups in need of socialization."[13]

Socialization groups also have many goals more limited than reentry into society. Youth groups are organized to increase social skills, reduce reduction of isolation and conflict, and enhance cooperation. Parents often seek agency peer groups that will provide creative and developmental opportunities for their children to supplement family and neighborhood life. The child, in this instance, is motivated to attend group meetings by the external stimulus of parents. Some agencies successfully create group experiences for such children over a period of many years.

Leadership of socialization groups is usually provided by a social worker with a bachelor's degree who is supervised by agency administrative personnel.

Therapeutic Groups

Greater leadership skill is typically required in therapeutic groups. "Therapy" is needed because of internal conflicts grounded in the past. In the group setting, conflicts and maladaptive social response patterns are exhibited in the presence of the therapist and the group. The leader uses the group to assist in "direct objective observation of the patient's behavior, his perceptions of situations, and expression of feelings, permitting explicit diagnosis of what his interpersonal needs and problems are, and setting the stage for the therapist and other group members to intervene directly in repetitive maladaptive social behavioral sequences."[14] Group treatment is often recommended after diagnosis by a mental health team. Group leadership may be provided by a social worker, psychologist, nurse, or psychiatrist. Often two mental health professionals co-lead a therapeutic group because they have differing skills.

In recent years, therapeutic groups have been utilized in a wider variety of agencies and institutions. Crisis intervention groups have been employed in emergency services in medical settings, public schools, protective service settings, and psychiatric institutions.[15] For example, a social worker may be called upon to meet with a patient ward group to openly discuss the feelings of grief and fright following suicide of a fellow patient. Saul and Saul suggest the potential value of group therapy sessions in nursing homes following the death of a resident to allow the elderly to express their feelings of loss. They believe that healthy, open discussion alleviates tension, eases depression, and helps residents deal with death as a phase of life.[16]

A Treatment Group Example of Behavior Modification

Walter: I guess I'm awfully nervous. Dad says I cry too much.
Larry: I get in lots of fights, so they kicked me out of school.
Greg: Just cause I won't do no chores, my ma always yells at me.
Bruce: I don't like rough kids, I don't like to get dirty or get picked on.
Alan: I don't like nothing at all, not you guys, not baseball, not anything.
Martin: No matter what they do, they can't make me go to school. Everybody makes fun of me.

These boys are receiving group treatment. If one watches through a one-way mirror, he observes the therapist responding to desirable behavior (such as one child's offering another a toy) by issuing poker chips or tokens to the giver (reinforcement). The therapist tends to ignore undesirable behaviors (extinction) such as whining or pushing which do not disrupt the group. Should a child get completely out of control, the therapist separates him from the others until he has calmed down (time out from reinforcement), then asks him to return to the group and continue as before. There are many group tasks of short duration during the ninety minute meeting. Some are school simulated activities, others are physical games, and still others are arts and crafts projects. During most of these activities tokens are awarded for specific achievements. At the end of the meeting, each child takes the tokens he has earned and cashes them in for food, small toys, pencils, books, and other items in a "store" in the corner of the room.

Toward the end of the meeting the boys are observed sitting in a circle and discussing what each will work on during the week. One child says he will do at least one chore every day. He signs an agreement (contract) to that effect. Another agrees that he will increase his homework time to thirty minutes a day; another writes in his contract that he will play with his schoolmates a game he learned in the group meeting. A fourth boy is being helped by the others to determine what he could do to make more friends. Each boy eventually receives a behavioral assignment which can be performed before the next meeting and which can be observed by a parent, teacher, or other person involved in his daily activities.[17]

Sheldon D. Rose, *Treating Children in Groups.*

Patient Governance Groups

In mental health programs organized around a therapeutic community approach, groups may be encouraged to seek creative solutions to problems of group conflict. Councils for patient government may provide the opportunity for patients and staff to work together to assert their rights as well as to remove obstacles impeding the therapeutic potential of the institution. Responsible social interaction achieved through problem-solving groups is a valuable therapeutic tool for development of skills for handling conflict and negotiation. Election of patients to serve on such representative councils often reduces the feelings of mistrust that patients have toward staff by allowing both to work together to remedy institutional problems. A self-government council in a home for the aged may be specifically aimed at developing the leadership of residents in defining activities and policies that will substantially enhance the agency's quality of care.[18]

Patient Self-Government

The groups which have been formed in our hospital are parallel to many found in the outside community. Such groups are essential in a psychiatric hospital, I believe, since one of the manifestations of the patient's illness is associated with a breakdown in capacity to cope with problems of community life. These groups offer voluntary opportunities for the patient which will strengthen his capacities to work, live and play with others in a socially acceptable manner.

In our hospital, the governmental group is called the Patient Council. Members are patients nominated and voted on by patients with whom they live. Their function is to assume responsibility for representing them in the council, which has as its assigned task that of calling to staff's attention matters of mutual interest and concern about daily problems of living. The relationship between staff and council is a reciprocal one. Being elected to represent one's fellow patients gives status to the patient member within his particular living unit and tends to strengthen his feelings of self-esteem. In the council, the patient's feelings toward authority are high-lighted around discussion of policy which affects their daily living. This occurs during each meeting as the patient seeks to establish a working relationship with the other members of the council. In the council, patient identification with the administration of the hospital begins to emerge, yet at the unit meetings this same patient may often be fearful of the angry feelings his group may express if he has not been able to accomplish his assigned task. The group worker's participation at unit meetings helps the patient to express the more positive side of his group's ambivalence and to appeal to the strength of his constituents in the unit meetings. In summary, the council provides the patient member three particular areas of relationship experience: (1) his relationship to the group in the council; (2) his relationship to the hospital staff; and (3) his relationship to those whom he represents.

The social worker's role in the council is to affect the total process so that it enhances both the individual patient's treatment and the treatment of the patient group as a whole. This group affords an opportunity for the staff to recognize and deal with the negative influences stemming from the natural associations of patients because many themes of their discussions become a part of the council meeting and thus provide a vehicle for working openly with them.[19]

Minnie M. Harlow, "Group Work in a Psychiatric Hospital: Today a Patient, Tomorrow—?"

Newer Types of Groups

Many social workers use concepts and techniques developed in encounter, sensitivity, transactional analysis, and gestalt groups. Such groups provide the setting and opportunity for persons to better understand the characteristic style and impact of their relationships with others. Immediate confrontation in the group is encouraged by the group facilitator and is used to further openness, authenticity in relationships, reduced defensiveness, and skill in giving and receiving feedback in the presence of others. As the social climate of the group encourages greater safety and mutual trust, members assume increased responsibility for their own personal growth and for the growth of others. Typically, perceptions and reactions to behavior of members provide the data for individual and group learning. Some intended outcomes include increased self-esteem, improved self-awareness, and the rewards of influencing the direction in which others grow. For some, vicarious learning about how others deal with personal and social problems is sufficient justification for participating in such groups.

GROUPS AS A RESPONSE TO MODERN LIFE

Many persons appear attracted to the potential intimacy of groups as a retreat from the monotony, complexity, and stress of life in a technological society. According to Martin Lakin, "in a technological world that threatens to dehumanize, people strive to remain human. In a social and educational system that threatens to homogenize, people seek ways of remaining distinct individuals. In a world where 'things' and the 'system' seem to conspire to make one feel insignificant, people still aspire to a feeling of community."[20] An interesting theory is proposed by John W. Bennett. The central problems of modern society are the disintegration of old ties and loyalties and the corresponding loss of personal identity.[21] "The large organization and its fabricated, impersonal milieu provides little of value for most people, and by the thousands people move into groups, seeking ties in common interests and rupturing the old class lines and social categories as they do." Psychologist O. Hobart Mowrer believes that the great masses of people no longer find in their everyday lives a sense of personal identity, emotional intimacy, and cosmic meaning. "The small-group movement represents an attempt to create not just a kind of 'therapy' but actually a new primary social group or institution which will compensate for these basic human losses."[22]

The objectives of current self-help, encounter, sensitivity, and marathon groups parallel those specified for many years in social group work—cooperative relations, sharing, trusting, responsibility for others, and mutual love and respect. Practitioners are committing themselves more fully to the need and potential of specially created groups. The combined experience and knowledge generated by practitioners and social scientists has enabled us to understand dynamics and processes as well as to create techniques and tools to enable groups to function more creatively and responsibly.

Despite the wide attention from the media and the literature of the helping professions, encounter and sensitivity groups remain controversial.

Some self-proclaimed leaders have been poorly qualified, members for groups often have been sought through direct and sometimes sensational advertising, physical intimacy is sometimes used as a come-on, members may be inappropriately selected, and the short term of some groups may serve to intensify personal problems rather than resolve them. Most leaders in the new group movement disclaim the use of encounter and marathon groups as a form of psychotherapy, but many persons seek out such groups to deal with emotional problems. Lieberman, Yalom, and Miles conclude from research on the impact of encounter groups:

> Encounter groups present a clear and evident danger if they are used for radical surgery to produce a new man. The danger is even greater when the leader and the participants share this misconception. If we no longer expect groups to produce magical, lasting change and if we stop seeing them as panaceas, we can regard them as useful, socially sanctioned opportunities for human beings to explore and to express themselves. Then we can begin to work on ways to improve them so that they may make a meaningful contribution toward solving human problems.[23]

SOCIAL WORK WITH YOUTH GROUPS

Paralleling the thrust of social workers and other professionals toward problem-solving around community problems has been the continuing effort to create relevant leisure-time services for children and youth. Whenever we hear of delinquency and crime among youth, the first excuse is that we do not have enough programs to "get the kids off the streets." The emergence of public playgrounds in 1889 in New York City marked a significant beginning of public concern around the needs of youth for viable, socially constructive activity centers. While almost all town and cities have developed after-school activity centers for youth, competitive sports programs, and day and residential camping, many children and youth still remain untouched, disinterested, and geographically distant from what is offered.

Boys' and Girls' Clubs, Scouts, 4-H Clubs, Young Judea, and B'nai B'rith Youth have flourished, but primarily for middle-class youth. Despite the outreach efforts of many agencies, children from lower economic groups still may find it difficult to pay the costs of participation.

Youth-serving agencies stress several program objectives.

1. Recreational and community service activities and informal education designed to encourage the development of spiritual and ethical values; love of home, family, and friends; concern for community and country; and the practice of responsible citizenship in a democracy.
2. Meaningful interpersonal relationships through participation in friendship clubs, special interest groups, out-of-doors living experiences, and competitive team sports.

3. Service to youth with special problems, such as learning difficulties in school, conflicts with police, and social isolation, to aid the child in his adjustment to the family, his peers, and the larger community.
4. The development of indigenous leadership through special training programs and representative councils.

Group services for the physically and educationally handicapped are still insufficient. For the past two decades, innovative youth agencies have identified the needs of these children and designed special programs or integrated them into groups with nonhandicapped children.[24] The use of group work to integrate delinquents into groups with prosocial children is another area that deserves more attention.[25] More programs of group work with youth in single-parent families[26] and services to children experiencing school difficulties are needed.[27] Much remains to be accomplished by agencies and professionals in aiding special populations who require socialization opportunities.

TOWARD GROUP TREATMENT

In the 1950s, the creative practice of social group work in institutional and clinical settings emerged as a significant contribution to the overall services of social workers. Group workers, as caseworkers had done years before, went into collaborative settings with psychiatrists, psychologists, nurses, and occupational therapists to offer their unique technology to further total patient and client care. Group workers defined a new area of social work practice concerned with the group-living problems of individuals confined in prisons, residential treatment centers, and settings serving the handicapped and the elderly.

The innovative work of Fritz Redl with emotionally disturbed children[28] and Minnie Harlow with adult mental hospital patients[29] exemplified a new era of concern for modifying institutional social structures that were considered antitherapeutic, oppressive, and dehumanizing. Group workers became agents to initiate and maintain diagnostic, therapeutic, and resocialization groups and helped create a social climate which maximized the healthy impact of peer group influence upon residents.[30] Institutional group work in many ways contributed to the objectives of the "therapeutic community" model, which was tested and conceptualized by the psychiatrist Maxwell Jones in England[31] and later popularized in the United States.

Now social workers serve treatment and resocialization groups in mental health centers, in-patient settings, day treatment programs, and aftercare programs. Group work is used to develop skills needed by patients who will be discharged from mental hospitals.

A perceptive discussion by Grace Coyle of the potential value of group experiences to individuals provides a suitable foundation for social workers in carrying out the profession's functions. Group experiences meet the needs of people in five distinct areas.

1 *The maturing process.* Just as the family group has remained vital in man's growth and development by providing the opportunity for closeness in human relationships, small face-to-face groups have become essential in man's maturational process. Children increasingly are provided opportunities for nursery school, preschool education, friendship clubs, team sports, dancing instruction, and other interactional activities. Most children choose involvement with acceptable neighborhood peer groups, but others are thrust into neighborhood gangs.

Parents value educational groups, creative workshops, competitive sports, and other group situations where children can gain social competencies, broadened horizons, and skills necessary for living fuller and happier lives.

After children have learned to use loosely organized and more structured play groups, adolescent cliques become important in continuing the development of independence from the parental family, the identification of sex role in company with others of the same sex, the attainment of social skills and attitudes acceptable to one's peers, and exploration and incorporation of the changing values needed as the individual grows from child to adult. As children and adolescents are able to gain acceptance and achievement with their peers in groups and to achieve satisfying relationships, they are better prepared to assume appropriate roles in social groups and to take on adult tasks and responsibilities. Traditional group-serving agencies stress mainly prevention of social dysfunctioning rather than restoration of impaired functioning.

In recent years increased attention has been given by social agencies to group experiences for older adults, to further growth and development and to enrich their lives. Group experiences tend to expand their sense of usefulness and their connection to useful life roles. Old age is seen as an opportunity for the development of interests and skills rather than as a time of retirement and rest.

2 *A supplement to other relationships.* When children and youth are denied the intimate and satisfying relationships of family life or of neighborhood and other peer groups, small-group experiences in agency programs are beneficial. Adults also require stimulation and experience beyond family and home to expand their outlook on life. Older adults need social group experiences and relationships when spouses and friends die and when children move away from home.

3 *Preparation for active citizenship.* Participation prepares members to exercise their rights and obligations as responsible citizens in a democracy. Groups have the potential for educating members about local, state, and national issues and involving them in social action. Members learn how to define common goals and engage in group deliberation and decision making. The concept of "self-government" becomes more visible. Through social action efforts groups become "other-directed" rather than overly concerned with personal needs.

4 *A corrective for social disorganization.* Group experience for dealing

with predelinquent and delinquent gangs in large urban areas has received wide attention. Social workers detached from social agencies have established relationship and maintained contact with gangs in their neighborhoods and hangouts. Through the years many group workers have attempted to penetrate the peer gang culture in order to influence antisocial norms of these groups as well as to provide socially constructive outlets for member interests.

Where differing racial, ethnic, or religious groups live in close proximity, group experiences and discussion may lessen tensions. Group work can be an effective instrument for the development of common interests where social differences and misunderstandings have disrupted normal community life.

5 *Treatment of intrapsychic maladjustment.* Specially formed treatment groups may provide restorative, remedial, or cathartic experiences in response to personal crisis or breakdown. Through the mutuality of the group, individuals provide and receive constructive attitudes and advice for dealing with stressful life situations. Groups may deter destructive behavior and yet allow persons to examine and test reality in a warm and receptive social climate. The member is aided by the group cohesiveness, realization that life's problems are universal, identification with others, and the hope generated within the group process.[32]

Group treatment provides within its complex interpersonal processes a corrective emotional experience for patients. Yalom feels that despite the potent "curative" potential of therapeutic groups, the group cannot change the patient/member. "Others will not change him for him. He is responsible for his past and his present life in the group (as well as in the outside world), and he is similarly and totally responsible for his future."[33]

PRACTICE PRINCIPLES FOR WORKING WITH GROUPS

Group work theorists and educators hold that the effective practice of group work, besides being based upon philosophical and value considerations, must be preceded by the acquisition of knowledge of the structure, function, dynamics, and development of small groups. Knowledge of the various processes by which individuals achieve change and developmental goals is also required. Social work practice with groups, regardless of theoretical orientation or school, follows an orderly sequence including fact-finding, planned group composition, assessment and reassessment of individuals and groups, recruitment and orientation of members, problem-solving or goal achievement, task specification, the work of the group members together, evaluation, and termination.

Decision-Making

The social worker in the group supports the worth, dignity, and uniqueness of all members and their right to participate to the extent of their capacities in making decisions about matters directly influencing their lives. The worker enables members to assume increasing responsibility and control in group deliberation and planning and supports the group's efforts at achieving a more optimum level of self-direction. Intended outcomes include an improved esprit de corps, achievement of leadership skills, and independence in social functioning. Members are helped to trust their capacities to make decisions and act upon them and are strengthened as group efforts are reinforced by the leader, agency, and community.

The group's purposes for coming together, together with the agency's purposes for offering services, are usually articulated and shared in the members' work together. Often the group worker shares his or her own hopes, aspirations, and perceptions of what the group and its members may accrue as well as what they need to accomplish if the experience is to be productive.

A *contract or working agreement*, negotiated early in the group's existence, serves to clearly define the respective roles and expectations of individual members and of the group worker. The contract also substantiates the agency's support of the negotiation. Since the terms of the contact may shift as the group gains experience together, it may be fruitful to reconsider the members' aims and roles as time goes on. Such an agreement lends direction and encourages movement toward change by strengthening commitment and motivation of the group. As members of organizations or committees, we know that when we are given latitude to contribute ideas toward.common purposes, we usually feel more strongly about the group and are more willing to get involved. Contracting within the group establishes an early norm of giving and receiving ideas, opinions, and feedback. Each member is helped to feel important to the group's collective sense of purpose.

Initial Concerns

Particular attention is given to the group's beginning concerns and resistances, usually by acknowledging that most beginnings tend to evoke conflicting feelings of hope and uncertainty, or of excitement and fear of the unknown. Members may unrealistically expect total change to occur quickly within the group, or conversely, may deny any possibility of achieving personal goals in the presence of others. According to Ruth Smalley, one should begin with the partialization, or breaking up and breaking down, of what can be felt as the total problem or global purpose into something that is small enough to be encompassed, and then get started on one piece of that problem or purpose.[34]

> The worker's responsibility is to help the other find a place to take hold, to begin with some aspect or part of his problem, need, or intent. . . . Nothing is so conducive to frustration and scatter as trying to do everything at once. . . . It cannot be overstressed that it is the worker's appreciation of the promise and problems in beginnings in general and his capacity fully to exploit this particular beginning for this particular client or clientele, to stay with the beginning in all its inevitable awkwardness and tentativeness, rather than to rush to try to solve all the problems in the first interview, group meeting, or conference, that embodies skill in this aspect of social work process.[35]

Individualization

Problems and needs of individual members lead to their participation in the group or may emerge as they seek identity with peers in the group. Often group members require special support, confrontation, limitations on behavior, or reinforcement for contributions to the group as a means of acknowledging movement toward change and self-actualization. The group worker may intervene to protect a member who is being used as a scapegoat by peers, or may cautiously counsel a withdrawn member around lack of responsiveness to the group and his or her own personal growth commitment. The worker is careful not to violate the group's integrity but often intervenes outside the group meeting with members. The worker individualizes when the group is unable to reach certain members or when, in the worker's judgment, a member is detracting from the group's ability to function.

Individualization in a clinical setting may take the form of an interdisciplinary team meeting to discuss the progress of certain patients/members, or possibly referral of a member to casework or another form of treatment. In a school, the child's teachers may be involved to offer reinforcement around behavioral change. A community center worker may discuss a child's behavior with the parents as a means of developing insights into his or her difficulties.

All individualization is based upon assessment through observations in the ongoing group. Most practitioners tend to make use of clinical or agency records, but members must not be prejudged on the basis of such records. Many health agencies tend to rely more upon pre-group and in-group diagnostic workups, while community centers and other socialization agencies vary in their demands for formal assessment statements. There is an advantage in making the effort to specify problem behaviors and group participation objectives to have a more objective means of evaluating what the individual has achieved, what he or she must yet do, and how the group can lend its strength to help.

As a general rule, it is not always possible or necessary to have all the facts about group members prior to their involvement. The medium of the group often provides the most valuable data upon which to construct verbal and written behavioral change contracts. It is the responsibility of the group member, the group, and the worker to periodically evaluate individual progress toward stated objectives and assess the impact of the intervention strategy. Likewise, observations by persons in the group members' natural environment—teachers, fellow employees, houseparents, family—may supply useful data to aid in the group work assessment of change and growth.

Group Assessment

Sociometry was developed more than two decades ago as a useful means of representing affiliations in groups. In the target figure at the beginning of this chapter, Northway assessed the acceptability of group members to one another and showed their choice patterns. Those with the highest acceptability occupy the bull's eye and the more peripheral members are placed in the outer rings on the basis of group judgments. Such results may be quite different from time to time, especially if different situations requiring a variety of skills are being measured. Sociometric data are often useful in the development of goals for both socialization and treatment groups.

Group Goals

Goal achievement or problem-solving is carried out by the group during what may be designated as its action, treatment, or work phase. During this time, the workers individualize the group, teach the members how to work together, challenge obstacles impeding the group's motivation, and facilitate the group's movement toward its declared aims. Leaders may, at times, offer their personal hopes and aspirations for the group, and strive to insure a serious purpose for the group coming together. If a group shows lack of commitment, the leader must confront this and reward progress toward cooperative relationships and treatment goals. Encouragement, exploration, direct advice, structuring of the activity, role-playing, behavioral rehearsal, and modeling are selectively employed to effect both personal and group goals.

Use of Programs

Selective use of program experiences is basic to mobilize constructive social interaction, develop diagnostic insights, enable members to learn and practice social roles, and ultimately advance the group's purpose. Selection of group activities should be based upon criteria consistent with the group's collective purpose as well as their impact upon participant behavior. Robert Vinter specifies six activity-setting dimensions relevant to all activities.

1. Prescriptiveness of the pattern of constituent performances
2. Institutionalized controls governing participant activity
3. Provision for physical movement
4. Competence required for performance
5. Provision for participant interactiveness
6. Reward structure[36]

James Whittaker has specified guidelines for programming for children.
1. The worker should become actively involved with activities as a means of modeling his enthusiasm.
2. Activities which are going well should be ended before participants tire of the program.
3. Timing and sequencing of activities should be considered so that children are not exposed to mass games when their egos are too fragmented.
4. Too much emphasis should not be placed on the "finished product" when children suffer from ego-damage.

5. The worker must be able to switch activities according to the pathologies of the individual child or the group mood.
6. In working with younger children it is better to begin with parallel activities, i.e., those which do not demand member-member interaction. For example, Whittaker believes that children should be given six individual model ships rather than one giant aircraft carrier until the group has matured.[37]

In social group work, as in other human relationships, communication of feelings enriches the group process. The worker values and uses the feelings of group members—excitement, spontaneity, loneliness, uselessness, anger, fear—to further connections between members and between him or herself and members. One view of this process suggests that "the worker's focus as he expresses feeling . . . cannot be his own need to be spontaneous, but must be centered on the group members' need to know and experience the reality of genuine emotion from another, if they, with the worker, are to create something valid for themselves through their participation."[38] One criterion of development is the movement of members toward positive regard for their peers. Program activities, and the skill of the worker in facilitating group cohesion, contribute toward the expression of genuine feelings.

Termination

Preparing the group for ending the experience together requires evaluating its progress toward original objectives. Both the social worker and the group members should take stock of positive changes and experiences and what remains to be done to achieve personal aims. Members must be helped to terminate on a positive yet realistic note, with some ideas as to what must still be accomplished. For some members, another program year may be forthcoming; for some, it is time to "make it" without the same group support, and for others it may be time to reevaluate the need for a group or some alternative service system. Attention to termination provides testimony about accomplishments as well as direction for further socialization or treatment goals.

EDUCATION AND JOB OPPORTUNITIES IN GROUP WORK

While group work was first taught in a school of social work at Western Reserve University in 1923, not until the 1950s did all schools of social work offer such courses. Many schools continue to offer a group work specialization, but the trend is toward generic methods courses stressing unitary concepts of the helping process in social work.

Bachelor's Degree Holders Needed

For many years, group workers with bachelor's degrees have been a vital force in the programming and services of settlement houses, community centers, youth clubs, Y's, residential and day camps, senior centers, and, more recently, community mental health agencies and homes for the aged. Many states have created new and exciting career opportunities for college graduates in human service programs. In-service training programs are widely available for bachelor's-level graduates who wish to enter social work and related fields.

Jobs continue to be available for graduates interested in youth services, Scouting, and community center and settlement house work. Opportunities exist for qualified persons at both program development and supervisory levels. Correctional, public welfare, and child welfare agencies also have openings for college graduates to work with groups.

SUMMARY AND APPLICATION

While social group workers do not have a corner on the group work market, they tend to play important roles in the management of a variety of group service programs and agencies. The development of bachelor's-degree social work programs is helpful for beginning group workers. Casework and group work skills in combination are in particular demand from social workers holding the master's degree. These personnel also fill planning and management jobs.

Social group work provides a means for people who are interrelated through a common environment or through common problems to gain skills to develop better ways of coping with life situations and to facilitate gaining greater autonomy.

—Gerald L. Euster

KEY TERMS

information giving	therapeutic groups
problem-solving	behavior modification
experience sharing	reinforcement
program activities	extinction
recreation groups	settlements
recreation-skill groups	contracts
education groups	individualization
self-help groups	assessment
socialization groups	

REFERENCES AND NOTES

1. Based on Mary L. Northway, "A Method for Depicting Social Relationships Obtained by Sociometric Testing," in J. L. Moreno (ed.), *The Sociometry Reader*, Free Press, Glencoe, 1960, p. 225.
2. Helen H. Perlman, "Social Work Method: A Review of the Past Decade," in *Trends in Social Work Practice and Knowledge*, National Association of Social Workers, New York, 1966, p. 84.

3. See Robert W. Roberts and Helen Northen, *Theories of Social Work with Groups*, Columbia University Press, New York, 1976.
4. Edward Lindeman, "The Roots of Democratic Culture," in Harleigh B. Trecker (ed.), *Group Work: Foundations and Frontiers*, Whiteside, New York, 1955, p. 13.
5. Ibid., p. 19.
6. Ruth R. Middleman, *The Non-Verbal Method in Working with Groups*, Association Press, New York, 1968, pp. 25–26.
7. Gertrude Wilson, "From Practice to Theory: A Personalized History," in Roberts and Northern, op. cit., p. 7.
8. Jane Addams, *Twenty Years at Hull House*, New American Library, New York, 1960, p. 98.
9. John W. Drakeford, *Farewell to the Lonely Crowd*, Word Books, Waco, 1969, p. 3.
10. Elizabeth McBroom, "Socialization Through Small Groups," in Roberts and Northen, op. cit., p. 271.
11. Ibid., p. 269.
12. Gertrude Wilson and Gladys Ryland, *Social Group Work Practice*, Houghton Mifflin, Cambridge, 1949, pp. 414–415.
13. Helen Northen and Robert W. Roberts, "The Status of Theory," in Roberts and Northen, op. cit., p. 389.
14. Jonathan A. Guttmacher and Lee Birk, "Group Therapy: What Specific Therapeutic Advantages?," *Comprehensive Psychiatry*, vol. 12, November 1971, pp. 546–547.
15. See Howard J. Parad et al., "Crisis Intervention with Families and Groups," in Roberts and Northen, op. cit., pp. 304–330.
16. Sidney R. Saul and Shura Saul, "Old People Talk About Death," *Omega*, vol. 4, no. 1, 1973, p. 28.
17. Sheldon D. Rose, *Treating Children in Groups*, Jossey-Bass, San Francisco, 1973, pp. 1–2.
18. Gerald L. Euster, "A System of Groups in Institutions for the Aged," *Social Casework*, vol. 52, October 1971, pp. 523–529.
19. Minnie M. Harlow, "Group Work in a Psychiatric Hospital: Today a Patient, Tomorrow—?," paper presented at the Annual Meeting of the National Conference on Social Welfare, 1960.
20. Martin Lakin, *Interpersonal Encounter: Theory and Practice in Sensitivity Training*, McGraw-Hill, New York, 1972, p. 4.
21. John W. Bennett, "Communes: The Oldest 'New' Movement in Western Civilization," *Washington University Magazine*, vol. 41, 1971, p. 21.
22. O. Hobart Mowrer, "Peer Groups and Medication, The Best 'Therapy' for Professionals and Laymen Alike," *Psychotherapy: Theory, Research, and Practice*, vol. 8, 1971, pp. 44–55.
23. Morton A. Lieberman et al., "Encounter: The Leader Makes the Difference," *Psychology Today*, vol. 6, 1973, p. 11.
24. Judith A. Lee, "Group Work with Mentally Retarded Foster Adolescents," *Social Casework*, vol. 58, March 1977, pp. 164–173.
25. Ronald Feldman et al., "Treating Delinquents in Traditional Agencies," *Social Work*, vol. 17, September 1972, pp. 72–79.
26. Jerry Wolkoff and Diane Applebaum, "The Jewish Community Center: A Group for Adolescents from One-Parent Families," *Journal of Jewish Communal Service*, vol. 53, 1976, pp. 179–184.

27. Gerald L. Euster, "Social Learning in School Groups," *Social Work*, vol. 17, September 1972, pp. 64–71.
28. Fritz Redl, *Children Who Hate*, Free Press, Glencoe, 1965, and *Controls from Within*, Free Press, Glencoe, 1952.
29. Harlow, op. cit.
30. Gisela Konopka, *Group Work in the Institution*, Whiteside, New York, 1970.
31. Maxwell Jones, *The Therapeutic Community*, Basic Books, New York, 1953, and *Beyond the Therapeutic Community*, Yale University Press, New Haven, 1968.
32. Grace Coyle, "Some Basic Assumptions about Social Group Work," in Marjorie Murphy (ed.), *The Social Group Work Method in Social Work Education*, Council on Social Work Education, New York, 1969, pp. 88–105.
33. Irvin D. Yalom, *The Theory and Practice of Group Psychotherapy*, Basic Books, New York, 1975, p. 158.
34. Ruth E. Smalley, *Theory for Social Work Practice*, Columbia University Press, New York, 1967, pp. 143–144.
35. Ibid.
36. Robert D. Vinter, "Program Activities: An Analysis of Their Effects on Participant Behavior," in Paul Glasser, Rosemary Sarri, and Robert Vinter (eds.), *Individual Change Through Small Groups*, Free Press, New York, 1974, pp. 235–237.
37. James K. Whittaker, "Program Activities: Their Selection and Use in a Therapeutic Milieu," ibid., pp. 255–257.
38. Helen U. Phillips, *Essentials of Social Group Work Skill*, Association Press, New York, 1957, p. 97.

FOR FURTHER STUDY

Paul Glasser, Rosemary Sarri, and Robert Vinter, *Individual Change through Small Groups*, Free Press, New York, 1974.
Margaret E. Hartford, *Groups in Social Work*, Columbia University Press, New York, 1972.
Robert W. Roberts and Helen Northern (eds.), *Theories of Social Work with Groups*, Columbia University Press, New York, 1976.
Carl R. Rogers, *On Encounter Groups*, Harper & Row, New York, 1970.
Harleigh B. Trecker, *Social Group Work: Practice and Principles*, Association Press, New York, 1972.
Emanuel Tropp, *A Humanistic Foundation for Group Work Practice*, Selected Academic Readings, New York, 1972.
Gertrude Wilson and Gladys Ryland, *Social Group Work Practice*, Riverside Press, Cambridge, 1949.

FOR DISCUSSION

1. What groups have you belonged to that were organized by a social group worker? By a lay leader?
2. Restate Perlman's observations about changes in group work using your own words.
3. Define group work.
4. What are some examples of situations in which group techniques would be most appropriate?

5. Illustrate: "Self-disclosure demands a high degree of trust of other group members."
6. Explain what is meant by a contract in group work.
7. How does a recreation group differ from a recreation-skill group?
8. Since self-help groups often reject professional leadership, who serves as leader?
9. What type of group would be most likely to provide increased self-confidence?
10. Explain when a patient governance group might be organized.
11. What rewards or reinforcers were used in the behavior-modification treatment group described in the chapter?
12. Research and report on the principles of one of the newer types of groups named in the chapter.
13. How was social reform related to the early development of group work?
14. Explain what Grace Coyle means by the use of group work as a "corrective for social disorganization."
15. Can groups change people? What evidence can you give for your answer?
16. How can group experience influence the ability to make decisions?
17. What are some examples of the use of individualization in group work?
18. Which of Whittaker's guidelines for programming for children's groups would you consider most useful? Why?
19. Describe a group situation and suggest what you would do to assist the process of termination.

PROJECTS

1. Five or six students develop a role-play in which they describe each member of the group briefly. Distribute the descriptions to the class. After the role-play has been presented, ask the class to identify the goals of the group. Compare the result with the group's goals written out in advance.
2. In the project above, prepare a brief record of the group session.
3. Make a special study of therapeutic groups and conduct a brief case conference about a hypothetical patient to illustrate the group activities involved in his or her treatment. If possible, use an experienced group worker as a consultant.
4. Organize a group to conduct a limited community project (such as repairing toys or rehabilitating a play area). Report on the process of organization and the outcome of the effort.
5. Organize a self-development group from your class to meet for four sessions. Determine goals and activities. Report on progress periodically to the class.
6. Prepare a series of questions that you could use as the basis for sociometric representation of a group. Include items involving general acceptance, such as "What two people would you want most as best friends?" and skill-related items, e.g., "If I had to camp out in the wilderness, whom would I choose to have with me?"

CHAPTER 5
Community Organization

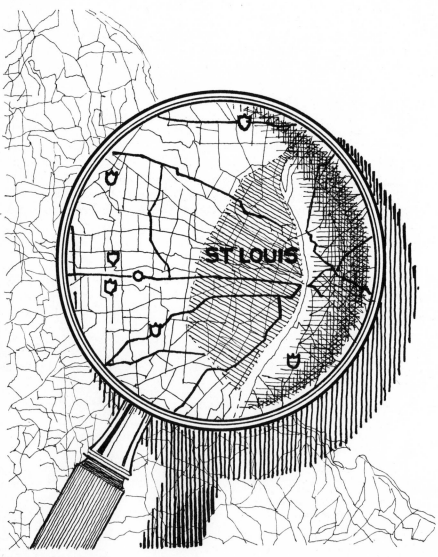

Focus on the community.

That I needed a home, and you gave me Food Stamps; That I needed a job, and you got me on the Welfare; That my family was sick, and you gave us your used clothes; That I needed my pride and dignity as a person, and you gave me surplus beans.

—Source Unknown

Community social work has developed out of a legacy of American protest. Organizers are catalysts for social change. They attempt to equip people who are "have-nots" with the skills to bring themselves a better life. This objective differs from casework or group work in that it concerns community change rather than individual or group change. The focus is on structural social change—changes in conditions for large groups of people.

THE RIGHT TO PROTEST

There are many different special groups: the unemployed, AFDC mothers, the handicapped, the culturally deprived, dropouts, the retarded, ghetto dwellers, minorities, addicts, the uneducated. They can be linked together because they all need organization if they are ever to pull themselves up and out of their poverty and ill health. Out of a tradition dating back to the founders of this country, Americans have been protesting with their voices, their votes, and their money. The *right to protest* has been used by citizens who sought relevant justice for groups of people. A theme appropriate for community organizers was stated by the abolitionist Frederick Douglass in 1857.

If there is no struggle, there is no progress. Those who profess to favor freedom, and yet deprecate agitation, are men who want crops without plowing up the ground. They want rain without thunder and lightning. They want the ocean without the awful roar of its many waters. This struggle may be a moral one; or it may be a physical one; or it may be both moral and physical; but it must be a struggle. Power concedes nothing without a demand. It never did and never will. . . . Men may not get all they pay for in this world; but they must certainly pay for all they get.[1]

Americans formed this nation by protesting the conditions imposed by British rule. The U.S. Constitution is replete with phrases which make the right to protest and the right to petition the government part of our national legacy.

Today, many issues lead to community action. Starting with small groups of activitists who form a core of protest, issues develop into national movements. We recognize these protests as the civil rights movement, the ecology movement, the antiwar movement, the movement for gay rights, the women's liberation movement, and the coalition of the elderly. These groups represent collections of citizens petitioning and protesting for social change.

Each group seeks certain goals for its membership—goods, services, or changes in opportunities in order to bring about increased equity. Pressure is brought on the nation to reorganize to meet these needs or adjust opportunity structures to include new groups in the American mainstream. Because of concerted community actions, citizens have acquired new health, welfare, and educational benefits. Social security, medical insurance, Aid to Families with Dependent Children, unemployment benefits, and opportunities for equal employment involving hiring and promotion all evolved out of our right to protest.

Community work has dramatic appeal to some young people because of its emphasis on challenging existing systems to reduce inequality in civil rights or social justice. Altruism, however, requires not only commitment to a cause but acceptance of varying degrees of risk which may result in loss of one's job. Community organization also provides the opportunity to study and perfect social service delivery mechanisms. It also provides the basis for a possible marriage of interests in research and social action.

EARLY CONCERNS OF COMMUNITY WORK

Like other social welfare activities, community work had its roots in the Charity Organization Society (COS) movement during the 1800s—the first major attempt in the United States to achieve some degree of rational order out of the chaos of emerging health and welfare services. The COS and the settlement movements represent the successful combination of the reforming zeal of the social worker with the philanthropic spirit and civic consciousness of well-to-do individuals.

The intensified social problems that accompanied industrialization became particularly evident in the twentieth century. For example, in 1900, twenty-four states and the District of Columbia had no minimum age for child labor, and other states had very inadequate provisions. There were few safety standards or sanitary facilities in factories and workshops; the employer was not considered liable for injuries to workers. Legal protection for women in industry was nil. Wages and hours were unregulated, and little organized interest was shown in the health or housing of the workers.

As the widening gap between the rich and the poor attested to the inequalities in wealth and income distribution, a few people were attracted by radical schemes for changing the prevailing system of individual business enterprise into state socialism, but the efforts of organized labor, social reformers, and social workers were mainly focused on easing the hardships of the working population rather than on changing the basic economic structure. These objectives were furthered after 1900 by more liberal and more honest administration in some state and local governments, and by growing competence and understanding on the part of social workers and social reformers. A spirit of optimism that the problems arising from the industrial era could be overcome began to replace the belief that poverty was a permanent and insoluble condition.

Supporters of progressive movements became convinced that social progress could be achieved only through legislative reform; such evils as child labor could be legislated out of existence, and government or industry could provide compensation for accidents and for involuntary unemployment. They also advocated the use of the state's taxing power to provide pensions for the aged and for mothers of dependent children. Social workers participated in the formation of the national Child Labor Committee in 1904 and the American Association for Labor Legislation in 1906.

After 1900 social workers constituted a growing, politically active element in American society. With the support of philanthropic foundations, they made intensive surveys of labor conditions, the causes of poverty, and means of alleviating distress. They envisaged use of state power to accomplish rearrangements of economic relationships. Professional social workers, students of labor problems, and leaders of advanced social opinion sought to affect national priorities on behalf of the powerless.

Progress toward enlightened welfare legislation to improve industrial conditions was beset with legal and other obstacles. In 1893 Illinois enacted the first enforceable eight-hour law for women, the result of the labors of Florence Kelley (associated with Hull House), only to have the State Supreme Court nullify the measure two years later. New York succeeded in enacting a similar statue in 1896, limiting women's work to sixty hours a week. In 1898 the U.S. Supreme Court, reflecting the rising liberal trend, affirmed that it was the duty of the state to protect the health and morals of its citizens through its police powers, thus making it constitutional to limit the hours of labor in dangerous occupations.[2]

COMMUNITY ORGANIZATION PRACTICE

The objectives of community organization practice in social work generally include the coordination of existing services, action to expand and modify services, and the creation and organization of new services. The development of new services in response to citizen demand has led to major growth of community work.

A community social worker may help a group to specify the nature of the problem; formulate effective, realizable goals; chart logical steps and program strategies to develop new models of service delivery; identify financial resources; and mount direct action campaigns to secure the service. Community organizers become involved in many social issues, including education, housing, health, leisure-time services, alienation of youth, economic and social control, labor relations, minority-group employment, and child care.

Social issues develop from citizen interest and concern about the imbalance between the needs of people and provisions to meet social ills. Often communications media define and clarify these issues. From issues, citizens who become caught in the necessity or even the morality of the cause develop programs for action. From issues, slogans often develop to promote a familiarity

Table 5-1 Community Social Work Opportunities

Agency	Voluntary Sector Organized Task
Red Cross	Establish a community blood bank
United Way	Open an emergency family shelter
Council on Aging	Form a militant group to protest for better health care for elderly
NAACP	Launch a movement to secure equal employment for minorities
Children's Home	Constitute a citizens lobby for improved children's services
Neighborhood Settlement House	Operate a food-buying cooperative

Agency	Public Sector Organized Task
Police Department	Organize a youth service bureau program
School District	Establish and develop a tutoring program for low-achieving youth
State Parole Office	Obtain community support for an adult halfway house for ex-offenders
Equal Employment Opportunity Commission	Create citizens task force to promote hiring of Indians
State College	Develop a plan for access to campus buildings for handicapped students
State Child Welfare Department	Plan and promote a statewide foster parents' training project
Public Housing Agency	Form a tenants council to improve recreation for residents

with the problem and its solutions. From issues, social agencies are created and financed after political sanctions define their social value.

Practice Settings for Community Social Work

Community social workers can choose from a variety of workplaces. There are many opportunities in both the voluntary and the public sector. Examples of settings and functions are shown in Table 5—some are more exciting than others, some will involve use of protest, others will not.

MAJOR ROLES OF THE COMMUNITY SOCIAL WORKER

The community social worker will use several models of operation. The model to be applied depends on the job to be accomplished. Four major roles can be differentiated; because a given situation may involve several roles, the distinctions are not always clear.

The Enabler

As *enabler* the worker helps people identify their needs, clarify their problems, and develop the capacity to deal with them more effectively. The emphasis is clearly on skill in developing relationships with community residents. The assumption is that self-motivated actions, growing out of a community's assessment of its own needs, have a value and permanence not found in actions imposed from the outside. The enabler must understand individual and group processes and use them as a central focus in practice. Community self-help is facilitated through the worker's assisting and enabling the participation of involved citizens.

The Broker

The *broker* acts as a guide in the "civilized jungle" of the service network to put people in touch with community resources that they need but do not know about. For instance, not all people who are eligible for public assistance actually get benefits. They may not know that they are eligible or how to apply. Many people may not know how to get food stamps, how to use the child guidance clinic, or how to qualify for public housing. Community organization workers playing the broker role either help people directly to locate needed resources or assist a citizens' group to provide an information and referral center to do the job.

The Advocate

Social workers in neighborhood community organization programs may find that the broker role is too indirect. Therefore, the role of *advocate* has been borrowed from the field of law. Often the institutions with which local residents must deal are hostile. Handling the issues brought to them by community groups, they sometimes conceal or distort information about rules, procedures, and office hours. By their own partisanship and practices, they create an atmosphere that demands advocacy on behalf of the poor or other clients. Productive interaction between community citizens and their institutions requires leadership and resources directed toward eliciting information, arguing the correctness of a position, and challenging the stance of a particular institution. The object is not to condemn the system but to modify or change particular institutions.

The community worker may be an advocate for the client group's point of view both to the community residents and to the institutional representatives. The advocate differs from the enabler and the broker by being a partisan whose expertise is available exclusively to service client interests. The impartiality of the enabler and the functionalism of the broker are absent. Other actors in a social conflict may be using their expertise and resources against the client. Thus the community organizer may argue the appropriateness of issuing a parade permit while the police argue its inappropriateness, or the worker and tenant may take the position that building-code violations warrant the withholding of rent while the landlord denies that violations exist. Social workers may be involved on both sides. A community organization worker may claim certain welfare benefits for a group of clients over the opposition of a social investigator. A community worker and a city housing authority worker may disagree over the criteria for eviction used by the housing authority.

The Activist

Social workers engaged in community organization produce partisan situations. The same logic that legitimizes the roles of broker, advocate, enabler, and social planner leads inevitably to the role of activist.

Morris and Rein establish a framework for the activist role.

> Political knowledge and skill to achieve one's ends have often been considered by social workers to be unprofessional. We have somehow believed that strong advocacy of a particular point of view and the development of techniques to achieve those ends violate our professional commitment to the democratic process. The question for us is whether our commitment to professional neutrality and noninvolvement is to continue to sustain our professional practice.[3]

The traditional neutrality of the social work profession has been exercised

(Drawing by Lorenz; © 1969 The New Yorker Magazine, Inc.)

to the detriment of certain client groups. If the policy of noninvolvement persists, the function of community organization practice will be limited to coordination, but if social workers are to find a role in community development, they cannot be exclusively neutral.

Except for the heroes of the American Revolution, this nation has usually had a culturally estranged view of political and social activists. Despite their ultimate vindication, abolitionists, suffragists, labor organizers, and pacifists are still viewed as deviants by the community at large. Activists are still characterized as "outsiders" and "agitators."

The activist role is legitimate for the social worker and especially for the community organizer. The passivity and objectivity of the service professions is, after all, something of a myth. People are urged to action of all sorts—to visit a dentist, curb their dogs, contribute to the Red Cross, and register to vote. In neighborhood community development, students are urged to stay in school, tenants to keep off the lawn, dropouts to join the Job Corps, and mothers to use well-baby clinics. Why should not tenants who are without heat be urged to confront slumlords, parents with grievances to boycott the schools, or citizens without franchise to take to the streets in legal public demonstration as a means to redress their grievances?

The selection from *Mau-Mauing the Flak Catchers* is an example of activism in San Francisco. Since jobs were being awarded on the basis of organizational power, the delegation had to make a strong impact. Obviously, they succeeded.

Activism Gets Summer Jobs

One morning about eleven o'clock a flamboyant black man in a dashiki turns up at City Hall. And this flamboyant black man, the Dashiki Chieftain, isn't running with any brothers from off the block. He is at the head of an army of about sixty young boys and girls from the ghetto.

. . . He comes marching up the stairs of City Hall and through those golden doors in his Somaliland dashiki, leading the children's army. And these kids are not marching in any kind of formation, either. They are swinging very free, with high spirits and good voices. The Dashiki Chief has distributed among them all the greatest grandest sweetest creamiest runniest and most luscious mess of All-American pop drinks, sweets, and fried food ever brought together in one place. Sixty strong, sixty loud, sixty wild, they come swinging into the great plush gold-and-marble lobby of the San Francisco City Hall with their hot dogs, tacos, Whammies, Frostees, Fudgsicles, french fries, Eskimo Pies, Awful-Awfuls, Sugar-Daddies, Sugar-Mommies, Sugar-Babies, chocolate-covered frozen bananas, malted milks, Yoo-Hoos, berry pies, bubble gums, cotton candy, Space Food sticks, Frescas, Baskin-Robbins boysenberry-cheesecake ice-cream cones, Milky Ways, M & Ms, Tootsie Pops, Slurpees, Drumsticks, jelly doughnuts, taffy apples, buttered Karamel Korn, root-beer floats, Hi-C punches, large Cokes, 7-Ups, Three Musketeer bars, frozen Kool-Aids—with the Dashiki Chief in the vanguard.

. . . The City Hall lifers can envision it already: a liver-red blob of sherbet sailing over the marble expance of the City Hall lobby on a foaming bile-green sea of Fresca, and the kids who are trying to rip the damned paper off the ice cream in the Drumstick popsicles, which always end up inextricable messes of crabbed paper and molten milk fat, mixing it up with the kids whose frozen Kool-Aids are leaking horrible streaks of fuchsia and tubercular blue into the napkins they have wrapped around them in their palms and mashing it all onto the marble bean of Mayor Angelo Rossi . . . and now Jomo Yarumba and his childstorm are swooping up the great marble stairs of the great central court toward the first gallery and the outer office of the Mayor himself, and the City Hall functionaires are beginning to confer in alarm. By and by a young man from the Mayor's office comes out and explains to Jomo Yarumba that the Mayor regrets he has a very tight schedule today and can't possibly see him.

"We'll wait for the cat to get through," says the Dashiki Chief.

"But he's completely tied up, all day."

"Hell, man, we'll stay here all night. We'll see the cat in the morning."

"All night?"

"That's right. We ain't budging, man. We're here to tend to business."[4]

Tom Wolfe, *Radical Chic and Mau-Mauing the Flak Catchers.*

CLIENT ACTION

Methods and roles can be combined as follows in the example from *Welfare Mothers Speak Out.* Self-help, activism, and advocacy were taken over by clients of a welfare agency. They had learned their techniques from community organizers.

Rights of the Poor

Me and my husband and our three children came to Milwaukee. We were migrant workers. We were looking for better jobs either in the factories or in the fields. When I say fields, I mean picking tomatoes and all kind of things . . . working on a farm. We came here to have a better living. We thought, "He can work and I can work and our children can work no matter what their age," because in farm work you can be just seven years old.

It is very, very hard when you don't have the education to get a job, especially when you been working all the time on the farm and you can't go to the city and talk to the people. You don't know where to go, what direction to take, what kind of job you can get. It's very hard to find a new job and get used to it because all the time you been working in the fields. You come home tired and that's it.

If you come to the city and get on welfare, you feel that you are doing nothing—just waiting for the money. We can't sit around because we been working all our life, the children, too. So I got in Welfare Rights.

I got on welfare when my husband left, and he left because there was three children in the family and he couldn't find a job to support them. This is the first of the Spanish-speaking people's problems—the father can get a job but it's not enough for the family. The rents would go high and the family has to pay for doctors and all these kinds of things, so he can't stay in one job.

Also, he can't have a job that he would like to have, so he just takes off. He is so mixed up and at the same time he would like to have everything that the family needs.

The men get tired of little or no work and just go from city to city because they just can't take it and keep looking for a job to support the family. There are a lot of people who come to Milwaukee looking for work and when they can't find it they move on. Some take their families, but some leave them. At least the family gets some help from welfare. The people in Welfare Rights can explain to them their rights. A mother can get a full-time job and still get some help from welfare, but many don't know. If the Welfare Department would tell the people their rights, it would be different, but it's not that way.

In the Latin community, it is very hard to get on welfare, because the people don't know what is going to happen. They think their children will be taken away and their husbands will be put in jail with no reason. There are many Latins who could be on welfare but aren't because they don't know their rights. They're afraid. Now some are on welfare, but they think that they don't have a right to this or that or even to see a man, or buy something. Like a mother spends the money on clothes for the kids and might not have it to pay the lights or gas, she is afraid she'll be cut off welfare.

I was afraid once, too, but not anymore. I was afraid that the caseworker would see my house and a few things would not be clean and she would drop me. In the first place she didn't understand me at all, because now I talk more English but I couldn't then and I was so shy because I had never talked to white people, because I had been working in the fields. When I first came on welfare, they didn't have any Spanish-speaking caseworkers at all. Sometimes, I would just move my hands; now I know more English because I have had more time in Milwaukee.

When I came on welfare, caseworkers came every week to my house and checked everything and asked everything. They went through my whole house and checked to see no man was around. When I joined Welfare Rights, that stopped—because I learned my rights. When you learn your rights, you feel more free; you're not afraid.

If they can't get a job, they still have a right to live. But someone will have to be at the Welfare Department with them to tell them what their rights are. And you got to keep telling them because they never heard that before. They have never been taught their rights.[5]

Here the right to protest is combined with the right to services. We observe client-centered organization among a cultural minority. The student preparing for such work must know the language (in this example, Spanish), the laws and policies of public welfare, the techniques of community organization. Each community organization job has its own particular set of skill requirements.

The writings of community residents will help an organizer to gain the flavor and develop an understanding of community issues. This example expresses the viewpoint of an Hispanic group.

Tierra Amarilla

"La tierra les pertenece a los que lo trabajan con sus proprias manos"
(The land belongs to those who work it with their own hands).

We, the people of Tierra Amarilla Merced (land grant) have formed a cooperative: COOPERATIVA AGRICOLA DEL PUEBLO DE TIERRA AMARILLA. We plan to work together this summer to grow such crops as beans, potatoes, wheat to grind for flour, onions, garlic and squash: just to name a few vegetables. We are going to work together so our children will not be hungry next winter.

Our people are hungry and have to practically beg for food from the government. We beg that same government which took our land or supported those who took it. We beg that same government which cuts down our right to the water in favor of the big cattle man, the rancher in Texas, the big growers in southern New Mexico. This government will not allow us to hunt all year round to feed our families . . . and instead will allow the Texan to come over and take his elk's head to put in his house as a trophy, while our children hunger for meat. We have to beg that same government which charges us a fortune to graze our cattle while at the same time it cuts down our grazing permits.

We don't want to beg anymore. We want to grow the food we need, so we don't have to go to welfare or to the store which robs us in credit charges. We will store the food we grow and next winter give it to those of our people who helped grow it and those who are hungry.

The world only knows Tierra Amarilla as a land of guerillas led by "fiery land grant leader, Reies Lopez Tijerina." The newspapers are always talking about the violence, vandalism and troublemakers of the North. What the world doesn't know is the history of the people of T.A., who have had the patience to match any saint. Surrounded for nearly a century by land-grabbing gringos, politicos, lambes,* state and federal governments, the people of Tierra Amarilla have always defended their right to stay on their land. For as one man has said, "The land is our mother. If we lose the land we are orphans. Where will we go?"

Before Reies Tijerina was born, the people of Tierra Amarilla were fighting for what is theirs by the Treaty of Guadalupe Hidalgo. "Ever since I was 4 or 5," says Senora Juan Martinex, "my daddy would explain to me how we came to be on the land and how it was ours by right. We have never stopped fighting for our land."

In the old way of life, whole villages of our people owned land together, because this was provided for in the laws of the Indies. They would farm together, build houses and prepare food for the winter together. These traditions have been crushed as our people have been driven off the land and onto welfare rolls. Under the anglo system of making a living, if a person wants to survive without being poor, he has to fight to "get ahead" and sometimes against his own people. When our communal way of life went, the trust our ancestors had to work the land and prepare the food together went too.

People seldom used to need money: they lived off the land. They worked their own leather and made boots and moccasins. They worked the wool, making blankets and clothes. And with the wood from the forest, they

*Lambes: Chicano Uncle Toms.

worked their own furniture. They grew their own crops and had enough water to irrigate the land. They used to dry or can the food without losing any of the vitamins. People say that eating the food this way made their bones and teeth stronger and people lived longer. Now the food they buy at the store has lost a lot of the food value and vitamins. The flour is bleached and they take out the healthiest part of the grain. El Senor Miguel Aguilar said during one of the co-op meetings, "In the factories they boil the vitamins out of the vegetables and sell them to us this way." Senor Nicolas Lopez added, "Yes, and then they sell us the vitamins."

What our people in Tierra Amarilla are going to do this year is to revive the old traditions of working together to feed our people . . . because this is the revolution also. What good is it to fight this long fight for the land, when our children grow up without food? Without a culture? Our children belong to the tomorrow, when our revolution will bring fruit.

The gringo doesn't understand the way we feel about the land. He used the land to make mon~y from. He doesn't care what he does with it, as long as he makes that money. And he does anything necessary for his profit: from stealing the land from us to making the laws—like the water laws—which benefit him and hurt us. The land for us is not to make money. Nor is the water or the trees. "ELLOS SON DE DIOS." He gave them to us to feed our families with, and not to make a whole lot of money. . . .

Spring has been here for more than a month in most of New Mexico, but for the people of Tierra Amarilla it has barely arrived. The rolling hills of this high plateau country are just turning green and every afternoon huge grey rain clouds move in and down from the somber mountains of Colorado that tower to the North. The adobe homes with their wooden outhouses and wells, standing in isolation across the landscape, look warmer and more comfortable now. The dirt roads are passable, after months of snow and mud. It is still a hard land, but the people have lived here for many generations and they are as strong as the land itself.

Out of that strength has been born La Cooperativa Agricola del Pueblo de Tierra Amarilla—the Agricultural Cooperative of the People of Tierra Amarilla.

. . . There have been many difficulties in getting the land plowed and planted. Daily rain-storms created delays, as did trouble with the 3 borrowed tractors. The land donated by the Aguilar family—Mrs. Gregorita Aguilar is President of the Cooperative—has not been worked in 35 years and was so hard that the tractor almost stood on end sometimes. Distances are long up here and you may have to go 175 miles or more to get one tractor part. But the people have lived with difficulties all their lives, and they keep moving, and the work gets done.

. . . I look around me. We have no running water, no electricity, no bathrooms. We have some farm equipment, a goat, cattle, a rabbit, a pregnant pig and ourselves. It is a good group of people; there have been no big personality hassles. We tease each other a lot, and get mad about little things, but we can always be free. The power of the people is growing stronger, the idea of having a harvest, of not selling our harvest to the exploiter merchants, of sharing it with the people, is becoming more real each day.[6]

ADELANTE UNIDOS

COMMUNITY ANALYSIS

Often, the community differs from the one in which the social worker grew up. Most likely, he or she will encounter cross-cultural experiences or find the new community strange in terms of racial makeup, social systems, economic structure, geography, or values. Thus, an exhaustive assessment of the community power structure is time well spent.

One way of looking at a community is to note its horizontal or vertical orientation.[7] The *horizontal* patterns are the structural and functional relationships of the community's various social units and subsystems to each other. Examples include an understanding of the relationships among racial and ethnic groups, or between capital and labor, within the community. How does the local setting—geography, streets, railroads, lakeshore—relate to community life. Where do the elected officials get their sanctions? Who are the principal decision-makers?

A second perspective is a vertical orientation. A community's *vertical* pattern is the structural and functional relationship of the community's social units to forces outside the community. Such assessment will assist the professional in learning the outside resources being granted to the community. What influence does the state or federal government have in your own town? There may be unusual difficulties in getting decisions made because the local saw mill is a branch of a company in another state.

A profile outline should enable the community work student to assess the relevant variables in a community. The following major topics should be included: (1) background and setting, including history, geography, and transportation; (2) demography; (3) communications; (4) economic life; (5) government, politics, law enforcement; (6) housing; (7) education; (8) recreation; (9) aids to family living; (10) religion; (11) associations and labor unions; (12) health facilities; and (13) environmental health.

PRACTICE PRINCIPLES FOR COMMUNITY SOCIAL WORKERS

In community social work practice, community *organization* is often distinguished from community *planning*. Others prefer to divide community organization into processes of directed social change, management of social conflict, and planning. Rothman considers "locality development, social planning, and social action."

Two examples illustrate the extremes and suggest the differences in the needed knowledge: A local health and welfare council plans for the distribution of funds to various member agencies within a community's voluntary network of services. In the course of activities a community social worker recommends additional services based on a survey of assessed need. Other recommendations may include agency mergers, improving accountability systems, interagency coordination and grant applications.

In such instances, planners and organizers need to understand the social fabric of society, community sociology, social problems, community psychology, social planning, and social policy in relevant areas such as health, housing, child care, mental health, and leisure-time services. Equally important is a knowledge of social welfare organizations, communications theory, fund raising, and public relations technology. Finally, skills in business management, social welfare law, and human behavior are useful tools.

At the other end of the spectrum are the activists employed in agencies, organizations, or governmental units in the business of social change. These practitioners should be prepared as social movement organizers. They need to know about community sociology, political organization, labor and industrial relations, group dynamics, political influence, social policy, and community planning. Subjects such as collective behavior, mass movements, history, and social psychology are also of benefit.

Table 5-2 develops Rothman's three approaches for twelve major practice variables.[8]

Whatever the model practiced in community social work, the professional is aware of community alienation. For each affiliation, there is usually a corresponding disaffiliation. For example, if a group of welfare recipients is critical of the welfare establishment, it follows that they may lose the support of some social workers.

JOBS IN COMMUNITY SOCIAL WORK

Employment opportunities are available on the basis of skill, experience, and educational achievement. While not increasing as rapidly as they were during the later 1960s, jobs are available for practitioners.

The concept of the community outreach worker was broadened during the last decade. Paraprofessional staff with little formal training are employed in their own neighborhoods as advocates, organizers, and referral agents. They may be attached to a neighborhood health center and organize a block health-education group or carry on a local campaign to urge residents to seek treatment for a particular contagious disease.

Programs organized by ACTION, the federal volunteer agency, such as University Year in Action, Volunteers in Service to America, and the Retired Senior Volunteer Program, employ staff for direct programming among low-income people. State agencies dealing with drug abuse, health, child welfare, and mental health also employ some paraprofessional staff to do community social work in the category of "community outreach" person, "neighborhood worker," or "area liaison" representative. New Careers programs sponsored by the Department of Labor developed training and placement programs for paraprofessionals in the field of community social work.

An innovative form of social work is the community collective movement. Collectives function as settlements of activists who do community organization work in neighborhoods. Often workers live together and share income from

Table 5-2 Rothman's Three Models of Community Organization Practice

	Model A (locality developppmental)	Model B (social planning)	Model C (social action)
1. Goal categories of community action	Self-help; community capacity and intergration (process goals)	Problem-solving with regard to substantive community problems (task goals)	Shifting of power relationships and resources; basic institutional change (task or process goals)
2. Assumptions concerning community structure and problem conditions	Community eclipsed, anomic; lack of relationships and democratic problem-solving capacities: static traditional community	Substantive social problems: mental and physical health housing, recreation	Disadvantaged populations, social injustice, deprivation, inequity
3. Basic change strategy	Broad cross section of people involved in determining and solving their own problems	Fact-gathering about problems and decisions on the most rational course of action	Crystallization of issues and organization of people to take action against enemy targets
4. Characteristic change tactics and techniques	Consensus: communication among community groups and interests; group discussion	Consensus or conflict	Conflict or contest: confrontation, direct action, negotiation
5. Salient practitioner roles	Enabler-catalyst, coordinator; teacher of problem-solving skills and ethical values	Fact-gatherer and analyst, program implementer, facilitator	Activist-advocate: agitator, broker, negotiator, partisan

employment. Sometimes they provide a specific service, such as a drug crisis center, hot line, emergency family shelter, or runaway halfway house, or they do more generalized community work.

Community social workers with a bachelor's degree are doing most of the tasks outlined in this chapter—the creation of new services, the coordination and realignment of programs, and issue-centered grass-roots organizing. Workers trained in a four-year social welfare undergraduate curriculum are prepared for entry-level positions. Many employment opportunities were developed by the antipoverty program and later became institutionalized by state and local governments.

Persons with the master's degree also engage in all types of community work. The M.S.W. in community organization can manage community council, health and welfare council, and United Way organizations. At the state or federal governmental level, they also supervise and manage large programs.

Table 5-2   (Continued)

	Model A (locality developpmental)	Model B (social planning)	Model C (social action)
6. Medium of change	Manipulation of small task-oriented groups	Manipulation of formal organizations and of data	Manipulation of mass organizations and political processes
7. Orientation toward power structure(s)	Members of power structure as collaborators in a common venture	Power structure as employers and sponsors	Power structure as external target of action: oppressors to be coerced or overturned
8. Boundary definition of the community client system or constituency	Total geographic community	Total community or community segment (including "functional" community)	Community segment
9. Assumptions regarding interests of community subparts	Common interests or reconcilable differences	Interests reconcilable or in conflict	Conflicting interests which are not easily reconcilable: scarce resources
10. Conception of the public interest	Rationalist-unitary	Idealist-unitary	Realist-individualist
11. Conception of the client population of constituency	Citizens	Consumers	Victims
12. Conception of client role	Participants in interactional problem-solving process	Consumers or recipients	Employers, constituents, members

They direct settlement houses or neighborhood centers. As community planners—employed, perhaps, by a union, a health planning council, an anti-delinquency board, or an area planning office for services for the aged—M.S.W.'s are involved in the development of new programs. In these jobs, a social worker may research legislation and program guidelines for new funding and develop proposals for foundation or government grants.

New agencies in the fields of women's rights, drug treatment, child welfare, public and mental health, and services for the elderly develop their programs with community social work personnel. The demands for workers vary with the political and financial support for social services.

Much of the work of community social workers is also done by other disciplines. Students gaining master's degrees in community psychology, recreation, urban and regional planning, health planning, or corrections planning and administration are competing with social workers for similar employment opportunities. Opportunities are especially promising for members of minority groups.

Only one out of every twenty professional social workers is employed in a community organization agency. Job opportunities in the new types of community work agencies vary. Some of them employ non-social workers as a matter of conviction, but many that prefer social workers with a master's degree have difficulty paying the higher entry salary that a person with a master's degree expects. They may then hire a B.S.W. or a paraprofessional. Some jobs require special knowledge about mental retardation, drug programs, or handicaps, for example.[9]

SUMMARY AND APPLICATION

The relationship between community work and social justice is clear. Participating in social change can be exciting. One of the major issues concerns the role of the social worker. Should staff members work as advocates and activists on behalf of a community or function mainly as enablers to train community residents to work on their own behalf? Both are necessary, but in what proportion? Many community groups organize, but many also are unable to sustain the gains that have been made. Leadership training may require more effort than direct advocacy and activism but may result in more commitment and sustained action efforts.

Community work, then, provides a wide range of objectives, strategies, and skills. One of the most important is to be able to work with a variety of people with differing backgrounds and attitudes—some of whom have come to distrust social workers as members of an insensitive establishment.

—*Arnold Panitch*

KEY TERMS

social change   horizontal orientation
right to protest   vertical orientation
enabler   community profile
broker   locality development
advocate   social planning
activist   social action
child labor laws

REFERENCES AND NOTES

1. Quoted in Lerone Bennett, Jr., *Before the Mayflower*, Penguin, Baltimore, 1966, p. 274.

2. *Holden v. Hardy*, 169 U.S. 366, 383 (1898).
3. Robert Morris and Martin Rein, "Emerging Patterns in Community Planning," in *Social Work Practice*, Columbia University Press, New York, 1963, p. 174.
4. Tom Wolfe, *Radical Chic and Mau-Mauing the Flak Catchers*, Farrar, Straus & Giroux, New York, 1970, pp. 144–147.
5. Clementina Castro, "Spanish-Speaking People and the Welfare System," in Milwaukee County Welfare Rights Organization, *Welfare Mothers Speak Out*, Norton, New York, 1972, pp. 66–69.
6. "Tierra Amarilla," from *El Grito* (1969), in Mitchell Goodman, *The Government Toward a New America*, Pilgrim Press, Philadelphia, pp. 232–233.
7. Roland L. Warren, *The Community in America*, Rand McNally, Chicago, 1963, pp. 240–246.
8. Jack Rothman, "Three Models of Community Organization Practice," in Fred M. Cox et al. (eds.), *Strategies of Community Organization*, Peacock, Itasca, Ill., 1974, pp. 26–27.
9. Alfred M. Stamm, "NASW Membership Characteristics, Development and Salaries," *Personnel Information*, vol. 12, May 1969, p. 49.

FOR FURTHER STUDY

Saul Alinsky, *Reville for Radicals*, Chicago: University of Chicago Press, 1946.
George Brager and Harry Specht, *Community Organizing*, Columbia University Press, New York, 1973.
Charles Grosser, *New Directions in Community Organization*, Praeger, New York, 1973.
A. Michael Washbum and Charles Beitz, *Creating the Future*, Bantam, New York, 1974.

FOR DISCUSSION

1. To what kind of change is community work directed?
2. What are some current examples of the use of the right to protest?
3. Choose a social program, such as social security or AFDC. Find out how its proponents organized to secure its adoption.
4. What are the three objectives of community organization?
5. Why are slogans often important to community organizations? Illustrate with examples.
6. Some people feel that the enabler role is the most difficult task of the community organizer? Do you agree? Why or why not?
7. Do you think that the techniques used in *Mau-Mauing the Flak Catchers* could be used next summer? If not, how do you explain the changes in attitude?
8. Explain "Community organization and planning continue to be *categorical*."
9. Legislative reform at the turn of the twentieth century focused on labor conditions. What two groups of the population were singled out for special projects?
10. If you study state and federal provisions as they affect your community, would such an analysis be considered *vertical* or *horizontal*?
11. Why would you include communications in a community profile?
12. List all of the associations in your community that offer programs for its residents. Can you identify at least fifty?

13. Differentiate the practitioner roles in locality development, social planning, and social action.
14. With what other disciplines is the community social worker likely to work?

PROJECTS

1. Make a list of the local community work agencies. Telephone the executive of each one and ask how he or she would define *community organization practice*. List the various responses and analyze the differences.
2. Survey the members of the class to determine how many of them have been involved in demonstrations, picketing, or other sorts of activism. How was each activity organized, and what success did it have?
3. Read *Reveille for Radicals* and present a report on the methods of community organization used by Saul Alinsky.
4. Have a small panel discuss the techniques used in *Mau-Mauing the Flak Catchers*. What elements are presented in the full text that are not included in the excerpt? What alternative techniques would you suggest?
5. Discuss the advantages and disadvantages of professional neutrality for social workers. What conflicts arise between their professional roles and their responsibility as citizens?
6. Interview the head of the local welfare council to find out its present role and how it has changed. Ask him or her to respond to the typical criticisms of such organizations. What innovations would he or she propose?

CHAPTER 6
Other Approaches to Methods

A famous generalist.

Our effort to intervene at the points where organism, personality, society, and culture intersect is essential for society, but tremendously difficult to accomplish. Yet from this noble perspective we have begun to fashion policies, programs, and principles of action. None of them is complete, satisfactory, or even moderately effective. But they exist; they are there to develop, use, and improve.

—Werner W. Boehm*

Social work has come a long way since the 1920s and 1930s. In that era, if you had a college degree, most schools of social work would grant you a professional degree in one additional academic year. The role of schools of social work was to turn out specialists. To be a medical social worker, you took one set of courses and received practical experience in a hospital or a clinic. To become a child welfare worker, you took a different set of courses and had field assignments with children. Psychiatric social work was a similar specialty, and casework was the sole method taught in most schools. Dissatisfaction resulted from this approach because a one-year professional program was considered too short. Also, the specialties had a common knowledge base, and people often moved from one specialty to another. Thus, social work took two steps simultaneously—the educational program became generic, and the time for the professional master's degree was lengthened to two academic years in all accredited schools.

THE GENERIC APPROACH

In a generic program, the student was expected to learn the basic principles and techniques of either casework or group work that would be applicable in work with medical patients, mental patients, children, offenders, the disabled, and the aged—to name but a few types of clients. Particular interests were accommodated in field placements, but academic courses tended to be broadly based, utilizing social science knowledge as well as psychoanalytic theory. The treatment methodology was still heavily psychosocial. Meanwhile, community work was developing, requiring a different knowledge base and a different array of skills.

In the last few years new tracks or majors have developed in addition to the original three methods. This chapter discusses several of them briefly—the generalist approach, involving all three methods; the fields of practice concept; the social problems approach; social policy development and analysis; management and administration; and research.

*Werner W. Boehm, "Social Work Education: Issues and Problems in the Light of Recent Developments," *Journal of Education for Social Work*, vol. 12, 1976, pp. 26–27.

THE GENERALIST

The generalist is usually well grounded in systems theory, which emphasizes the importance of interaction and interdependence. The social work client functions in many systems—including the agency, the family, the workplace, and the community. Inputs are made in each, and the individual is in turn affected by each. A single event can often have far-reaching effects. If a person takes a position in another city, whatever service he or she gets from a given agency will be terminated. There will be a move to a new neighborhood and transfer of the children to new schools. There will be a different constellation of factors at work, and a different group of community organizations. The move may profoundly affect the person's roles and role satisfactions. Social services may involve influencing the various systems of which the individual is a part. The generalist should understand systems models and use them in problem-solving.

Solving Human Problems   Until social work developed, solutions to human problems were never thought of in terms of casework, group work, or community work. The individual, his or her family group, other people, and the community have been there for centuries, and they have always had to be reckoned with. As the efforts of the nonprofessional helpers and the social reformers were described and analyzed and social science knowledge increased, systematic methods for helping individuals resulted. As the discussion in Chapter 3 suggested, eventually a marriage with psychiatry was consummated, and casework adopted a medical model that emphasized personality change through psychosocial treatment. But many social workers were not influenced much by the medical model. They continued their concerns with helping a person get more marketable skills and a better job, reducing family conflict by talking with other family members, trying to provide child care, and improving housing. These activities, however, were usually considered secondary to treatment, which has centered directly on a better self-concept or an increase in ego strength.

Use of Groups   To help people in their personality development, groups were used increasingly. Learning to share with others in organized activities provided transferable skills for learning to work with others. Recreational skills enhanced personal satisfaction and group acceptance. Cooperative projects under effective leaders taught skills in personal interaction. People with particular problems or handicaps were able to see that others had the same difficulties and that better means of coping could be learned from each other as well as from a leader. Groups could plan to do things together that their members never would have considered doing as individuals. The family was discovered by both caseworkers and group workers as the most significant small group. Goals for the individual were often facilitated or constrained by other family members, so caseworkers began working with total family groups.

Agencies with group services also hired caseworkers to supplement group sessions.

Community Work   Meanwhile, as we have seen, social work was developing its own organizational structure. Welfare councils did community planning and coordinated agency programs. Neighborhood improvement groups were formed to obtain concessions from the city council, to put pressure on local property owners, to sponsor or oppose political candidates, or to apply for grants. Often the major task was to work not with the whole community but with subgroups. To affect decision-making, the community worker also had to single out individuals to try to change their values and to change their minds on issues.

A Combination of Skills   A variety of skills are often needed in the same person. Just as social workers did not want to be limited to one field, they also began to see one method as too limiting. Schools of social work looked for new ways to skin the cat—to somehow combine the skills and experiences required for the three methods in a more adequate package. Sometimes the attempt was complete; in others it was partial.

One approach was to skin the old cat very carefully and to skin another one or two quickly—to concentrate on a major method and supplement it with a survey of the others. Casework students, for instance, were expected to have knowledge of group work or community work for caseworkers, or both. Students who were critical often felt they got only a smattering of the "minor" methods unrelated to the primary method.

Another approach was to cross-breed the three cats into two. Casework and group work were put together as "social treatment." Group work and community work were combined into "intervention with groups and communities." These two are also known as "micro" and "macro" methods.

The generalist model was new and exciting. It involves identifying and analyzing the interventive behaviors appropriate to social work and providing experience with them. The worker must perform a wide range of tasks related to the provision and management of direct service, the development of social policy, and the facilitation of social change. As persons with a bachelor's degree perform more of the direct service tasks, professional social workers are encouraged to move into middle-level management of the social services, thus enhancing their role as generalists.

This discussion suggests that a specific definition of a social work generalist is difficult. Just as "intelligence is what the intelligence test measures," a generalist is defined by what a generalist does.

The Generalist Is Not New

The generalist label is new, but the generalist is not. Especially in rural areas, social workers have been expected to undertake a range of intervention strategies. Their own inventiveness has extended that range. Their roles have included services to individuals and groups. Community planning and advocacy efforts have often been born of necessity more than design. Workers gained versatility and competence through practical experience and an occasional short course or workshop. These generalists have most often been women who changed jobs infrequently and had deep roots in the community. They knew everyone, and everyone knew them. They were publicly identified with social work practice and had no desire to hide in a bureaucracy. As client advocates, they expected to be equally effective with clients and with the power structure. They did not hesitate to enlist other agencies on behalf of a client and often called staff members of several agencies together to plan jointly on a case. Organizing and leading groups, developing new resources and facilities, promoting better schools and improved housing was their responsibility, too. Hours were spent in meetings outside traditional work time. Roles as agency employees and as concerned citizens were seldom clearly separated. What these social workers did and how they did it were highly individual. There was little documentation of methods or outcome. Although the home-grown generalists work mainly in rural areas, a similar need exists in urban communities. Service advocacy that pushes all relevant community institutions to meet a client's needs is essential and is especially congruent with the generalist approach.

Family treatment typically requires the application of both individual and group principles. Community centers find that individual counseling is needed to supplement work in groups. The leader in many instances may also work best with individuals from the group. In affecting the behavior of an individual or of a group, changes in the environment or the opportunity structure may be required to make individual change possible. The worker serving the client may be best equipped to carry out this role. This suggests the close linkages among individual, group, and community intervention. Living in the community where one works helps. Then the worker's skills and concerns may both be much more sharply focused.

To tie one's expertise to a single method may be uneconomical and unpromising. The small voluntary agency finds that it cannot afford a variety of specialists, and the large public agency has learned that to be effective it cannot separate individual and family improvement from societal change. For those who see the world in holistic terms, the generalist has come to represent a promising solution.

Educational Formats

The Bachelor of Social Work* program is seen by some social workers as the most appropriate point to emphasize generalist preparation. The generalist

*The terms for the degree may differ but should be considered to be interchangeable. Bachelor of Arts in Social Work, Bachelor of Science in Social Work, and Bachelor of Social Service are common titles. Bachelor of Social Work (B.S.W.) is used here because it is probably the most common term. From a similar variety of terminology for the master's degree, we have chosen to use Master of Social Work (M.S.W.).

must learn to make a diagnosis, that is, an accurate assessment of a given situation, and must be competent to deal with the more usual forms of dysfunctioning while working with different targets: individuals, groups, organizations, and communities.[1] Ideally, the generalist at the entry level should have a widely varied practice dealing with common problems and should have careful supervision.

The Southern Regional Education Board defines the core of competence of social welfare as "all of that area of human endeavor in which the worker uses himself as an agent to assist individuals, families, and communities to better cope with social crises and stresses, to prevent and alleviate social stresses, and to function effectively in areas of social living." The following areas are included: public welfare, child welfare, mental health, corrections, vocational counseling and rehabilitation, community action, and community development.[2]

Other Variations   The generalist emphasis can provide a foundation for later specialization. The generalist B.S.W. may be followed by a specialized M.S.W. a generalist program for the first year of graduate education and a second year that involves specialization is popular. Another format begins with the more tangible specialization and follows it with generalist content and experience. The two-year M.S.W. generalist program at the University of Chicago was based on this rationale:

> We believe that such a practice must be marked by a solution-seeking emphasis as opposed to the methods orientation of traditional practice or combined methods. A generalist practice could be developed, we concluded, by (1) being responsive to leads from practice; (2) utilizing a problem-solving approach as the major organizing principle; (3) turning to the practice literatures and skills of all three practice methods for intervention, planning, and implementation; and (4) focusing on the relationships between change and stability that are germane to each problem situation.
>
> Our particular approach to generalist practice as it finally evolved was developed in response both to renewed and changing awareness of the dynamic interrelationship of the individual to his total environment and to an increased awareness of the limitations imposed on the worker's role. We contended that a strict adherence to a methods orientation limits the perceptions and activity of social work practitioners. This point of view gave us a new feeling for the long-held social work principle that human problems, multi-caused and multi-faceted as they are, result in far-reaching cause-effect spirals. We also believed that agency structure, policy, and procedures too often hinder problem-solving activity rather than encourage or support it. The nature of the problem is the crucial determining factor in interventions. It follows that solutions to and prevention of problems frequently require a multiplicity of methods in the interventions; agency flexibility and expanded community effort are essential to support practice that is guided by the nature of the problem.
>
> Our conception of generalist practice requires a worker to assist individuals, families, small groups, and larger social systems to work on change that promotes

the best possible relationship between people and their environment. In this process, all social work methods, traditional and innovative, are utilized singly or in combination to meet reality needs and to alleviate stresses in ways that enhance or strengthen the inherent capacities of client systems. Generalist practice is addressed to the solution and/or prevention of problems at all levels of intervention—intrapersonal, familial, interpersonal, organizational, community, institutional, and societal. Commonly, more than one aspect of a given problem may be dealt with simultaneously. There is an effort to establish and review the necessary balance between change and stability in every situation and to identify areas that may require stabilization if the desired change is to take place and to survive.

The generalist social worker is a practitioner who usually is first involved in the problem-solving process with individuals or groups who are having problems in social functioning. Social functioning refers to the life-tasks required of people and their efforts to cope with them. Exploration of these problems focuses on those social, cultural, and institutional antecedents in the larger social system that are adversely influencing the clients' lives and coping efforts. This process of problem identification and definition is the joint endeavor of client and worker. Plans are also formulated collaboratively and interventions leading to solutions are outlined. In these two stages of the problem-solving process (problem identification and problem assessment) the worker has two judgments to make. One is the level or levels at which intervention should take place. The other is the specific plan of action to guide the actual interventive efforts. Systematic assessment guides the first decision in ways that avoid premature closure on the object of change (problem) and the means to be employed. Assessment also assists in the determination of the social problem context in which the problem-solving will be done.

A specific assessment and plan for action may be drawn from any one or any combination of the practice methods. Each practice method is seen as a repertoire of specific approaches. To analyze and address each problem situation, the worker attempts to match specific approaches to the problems. In this way, already established knowledge is eclectically utilized, and additional modes can be developed to meet new challenges to the profession.[3]

The key differences among generalist educational programs come in the independence or integration of generalist and specialist training, the extent of versatility expected in role behaviors, and the terminal level of skills considered to constitute successful outcomes of professional education.

The Worker as Advocate

Social workers and students often see the generalist concept as the essence of social work. They see the worker as an advocate who should make societal systems responsive to the needs of those served. The worker deals with the client's feelings and instills confidence and helps clients define problems and priorities. Social workers may need to bring clients together for better understanding or for the greater power that comes from group membership. The generalist represents the client in dealings with other agencies or groups—not with vague or routine referrals but as one who helps negotiate the system and looks at the adequacy of existing services and their implied values and operating policies. Often the major goal is to make existing services more accessible or more responsive. When there are significant gaps, generalists help organize new programs and negotiate their acceptance by power groups and by the public. When policies are unfair, they may be able to break down the barriers. When money is needed, they have to find it. When a program is inefficient, they can make that judgment accurately and determine the reasons why.

Like the early founders of American social work, the generalist sees the environment as the major target for change, and environmental change as often preceding changes in the psyche. As a citizen away from the job, the generalist is active in a range of organizations that can use both knowledge and energy. Protest is often useful, but more subtle forms of persuasion are also used. Generalists are critical of their own organization as well as others. They must also be able to challenge the effectiveness of efforts. When there are ethical conflicts, they may have to risk their job for what they believe.

The Right to Have an Advocate;
The Right to Be an Advocate

Advocacy, a new emphasis in social work, encourages active and sometimes aggressive responses to assist the people whom a social worker serves. The social worker makes a clear commitment to the client to help get whatever may be required. Those who see social services as providing minimum effort at minimum cost often question the right of people with special problems to have an advocate and question advocacy as an appropriate activity for a social worker. If no more is done than what the law requires, only a few social workers are needed for many clients. Personnel costs are kept down, and there is little confrontation to provide more or better services. After all, say the critics, a client is supposed to accept the services given with gratitude. The advocate rejects all of these limitations.

Advocacy covers a broad spectrum. Piven and Cloward were among the first to press for active support of welfare clients in their struggle to obtain basic rights.[4] Some social workers became organizers of tenant unions and led rent strikes to help improve housing. Others have lobbied for new programs or new facilities. Many take an active role in referral—going with the client to other agencies, helping answer questions, and when necessary pleading the client's cause.

When advocacy involves the political process, employees of public agencies may find themselves limited by the Hatch Act and other laws intended to restrict the political activity of civil servants. Such laws regulate use of time off the job and constitute a major restriction of personal freedom.

The most difficult conflict may result when a worker finds that the policies of his or her agency serve the client badly. When agencies conducted midnight raids to see whether welfare mothers were living with a male friend, an employee refused to participate in such a raid and was fired. As a result, the worker had to sue to get the job back.[5] Meanwhile, the federal government outlawed such raids as an invasion of privacy.

A generalist is often the best advocate because of the combination of skills with individuals and groups that are required. In school social work, the worker must challenge the school's evaluation and discipline policies if they contribute to the behavior problems of children and may also become involved in promoting job programs outside of school hours. The worker will often represent those who are in trouble with the law and at the same time help to make the students' behavior more acceptable.

The advocate stands in sharp contrast to the social worker who sees the content of the job as one of "adjustment." The advocate must be able to take criticism for being "too much of an activist."

Field Experiences for the Generalist

The development of accredited B.S.W. programs makes it easier to provide a generalist foundation, including an appropriate field placement. In many graduate schools of social work, students are able to complete a master's degree in one additional year and have the range of experiences needed to meet the goals of the generalist model.

Types of Placement   For the generalist a *block* field placement—in which the student is available virtually full time to work intensively with the social services of the community—is preferable to a placement operating concurrently with classroom work. Availability of the student to meet crises is especially important. If placements are *concurrent* with classroom work, the student does not have the same opportunity for sustained effort, and there may be tension between field and classroom demands. Most concurrent programs do not succeed in integrating classroom and field experience, although integration is a potential advantage.

A Key Element   Perhaps the greatest test of generalist programs comes in the available field placements. Whereas students may see themselves as potential agents of social change, their practical experience may still be limited to one traditional social work method. Then the experience is inadequate.

The content of field instruction is important. Special faculty skills are needed to provide the necessary variety of experiences, often beyond the limits of a single agency. Schools of social work have found that operating their own service units or having direct control over an agency program may make it possible to provide a better generalist learning experience, although such a system is costly. Schools have also provided student placements in their own service projects operated through grants. Sometimes a faculty member is responsible for directly planning and monitoring the learning experiences of the student in an agency. With several students, the agency outpost may become a learning center.

FIELDS OF PRACTICE

Many agencies, faculty, and students have not been fully satisfied with the emphasis on one of the three traditional methods or with a generalist approach—especially for graduate social work education. By emphasizing specialization in a field of practice, the experience can be more directly relevant to the type of setting in which the student would like to work upon graduation. Although this approach may seem to resemble the narrower specialties with which the profession started, it involves many more options and often a combination of methods. Typical fields of practice include children and families, mental health, health and rehabilitation, school social work, income maintenance, aging, corrections, employment programs, and social work in business and industry. At the same time research, management and planning, and social policy may be offered as distinct specialties.

Fields of practice programs appeal to agencies. A mental health program, for example, can then hire a student who has spent a year or more with a concentration in mental health, including experience in an agency in that field. A generalist placement in the first year and a placement in a specialty in the second is quite common.

The fields of practice or areas of specialization chosen by any school should be based on student interest, field placement resources in the specialty, and employment opportunities after graduation.

THE SOCIAL PROBLEM APPROACH

Some schools of social work have built their curricula around the study of intervention in selected social problems. Problems selected may be broad or more narrow. Examples include (1) poverty and income security, (2) delivery of health services, (3) corrections, and (4) the unmarried mother and her child. The social problem approach may be used either for development of generalists or for students who are interested in the traditional social work methods.

In a fully integrated curriculum, courses in social policy and planning, human behavior and social environment, social work intervention, research, and administration might all concentrate on the same social problem.

An Illustrative Problem

With the unmarried mother and her child as the social problem, for example, social policy courses may concentrate on legal rights and constraints and on service issues, with particular emphasis on school attendance policies and provisions of medical care. In connection with human behavior, the differing problems of the fifteen-year-old and the twenty-five-year-old unmarried mother can be compared. Nutrition and prenatal development is a major topic, involving possible mental retardation. Maternal employment and day care are important too, especially when the unmarried mother is likely to want to keep her child. Obviously adoption is another relevant subject for those who surrender a child.

Research   Projects can be developed to study the client group, the provision of service, or public attitudes toward unmarried motherhood. One group of students found that their social action efforts could also be effective; over a two-year span they were able to eliminate a regulation that had barred women with more than one illegitimate child from being accepted for public housing.

Intervention   Extended examples of help required by unmarried mothers can be developed for courses in intervention—work with the pregnant women individually and in groups; ways to deal with family concerns related to the pregnancy and to possible marriage; goals and techniques for involving the girls and sometimes their boyfriends in groups; access to the medical care system; preparental education; school policies and peer-group reactions to pregnancy; and facilitation of independent study if the woman is to receive home instruction.

Administration   In administration courses, unmarried motherhood can be studied in terms of the major decisions faced by administrators in public assistance, foster care agencies, maternity homes, and group-serving agencies. Administrative decision making is particularly interesting because maternity homes are slowly disappearing or finding other roles. A community analysis can be made of the barriers to service faced by the girls. The findings can be presented to city officials, school personnel, public health nurses, and other interested groups, with the social worker acting as advocate.

Field Instruction   The social problem approach has special implications for field instruction.[6] Field placements are selected so that the group will gain experience working on aspects of the problem, although they may not (and perhaps should not) serve unmarried mothers exclusively. The social problem model makes the assumption that students will generalize from this problem to others, since by no means all of them will be employed to serve unmarried mothers. Although poverty and health care are broader topics, a program using these problems relies on the same assumptions concerning generalization of experience.

POLICY ANALYSIS AND DEVELOPMENT

A major interest of contemporary social workers is changing ineffective social policies and developing new ones. As a result, some programs at the master's and doctoral levels seek to produce policy specialists.[7] These tracks emphasize the need for increasing knowledge from the social sciences—especially economics and political science. Courses also help students to become familiar with major policy issues and techniques of analysis and evaluation. Block field placements are often available to governmental agencies at the state and federal levels concerned with public policy and the development of regulations to implement it. Students may obtain interesting jobs with social agencies and as policy advisers to legislators, or as social welfare reporters for larger newspapers and magazines. They are encouraged to act as advocates for new policies. Demand is increasing for policy specialists for the faculties of schools of social work and for public administration, but positions are still very limited.

SUPERVISION, MANAGEMENT, AND ADMINISTRATION

Recently many efforts have been made in the schools of social work to include supervision, management, and administration to accelerate the career line of interested students. In the past, leadership positions covering a wide range of autonomy and authority have been filled by promoting people who have provided direct services. Especially with developments in administrative science and management that involve specialized knowledge and skills unavailable to the traditional social worker, the apprenticeship system is inefficient as a means of leadership training. Only recently have students considered work measurement, cost analysis, and planning techniques. Along with efforts to train administrators, emphasis is put on educating students to become supervisors or team leaders—managers of direct service activities.

Management Roles

People who have responsibility for the work of others exercise a management function and must constantly evaluate the efforts of the work group in terms of the purposes and goals of the organization. Schools of social work and agencies are interested in training social workers to be responsible for the direct service efforts of teams of employees involving a variety of skills, educational levels, and job titles. By serving as assistant team leaders and gradually assuming greater responsibility during their field placements, they learn to supervise others. These career objectives are realistic, since most of the M.S.W. graduates are offered opportunities to serve in a supervisory role within two or three years after graduation, if not sooner. The service management curricula include special attention to decision-making, the effectiveness and efficiency of work, work measurement, and work satisfaction. Their study of group techniques is focused on both client groups and staff teams.

Training for middle-range management includes the development of staff specialists, program planners, and consultants. Especially in large public agencies, recent graduates are not expected to direct programs for adoption, homemaker services, institutional care for the aged, and many other similar specialties. Special courses and field placements involving work with comparable specialists are included.

Curriculum Content   Schools of social work have long had administration courses, but now students interested in executive management are encouraged to take courses in organizational sciences, the functioning of bureaucracies, and fiscal planning and budgeting. The administrator will require detailed knowledge of many laws, skills in personnel management and negotiations with unions, and use of data processing, as well as general courses in management. Schools of social work are increasingly involved in cooperative arrangements with other professional schools and academic departments to provide an enriched program. In their field placements, students serve as assistants to top-flight administrators in federal, state, or local agencies.

RESEARCH

Some schools of social work offer a research major to provide advanced education in research methods and statistics, with an appropriate specialized field placement. Welfare councils and other planning groups have been the major employers of such social workers. Researchers in individual service agencies have been limited mainly to projects. Research training is of special importance to social work students who expect to go on to the doctorate. The vast majority of dissertations are experimental studies that require skills in problem formulation, data gathering, and analysis. With modern computer technology, much of the "busy work" can be eliminated. At the same time, schools of social work are interested in providing an understanding of research for B.S.W. students so that they can read and understand published studies and participate intelligently as subjects. For both doctoral and master's programs in research, the resources of other academic departments are essential.

FOR MORE INFORMATION

Social work is more than casework, group work, and community work. New opportunities are available for those who want more versatility as generalists or who want to study social problems in considerable depth. There is a need for more "movers and shakers" concerned with social policy and social change. Vast new opportunities present themselves for team leaders, specialists, and administrators. The researcher has challenging problems and much more efficient tools to use in dealing with them.

Except for the generalist, most of these opportunities involve a graduate degree. Some of the block placement programs offer paid field experiences as a financial incentive.

New programs are developing rapidly in agencies. Schools of social work have many new approaches in their course offerings and field placements— some so new that their catalogues may not list them. A directory of accredited school of social work offering B.S.W. and M.S.W. degrees is available from the Council on Social Work Education, 345 East 46th Street, New York, N.Y. 10017. Also, inquire at the admissions offices of the schools that interest you.

SUMMARY AND APPLICATION

You have the opportunity to explore many different educational programs in social work. Through advocacy you have the chance to be an agent of change for both individuals and groups. If you choose social work as a professional field, both your academic courses and your field instruction can give you a foundation for later employment. The earlier you determine your career goals, the more efficient will be your educational plan. Both the generalist roles and the newer specialties should be considered along with the more established social work methods.

—Donald Brieland

KEY TERMS

specializations
generic programs
the generalist
micro and macro methods
service advocacy

fields of practice
social problems approach
policy analysis
management

REFERENCES AND NOTES

1. Paul L. Schwartz, "Curriculum for Undergraduate Social Welfare," in *Curriculum Building for the Continuum for Social Welfare Education*, State University System of Florida, Tallahassee, 1972, pp. 39–40.
2. Harold L. McPheeters and Robert M. Ryan, *A Core of Competence for Baccalaureate Social Welfare*, Southern Regional Education Board, Atlanta, 1971, p. 13.
3. Ian Westbury, Bernece K. Simon, and John Korbelik (eds.), *Generalist Practice: Description and Evaluation*, University of Chicago, Chicago, 1973, pp. 24–26.
4. Frances Fox Piven and Richard A. Cloward, *Regulating the Poor: The Functions of Public Welfare*, Pantheon, New York, 1971; see also Piven and Cloward, "Reaffirming the Regulation of the Poor," *Social Service Review*, vol. 48, 1974, pp. 147–169.
5. *Parrish v. Civil Service Commission of County of Alameda*, 66 Cal. 2d. 260.
6. Howard W. Borsuk, "Agency-School Communication: The Influence of Changing Patterns of Education," in Betty Lacy Jones (ed.), *Current Patterns in Field Instruction in Graduate Social Work Education*, Council on Social Work Education, New York, 1969, pp. 51–59.
7. The Policy Institute Program at the University of Chicago is an example of the concentration in policy analysis.

FOR FURTHER STUDY

Curriculum Building for the Continuum in Social Welfare Education, State University System of Florida, Tallahassee, 1972.

Carol H. Meyer, *Social Work Practice: The Changing Landscape*, Free Press, New York, 1976.

Robert J. Teare and Harold L. McPheeters, *Manpower Utilization in Social Welfare*, Southern Regional Education Board, Atlanta, 1970. This publication presents a generalist model for the B.S.W.

Harold H. Weisman (ed.), *The New Social Work*, Association Press, New York, 1969.

FOR DISCUSSION

1. What specialties characterized the curricula of schools of social work in the 1920s and 1930s?
2. How did the generic program differ from the specialized programs?
3. Why is systems theory especially useful to the generalist?
4. Rural social workers sometimes say that they are "generalists by necessity." Amplify this statement.
5. Why is a generalist program especially appropriate for B.S.W.'s?
6. Give several examples of advocacy.
7. What is a *block* field placement?
8. Why does an emphasis on fields of practice appeal to employing agencies?
9. Choose a social problem not mentioned in the textbook and indicate how you could use it as the basis for a social work curriculum.
10. Discuss the employment possibilities for students who have specialized in policy analysis. What kinds of field placements would be most desirable?
11. What are some examples of the successful use of social work teams?
12. What supporting areas of study would be useful for a student who wants to be a specialist in social work research?

PROJECTS

1. Develop and compare a course of study for social work generalists at the B.S.W. level. Assume that thirty semester hours of social work sources were required. What courses would you require from other departments?
2. Find out from the local welfare council which agencies employ generalists. Interview several of the staff members, preferably from different agencies. Compare their roles. What proportion of their efforts would be classified under each of the three traditional methods?
3. Discuss the fields of practice approach in class. Identify those fields in which there is the greatest demand for personnel and the special skills required in each one. Discuss the question of moving from one field to another when the educational plan emphasizes specialization for a given field of practice.
4. Organize a panel discussion on how the management of nonprofit agencies differs from that of businesses making a profit. Previous chapters in this book will suggest some of the specific issues.

5. Get examples of annual reports of agencies. What kinds of data are reported? Are any of the agencies conducting special research studies? Find out more about them. Are social workers in charge of the studies? If so, what are their qualifications?
6. Poll several agency executives to find out what kinds of research they would like to see carried out. Determine whether the questions proposed are significant and reasonable.
7. Organize a faculty panel to describe and assess new developments in curriculum formats, including those in the chapter. Compare their responses with your own ideas.

PART THREE
Fields of Practice

The major opportunities to practice social work are found in a limited number of specialized areas called fields of practice. Social work education tends to provide courses that deal with social policy and practice in several such areas.

To be considered a specialty, a field of practice must involve a considerable number of social workers. It may or may not involve management of the program by social workers.

In public assistance and family and child welfare, social work is the dominant element. In the public schools, health, mental health, and rehabilitation, social work is practiced in a "host setting" under the direction of educators or physicians. There is usually less power to affect planning and program development in host agencies.

Part Three concentrates on social work roles to provide a more specific idea of social work practice in each area than is provided by a general discussion of methods. It focuses on unique problems as well—poverty, dependency and neglect, family breakdown, learning disabilities, illness and disease, emotional stress and disability. It concentrates on the programs that address these issues. It may suggest an answer to the question, "Where would I fit in social work?"

CHAPTER 7
Public Assistance

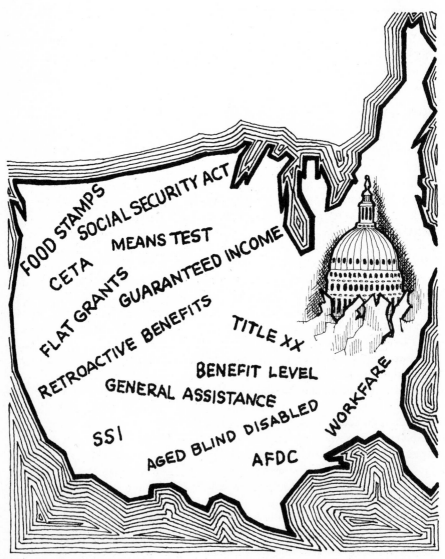

Learning the language of "welfare."

People who are much too sensitive to demand of cripples that they run races ask of the poor that they get up and act just like everyone else in the society.

—Michael Harrington*

Social work has played various roles for many years in administering assistance programs for the poor. The current structure of modern public assistance and the characteristics of recipients are described in this chapter. The right to an adequate income is highlighted, and establishment of adequate benefit levels is emphasized as a focal point for reform.

RATIONALE FOR SOCIAL WORKERS IN PUBLIC ASSISTANCE

One of the earliest responsibilities of social work was the organization of resources to aid the poor. The leadership of social workers in programs for the poor, however, has not been consistent or strong. The effectiveness of social services and counseling for low-income families has been strongly questioned both in Congress and in the executive branch of the federal government. Social workers have been struggling to defend and redefine their role in public assistance. Yet the number of individuals and families participating in assistance programs has grown dramatically, creating new demands to work with clients in a variety of roles. Career opportunities for social workers holding a B.S.W. degree have expanded, while openings for M.S.W. personnel are apparently declining.

A debate on welfare reform has gone on for the past two decades. Social workers have been especially concerned about the adequacy of benefits for the poor and their right to obtain them through a humane, flexible administrative framework. In examining the changes necessary in this system, the types and evolution of public support mechanisms and related roles of the social work profession should be considered.

IMPROVING INCOMES OF THE POOR

Three major means are used to improve the adequacy of individual incomes. People can find a better-paying job; they can learn new skills through manpower training; and they can receive unearned income or cash transfer payments through public programs.

Traditionally, the most effective and dramatic means of improving income adequacy has been through industrial expansion and economic growth that

*Michael Harrington, *The Other America*, Macmillan, New York, 1962, p. 75.

generates new opportunities for employment and higher wages, but recent criticisms of corporate behavior make clear that economic growth is not without its cost in terms of pollution, congestion, industrial disease, and stress. On the other hand, improved incomes have permitted millions to raise their standard of living since 1900. Higher productivity in the national economy over the past eighty years has meant that people have been able to purchase more goods and services at prices within their budget. Poverty, by most measures, has decreased since the turn of the century because until recently the American economy was successful in expanding business activity without excessive inflation.

Between 1959 and 1969, the number of people living in poverty declined from 39,490,000 to 24,147,000. However, few gains were made in the 1970s, and by 1976, nearly 25,000,000 were still living at below-subsistence levels.[1]

In addition to economic growth, training programs have grown rapidly since 1973 under the Comprehensive Employment and Training Act (CETA). However, with an estimated 25 million people living in poverty, the 1.5–2 million jobs provided under CETA are not adequate.

Employment is not always a feasible answer. Many individuals cannot work either temporarily or permanently—the aged, ill, unskilled, dependent, or socially rejected members of our communities; the casualties of our mistakes in foreign policy—Vietnamese refugees for example; and victims of technological change and resource depletion, including the families living around exhausted coal mines in Appalachia. Workers have been ousted from their jobs during localized or national business recessions, particularly in the auto, steel, and garment industries; others are targets of job discrimination, notably young blacks, Hispanics, and Indians. Increasingly, families suffer from absence or incapacity of the breadwinner.

Individuals outside the labor market cannot expect to benefit from industrial growth. The seventy-three-year-old widow with failing eyesight and the truck driver with a spinal abscess are not in need of training. They require support and maintenance of income at a level which permits some choice, personal satisfaction, and material sufficiency.

Even for those whose problems stem from bankruptcies, recessions, low wages, limited personal competency, industrial innovation or relocation, employment discrimination, or other market-related variables, maintenance of income is a necessary first step to restoration of family equilibrium and problem-solving ability.

Government programs of direct cash grants to individuals and families will always function as an essential adjunct to employment in the private sector in maintaining the income of American citizens. Programs designed specifically to benefit the poor have traditionally been referred to as "public assistance." They are of primary concern to social work, because income—along with housing and health—is a fundamental determinant of well-being.

Poverty is society's oldest and most persistent problem. The capacity of human beings to change, grow, and realize their potentialities requires material resources. At a broader level, the progress of any society is always constrained by the condition of those least well-off. A nation which seeks to develop without making provision for the basic needs of all its citizens ultimately faces the penalty of social unrest. Democracy has economic as well as political implications. When, for various reasons, the private sector cannot meet peoples' needs for income, public assistance has been a cornerstone of protection against destitution. Our nation's social security programs also play a part in preventing and reducing poverty, but they are beyond the scope of this chapter.

Public assistance and the emergence of professional social work were intimately intertwined. Features of modern public administration still reflect this early connection between service-giving and the payment of benefits to persons in need. A brief examination of the social service tradition in public assistance is important.

THE SOCIAL WORK TRADITION IN AMERICAN PUBLIC ASSISTANCE

The Charity Organization Society: Rationalizing Services to the Poor

We now look at the Charity Organization Society from a different vantage point.[2] The COS was first set up to deal with two difficult social problems: (1) provision of adequate assistance to the destitute; and (2) rational management and coordination of a multiplicity of programs providing relief.

The society emerged during a period of great turbulence in American life. Industrialization and a stream of European immigrants brought rapid urbanization and poverty on a scale never experienced before. Hostility toward the poor among the general public was widespread, while philanthropists worried about the proliferation of need and suffering in the cities. Long lines at soup kitchens were a daily occurrence. Businessmen were besieged by beggars, church representatives, and charities requesting resources. On every side evidence of corruption and fraud permeated public provisions for relief.

In the midst of this confusion the COS offered a plan for bringing efficiency and reason to the distribution of benefits, without resort to government. This philosophy meshed well with the *laissez-faire* economic ideas of the nineteenth century.

The methods used by the COS established the basis for early professional casework. In its initial years, the COS was determined not to become a relief-giving agency itself. It investigated requests for assistance, helped the family discover potential resources within itself, and mobilized help from appropriate charities in the community. A *paid agent* or staff person from COS made an individual evaluation of each family through a home visit. The organization tried to form a rational concept of family budgets and standards of sufficiency which could be used in making an objective assessment. While not entirely successful in maintaining detachment in the assessment, the COS was nonetheless the first to adopt a systematic nonsectarian approach to the question of assessing need and determining eligibility for community services.

After the evaluation by a paid staff member, the COS assigned a volunteer to act as a "friendly visitor" to destitute families. The visitor's role was to educate poor families in becoming better parents, home managers, and more adequate individuals. Employment and sobriety were stressed. The relationship between friendly visitor and family was conceived of as a continuing, perhaps permanent, bond. The destitute family was expected to gradually shift its social aspirations and grow more conforming in its social behavior. Role-modeling or "resocialization" remains part of the basic intervention strategy of the social work profession, although the patronizing tone of the COS has generally disappeared.

Strengths and Weaknesses of the COS Approach   Income maintenance programs were coupled with social rehabilitation in the COS approach. No person was to receive relief in the absence of a relationship with a helping person.

As with all organizations, the COS departed in practice from its formal goals. The volunteer pool never grew large enough to provide visitation for more than 15–20 percent of all clients. The responsibility for visitation fell increasingly to the paid agent, who combined eligibility determination and provision of advice, support, and surveillance for the family in one role. The COS was also drawn into direct relief-giving itself, as other resources often proved insufficient or inappropriate. "Preventive charity" and personal services frequently took a back seat to judgmental and exclusionary treatment of needs. The goal of case-by-case, individualized treatment of clients was sometimes synonymous with witch-hunting for frauds and cheaters. Middle- and upper-class attitudes permeated the COS; agents and friendly visitors took their social superiority to clients for granted.

Moralizing and demands for social conformity have always characterized programs for the able-bodied poor. This was eminently true prior to the nineteenth century; the COS maintained this pattern, and it is still present in our modern public assistance program for families with dependent children (AFDC).

The COS movement made several important contributions to modern public assistance practice. While generally supporting the use of an institutional or workhouse setting for the poor, the COS also pushed for the provision of money payments, rather than in-kind gifts or supplementation, for the relief of persons living in their own homes. The organization helped set up standards for a minimum subsistence budget by which a family's income deficiencies might be gauged. The COS was more scientific and fact-oriented than earlier philanthropic groups. The effort made by these agencies to assist the poor toward greater self-sufficiency remains a major objective in modern public assistance policy.

Provision of material assistance on the condition of a caseworker-client relationship is still widely accepted, but now the relationship is supposed to be more egalitarian. The client should be given a voice in the selection of services.

Professional Casework Services for the Poor   The professionalization of the COS movement progressed rapidly in the early 1900s and much of the initial paternalism and moralizing dropped out of its literature and philosophy. The tendency to categorize families as "deserving" or "undeserving" persisted, however, until after the depression of the 1930s.

In 1917 the first textbook on social casework was published by Mary Richmond, a lifelong COS worker. Entitled *Social Diagnosis*, the book was devoted to techniques for collecting and evaluating data which would permit the worker to make a careful and systematic study of individual needs. This perspective was derived from COS principles. With the introduction of *Social Diagnosis*, followed by the incorporation of Freudian psychology as the governing theory of personality in the profession, the COS completed its transition to the family welfare agency staffed by professional caseworkers.

Failure of Local Programs for the Poor

Nearly a third of the nation was unemployed after the Great Depression overtook this country in 1929. Family welfare agencies were drawn into full-scale relief administration. There was a rapid breakdown in traditional local methods of giving to the poor. No one, including taxpayers, had resources.

A social worker from Iowa, Harry Hopkins, was appointed by President Roosevelt to oversee national emergency assistance and employment programs. Hopkins remained one of Roosevelt's closest advisers and exerted influence on major reforms of public assistance which were enacted in 1935 through passage of the Social Security Act.

The Social Security Act and Administration of Benefits to the Poor

The Social Security Act of 1935 created a two-pronged national system for income maintenance, designed to prevent poverty by providing minimum benefits for retired workers and their dependents, with special programs included for the aged, the blind, and dependent children.*

Old age and survivors' insurance was later expanded to include health coverage and disability coverage. The Old Age Survivors, Disability and Health Insurance, (OASDHI) program is administered by the Federal Social Security Administration and financed by a payroll tax on workers and employers. Participation carries no stigma. Almost everyone regards social security benefits as an earned right. One in six Americans is presently receiving benefits in some form through various insurance provisions.

*The latter program was originally called Aid to Dependent Children (ADC). Since 1962, states have been able to include families with unemployed fathers, and the name was changed to Aid to Families with Dependent Children (AFDC). The latter term is used throughout this chapter.

Congress restructured the administration and financing of public assistance to permit, for the first time, a much-expanded role for the state and federal governments. The Social Security Act encouraged states to take over the administration of public relief, with matching grants from Washington. Harry Hopkins summarized the immediate impact of the Social Security Act: "America has spent the last few years in the counting house. From our inventory we have emerged, as a nation, with the conviction that there is no need for any American to be destitute, to be illiterate, to be reduced by the bondage of these things into either political or economic impotence . . ."[3]

Many of the administrative requirements in public assistance established under the Social Security Act were an outgrowth of the COS experience, pressures by Hopkins, and the testimony of social workers in public hearings before Congress. States were expected to designate a single agency to make money payments and determine eligibility for benefits. Every county in the state was to provide assistance, not just those jurisdictions that wished to do so. States were expected to pay part of the cost of public assistance from their own revenues, rather than rely on the traditional method of local taxation. Applicants were to be given an opportunity for a "fair hearing" if claims were not acted upon promptly by the agency, or if benefits were denied.

Most significantly, payments were to be made in the form of direct, unrestricted cash grants. The time-honored method of giving in-kind assistance alone—e.g., bags of groceries or free shelter—was prohibited from any assistance program that was to be eligible for federal reimbursement. This meant, however, that all states had to create standards for assistance to determine how much families and individuals might receive. Public assistance agencies were implicitly asked to set a minimum standard for the community—a problem of great potential social and political divisiveness.

This concept of public assistance administration was born in the COS tradition, and the state assistance offices which opened after 1935 were staffed principally by social workers from the Family Welfare Association and other successor agencies to the COS.

The Social Service Amendments of 1962

After 1935 the social work profession continued through schools of social work to provide manpower for the management of public assistance programs and for direct services to recipients. The profession as a whole, however, became preoccupied, following the war years of the 1940s, with the problems of middle-income families and with mental health. Careers in public assistance agencies were seen as less attractive than those in private, nonprofit agencies or in other public agencies. The profession, in fact, abrogated much of its traditional responsibility for the poor.

However, from the efforts of some social workers who did remain actively committed to experimentation and policy development in public assistance, in 1962 a major opportunity arose for an impact upon national legislation. Congress heard testimony from social workers that reduction in caseloads and increased social services to families would help clients leave the AFDC program. Congress agreed and the 1962 Social Service Amendments to the Social Security Act were adopted, permitting the federal government to reimburse states for three-quarters of a social service worker's salary. Caseloads were not to exceed sixty clients per social worker to give maximum opportunity for interaction between worker and recipient. A list of priority social services was drawn up for the states. Other types of service could be provided at the state's option. Congress expected that this legislation would improve the quality of the social service workforce and slow the growth of public assistance rolls.

Passage of the 1962 amendments, however, coincided with a dramatic rise in applications for the AFDC program. The rise, which had already been observable in 1958, continued at an increasing rate until 1975. The social service strategy, under the best of circumstances, could have produced only marginal results in limiting expansion of AFDC. Too many other determinants of poverty also have their effects. Age discrimination, for example, prevents an individual from obtaining work even if the social worker is highly effective in increasing the job-seeker's motivation to find employment. As matters developed, the social services approach never had a chance of stemming the AFDC floodtide of the 1960s.

For its part, Congress was heartily disappointed and turned to other devices. All of these factors made the new War on Poverty, which began with the Economic Opportunity Act of 1964, distinctly antiprofessional in outlook. Public assistance caseworkers also tended to lack professional training. In the 1960s they were scorned for invading clients' privacy, arbitrary decisions, misuse of the budgeting process to manipulate poor people's behavior, judgmental attitudes that deterred the poor at intake from applying for assistance, and poor management of public welfare programs.

Separation of Social Services and Eligibility Determination

The Department of Health, Education and Welfare (DHEW) recommended in 1968 that social services be separated administratively from determination of eligibility for public assistance. DHEW argued that review of an applicant's income and resources was a routine clerical function in which the goal was to minimize discretionary judgments. In a profound break with the COS tradition, DHEW maintained that services and social rehabilitation should *not* automatically be linked with money payments. The client should be allowed to express a preference. Refusal of services should not affect eligibility.

Since 1969 federal and state agencies have reorganized to implement this new distinction between the administration of income maintenance payments and the administration of social services. In 1977 President Carter created the Public Service Administration (PSA) in the Department of Health, Education and Welfare. PSA has responsibility for social services to low-income families and to other groups, such as the aged, the handicapped, and children. State departments of public welfare similarly created separate "income maintenance" and "social service" units for the AFDC program. Income maintenance workers interview the client to establish eligibility, set the benefit level, and refer the client for any additional services. Social service workers arrange for a diverse array of programs, including educational grants, day care, home-delivered meals, homemaker service, and nutrition or budget counseling. Social service workers in larger communities are also sometimes organized into special counseling teams to deal with multiproblem, severely disorganized families. Rural public welfare offices tend to be less specialized and functionally differentiated.

Title XX: Decentralized Planning for Social Services

The 1962 Social Service Amendments have also been superseded by another amendment, Title XX of the Social Security Act, passed in 1975. Title XX gives much more power to the states in deciding what social services may be provided but limits the total amount the federal government may spent in any one year. It also permits non–assistance recipients to participate in Title XX–funded programs upon payment of fees based on financial ability.

The social worker in public assistance today must struggle harder to defend the value of social service to clients. The provision of adequate income to poor families and individuals requires the understanding of legislative and administrative processes which professionals within the agency can bring. The social worker's role of articulating the needs of America's poor remains as crucial as ever.

Prior to the passage of the Social Security Act, the legislative framework and structure for financing public assistance evolved separately from social service. A brief review of these developments will point up the influence of tradition which affects options for change in the entire welfare system.

THE CURRENT LEGISLATIVE FRAMEWORK FOR PUBLIC ASSISTANCE IN AMERICA

General Assistance

General assistance is designed to serve persons who are ineligible for other assistance programs and has functioned as the only major source of support for migrating families, the working poor, and healthy adults without children.

Before 1935 local property taxes were used in part for assistance to the poor. General assistance still provides over $100 million a year to about 1 million individuals. In such cities as New York City and Chicago, general assistance benefits today represent an important component of the total welfare package for low-income families. Outside major metropolitan areas, general assistance benefits are more often paid in "kind," goods rather than cash. Sometimes, the agency makes payments directly to physicians, landlords, grocers, and other suppliers.

Provisions for Families with No Breadwinner: AFDC

The depression of the 1930s demonstrated that locally financed, locally administered relief programs were not viable under conditions of widespread unemployment and need. Taxpayers were unable to meet assessments against their property. Demands for aid surpassed the fiscal capacity of local communities under the best of circumstances. There were not enough personnel to administer benefits and determine eligibility. The Social Security Act built instead upon fledgling programs of state pensions for mothers and for the destitute aged. These programs had sprung up in a haphazard manner after the turn of the century in order to protect certain groups from the harshness and degradation of assistance under the poor laws. The Social Security Act of 1935 excluded general assistance from its provisions.

In 1911 Illinois was the first state to pass a law providing financial support to fatherless families. As Grace Abbott, a distinguished social worker, put it:

> Prior to 1911 we had, in effect, said to the widow of a workingman who left her without means for the support of her children through the school period that she had two courses open to her; she could surrender her children to a public or private orphanage (in some places it was the poor farm); or she could attempt to run a boarding house or do some work outside the home to support herself and her children. The bereaved mother was not told that the records showed that her health would probably break under the double strain of serving as a homemaker and wage-earner; that she would be able to give only very inadequate supervision to her children, and, if they became demoralized and delinquent in consequence, as the records showed frequently happened, society would then take the children by legal process and begin a costly program for their reeducation in an institution for delinquent children.[4]

Mother's pensions—and the rationale for them—were the foundation in 1935 for our modern Aid to Families with Dependent Children program (AFDC). No one ever anticipated that the program would grow to include nearly 12 million people, two-thirds of whom were children. The rise in recipiency rates was spurred by the South to North migration of low-income families during and after World War II.

Help for Adult Aged, Blind, and Disabled: SSI

In addition to AFDC, aged poor over sixty-five years old and blind destitute adults could be assisted with federal/state funding under the Social Security Act. Another group of adults was added by Congress in 1955 when Aid to the Permanently and Totally Disabled (APTD) was added.

An even more significant change occurred in 1974. Assistance for the needy, blind, aged poor, and disabled was combined to form one new program: Supplemental Security Income, or SSI. The Social Security Administration, which administers our national social insurance programs, was given control over SSI to the extent that each state was willing to relinquish authority. By 1978 only thirty-seven states had agreed to permit the Social Security Administration to operate SSI. In the remaining states administrative arrangements remained in state departments of public welfare. Some states were fearful that the federal government would not administer assistance programs well and have taken a "wait-and-see" attitude.

In the changeover to SSI, Congress used two devices to lure the states into surrendering control over assistance programs. First, the federal government agreed to pay 100 percent of the cost of basic cash benefits in SSI. Second, the federal government promised to pay all costs of program administration, provided a state permitted the Social Security Administration to take over program management.

SSI is particularly interesting because it demonstrates how slowly and awkwardly we move toward welfare reform. A federated political system, in which the states share power with the central government in Washington, permits no sudden, overnight restructuring of public assistance provisions.

The legislative framework for public assistance has come under increasing scrutiny during the past two decades. The pressures for revision of public relief have intensified as caseloads have expanded in spite of rising prosperity, as the number of able-bodied recipients has grown, and as the proportion of minority-group recipients has become more visible in the nation's large cities.

DISTINGUISHING FEATURES OF PUBLIC ASSISTANCE PROGRAMS

Publicly financed programs to assist the poor have traditionally displayed several characteristics.

Programs Have Been Means-Tested   The means test is applied to be sure that a person does not have too much income or assets to qualify for assistance. Resources include both earned and unearned income. Earned income is money received in the form of wages or salary. Unearned income is financial support in any other form—benefits from other public and private programs, prizes, life insurance annuities, gifts from neighbors, support payments from relatives, inheritances, rental income, dividends from stocks, and so on. Few poor families enjoy income from assets, but many do rely on social security or other public programs. Many also have income from work. The means test is supposed to ensure that individuals receiving assistance do not already have sufficient resources for a minimum level of subsistence.

Eligibility and Benefit Levels Have Been Determined on a Case-By-Case Basis   Although federal and state regulations specify what types of people may receive benefits and how much is allowable as a benefit for eligible persons, substantial discretion has operated in eligibility determination. The staff who administer public assistance have some latitude in deciding whether a client will receive special allowances in addition to basic benefits, what social services may be made available, and what resources outside public assistance might be mobilized on behalf of the client. The general trend in recent years has been to

"I'm terribly sorry, sir, but in the process of cutting out programs for the poor we inadvertently cut out a program for the rich." (Drawing by Dana Fradon; © 1979 The New Yorker Magazine, Inc.)

reduce caseworker discretion so that clients will be treated more uniformly. However, the extraordinary needs, emergencies, and anomalous life situations of poor people have led some social workers to argue for the retention of flexibility in the decision-making process.

Entitlement to Benefits Has Not Been Established as an Individual Right   In the United States no poor person has a constitutionally established right to a minimum income. The taxpayers, through their elected representatives, have a responsibility to promote the general welfare, but only in this sense is public assistance an obligation. In repeated court tests, states have affirmed that money received by an assistance recipient is charity, or taxpayer largesse.[5] By contrast, the legal entitlement of American citizens to social security benefits is well recognized. Some foreign countries, such as Great Britain, recognize the right of those in poverty to be protected and maintained by government. The United States has not accepted this principle, possibly because of the emphasis on work and the feeling that all people should be self-reliant.

Program   Benefits   Have   Been   Paid   from   General   Government Revenues   Public assistance benefits have always been financed through taxes on personal income or property at the local, state, and federal levels. Since the passage of the Social Security Act in 1935, the states and the federal government have shared the cost of payments to aged, blind, and disabled poor and to families with dependent children. In some states like New York, local governments also contribute to the cost. All local units of government put aside part of their revenues from property taxes for "general assistance," or temporary aid for individuals and families who are unable to find help from state and federally supported assisted programs, but many small units expend no general assistance funds.

In the federal budget, expenditures for all assistance programs now represent about 10 percent of allocations. Between 1950 and 1975 public assistance expenditures grew principally because of the introduction of medical care for the needy through Medicaid, new training programs in the Work Incentive Program (WIN), wider utilization of food stamps, and liberalization of benefits for the aged, blind, and disabled poor from Supplemental Security Income.

The Constitution Reserves Power to the States for Control and Funding of Assistance Programs   The federal government cannot directly initiate an overhaul of our assistance system without state consent. No state, for example, was mandated to set up an AFDC program, although all eventually did in order to obtain federal help with assistance payments. Of course once states accept federal funds, federal regulations become binding. Complete federal control over the system would possibly bring greater uniformity in eligibility criteria and minimum benefit standards. However, state administration may be more efficient and responsive to local conditions. The tension between the states and the federal government is a persistent and distinctive feature of our assistance system.

SOCIAL OBJECTIVES OF PUBLIC ASSISTANCE

One purpose of public assistance programs has been to provide benefits to certain categories of poor individuals and families—income for persons with no earnings to ensure that highly vulnerable groups are able to live at some minimum standard of health and decency. This is the *income maintenance goal.*

A more complicated problem arises for low-income families with working members or for those able-bodied persons who are not in the labor market. It is more desirable for people to be self-sufficient than entirely dependent upon government support. A second goal of modern public assistance is, therefore, *to promote labor force participation to improve capacity for self-support.*

Some people live in poverty because they lack effective interpersonal skills or are unable to succeed in the competition for scarce resources such as housing or education. These individuals can be helped not only by cash payments but through social services designed to strengthen family functioning or to improve competence in dealing with social institutions. A third social goal of public assistance is *to change or rehabilitate families and individuals so that they can achieve more satisfying and stable relationships within the community.* With improved social functioning may also come enhanced ability to seek and hold a job.

Unfortunately the goals of income maintenance, labor force participation, and rehabilitation are not always compatible. To encourage people to stay on a job, or to enter the labor market if they have not done so, a public assistance program should pay low benefits. However, if a mother cannot work because she does not wish to leave her infant at home or another parent must limit activities because of severe emphysema, then low benefit levels are an undeserved penalty. Persons unable to enter the labor market who need to have their income maintained suffer. Moreover, even where people are willing to work, jobs are not always either available or accessible.

Similarly, not all persons who apply for public assistance benefits require social services. Many have experienced a short-term reversal in their economic status due to a lay-off, temporary desertion by a spouse, lack of sick pay at work, or a crisis involving another family member which demands that the breadwinner remain at home for a while. This group best profits from a public assistance system which is administered in a uniform, impersonal manner, with a maximum of special requirements for reporting.

On the other hand, geriatric patients discharged after years of institutionalization in mental hospitals, isolated, depressed, and marginally functioning adults, drug addicts, severely disorganized families, refugees and new migrants to the city from rural areas, and similar socially disadvantaged groups require a system which is capable of responding to special needs and circumstances. A social service–oriented approach to these individuals recognizes their psychological and social vulnerability, in some cases their need for protection, and the insufficiency of cash payment systems alone as a means of improving their well-being.

The great struggles over welfare reform since the early 1960s have been over which goals should prevail. All the new proposals placed before Congress have sought a system of minimum income guarantees tied closely to work requirements, provisions for helping the working poor to retain eligibility for income supplements, and training for the unskilled. Social services have had a much lower priority and Congress has placed a ceiling on the total amount of money which may be appropriated in any one year for social services to low-income recipients.

The structure and goals of public assistance must inevitably depend upon who will be participating in assistance programs. (After all, these programs are operated to benefit the client, not minimize the taxpayer's discomfort.) How many people are likely to participate in assistance programs? How will they respond to work opportunities or high benefit levels? Are persons receiving assistance psychologically different from those who never make application? Answers to these questions may help to determine which goals should be most emphasized in future policy development.

Characteristics of Recipients

Of the approximately 25 million persons with below-subsistence incomes in the United States, over 10 million receive AFDC benefits.[6] Approximately 5 million others are participating in the SSI program. In addition, some low-income families are neither AFDC nor SSI recipients but qualify for such means-tested assistance as food stamps, public housing, or medical assistance. In a period of sharp recession, during 1972–74, nearly 1 million individuals were found eligible for general assistance, particularly in large urban areas.

Among the poor, several million at any one time receive no direct cash benefits under public assistance. Participants in the food stamp, public housing, medical assistance, and/or general assistance programs may receive no other subsidy and often are only temporary users of these benefits. The assistance system includes people with highly diverse characteristics, ranging from severe disability or old age in SSI to dependent children in families with an absent, incapacitated, or partially unemployed breadwinner in AFDC.

In the public mind, the words "welfare recipient" now mean someone who receives AFDC. Most of the controversy in welfare reform efforts has centered on this group, while only sporadic attention has been paid to users of SSI, GA, or food stamps, yet the problem of poverty is considerably greater than the issue of improving or revising AFDC benefits and eligibility criteria.

COURT DECISIONS INVOLVING WELFARE RIGHTS

Until the late 1960s few welfare rights were guaranteed by law. Some of the early cases reveal the callousness with which the poor were treated. The Iowa

Supreme Court decided in 1911 that damages could not be collected from the county even though a plaintiff lost both feet through the negligence of relief officials. After freezing his feet while examining timber that he expected to be hired to cut, the man appealed to the county for medical help. He was given "emergency care" and passed on to the next county. The process was repeated until he reached Cerro Gordo County. By that time both feet had to be amputated. The court held, "there can be no liability to a pauper for failure to furnish relief no matter how grievous the consequences."[7]

With the development of legal aid services, a number of suits were filed to establish welfare rights. Several reached the U.S. Supreme Court. Decisions between 1968 and 1971 by the "Warren" Court were generally favorable to clients. Later decisions by the "Burger" Court tended to be unfavorable.

The Warren Court agreed that living in a AFDC household did not make a man responsible for the support of children for whom he had no parental responsibility,[8] that the right of freedom of travel invalidated residence requirements for public assistance,[9] that AFDC recipients were entitled to a fair hearing before they could be removed from the rolls,[10] and that flat grants which eliminated allowances for special needs could not be used as a means of reducing welfare costs.[11]

Decisions unfavorable to clients included the legality of maximum grants based on family size,[12] home visits as a legal requirement for receiving benefits,[13] the right of the state to impose more stringent work requirements than those required under WIN,[14] no responsibility to pay retroactive benefits to cover the time from date of application to determination of eligibility,[15] and no mandatory responsibility to provide AFDC benefits for unborn children.[16]

Because of the recent unfavorable findings of the court, few cases dealing with clients' rights have been filed in the last several years.

MYTHS OF PUBLIC ASSISTANCE

Because AFDC is such a controversial program, the characteristics of recipients are of more than passing interest. One approach is to look at some widely held beliefs about AFDC families and examine the extent to which these notions conform with available evidence from program data and research.

AFDC Mothers Become Pregnant to Increase Their Public Assistance Benefits

The size of families on AFDC has actually been declining, particularly since 1967, reflecting a general trend in the birth rate for the population as a whole. In 1977 the majority of AFDC families consisted of a mother and one or two children. Average family size was 3.6 persons for the AFDC population, exactly the same as the national average for all families.[17]

The majority of children in AFDC families are older than age two (63.6 percent), but half of these families include children of less than two years. For this group the evidence is not convincing that conception occurred to establish eligibility status. For those children born after a family is receiving benefits, lack of appropriate family-planning technology may be principally responsible.

Finally, how much does a mother actually receive if she adds another child to the recipient unit? On the average, a family will experience a boost of $900 per year for each additional child. However, in states with a "flat grant" system of payments, the family will not be given any extra funds to pay for special expenses arising from the baby's needs: baby clothes, diapers, equipment such as crib or high chair, expensive baby foods and formulas, vitamins, furniture to hold the baby's possessions, car seats—the list is long, costly, and a strain on the budgets of families with much higher income. The amount of "profit" which a mother might expect to realize is minuscule and probably not a genuine motivating factor.

Most Welfare Recipients Are Cheaters and Frauds

The amount of fraud on AFDC appears to be low, where fraud is defined as a deliberate and knowing attempt by a client to deceive the agency. The experience of Illinois in catching "cheaters" may be illustrative. In its 1976 *Annual Report*, the Illinois Department of Public Aid wrote: "During 1976 approximately 10,000 calls were received by the department's toll free fraud hotline. After thorough investigation, 189 cases were referred to the Attorney General, 183 grants were cancelled, and 55 grants were reduced."[18]

Surveys conducted by the government since the early 1970s seem to indicate that the greatest difficulty concerning recipients is not fraud, but error—mistakes unintentionally made either by the agency or by the client. Mistakes may lead to a determination of eligibility when a client does not in fact meet the criteria. Or a client may be paid an incorrect amount, either too little or too much.

The error rate in AFDC has indeed been high by almost anyone's standards. In 1972 the Undersecretary of the Department of Health, Education and Welfare testified before a special congressional subcommittee investigating our welfare system. The Undersecretary reported on a national survey of AFDC records, and concluded:

> We found one out of every 20 welfare recipients getting checks were ineligible for that month. And one out of four were being paid the wrong amount—either too much or too little. . . .
>
> If that survey indicated anything, it showed that it is not welfare recipients cheating the system that constitute our big problem. It is the chaotic do-it-yourself system that is cheating the whole nation.[19]

The need, as most persons have come to agree, is to streamline the management of AFDC and reduce mistakes. The complexity of the rules governing eligibility and benefit determination makes this process resistant to uniform administration. While fraud remains dramatic news, the real dilemma—still unsolved—is the provision of benefits in a humane, consistent manner according to verifiable and reasonable criteria.

AFDC Recipients Do Not Want to Work

Over 500,000 AFDC mothers were working in 1977—most at half-time jobs. This number represents about 16 percent of the 3.1 million adult women recipients. An additional 13 percent were actively seeking work, waiting to be called back after a lay-off, or in school. In the remaining three-fifths of female-headed AFDC households, most did not work because of a disability (7.3 percent) or the presence of dependent family members needing care (40 percent).[20]

Twenty-two of the fifty states have no provision for AFDC benefits if there is a father in the home. The program for unemployed or partially unemployed fathers (AFDC-UP) has always remained small, comprising about 6.6 percent of total recipients in 1977, or 343,000 men. More of this group were expecting to go back to work after lay-off or actively seeking a new job (25 percent); 12 percent were employed part-time; and 2 percent were enrolled in school. The remaining half were incapacitated or staying at home to take care of dependent children.[21]

These statistics show that an important minority of the AFDC population retain a connection with the labor force. Unfortunately, most AFDC recipients are unlikely to be successful in job-seeking. One-third are under age twenty-four, where unemployment rates in this country are highest. Most recipients are women, who suffer as a group from limited employment opportunities. Only one-third of women AFDC recipients and one-fifth of the men on AFDC have graduated from high school. Even with high motivation, these individuals would be competitively disadvantaged and failure-prone in the labor market.[22]

Available research generally tends to support the argument that AFDC recipients would like to work, and prefer employment to assistance.[23] An AFDC recipient's decision about working may be based on the likelihood of finding a job, expected rates of pay, and the importance to other family members of the parent remaining at home. While some recipients are anxious to work, they are not attracted by undesirable jobs with poor compensation. The costs of going to work—transportation, child care, new clothing, and tooling—often exceed the wage level for unskilled persons. Full-time employment is not a viable alternative to AFDC in these circumstances. One study which attempted to evaluate the attachment to work by low-income families concluded that virtually all poor adults believe in work. However, those with lowest incomes do not seem to derive much self-esteem from what they do.

AFDC Recipients Are Likely to Spend a Lifetime on Welfare

About half of recipient families remain on AFDC for two and a half years. An additional 15 percent receive benefits for three years or longer. Only 10 percent of the households receive benefits for at least ten years. At the other extreme, 17 percent of the families are off the rolls in from one to six months.[24]

The reasons which provoke applications partially determine whether a family will continue to need benefits for a short while or a long time. Family instability is most common. Women have been deserted, are themselves seeking a means of separation, or fear a breakdown of their marital relationship. If a family should reconcile or the wife terminate the relationship by divorce, it is likely that the period of recipiency will be short. However, the more ambiguous or indeterminate the nature of the parental relationship—e.g., extended separation or absence—the more likely the family is to remain on the rolls.

RECIPIENTS VERSUS NONRECIPIENTS

Limited research evidence shows that AFDC recipients and nonrecipients are similar in valuing education and upward occupational mobility for their children. Mothers in nonrecipient families are more likely to work. Welfare families are apparently no more psychologically dependent in their orientation toward life than other groups. A study by Stone and Schlamp[25] in 1965 showed a basic similarity in the life patterns of poor persons never receiving assistance, short-term recipients, and long-term recipients. However, long-term recipients had multiple problems in social economic, and psychological functioning—some perhaps induced by extended reliance on below-subsistence benefits. Several factors may make families economically vulnerable: health, sex of family head, average annual income in relation to the poverty line, racial status, availability of relatives and friends as resources, ability to deal with crisis, and willingness to accept assistance. These criteria, more than innate deficiencies or psychological problems in the individual, are likely to account for whether a person applies for assistance and remains on the rolls.

The conventional wisdom about AFDC recipients is a mixture of approximate truths and doubtful assumptions. Many poor families value the economic security of AFDC in times of personal hardship, but most feel stigmatized and uncomfortable and would prefer to be independent.

Characteristics of SSI Recipients

The characteristics of SSI recipients have attracted little general concern, in contrast to AFDC families. In 1975, 4.3 million individuals were participating in this program, of whom slightly over half were aged, and almost all the remainder severely disabled. Only 74,000 were blind, reflecting the decline of this problem in society and the availability of other social supports for this group. Four-fifths of the SSI recipients lived independently in their own homes. Only 3 percent were employed, but the majority received income from social security in addition to SSI payments. Those who worked earned an average of $81 per month. Social security benefits were usually about $130 per month.[26]

Most aged recipients were women, of whom half were seventy-five or over. If one puts together a composite picture of age, sex, and living circumstances, a picture emerges of very old, isolated, and poverty-stricken females with no outside resources other than social security benefits.

The general public and Congress rarely debate whether SSI recipients work if able, maintain family relationships, have children outside marriage, or remain for long periods on the rolls. The aged, blind, and disabled poor seem "deserving," and fewer obstacles are raised to their entitlement for public support. However, incentive problems are present for this group, too. For example, SSI benefits may encourage some ill persons to resist recovery, since disability status "pays."

A 1972 survey of the disabled conducted by the Social Security Administration showed the adverse effects on family life caused by a long-term, severe physical impairment. The study concluded:

> Although the disabled were about as likely to have married as persons in the general population, the stability of their marriages was more limited. The extended families of disabled persons generally provided no greater support through financial or household assistance or visits than did the relatives of healthy persons. Within the nuclear family, contraction of activities—rather than compensatory shifts in sex roles—and decreased participation in most aspects of living were the major consequence of disability.[27]

The study further showed that the disabled were disproportionately nonwhite, less educated on the average than the general population, and live more commonly in rural areas or less affluent regions of the country—particularly the South.

ADEQUATE BENEFIT STANDARDS IN PUBLIC ASSISTANCE

Social workers as a profession have supported the *right to adequate income* for all members of our society. The concept of "adequacy" generally refers to the minimum level of goods and services necessary to maintain health and dignity at some culturally defined standard. The standard of adequacy changes over time in keeping with rising wages and national affluence.

The standard of living, or the total amount of goods and services which the average family can purchase, has risen steadily throughout this century in the United States and now exceeds that of many European nations and all developing countries. However, the government has still failed to guarantee an adequate minimum living standard for all members of society.

Individuals have a right to sufficient income in their own generation at the level established by their own culture. The concept of adequacy must be fluid to expand as times and social expectations change.

To maintain families at a level of minimal adequacy may be costly if the family has no earnings. For example the poverty threshold for an urban family of four stood at $5,500 in 1978. This amount is greater than the total annual income of a full-time worker in many low-wage occupations—e.g., gas station attendant, nurse's aide, or common laborer. Raising benefit levels in public assistance to some standard of minimal sufficiency for families with no earnings would mean even greater direct competition with private industry or agriculture. Some decline in labor-force participation in low-wage industries might result.

Liberalization of benefits also makes more people eligible for assistance, raising program costs. Eligibility for an assistance program partly depends upon whether income is less than the benefit standard. When standards are raised, more incomes automatically become "deficient."

The value of allowing more people to participate in the assistance program gives a broader base of social support for the program. Currently only some categories of poor are eligible while other low-income families, taxpayers themselves, are excluded from the system.

Arguments for raising benefits have been convincing. Negligible social investment in the children of poor families means that these youngsters may contribute too little to the nation's productivity as adults. Low benefit levels force families to liquidate most of their resources, and the chances for future economic rehabilitation of the family unit diminish. For persons who are short-term recipients under the system, high benefit levels may actually preserve and protect the family's living standard, thus reducing the chances of future dependency. Undeniably, considerable suffering and deprivation is likely for a family forced to live below the subsistence level.

A relatively new problem in benefit standards has arisen over the past fifteen years as a result of the proliferation of means-tested programs sponsored by the government. A growing number of individuals and families now receive benefits from more than one source. For example, in a large metropolitan environment, an ambitious and assertive poor family might establish eligibility in the following programs: AFDC, food stamps, public housing, Medicaid, free school lunches, Headstart, and community day care. The total value of the benefits to one hypothetical AFDC family in New York City who participated in all these programs would equal the purchasing power of a worker with a gross income of $11,500 per year. On the other hand most American communities do not have all these resources nor are most assistance recipients knowledgeable and confident enough to pursue all the opportunities for public support. For example, only about 14 percent of public housing is presently occupied by AFDC or SSI recipients; most have to find accommodations in the private market.[28]

The problem of overlapping benefits and different benefit reduction formulas is especially serious if one looks at the social objectives of public assistance. Given multiple means-tested programs, it is no longer possible to assess the effects of the benefit standard on adequacy of income, labor force participation, or rates of family saving.

Benefits to families with able-bodied workers have always posed a vexing problem. Conservatives claim that the government already oversubsidizes employables at unconscionable social expense, and liberals assert that many poor families are not provided with sufficient income to maintain human dignity. Social workers have tended to insist that social and personal change is nearly impossible in families that live daily from crisis to crisis, growing out of too meager material resources.

Variations in Benefit Levels

Despite recent attempts to achieve more uniformity, benefit levels in all assistance programs remain highly variable across the country. While SSI has set a uniform national *minimum* benefit, many states pay well over this amount. The differences in AFDC benefit levels among the states are even greater. All maximum cash payments in the AFDC program are presently below the poverty standard.

Many factors produce differences in benefit standards between states. Certainly public assistance benefits can be more efficiently administered to greater numbers of clients in an urban setting. The agency is likely to be somewhat more accessible to the client who wishes to make application. Family supports as a substitute for assistance income are likely to be fewer in the city. One could expect utilization of the program to increase in urban centers for these reasons alone. However, some people also argue that benefits are higher where society has its worst social problems. Handing out subsistence checks to poor families may "keep the peace," especially where minorities live in densely compacted and potentially explosive areas like the inner cities.

The present variation in benefit standards makes it difficult for public assistance applicants to anticipate how much they are likely to receive. A major equity problem is also created when persons in similar economic circumstances throughout the country are subject to very different benefit standards.

Citizens of the United States should receive similar treatment at the hands of public agencies, irrespective of where they happen to reside. Social workers have long urged that benefit standards in public aid should be more uniform. The usual counter-argument stresses that states participate in financing AFDC programs; therefore, the federal government has no right to dictate policies which may affect state treasuries adversely. Some have contended that uniformity in benefit standards could be achieved by federalizing the funding and administration of AFDC programs. However, with federalization might actually come a reduction in benefit levels, because many congressmen would not approve high standards in a nationalized program. The drain on the federal budget would seem potentially very high if liberal benefits were authorized. Some states might supplement a federalized program, while other states would not—recreating interstate differences all over again. The main gain from a federal takeover of AFDC would be a minimum benefit standard throughout our country, with centralized direction and federal initiative.

SUMMARY AND APPLICATION

What will be the direction of future welfare reform? Several trends have emerged from the debate over welfare reform since 1968 that suggest the direction of amendments to the Social Security Act and to related legislation. The changes will reflect demographic shifts in the nation's age structure, concern over maintaining high economic productivity, reducing inequities in eligibility and benefit criteria created through piecemeal changes in welfare laws, and shifting the financial burden for the support of welfare programs to a broader tax base.

The experience with WIN and similar programs indicates that public service employment must be expanded as a real option for welfare recipients. Neither families receiving AFDC nor individual SSI recipients are generally competitive when vying with others for jobs in the private sector. Inner cities have a limited supply of opportunities available even for the most eager applicants. The government must become the employer of last resort. New public service positions are likely to be targeted for the economically disadvantaged, particularly current public assistance recipients. Training programs under WIN and CETA will expand concurrently, to prepare more recipients for future employment in the private sector. Training solutions to the problem of economic self-sufficiency will be stressed.

To achieve greater equity for the system, proposed legislation has aimed at standardization of eligibility and rules for participation in the AFDC program, with extension of AFDC-UP to all states. Controversy still flares over further universalization of this program, however. Rather than make further alterations in the AFDC program structure, this country will probably use the tax system as a method for providing money to low-income wage earners.

The federal government will probably take wider responsibility for financing public assistance programs. The federal reimbursement rate may be increased from 75 percent to 100 percent for AFDC. At the same time, Congress is considering a proposal to lower the minimum age for SSI benefits from sixty-five to fifty-five years to cover people experiencing age-specific income-related problems for which no remedies now exist. Federal support for SSI is already at 100 percent.

Pilot studies of more comprehensive reforms will be carried out to give Congress a basis for considering far-reaching changes. The social security system may also be used as a vehicle for improving the system of supports for low-income families—principally by widening the range of risks covered.

The role of social services in income maintenance problems will apparently expand, but largely in areas which are related to support of work or training. A piecemeal, incremental approach will continue to characterize the approach of this country in modifying its basic mechanisms for support of the poor.

Positions for social workers in public assistance will depend mainly upon the utilization of purchase of care and service. The greater the use of purchase, the fewer services will be offered by public assistance agencies directly. Eligibility determination and other basic tasks in such agencies have been unappealing to social workers because they provide an inadequate opportunity for the use of professional skills.

Meanwhile, the right to an adequate income and the responsibility to work to earn it continue to be a source of philosophical and political conflict. As individual productivity increases and the cost of living increases, the conflict may become more acute.

—*Marilyn Flynn*

KEY TERMS

Comprehensive Employment and Training Act
friendly visitor
social diagnosis
Social Security Act
fair hearing
standards for assistance
in-kind assistance

cash grants
Title XX
general assistance
AFDC
SSI
means test
WIN
residence requirements

REFERENCES AND NOTES

1. U.S. Senate, Committee on Finance, Subcommittee on Public Assistance, *Staff Data and Materials on Public Assistance*, U.S. Government Printing Office, Washington, D.C., 1978, p. 5.
2. Verl S. Lewis, "Charity Organization Society," *Encyclopedia of Social Work*, 1971, vol. 1; Blanche Coll, *Perspectives in Public Welfare: A History*, U.S. Government Printing Office, Washington, D.C., 1970; Walter I. Trattner, *From Poor Law to Welfare State: A History of Social Welfare in America*, Free Press, New York, 1974; Winifred Bell, *Aid to Dependent Children*, Columbia University Press, New York, 1965; Grace Abbott, *The Child and the State: The Dependent and the Delinquent Child*, vol. 2, University of Chicago Press, Chicago, 1938; Amos G. Warner, *American Charities*, Crowell, New York, 1908.
3. Harry L. Hopkins, *Spending to Save: The Complete Story of Relief*, Norton, New York, 1936, pp. 179–180.
4. Grace Abbott, *From Relief to Social Security: The Development of the New Public Welfare Services and Their Administration*, University of Chicago Press, Chicago, 1941, p. 231.
5. Hilary M. Leyendecker, *Problems and Policy in Public Assistance*, Harper & Brothers, New York, 1955; see also Coll, op. cit., p. 19.
6. U.S. Department of Health, Education and Welfare, Social Security Administration, *Social Security Bulletin*, U.S. Government Printing Office, Washington, D.C., October 1978, p. 60.
7. Leyendecker, op. cit.
8. *King v. Smith*, 392 U.S. 306 (1968)
9. *Shapiro v. Thompson*, 394 U.S. 618 (1969)
10. *Goldberg v. Kelly*, 397 U.S. 257 (1970)
11. *Rosado v. Wyman*, 397 U.S. 397 (1970)
12. *Dandridge v. Williams*, 397 U.S. 471 (1970)
13. *Wyman v. James*, 400 U.S. 309 (1971)

14. *New York Department of Social Services v. Dublino*, 413 U.S. 405 (1973)
15. *Edelman v. Jordan*, 415 U.S. 651 (1974)
16. *Burns v. Alcala*, 420 U.S. 575 (1975)
17. U.S. Senate, Subcommittee on Public Assistance, op. cit., p. 11.
18. Illinois Department of Public Aid, *1976 Annual Report*, Springfield, Ill.
19. U.S. Congress, Joint Economic Committee, Subcommittee on Fiscal Policy, *Issues in Welfare Administration: Welfare—An Administrative Nightmare*, Studies in Public Welfare, Paper no. 5, pt. 1, U.S. Government Printing Office, Washington, D.C., 1972, p. 35.
20. Sar A. Levitan, *Work and Welfare in the 1970s*, Welfare Policy Project, Institute of Policy Science and Public Affairs of Duke University, Spring 1977, p. 16; See also, U.S. Senate, Subcommittee on Public Assistance, op. cit., p. 42.
21. Ibid.
22. Leonard Goodwin, *What Has Been Learned from the Work Incentive Program and Related Experiences: A Review of Research with Policy Implications*, U.S. Department of Labor, Employment and Training Administration, Washington, D.C., February 1977.
23. Adverse effects on labor force participation and family stability have also been reported in some research on AFDC caseloads. For a good summary of these data, see David W. Lyon, *The Dynamics of Welfare Dependency: A Survey*, Welfare Policy Project, Institute of Policy Sciences and Public Affairs of Duke University, Spring 1977.
24. U.S. Department of Health, Education and Welfare, *Findings of the 1973 AFDC Study: Part I*, National Center for Social Statistics, Washington, D.C., June 1974, p. 80.
25. Robert C. Stone, and Frederic T. Schlamp, "Characteristics Associated with Receipt or Nonreceipt of Financial Aid from Welfare Agencies," *Welfare in Review*, vol. 3, July 1965, pp. 1–12.
26. U.S. Department of Health, Education and Welfare, *Social Security Bulletin*, October 1978, p. 53.
27. U.S. Department of Health, Education and Welfare, Social Security Adminiatra- tion, *Social Security Survey of the Disabled*, U.S. Government Printing Office, Washington, D.C., 1972.
28. U.S. Senate, Subcommittee on Public Assistance, op. cit., p. 5.

FOR FURTHER STUDY

Robert M. Ball, *Social Security: Today and Tomorrow*, Columbia University Press, New York, 1978.
Alan B. Batchelder, *The Economics of Poverty*, Wiley, New York, 1966.
Philip Booth, *Social Security in America*, Institute of Labor and Industrial Relations, Ann Arbor, Mich., 1973.
Irwin Garfinkel and Felicity Skidmore, *Income Support Policy: Where We Have Come From and Where We Should Be Going*. Institute for Research on Poverty. University of Wisconsin, Madison, 1978.
Irwin Garfinkel, "What's Wrong With Welfare," *Social Work*, vol. 23, 1978, pp. 185–191.

Sar A. Levitan and Robert Taggart (eds.), *The Promise of Greatness*, Harvard University Press, Cambridge, Mass., London, England, 1976.

David Macarov, *The Design of Social Welfare*, Holt, Rinehart, and Winston, New York, 1978.

Richard L. Morrill and Ernest H. Wohlenberg, *The Geography of Poverty in the United States*, McGraw-Hill, New York, 1971.

Robert D. Poltnick and Felicity Skidmore, *Progress against Poverty*, "Poverty Policy Analysis Series," Academic Press, New York, 1975.

Isabel V. Sawhill, et al. (eds.), *Income Transfers and Family Structure*, The Urban Institute, Washington, D.C., September 1975.

Bruno Stein, *On Relief*, Basic Books, New York, 1971.

Welfare Reform: Issues, Objectives, and Approaches (Washington, D.C.: Congressional Budget Office, 1977).

Sidney E. Zimbalist, "Comparison of Social Welfare Values: A Semantic Approach," *Social Work*, vol. 23, 1978, pp. 198–202.

FOR DISCUSSION

1. What three ways may be used to increase individual incomes?
2. Identify groups of people for whom employment is not a feasible solution to their income problems?
3. How is poverty related to societal progress?
4. What were the key problems addressed by the Charity Organization Society?
5. What two types of COS representatives worked with families?
6. What were major problems in the COS approach?
7. Why did local programs for the poor fail in 1929?
8. What are the "two prongs" of the provisions in the Social Security Act for income maintenance?
9. What was the outcome of lowered caseloads and increased social services provided in the 1962 amendments to the Social Security Act?
10. What were the major criticisms of social services staffs in the 1960s?
11. What was the change in 1969 involving income maintenance payments and social services?
12. Whom does general assistance serve?
13. What programs were the forerunners of AFDC? How effective were they?
14. What inducements did the federal government use to get states to cooperate in SSI?
15. Why is it said that an assistance recipient must "fail" a means test to "pass"?
16. Explain the concept of the right to welfare benefits.
17. How are federal and state responsibilities for public assistance shared?
18. What are the social objectives of public assistance.
19. How does the number of AFDC requests compare to those in SSI?
20. Why were residency requirements for public assistance declared invalid by the Supreme Court?
21. Which myth regarding public assistance surprised you most? Why?
22. Of the three groups receiving SSI, which is the largest?
23. What major suggestion does the chapter make concerning AFDC benefits?
24. What major changes in public assistance are suggested for the future?

PROJECTS

1. Use the *Social Security Bulletin* to get the latest data on public assistance costs. Are total expenditures rising or falling? Are per capita payments rising? What is the relative standing of your state on a per capita payment basis? Report to the class on your findings.

2. Choose a European country and compare its income maintenance program to that of the United States. Is modern capitalism "highly impersonal"? Cite examples in your answer.

3. Present a panel of two or three members of the local welfare rights organization to hear their concerns about public assistance. Include a student as chairperson and another as a discussant. Tape the panel as it is being presented to the class.

4. Ask a local public assistance administrator to listen to the tape prepared for No. 3 above, and discuss his or her reactions with the class.

5. Present this debate: "Resolved, that the present system of public assistance should be replaced by a guaranteed annual income."

6. Make a detailed study of the poor laws in England. Prepare two or three role-play situations. One example would be bringing a "sturdy beggar" before a local magistrate.

7. Nutritional deficits are most serious for pregnant women. Study the nutritional programs that are available, and indicate the benefits and shortcomings of each for pregnant teenage girls, considering that the first trimester of pregnancy is most critical in terms of mental development of the child. Distinguish between malnourishment and undernourishment.

CHAPTER 8
Child and Family Welfare

Complications in the changing family.

"Family" conjures up visions of God, motherhood, and apple pie. Yet God has been proclaimed deceased, motherhood has been attacked as a form of slavery, and apple pie contains cholesterol and calories dangerous for human consumption. The family has been disdained as outmoded by some.

Even more important, Americans have reserved their family lives as last preserves of privacy. To consider public policy toward the family might enlarge the domain of government beyond the limit of a freedom-loving people's endurance. "The family is one place where the government should have a hands-off policy" is a repeated cocktail-party comment. Few, it seems, would wish their personal lives to be further regulated by an intrusive government.

—Robert M. Rice*

T his country lacks a formalized national family policy. As used here, "social policy" means the official decisions by legislative bodies, courts, or other governmental agencies about social issues. The result is a broad principle of operation for carrying out a specific social welfare program. Policies define the nature of the service or aid, who will receive the agency service, the standards of practice, and specific principles and procedures for carrying out a social welfare program.

NEED FOR A NATIONAL FAMILY POLICY

Varying state and federal programs have an impact upon family life even though family concerns were not a reason for their invention or directly considered in the formulation of their policies. For example, when government acts ineffectively to prevent the pollution of lake waters by the discharge of industrial waste, scarce recreational areas which are important to family life are lost. Some urban renewal programs have cleared unsightly and overcrowded areas of a city and constructed modern buildings, but in doing so have ignored the established patterns of neighborhood life. In effect, most family policy in the United States occurs by default. In contrast, by testing its policies of taxation, energy, transportation, housing, education, and income security for their effects on family life, government could add to the stability of the family.

In many ways, family policy is our policy toward children; thus family and child welfare are considered together in this chapter. Successful family and child policy will require a balancing of the interests of children, their parents, and government. If this kind of collaboration were combined with a belief that children are helped most effectively through their parents, the result would be more services to the family and more power for social agencies to work in behalf of children *with* parents, not *against* them.

*Robert M. Rice, *American Family Policy: Context and Control*, Family Service Association, New York, 1977, p. 3.

Alvin Schorr provided a challenge in his answer to the question: "How can it be that children are abused or neglected, or starved or exploited and decent people do no better?"

> First, we are not wholly decent. . . . We love our children and do much for them, but we do not love them all or in every circumstance, and often we turn on them angrily *because* they are in difficulty. Second, when we do attempt to serve them, we find ourselves politically divided, and other issues (demographic, religious, racial, and professional) become more important than the outcome for children. Third, possibly without intending it, we have perfected a system that rations service and contains its own adulterated standards of performance. . . . Fourth, we are for various reasons committed to duplex programming—that is, separate programming for the poor and non-poor. The system joins relatively low-status professionals to low-status clients, as if designed for impotence. The system works out badly—a point to which we resolutely do not pay attention—and leaves vaguely confirmed a feeling that the problems are inevitable. [1]

The Family Service Association of America sponsored a family policy statement:

> Family policies should emphasize support of, rather than substitution for, family functions.
>
> 1. Marriage should be satisfying and, when it is not, termination of the marriage is an appropriate solution. Regulatory measures to stem the divorce tide appear to be ineffective. Services must be available to ameliorate the disadvantages of the high-risk single-parent family. More consistent state laws are also recommended.
> 2. Family policy should support individuals in making satisfying choices of familial life-styles which are compatible with the requirements and commitments necessary for the maintenance of the society. The trend toward acceptance of varieties of sexual attachment between consenting adults should continue to be reflected in law.
> 3. Pluralism should be a guiding principle in framing family policy. Family concerns cannot safely be left to the widely varying state laws in an age of ease and frequency of travel. Consistency in law should not require uniformity in family performance.
> 4. Family policy must be based on knowledge. Data on attitudes and underlying structural changes are especially needed. Financing of needed research is essential.
> 5. Ways should be formed for industry to better support family life. Geographic mobility and transfer of workers are special problems. Industrially sponsored day care and expanded options in regard to laws of work are needed. Housing should be considered in terms of a physical environment for families.
> 6. An income standard of decency should be promulgated for all families. Family household work should be considered as an aspect of national product. A trade-off must be considered—the social value of employment against the value of child care.
> 7. The health delivery system should be comprehensive and integrated and should offer improved family-oriented services.
> 8. Administrative structures need to be designed to coordinate family-oriented

services provided by multiple organizations. These structures must make possible rational administration, serve the peculiar purposes of the individual human service situation, and seek and utilize citizens' input. Especially important is sensitivity to administrative accountability, to the conditions necessary for providing good direct services, and to citizen interests.[2]

Since the major concern of the social work student in family and child welfare is to deal with stressful family conditions, commitment to rational policy development is essential. It is a commentary on the status of national family and child policy that a White House Conference on the family was set for 1980; but conflict over major issues led to its cancellation by the Carter administration.

> Daniel Yankelovich looked at the family values of the "New Breed" and the "Old Breed." In a sample of 1,230 households with one or more children under 13 years of age, 43 percent were defined as the New Breed, viewed as stressing freedom over authority, self-fulfillment over material success, and duty to self over duty to their own children and others.
>
> Half of parents were committed to stricter child rearing and older American values—"We will sacrifice for you and be repaid by your success and sense of obligation." The New Breed message is "We will not sacrifice for you because we have our own lives to lead. But, when you are grown, you owe us nothing.[3]

WHY SOME FAMILIES AND CHILDREN NEED SOCIAL SERVICES

Child and Family Population   The 66 million children under eighteen years of age make up over 30 percent of the nation's population. Over 80 percent of the children live with two parents, a decline from 85 percent in 1970. Another 15.5 percent of the children live with their mothers as the single family head. One and a half percent of children live with their father only. The remaining 2.7 percent live with neither parent but have some form of substitute care.[4]

During the past decade families headed by women have increased ten times as fast as two-parent families, a result of higher rates of marital instability and births out-of-wedlock.[5] The growth rate is shown in Figure 8-1. Between 34 percent and 46 percent of children will be living in single-parent homes for an average of five or six years.[6]

The greatest increase in single-parent families is among the youngest women and among nonwhite female-headed families. Since 1960 the latter group has increased twice as fast as its white counterpart. Among nonwhites, the rate of out-of-wedlock births is higher; smaller proportions of children are placed for adoption; and levels of marital disruption are higher. The risk of widowhood is also higher for nonwhite women.[7]

The fertility rate in this country, which began to decline in the late 1960s, dropped to a record low in 1977, 1.8 children for each woman. The decline was highly significant since the number of women of childbearing age, i.e., from fifteen to forty-four, had increased at more than twice the rate of the total population.[8]

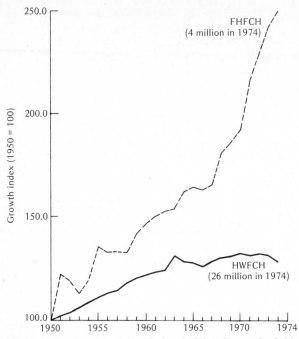

Figure 8.1 Growth of female-headed families with children (FHFCH) and husband-wife families with children (HWFWC), 1950–1974, (1950-100). (SOURCE: *Current Population Reports*, Series P-20, "Household and Family Characteristics," U.S. Bureau of the Census, Washington, D.C.)

Vital Statistics From 1966 to 1975 the rate of illegitimacy among girls fifteen to seventeen years increased by nearly 50 percent. Illegitimacy rates dropped for women in their twenties. The increase occurred at the same time that inexpensive contraception and legal abortion became widely available. Increased sexual activity without contraception was apparently a major cause.

The upward trend, both in birth rates and illegitimacy rates, occurred only among white women. Rates for black women declined; however, birth rates for young black women are still three times higher, and the rate of illegitimacy is still eight times that of the white race.[9] The trend toward increased births among young teenagers is alarming because pregnant teenagers tend to receive inadequate prenatal care, thus increasing the risk to themselves and their babies. They are also less likely to be prepared for the responsibilities of parenthood.

The Single-Parent Family

Economic Problems On the average, families headed by women have much lower incomes than those headed by a male. The median annual income of families headed by a women was $6,844 in 1975. Families headed by men reported a median income of $14,816. In black single-parent families, the level of income is lower. For example, only 46.2 percent of persons in families with a nonwhite female head are above the poverty line, compared with 73.7 percent of comparable white families.[10] The extent of the financial problems is further highlighted by the following facts:

1. About two-fifths of the divorced, separated, and single women eligible to receive financial support from the children's fathers have never received a single payment.
2. Fathers who make some support payments typically pay irregularly; one-third make none at all.
3. If families headed by women were forced to rely solely on child support/alimony payments, only 3 percent would be above the poverty level.
4. About 12 percent of the earnings of absent fathers who provide financial assistance goes for child support or alimony.
5. Families actually receiving support get payments supplying only half of the child's basic needs.[11]

Role Conflict   Role conflict is often a source of problems in the single-parent family, especially when the parent is employed outside the home. School schedules and child illnesses tend to highlight the complexity of the parental roles and the difficulties in fulfilling them.

Adequate child-care arrangements are among the most important supports for single-parent families. For mothers of preschool children, employment depends on child-care resources. While social workers tend to prefer day care centers, single parents more often choose relatives or neighbors who come in or take children to their homes. Such arrangements are both less costly and more convenient. Also, an in-home baby-sitter does not have to be licensed. For low-income jobs, child care costs make it uneconomical for the mother to work. We will return to day care later.

In addition to role conflict resulting from the need to combine parental responsibilities and employment demands, a desire to fulfill other roles creates tensions. The single parent usually wants to be able to go out with friends, to find adult companionship or marriage. This may require a renewal of social skills. Sometimes mothers feel guilty at being away from their children to seek personal pleasure. A mother who is a widow may be concerned that her children will interpret her interest in another man as a betrayal of their father.

Special Situations of Single-Parenthood

The School-Age Parent   Mothers who give birth to children and choose to raise them without getting married include many school-age parents. The stigma attached to childbearing out of wedlock has eased. However, school-age mothers often lack the education, job skills, and family supports needed to keep the child. Neglect and abuse may result if the child becomes an obstacle to social activities. Even the father who is willing to support the child usually has limited resources. Thus, foster care or adoption may become the solution.

The Single-Adoptive Parent   The single adoptive parent—a special type of unwed parent—is often omitted from consideration because the status is usually attained voluntarily. While most single-parent adopters are economically self-sufficient, they often need day care and other supporting services, including sex-role models for their children. Single parents frequently are more willing to adopt handicapped children who may need special provisions for health care or surgery. Agency financial subsidy is helpful to meet such expenses. Nationally, between 1,000 and 2,000 single-parent adoptions have been finalized.[12] The women's movement has helped to extend the idea of children being reared by a single adult.

Death of a Spouse   Nine million widows with over 1.25 million dependent children and 1.8 widowers with about 175,000 children under their care make up another group of single parents.[13] Generally, being a widow or widower is more respected than being divorced or separated. As a result, societal supports are more readily available. The length and quality of the marriage relationship will influence how well a family can recover to carry on its economic, emotional, and child-bearing tasks. Financial decisions must often be made under severe emotional stress.

Desertion   Desertion as a substitute for divorce represents a drastic way to terminate a marriage. It involves no visitation and no support payments without legal compulsion, but desertion does not terminate the obligations of marriage.

> Mrs. Y., fifty years old, came to the Legal Aid agency to get a divorce from her "husband" of ten years. In the intake interview with the staff social worker, it was revealed that Mrs. Y. had been married in Mississippi when she was eighteen years old and after four years, her husband left home. The next year, she moved north. Mrs. Y. had not heard from her husband, and he had not contacted her or offered support for her daughter from that marriage. Therefore, Mrs. Y. concluded that she was free to marry again. Now she wanted a divorce, but her second marriage was never legal because it was bigamous. She needed the divorce from her first husband.

Divorce   Divorce is the legal termination of a marriage allowing both parties the right to live separately and to marry again. Divorces increased sixfold between 1920 and 1975.

Bohannon identifies six "overlapping" experiences in divorce.

1. *Emotional divorce* or the experience of a deteriorating marriage.
2. *Legal divorce* or divorce based on grounds established by laws.
3. *Economic divorce* or the experience of dealing with money or property.

4. *Coparental divorce* or the experience of custody, single parent homes and visitation.

5. *Community divorce* or the experience of changing friends and community.

6. *Psychic divorce* or the problem of reestablishing one's individual autonomy.[14]

Generally, the courts no longer try to maintain the guarantee of the sanctity of marriage. Most grant a divorce routinely without testimony regarding fault when a property settlement has been agreed upon. The court is interested in the proposed settlement—particularly as it affects the custody and care of children. To discharge the responsibility to the children, courts now often appoint a *guardian ad litem*, a lawyer to represent the interests of the children. The court also may request a social work investigation and recommendations on child custody. In some states in a custody battle, social workers may be retained by either or both sides to provide testimony.

Social workers who have served families where divorce was being considered are familiar with the multiple impact on both parents and children. In California, conciliation courts have been established to protect the rights of children and promote the public welfare by preserving, promoting, and protecting family life and the institution of matrimony, and to provide means for the reconciliation of spouses and the amicable settlement of domestic and family controversies. Social workers are employed by the courts to help provide counseling services. The conciliation conference is planned short-term counseling. While some pressures can be relieved immediately, severe situations are referred to community agencies for continued treatment. A similar service for families is offered by the Family Mediation Center of Atlanta, Georgia, where divorcing couples can work out the details of their settlement outside the traditional adversary system.

Major issues for the female parent are adequate financial support and assistance in the child-rearing process which may be provided in part through visitation by the natural father or by remarriage.

Major issues for the father in and after divorce concern financial obligations, custody awards, and visitation privileges. Men have organized several groups, including Fathers United for Equal Justice, which advocate the rights of single fathers and fathers in divorce proceedings in relation to custody and visitation.

The women's movement has resulted in greater attention to the rights of fathers in marital break-ups because there is an interest in sharing child care responsibilities. Sometimes the child may have to be placed in foster care at time of the divorce or removed from the home later because of neglect or abuse.

Child snatching by a divorced parent has become a major issue. In order to get custody, a parent simply picks up the child in the neighborhood or does not return the child after visitation. Flight to another state is common because the matter may be reopened in another court. A proposed Uniform Child Custody Jurisdiction Act automatically denies legal remedies to any parent who has illegally obtained the child from another state.[15]

As social workers are granted greater involvement in policy and decision-making activities related to custody, agencies will necessarily have to give closer attention to staff recruitment, training, and procedural operations.

Remarriage after Divorce

The vast majority of people who divorce remarry. Therefore the role of stepchild and stepparent often requires major adjustment, a new physical environment, new authority figures, and stepbrothers or stepsisters.

Mr. and Mrs. T. were married about six months when they sought help. Mrs. T. had a boy nine and a girl twelve. Mr. T. had a girl ten and a boy seven. Mr. T. moved into Mrs. T's home after their marriage. His children visit for the summer months. During their visits, they share rooms with the other children. Mr. T's children complained that they do not feel welcome when they visit and that Mrs. T. always does much more for her children and virtually leaves them out. Mr. T. has been reluctant to discuss this with Mrs. T. He feels that he doesn't have much influence since he is living in Mrs. T.'s home. Mrs. T.'s children have complained about having to share their rooms. Mrs. T. does not discuss the problem because she does not want to be a "wicked step-mother." Mr. T. does not really want his children to stay with them next summer. He feels that he has to be a good father to Mrs. T.'s children.

Remarriages sometimes succeed better than first marriages because people may be more realistic about marriage, work harder at succeeding, be less likely to "outgrow" each other, and be more prepared to deal with crisis situations. However, remarriages often bring acute economic stress to both families.

Mr. and Mrs. C. had been married about six months. They had agreed that they would not argue about money since they knew what their financial obligations would be. Mrs. C. told Mr. C. that he should stop making house payments on his former wife's home since she now has a man friend who spends time there. Mr. C. complained about having to support Mrs. C.'s children because her ex-husband made occasional child support payments. He told her to take her ex-husband to court so that payment obligations can be enforced. Both Mr. and Mrs. C. expressed deep concern about repeated arguments over money.

Specialized counseling programs for second or subsequent marriages are especially needed. Financial planning usually is essential.

Self-Help and Professional Help for Parents

Parents Without Partners provides self-help services for single parents. Professional family agency services include self-help groups, individual therapy, and family counseling. While many receive help through sharing their own experiences, some get depressed and discouraged by hearing reports of tragic situations faced by others. Some agencies develop programs to help in adjustment to widowhood. The needs of various members may differ considerably. Parents who have recently lost their spouse may be dealing with the grieving process while those who have adjusted to the loss are ready to make future plans for employment, social activities, and marriage. Even when programs exist, people may remain unaware of them—especially if they have not used social services previously.

Homosexual Family Life

Approval of homosexual marriage and the adoption of children by homosexual couples is a test of one's tolerance of diversity of family structures and life-styles. The courts have tended to disallow homosexual marriages[16] but have permitted adoptions of one partner by the other. Agencies have been reluctant to approve adoptions of children by homosexuals; the question of a parent's fitness to have visits from or to retain custody of his or her own children while participating in a homosexual living arrangement is also controversial.

CHILD WELFARE DEFINED

Child welfare is concerned with the well-being of individual children, the strengths of family life, and the rights of all children and young persons. In the last decade other groups, including the aging, childless adults, handicapped adults, and minorities, have brought pressure upon governmental planning groups and social agencies for attention to their particular needs and a greater share of social services; thus child advocates face heightened competition for allocation of resources. By no means can they count upon children's needs being given a clear priority in social welfare planning and financing.

Now we shall consider children in need of protection from a broad perspective of programs and public policy issues directly related to the fulfillment of the rights of all children. A narrow definition of child welfare that has persisted in many communities stresses long-term care of children outside their own homes in cases of parental neglect, abuse, and poverty. Child welfare involves the needs of children in their own homes as well as those whose homes are so unsuitable that they require placement.

EFFECTIVE CHILD WELFARE POLICY AND PRACTICE

Children and families with serious problems need social services to support and strengthen their family life, to supplement parental care of children, or to substitute for inadequate or unavailable care by a child's own parents. In addition to these forms of care and social service, child welfare services must be directed toward social conditions that are unfavorable to family life and infringe on the needs and rights of children and youth.

Social Services Are Not a Substitute for Inadequate Income   For children and their families, obtaining food and clothing, keeping a place to live, and getting medical service for emergency health problems must receive first attention. When families are continually bound down to meeting these daily demands, it is unrealistic to expect social services to overcome the loss of a reliable income, decent housing, the acquisition of marketable skills, and employment opportunities free of discriminatory practices.

An early child welfare reformer, Julia Lathrop, who gave leadership to the establishment of juvenile courts and later became the first chief of the United States Children's Bureau, recognized the importance of adequate income to families if child welfare services were to succeed in their purposes. In an address to the National Conference of Charities and Correction in 1919 she commented, "Children are not safe and happy if their parents are miserable, and parents must be miserable if they cannot protect a home from poverty. Let us not deceive ourselves. The power to maintain a decent family living standard is the primary essential of child welfare."[17] Yet the effects of poverty on children and their families continue to manifest themselves throughout the child and family welfare service system and prevent the full attainment of social service goals.

Social Services for Children Must Be Reexamined to Identify and Remove the Influences of Long-Standing Racism and Sexism From a study of black children and child welfare by Billingsley and Giovannoni, racism manifested itself in three ways: (1) The kinds of services available are not sufficient to the special situation of black children, who should be seen as members of black families and black communities in all their variety and complexity; (2) within the system of services that exists, black children are not treated equitably; and (3) efforts to change the system have been incomplete and abortive.[18]

Adoption resources for children of unwed mothers provide another example of racial and socioeconomic discrimination. Social workers showed ambivalence when they attempted to come to terms with the racial component of the illegitimacy problem. Ruth Reed found that black families were more likely to keep an illegitimate child and that social workers believed that a black unmarried mother was less likely to wish to surrender the child, because of her "natural affection," fewer social pressures, and the presence of relatives who were likely to be willing to help her. At the same time, social workers acknowledged that facilities existing for the care of the dependent black child are far less adequate than the same facilities for the dependent white child, and that, even if the black unmarried mother should wish to surrender her child, she would have more difficulty in doing so.[19]

For a long time it was assumed that black illegitimate children were accepted in a matter-of-fact way, that they were not faced with social ostracism, and that the black community's readiness to care for illegitimate children should be seen as a positive innate characteristic rather than as a response to a lack of social services. Social workers now question these generalizations.

Sexist influences abound in our social insurance system. Its benefits still reflect the obsolete concept of a woman as dependent on her husband rather than as an economic partner—her role in over half of the marriages today.

Recent studies have documented the ways in which the juvenile justice system—police, judges, prosecutors, and correctional officers—treats girls differently than boys. Girls are more likely than are boys to be referred to court by parents and by police. They are referred for less serious offenses. Girls are routinely referred to court for sexual misbehavior while boys are not. More girls risk detention, and in the disposition hearing of the court are less likely to be enrolled in community programs and more likely to risk institutionalization in a severely restricted environment. Fewer alternative programs have been developed for girls than for boys, increasing the chance that they will be removed from their own homes. Once institutionalized, girls are afforded fewer services and learning opportunities.[20]

Recipients of Child Welfare Services Should Have a Part in the Plan for Social Services   The importance of "consumer involvement" has become recognized in the delivery of all social services. Social workers adhere to the principle that solutions to problems cannot be enforced upon persons affected by those problems; people must be helped to help themselves. Their individual capacities must be identified and strengthened to cope with their particular personal and social problems. In addition, children and adults can sometimes help each other. Sixth-grade children can successfully tutor lower-grade elementary children who are not achieving well in school; older teenagers can best identify recreational interests and readiness to participate in activities on the part of younger adolescents; parents with common problems in relation to their children can frequently help each other, particularly if skilled professional direction is available.

Parents should be given a responsible role in program development and policy-making in matters that affect their children. Groups of adoptive applicants and successful adoptive parents came together in councils for adoptable children or open door societies to persuade adoptive agencies to modify their perceptions of the readiness of many couples to care for "hard-to-place" children. Representatives of the black communities have organized to lobby in Congress for day care programs with a child-development focus that requires attention to neighborhood patterns and life-styles and parental preferences in child care. Foster parents have also come together in organizations that sometimes make demands on sponsoring agencies.

Effective Child Welfare Services Should Be Available to All Children and Families Who Need Them—Universally, Not Selectively   Most social services are geared toward certain groups identified by categories of income or special need. Services continue to be "residual," and they are provided only after the family or the market economy has failed to meet the needs of an individual or group. Services rest on an underlying assumption—often denied or unacknowledged—that adequate and competent families do not need help. As a result, services have been provided only after the family has endured hardship and trouble, and the community has stood by while breakdown or family disintegration goes on. The residual approach to social services, then, focuses on breakdown, economic depression, pathology, inadequacy, and need for treatment.

By contrast, an "institutional" conception of social welfare holds that many normal and adequate families have common human needs and require help at various times. Therefore, services for children and families should primarily be preventive, easily available without stigma, and aimed toward supporting and holding families together and helping parents and their children toward self-fulfillment. This conception of child welfare services necessitates a much fuller development of supplementary services, i.e. social supports or "social utilities" necessary to help families meet the realities of family and community living.[21] Social services should be made generally and easily available to all families at the points of normal stress in the family life-cycle rather than only to those who are casualties of modern life and in need of protective or therapeutic services.

Experience shows the wisdom of planning services with the needs of all the population in mind. Services for poor children tend to be poor services. Services designed for the middle and upper classes tend to be services of higher quality.

Social Services for Children and Families Should Be Comprehensive Rather Than Islands of Services that Result from Fragmentation Although child welfare services vary greatly, no community in this country can claim a truly comprehensive child welfare service. Early historical influences prompted private citizens to establish social service agencies to protect special groups of children and special adult interests. For example, numerous sectarian children's agencies emerged from the foster care movement. In addition to the humanitarian motive to provide rescue and care to homeless children, the founders of these early agencies intended to ensure that children needing care outside their own families should be guaranteed their religious faith. Such agencies have provided a volume of service for many children, but, depending upon their religious identification, not all children have been eligible for service, nor has equal service always been available elsewhere in the community.

Fragmented child welfare services exist in day care as well as in the care of emotionally disturbed, physically handicapped, and mentally retarded children.

Still another example of the adverse effects of this nation's fragmented approach to child welfare is services to unmarried mothers. Frequently, the only help available is abortion counseling, or during pregnancy, and adoptive placement of the baby. Yet the majority of unmarried mothers keep their children.

Fully Effective Social Services for Children and Their Families Will Require a Commitment to the Rights of the Child and the Importance of the Child's Own Family and an Active Role for Government in Protecting Children Against the Hazards of Life For many voters, the extent to which government should intervene in the affairs of children is debatable. In this country not all areas of national life are considered equally suitable for social planning. There is a wide difference of opinion as to the role the government should assume for a comprehensive approach to family policy.

Governmental Programs on Behalf of Children

In what ways does government have the right and responsibility to exercise authority in behalf of children?

(1) It can set up regulations for the protection of children generally. By exercising its regulatory powers, it can compel parents to send their children to school or impose restrictions on employers who hire children to perform certain kinds of work. It may also apply regulations to foster parents and social welfare agencies that give care to children. These regulations consist of prescribed standards of care and treatment to which all foster parents of child care agencies must adhere. The intent in the state's use of its regulatory authority is to represent society's interest in all children by setting standards which apply to all children or to all parents or to other adults acting in relation to children.

(2) The state can also intervene in the relationship of parent and child in the life of a particular family. When parental care falls below a level allowed for by law, or when a child or young person engages in delinquent acts prohibited by law, the state has a responsibility to intervene and exercise the ancient principle of *parens patriae*, under which the court, acting as a protector of the dependent child, uses its power to require a better level of care or treatment for a particular child. This can result in the removal of the children from their own homes to a foster home or institution.

(3) The state has the authority to legislate for the development of various child welfare services. The federal government provides grants-in-aid to the states so that they can develop their own plans of social services to children and their families. State governments have the power to adopt statutes which provide for the development and financing of a range of social services on behalf of children. The importance of the state's authority to legislate for the development of social services to children and their families cannot be overemphasized. How successfully children are helped often depends upon the extent to which the statutes of a state reflect modern knowledge about children, respect for their rights, and readiness to tax and appropriate money for professional services and facilities to meet the needs of children.

Providing basic support for children in need of protection is a public responsibility. Furthermore, only government has the resources to make a significant impact on poverty and to extend basic child welfare services to all children who need them.

SUPPORTIVE SERVICES FOR CHILDREN IN THEIR OWN HOMES

The conception of child welfare services has been broadened to emphasize support for the normal growth and development of children within their own families. The goal is to help preserve, strengthen, and enhance family life and the quality of the child's environment.

Counseling and therapy in various forms are a major means of helping children in their own homes, including casework with individual parents to help them use their own strengths for the solution to family problems. Children may be provided individual or group therapy. Sometimes distress about a particular child in a family lends itself most effectively to a form of family therapy, a shift from traditional casework practice to a focus on the interaction of all family members. Group experiences for children in summer camps, group programs for handicapped children, and a variety of services to teenage mothers also are among the supportive services for children living in their own homes.

Day care services and homemaker services constitute a highly significant segment of supportive services and have been selected for fuller discussion.

Day Care

Some children require planned experiences outside their own homes. Many others can benefit from them. Day care encompasses a variety of provisions for children's daytime care and development. The perceived need for day care, terminology, auspices, and parents' reasons for using it differ. Nevertheless, all day care programs should include: programs based on understanding a child's individual needs and stage of growth, consistent nurture, supportive emotional response, attention to health and physical progress, and a stimulating experience to contribute to cognitive and social development.

Auspices   A variety of sponsors plan and administer day care programs in family or group settings. Some are under the direction and control of state or local public welfare agencies, using tax funds made available through the Social Security Act. Public funds are also used in the Head Start program. In some localities public health departments or teaching hospitals have developed day care centers for the care of children with special health problems. Many of the experimental group programs of compensatory education are sponsored by colleges or other centers for the study of child development.

Voluntary family and children's agencies may provide group care centers or family day care homes, or both, financed from voluntary contributions, public funds through a purchase of care, and parents' fees. Churches sometimes provide day care. Parents who want additional opportunities outside their homes for their children's development may choose to operate nursery schools cooperatively.

Thousands of children receive day care under commercial auspices—

"My mother goes to work and my father takes care of the house. At the moment they're both at the hospital. One of them is having a baby." (*Saturday Evening Post*, March 1979.)

centers operated as a business or day care homes where a woman takes one child or more into her home during the day for pay. Other types of commercial day care have appeared. Some employers operate day care programs to attract women employees and reduce absenteeism. Franchised businesses guided by companies of stockholders have developed day care centers on a regional or national basis, carrying such names as Mary Moppet's Day Care School, or Alphabetical Pre-School Center. Their intent is to plan more extensive operations than the family or individual owner, to develop a clientele among the better-paid working women, and to operate on a contract basis with industry, labor, and public welfare. Franchised centers have encountered problems of financing and criticisms about motives and quality of program. As a result, their potential for growth in the future is not clear.

Federal funding sources with different eligibility criteria and program standards have caused confusion. Overall, the financing of day care has depended heavily upon parent fees, an inadequate financial base that has retarded growth in quality day care services.

Children of Working Mothers   The most frequent need for day care comes from working mothers. The numbers and proportions of working mothers have increased markedly for a quarter century. Half of all mothers with children under age eighteen are employed outside their homes.[22] Recent increases have come from mothers of young children joining the labor force. Almost 6.5 million preschool children have working mothers, a growth of more than 60 percent over 1960.[23] Given the decline in the birth rate in the same period, the rapid rise is all the more significant.

Value attached to achievement and recognition outside the home, a means of self-fulfillment, desire to use special skills—all these induce mothers to work. Some work just because they enjoy the variety it adds to their lives, or they want to be with adults. Nonwhite mothers work in higher proportions than white. The higher the mother's education, the more likely she is to have a high commitment to her work. Marital status is another factor. Mothers who are widowed, separated, divorced, or single are more likely to work.

Child Care Arrangements   Day care for the children of working mothers is most often an informal arrangement between private individuals, with no organized community involvement or sanction. Seventy-two percent of the children of working mothers are cared for in their own homes, usually by their fathers, siblings, grandparents, or baby-sitters. In 10 percent of instances, children look after themselves. The remaining children are cared for outside the home—by relatives, neighbors, or friends in unlicensed family homes, in centers and nursery schools, or at playgrounds or recreation facilities. Only 1.7 percent of the children of mothers in the labor market are in day care centers.[24] Existing day care programs differ widely. The majority of day care facilities are proprietary. The generally unsatisfactory level of day care has been documented.[25]

Kahn argues for the provision of day care as a service to which a child has a right by virtue of status rather than special problems. The child would become eligible on the basis of age, health, local residence, innoculation, but the family would not have to establish in an intake evaluation that day care is "good" for one or "necessary." Day care in an advanced industrial society, Kahn says, should be a social utility.[26]

In any event, several issues must be resolved. What is the real need for new day care facilities? Do projections of need take into account the substantial amount of unlicensed family home care now in use which is not entirely unsatisfactory, or are the projections only in relation to existing licensed facilities? What shall be the sources of funding? At what income level will parents be required to pay part or all of the cost? What governmental or voluntary agencies shall qualify as sponsors for receipt of federal funds? To what extent should day care become an extension of a tax-financed school system, considering the problems with which the public schools are presently faced? How can child care personnel be trained to enhance child care as an occupation to the benefit of children? Considering the variety of forms of day care which parents seek, how can a national day care policy allow for a pluralistic system and a role for parents in planning the day care program? Can day care become an economical way of freeing low-income mothers with limited skills and education for work or should it be viewed as a public investment for the development of all the nation's children?

Inevitably public child care programs will increase, and some fixed public policy will come, either by rational planning or by default.

Homemaker Service

Homemaker service in behalf of children is provided by a governmental or nonprofit health or welfare agency to enable children to receive adequate care in their own homes when their mother for any number of reasons cannot fully meet her maternal and homemaking responsibilities. In such instances, the agency provides a "homemaker" (sometimes called a home-health aide), a woman trained in child care and home management who comes into the home for a few hours or more a day, or perhaps twenty-four hours a day, to perform a variety of tasks to help the family maintain itself in wholesome family living. The service goes beyond housekeeping per se, being concerned with the social and emotional effects of the mother's inability to care for her home and children. Consequently, in addition to the help provided by the homemaker, the sponsoring agency tries to facilitate use of other social or health services by family members as may be needed.

When Homemaker Service Is Appropriate   Homemaker service can be helpful in a variety of situations. In some the mother is absent from the home. In others she is present but unable to meet her responsibilities fully.

The mother may be absent because of physical or mental illness which makes hospitalization necessary. Or she may find it imperative to be away from home because of the illness of a close relative, perhaps her own parent, where she is needed to give solace or nursing care. Sometimes a mother temporarily deserts her family because of marital discord or discouragement with continuing and overwhelming burdens. A capable and accepting homemaker may serve to hold the family together and minimize the stress felt by the children until the mother has returned or the father has made other arrangements for their care.

Homemakers have also been used most benefically when a mother dies, to enable a father to hold his family together within its own home, particularly during the difficult period of adjustment to a way of life without the mother.

Homemaker service is also a useful resource in homes when a mother needs to learn better household practices or child care. She may lack the knowledge or motivation needed to meet her responsibilities; an accepting and competent homemaker can demonstrate ways of fulfilling her role more effectively and, in so doing, provide support and encouragement which nourish her motivation. Sometimes a mother's excessively poor housekeeping threatens the family with eviction: a homemaker can stave off this action while she teaches the mother to perform more adequately.

Assessment   Homemaker service has been in use since the turn of the century, and has demonstrated its value. States have been given authority to purchase such service or to develop their own. Nevertheless, homemaker service is still insufficiently provided. Even though homemaker service has been shown to be feasible in rural areas, it continues to be primarily an urban service. Moreover, services tend to be concentrated in a relatively few areas. Although, in principle, homemaker service is applicable to all socioeconomic groups, in the face of personnel shortages it continues to be offered mainly to low-income groups. Homemaker service can be provided at less cost in terms of both money and human stress than can foster care, particularly when there are several children in the family. It is unfortunate, therefore, that the service is so insufficiently supplied to all segments of the population.

CHILD PROTECTION FROM NEGLECT AND ABUSE

Neglect, abuse, and exploitation of children by parents are the most frequent problems to come to the attention of child welfare agencies. Children who are found to be neglected, abused, or at high risk in their family situations require specialized protective services from the community and its social agencies. Even though the intent of protective services is to help parents improve their level of care and keep the family together, neglect and abuse constitute the major reason for placement of children in foster care.

Neglect is the failure to perform expected child care tasks; abuse is nonaccidental injury inflicted on the child's person. A child may often be the victim of both neglect and abuse.

Child Protective Services Are Involuntary   The protective agency initiates the service by approaching the parents about a complaint from someone in the community—police, schools, public health nurses, neighbors, relatives, or other persons. Thus, the service is involuntary for the parents. That the agency approaches a family about its problems without a request from the family implies some invasion of privacy, however well motivated the services may be.

Child Protective Services Carry Increased Social Agency Responsibility, Since They Are Directed Toward Families Who Have Children at Risk   Children cannot make effective claims by themselves for the enforcement of their rights; if prompt and effective initiation of services does not follow a complaint from the community, a child may experience lasting harm through physical abuse or continued neglect. Moreover, the social agency cannot withdraw from the situation if it finds the parents uncooperative or resistant (as it can when individuals have voluntarily sought help).

Child Protective Services Involve a Special Mandate to the Agency From the Community   Statutes or terms of their charters charge particular agencies to receive complaints about alleged neglect and abuse of children, to investigate those complaints, and if necessary to initiate service to the parents. A voluntary agency sometimes has a sanction in its charter to give protective services, but even when voluntary services are offered, the provision of child protective services is a fundamental public· agency responsibility, one as essential for children as the provision of education.

Protective Services Require an Effective and Just Balance in the Use of the Agency's Authority   The social worker who extends child protective services is given authority by law to act to protect children from neglect and abuse. Parents usually feel this to be a threat. An agency representative has come without being asked and has reported a complaint about their child care. When the complaint is well founded, parents must either seek ways to improve the level of child care or face the possibility of the child's removal from their home through a court order.

Incidence

No accurate figures are available on the rate of child neglect and abuse. However, the incidence of reported child neglect surpasses that of child abuse by at least ten to one. As the statistics on child neglect become more accurate, the rate of neglect will probably be found to vary from state to state in response to per capita income, crimes of violence against adult persons, and other social indicators.[27]

Estimates of the incidence of child abuse vary widely, depending particularly upon the effort made within a state to enforce child abuse reporting statutes, and the common reluctance of physicians to report. When national attention was directed to the battered child syndrome in the early 1960s, the American Medical Association held that child abuse was likely to be a more frequent cause of death or acquired disturbances of the central nervous system than the well-recognized diseases of childhood or automobile accidents.[28]

Gil has taken a more moderate perspective out of his study of legally reported instances of child abuse. He acknowledges the strong emotional impact and tragic aspects of each instance of child abuse but sees the scope of physical abuse of children as less of a major social problem than the serious social problems that undermine the development of millions of children—poverty, malnutrition, racial discrimination, and inadequate medical care and education.[29]

Causes of Child Neglect and Abuse

The conditions leading to the neglect or abuse of children are multiple and interacting. Some families demonstrate individual or group psychopathology in the neglectors or abusers and other family members. In other instances neglect and abuse are more directly traceable to the social conditions and environmental stresses that bear harshly upon parents. Usually elements of both psychopathology and of stressful social conditions can be identified.

Parental Experiences In most cases of abuse and neglect, the effects of the parents' own deprived childhood and their lack of relationships to caring, reliable adults can be traced. They may try to cope with these early experiences by withdrawing from parental responsibility or by striking out against their children, who are vulnerable symbols of their own deprivations and failures. Other factors are the added stresses which accompany untreated poor physical health, unwanted pregnancies, or lack of supports which more fortunate parents take for granted—e.g., adequate income or helpful and reliable relatives.

Environmental Conditions Lack of parental control over some situations also contributes to child neglect and abuse. Negative influences exist within a community's system of social services; for example, there may be a lack of social utilities, so that families and children receive attention long after the onset of trouble or stress, or agencies may fail to follow through on referrals or to establish effective communications when referrals are finally made. Serious social problems in our communities increase the incidence of child neglect and abuse—problems such as large-scale incidence of mental ill health, unequal medical services, poverty in the midst of affluence, lack of jobs for youth and heads of families, deplorable housing for many families, high rates of delinquency, or inadequate or irrelevant education for the nation's youth who become the new young parents.

Symptoms of Child Neglect
The label "neglect" is attached to those symptoms which suggest the failure of the parents to adequately perform essential child care tasks. Children may be poorly fed, resulting in lack of proper growth, low energy levels, apathy, restlessness, or susceptibility to chronic infections. They may be shabbily clothed or dirty. Sometimes neglect involves a failure or refusal to obtain essential medical care. Frequent and persistent absence from school may be a symptom of parental failure to get children up on time in the morning, to start them off feeling prepared for the day's demands, or to support them in their school life with interest and approval. Preschool children who belong to multiproblem, disorganized families often show distinctive and handicapping deviations in their psychological development. Some infants and young children show a general failure to thrive even when no organic basis can explain their lack of healthy growth and development. Children of all ages may reveal parental neglect through a range of maladjusted behaviors and emotional disorders.

A child's neglect may be directly observable in adverse home conditions, including dilapidated housing and lack of privacy. Children may also experience eviction and homelessness. The family may live in squalor. Children may not have an adequate place to sleep. If they are young, they may be left alone or be poorly attended when the parents are away. The home may contain physical hazards to children's safety or unwholesome or demoralizing circumstances—

violence, excessive quarreling, parental dishonesty, defiance of authority in society, or lack of love and concern for each other's welfare among family members.

As Polansky has observed, "Although child neglect sometimes has striking and bizarre aspects, it most often takes place silently and routinely in the lives of children who are reared by their own mothers in their own homes."[30]

Symptoms of Child Abuse

With its connotations of violence and injury inflicted upon the child's person, child abuse has medical, social, and legal significance. Each year in this country large numbers of children are beaten, cut, or burned by their caretakers in circumstances which cannot be explained as accidents. Moreover, their injuries usually result from recurring acts of violence rather than from a single expression of anger or loss of control by the adults who care for them. The severity of such injuries ranges from mild forms of abuse, which may not come to the attention of a doctor or other persons outside the home, to an extreme deviancy in child care which results in extensive physical damage or even death to the child.

How Children Are Abused   Children are severely and repeatedly hit with a hand, hair brush, or fists, or are beaten cruelly with sharp or heavy objects, or straps, electric cords, ropes—sometimes baseball bats. They are cut with knives and broken bottles. They are assaulted by adults who sexually molest them or administer overdoses of drugs or expose them to noxious gases or other toxic substances. Sometimes infants are thrown against a wall or downstairs or are held by their legs and shaken hard. Children of all ages may be viciously yanked or shoved. They are burned by having hot coffee or scalding water thrown at them. Their limbs may be held over open flames or pressed against steaming pipes. Sometimes they may be burned systematically by lighted cigarettes. Sexual abuse of children occurs even more frequently than other forms of abuse and is ignored for the most part by families and communities.

The Social Worker's Role in Protective Services

Working with the seriously disorganized families referred for protective services places special demands upon social workers. Requirements include understanding the state's legal definition of abuse and neglect as well as the community's own definition reflected in the kinds of situations that result in a "complaint" about child care. It is also important to understand the source and use of the authority implicit in the nature of "protective" services. To give social workers support and to be fair to parents complained about, the agency must establish clear and objective criteria as a basis for intervention into the privacy of family life. The social worker must be prepared to use a broadly based treatment approach with attention to individual, family, and neighborhood dynamics.

Do Protective Services Improve Family Functioning?

Child abuse and neglect have become a major cost to agencies, yet protective services do not achieve their goals very well. Many social workers engaged in work with neglecting and abusing parents believe that they effect improvement with a number of these families, and this encourages them to continue. Their cautious optimism is borne out by studies of protective caseloads in some agencies. Whether the gains occur mostly in cases of moderate rather than severe neglect or abuse is not clear. Certainly helping the multiproblem family or the severely abusing family out of its problem-producing cycle is extremely difficult. A disturbing fact is the lack of follow-up studies of abused children who have come into protective foster care and are then returned to their parents.

Protective intervention through social services comes very late in a family's problems, after heavy stresses have led to neglect or abuse. New ways of "reaching out" are needed to help parents use help voluntarily, requiring auxiliary services adapted to the needs of these deeply troubled families such as birth control, day care, homemaker service, recreation centers, and family life education.

Finally, an agency's protective service must be defined and organized in relation to all of a community's social, medical, and legal services, with attention to coordinating these services effectively for the community's most vulnerable children.

PROVIDING A SUBSTITUTE HOME

Foster Care

As a child welfare service, foster care is arranged by a public or voluntary social agency (although an unknown number of children are living in foster homes or institutions under arrangements made by their parents independent of a social agency). Responsibility for the child's daily living usually has been transferred from the parents because of some serious situation—a set of conditions or parental characteristics which leaves them unable to continue to care for their child and thus necessitates community assumption of responsibility.

Foster care is full-time care, twenty-four hours a day, outside the child's own home. It may be given within a foster family home, a small group home, or an institution.

In contrast to adoption, foster care implies a temporary arrangement—an expectation that the child may be enabled to return to the parents' home. Using social work methods, the agency intends to play a major role in planning and carrying out the child's care as long as it is needed.

To be effective, this broad child-rearing responsibility has to be shared with the parents, the court, and other institutions of the community.

As a consequence of the difficult experiences of children who enter foster care and the unresolved conflicts in relation to their parents, effective foster care is not supplied by a change of setting alone; attention must be given to the child's previous experiences and continuing total development.

Incidence of Foster Care   By analyzing a variety of social statistics and studies, Kahn determined that in 1975 there were 250,000 children in foster home care, 100,000 to 125,000 in institutions for dependent, neglected, or delinquent children, 95,000 retarded and handicapped children in institutional care, and an additional 27,000 children in psychiatric residential care.[31]

The increase in the number of children in foster care in the United States between 1960 and 1970 was dramatic. In 1960, 3.7 per 1,000 children were in foster care. By 1970 the rate had risen to 4.7. New York State in 1971 had 7.6 per 1,000.[32]

Conditions Leading to Foster Care

The parental characteristics and social conditions that precede foster care in most instances are not easily corrected by existing services. Although the child welfare concept of foster care emphasizes its temporary nature—substitute care until the child's own parents can be helped to restore their home—foster care often is long-term. Furthermore, children may experience a series of foster living situations.

Contrary to popular belief, most children in foster care are not orphans; at least they have not lost their parents through death. Their biological parents may or may not visit them or assume any responsibility for them. As a result, children in foster care have been termed "orphans of the living" to emphasize the emotional, social, and legal limbo in which these children frequently live. Too often they are tied to their parents by unmet needs and unresolved conflicts, with a future which promises only a succession of foster homes or institutions.

The Child's Identity

As children move into foster placement, many show an intense need to understand the circumstances of separation from their parents. Their feelings tend to be most accessible early in foster care, offering the social worker an opportunity to help them talk about their experiences so they can begin to understand and accept them. Leaving the child alone with feelings of confusion and rejection over what has taken place or avoiding the child's stressful feelings by giving too ready reassurance about the future will fail to alleviate the child's real hurt. Also, the social worker is apt to lose a critical opportunity to forestall the hazards of denial or repression of the true situation or of the child's fantasy about his or her troubled parents.

The need to help children connect their present life in foster care to their past experiences with their own parents has not always been recognized in social work practice. In earlier years, agencies sought to break all continuity with the child's parental home when a child was moved into a foster home. But physical separation of a parent and child does not necessarily interrupt the influence of the parent. Children can modify their relationships to parents more effectively if their parents continue to see them and if their parental ties are openly discussed by the social worker and the foster parents.

Foster Care Facilities

Family foster homes offer the child experiences of family living. In the foster home, the child has a chance to form emotional relationships with substitute parents and the rest of the family and their friends as well as to learn about modes of behavior and family roles and responsibilities. Mainly for these reasons, the foster home has been the preferred form of care when children cannot live with their own parents.

Foster parents are selected by means of a social study from persons in the community who apply to give care to children. They usually receive payment for their service, but the payment in most cases is low, especially in view of the service they provide.

A wide gap is evident between the quality of foster homes needed and those that are available. Although children's agencies can all cite gratifying examples of effective, reliable foster parents who give good care to children, the average foster home falls far short of what is needed. Studies have shown that foster parents are recruited generally from lower socioeconomic groups. They are persons with limited education who are older than the foster children's own parents. They often show ambivalent attitudes toward the disturbed children they care for and may be unable to withstand the impact of aggression that is common among foster children. Foster parents do not have a clear understanding of their role because of lack of foster parent training, and they frequently are without constructive techniques to use in child rearing. Amid great obstacles and little reward from the community, foster parents give an essential child care service, but overall they lack the qualifications necessary for an effective foster care program.[33]

Foster parents are beginning to develop and use their own power. We have already mentioned foster parent organizations. Foster parents are also more likely to use legal means to assert their rights. Suits have been filed to prevent children under their care from being placed with others for adoption without according the foster parents due consideration.

Institutions   Foster care institutions have existed in this country for more than 200 years. Today they are being asked to provide specialized care and treatment for more children and young persons who are handicapped emotionally, socially, or intellectually. The shortage of good foster homes for children has been a factor in the widespread use of institutions.

Because of their characteristics, some children who enter foster care today are able to make better therapeutic use of a group living experience than of the more intimate and autonomous foster home setting. The successful use of different forms of group care for child rearing in other countries has led to interest here in new forms of institutional care. Also, research findings have seriously questioned the traditional view that living in an institution necessarily has devastating effects upon children.

Group Homes Many children who need foster care have characteristics which make them unsuited for either foster homes or institutions. Serious unresolved conflicts in relation to their parents may make it difficult for them to accept the traditional foster family setting; yet they need opportunities for more informal living and casual community experiences than institutions permit. To meet this need, some agencies have developed small group homes for preadolescents and adolescents.

The group home is usually a home or apartment, owned or rented by an agency, and located in a residential area. From four to twelve children are usually cared for. Child care staff are viewed as counselors rather than foster parents. Other professional personnel are also involved—social workers, psychiatrists, psychologists, tutors, among others. In view of their potentiality for effective care and treatment, many more group homes are needed.

For older adolescents, independent living arrangements are increasingly common. The young person obtains a room in a private home, at the "Y," or in an apartment with age-mates. A social worker or an older lay advocate provides help and minimal supervision. This plan is superior to a group home for some adolescents who are self-motivated and responsible.

THE CHILD'S RIGHT TO A PERMANENT HOME

A study of foster care practice in nine communities marshaled concern about the plight of children who are in danger of staying in foster care throughout their childhood years. How to decrease the numbers was a challenge recognized throughout child welfare. Yet despite some gains, the central problems are still unsolved: (1) the limited use of evaluation by agencies while children are in care or after they are discharged; (2) the limits on effectiveness because of staff shortages and turnover; (3) maladaptive ways for the court and social agency to meet their mutual responsibilities for children; (4) minimal professional concern about certain groups, including young persons in correctional institutions, children in private boarding schools, and American Indian children who must live away from their parents because of critical social and educational deficits in their own communities; (5) the acute shortage of foster parents who can effectively serve children with emotional, educational, and physical handicaps; and (6) the confused identity that is characteristic of many foster children.

The availability of permanent homes—continuity of relationships in their living arrangements—is a criterion now being emphasized in assessing agency service to children. In testimony before the Senate Subcommittee on Children and Youth, Fanshel said that "the notion that all children should be living with their biological families or adoptive families and that foster care should not be a permanent status has taken on such force in recent years that we face the prospect of a small revolution in child welfare as a result. "The first revolution in child welfare was the closing down of the mass congregate institutions and the development of foster family care as a major alternative living arrangement. The second revolution may soon be upon us: a massive effort to limit the duration of foster care status."[34]

Characteristics of parents and their children as well as characteristics of the service delivery system act as difficult barriers to permanent planning for children. For example, the longer a child stays in poorly defined foster care arrangements, the greater the barrier to a permanent home. A child's age influences length of stay in foster care. Younger children and minority children tend to stay in foster care longer. Characteristics of the biological mother may also constitute a barrier to a permanent home—particularly the adequacy of her mothering ability, her degree of disturbance, and the outlook for the social worker to work with her successfully. Whether parents visit and how often they visit their child in foster care was found by Fanshel to be the major correlate of discharge from foster care. Lack of parental visiting is a significant barrier to children having a permanent home outside the foster care systems.[35]

But not all barriers to permanent homes for children can be attributed to child- and family-centered characteristics. Equally influential are institutionally centered barriers—e.g., those resulting from a failure by the agency staff to arrive at a sufficient understanding of the serious family and environmental conditions that brought children into care. Barriers include maintaining a foster care program without links to preventive supplementary services and failure to develop alternatives to foster care as a remedy for family problems; "drift" characterized by social workers' indecisiveness about goals and pessimistic attitudes toward certain children and their parents; failure to set goals at key decision points and to monitor progress toward attainment of a permanent home for a particular child; and failure on the part of agency directors and staff to move assertively toward termination of parental rights even when children remain in foster care and are unvisited by their parents.[36]

As a result of a new awareness of such barriers to permanent homes for children, attention is being given to more effective service to parents. "Contracts" with parents of children in foster care are used to encourage parental participation in planning and decision-making about the future of their child in foster care. Periodic court or agency case reviews are used as a monitoring process to assure that children are not cast adrift in the foster care system but are moved out into permanent arrangements. Computerized management information systems are employed to help provide child welfare services and achieve permanent homes for children. An Interstate Compact on the Placement of Children has been adopted to reduce the injustices to "banished children"—those placed in foster care outside their state of origin without adequate supervision and planning for their future.

One result of the new effort to assure children a permanent home is a realignment in foster care and adoption practice. Today foster care and adoption services are more like "two sides of a coin" in agency practice rather than separate services.

ADOPTION

Adoption is a social and a legal process whereby the parent-child relationship is established between persons not so related by birth. By this means a child born to one set of parents becomes, legally and socially, the child of other parents and a member of another family, and assumes the same rights and duties as those that exist between children and their biological parents.

Incidence of Adoption

Accurate annual statistics on adoption in the United States have not been available since 1971 because of a lack of standard and mandatory reporting by states. Of the children adopted in the United States in 1971, 51 percent (86,200 children) were adopted by stepparents or other relatives, and 49 percent (82,800) were adopted by nonrelatives. Of the nonrelative adoptions, 79 percent (65,400 children) were placed by social agencies, and 21 percent (17,400) were placed independently. Of those placed by social agencies, 46 percent were arranged by public agencies, and 54 percent were arranged by voluntary agencies.[37]

The shortage of infants for adoption, as a result of the lowered rates of illegitimacy and the practice of single mothers keeping their babies, has also led agencies to consider adoptive placement of older children and children with special needs. Yet despite the gains derived from a more liberal definition of "adoptability" and "suitable adoptive parents," agency efforts to find adoptive homes for certain groups of children have not been sufficient.

The Older Child   Children beyond infancy are highly likely to be passed over in adoptive practice. Moreover, the condition of being an "older" child is often linked to other deterrents to adoption, especially nonwhite status and medical problems or handicaps. But despite difficulties, social agencies have demonstrated that older children can be given permanent homes through adoption, although doing so requires additional agency services at each stage of the adoptive process. Significantly, Kadushin's investigation of the outcomes of placements of older children provided evidence of a level of success nearly parallel to that for infants placed in adoption.[38]

Children with Medical Impairments   As long as the definition of an adoptable child was focused on favorable heredity and good physical development, children with various mental or physical handicaps were viewed as unwarranted risks for successful adoption. However, the growing flexibility of both public and voluntary agency practice has brought progress in the placement of children with physical handicaps. An important study of the outcome of adoptive placements of 314 children with diagnosed medical impairments, using a control group of adopted children without medical conditions, found that children with medical conditions of all degrees of severity and correctability can be successfully placed and reared in adoptive homes.[39] Furthermore, delay in permanent placement of children with medical impairments until a prognosis is established or corrective treatment begun was shown to be unnecessary; adoptive parents on the whole would have preferred to accept the child at a younger age and see him or her through corrective treatment from the beginning.

Racial Minorities   The number of children of racial minorities who need permanent homes through adoption is high despite special efforts in the past two decades to recruit adoptive homes for them. Minority adoptive applicants often have limited income and inadequate housing, lack of knowledge about adoption services, and fear of rejection. It is reasonable to expect, however, that minority adoptions may increase as a result of mandated case review procedures in foster care and more widespread and creative use of financial subsidy.

Intercountry Adoptions

Since World War II there has been a substantial movement into the United States of children who are adopted across national boundaries. In 1975 foreign children placed in American adoptive homes came mainly from Asia. Factors contributing to intercountry adoptions include the mobility of families around the world; the increase in international marriages; the greater ease of communication between countries; the continuing large numbers of American servicemen stationed abroad, many of whom seek to adopt children during their residence in another country or father children illegitimately with no means to care for them; and a humanitarian concern by many persons for the plight of refugee and other homeless children, many of whom are grossly neglected or discriminated against in their own country because of illegitimacy or mixed racial background.

People in this country become interested in adopting a child from another country in various ways. Often they are related to the child whom they want to bring to this country. Sometimes they seek to adopt a child with an ethnic background and cultural ties like their own. In some instances they want to adopt a child whom they met during a temporary stay abroad.

The legal adoption of children from other countries requires the cooperation of social agencies in two or more countries. International Social Service American Branch, a voluntary nonsectarian organization, is the principal agency recognized by the United States government to assist in the adoption by U.S. citizens of children from other countries. There are some sectarian agencies as well. The cooperation of child welfare agencies at state and local levels is also required.

Transracial Adoptions

Another development in adoption is the placement of children across racial lines. The term "transracial placement" refers to a family constellation in which a child with mixed racial background (usually a child with one white parent and one Asian, American Indian, black, or Puerto Rican parent) is adopted by a white couple.

A nationwide survey on transracial adoption in 1972 indicated that since 1967, when agencies had begun to increase substantially their efforts to make such placements, about 10,000 black children had been placed in white homes across the country. Figures for 1971 were then incomplete but were expected to be similar to those for 1970, when more than one-third of the adopted black children went into white homes.[40] Social workers, although not unanimous in their approval, for the most part seemed to endorse the practice as a means to provide homes for children who were otherwise likely to grow up in foster homes and institutions.

In the early 1970s, however, the climate of opinion about the appropriateness of transracial adoption began to change sharply as minority groups stressed the fostering of racial and cultural identity. At their 1972 meeting, the National Association of Black Social Workers came out "in vehement opposition" to the practice of placing black children with white families and called upon public and voluntary agencies to "cease and desist" transracial placement, which were termed "a growing threat to the preservation of the black family." The association directed much of its attack toward the CWLA for sanctioning placement of children across racial lines in its standards and for undertaking research on transracial adoption.[41]

The position taken stirred heated responses from professionals and parents involved with the relatively recent development of transracial adoptions. Even among black social workers, opinion was divided as to whether transracial placements should be eliminated completely or continued and used under the direction of a black social worker as an available alternative for children who might otherwise grow up without a permanent home.[42]

In any case, the practice of transracial placement of black and American Indian children fell off sharply and in some agencies virtually ended. A renewed effort was made to recruit more black and Indian adoptive homes. Given the lack of clear and mandatory reporting of adoptions, precise data on which to judge the results are lacking. The CWLA's semiannual report in 1974, based on statistics from forty-nine voluntary and eighteen public agencies, concludes:

> The recent stability of nonwhite homes is somewhat discouraging; it has varied from 49 to 67 homes per 100 children over the past 2 years, even lower than during the three earliest periods of the series (begun in 1971), when it ranged

between 74 and 85. Recruitment of nonwhite homes has a long way to go to match or exceed the number of nonwhite children accepted.[43]

Subsidized Adoption

Another development designed to expand adoption resources is subsidized adoption, in which a social agency makes financial payments to a set of adoptive parents beyond the point of their legal consummation of the adoption.

Subsidies are of three general types: those for specific services, such as medical care, legal services, or special education; time-limited subsidies, to be agreed upon by the family and the agency, to help absorb the costs of transition of an additional member into a family, and long-term subsidies in the form of monthly payments until the child is grown.[44]

Subsidies have several advantages. They can open up new possibilities for children who have handicaps or medical problems, those who are "older," and those who are black or have mixed racial parentage, for whom the prospects for attaining a permanent home through traditional forms of adoption have been bleak. They can obtain greater security, continuity of care, and clearer status for children with close ties to foster parents who have all the essential qualifications for adoptive parenthood except an adequate financial base. In addition, they have the potential for providing considerable financial saving in comparison with the costs of long-term foster care, as shown by a study in four Illinois agencies.[45]

Gary L. Shaffer examined the subsidized adoption program in Illinois, a state that has used this alternative extensively.[46] The number of subsidized adoptions approved each fiscal year increased appreciably from 70 in 1970 to 508 in 1976. The Illinois program was successful in that a large number of children viewed as "unadoptable" found permanent adoptive homes, including children who were physically or mentally handicapped and had been in foster care for long periods of time. Not only were children moved out of foster care after five or more years; many of them also had already experienced relatively stable relationships with foster parents, who were now enabled to adopt them.

Single-Parent Adoption

In the search for permanent homes for children, legal adoption by single parents (unmarried, widowed, or divorced) has gained ground—further evidence of the dearth of foster homes or two-parent adoptive homes for certain groups of children and a greater readiness by social workers and the public to question old practices and discard artificial barriers which keep children from having their "own homes."

In the late 1960s, the practice of single-parent adoption was given considerable publicity in newspapers and popular magazines through appealing photographs and stories of successful adoptions. No laws in any state prohibit adoption by single adults. Although there is no central tabulation of the total number of such placements, social agencies in at least ten states and the

District of Columbia have placed adoptive children with single adults or have publicized their willingness to accept applications from single adults.

Social workers have reported instances in which they have been highly impressed by the positive development of children placed with single mothers and the recognizable "good parenting" which followed placement. Placements with single males also have been made, but more rarely.

Identity in Adoption

The need to know about one's birth origins and to connect one's present life to biological beginnings is illustrated in child adoption. From time to time agencies received such inquiries from adopted adults, but only occasionally. Little mention in the literature was given to the right of adult adoptees to such information. In the past decade, however, a national movement was initiated by adult adoptees, and it gained support from a number of social workers, lawyers, and other professional persons.

Among adopted adults who embark upon a search of their past, some want only information, e.g., the personal, social, or physical characteristics of their biological parents. They believe such information will add to their understanding of themselves and to their sense of identity. Practical considerations, such as obtaining security clearance for a job or obtaining medical history, may also be factors that prompt the search. Some others want to locate their first parents, meet them, and attempt to establish a relationship with them. In a study of the sealed record controversy, Jones concluded that 60 percent of the small proportion of adoptees who return to an agency or the court for the information actually want to locate their biological parents.[47] The right to information of the adopted adolescent, who may be facing severe problems of self-identity, has scarcely been mentioned.

SUMMARY AND APPLICATION

Both family policy and child welfare services have many gaps. An assessment must take serious note of the continued fragmentation of social services for children and their families and the lack of comprehensive social planning.

While steps have been taken to integrate public child welfare services with social services extended to AFDC families, this has not been fully effective. The United States continues to be the only industrialized nation that has not legislated a program of children's allowances—financial benefits to parents regardless of need—to act as a base of protection for children. Family and child interests are only sporadically represented when public social policy is formulated which explicitly or implicitly affects family life.

Some positive trends brighten the outlook for children and make child welfare an attractive field of practice for new professionals to enter. Child welfare services have always drawn a large proportion of social workers into employment. It is an expanding field of practice, not only in quantity of services but in variety. Persons entering the field can expect to find opportunities to work in newer ways intended to be especially responsive to the needs and interests of minority groups and parents. We all need to work to extend the rights to which children and young persons are entitled.

—*Lela B. Costin*
Ruppert Downing

KEY TERMS

family policy
single-parent family
custody and visitation
"residual" services
social utilities
fragmented services
parens patriae

day care
child neglect
child abuse
protective services
permanent planning for children
subsidized adoption
supportive services

REFERENCES AND NOTES

1. Alvin L. Schorr, "Family Values and Real Life," *Social Casework*, vol. 87, 1976, pp. 403–404.
2. Robert M. Rice, *American Family Policy: Context And Control*, Family Service Association, New York, 1977, pp. 99–113.
3. D. Yankelovich, "Family: New Breed v. the Old," *Time*, vol. 109, May 2, 1977, p. 76.
4. U.S. Bureau of the Census, *Statistical Abstract of the United States*, 97th ed., Government Printing Office, Washington, D.C. 1976, p. 44.
5. Heather L. Ross and Isabel V. Sawhill, *Time of Transition: The Growth of Families Headed by Women*, Urban Institute, Washington, D.C., 1975.
6. Mary Jo Bane, "Marital Disruption and the Lives of Children," *Journal of Social Issues*, vol. 32, no. 1, 1976, pp. 103–110.
7. Ross and Sawhill, op. cit.
8. "Around the Nation. U.S. Fertility Rate Drops to 1.8, a Record Low," *New York Times*, February 11, 1977.
9. Robert Reinhold, "Birth Rate Among Girls 15 to 17 Rises in 'Puzzling' 10-Year Trend," *New York Times*, September 21, 1977.
10. "Money Incomes and Poverty Status of Families and Persons in the United States," *Current Populations Reports*, U.S. Bureau of the Census, series P-20, no. 103, 1976.
11. Bob Westgate, "Single Parent on the Hill," *Single Parent*, no. 44, September 1977, p. 25.
12. William Feigelman and Arnold R. Silverman, "Single Parent Adoption," *Social Casework*, vol. 58, July 1977, pp. 418–425. See also "Solo Parents and Adoptions," *Human Behavior*, vol. 7, January 1978.
13. "Easing the Plight of America's 1.8 Million Widowers," *U.S. News & World Report*, December 12, 1977, pp. 48–50.

14. Paul Bohannon (ed.), *Divorce And After: An Analysis of Emotional and Social Problems of Divorce*, Doubleday, Garden City, N.Y., 1970, p. 34.

15. Brieland and Lemmon, *Social Work and the Law*, West Publishing Co., St. Paul, 1977, pp. 243–244.

16. *Baker v. Nelson*, 291 Minn. 310, 191 N.W. 2d. 185.

17. Julia Lathrop, "Child Welfare Standards: A Test for Democracy," *Proceedings of the National Conference of Social Work, Atlantic City, New Jersey, 1919*, Rogers & Hall, Chicago, 1920.

18. Andrew Billingsley and Jeanne M. Giovannoni, *Children of the Storm: Black Children and American Child Welfare*, Harcourt Brace Jovanovich, New York, 1972.

19. Ruth Reed, *The Illegitimate Family in New York City*, Columbia, New York, 1934.

20. Rosemary Sarri and Yeheskel Hasenfeld (eds.), *Brought to Justice? Juveniles, the Courts, and the Law*, University of Michigan National Assessment of Juvenile Corrections, Ann Arbor, 1976; Catherine H. Milton et al., *Little Sisters and the Law*. Female Offender Resource Center, Washington, D.C., 1977, p. 1.

21. Alfred J. Kahn, *Social Policy and Social Services*, Random House, New York, 1973, pp. 74–76.

22. *Working Mothers and Their Children*, U.S. Department of Labor, Women's Bureau, Employment Standards Administration, 1977, p. 1.

23. "Annual Study Shows Increase in the Number of Children Whose Mothers Work," U.S. Department of Labor, Release no. 77-165. February 25, 1977.

24. *Working Mothers and Their Children*, op. cit., p. 11.

25. Mary Dublin Keyserling. *Windows on Day Care*, National Council of Jewish Woman, New York, 1972.

26. Alfred J. Kahn, "Therapy, Prevention and Developmental Provisions: A Social Work Strategy," in *Public Health Concepts in Social Work Education*, Council on Social Work Education, New York, 192, pp. 146–147.

27. Norman A. Polansky, Carolyn Hally, and Nancy F. Polansky, *Profile of Neglect: A Survey of the State of Knowledge of Child Neglect*. U.S. Department of Health, Education and Welfare, Social and Rehabilitation Service, Community Services Administration, (SRS) 76-23037, 1975, pp. 3–5.

28. "The Battered-Child Syndrome," *Journal of the American Medical Association*, vol. 181, 1962, p. 42.

29. David G. Gil, *Violence Against Children: Physical Child Abuse in the United States*, Harvard, Cambridge, Mass., 1970, pp. 7–8.

30. Normal Polansky et al., "Child Neglect in a Rural Community," *Social Casework*, vol. 49, 1968, p. 468.

31. Alfred J. Kahn, "Child Welfare," in *Encyclopedia of Social Work*, 1974, p. 101.

32. Mary Ann Jones, Renee Neuman, and Ann W. Shyne, *A Second Chance for Families: Evaluation of a Program to Reduce Foster Care*, Child Welfare League, New York, 1976.

33. Zira De Fries, Shirley Jenkins, and Ethelyn C. Williams, "Foster Family Care for Disturbed Children—A Nonsentimental View," *Child Welfare*, vol. 44, February 1965, pp. 73–84; Leon Eisenberg, "The Sins of the Fathers: Urban Decay and Social Pathology," *American Journal of Orthopsychiatry*, vol. 32, January 1962, pp. 5–17; David Fanshel, "The Role of Foster Parents in the Future of Foster Care," in Helen D. Stone (ed.), *Foster Care in Questions*, Child Welfare League, New York, 1970, pp. 228–240; and Delores A. Taylor and Philip Starr, "Foster Parenting: An

Integrative Review of the Literature," *Child Welfare*, vol. 46, July 1967, pp. 371–385.

34. Testimony presented before the Subcommittee on Children and Youth of the Senate Committee on Labor and Public Welfare and the House of Representatives Select Subcommittee on Education, December 1, 1975.

35. David Fanshel and Eugene B. Shinn, *Children in Foster Care: A Longitudinal Investigation*, Columbia, New York, 1978.

36. Arthur Emlen et al., *Overcoming Barriers to Planning for Children*, Government Printing Office, Washington, D.C., 1978; Deborah Shapiro, *Agencies and Foster Care*, Columbia, New York, 1976; Shirley Jenkins and Elaine Norman, *Beyond Placement: Mothers View Foster Care*, Columbia, New York, 1975.

37. *Adoptions in 1971*, U.S. Department of Health, Education and Welfare, Social and Rehabilitation Service, National Center for Social Statistics, 1973.

38. Alfred Kodushin, *Adopting Older Children*, Columbia, New York, 1970.

39. David S. Franklin and Fred Massrik, "The Adoption of Children with Medical Conditions: Parts I, II, and III," *Child Welfare*, vol. 48, nos. 8–10, October–November–December 1969, pp. 459–467, 533–539, 595–601.

40. Judy Klemesrud, "Furor Over Whites Adopting Blacks," *New York Times*, April 12, 1972, p. 38.

41. C. Gerald Fraser, "Blacks Condemn Mixed Adoptions," *New York Times*, April 10, 1972; Grow and Shapiro, op. cit., pp. ii–iii.

42. Klemesrud, op. cit. For a black perspective on American adoption practices, see also Billingsley and Giovannoni, op. cit.

43. *CWLA Adoption Statistics—January–June '74, Compared With July–December '73: Summary of Findings*, Child Welfare League, New York, October 1974.

44. *Subsidized Adoption: A Call to Action*, Child Care Association, Moline, Ill., 1968.

45. *Subsidized Adoption: A Study of Use and Need in Four Agencies*, Child Care Association, Springfield, Ill., 1969.

46. Gary L. Shaffer, "Subsidized Adoption: A Fifty-State Survey," unpublished research paper, 1976, reported in Gary L. Shaffer, "Subsidized Adoption: An Alternative to Long Term Foster Care,"D.S.W. dissertation, University of Illinois at Urbana-Champaign, 1977.

47. Mary Ann Jones, *The Sealed Record Controversy: Report of a Survey of Agency Policy, Practice and Opinions*, Child Welfare League, New York, 1976, p. 16.

FOR FURTHER STUDY

Andrew Billingsley and Jeanne M. Giovannoni, *Children of the Storm: Black Children and American Child Welfare*, Harcourt Brace Jovanovich, New York, 1972.

David Fanshel and Eugene B. Shinn, *Children in Foster Care: A Longitudinal Investigation*, Columbia, New York, 1978.

Joseph Goldstein, Anna Freud, and Albert J. Solnit, *Beyond the Best Interests of the Child*, Free Press, New York, 1973.

Ray E. Helfer and C. Henry Kempe (eds.), *Child Abuse and Neglect: The Family and the Community*, Ballinger, Cambridge, Mass., 1976.

Robert B. Hill, *The Strengths of Black Families*, Emerson Hall, New York, 1972.

Kenneth Keniston, and the Carnegie Council on Children, *All Our Children: The American Family Under Pressure*, Harcourt Brace Jovanovich, New York, 1977.

National Academy of Sciences, Advisory Committee on Child Development, *Toward a National Policy for Children and Families*, Washington, D.C., 1976.

Norman A. Polansky, Carolyn Hally, and Nancy F. Polansky, *Profile of Neglect: A Survey of the State of Knowledge of Child Neglect*, U.S. Department of Health, Education and Welfare, Social and Rehabilitation Services, DHEW Publication no. (SRS) 76-23037, 1975.

Heather L. Ross, and Isabel V. Sawhill, *Time of Transition: The Growth of Families Headed by Women*, Urban Institute, Washington, D.C., 1975.

Gilbert Y. Steiner, *The Children's Cause*, Brookings, Washington, D.C., 1976.

FOR DISCUSSION

1. What is meant by family and child policy? Give examples in addition to those mentioned in the text which directly or indirectly affect child and family life. Draw from knowledge of your own community.
2. Discuss the consequences of the trend toward increased births among young teenagers. What kind of social services might help to reverse this trend or reduce the risks to mothers and babies?
3. In divorce, how might the father's continuing rights and responsibilities to his children be better protected and enforced?
4. Should two persons of the same sex be permitted to marry? Should homosexuals be permitted to become foster parents or adoptive parents? Give reasons to support your point of view.
5. Why are girls more likely than boys to be referred to courts by parents and by police and to be referred for less serious offenses?
6. Why are supportive services to children in their own homes less well developed than foster care and adoption?
7. Where are most children cared for when their mothers work? Discuss the advantages and disadvantages of the various child care arrangements.
8. Give some examples of useful social utilities that could be developed to strengthen family life.
9. Given its proven usefulness in a variety of situations, why is the amount of homemaker service still insufficient to meet needs?
10. Explain how child protective services differ from other social services.
11. Discuss the various kinds of foster care facilities. How is each one different? For what children is each one often most appropriate?
12. What is meant by "permanent planning for children?" Why does it currently have a high priority?
13. How does foster care differ from adoption? What kinds of children are most available for adoption?

PROJECTS

1. Develop a role-play involving a short interview with a family. Choose and develop a typical family problem. Have one of the students serve as the social worker. Repeat the role-play with the instructor in the social worker's role.
2. As the administrator of a local family and children's agency to discuss the current

program and the funding of the agency. What changes have taken place recently? What directions would he or she like to see followed?

3. Assign several students to interview one of their grandparents and make brief talks on the family life-cycle as the grandparent revealed it.
4. Organize a class debate on the right of adopted adults or young persons to gain access to their own adoptive records.
5. Prepare a schedule of questions and arrange to interview personnel in a child welfare agency to learn more about barriers to planning for permanent homes for children and about the progress being made.
6. Visit a children's institution. Interview the executive director or the head of social services about the purposes and methods of the program. Interview several of the children served. What is the content of a typical day? Is the program custodial or treatment-oriented? Do the perceptions of the staff and of the children differ?
7. Obtain the latest statistics of child abuse for your state from the local or state child welfare office. Report on trends over a period of time, program changes, and future plans.
8. Describe the possible family structures for a child who is placed in foster care after the parents get a divorce. At a given time, how many "parent figures" maximally is such a child likely to have? (Most students have said seven; why?)
9. Invite a judge to talk about the role of the public child welfare program in his or her jurisdiction. Tape the talk, and ask a child welfare supervisor to listen to it and indicate areas of agreement and disagreement.
10. Make a chart listing all the child welfare services mentioned in the chapter. Identify where each one can be found in your community. Indicate the gaps.
11. Prepare a discussion or debate on this topic: "Resolved, that foster parents should be given first consideration when the child they are caring for becomes available for adoption."
12. Obtain and evaluate the annual report of a public child welfare agency. Suggest any changes in program emphasis, and indicate your reasons.

CHAPTER 9
Social Work
in the Schools

The school bridges family and community.

The role of the school social worker is ambiguous; there is typically little supervision and often much misunderstanding by the educators who fill the school system. Yet it is in school social work that one effective worker can have an enormous impact. It is in schools that the otherwise hard-to-reach population abounds. . . . There is enough flexibility in the system today for one creative, energetic social worker to make a significant difference in the lives of thousands of children.

—Norma Radin[*]

Most citizens have strong opinions about the public schools, perhaps because the school was an important influence and still looms large in the memories of their childhood. One's own experience as a child in school, however, may have only limited usefulness today in understanding public education as a part of the social welfare structure, particularly when schools are inadequate, crowded, regimented, and nonmotivating.

America has long maintained a belief in the power of the school and a faith in education as a means of solving social problems. Since the early part of the nineteenth century, when the states began to pass compulsory attendance laws, the school has been given additional responsibilities in each succeeding generation. Today we have an elaborate system of public education supported by taxation with a continuum of preschool, elementary, and secondary education, continuing education for adults, and institutions of higher learning. Yet at no time in our history has public education been the object of more dissatisfaction.

This chapter will focus on elementary and secondary public school education. Attention will be given to costs, enrollment rates, and special problems attached to school financing. The often contradictory functions of public school education, current school problems, and the changing role of the school social worker will be considered.

SCHOOL FINANCES

A higher percentage of older youth are in school in America than in any other country of the world. About 75 percent of seventeen-year-olds are in school here compared with about 55 percent in Japan and 40 percent in Sweden. Our higher attendance is due to a later legal school leaving age—sixteen in most states—and to emphasis on the importance of a high school diploma.[1]

The expenditures for education in developing nations are less than 10 percent of those in industrialized nations. Yet industrialized countries have

[*]Norma Radin, "A Personal Perspective on School Social Work," *Social Casework* vol. 56, 1975, p. 605.

227

only about one-third of the world's population. For hundreds of millions of illiterate people in the world, school can no longer be of help. In ten years the number of potential school pupils between ages five and nineteen in developing countries increased by 36 million more than the number of school enrollments. Moreover, in the developing countries nearly half of the children of primary school age today are condemned, no matter what happens, to grow up without ever having attended a class.[2]

Costs of American Education

Concern has grown about the current and projected costs of education in the United States. The total expenditure for public elementary and secondary education in the 1976–77 school year was estimated at over $66 billion.[3] By 1983–84 the figure will be over $81 billion.[4] If prices continue to rise, costs will be even higher.

Education and Property Taxes

In most states, the major costs of elementary and secondary public schools are still paid by local government, mostly from property taxes. Since the establishment of this country, support of schools has been a local responsibility. Income taxes were virtually unknown until this century.

The public educational opportunity available to children and young persons rests upon two key questions: What is the total value of the property on the tax rolls, and how many pupils are there in the district? The rate of assessed valuation of real property determines the funds available for educational programs.

The movement of population and variations in concentration of industry and natural resources make for gross disparities in property values. For example, within a state, the taxable property per pupil in one district can exceed the resources of another district by sixty-fold. Furthermore, where property values are high, a moderate tax rate will produce sufficient revenues. Where assessed valuations are low, the people have to tax themselves heavily to produce a minimum amount of money per pupil.

Schools in areas with low property values are disadvantaged further in supporting new school construction because statutes stipulate the maximum percentage of assessed valuation for which each district can issue bonds. Differences also exist among the states in average per-pupil expenditures. In 1976 New York spent an average of $2,179 per pupil, and Arkansas spent $881.[5]

Following World War II, states passed legislation to attempt to equalize the tax burden between school districts and assure every pupil at least a minimum educational program. State aid was needed to supplement the proceeds of local property taxes so that a "foundation" or minimum financial backing per pupil would be possible in every district. The federal Elementary and Secondary Education Act and the Economic Opportunity Act provided additional funds to selected school districts with special problems. Nevertheless, as equalizers these measures have been disappointing.

The power to control public education and its quality for every pupil continues to rest mainly with the states. But even in states that provide the bulk of the money, the local district usually exercises its autonomy, contradicting the traditional belief that power resides with the holder of the purse.[6]

Challenges to the Property Tax

The dissatisfaction of taxpayers with the traditional system of school financing has become widely apparent. In the 1970s nearly half of the school bond issues and referendums for tax rate increases were voted down because property taxes were rising so fast. This trend was a forerunner of the more generalized taxpayers' revolt that led to tax limitations through referenda in many states.

Inequities in educational opportunity as measured by expenditure per pupil led to a strategy for challenging the local property tax as a basis for school financing. The path to social reform of school financing began a decade ago when a group of young lawyers became interested in altering an indefensible and unequal system—spending significantly more on educating a child in one district than in another.[7] Together with a social worker, John Serrano, active in educational affairs in the Mexican-American community of Los Angeles, they filed a class action suit against the state officials who dispensed public education funds. As a result, a decision by the California Supreme Court in *Serrano v. Priest* held that the state's reliance on local property taxes for school financing was unconstitutional.[8] It discriminated against the poor by making the quality of a child's education a function of the wealth of his or her parents and neighbors.

Rodriguez Decision   Another case was decided in 1973 by the U.S. Supreme Court in *San Antonio Independent School District v. Rodriguez.*[9] Demetrio Rodriguez, who became prominent as a leader in his Mexican-American community, lived in one of the poorest school districts. The state and local property tax allocated for each pupil in his district provided one of the lowest per-pupil incomes in the country and less than 5 percent of that allocated in some other Texas communities. In addition the Rodriguez case emphasized racial discrimination.

By a vote of 5 to 4, the Supreme Court ruled that the Texas system of financing public school education through primary reliance upon the property tax was not unconstitutional "merely because the burden of benefits falls unevenly." The equal protection clause of the Constitution, the majority decision said, "does not require absolute equality or precisely equal advantages." In other words, the court held that the states could finance their public school systems with property taxes even though this provides more money and better educational facilities for pupils who live in wealthier districts.

The decision criticized the property tax as a means of financing public school education but said that ruling against that system would produce "an unprecedented upheaval in public education." The Supreme Court, in effect, gave a breathing spell to the states that had been under pressure to reform their system of school financing.

Efforts persist across the country to eliminate or modify the present financing. The Supreme Court decision delayed but did not turn back reforms.

Although reform may be slowed, a basic change in school financing seems inevitable in view of the growing awareness that current financing is unjust for children and for taxpayers. Before the Supreme Court decision, a variety of alternative methods of school financing were proposed, e.g., a statewide property tax, combining school districts, improving programs for state aid, and a national sales tax. By 1978 taxpayer dissatisfaction with high property taxes had led some states to legislate ceilings on property taxes, posing a new threat of more limited financing for public education.

All of the alternative proposals raise questions about the relationships between federal, state, and local units of government for policy-making, curriculum planning, and accountability.

FUNCTIONS OF PUBLIC SCHOOL EDUCATION

Public education is closely interwoven with other major social institutions. The cost is very high, and society's commitment is great. The public school has multiple and sometimes contradictory societal functions. Some are explicit and other are not, though they bear directly upon pupils and their parents in adverse ways.

Facilitator of Education

A major manifest function of the school is to facilitate and guide the process of education. We expect the public school to play a major role in directing and helping children integrate their learning. The school indoctrinates the children in the life of our society and trains them in the use of the implements of civilization. Public education is the medium for a many-sided interchange of attitudes and definitions of situations, techniques, and knowledge about the culture.

Censor and Judge

The school performs a normative function as a censor and judge of society. It orders its curriculum and procedures in harmony with norms and values. In so doing it passes judgment on the actions of other institutions and seeks to control both the direction and extent of social change. In its discharge of the normative function, what scale of values should the school adopt? It usually conforms to the interests and beliefs of those people who control the school. Individual schools break away to experiment and innovate, but generally the school tends to conserve the existing social order rather than foster change. One can acknowledge the need for these conservative functions of the school and still hold that citizens and school personnel need to shape the school into an effective agency for social progress.

Sorter and Socializer

The school's less explicitly endorsed functions are pervasive and interactive. They remove from young persons a significant amount of self-direction and control of their own fate. The school sorts out individuals for fitness for certain occupations and social positions but does not subject all children to the same kind of sorting. The process is influenced by the child's socioeconomic status, race or ethnic group, initial adjustment to school entrance, behavior in the classroom and on the playground, the relationship of the child's parents to the school, and the reputation the child acquires among school personnel and other pupils. By testing procedures, record keeping, reputation diffusion, counseling practices, and disciplinary practices, the school becomes a testing, selecting, and distributing agency—a gatekeeper. Americans have chosen to view the school as an avenue for vertical mobility and as an open environment of fair competition. While it has served this function for some students, for large groups of pupils the school provides limited opportunity and keeps them at the same relative position in society which their parents occupy.

The school socializes children into age, sex, and race roles. Sex and skin color are likely to be the dominant variables in their social relationships. Schools prescribe roles when they use age as a criterion in organizing classes and group activities and in giving various kinds of rewards and recognitions. They withhold opportunity for certain kinds of learning until the pupil reaches a predetermined age. Age in and of itself carries limitations and rewards.

Girls and boys are also taught to see themselves in predetermined sex roles and statuses prescribed by segregated activities, adult expectations of certain behavior, and curriculum materials. Teachers' and counselors' attitudes also are influential, particularly when children violate traditional sex roles.

Pupils' awareness of race and expectations for prescribed race roles are introduced and reinforced by subtle or overt cues from teachers and other pupils, choice of curriculum materials, and participation of selected groups of parents in school policy matters.

Overall, "the favored role model becomes the twenty to twenty-five-year-old, white, university-educated male who has had an outstanding career in athletics. Implicitly and explicitly students are taught that Western culture is a male-oriented, white-based enterprise."[10]

The school may socialize children for failure by using only white middle-class teaching materials, putting troublemaking pupils in low-status schools or curricula, and viewing children as "incompetent" and incapable of helping to direct their own development. Differential counseling in relation to occupations or higher education and disciplinary practices concerning absenteeism also may socialize for failure.

Care Giver

The school performs a child care function for parents both during the school day and in afterschool extracurricular activities. Maternal employment would be restricted if the school did not provide care and supervision. Our

Table 9-1   Values Versus Reality in American Education Today

Value		Reality
Education provides the means for all individuals to improve their status.	vs.	Schools educate children to function in about the same social and economic stratum as their parents.
Public education is a channel for social change	vs.	The schools preserve and pass on the existing system.
Students have the right to participate in their own education.	vs.	Students are often powerless to share in their own educational planning.
Approval is appropriate to reinforce desired pupil behavior.	vs.	Corporal punishment is a major social control within the school.
All children have a right to an education to achieve their full potential.	vs.	Too many children are excluded from the school.
An open environment within the school promotes learning.	vs.	The schools are preoccupied with "order and control."

society has not developed day and afterschool care for children on any adequate scale. Thousands of "latch-key" children are left on their own. Furthermore, public education frequently serves as a holding action for young persons whom society is not prepared to absorb into the economy.

SCHOOL PROBLEMS AND PUPIL CHARACTERISTICS

In the last decade, many articles have questioned the quality of education in the face of our serious social problems. Concern has developed about the ability of the schools to educate the children of the poor or the affluent. This concern has been coupled with a renewed emphasis on the capacity to learn and to provide tools for future education, skills for earning a living, and a mentally healthy adulthood.

Modern theories have brought useful knowledge about how children learn, and this knowledge has focused attention on conditions within school systems that either enable students to grasp the opportunity for education or cause them to be pushed aside and to fail. The family and the community also contribute to poor scholastic performance, a factor long recognized in pupil failure. Now increasing evidence suggest that the schools themselves contribute to the educational failure of many children and youth. Because of deficiencies in many school systems, large groups of children are not dealt with effectively, and their life experiences are not utilized in a logical and meaningful way. Harmful school conditions and practices, interacting with pupil characteristics, result in recognizable problem situations.

Racial and Economic Segregation

Segregation by race or class in the public schools is still widespread and has even increased in the central cites of major metropolitan areas. As middle-

and upper-income families have moved out of the inner cities, economically segregated groups have remained. The result is that pupils are highly likely to attend schools composed largely of students like themselves, both racially and economically.

The Supreme Court in 1954 struck down the doctrine of "separate but equal," holding that racial segregation of schools was inherently unequal.[11] The search for means to integrate the schools was given impetus by the Coleman Report, a national study under the auspices of the Office of Education. Pupil aspirations and achievements are strongly related to the educational backgrounds and performances of other pupils in the same school, this study said. Children attending schools where the level of student achievement is low are more apt to have low achievement than those in schools where overall achievement levels are higher. Nonwhite or low-income pupils (and they are frequently the same) can be expected to attain higher levels of educational performance if they attend schools that are predominantly middle-class or white. Not only does racial and economic balance in schools increase the achievement of minority group children from homes without much educational strength, it does so without reducing the other children's achievement.[12]

Busing

Because prevailing segregated housing patterns do not bring about integration in neighborhood schools, busing of children to other schools out of their neighborhoods was introduced to achieve racially balanced school populations. Busing has been a highly controversial political issue. In some school districts integration of schools through busing has proceeded with minimal difficulty. In others there have been militant protests, parent boycotts of schools, and episodes of disorder.

The issue of busing is affected by a number of factors. Racial integration is no longer a core goal of the black movement. Greater emphasis is now given to such issues as equal opportunity in employment and housing, community control of schools, and recognition of the merits of black identity. White people who supported the movement for civil rights and racial integration in relation to employment, housing, voting privileges, public transportation, and college admissions have been divided on the busing of young children away from their neighborhood schools. Leaders in the legislative and executive branches of government display negative attitudes toward busing. Courts more frequently grant delays in connection with busing plans. Some cities are beginning to cut back busing or to hold off plans to expand it.

Records, "Tracking," and Special Education

Many school systems still have a stereotyped view that most low-income and nonwhite pupils have limited capabilities or are "slow learners," and that not much can be done with them. This belief is usually coupled with an expectation that certain school programs and services will be used by certain groups of students. Academic goals are lowered because it is assumed that children are not interested in learning. Children and youth, responding to this negative perception on the part of the school staff, give the substandard performance that is expected.

Testing   When ability and achievement tests are used as measures of innate potential without regard for past learning opportunities and experiences and the familiarity of those taking the tests with the kinds of tasks expected, they underestimate the abilities of particular children and lower the expectations for their performance.

Grouping   The negative effects of ability grouping or "tracking" are apt to be crucial during the elementary years as the distance between the "slow" and the "fast" learners widens rapidly. In secondary schools students are often grouped in one of several curricular tracks. Criteria for placement include test scores, teacher and counselor judgments, expressed parental preferences, and assessment of student aspirations. Low-income parents frequently do not feel as free as middle-class parents to object to the decisions made.

Tracking affects the chance to go to college or enter certain occupations. Lower tracks lead to lower status among peers and teachers. Special education rooms for mentally retarded children may fail to achieve the educational purpose for which they were established. Often they become catchalls for children—frequently minority-group children—with different characteristics and needs who are not retarded but may demonstrate varying manifestations of emotional disturbance.

Parents and some school personnel have begun to raise critical questions about the rights of children as a result of testing and tracking. Evaluation and judgments are often made on unspecified criteria. Without a hearing children are labeled, categorized, and locked into special education tracks which may unfairly limit future opportunities.

With the help of legal services for low-income parents and of civil liberties groups, court cases have focused attention on pupil and parent rights in relation to educational placement. California has prohibited group IQ tests for children from non-English-speaking countries until they have resided in the United States for two years.

Student Nonattendance

Absenteeism   Sporadic school attendance results when pupils are beset with demands they cannot meet adequately. For example, older children are still kept out of school to supervise young siblings. Children of all ages miss school frequently because preventive health care is not available and they have one illness after another, or because their parents are disorganized and there is no reliable adult support for their school attendance. Secondary school pupils may come to school but roam the building during school hours to evade teachers and classes. These pupils find little satisfaction in school and are alienated from the school environment and isolated from their peers, except perhaps from chronic absentees like themselves.

Truancy Nonattendance of longer standing is officially identified as truancy. Truants resist the school attendance officer's efforts to return them to school, often leading to a court referral. Difficulties in consistent enforcement of school attendance laws are exacerbated in crowded urban neighborhoods because of insufficient staff, high population mobility, and crime rates that make attendance officers reluctant to make home visits. Persuasion, warning, coercion, and threats have seldom improved attendance very long. Attendance can be expected to improve only with changes in the school-community-pupil relations that produce the problem.

Exclusion Many children and young persons are absent from school because they have been formally excluded or strongly discouraged from attending. Excluded children may be allowed to leave school or never to enroll because the district has no educational program for them. These children are often from minority groups who do not speak English. Some have physical handicaps or epilepsy and are not allowed to participate in the regular program even though there has been no determination of their abilities. Mentally retarded, emotionally disturbed, and perceptually handicapped children are often excluded, even though no other special education facility exists for them. Any child who is culturally, physically, mentally, or behaviorally different risks arbitrary labeling and exclusion from school in many communities. Although by no means fully implemented, the Education for All Handicapped Children Act (PL-94-142) promises greater educational opportunity for those it covers.

Pregnancy Girls who become pregnant are still systematically excluded from many schools either for the period of the pregnancy or permanently. Some districts have recognized the importance of enabling these girls to continue their education, in the regular classroom, a special classroom, or a program of home-bound instruction. Other districts have given up arbitrary exclusion only after a court has ruled that the policy violates the equal protection clause of the Fourteenth Amendment. Yet despite awareness of the unwed mother's need to complete her education, she is still excluded from many schools.

Other Controls on Students

Attempts to restrict pupil behavior include denial of privileges in extracurricular activities or compulsory counseling interviews. Misbehavior is assumed to result from some problem with the child or from family problems that have affected the child's personality. Such methods tend to ignore conditions in the school or classroom which produce the so-called "emotional problems."

"Dress codes" have prescribed the types of clothing pupils must wear on school premises. If these rules are challenged, they must usually meet the test of reasonableness to be enforced. For example, prescribing certain clothing for physical education classes or "shop" classes may be defended as necessary for the safety of pupils. Forbidding the wearing of metal heel plates is justified on the basis that it damages floors in the school building. Schools pass rules about length of hair or beards on the claim that a student's appearance may be distracting and disturbing to others in the classroom. Yet students claim that the right to wear one's hair at any length or in any style is a personal choice. When challenged the school usually has to provide evidence that the nonconforming appearance has an adverse effect on the educational process.

Many of the criticisms revolve around aspects of the school's climate that fail to promote and enhance self-discipline and self-direction for the student's continued learning. For example, many classroom teachers carefully avoid all but neutral topics; honest expressions of feelings are avoided. Docility and suggestibility are prized and curiosity repressed. Many pupils fear failure in a world of confusing demands and irrelevant materials; other pupils are continually bored with an unstimulating, pedantic learning pace.

In such schools conflict among pupils is common. Police are frequent visitors. Pupils tend to move in segregated groups, racially and economically, even though they attend an "integrated" school. The probability of low achievement and failure for large numbers of children and young persons is increased.

Social Distance between School and Community

Lack of communication between the school and the community and between the school and the home increases the probability of school failure. Schools that serve middle-class families are more apt to be relatively "close" to the community and neighborhoods of their pupils. Middle-class parents are ready to speak for themselves, and generally supportive of education, and often are in reasonably close communication with school personnel. School expectations in relation to parental involvement may be the same for the poor, without recognition that low-income parents more often see the school as alien, cold, and unwelcoming. Even though studies have shown that these parents place a high value on school achievement for their children, they usually communicate less easily or effectively with teachers, principals, and counselors. When schools make insufficient attempts to understand the surroundings in which their pupils live and the desires of their parents, social distance between home and school is increased.

Parental Participation   In some communities, parents have demanded greater participation in the school's decision-making and policy-formulation processes. Black ghetto residents of New York City have given leadership in greater community control of schools, and groups of minority parents in other parts of the country have also pressed for a fuller share in planning their children's education.

Even when school-community distance has been lessened through more community control, problems remain. For example, educational issues may be subordinated to political issues and to implicit racial issues. It is also difficult to coordinate the variations in the specific educational desires, expectations, and concerns of the subgroups of parents within the community.

Attendance Policies

Effective enforcement of attendance statutes has demanded the attention of administrators since compulsory education was first legislated. An early study of nonattendance problems endorsed the need for social workers to serve as school attendance officers. Nonattendance, the investigators said, resulted from the social ills of the community, such as poverty, lack of adequate adult wage levels, illiteracy, and ill health—conditions that existed in many families not known to any social agency.[13] The problem of nonattendance has not been solved. Superintendents or principals in large inner-city schools still designate absenteeism and truancy as their most difficult problems.

Behavior Problems   Pupils identified as "troublemakers," particularly at the secondary level, are frequently suspended or expelled. Student unrest and dissent have resulted from political issues, smoking rules, the curriculum, athletics, dress and hair regulations, and racial conflict, for example. Many disruptive incidents have resulted in use of suspension (for a defined and limited period) or expulsion (for the rest of the term or permanently). Sometimes no actual disturbance occurred, but school officials evaluated pupil actions as likely to produce disruption. In other instances disruption ranged from scuffling to serious injuries, from assault to attempted arson. The destruction or theft of school property is another area of concern.

School principals have also used repeated suspensions to cope with individual students who distract others in the classroom, come late to class, fail to learn, annoy teachers, provoke peers, or otherwise express their dissatisfaction with the school.

DISCIPLINE IN THE SCHOOLS

Student Rights

Until recently, the right of school boards to suspend or expel pupils was rarely challenged. Courts showed little interest in examining school actions. However, concern with legal rights brought greater attention to such procedures. In general the courts have said that the schools do have the authority to regulate conduct likely to cause disorder and interfere with educational functions, but students must be treated fairly and accorded due process of law under the Fourteenth Amendment.

Freedom of expression has been the subject of court cases. Some were challenges to freedom of verbal expression. One group of students attempted to organize a boycott of the school cafeteria. Some involved freedom of written expression, most often the distribution of underground or unauthorized newspapers or pamphlets. Others concerned symbolic expression. Upon learning that students were planning to wear black armbands to express sympathy for the victims of the Vietnam war, school officials in one city passed a resolution forbidding such symbolic expression on school premises. Five students later wore armbands and were sent home, although no disruption had occurred. Three students and their parents sought court action. The Supreme Court finally reversed two lower court actions on the basis that the symbolic wearing of armbands had not been disruptive and had not interfered with discipline nor implied reasonable anticipation of disruption.

In the majority opinion, Justice Abe Fortas said: "First Amendment rights, applied in the light of the special characteristics of the school environment, are available to teachers and students. It can hardly be argued that either students or teachers shed their constitutional rights to freedom of speech or expression at the schoolhouse gate."[14]

Suspension and Expulsion

Suspension and expulsion have been traditional means to maintain discipline. But do suspensions help children? With school desegregation have come charges that suspension and expulsion are used for purposes of race and class discrimination.

An analysis of suspension data in nine states and the District of Columbia, using interviews and surveys with children, parents, school officials, community leaders, and families, revealed:

> The use of suspensions in the public schools is of mammoth proportions. School districts serving a little over half the total school-age population in 1972–73 suspended over one million pupils, representing a loss of four million school days.

1. Most suspensions were for offenses that were not dangerous or violent or did not seriously disrupt the educational process, for example: truancy, tardiness, minor violations of dress codes, and failures to purchase required materials or equipment. Only three percent of the suspensions were for the destruction of property, the use of drugs or alcohol, or other delinquent activity.
2. Fighting made up a third of the offenses leading to suspension, but the fighting generally was among pupils rather than acts of violence against teachers or other school personnel.
3. Black students were suspended at twice the rate of others. The largest number of suspended children were white, but a disproportionate number of suspensions involved the black, poor, older male pupil.
4. The grounds for suspension, the procedures used, and the frequency and length of suspensions varied widely among schools within the same district and between school districts.[15]

Clearly suspensions do not serve any demonstrated valid interests of children or schools. Instead they are harmful in that they jeopardize chances for children to secure a useful education.

In two companion cases the Supreme Court found public school students entitled to due process safeguards prior to being suspended. Such procedures of due process must precede a suspension irrespective of its length. The only exceptions involve behavior that poses a continuing danger to persons or property or an ongoing disruption of the educational process. Otherwise, even in simple short-term suspension, students are now entitled to written or oral "effective notice of the charges," an explanation of the evidence supporting the charges, and an opportunity to present their version of the charges. Further, school board members can be sued for damages if they violate a student's constitutional rights in the use of suspensions.[16]

Corporal Punishment

Paradoxically, children sometimes need legal protection from their teachers. Any consideration of corporal punishment in the schools requires attention to issues of values and of civil liberties. The status of children on both counts began to change in this century. The pace was accelerated in the turbulent 1960s by the realization that children were no longer subject only to the control of their parents. Indeed, children and young persons had become subject to control by a range of community institutions—schools, courts, health, social, and recreational agencies, employment offices, and other agencies of the state. Too often the protection these agencies provided had become restrictive, raising questions about the necessity to obtain for children the rights that adults take for granted. Yet child advocates have faced particularly difficult obstacles in their attempts to limit corporal punishment in the schools.

Corporal punishment can be defined as pain inflicted upon the body of a school pupil by a teacher, principal, or other school employee who does not approve of some behavior of the pupil, but this definition does not cover using force to obtain possession of a weapon or other dangerous object or for other reasons to protect oneself or others from physical injury.

Perhaps corporal punishment persists because it is practical. "It can be applied by anyone in any setting, there is no need for specialized training or special equipment other than a paddle, and there is no dollar cost. The fact that most school personnel are physically stronger than children also makes corporal punishment especially attractive."[17] In addition it provides a prompt response to a variety of frustrating conditions. As a result school personnel are spared the necessity to assess situations individually or to identify the factors that have prompted a pupil to act in a way that is disapproved. The myth persists that corporal punishment is administered for the benefit of the child. Corporal punishment is used because "it serves the immediate needs of the attacking adult who is seeking relief from his uncontrollable anger and stress."[18]

Corporal punishment of children and young persons at school has been so severe that had it been administered by a parent, it would have constituted a basis for an official report of child abuse. David Gil, who studied violence against children, has called attention to a curious contradiction—several state legislatures enacted laws permitting teachers to use corporal punishment, and in the same session passed laws mandating the reporting of physical abuse of children.[19] Another such contrast is an increase in policy statements and guidelines for use of school personnel in reporting suspected parental child abuse[20] but an unwillingness to give up their own form of child abuse under the label of "a legitimate and necessary disciplinary action." We give children and young persons conflicting signals: violence is sometimes good and sometimes bad.

Effects upon Children and Young Persons   Physical injury is an obvious hazard. Psychological injury is also common as a concomitant of the humiliation and loss of self-respect that most children feel when punishment is inflicted, often in the presence of classmates or other adults.

Corporal punishment also provides a model of aggressive behavior which children are prone to imitate. Arbitrary and unreasonable methods of control teach children a direct lesson—that aggression is a legitimate method of problem-solving. Furthermore, in our society, aggression is circular.[21] When a child is aggressive and a teacher retaliates, the child is further frustrated or angered and becomes more aggressive, which in turn heightens the stress felt by the teacher and leads to further aggressive acts against the pupil. Increasingly hostile interpersonal behaviors between pupils and teachers follow. And because children seldom can win a game of physical force between themselves and adults, they are likely to choose other children or school property as objects for further retaliation.

Corporal punishment in schools negatively affects the educational opportunities for children. "To grow up successfully, children require a sense of security that is inherent in nonarbitrary structures and limits. Understanding adults can establish such structures and limits through love, patience, firmness, consistency, and rational authority. Corporal punishment seems devoid of constructive educational value, since it cannot provide that sense of security and nonarbitrary authority."[22]

Fear and anxiety among pupils is generated, and that interferes with the learning process among both those who are punished and those who only observe the adult's aggression. Especially among young children, "harsh treatment of one of their number produces a 'ripple' effect, which sends emotional disturbance and anxiety through the whole group."[23]

Physical punishment strongly influences children to avoid the punishing environment or person. Corporal punishment can destroy or prevent the development of constructive teacher-pupil relationships and often is a factor in pupils' increasing absenteeism, truancy, or complete withdrawal from school. Not only do general societal conditions have a substantial effect on children's school behavior; a variety of "in-school" conditions also contribute to youthful disorder in and out of school. Extreme and ineffective school disciplinary practices are primary contributors. A range of school situations interact— exclusion from school through repeated suspensions, absenteeism and truancy, corporal punishment and violence and vandalism in schools.[24]

The Present Legal Status of Corporal Punishment   The United States does not compare well with other nations. Countries that have abolished corporal punishment include Italy, Austria, Portugal, France, Belgium, Holland, Luxembourg, Finland, Norway, Sweden, Denmark, and all the Communist bloc countries in Europe, as well as Cyprus, Japan, Ecuador, Iceland, Jordan, Qatar, Mauritius, Israel, and the Philippines.[25]

A recent survey shows that only two states, Massachusetts and New Jersey, completely ban corporal punishment. Three other states have imposed strict limitations on its use. Twelve states remain silent, which acts as an implicit sanction of the practice. The remaining thirty-three states allow corporal punishment or even specifically endorse it as a means of disciplining schoolchildren. On a more positive note, the school systems of many cities have banned the use of corporal punishment, including Chicago, Washington, D.C., and New York City.[26]

In a 1975 case reviewed by the Supreme Court, some restrictions were placed on the use of corporal punishment in schools (except in instances where the misbehavior was "so disruptive as to shock the conscience") by specifying a warning, a hearing, and another teacher as witness to the physical punishment.[27] Reactions to the ruling by civil libertarians were mixed— disappointment that corporal punishment was not prohibited but satisfaction with the limited provisions of due process.

When the Supreme Court agreed to consider a second case of corporal punishment, advocates of child rights saw an opportunity for advances in relation to two fundamental violations of constitutional rights: "Whether the paddling of students as a means of maintaining school discipline constitutes cruel and unusual punishment in violation of the Eighth Amendment," and "whether the Due Process Clause of the Fourteenth Amendment requires prior notice and an opportunity to be heard."[28] A five to four decision sanctioned corporal punishment and provided a defeat for children's rights.

Two junior high school boys had required medical attention following severe physical punishment by school officials. "Because he had been slow to respond to his teacher's instructions, Ingraham was subjected to more than 20 licks with a paddle while being held over a table in the principal's office. The paddling was so severe that he suffered a hematoma requiring medical attention and keeping him out of school for 11 days. Andrews was paddled several times for minor infractions. On two occasions he was struck on his arms, once depriving him of the full use of his arm for a week."[29]

The Supreme Court held that the protections of the Eighth Amendment against cruel and unusual punishment applied only to persons who were convicted of criminal offenses and incarcerated. "The school child has little need for the protection of the Eighth Amendment," the court said. "Though attendance may not always be voluntary, the public school remains an open institution. . . . The openness of the public school and its supervision by the community afford significant safeguards against the kinds of abuses from which the Eighth Amendment protects the prisoner."[30]

Does corporal punishment merit the requirement of due process? The court said that "the traditional common law remedies are fully adequate to afford due process." A universal constitutional requirement of hearings, even informal hearings, would significantly burden the use of corporal punishment as a disciplinary measure.[31]

Significantly, the court said further that "elimination or curtailment of corporal punishment would be welcomed by many as a societal advance." But it should result from the normal processes of community debate and legislative action rather than the court's determination of a right to due process. "Imposing additional administrative safeguards as a constitutional requirement . . . would . . . entail a significant intrusion into an area of primary educational responsibility."[32] Thus corporal punishment, as a civil literties issue, was turned back to the state legislatures and local school boards.

Social workers should take a clear position against the use of corporal punishment.

1. Corporal punishment is educationally ineffective. Its use generates fear and anxiety on the part of children and young persons, widens the social distance between teacher and pupil, and contributes to a withdrawal and rejection of the school environment—all factors detrimental to successful learning.
2. Corporal punishment does not instill self-discipline or socialize for constructive societal roles. The punisher becomes a model for aggressive behavior and gives endorsement to the use of aggression for problem-solving. Corporal punishment fosters attitudes of resentment and hostility, and lays the groundwork for related antisocial acts on the part of school pupils.
3. Corporal punishment in schools is one of a set of interacting practices and patterns of control that deprive children of educational opportunity and lead them into the path of failure.
4. Corporal punishment falls disproportionately on children and young persons already subject to other forms of societal neglect and abuse, e.g., poverty, racial discrimination, poor housing and health care.
5. Finally, apart from the legal status of corporal punishment and its demonstrated educational ineffectiveness, to use corporal punishment as an attempt to control children and young persons is directly antithetical to the values of the social work profession, e.g., a commitment to measures that support and enhance the dignity of each person and a respect for individual differences among children and their parents.

What, then, can social workers do about corporal punishment in schools? They can refuse to ignore excesses in disciplinary measures and can reject the myth that for some unruly children, corporal punishment is the only thing that will work. Social workers can become facilitators of change by interpreting and demonstrating acceptable and constructive disciplinary measures.

Alternatives to Corporal Punishment
A Task Force on Corporal Punishment of the National Education Association has developed alternative techniques based on the principle of "the

least restrictive alternative." Proposed alternatives follow a continuum ranging from negligible to considerable intervention in the child's school life. One set of techniques offers short-range solutions to use while longer-range programs are being developed. Another group of alternatives provides intermediate-range solutions. Long-range solutions within schools and in collaboration with community agents are proposed.

Another resource is the Center for the Study of Corporal Punishment and Alternatives in the Schools at the Temple University Department of School Psychology. The center has developed educational strategies to serve as alternatives to corporal punishment as well as in-service training materials to help teachers and administrators use more constructive methods of discipline.

One of the most important contributions social workers can make in public school education is a steady and persistent interpretation of the need to clarify and extend the rights of the child. Another is to interpret the need to maintain and nurture the inherent dignity of the child. Planning new social work tasks and roles that will help end the use of corporal punishment is essential if these social work contributions to education are to be truly valid.

SOCIAL WORK IN THE SCHOOLS

School social work is an application of social work principles and methods to the major purpose of the school. Goals center upon helping pupils attain a sense of competence, a readiness for continued learning, and an ability to adapt to change. Increasingly, the focus of school social work is on cognitive areas—learning, thinking, and problem-solving—as well as the traditional areas of concern, i.e., relationships, emotions, motivation, and personality.

School social work is related to a particular school system, the outside community, the characteristics of the pupils, and the social conditions they face. Within this framework school social workers endeavor to aid the school to give attention to pupils' individual needs and to offer each pupil an opportunity for success and achievement. In addition, school social workers must be concerned with the relationship of the school to other social institutions in the community.

Historical Development

Early Influences   School social work began in the early twentieth century. It originated outside the school system. Private agencies and civic organizations supported the work until schools agreed to administer and finance it.

Social work in the schools represented a response to the passage of compulsory school attendance laws, new knowledge about individual differences among children, a realization of the strategic place of school and education in the lives of children, and concern for the relevance of education to the child's life at home and in the community.

Social workers in the settlement houses contributed significantly to the methods of school social work and frequently pointed up the necessity for the school to relate more closely to the lives of its children. For example, from the Henry Street Settlement in New York City came the comment: "Intelligent social workers seize opportunities for observation, and almost unconsciously develop methods to meet needs. They see conditions as they are, and become critical of systems as they act and react upon the child or fail to reach him at all. . . . Where the school fails, it appears to the social workers to do so because it makes education a thing apart—because it separates its work from all that makes up the child's life outside the classroom."[33]

School social work underwent rapid growth in the 1920s following demonstrations in various communities financed by the Commonwealth Fund. The focus was on the prevention of juvenile delinquency.

Home-school-community liaison continued to be the principal focus of school social work throughout most of the 1920s. Modifications in practice began to emerge in response to the mental hygiene movement: Social workers increased their efforts to develop and define their own method of social casework in the schools, and they began to turn more attention to work with the individual maladjusted child at school.

Developments from 1930 to 1960   A retrenchment in school social work practice came with the depression of the 1930s, but with its end, services were extended rapidly and school social work was accepted as an integral part of pupil services.

During the 1930s truancy and delinquency were given less emphasis. Social workers increased their attention to the individual child in the existing school environment and to the refinement of professional methods and techniques.

By 1940 the transiton appeared complete—from the early focus on school and neighborhood conditions and social change to a clinical orientation in relation to individual personality needs. Social casework was the method used, the development of effective relationships the essential technique.

Developments from 1960 to 1970   Beginning in the 1960s, school social work literature began to urge a transition to new goals and methods of work in response to the urgent social problems affecting many schoolchildren and youth. A new awareness of the school as a social system was reflected, and the professions of education and social work began to collaborate more effectively on behalf of pupils who were unable to utilize educational opportunities because of social and cultural problems. Group work appeared and was used increasingly by school social workers. Some demonstrations of new approaches to working with the community also resulted. Considerable confusion arose about the roles of the various pupil specialists in the school, underscoring the responsibility of each specialty to clarify its function and measure it against the critical needs of schoolchildren.

Developments in the 1970s

Legislation for the education of handicapped children passed by Congress in 1975 (P.L. 94-142) has greatly extended the obligation of the public schools to offer opportunities for children with a range of handicaps. Children with speech impairments, mental retardation, hearing and visual impairments, orthopedic disabilities, learning disabilities, and emotional disturbances can no longer be excluded from education for lack of a suitable program. Furthermore, relying on the concept of "mainstreaming," handicapped children must be offered an appropriate education in the least restrictive educational environment.

The legislation has opened up a variety of new roles for social workers in schools. They participate in the search for handicapped children in the community who may have been denied attendance at school because of their handicap, or for children in school but inappropriately placed in educational programs. Social workers are members of the evaluation team that develops a child's educational program. The traditional role of liaison between school and parent has been intensified, with the requirement that parents be given full opportunity to participate in the development of their child's "individual educational plan." Social workers also serve as mediators in administrative hearings when school personnel and parents are unable to agree on the child's educational program.

Organization and Support

School social workers usually are employed by and accountable to local school districts. In the more populous states, departments of education coordinate and supervise a range of pupil services in the public schools—e.g., guidance, psychology, social work, health, attendance, speech—through "pupil personnel services" or "special services."

By no means do all schools have social workers on their staffs. They are about as numerous as school psychologists or attendance officers. There are far more elementary and secondary school guidance counselors than other "pupil specialists."

Social work is one of the disciplines which may be represented in a state department of public education. When this is so, social workers employed in the public school usually will be required to have a master's degree. In some states, social workers with baccalaureate degrees may be employed. The most desirable staffing pattern involves teams including social workers with different levels of training—master's degrees, baccalaureate degrees, and diplomas from two-year college programs.

In the last decade, state and regional associations of school social workers have flourished. State and regional conferences planned by these associations attract many school social workers in search of collegial support and new learning. In 1978 the National Association of Social Workers adopted Standards of Practice for Social Work Services in Schools.[34]

Background for Change

School social work has undergone changes in working with pupils, their parents, and school personnel. Early leaders were keenly aware of the strategic place of the school among a community's institutions. They saw the pivotal position for leadership open to school social workers because they were able to move between the institutions of public education and public welfare. They emphasized work in the community and in the neighborhood in an effort to bring school and home closer together.

As casework theory developed and the social work profession became more responsive to the search for psychological causes for their clients' problems, school social workers moved toward a clinical orientation—working with the individual schoolchildren in relation to their personal problems. In doing so, they moved away from their focus on school and neighborhood conditions and the need for social change. An analysis of the tasks in school social work primarily favored casework with individual children in relation to emotional problems and personal adjustment.[35] The problems of children in school were viewed as arising mostly from personal characteristics or those of parents. The impact that school policies and community conditions had on pupils was almost unrecognized. School social workers minimized the importance of their responsibilities for leadership in modifying school and community conditions. They also were reluctant to delegate tasks to persons with less than the master's degree in social work. These findings provided impetus to school social workers to reexamine their goals and their staffing patterns.

A recent replication of this analysis of tasks indicated that school social work is a field of practice in transition. School social workers had moved away from a primary emphasis upon the individual child and parents in relation to personal or emotional problems toward an approach more indicative of an emphasis on facilitating home-school-community relations and educational counseling for children. The service remained individualistic, however. There was no evidence of a strong emphasis on identifying target groups of children experiencing similar difficulties, e.g., truancy, behavior, or need for alternative educational programs.[36]

Present Practice

The traditional clinical model of school social work has been widely criticized as outmoded. Yet it is still the predominant mode of school social work practice in the United States today. School administrators view it as benign intervention and thus acceptable, emphasizing as it does the individual student's need to adapt and adjust to the normative conditions with the school.[37]

In addition, educational systems faced with budget cut-backs view pupil personnel services as more expendable than classroom teachers. Under such circumstances school social workers may be reluctant to undertake a new role in the system which employs them.[38] Experienced school social workers who have been trained in casework and have successfully helped individual children may understandably find new models of school social work difficult.

The School as a Social System

A new model being demonstrated is broadly focused on school-community-pupil relations. The school is regarded as a social system, a unity of interacting and interdependent personalities and functions. The social work tasks given greatest priority are to:

1. Facilitate the provision of direct educational and social services and provide direct social casework and group work services to selected pupils.
2. Act as a pupil advocate, focusing upon the urgent needs of selected groups of pupils.
3. Consult with school administrators to jointly identify major problems toward which a planned service approach will be aimed; aid in developing cooperative working relationships with community agencies; and assist in the formulation of school policy that directly affects the welfare of children and young persons.
4. Consult with teachers about techniques for creating a climate in which children are freed and motivated to learn by interpreting social and cultural influences in the lives of pupils, facilitating the use of peers to help a troubled child, or assisting in managing relationships within a classroom.
5. Organize parent and community groups to channel concerns about pupils and school and to improve school and community relations.
6. Develop and maintain liaison between the school and critical fields of social work—child welfare, corrections, mental health, and legal services for the poor. Such liaison facilitates more effective community services for school children and their families, assists with planned change in the community's organizational pattern of social welfare programs and resources, and acts as a catalyst to change the pattern of the social structure.
7. Provide leadership in the coordination of interdisciplinary skills among pupil services personnel, e.g., guidance counselors, psychologists, nurses, and attendance officers.

These tasks require adaptations in practice on the part of social workers already in the schools. They must assume greater responsibility for identifying target groups of pupils who present interrelated problems and reactions to strain, failure, or dissatisfaction in the learning situation. They must focus diagnosis and treatment on an understanding of the larger problem complex rather than on the individual case. School administrators need to establish a contract for service-giving in relation to specified problems. Staff should be assigned for schools where problems are greatest and contracts made with principals regarding the use of staff resources. Service will be most effective if multidisciplinary teams are assigned to particular schools so that the full range of skills among pupil personnel specialists can be brought to bear on major problems.

The pupil-welfare team is focused on the public school as a vital and strategic social institution that affects all children during their formative years. This model is geared to the basic purpose of the school—that is, not to serve as a therapeutic center but to provide a life setting where competence can be acquired.

SUMMARY AND APPLICATION

As the school social worker's role expands from that of case worker for individual children to specialist in the impact of the educational system on children, many more opportunities will be provided for recommending changes that serve numbers of children. However, the financial pressures on some school systems lead to a reluctance to expand school social work services and also give social workers a conservative view of their own roles because of the possible elimination of their jobs.

Students who choose school social work will have the opportunity to work with large numbers of children and teachers with a variety of needs. They will have the task of adapting to a non–social work setting, and they will need to be expert in work with both individuals and groups. Some school systems are much more willing than others to hire bachelor's-degree social workers.

As an advocate for children you will want to give special attention to disciplinary practices, including safeguards of rights concerning corporal punishment as well as due process related to suspension and expulsion.

—Lela B. Costin

KEY TERMS

assessed property valuation

absenteeism

truancy

suspension

expulsion

in loco parentis

corporal punishment

tracking

community control

school-community-pupil relations

change agent

social system

pupil advocate

standards for school social work.

REFERENCES AND NOTES

1. *Times*, (London), July 23, 1970, p. 9.
2. Edgar Faure et al., *Learning to Be: The World of Education Today and Tomorrow*, UNESCO, Paris, 1972, pp. 40–49.
3. U.S. Bureau of the Census, *Statistical Abstract of the United States, 1977*, Government Printing Office, Washington, D.C., 19, p. 128.
4. Kermit A. Simon and Martin M. Frankel, *Projections of Educational Statistics to 1983–84*, Department of Health, Education and Welfare, National Center for Educational Statistics, Washington, D.C., 1975, p. 10.

5. U.S. Bureau of the Census, *Statistical Abstract of the United States, 1975*, Government Printing Office, Washington, D.C., 19, p. 139.
6. President's Commission on School Finance, *Schools, People, and Money: The Need for Educational Reform*, Government Printing Office, Washington, D.C., 1970, p. 11.
7. John E. Coons, Stephen D. Sugarman, and William H. Clune III, *Private Wealth and Public Education*, Belknap Press, Cambridge, Mass., 1970.
8. *Serrano v. Priest*, 5 Cal. 3d 584, 96 Cal. Rept. 601 (1971).
9. *San Antonio Independent School District v. Rodriguez*, 411 U.S. 1 (1973).
10. Normal K. Denzin, "Children and Their Caretakers," *Trans-Action*, July–August 1971, pp. 62–72.
11. *Brown v. Board of Education of Topeka*, 74 U.S. S. Ct. 686 (1954).
12. James B. Coleman et al., *Equality of Educational Opportunity*, Government Printing Office, Washington, D.C., 1966, pp. 22, 302.
13. Edith Abbott and Sophonisba P. Breckinridge, *Truancy and Non-Attendance in the Chicago Schools: A Study of the Social Aspects of the Compulsory Education and Child Labor Legislation of Illinois*, University of Chicago Press, Chicago, 1917, p. 241.
14. *Tinker v. Des Moines Independent Community School District*, 89 U.S. 733 (1969).
15. The Children's Defense Fund of the Washington Research Project, *School Suspensions: Are They Helping Children?* Cambridge, Mass., 1975.
16. *Goss v. Lopez*, 95 S. Ct. 992 (1975). *Wood V. Strickland* 95 S. Ct. 992 (1975).
17. Irwin A. Hyman et al., "Paddling, Punishing and Force: Where Do We Go From Here?" *Children Today*, vol. 6, no. 6, 1977, pp. 17–23.
18. David G. Gil, *Violence Against Children: Physical Child Abuse in the United States*, Harvard, Cambridge, Mass., 1970, p. 144.
19. Ibid., p. 10, fn. 6.
20. *American Teacher*, vol. 62, February 1978, p. 3.
21. Boyd R. McCandless, *Children: Behavior and Development*, 2d ed., Holt, New York, 1967, p. 152.
22. Gil, op. cit., p. 144.
23. Alan Reitman, Judith Follman, and Edward T. Ladd, *Corporal Punishment in the Public Schools: The Use of Force in Controlling Student Behavior*. American Civil Liberties Union, New York, March 1972, pp. 16–17.
24. Committee on the Judiciary, U.S. Senate, 94th Congress, 1st Session, Preliminary Report of the Subcommittee to Investigate Juvenile Delinquency, "Our Nation's Schools—A Report Card: 'A' in School Violence and Vandalism," April 1975, pp. 8–13.
25. Hyman et al., op. cit., p. 19.
26. R. Friedman and I. Hyman, "An Analysis of State Legislation Regarding Corporal Punishment," paper presented at the Conference on Child Abuse, Children's Hospital National Medical Center, Washington, D.C., February 1977.
27. *Baker v. Owen*, 423 U.S. 907 (1975).
28. *U.S. Law Week*, 1977, p. 4364.
29. Ibid., p. 4366
30. Ibid., p. 4369.
31. Ibid., p. 4372.
32. Ibid.
33. Lillian D. Wald, *The House on Henry Street*, Hall, New York, 1915, p. 106.

34. NASW Policy Statement 7, *NASW Standards for Social Work Services in Schools*, National Association of Social Workers, Washington, D.C., 1978.
35. Lela B. Costin, "An Analysis of the Tasks in School Social Work," *Social Service Review*, vol. 43, September 1969, pp. 274–285.
36. Paula Allen Meares, "Analysis of Tasks in School Social Work," *Social Work*, vol. 22, May 1977, pp. 196–201.
37. John Alderson, "Models of School Social Work Practice," in Frank F. Maple and Rosemary Sarri (eds.), *The School and the Community*, Washington, D.C.: National Association of Social Workers, 1972, pp. 57–74.
38. Sam Negrin, "Foreword," in Maple and Sarri, op. cit., pp. 5–6.

FOR FURTHER STUDY

Rosemary Sarri and Frank F. Maple (eds.), *The School in the Community*, National Association of Social Workers, Washington, D.C., 1972.

Charles E. Silberman, *Crisis in the Classroom: The Remaking of American Education*, Random House, New York, 1970.

Neal S. Bellos, Gerald M. Gross, and Joseph R. Steiner, *Innovative Projects in School Social Work Practice*, Division of Continuing Education and Manpower Development, Syracuse University School of Social Work, Syracuse, N.Y., 1977.

Benjamin S. Bloom, *Human Characteristics and School Learning*, McGraw-Hill, New York, 1976.

Lela B. Costin, "A Historical Review of School Social Work," *Social Casework*, vol. 50, October 1969, pp. 439–453.

Ruth G. Newman, *Groups in Schools*, Simon and Schuster, New York, 1974.

FOR DISCUSSION

1. Compare the proportion of youth in school in the United States and in other developed nations.
2. Why have property taxes provided the major means of school financing?
3. Developing countries face what major problem in the growth of education?
4. What is the purpose of state aid to local school districts?
5. Since *San Antonio v. Rodriguez*, will attempts be continued to equalize incomes of schools? Why?
6. What are two major functions of the public school system?
7. Explain how the school also has a sorting function.
8. Evaluate the values and realities set forth in the chapter in relation to your own school experiences.
9. Differentiate between absenteeism and truancy.
10. Consider the policies and procedures concerning suspension and expulsion. Draft an equitable policy.
11. In view of the power of state government, why do local school districts exercise basic autonomy?
12. What does *in loco parentis* mean in relation to the school's authority?
13. Discuss the use of corporal punishment. Should parental consent be a condition for corporal punishment?

14. What is meant by *tracking?* What are its advantages and difficulties?
15. Contrast the newer newer model of school social work with the traditional clinical model.

PROJECTS

1. Ask a school administrator to respond to questions on (1) dress codes, (2) underground newspapers, (3) programs for pregnant girls, (4) expulsion and suspension policies in the school. How does the administrator see the issue in *Tinker v. Des Moines Board of Education* concerning the wearing of black armbands?
2. Choose the center city and several differing suburbs. Find out how much money is available to the schools on a per-pupil basis from local taxes and from other aid. Do the findings suggest inequities?
3. Invite a school social worker to discuss school rules and policies that need study because they contribute to student problems. Is this change process part of the social worker's role?
4. Discuss or debate: "Resolved, that the age for compulsory school attendance should be lowered."
5. If students in your community are participating in a free school or programs of more "open" education, invite them to describe the programs to your class and to respond to questions.
6. Devise a plan for a day care center for the children of school-age mothers. Consider costs, community acceptance, program, educational goals for the mothers, possible involvement of school-age fathers, and location and auspices.

CHAPTER 10
Health

Making sense out of the dollars for health.

Health policy is pathological because we are neurotic and insist on making our government psychotic. Our neurosis consists in knowing what is required for good health (Mother was right: Eat a good breakfast! Sleep eight hours a day! Don't drink! Don't smoke! Keep clean! *And* don't worry!) but not being willing to do it. Government's ambivalence consists in paying coming and going: once for telling people how to be healthy and once for paying their bills when they disregard this advice. Psychosis appears when government persists in repeating this self-defeating play.

—Aaron Wildavsky*

Social workers in health settings are concerned with the treatment of illness and the maintenance and promotion of health in hospitals, clinics, and various public and private agencies. Social workers collaborate with physicians, nurses, and members of other professions in the care of patients and their families. Social workers need an understanding of the psychosocial implications of illness, including an appreciation of the factors contributing to sickness and disability. At the same time health delivery systems have become more complex and impersonal, making it more difficult for patients to receive individualized attention. In the past physicians and nurses were primarily concerned with the physical needs of patients, and social workers tended to emphasize social needs. Today other health professionals are also becoming more sensitive to the psychological needs of patients. New disciplines, such as medical sociology, are also adding knowledge to the field. However, the social worker's special contribution is in the restoration of maximum social functioning to the individual who is ill, and also in the development of the services required to achieve that goal.

HEALTH CARE IN THE UNITED STATES

Health care services in the United States constitute a "sick care" rather than a "health care" system. As a result, the United States has had a disappointing record in maternal and infant health. In addition, health services have suffered from severe economic inflation, geographical and income-based variability of care, maldistribution of medical personnel, lack of clarity of responsibility, leading to the shunting of people from one facility to another, depersonalization, and uneconomic use of hospital beds and expensive equipment.

*Aaron Wildavsky, "Doing Better and Feeling Worse: The Political Pathology of Health Policy," in John H. Knowles (ed.), *Doing Better and Feeling Worse: Health in the United States*, Norton, New York, 1977, p. 124.

Factors Affecting Health Status

Income   Good health and high income are positively related. Even though medical resources vary in quality and quantity for the more affluent, the poor suffer acute deficiencies in health care.[1] Poor people have a higher rate of illness, yet services are less accessible to them. Impersonal, grudging attitudes of health staff also discourage use of the services that exist. The poor are usually denied the opportunity to establish a continuing doctor-patient relationship. Without the financial resources to pay for medical care, they tend to postpone seeing a doctor until their condition is serious. They are less likely to have insurance, so they enter a hospital at the point of emergency, resulting in a longer stay. Low-income families tend to have several hospitalizations per year, suffer from chronic conditions, and have their activities restricted. They also lose more days from work because of illness than the rest of the population.[2]

Understanding of Symptoms   Whether or not people consider themselves ill depends upon their understanding of the cause and course of their symptoms, their expectation of the outcome, and the financial consequences of illness. A college professor or a bookkeeper with a severe headache may be too ill to work, yet a miner with an advanced case of emphysema or black lung disease still may continue on his job. To define himself as ill is to cut off his means of livelihood. Researchers also report that the symptoms taken seriously vary by social class.[3] Lack of recognition of the importance of major symptoms in lower-class groups may result from inadequate experience with medical services as well as insufficient general knowledge.

Race   Infant mortality is nearly twice as high for nonwhites as for whites, and life expectancies for both sexes are about six years shorter for nonwhites—63.6 years compared to 69.4 years for males and 72.3 to 77.2 years for females. The nonwhite poor have a shorter life, greater maternal mortality, and a higher rate of death from tuberculosis, influenza, pneumonia, vascular lesions, and cancer of the cervix.[4]

Age   People over sixty-five now make up 10 percent of the population, and the percentage is increasing each year. The aged are more likely to be poor and get sick more often than younger people. They have more serious illnesses, are admitted to the hospital more often, and stay longer. They spend three times more on health per capita than younger persons, mostly for hospital or nursing home care. Their illnesses are characterized by disability and complexity—arthritis, rheumatism, heart disease and high blood pressure, and deficits of hearing, vision, speech, and memory.[5]

Costs and Access
The federal government declared a "new national health strategy" in 1971, no doubt motivated by the striking rise of over 170 percent in medical costs since the beginning of the 1960s.

From August 1971 to April 1974, medical-care prices were controlled

Table 10-1   U. S. Health Costs for 1976

Health Costs	Percent (1976)
Hospital care	39.8
Doctors' services	18.9
Drugs	8.0
Dentists	6.1
Construction	3.5
Nursing homes	7.6
Research	2.3
Public Health	2.4
Other	11.4

under the economic stabilization program. However, with the lifting of controls, expenditures rose 31 percent in two years while the gross national product increased 18 percent. By 1976 the United States was spending $139.3 billion for health (8.6 percent of GNP) as compared to $75 billion in 1971. This sum was apportioned as shown in Table 10-1.[6]

The per patient costs of hospital service in the United States rose from $44 per day in 1965 to $81 per day in 1970, and $151 in 1975.[7] The employment of more highly skilled personnel, rising construction costs, the use of sophisticated therapeutic procedures, and the persistence of many inefficient small units have been partially responsible. Third-party financing through private insurance, Medicare, and Medicaid also increases costs, since health-care vendors know that the money is there, and the demand for services also increases.

Until recently, hospitals have had little incentive to control costs. Insurance programs cover in-patient rather than out-patient services, resulting in serious overuse of hospital services. As nonprofit organizations in a noncompetitive market, the hospitals have expanded, duplicated, and added to the consumer's bill. Hospitals are now being faced with community criticism because of consumer demands, high costs, overuse, and tension between physicians and hospital administrators. External controls are increasing. Control of hospital costs is seen as a key element in developing a viable national health insurance system.

MAJOR COMPONENTS IN HEALTH CARE

Physicians, nurses, technicians, and other medical professional and paramedical personnel, private and public hospitals, convalescent and nursing homes, insurance companies, manufacturers of drugs and technical equipment, and governmental agencies concerned with research and direct and indirect health care for special groups are all involved in providing health services.

Hospitals and Nursing Homes

Health care in the United States is delivered through a variety of facilities—in-patient and out-patient, private and public. In-patient facilities include hospitals, and nursing homes. Out-patient facilities include hospital emergency rooms, private offices of physicians, and clinics supported by private or public funds. Prepaid comprehensive health programs, known as health maintenance organizations (HMOs), have been developed to provide complete health care financed by an annual fee.

Because of the lack of access to primary health care, hospital emergency rooms have often been the major facility used by poor people needing medical care. Home health services, supported by Medicare and Medicaid legislation, and the nursing home industry have been expanding.

The development of medical technology has made the hospital the center of medical care for in-patient and out-patient services and community health services and planning. Medical schools are combining with community hospitals to take responsibility for teaching, research, and outreach programs. Hospitals are increasingly becoming associated with extended-care facilities where less expensive services can be provided for recuperation and rehabilitation.

Federal programs for medical care and the increasing number of aged have focused attention on nursing homes as resources for patients who do not need full hospital services. Medicare pays for post-hospital care in skilled nursing home facilities for eligible patients for up to sixty days. Medicaid payments are made for needy individuals requiring a range of care from skilled to custodial. Unlike hospitals, about nine out of ten nursing homes are established to make a profit.

Many states have investigated complaints of malnutrition, neglect, and physical abuse in nursing homes.[8] In view of the variations in the quality of care, licensing regulations are of particular importance. More emphasis should be placed on the social needs of the long-term patients who have chronic problems which are of little interest to most physicians. Routine medical care can be given by trained nurse practitioners.

In 1965 social work services in nursing homes were required as part of Medicare regulations. This requirement was deleted in 1972. However, social services are reimbursable when they are available. A 1974 study showed that only 26.3 percent of skilled nursing facilities had full-time social work staff.[9]

Physicians

Until World War II, medical service was dominated by physicians in individual practice. Hospitals assumed a relatively minor role because ill people were generally cared for at home. In the past thirty-five years, technology has emphasized the treatment of acute illness for which hospital facilities are essential. The role of the general practitioner has been devalued. Physicians today are increasingly specialized, and many engage in group practice. The specialized health system has deprived many patients of personalized care. Physicians rarely make house calls, and the emergency room has become the center for crisis care and a variety of out-patient services.

As a group American doctors are the highest paid professionals, earning an average of $47,520 in 1975 if self-employed physicians and $76,300 if shareholders in medical corporations.[10] Physicians are concentrated in the high population areas. In 1975, of the 340,280 active physicians in the United States, only 16 percent were in general practice: 75 percent were engaged in specialized practice, and 9 percent were involved in teaching, research, and administration.[11] Specialization in medical education means that doctors are staying in training longer. Large teaching hospitals have attracted the most skilled and ambitious physicians. To meet the need for primary care, the new specialization of family medicine is being emphasized, and family practice residencies are being developed all over the country.

Allied Health Personnel

Pressures on the health delivery system have brought about changes in the personnel of the health team and its services. Medical technicians trained by the armed forces take further training and serve in hospitals and clinics. "New careerists," many of them women and minority-group members, have been trained as nurse's aides, social work aides, home health care workers, and community health workers. Indigenous persons have found jobs in neighborhood health centers.

The health team is no longer limited to the doctor and nurse. Physical therapists, occupational therapists, midwives, surgical assistants, pediatric assistants, social workers, and various other health workers are important. Teams must be task-oriented and offer services appropriate to the needs of the clients. How social workers participate in these services will be discussed later in this chapter.

Until recently the federal government encouraged the expansion of professional schools, the training of allied health personnel, the preparation of supervisors of subprofessional workers teachers of allied health professions, and the development of new types of allied health workers through grants and loans. Many federal training programs have been curtailed.

Consumers

The consumer is a relative newcomer to policy-making for health. However, with the recognition of the principle of "maximum feasible participation" for affected groups, and the increasing interest of organized community groups in influencing the delivery of services, the health system has been penetrated by consumer interests. Consumer representatives are now included on advisory boards of hospitals, neighborhood health centers, and health planning bodies to assist institutions to understand the dissatisfactions of the public and help consumers to deal with the complexity and limitations of the programs. Struggles often develop over the power of such boards and the issue of medical versus nonmedical control.

Increasing recognition of the importance of self-care and decision-making on the part of patients involves consumers in another role in health care. Smoking, alcohol and drug abuse, poor nutrition, and lack of physical exercise are all recognized as contributors to poor health over which the individual has an opportunity to exercise control. Health education is used more effectively, and social workers are becoming part of this movement.

Also, greater recognition is given to patients' rights. Patients expect to be informed about their condition, to understand as much as possible about treatment procedures, and to be given sufficient information to participate in decision-making. These expectancies have culminated in a bill of rights.

Patients' Bill of Rights

The patient has the right to

1. Considerate and respectful care
2. Obtain from his/her physician complete, current information concerning his diagnosis, treatment, and prognosis in terms he/she can reasonably be expected to understand
3. Receive from his/her physician information necessary to give informed consent prior to the start of any procedure and/or treatment
4. Refuse treatment to the extent permitted by law, and to be informed of the medical consequences of his/her action
5. Every consideration of privacy concerning his/her medical-care program
6. Expect that all communication and records pertaining to his/her care should be treated as confidential
7. Expect that within its capacity a hospital must make reasonable response to the request of a patient for services
8. Obtain information as to any relationship of his hospital to other health-care and educational institutions insofar as his/her health is concerned
9. Be advised if the hospital proposed to engage in or perform human experimentation affecting his/her care or treatment
10. Expect reasonable continuity of care
11. Examine and receive an explanation of his/her bill regardless of the source of payment.[12]

The proliferation of malpractice suits in the health field has been attributable to a sense of alienation felt by patients toward their health providers. Closer attention to informing and sharing in decision-making between physician and patient could help alleviate this conflict.

FINANCING OF HEALTH SERVICES

Health services are financed by direct payments from the individual to the health provider, by private insurance, and through governmental programs. Of the total expenditures for personal health care in 1976, the consumer paid one-third, private insurance 26 percent, and the government almost 40 percent.[13]

Figure 10-1 shows that contributions vary according to the category of care. Individuals contributed only 8.9 percent of costs directly for hospital care,

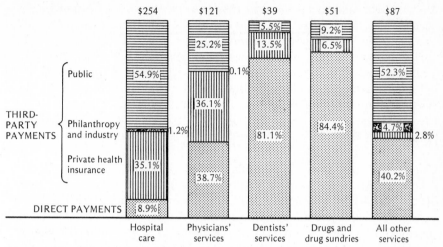

Figure 10-1 Percentage distribution of per capita personal health care expenditures, by type of expenditure and source of funds, fiscal year 1976.

38.7 percent to physician's services, 81 percent to dental service, 84 percent to drugs, and 40 percent to other services. Despite increased contributions by government and insurance to health care, individuals still continue to make large cash expenditures because of co-payments and other restrictions in various insurance plans.

Private Insurance
Problems of private health insurance include:

1. High-risk groups who most need insurance—the poor, aged, and chronically ill—cannot get it economically.
2. Health insurance premiums are too high.
3. Coverage is inadequate for preventive or out-patient care, encouraging overuse of hospitals.
4. Most policies have a deductible provision requiring considerable cash outlay despite benefits.
5. Private insurers exercise little control over rising costs.
6. Programs do not cover the costs of long-term chronic illness.
7. Advertising by commercial companies is often misleading to consumers.

   Three types of private health insurance plans can be differentiated: Blue Cross and Blue Shield, commercial companies, and independent plans.

Blue Cross and Blue Shield   In 1929 Blue Cross was created when a group of schoolteachers insured themselves against hospital bills through a prepayment plan. Plans developed in a number of cities and were endorsed by the

American Hospital Association. In 1939 Blue Shield was established to cover doctors' bills. Blue Cross became a separate organization in 1972. The Blue Cross and Blue Shield programs are not-for-profit organizations monitored by various state insurance commissioners. They began the pattern of reimbursing for health costs in the United States. In 1975, 83 million people were covered by Blue Cross, and 2.5 million by Blue Shield.[14] The "Blues" have a record of low expenditures for administrative costs (about 5 percent of premiums). They have had an important role as intermediaries for the government in handling payments for Medicare and Medicaid.

Commercial Companies   The health insurance business attracted commercial companies in large numbers particularly as a result of organized labor's demands for health benefits. In 1975, 79 percent of the population had hospital care, and about 75 percent had protection against physicians' costs. Most of this coverage was through group plans written with insurance companies.[15] Commercial carriers receive 50 percent of subscriptions, as compared to 43 percent for Blue Cross and Blue Shield. In 1974, while the Blues returned 94 percent of the money taken in, commercial carriers returned 80 percent in payments.[16]

Independent Plans   In addition to Blue Cross and Blue Shield, and the commercial companies, there are a number of prepaid health-financing plans, such as the Kaiser-Permanente Program on the West Coast and the Health Insurance Plan of Greater New York. They made up 4 percent of total enrollment under private health insurance in 1975.[17] Plans are community sponsored, employer-employee–union sponsored, or involve private group clinics.

No Health Insurance

Some weeks ago, my father survived a heart attack. My father is among the estimated hundreds of thousands of Americans who have no health insurance. . . .

He spent eight days in a coronary-care unit at a cost of $200 per day and another two weeks in a semi-private hospital room at approximately $100 per day. If my arithmetic is correct, he can expect a hospital bill of about $3,160. This, of course, does not include diagnostic costs or his cardiologist's fee. I figure that a conservative estimate of my father's medical expenses should total about $5,000. And he may still need an operation!

To some people that amount may not seem like much money. But to a 58 year-old man who is a self-employed barber in rural Dutchess County, N.Y., that amount is enough to make one worry. I see the worry in my father's face. Self-employed barbers in rural Dutchess County don't make that much money.

My father—like a good number of other self-employed, working-class Americans—falls into an unhappy category of many thousands who can neither afford the escalating costs of the monthly private health insurance premiums, nor meet the required means test of Medicaid. Financially, my father and others like him find themselves in the unenviable situation of being in a "no-man's land" when it comes to affording adequate health care for their families.[18]

John P. Allegrante, letter in *New York Times.*

Government Health Programs

Currently the government pays 40 percent of the country's health care bill. It participates in the health insurance of federal employees and provides medical programs for families of members of the armed forces and, through Veterans Administration hospitals, for those who have had military service. Government funds are also expended on beneficiaries of Medicare and Medicaid.

Historical Highlights   Other countries began to develop insured health care in the latter part of the nineteenth and the early twentieth century. Interest in national health insurance was evident in this country in 1912, when the Progressive Party, under Theodore Roosevelt, included a national health insurance plan in its platform. Social workers played a key role in the adoption of the platform plank. Although a national health insurance program was urged in the Social Security Act of 1935, health insurance was finally omitted because it might have endangered the passage of the act.

Legislation for national health insurance has been introduced in each session of Congress since 1939. In 1949 President Harry S. Truman, with strong liberal support, urged the enactment of a compulsory system in his State of the Union message. No law resulted. Medicare was passed in 1965 as Title XVIII of the Social Security Act because lack of health care for the aged had become intolerable.

Current Programs

Medicare   This is a dual program financed by payroll taxes on employers and employees. Part A includes coverage for hospital service, extended care aid, and some home health care. Initially patients were required to pay the first $40. In 1979 they had to pay the first $160, and $40 per day after they had been hospitalized more than 60 days (61–90 days); after 90 days the co-insurance charge was $80 per day (91–150 days).

Part B, covering physicians' fees, hospital out-patient services, home health care, physical therapy, and diagnostic X-rays, is voluntary. Originally, participants paid $3 a month for this coverage; in 1978 it cost $7.70 a month. Since 1973 the deductible provision has required the patient to pay the first $60 of medical expenses and Medicare covered 80 percent of the remaining charges. Rates may well rise. The local social security office can give information about current rates. Some people meet costs not covered by Medicare with private insurance. Otherwise, Medicaid funds have been used to fill the gaps for poor people.

The federal government was careful not to interfere with the existing health delivery system. While the Social Security Administration has overall responsibility for the program, intermediaries, such as Blue Cross, private insurance companies, and other organizations, are chosen by hospitals or physicians to carry out the bookkeeping and payments. This has served to increase the power of the Blue Cross groups, since they make payments to the health providers and set "reasonable" fees.

The advantages of Medicare include participation in coverage of the aged as a right, elimination of negative feelings about health insurance, better benefits than those of private health insurance plans, and improved services to the aged, such as home care and extended care.

The problems involve greatly expanded demand for services already in short supply, increased health costs, lack of consumer participation in decision-making, overutilization of hospitals, exclusion of drugs and long-term care, and the deductible provisions, resulting in the need for additional private insurance and use of Medicaid funds.

In 1973, through an amendment to the Social Security Act, younger permanently and totally disabled people and persons with chronic kidney disease were also included in the program. However, all the aged and poor persons with long-term disabilities are still not covered.

Medicaid   With the passage of Title XIX of the Social Security Act in 1965, the federal government provided benefits for the medically indigent through Medicaid. Medicaid differs from Medicare in almost every respect. Medicare is based on worker-employment taxes to make it generally self-supporting. Medicaid, like other public assistance programs, is financed by appropriations from general tax revenues. One must pass a means test to qualify. The benefits vary from state to state. Generally they are available to persons on public assistance. The original legislation encouraged states to include coverage of self-supporting persons whose marginal incomes made them unable to pay for medical care. However, this inclusion was not mandatory, and the definition of "medical indigence" was left to the states.

By 1967 the program had developed severe administrative problems. Guidelines were established requiring the states to review the costs, administration, and quality of medical care. A program was added requiring Early and Periodic Screening, Diagnosis and Treatment (EPSDT) of children under twenty-one eligible for Medicaid.

In 1972 provisions were enacted which would permit withholding funds if the states were remiss in utilization review and EPSDT programs. To improve the quality of care, professional standards review organizations (PSROs) of physicians were created to monitor medical care under Medicaid and Medicare.

In 1976 a ten-year review identified basic difficulties in the Medicaid program: (1) complexity of eligibility requirements and gaps in coverage; (2) a small federal staff to oversee fifty-three different programs; (3) the incomplete coverage of long-term care by Medicare, which requires Medicaid to devote 40 percent of its funds to long-term care; (4) inequities between the states.

While costs have accelerated far beyond anticipation, Medicaid has remained 2 percent of the federal budget, and 2 percent of state and local budgets. The increased cost has been due to the larger number of people on AFDC, rising medical costs in general, and the rising cost of maintaining elderly and disabled persons in nursing homes.[19] Payments for white recipients are larger than for black recipients, and payments for urban dwellers are larger than for rural residents. Medicaid has greatly increased access to health care for poor people but has involved high costs and much inequity. The federal government needs improved methods of reviewing costs, administration, quality of medical care, and action against fraud and abuse.

Public Health

Public health services operate at the federal, state, and local levels. They are dependent upon the authority of the state and federal government to intervene in many ways. Nationally, the emphasis has been on research and education, the monitoring of the safety of drugs, and the purity of food. The U.S. Public Health Service has become involved in more direct services since the creation of the Department of Health, Education and Welfare in 1953.

The first state health department was established in Massachusetts in 1869. On a state and local level, major concerns include water supply, sewage disposal, environmental hazards, control of communicable diseases, and regulation of health facilities through licensing. Public health experts have virtually eliminated a number of communicable diseases, such as tuberculosis, polio, and smallpox. Existing clinics generally have been limited to specialized programs, such as well-baby care, treatment of venereal disease, and detection of such diseases as tuberculosis, glaucoma, and more recently sickle-cell anemia. A network of community public health clinics, staffed by teams of public health nurses, social workers, public health educators, and paramedical personnel, could help meet the present crisis in medical care. Public health education in relation to nutrition, smoking, accidents, suicide, and drug use has been given limited support.

New Models of Health Delivery—The Right to Access

The foregoing discussion suggests that the United States has a multifaceted and fragmented system of health delivery.

Essential Conditions   Ann R. Somers has identified four conditions essential to a comprehensive system of care.

> Every individual must have access to the whole spectrum of health services through referral channels that do not break the primary personal

relationship, and do not require unnecessary duplication of diagnostic tests or other services, but provide complete records of all medical and other health-related information.

Every individual must have access to a meaningful personal relationship with at least one health professional, preferably a physician or a specialist who can provide the necessary general coordination and continuity.

The supply of doctor, nurses, and other health personnel must be adequate.

Health professionals should be subject to an organized system of professional discipline or peer review involving the quality, quantity, and price of services rendered. Every health institution must be subject to some form of price discipline—through market competition, public regulation, or a combination of both.[20]

With these essential conditions in mind, we will consider some models for the delivery of health care.

Prepaid Health Plans   Congress passed Public Law 93-222 in December 1973 to assist in the development of prepaid health plans known as health maintenance organizations (HMOs). The program is intended to encourage comprehensive health programs for "underserved populations" for a five-year period. The bill provides financial assistance for feasibility surveys, planning, initial developmental costs, and research, but not construction costs or subsidies to permit the medically indigent to join HMOs. It removes obstacles of restrictive laws, and mandates employers of over twenty-five people to include in their health benefits plans the option of membership in "qualified health maintenance organizations" where they exist. To quality, minimum services include physicians, hospitalization, mental health visits, alcoholic and drug abuse treatment and referral, diagnostic laboratory and radiology, home health services, preventive health services, health education, and medical social services—more than any prepaid health plan provided.

Prepaid health plans offer many attractive features—ability to anticipate income, incentives to offer preventive services, removal of barriers to entrance into the health system as a result of financial hardship, and opportunity for quality and cost control. However, administration of these programs in a financially feasible manner requires a careful balance of membership among socioeconomic groups. Previous successful programs have catered essentially to families of employed workers. Research indicates that low-income families are apt to have an initial period of increased usage and that premium structures should reflect this difference. It was also considered essential that support services needed to be included to assure utilization by these clients.[21]

Community Health Centers

Community health centers have been developing since the 1960s, when neighborhood health centers were funded under the Office of Economic Opportunity as part of the War on Poverty. These neighborhood health centers emphasized community involvement and the training of paraprofessionals. The objective was to provide family-oriented ambulatory care in areas where there were inadequate health care facilities or special health needs. Physicians, nurses, social workers, and other trained professionals worked in teams with paraprofessionals and indigenous outreach workers to provide care that recognized the social as well as the medical implications of illness.

By 1974, 104 neighborhood health centers had been developed. In 1974 the centers were told by the federal government to seek alternative funding, which proved to be unrealistic. In 1975 a new emphasis was placed on the development of community health centers in rural and urban areas. By 1978 574 centers were serving over 3 million people.[22] Special attention is being focused on the health needs of migratory workers as a target group. Community health centers developed under various auspices. Some had hospital affiliations and some did not. Those without affiliations have had more difficulty providing comprehensive care. Some have become combined health and mental health centers. Overall, community health centers have proved to be a successful innovation in meeting the needs of medically underserved communities. Their future depends upon the development of a national health policy.

PLANNING OF HEALTH CARE

The Hill-Burton Hospital and Construction Act of 1946 was the first national legislation requiring each state to study its hospital facilities, establish its priority needs, and plan for expansion. Through this legislation hospitals have been expanded and nursing homes, clinics, and public health and rehabilitation centers built.

Health care planning was greatly stimulated by the 1966 Partnership for Health Act, which attempted to aid states in establishing health-planning organizations. The act included advisory councils having a majority of consumer representatives, aid to the development of regional health plans, also requiring consumer representation, and grants for the development of health and mental health programs.

This legislation sought to reach every level of government, to relate to both private and public sectors, and to assure the highest level of health for every individual, "without interfering with existing patterns of private practice."

Public Law 89-239, passed in 1965, authorized grants to aid in the planning for regional programs related to heart disease, cancer, and stroke. Included were projects affecting nonprofit universities, medical schools, research institutions, hospitals, and health agencies engaged in training and research. Model Cities funds were also provided to assist cities in the planning and construction of hospitals and other facilities.

The National Health Planning and Resources Act of 1974, which superseded all previous planning programs, provides a network of local health-planning agencies across the nation called health systems agencies (HSAs), state planning and development agencies (SPDAs), and state health-coordinating councils (SHCCs). A National Council for Health Policy within the Department of Health, Education and Welfare sets guidelines.

The bill was intended to develop a national health-planning policy, augment state planning for health services, personnel, and facilities, and develop resources to further that policy.[23]

The health systems agencies are intended to:

1. Improve the health of residents,
2. Increase accessibility, acceptability, continuity, and quality of health services,
3. Restrain increases in costs,
4. Prevent unnecessary duplication.

Emphasis is placed upon local planning agencies representing all segments of the health system—providers, consumers, and third-party payers—to carry on specific functions in addition to preparing health plans. These include:

1. Review and approval or disapproval of applications for federal health program funds,
2. Periodic review of existing institutional health services,
3. Administrative certification of need programs to prohibit development of unneeded services.

A new title provides for the development of new facilities, and encouragement is given to experimentation in rate regulation and other cost-saving efforts. Should a national health insurance bill be passed, the national network of health-planning agencies could well become part of an overall system.

Need for Health Insurance

National health insurance is long overdue in the United States. Even though insurance coverage is increasing, and 91 percent of hospital care is covered, 39 percent of physicians' services, and only 20 percent of other health needs, such as medicine and special glasses, are covered. The poor, who are most at risk, have no insurance. Even the aged, covered by Medicare, have no resources for long-term chronic illnesses. In addition, the possibility of serious or extended illness is a critical economic threat to people in the middle-income groups. To begin to meet the present crisis in health care, any national insurance plan must include provisions not only for financing but also for regulating and redistributing health care, training health personnel, and prevention.

The uncontrolled rise in health costs has led to increased support for broad-scale national health insurance programs. Without governmental insurance, many Americans cannot cover the cost of hospitalization for an extensive illness. Hospitals cannot survive without assured income. Physicians also have benefited from insurance. Proposals for national health insurance programs are being made by Republican and Democratic spokesmen, the American Medical Association, the American Hospital Association, representatives of private insurance companies, and organized labor.

Approaches   The proposals embody four major approaches. In the mixed public-private approach, health insurance funds would be collected by the federal government and disbursed by private insurance companies, which would handle the claims and pay the providers. In the public approach, governmental agencies would not only collect funds but also pay the claims. Tax credits for the purchase of private health insurance are another possible system. The catastrophic approach involves governmental participation only when medical expenses exceed a certain amount. Several criteria may be applied:

1. Will the proposal make adequate health care accessible to all?
2. Will the proposal improve health delivery for those whose needs are not presently being met?
3. Does the proposal provide for a comprehensive view of health care, including prevention and mental health services?
4. Is the proposed method of financing equitable?
5. Does the proposed system provide mechanisms for controlling costs?
6. How does the proposed plan affect other government programs?

Expectations vary as to the direction national health insurance will take in the United States. While considerable support for some kind of program is found in almost every segment of society, the unpredictable continuous rise in health costs has made the federal administration wary of proceeding too rapidly. There is some sentiment to move incrementally, including putting new groups with special needs into the existing framework of Medicare. Examples would be children or pregnant women. Differences of opinion exist as to the role that private insurance companies should play. Another issue is cost sharing by persons with higher incomes. There is concern about perpetuating a system which is different for the poor and the nonpoor. Quality of care must be protected. Experience with Medicare and Medicaid has illustrated the importance of planning if large amounts of money are to be funneled into the health system. Further, a national health insurance program should take into consideration the problems of long-term care and preventive care, both of which have so far been neglected.

HEALTH CAREERS IN SOCIAL WORK

Social workers in the health field are most likely to work in hospitals and clinics. They also serve in various capacities in federal, state, and local public health agencies, the Veterans Administration, and the armed services, and as health consultants to public welfare agencies. In addition, social workers work with physicians in private medical practices, home health care teams, nursing home staffs, and health-planning agencies. Social workers are on the faculties of medical schools and schools of public health across the country.

Employment

The health field offers expanding opportunities for social workers at all levels of professional training. In 1974, 28,000 of the 3.8 million people employed in the health industry were social workers. This number has been increasing.[24] Phillips reported that while only 35 percent of the registered hospitals had social service departments in 1970, 55.6 percent had social service departments in 1974.[25] The decision of the Joint Commission on Accreditation of Hospitals, in 1971, to require social services as a condition for accreditation, has done much to encourage the development of social service departments in hospitals.

Historical Development

Dr. Richard C. Cabot and Ida Cannon, a social worker, introduced social services into the Massachusetts General Hospital in Boston in 1905. They recognized the importance of the environment to the patient's recovery and believed that consideration of patients as individuals would enable them to make better use of the medical care being offered. By 1915 social workers were employed in over 100 hospitals. Medical social work followed the trends of the profession as a whole. It began with a commitment to the rehabilitation of the ill client and moved into involvement with psychosomatic medicine and concern about the psychological components of illness. Now the concept of practice is broader. It includes the internal and external needs of the client and concern for the total care system. Whereas the traditional focus was primarily on direct casework with the individual and his family, medical social workers have also introduced group work, community organization, and planning into their practice. Originally they took subservient roles as members of a "guest" agency within the "host" medical agency. However, social workers have become increasingly versatile members of the health team. They provide consultation, training of other professionals, and policy development within various health agencies.

SOCIAL WORKERS' ROLES

The social workers' tasks in health settings can be divided into the following general areas: direct services to patients and their families; management, administration, and planning activities; community work; research and scholarly pursuits; and education of other professionals.

Services to Patients and Families

The social worker in a medical setting is responsible for assisting patients and their families to cope with the pressures brought about by illness and to help the patient achieve maximum recovery and social functioning. The nature of being a patient implies an inability to carry out normal activities. The patient is expected to seek medical care, follow medical instructions, get better, and resume normal functions. Sometimes the patient cannot do so because of the disabling nature of the illness, lack of scientific knowledge of curative measures, or inability to utilize the treatment offered for a variety of social or psychological reasons. The social worker individualizes the patient, assesses the nature of personal needs, and contributes this knowledge to the medical social planning process.

This can be illustrated in the care of an elderly stroke patient who cannot return to the home he had lived alone in prior to hospitalization. The social worker assesses the patient's former life-style, his relationships with his family and friends, his reactions to his illness, possible resources available to him, and then plans with the physicians and other concerned with his medical care toward the best possible plan for restoration and rehabilitation.

In working with patients, the social worker evaluates their concerns about the illness and the treatment being offered, their psychosocial capabilities, the effects of familial, cultural, or economic factors on their adjustment, financial or other needs with which patient or family requires assistance, and how well patient and family deal with their fears and anxieties.

Patients are referred to social service by physicians, nurses, or other personnel, or they are identified by the social worker as being potentially vulnerable. These are patients or families of patients who have indicated signs of undue stress, crises, inability to follow the medical regime, anxiety about the future, or other special problems of adjustment to their illness or disability. The social worker explores and assesses the client's situation, in collaboration with the physician and other involved professionals. The social worker must integrate the medical information provided by the physician and the nurse into the assessment. As the physician plans medical treatment, the social worker plans social treatment, each sharing information significant for the other. Through transfer of information between professionals the best interests of the patient are served. The social worker relates to the patient and the patient's family and to the members of the medical team. The social worker has the responsibility to be well informed about the patient's medical condition and about the psychosocial implications of disease processes in general. In this way, medical and social planning are coordinated. Sometimes the social worker must act as an advocate to assure that the patient's needs are best served.

Death and Dying

Social workers in hospitals are constantly interacting with patients who are dying and relatives who are grieving. Many conflicting feelings are aroused by the threatened loss of life. One of the possible reactions to imminent death is to disassociate oneself from the dying person. This is true not only of relatives who sometimes retreat from visiting, but of the professionals as well. There are also feelings of shame and guilt. Losses beget reactions to past losses so that each person faces death in a unique way. To assist the survivor who is grieving, it is necessary to have an understanding of the nature of the relationship with the deceased person. Colleagues as well must deal with feelings aroused by the death of a patient. To physicians death may be seen as a failure and a threat to their capacity to help. The social worker can help the family to remain involved with the dying patient and to bear the loss and grief associated with death.

Management, Administration, and Planning Functions

The social worker has management tasks in relationship to the hospital, clinic, or health agency and as a member of a social service department. The social worker participates with others in planning programs, identifying the needs of certain high-risk groups, improving patient care, utilization review, and allocation of resources. Social workers play an important role in the development of policies relative to the improvement of patient care within health agencies. They can contribute to organizing services for such problems as child abuse, unwed motherhood, drug abuse, rape, and high-risk infants. Social workers are in a position to alert the institution to problems of depersonalization, long waiting periods, lack of attention to culturally different groups, and other human needs.

The social service department within the health organization requires administration, program planning, policy-making, hiring, supervision of staff, and the evaluation of services. The right of social workers in host health agencies to do their own case finding has been of considerable concern. Without this right, the social service department is unable to set its own priorities.

Community Work

Helping families through a crisis often requires up-to-date information on resources available in the community, and a network relationship to ensure that clients receive their rightful benefits and services. The social worker in the health agency has the responsibility to maintain community relationships, both as a member of the hospital or clinic staff and as a member of the social service department. The social worker can assist in developing needed services inside and outside of institutions.

Research and Scholarly Activities

Social workers in health settings conduct research contributing to increased understanding of the impact of illness and disability on individuals and families.[26] They also study organizational problems. While this area has not been sufficiently stressed in the past, the importance of research is being recognized through the development of two new journals on social work and health, *Health and Social Work*, published by the National Association of Social Workers, and *Social Work and Health Care*, published by Haworth Press.

Teaching

Social workers in practice help to teach undergraduate and graduate students from schools of social work. In addition, they participate in the training of other professionals and paraprofessionals within the health agencies. Social workers are at present employed in 80 percent of the schools of medicine in the United States, where they teach courses on such subjects as the psychosocial implications of hospitalization, the psychosocial aspects of illness and rehabilitation, death and dying, family dynamics, health care of minority groups, alcoholism, drug abuse, and child abuse. Social workers often teach in collaboration with faculty in other disciplines.[27] Indications are that there will be increasing opportunities in medical education in the future.

Teamwork

The social worker in the health setting collaborates with other health professionals in a variety of ways. Sometimes the collaboration is very informal; at other times it is highly structured.

Kane found that social workers were assigned to multidisciplinary teams more frequently than any other professional. Teamwork necessitates the development of trust between members, the capacity to set mutual goals, and the ability to share information.[28] However, studies indicated considerable confusion in relation to role performance and role expectation among professionals attempting to work together in the health field.[29] Physicians have been seen as the highest-status health professionals, and other professionals, including social workers, compete to achieve recognition.

A strong contribution to the health team requires not only practice skill, but also respect for the contributions of other professionals, the ability to communicate effectively, and the capacity to engage in decision-making as a member of a group. Team practice is an essential for offering comprehensive care in the health field. Teamwork has become increasingly important in solving such dilemmas as the selection of transplant and dialysis candidates, whether to extend life with technical supports, and planning for the treatment of severely disabled newborns. All these issues require team judgments. Social workers are also participants in utilization review teams to evaluate appropriate use of institutional facilities.

Group Work

Group work has become an increasingly significant method of aiding persons who are going through a trying adaptation to a chronic disease or disability. This method provides opportunities for patients to share fears, anxieties, and experiences in a supportive, constructive manner. The group experience permits reality testing, which helps patients to face their situation and gain better understanding of the nature of their abilities and limitations. Practical experience can be shared, and patients are relieved of feelings of isolation and withdrawal. Group work is not only effectively carried out with patients themselves, but with significant family members as well. Recent work has been reported on group work with patients who had experienced strokes, kidney dialysis, or sickle-cell anemia, and with parents of multihandicapped children.

Prevention

Social workers can play a preventive as well as a therapeutic role. Through an understanding of the implications of various high-risk situations, the social worker can aid patients and families to anticipate problems and cope more effectively. Examples of high-risk groups are premature babies, teenage mothers, women requesting abortion, persons attempting suicide, persons addicted to drugs or alcohol, patients on kidney dialysis, persons undergoing organ transplant, and amputees. Other groups who should also be expected to require assistance would be the chronically ill and repeated users of emergency rooms. The social worker's role is to emphasize the functioning capacities of the patient, help reduce pressures, promote rehabilitation, and prevent unnecessary dysfunctioning. The family is aided to support the patient and to move in the most constructive direction possible. The author of this chapter was engaged for some years in a program for parents having their first child. The focus was on preventing disorders in the parent-child relationship by helping the young families to cope with the strains that arose during the pregnancy and early infancy. The team consisted of an obstetrician, a public health nurse, a dietitian, a pediatrician, and a social worker, with a psychiatric consultant.[30]

Expanding Role

The development of general community clinics and specialized clinics for family planning, genetic counseling, abortion counseling, the treatment of alcoholics, drug abusers, mothers and infants, and the elderly has created new opportunities for social workers in the health field. Medicare and Medicaid have brought increased attention to the medical-social needs of the elderly. More recently, with the trend to deinstitutionalization, aged and severely disabled persons in nursing homes require extensive assistance. Many elderly people lack the social and emotional resources to cope with the changes that have taken place in their lives. In addition to working directly with patients and families, social workers are acting as consultants to extended-care staff.

Private Practice of Social Work

Private practice of social work has only recently achieved legitimacy in the profession. However, with increased purchase of service, insurance coverage, and diminishing private agency support, social workers interested in clinical casework services are increasingly moving into part-time and full-time private practice. One promising area for practice is primary health care. Social workers are reporting associations with group medical clinics, individual practitioners, family practice clinics, and prepaid health clinics, as well as extended-care facilities.

SUMMARY AND APPLICATION

Accountability is the goal in the entire health field. With pressure to reduce costs, each patient's hospital stay is being closely monitored. Social workers are participating in utilization reviews and being pressed to move patients swiftly out of hospitals into less costly institutions. The provision of adequate home health care for elderly, single, or other needful individuals is one of the community-organization challenges for the health social worker. Financial pressures on families as a result of inflated health costs are prevalent. Social workers are finding themselves in overlapping roles with other professional groups, such as psychologists, nurses, chaplains, occupational therapists, and patient representatives. Consideration must be given to effective and differential use of social workers with varying degrees of training. With the new emphasis on health planning, social workers will need to develop increased knowledge in this area. Other skills needed include training of indigenous workers and paraprofessionals, and understanding of effective methods of advocacy.

The employment outlook for social work in the health field is good. As the third-largest employer in the United States, the health care industry offers opportunities at every level of service. As we have seen, the Joint Committee on Accreditation requires social service as a condition of accreditation of hospitals. A federal health insurance program will provide additional demands for social workers not only in direct service to patients, but in managerial and planning roles as well. To meet these demands, the profession has taken the initiative that will assure quality of social work performance in hospitals and has encouraged licensure and professional certification. Increasingly, schools of social work are developing concentrations in the health area and expanding training to the undergraduate and doctoral levels. With this expansion of training should come increases in knowledge.

Medical social work should make a significant contribution to the development of a comprehensive, humane health delivery system for all.

—Shirley H. Wattenberg

KEY TERMS

"sick" care system
maximum feasible consumer participation
Blue Cross/Blue Shield

Medicare
Medicaid
HMOs
national health insurance

REFERENCES AND NOTES

1. Ann R. Somers, "Health Care in Transiton: Directions for the Future," *Hospital Research and Educational Trust*, 1971, p. 23.
2. Department of Health, Education and Welfare, Social Security Administration, *Delivery of Health Services for the Poor: A Program Analysis*, 1969.
3. E. Koos, *The Health of Regionsville: What the People Thought and Did About It*, Columbia, New York, 1954.
4. *Statistical Abstract of the United States, 1977*, Department of Commerce, Bureau of the Census, Washington, D.C., 1977, p. 65.
5. Elaine M. Brody, "Aging," in *Encyclopedia of Social Work*, 1977, p. 63.
6. Robert M. Gibson and Marjorie Smith Mueller, "National Health Expenditures: Fiscal Year 1976," *Social Security Bulletin*, April 1977, pp. 4 and 5.
7. *Statistical Abstract 1977*, p. xiv.
8. Claire Townsend, *Old Age: The Last Segregation; Ralph Nader's Study Group on Nursing Homes*, Grossman, New York, 1971.
9. *Social Work Consultation in Long-Term Care Facilities*, Department of Health, Education and Welfare, Public Health Service; Department of Commerce, National Technical Information Service, HRP 0023851, 1971, p. 11.
10. *Statistical Abstract, 1977*, p. 102.
11. Ann R. Somers and Herman M. Somers, *Health and Health Care: Policies in Perspective*, Aspen Systems Corp., Germantown, Md., 1977, p. 496.
12. Ruth I. Knee, "Health Care Patients Rights," *Encyclopedia of Social Work*, 1977, pp. 542–543.
13. Gibson and Mueller, op. cit., p. 15.
14. Marjorie Smith Mueller, "Private Health Insurance in 1975: Coverage Enrollment and Financial Experience," *Social Security Bulletin*, June 1977, p. 8.
15. Ibid., p. 4.
16. Ibid., p. 7
17. Ibid., p. 3
18. John P. Allegrante, letter in *New York Times*, April 27, 1977.
19. *Public Health Reports*, vol. 91, no. 4, July–August 1976, pp. 303–316, p. 18.
20. Ann R. Somers, op. cit., p. 100.
21. Gerald Sparer and Arne Anderson, "Experience of Low Income Families in Four Pre-paid Group Practice Plans," in Robert L. Kane, Josephine M. Kasteter, and Robert M. Gray (eds.), *The Health Gap*, Springer, New York, 1976, pp. 202–214.
22. Senate Report 95-860 on S. 2474. Reauthorization for Community and Migrant Health Centers and Other Programs submitted by Senator T. Kennedy, April 24, 1978, p. 10.
23. Public Law 93-641, p. 3.
24. Milton Wittman, "Social Work Manpower for the Health Services," *American Journal of Public Health*, vol. 64, no. 4, April 1974, p. 371.
25. Beatrice Phillips, "Health Services: Social Workers," in *Encyclopedia of Social Work*, 1977, p. 616.
26. David M. Kaplan, Rose Grobstein, and Aaron Smith, "Predicting the Impact of Severe Illness in Families," *Health and Social Work*, August 1976, p. 71–82.
27. Richard M. Arennell, Jr., et al., "The Status of Graduate Level Social Workers Teaching in Medical Schools," *Social Work in Health Care*, vol. 1, no. 3, Spring 1976, pp. 317–324.

28. Rosalie A. Kane, *Interprofessional Teamwork*, Division of Continuing Education and Manpower Development, Syracuse University School of Social Work, Syracuse, N.Y., 1975, p. 50.
29. Katherine M. Olsen and Marvin E. Olsen, "Role Expectations and Perceptions of Social Workers in Medical Settings," *Social Work*, vol. 12, no. 3, July 1967, pp. 105–118.
30. Florence E. Cyr and Shirley H. Wattenberg, "Social Work in a Preventive Program of Maternal and Child Health," *Social Work*, vol. 12, no. 3, July 1957, pp. 32–39.

FOR FURTHER STUDY

Boston Womens' Book Collective, *Our Bodies Ourselves; A book by and for Women*, Simon and Schuster, New York, 1973.

Neil F. Bracht, *Social Work in Health Care*, Haworth Press, New York, 1978.

Elaine M. Brody, *Long-term Care of Older People*, Human Sciences Press, New York, 1977.

Pauline Cohen, "Family Adaptation to Terminal Illness and the Death of a Parent," *Social Casework*, vol. 58, April 1977, pp. 223–228.

Zelda Foster, "Standards for Hospice Care: Assumptions and Principles," *Health and Social Work*, vol. 4, February 1979, pp. 118–128.

Nina Millett, "Hospice: Challenging Society's Approach to Death," *Health and Social Work*, vol. 4, February 1979, pp. 131–150.

National Association of Social Workers, *Stancards for Hospital Social Services*, Washington, D.C., 1976.

Georgia Travis, *Chronic Illness in Children*, Stanford University Press, Palo Alto, Calif., 1976.

FOR DISCUSSION

1. What have been some of the major problems in health care in the United States?
2. How does life expectancy differ by race?
3. What complaints have been made against conditions in nursing homes?
4. What type of service dominates health care costs?
5. What medical speciality has developed to meet the need for primary health care?
6. How are consumers of health services given a voice in community decision-making?
7. Who pays the largest proportion of the costs of personal health care?
8. Would you choose Blue Cross and Blue Shield or a commercial health insurance company? Why?
9. Contrast the purposes of Medicare and Medicaid.
10. What are HMO's?
11. Explain the need for national health insurance.
12. What are the employment trends in the use of social workers in health settings?
13. What services do social workers provide to patients and their families?
14. Why has social work taken a leading role in death and dying?
15. What are the management tasks of the social worker in the health field?
16. What are the roles of social workers who teach in schools of medicine?

PROJECTS

1. Use the latest *Statistical Abstract of the United States* to give a picture of the costs of health services, the number of health personnel, and other data that you consider important in understanding the health delivery system. Do any of your findings present a different picture from those in the text?
2. Identify the health planning bodies in your community. Make a study of their roles. Attend at least one meeting of each group and report on the discussion. Who was involved? What is your impression of the power structure? Did social workers take any role?
3. Invite one or more directors of social services of local hospitals to talk about the roles of social work and to assess manpower needs. Ask a medical social worker who is not an administrator to make the same assessment. Do their observations differ? If so, how?
4. Interview a representative of Blue Cross-Blue Shield or some other large private health insurance plan. Ask him or her to explain the benefits available, including their relationship to Medicare. What is the attitude expressed toward comprehensive planning for health services?
5. Ask students in your class who have had extensive medical services to discuss the care given, the costs, and the general outcomes of their experience. What role did medical social workers play? Were the social workers effective? What improvements can be suggested? Was the experience of students who had acute illness different from those who are disabled?
6. Report on the current status of National Health Insurance proposals in Congress.

CHAPTER 11
Mental Health

Mental health became a presidential concern.

Professionals should move beyond their traditional commitment to help people help themselves and become personally involved with their clients' causes and concerns. This can best be done by learning how to remove the barriers to authentic human interaction that often exist between the helper and the helped.

—Anthony J. Vattano*

Mental illness is a major concern to individuals under stress and to society as well. This chapter will review the current situation, using the report of the President's Commission on Mental Health. It will trace trends, from institutionalization to community-based mental health services to self-help groups and finally to an aggressive policy of deinstitutionalization. Three revolutions in attitudes toward patient care and service have characterized the mental health movement. Some of the new trends will be identified, as well as policy issues that remain unresolved. Finally, social work roles will be discussed.

EMOTIONAL PROBLEMS IN PERSPECTIVE

President Jimmy Carter established a Presidential Commission on Mental Health charged with assessing the current mental health needs of the nation. Twenty commissioners and 450 people served on thirty-two task panels. The commission found that at any one time, approximately 15 percent of the population is in need of some type of mental health service. In a given period, up to 25 percent of the population may suffer from anxiety, depression, and other symptoms of emotional disorder.[1] In addition, most people in our society encounter serious emotional difficulties at some time in their lives. For example, some individuals are caught up in personal or interpersonal conflicts or cannot cope with the effects of environmental stress. Others are victims of racial or sexual discrimination which impairs identity and self-esteem. Still others suffer from addictions or from serious distortions in their relationship to reality. Such problems require professional mental health personnel. Social workers with undergraduate or graduate training constitute approximately one-half of that labor force. Before assessing our current mental health services, we need to know how the services developed.

THREE REVOLUTIONS IN MENTAL HEALTH

Three revolutions have involved different views of the mentally ill and their treatment. In earliest times individuals with behavior disorders were consid-

*Anthony J. Vattano, "Power to the People: Self-Help Groups," *Social Work*, vol. 17, July 1972, p. 15.

ered to be possessed by the devil. The accepted treatment in many parts of the world was to isolate and punish those who were "possessed." The first revolution was typified by the "striking off of the chains" of the patients at the Bicòtre Hospital for the Insane in Paris in 1793 by its director, Philippe Pinel—a symbol of a new period of humane treatment for the mentally ill.

From Moral Treatment to Institutionalization in Large Facilities

The humanistic concerns of Pinel and workers in other countries led to the era of "moral treatment" and the substitution of an accepting human relationship for punishment in treating behavior disorders. The major characteristic of moral treatment was the creation of a total therapeutic environment where patients received hope, guidance, and support. The staff viewed patients as having problems in living, treated them with acceptance and respect, and provided good examples. Improved social functioning was expected and reinforced. This emphasis was the forerunner of the modern-day "therapeutic community." Most institutions were relatively small, chronic patients were rare, and the staff came to know the patients and their families quite well. Moral treatment flourished in Europe and the United States for sixty years, until about 1855, prior to the large migration of immigrants from central and southern Europe to the United States. Thus, the staff and patients shared a common language and culture that enhanced their communication and interpersonal relationships, leading to a relatively high "cure" rate.[2]

Not all the mentally ill obtained the benefits of moral treatment. The thousands of emotionally disturbed people who were kept in jails and almshouses under deplorable conditions became the object of reform for Dorothea Dix,[3] a crusader who was remarkably successful in convincing state legislatures to expand existing hospitals for the mentally ill and build new ones. She made periodic inspection tours of the hospitals and was influential in appointing their directors. Her efforts resulted in the transfer of most emotionally disturbed people from jails and almshouses to the new hospitals by the 1880s. Unfortunately, the effectiveness of treatment was diminished by the combination of large institutions, an influx of many chronically ill patients, and immigrants whose ability to speak English was limited. The atmosphere changed from hope and enthusiasm to concern about management and routine. Along with the change, moral treatment gave way to a new emphasis on medical diagnosis and treatment. As recovery rates decreased, mental illness was seen as an organic disease with an unknown origin and poor prognosis. Since that time, state hospitals have generally served a custodial rather than a treatment function.

The chronically mentally ill, the aged, and the poor who are unable to afford other resources were sent to state mental hospitals as a last resort. Unfortunately, the "treatment" in many of these hospitals was often inadequate due to overcrowding and insufficient numbers of trained personnel. Some people went to state hospitals to avoid problems in community living, only to encounter equally stressful conditions. On the other hand, Paul and Lentz report that institutional programs can facilitate the return of chronically ill patients to the community.[4]

Individual Treatment Based on Freudian Theory

The second revolution in mental health began in 1893, when Sigmund Freud evolved the technique of free association to enable people to speak freely about their troubled feelings. He analyzed the verbalizations of patients and constructed a theory of *psychoanalysis* and a method of treatment. His experiences led him to hypothesize the existence of psychic energy and tensions related to inborn biological drives. Freud proposed a psychosexual view of human development emphasizing oral, anal, phallic, latent, and genital states. He viewed neurosis as the symptom of a struggle between the instinctual demands of the *id* and the learned prohibitions of the conscience or *superego*. In this struggle, the mediator of the mind, called *ego*, employs a variety of energy-depleting defenses. These defenses consist of exaggerated forms of behavior which appear as the symptoms of neurosis. Phobias, for example, are displaced fears which result in unrealistic efforts to avoid the feared object. Freud concluded that much of our behavior is due to the workings of the unconscious. He devised a systematic method for analyzing unconscious mental conflicts and employed this method to help patients achieve awareness of how early life experiences determined their current behavior.[5]

Since Freud was trained in medicine, his theory of behavior followed the medical model of diagnosis and treatment of underlying causes. Nevertheless, Freud believed that psychoanalysis should not be restricted to the profession of medicine. As a result, many European followers of Freud were nonmedical analysts. In the United States, the professions of psychology and social work embraced many of Freud's ideas and integrated them into their practice beginning in the 1930s. Today some people consider that to be a mistake, because social workers concentrated on their clients' intrapsychic conflicts rather than on the need for social and institutional change. However, because social work must deal with both personal and public concerns, the profession was influenced by the psychoanalytic theory of human functioning and treatment, which went far beyond the previous limited state of knowledge.[6]

Psychodynamic approaches assume that the behavioral symptoms of mental illness can best be treated by determining and dealing with their causes—causes presumed to be rooted in unresolved past experiences of which the patient is often unaware. A major goal of diagnosis is to identify and understand the meaning of the patient's conflicts and ego defenses. Treatment is aimed at increasing insight into these conflicts and defenses. Insight presumably leads to modification of attitude, which is seen as a necessary condition for behavior change. Problematic behavior is thus thought to be a symptom of underlying emotional difficulties. Therefore, changing behavior without dealing with its causes may produce a new set of symptoms.

Although Freud died in 1939, his ideas still enjoy considerable accept-

"I'm *terribly* sorry, Mrs. Crumett, but all at once I've had it up to here with psychiatry."
(Drawing by Weber; © 1978 The New Yorker Magazine, Inc.)

been criticized by client groups and by organizations of "radical therapists" who propose social action to bring about necessary changes.[12]

The recommendations of the President's Commission on Mental Health were focused on providing a more responsive service system for the chronically ill and for those who are most in need. Three population groups require special attention: (1) the *underserved,* including racial and ethnic minorities, children, adolescents, and the elderly; (2) the *unserved* in rural areas, small towns, and poor urban communities; and (3) the *inappropriately served*—people with different cultural values or life-styles.

The commission called for federal support in three new directions: (1) a grant program for community-based services beyond those provided by community mental health centers; (2) a major effort at preventing mental illness; (3) increased use of community support systems, such as families, churches, schools, and volunteer organizations. Continued phasing down and closing of large state hospitals, more systematic research on mental health problems, and correction of the geographic maldistribution of mental health personnel were highlighted.[13]

VIEWS OF MENTAL ILLNESS AND MENTAL HEALTH

Psychiatry has been charged with primary responsibility for defining mental illness and for designing and delivering mental health services. Its traditional "medical model" views serious emotional problems as manifestations of mental illness caused by brain dysfunction or "intrapsychic" conflicts. The assumption of underlying internal causes has been extended to less serious emotional problems in living, such as marital and parent-child maladjustments. However, in recent years, authorities have questioned the concept of mental illness.[14]

They suggest that the medical model be reserved for behavior disorders which demonstrate direct pathology of the brain. This newer view of emotional problems brings them closer to the psychosocial orientation of social work. Indeed, the subspecialties of community psychiatry and psychology increasingly emphasize social work's traditional concern with the mental health aspects of social and environmental problems, the importance of the family and community, and the delivery of services to minorities and other disadvantaged members of society.

Paradoxically, the nonmedical approach to mental health has accompanied new discoveries about the genetic and biological bases of certain behavior disorders. Since current literature and practice still make use of the terms "mental illness" and "mental patient," they will be retained here. Nonetheless, the orientation in this chapter is psychosocial rather than medical.

The terms "mental illness" and "mental health" are both poorly defined. Freud proposed that the mentally healthy person is one who is capable of working and loving. Not everyone would consider these characteristics sufficient indicators of sound mental health. For example, anthropologists have documented the wide variety of behaviors considered normal or abnormal among different societies of the world. Moreover, our recent cultural and sexual revolutions have produced increasing recognition of the effect of diverse life-styles on fundamental aspects of behavior and standards of normality. These events contrast sharply with an earlier period when nonacceptance of individual and cultural diversity involved a commitment to rigid sex roles and a melting pot ideology. Today we accept the options of a pluralistic society. However, we still limit behaviors considered inappropriate. For example, while it is acceptable to pray to God, it is not "normal" to act as if God were talking to us.

From one perspective, mental health is the ability to be personally and socially effective within a particular society. Effectiveness is revealed by one's performance in carrying out significant life-roles in the family, school, employment, and the community. On the other hand, the problems of mental illness are manifested in maladaptive behavior which impedes role performances, necessitating the intervention of a mental health speciality. So-called psychotic behavior, which demonstrates poor contact with reality, is the hallmark of mental illness. This includes *hallucinations* (perceiving stimuli in the absence of objective reality) and *delusions* (maintaining false beliefs in the absence of fact).

Researchers supported by the National Institute of Mental Health and other agencies are attempting to assess the incidence and prevalence of behavior disorders in society. However, the absence of precise criteria makes this task difficult. Despite widespread use of psychological tests, social histories, and clinical assessments, there is little professional agreement on any but the grossest deviant behavior.

A dramatic illustration of problems which occur in the assessment of abnormal behavior was provided by psychologist David Rosenhan. He discovered that the professional staff in psychiatric hospitals could not distinguish sane people from insane patients.[15] Rosenhan and seven "normal" associates walked into twelve psychiatric hospitals in five different states on the East and West Coasts. All eight were admitted to the hospital by feigning the same symptom of hearing voices. After admission, the pseudopatients reverted to their normal behavior. The psychiatric staff was unable to distinguish the pseudopatients' sane behavior from that of the "insane" patients. Rosenhan and his associates remained hospitalized for periods ranging from seven to fifty-two days, with an average of nineteen days. All of the pseudopatients were discharged with a diagnosis of "schizophrenia in remission."

Since very few state hospitals have such programs, there is growing concern about the nontherapeutic conditions disadvantaged people experience in these institutions. As a consequence, many state hospitals are being closed. Social workers and other professionals are actively involved in attempting to prevent mental disorders and to provide community-based services to all elements of the population.

VIEWS OF BEHAVIOR DISORDERS

What are the major approaches employed in current practice? Mental illness is most often caused by the interaction of genetically determined predispositions and environmental or experimental factors. Mowrer has conceptualized a fourfold approach to mental illness based on heredity, social processes, reeducation, and existential factors. His approach has been instrumental in promoting interdisciplinary cooperation and the team concept in treating the mentally ill.[16]

Heredity

Heredity plays a part in mental illness. Research has repeatedly shown higher percentages of schizophrenia and manic-depressive disorders in monozygotic (identical) twins over dizygotic (fraternal) twins. Carefully designed studies in Europe and the United States over the past twenty-five years have led to the conclusion that complex genetic factors are instrumental in transmitting the potential for both of these disorders.[17]

Research since 1961 has reported that inmates of penal and mental institutions have a higher prevalence of an extra Y, or male-determining, chromosome than persons in the general population.[18] The next few years may provide additional data to clarify the effects of heredity and chromosomal abnormality on deviant behavior.

Biochemistry

Drugs can influence behavior. Interest in the use of medication to treat behavior problems was dramatically awakened in 1954 with the introduction of the tranquilizers chlorpromazine and reserpine. These drugs initiated a new era of drug therapy because of their dramatic ability to ameliorate excited behavior without marked impairment of motor function or consciousness. The increasing use of tranquilizers and other drugs made it possible to calm large numbers of disturbed patients so they may function more adequately. The marked decrease in the number of resident patients in state hospitals, from a peak figure of 555,000 in 1955 to 191,000 in 1975,[19] was due largely to the employment of psychotropic drugs.

Antipsychotic drugs are especially useful in treating schizophrenia. The antidepressant drugs have been less impressive. Antianxiety drugs have been used alone and in conjunction with other forms of treatment to modify incapacitating tension.

People in our society commonly make extensive use of prescription and over-the-counter drugs. Unfortunately, drug use often leads to drug abuse. For example, many people use alcohol occasionally and in moderation, with few adverse side-effects. However, the 10 to 12 percent of drinkers who become addicted to alcohol suffer extensive physical, mental, and social harm. Likewise, while minor tranquilizers, such as Valium, Librium, and Equanil, are widely used and accepted as valuable therapeutic agents, many people have developed physical and psychological dependence on these drugs. Most general practitioners prescribe tranquilizers for the large number of patients who complain of emotional upset. "Popping pills" has become fashionable in American society. Therefore, it is difficult to obtain accurate data on the growing number of people who depend on such drugs to cope with their usual problems of living.

Unsupervised use of drugs to alter perceptions of life experiences is less easily managed. The increasing use of "recreational" drugs provides an illustration of cultural changes that affect the definition of acceptable behavior. The growing problem of drug abuse through the use of tranquilizers, hallucinogens, barbiturates, amphetamines, sedatives, and opiates is the consequence of the biochemical advances of the past few years. The general availability and acceptance of mind-altering substances has led people of all ages and social classes to experiment with a variety of drugs. As a consequence, the use of some previously illegal, controlled substances is gradually being decriminalized.

Social Processes

Over the past twenty-five years, the importance of social and environmental events in the cause and treatment of mental illness has been increasingly recognized. Accumulating evidence about the damaging effects of racial and sexual discrimination, urban blight, and advancing technology helped shift the emphasis from intrapsychic to psychosocial causes of stress. The cultural and civil rights revolutions in American society gave added emphasis to the importance of social and environmental factors in determining emotional problems.

The investigation of poor communication patterns in disorganized and disadvantaged families and in the families of schizophrenic patients was stimulated by the hypothesis that the developing infant who is repeatedly exposed to contradictory messages about love and acceptance from a rejecting mother has more difficulty in accurately discriminating the message it receives.[20] Perceptions and concepts of self and the world become distorted, thus forming the potential nucleus for eventual schizophrenia. This hypothesis has influenced family therapy even though research evidence for its support is lacking. Researchers continue to explore the importance of family relationships in producing a variety of emotional problems.[21]

In the 1960s, a new line of investigation highlighted the antitherapeutic effects of labeling and hospitalizing the mentally ill. Irving Goffman,[22] Thomas Scheff,[23] and other sociologists made use of symbolic interaction theory to analyze the initiation and maintenance of the mental patient's career. The symbolic interactionists emphasize that one's self-perception is influenced by the definitions of others. The imprecise concepts of mental health and illness result in a subjective designation of certain less common behaviors as deviant. Once people demonstrate these behaviors, they are labeled mentally ill, given the status of mental patients, and hospitalized. They react to the dehumanizing environment of the hospital, and their behavior then confirms the negative expectations of others. People respond to them accordingly and reinforce their deviant behavior.

The concepts of social and family interaction, deviancy, and labeling have made a significant contribution to our understanding of mental illness. However, they do not account sufficiently for the effect of the mental patients' own behavior on the way others treat them.

Existential Factors

The experience of existence is an important dimension of mental health and illness. No matter how much guidance or support we receive from others, each person must take ultimate responsibility for the way he or she lives and dies. The existential approach to treatment, through individual counseling or group psychotherapy, focuses on human values, purpose, responsibility, will, and courage in the face of adversity.[24]

Reeducation

Reeducation employs a human relationship and psychological methods and techniques to bring about more effective and satisfying behavior. People function and interact with one another by thinking, feeling, and acting, but many psychological approaches to human functioning and behavior disorders typically emphasize one of these components rather than their integration. The best-known approaches are derived from psychoanalytic theory, learning theory, and techniques for enhancing personal growth and consciousness.

The early learning theory approaches of Ivan Pavlov and American psychologists like E. L. Thorndike and John B. Watson in the 1920s and 1930s were not initially seen as having broad human applications. However, systematic research by B. F. Skinner and other behaviorists during the past forty years has demonstrated the powerful effect of social learning in modifying all sorts of maladaptive behavior. This has been particularly evident in work with the severly retarded and the mentally ill. Applications of the research on learning have resulted in the technology of behavior modification, which now provides a major alternative to psychoanalytic methods.

Behaviorists avoid "mentalistic" concepts, and emphasize the connection between an environmental stimulus and a behavioral response. In many respects, this orientation is more congruent with the psychosocial commitment of social work than is psychoanalytic theory, with its emphasis on underlying causes of behavior. Behaviorists distinguish no qualitative difference between normal and abnormal behavior, since all behavior is learned.

Learning can take place in three ways. First, according to classical Pavlovian respondent conditioning, a stimulus precedes and elicits a response. A classic example of conditioning was described by Watson and Rayner in 1920.[25] They determined that an eleven-month-old child named Albert was not afraid of a white rat. They knew that children his age were frightened by loud noises. The white rat (a neutral stimulus) was given to Albert, followed immediately by a loud noise (unconditioned stimulus). After this sequence was repeated several times, the rat without the noise became a conditioned stimulus and elicited a fear response from Albert. This type of learning occurs in many common experiences. For example, an accident may elicit fear of riding in automobiles.

Second, in Skinnerian instrumental, or operant, conditioning, the situation is reversed. Here a person first responds to a situation, then an environmental event happens which is contingent upon the behavior. If an event following some behavior increases the rate at which the behavior is emitted, it is called a reinforcer. A child has a temper tantrum and its mother gives the child attention. The child then engages in frequent tantrums. Behaviors that are reinforced are likely to increase in frequency. Thus, the mother unwittingly reinforces tantrums by her attention.

Third, observational or vicarious learning, or modeling, occurs when a person learns behavior from merely watching a model. Albert Bandura and other researchers have demonstrated how children may learn aggressive responses from observing films of adults hitting and kicking a large doll. There has been growing concern about the exposure of children to models of aggression on television. On the other hand, modeling is being used therapeutically to help children and adults learn a variety of prosocial behaviors, such as speech, interpersonal relations, and social skills.[26]

From such research-based concepts, behavior-change techniques have evolved that focus on increasing desired behavior or decreasing unwanted behavior. The wide variety of strategies include various kinds of reinforcement, systematic desensitization, and assertiveness training. For more than fifteen years, behavior modification has been employed to help people with a variety of problems, ranging from socializing an autistic child to quieting a classroom of unruly adolescents. "Token economies" have been established in institutions for the mentally ill, delinquents, and the retarded where prosocial behaviors are used to earn tokens which can be exchanged for material rewards. The primary reinforcers are gradually phased out, and residents are taught to modify their behavior in response to verbal praise and attention. The efficacy of behavior-modification techniques is demonstrated by single-case experimental designs which compare client behavior before and after treatment.[27]

Nonbehaviorists are particularly concerned about the amount of control the behavior modifier may exert over people. However, research indicates that more traditionally oriented therapists also shape the verbalizations and behavior of their clients. Moreover, rather than exert unilateral control, most behaviorists employ specific goal-oriented contracts; while behaviorists are primarily interested in observable stimuli and responses, some have recently been exploring the "inner world" of private events, cognitive processes, and self-control.[28] Social workers increasingly employ behavior modification techniques with individuals, families, and groups in the home, community, and institutions. Despite continued debate between psychodynamic therapists and behaviorists, carefully designed research indicates that both are equally capable of helping troubled people.[29]

OTHER APPROACHES TO MENTAL HEALTH INTERVENTION

Concern with the feeling aspects of behavior is not new. Psychoanalytically oriented therapists and behavior modifiers certainly take feelings into account. However, fostering human awareness and interpersonal encounter as a response to the alienation experienced by large numbers of Americans has also become a major goal. A means to perceive oneself and communicate on an authentic feeling level is considered essential to help people achieve self-actualization and an interpersonal competence. The theoretical methods and techniques for accomplishing this goal are varied. They range from the gestalt therapy of the late Fritz Perls[30] to the encounter groups of Carl Rogers[31] and the varied programs of the Esalen Institute. Also important are such new procedures as biofeedback, EST, Arica, meditation, bio-energetics, and psychosynthesis, to name a few. They all share the goal of plumbing the senses and emotions to achieve greater awareness.

Increasing human consciousness and interpersonal communication is often achieved through group interaction. A leader or facilitator teaches group members how to modify their behavior by experimenting with a variety of sensory experiences. Feedback is provided through unrestrained dialogue, games, touching, and marathon sessions. Group members achieve a new depth of self-understanding and intimate communication with others.[32]

Encounter and awareness groups are for ostensibly "normal" people who wish to develop their human potential. The emphasis is on training rather than treatment. However, people with serious emotional problems find their way into such groups—occasionally at some peril to themselves. While most groups are led by professionals, such as psychiatrists, psychologists, and social workers, untrained leaders also operate groups. The American Psychiatric Association, the American Psychological Association, and the National Association of Social Workers are concerned about the absence of standards for leaders or facilitators.

Continued research is needed on the effects of such experiences. A detailed study of encounter groups shows that people can learn how to experience many deep feelings and relationships in these groups. However, evidence indicates that such experiences may not produce lasting changes. Despite these findings, techniques from the human potential movement have contributed much to our understanding of the importance of feelings and emotions. Many of the techniques from this movement have been incorporated in the treatment approaches to people with serious emotional problems. As further research becomes available, we should learn more about the interrelationship of thinking, feeling, and behavior.

Mowrer's integrity groups, for example, are a support system designed to help people deal with the growing problems of personal alienation, isolation, loneliness, and the generalized lack of community in our society.[33] Problems are presumed to be associated with the significant changes that have occurred in the previously stable institutions of the family, the church, the school, and the neighborhood. Group members are helped to overcome their identity crisis by learning how to grow in honesty, responsibility, and involvement, thereby developing personal autonomy and a sense of community with others.

The newer approaches often utilize earlier conceptualizations. In transactional analysis, understanding of superego, ego, and id is replaced by analysis of one's parent, adult, and child "ego states." The goal of treatment is not to develop ego strength, but to accelerate the appropriate operation of the adult state in transactions with others.[34] In gestalt therapy, the therapist encourages self-expression, fantasy, and dream reporting to help the client discover and resolve underlying conflicts.[35] The therapist in rational-emotive therapy helps clients achieve insight into their irrational, self-defeating attitudes in order to facilitate more realistic ways of thinking and behaving.[36]

Self-Help Groups
Some people do not depend on professional leadership for help with such emotionally upsetting problems as alcoholism, drug addiction, alienation, mental and physical illness, obesity, child abuse, and impairment of sexual or personal consciousness. Instead, they turn to self-help or mutual aid groups operated by people who have experienced the problem. They employ self-disclosure, confrontation, and support—all aimed at behavioral change. Social workers refer clients to self-help groups and maintain liaison with them. To do so, they must recognize the mistrust some self-help groups have for professionals. Trust can be generated if professionals are willing to engage in self-disclosure, confrontation, and support. After winning group acceptance, professionals may be permitted to initiate and facilitate group interaction, do research on the group's helping procedures, and provide ideas for further

development of the self-help group. Such groups augment professional mental health services by providing important community-based support systems.[37] The best-known and perhaps most successful self-help group is Alcoholics Anonymous. Its program has been described:

> In Alcoholics Anonymous (AA), there is a recognized acknowledgment of the individual's responsibility for behavioral change and faith in the group's power to help accomplish this goal. Although AA recognizes the external or environmental events or circumstances that contribute to an individual's problem or need, it emphasizes his responsibility to change his own behavior and deal with situations himself. This orientation was the basis on which AA was created in 1935 by two chronic alcoholics. AA was perhaps the first of modern-day clinical self-help groups. Its emphasis on individual and group responsibility and a structured value system served as a model for many of the later approaches to other problem behaviors. The Twelve Steps of AA, which provide a philosophy and guidelines for behavior, maintain that although the individual is powerless over alcohol, he can overcome his problem through self-appraisal, disclosure, and responsible behavioral change. Through regular group meetings and individual helping activities, members assist and encourage each other by mutually supporting nondrinking behavior. Much of AA's success derives from the notion that one can help himself by helping others who have the same problem.[38]

LEGAL CONSIDERATIONS AND CIVIL RIGHTS

In 1964 Congress established a statutory right to treatment in the Hospitalization of the Mentally Ill Act. However, despite the progress made in understanding and treating mental illness, our laws still permit the involuntary curtailment of a patient's liberty. Infringement of civil rights for the mental patient usually occurs in relation to enforced hospitalization. While state laws differ, in many jurisdictions people may be hospitalized for many years without due process. They may be sent to a mental hospital for "treatment" on the statement of a physician. However, they often receive no adequate treatment even after several years of confinement.

A particular irony is seen in comparing the staff and patient populations in today's state hospitals. One of the reasons for the decline of moral treatment was the breakdown in communication between American psychiatrists and an increasing population of immigrants with different cultures and languages. Today, most of the patients in state hospitals are American-born. However, in many instances their "treatment" is provided by a "psychiatrist" who may be a foreign-trained physician and a recent immigrant to this country.

Decisions about treatments such as electroconvulsive therapy pose a real dilemma for the seriously disturbed, who are often unable to make rational choices for their own welfare. In such instances, the permission of relatives is obtained. Nonetheless, this still denies patients their fundamental rights.

Enforced hospitalization and treatment are often imposed on elderly people who might be more appropriately cared for outside of state hospitals.

These problems caused the President's Commission on Mental Health to focus attention on the need for due process for all of our citizens, irrespective of their behavior.[39] Recent federal court decisions have reflected this concern. They have held that mental illness alone is not a sufficient basis for denying liberty, and hospitalized mental patients have a right either to adequate treatment or to release.[40]

Major Issues in Mental Health

From the preceding discussion, it becomes apparent that the medical model is a major issue in mental health. Dependence on this model often makes it necessary for a social worker to be nominally supervised by a psychiatrist—especially if the social services are to be paid for by health insurance. Social workers feel that they should be considered capable of providing mental health services without any certification from a physician. The medical model acts as a major restraint on social workers in private practice who serve many patients who are covered by private insurance plans.

The use of drugs is a matter for controversy because of the drug dependence that may result.

One of the most serious questions concerns the movement of people with serious emotional problems into nonspecialized community facilities—either foster homes or "independent" living. The following letter indicates some of the problems:

> Dear Phil:
>
> I couldn't sleep Friday night.
> I believe you too were deeply affected by the visit to so-called foster homes.
> The list of deficiencies is long—no one of responsibility present—no fire evacuation procedure or drills—untrained sponsors—no medical, dietary, social services, etc.
> There was stench. There was the man who could only remember his name yet had bottles of Stelazine [a tranquilizer] and Dilantin [for epilepsy] in his own keeping. There were forlorn patients who answered the doors.
> This is not outplacement care. It is no care.[41]

SOCIAL WORK ROLES IN MENTAL HEALTH

Social workers began obtaining social histories from relatives of patients newly admitted to Manhattan State Hospital in 1906. Since then, social workers in mental health settings have provided a variety of preventive, diagnostic, and treatment services. For example, social workers were instrumental in originating foster home care for discharged mental patients. They continue to furnish the major supervision in these programs. In the 1920s, social workers first became an integral part of the mental health team with psychiatrists and psychologists in the child guidance clinics established by the Commonwealth Fund. The psychiatrist coordinated the services and treated emotionally disturbed children. The psychologist provided projective and intelligence tests. The social worker interviewed the child's mother to obtain a social history. The social worker also dealt with the family's social situation and helped the mother modify her behavior in relation to the child.

Over the years, the treatment emphasis has moved from the individual to the total family unit. Psychiatrists, psychologists, and social workers now function interchangeably as individual, family, and group therapists. They also share responsibility for designing and administering mental health programs. The experienced clinical social worker operates both autonomously and in collaboration with the other mental health personnel. The resulting role diffusion in the psychiatric team has been accentuated in recent years with the addition of nurses and other professionals as well as nonprofessionals. Social workers are equipped by training and experience with particular knowledge about family relationships and community resources. Thus, social workers continue to provide specific services related to these important dimensions of the mental patient's life.

Since one-half of the people who provide mental health services in the United States today are social workers, the future of clinical social work looks promising as education and practice continue to keep pace with changing client needs and new developments in helping methods.

Many social agencies and institutions, including schools, courts, public welfare offices, hospitals and clinics, and the military deal with emotional stress. Social workers are employed in these agencies because of their ability to handle a wide range of psychosocial problems.

Comprehensive community mental health centers provide a broad package of preventive and treatment services for an increasing number of Americans. These centers employ both professional and nonprofessional workers.

Emotional difficulties that seriously interfere with an adult's or child's functioning are usually treated by psychiatrists, psychologists, social workers, and other personnel in community mental health clinics or psychiatric hospitals. These agencies provide individual and group psychotherapy, behavior modification, pharmacotherapy, and many other intervention strategies. Less serious emotional concerns, such as reactions to interpersonal and environmental stress, are dealt with through individual counseling and family therapy in family service agencies. However, this division of responsibility does not always apply. A study by the Illinois Department of Mental Health and the Family Service Association of America demonstrated overlap in the kinds of problems treated and the services provided by mental health clinics and family service agencies.[42]

Psychiatrists and psychologists furnish individual, family, and group therapy for a variety of emotional problems. An increasing number of clinical social workers in full- or part-time private practice also provide similar services. Since private practitioners usually charge relatively high fees, they do not treat many poor people. However, the payments from public and private insurance plans reimburse social workers for providing clinical services on a private basis. As a consequence, private practitioners are becoming involved with a broader cross-section of the population.

The National Association of Social Workers has been actively involved in promoting state registration and licensing requirements to ensure that practitioners meet high standards of competence. The association has established a national Registry of Clinical Social Workers. Requirements for membership are:

> A master's or doctoral degree in social work from a graduate school of social work accredited or recognized by the Council on Social Work Education; two years or 3,000 hours of post-master's clinical social work practice under the supervision of a master's degree level social worker, or, if social work supervision could be shown to have been unavailable, supervision by another mental health professional with the added condition of giving evidence of continued participation and identification with the social work profession; at least two years or 3,000 hours of direct clinical practice within the last ten years; be a member of the Academy of Certified Social Workers (ACSW) or be licensed in a State at a level at least equivalent to ACSW standards. The clinical social worker has specialized knowledge of human growth and behavior and of internal, interpersonal and environmental stress on social functioning. This knowledge must be combined with practice skills in treatment modalities which alleviate such problems.[43]

As we have seen, many emotional problems are unrelated to organic dysfunction. Help for people with any of these disorders is oriented to the psychosocial well-being of the patient and the patient's family. Marital and family problems are probably treated more often by social workers than by any other professional group. Job finding, job adjustment, and financial provision for the unemployed are also social work concerns.

The social worker's efforts are usually directed toward mobilizing the motivation and capacity of the patient and the family and the resources in the community. A systematic assessment of the patient and his or her situation is followed by the skillful employment of a variety of intervention techniques. These range from reinforcement of self-control activities by the patient to serving as the patient's advocate with community agencies and society at large. The nature and severity of the patient's problems will determine the specific treatment. The overall social work goal is to enable the patient to achieve and maintain the highest possible level of psychosocial functioning within the family and the community.

Employment Opportunities

Until a few years ago, social work in the mental health field was practiced in relation to psychiatry, but since the problems of mental health are problems in living, they transcend the boundaries of traditional psychiatry. The social worker interested in this field now has a broader opportunity for service.

Numerous employment possibilities are found in hospital and clinical settings, particularly in large urban areas. Outside of state hospitals, this type of practice is usually centered in programs for verbal upper- and middle-class children and adults.

The social worker will usually be able to provide individual, group, and family therapy. Treatment approaches differ among agencies. Most employ a psychodynamic approach or behavior modification in combination with a variety of methods, such as transactional analysis, rational-emotive therapy, gestalt, and reality therapy.

The community-based programs, under the ill-defined mantle of comprehensive community mental health services, are often more challenging. The emphasis is on providing services to a more heterogeneous population, including the underprivileged, the retarded, the chronically mentally ill, and the aged. The commitment to continuity of care enables the social worker to provide in-patient and out-patient services, partial hospitalization, emergency consultation and education, prevention, and aftercare. Also available are hotline services, runaway shelters, and drop-in services for youth. The mental health team in these settings is made up of many different professionals and nonprofessionals. Treatment methods are more varied and eclectic than in traditional settings, with less emphasis on psychodynamic concerns, and greater concern with the social antecedents and consequences of observable behavior.

SUMMARY AND APPLICATION

The social worker in the mental health field today is operating from the standpoint of both yesterday and tomorrow. The concepts and terminology of yesterday's medical model are being transformed by new discoveries about learning, human awareness, small groups, and psychosocial forces that will emphasize education and prevention. Everyone needs to learn more about the mental health consequences of life circumstances and behavior and the way in which social forces affect emotional well-being. Social workers have an important role to play in helping people cope with the emotional problems of living.

—Anthony J. Vattano

KEY TERMS

mental health	community mental health center
mental illness	self-help groups
psychoanalytic theory	respondent conditioning
behavior modification	neuroses
social processes	psychoses
symbolic interaction	personality disorders

REFERENCES AND NOTES

1. *The President's Commission on Mental Health*, vol. 1, Government Printing Office, Washington, D.C., 1978, p. 8.
2. J. S. Bockhoven, *Moral Treatment in American Psychiatry*, Springer, New York, 1963.
3. Helen E. Marshall, *Dorothea Dix: Forgotten Samaritan*, University of North Carolina Press, Chapel Hill, 1937; Francis Tiffany, *Life of Dorothea Lynde Dix*, Houghton Mifflin, Boston, 1892.
4. Irving Goffman, *Asylums*, Anchor Books, Garden City, N.Y., 1961, p. xiii.; Gordon L. Paul and A. S. Lentz, *Psychological Treatment of Chronically Institutionalized Patients*, Harvard University Press, Cambridge, Mass., 1977.
5. Calvin Hall and Gardner Lindzey, *Theories of Personality*, Wiley, New York, 1970.
6. Merlin Taber and Anthony Vattano, "Clinical and Social Organizations in Social Work: An Empirical Study," *Social Service Review*, vol. 44, March 1970, p. 35.
7. Patrick Mullahy, *Psychoanalysis and Interpersonal Psychiatry: The Contributions of Harry Stack Sullivan*, Science House, New York, 1970.
8. *Directory: Federally Funded Community Mental Health Centers*, National Institute of Mental Health, Rockville, Md., 1975, p. 1.
9. Franklin D. Chu and Sharland Trotter, *The Madness Establishment*, Grossman, New York, 1974.
10. "Special Report: Schizophrenia, 1976," *Schizophrenia Bulletin*, vol. 2, no. 4, 1976, pp. 44–45.
11. Chu and Trotter, op. cit.
12. Paul Lowinger et al., "Radical Psychiatry," *International Journal of Psychiatry*, vol. 9, 1970–71.
13. *The President's Commission on Mental Health*, vol. 1.
14. Thomas Szasz, *The Manufacture of Madness*, Harper & Row, New York, 1970. Also see Thomas Scheff, *Being Mentally Ill*, Aldine, Chicago, 1966.
15. D. L. Rosenhan, "On Being Sane in Insane Places," *Science*, vol. 179, 1973, pp. 250–257.
16. Hobart Mowrer, "Integrity Groups: Basic Principles and Objectives," *The Counseling Psychologist*, vol. 3, No. 2, 1972, p. 25.
17. David Reiss, "Competing Hypotheses and Warring Factions: Applying Knowledge of Schizophrenia," *Schizophrenia Bulletin*, vol. 8, Spring 1974, pp. 7–10; also see D. Rosenthal, *Genetics of Psychopathology*, McGraw-Hill, New York, 1971.
18. National Institute of Mental Health Center for Prevention of Crime and Delinquency, *Report on the XYY Chromosomal Abnormality*, Government Printing Office, Washington, D.C., 1970; also see B. J. Culliton, "Harvard Researcher Under Fire Stops New Born Screening," *Science*, vol. 188, 1975, pp. 1284–1285.
19. U.S. Bureau of the Census, *Statistical Abstract of the United States, 1957*, p. 79; also see *Statistical Abstract, 1977*, p. 109.
20. Gregory Bateson et al., "Toward a Theory of Schizophrenia," *Behavioral Science*, vol. 1, 1956, pp. 251–264.
21. Salvador Minuchin, *Families and Family Therapy*, Harvard, Cambridge, 1974.
22. Goffman, op. cit.
23. Scheff, op. cit.
24. Irvin Yalom, *The Theory and Practice of Group Psychotherapy*, 2d ed., Basic Books, New York, 1975, pp. 84–91.

25. J. B. Watson and R. Rayner, "Conditional Emotional Reactions," *Journal of Experimental Psychology,* vol. 3, 1920, pp. 1–14.
26. Albert Bandura, "Psychotherapy Based upon Modeling Principles," in A. E. Bergin and S. L. Garfield (eds.), *Handbook of Psychotherapy and Behavior Change,* Wiley, New York, 1971.
27. Michael Herson and David Barlow, *Single-Case Experimental Designs: Strategies for Studying Behavior Change,* Pergamon, New York, 1976.
28. Donald Meichenbaum, *Cognitive Behavior Modification: An Integrative Approach,* Plenum, New York, 1977. Also see Richard Stuart (ed.), *Behavioral Self-Management,* Brunner/Mazel, New York, 1977; Anthony Vattano, "Self-Management Procedures for Coping with Stress," *Social Work,* vol. 23, no. 2, March 1978, pp. 113–118.
29. R. Bruce Sloane et al., *Psychotherapy versus Behavior Therapy,* Harvard, Cambridge, 1975. Also see Paul Wachtel, *Psychoanalysis and Behavior Therapy: Toward an Integration,* Basic Books, New York, 1977.
30. Fritz Perls, *The Gestalt Approach: An Eye Witness to Therapy,* Science and Behavior Books, Ben Lamond, Calif., 1973.
31. Carl Rogers, *Carl Rogers on Encounter Groups,* Harper & Row, New York, 1970.
32. Jane Howard, *Please Touch,* McGraw-Hill, New York, 1970.
33. O. Hobart Mowrer and Anthony Vattano, "Integrity Groups: A Context for Growth in Honesty, Responsibility and Involvement," *Journal of Applied Behavioral Science,* vol. 12, no. 3, 1976, pp. 419–431.
34. M. James and D. Jongeward, *Born to Win: Transactional Analysis with Gestalt Experiments,* Addison-Wesley, Reading, Mass., 1971.
35. J. Fagen and I. Sheppard (eds.), *Gestalt Therapy Now,* Science and Behavior Books, Palo Alto, Calif., 1970.
36. Albert Ellis, "Rational-Emotive therapy," in R. Corsini (ed.), *Current Psychotherapies,* Peacock, Itasca, Ill., 1973.
37. Alan Gartner and Frank Riessman, *Self-Help in the Human Services,* Jossey-Bass, San Francisco, 1977. Also see Anthony J. Vattano, "Power to the People: Self-Help Groups," *Social Work,* vol. 17, July 1972, pp. 7–15; "Special Issue: Self-Help Groups," *Journal of Applied Behavioral Science,* vol. 12, no. 3, 1976.
38. Vattano, "Power to the People," p. 10.
39. *The President's Commission on Mental Health,* vol. 1, Government Printing Office, Washington, D.C., 1978, pp. 69–72.
40. Chu and Trotter, op. cit., p. 40.
41. Ibid.
42. William C. Hill, Joseph B. Lehmann, and Elizabeth Slotkin, *Family Service Agencies and Mental Health Clinics: A Comparative Study,* Family Service Association, New York, 1971.
43. *NASW Register of Clinical Social Workers, Supplement to the First Edition,* National Association of Social Workers, Washington, D.C., 1977, p. x.

FOR FURTHER STUDY

Frank Costin, *Abnormal Psychology,* Learning Systems Co., Irwin, Homewood, Ill., 1976.

Gerald C. Davison and John M. Neale, *Abnormal Psychology: An Experimental Clinical Approach*, Wiley, New York, 1974.

Lawrence C. Kolb, *Modern Clinical Psychiatry*, 8th ed., Saunders, Philadelphia, 1973.

Theodore Millon, *Theories of Psychopathology and Personality*, 2d·ed., Saunders, Philadelphia, 1973.

Stephan P. Spitzer and Norman K. Denzin, *The Mental Patient: Studies in Sociology of Deviance*, McGraw-Hill, New York, 1968.

FOR DISCUSSION

1. Why do mental health centers and family agencies see similar clients?
2. Why has mental health treatment been a medical specialty?
3. Contrast the "melting pot" and pluralistic ideologies.
4. Criticize: "One out of every ten people needs mental health treatment."
5. What are the implications of Rosenhan's findings about the difficulty in identifying psychiatric patients?
6. Why was moral treatment successful?
7. What were the three revolutions in mental health?
8. Identify the components of comprehensive community mental health service.
9. Explain the dramatic decrease in the number of mental hospital patients.
10. What are the shortcomings of the Freudian emphasis in social work?
11. How is conditioning used to alter behavior?
12. What knowledge and skills do social workers bring to the mental health field?
13. How are the mentally ill denied due process of law?
14. What are the employment opportunities for social workers in mental health?

PROJECTS

1. Compare the services of mental health and family agencies in your community. How are they alike and how do they differ?
2. Prepare a report on hospitalization for mental patients in your state since 1950. What trends are shown in admission rates, length of stay, and cost of care?
3. A Long Island community recently passed an ordinance to try to prevent mental patients from living there. What would lead a community to take that action? If you were a mental health professional, how would you respond?
4. Invite representatives from Recovery Incorporated (or a similar program for former mental patients) to discuss programs for self-help. How are social workers involved, if at all?
5. Reserve two class sessions. Ask a social worker from a mental hospital to describe the hospital program in the first meeting, and a worker from a community mental health center to make a similar presentation on the center at the second meeting. Be sure they discuss their professional activities. How do the two programs differ?
6. Debate this topic: "Resolved, that serious emotional problems are best described and treated from a medical viewpoint."
7. Interview the local representative of the state mental health association. How is it funded? How do its activities relate to mental health programs in the community?

CHAPTER 12
Rehabilitation

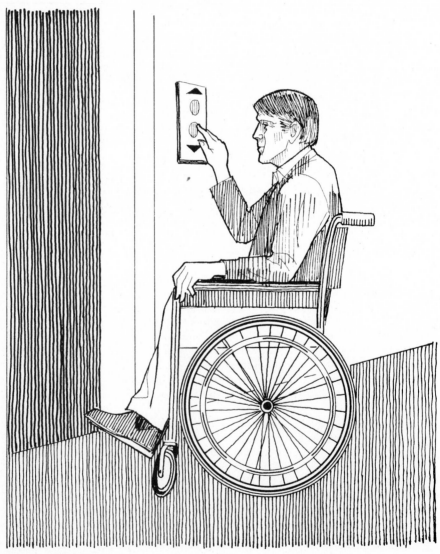

A lift for the handicapped.

Take the most hideous, repulsive, complete physical deformity; place it where it will be most striking—at the lowest, meanest, most despised stage of the social edifice; light up that miserable creature from all sides with the sinister light of contrast; and then throw into him a soul, and put into that soul the purest feeling given to man. . . . The degraded creature will then transform before your eyes. The being that was small will become great; the being that was deformed will become beautiful.

—Victor Hugo*

In the late 1960s and early 1970s, a new minority group began to emerge. Persons with physical disabilities began speaking up, marching forth, sitting in, and filing suits to demand their rights. They were seeking an end to limited educational opportunities, job discrimination, societal discrimination, and architectural barriers. Joining forces, national groups representing the blind, the deaf, the mentally retarded, those with spinal cord injuries, and disabled veterans put pressure on the White House for action. In 1973 Congress passed a section of the Vocational Rehabilitation Act prohibiting discrimination against the handicapped by any program or activity receiving federal funds. Unfortunately, it took four more years of pressure before the Department of Health, Education and Welfare, in June of 1977, passed guidelines for the enforcement of these provisions. The principle of equal rights for the physically handicapped is finally being addressed.

WHO ARE THE DISABLED

The exact number of people in this country with disabilities is not known. Obtaining accurate figures involves both definitional problems and getting access to information. The 1970 census was the first to gather information about disabilities. According to this census 40 million people have disabilities. However, this figure does not include handicapped persons in institutions or persons with heart disease, cancer, diabetes, epilepsy, or a history of emotional illness. In addition, many people responding in the census may have failed to mention their disabilities.

The totals below are provided by the National Arts and the Handicapped Information Service from several sources, including the National Center for Health Statistics.

11.7 million physically disabled (including people in wheelchairs, people who use crutches, canes, braces, or walkers, the mobility-impaired elderly,

*Quoted by Ashley Montagu, *The Elephant Man,* Ballantine Books, New York, 1971, pp. 145–146.

amputees, and people with illnesses such as chronic arthritis, severe cardiovascular disorder, and cerebral palsy)

12.5   *million temporarily injured* (broken limb, injury to back or spine, severe burns)

2.4   *million deaf*

11.0   *million hearing impaired*

1.3   *million blind*

8.2   *million visually impaired*

6.8   *million mentally disabled* (retarded, severely emotionally disturbed, brain damaged, severely learning disabled)

1.7   *million homebound* (chronic health disorders, degenerative diseases like multiple sclerosis)

2.1   *million institutionalized(* mentally disturbed, mentally retarded, terminally ill)

It can be conservatively estimated that there are over 50 million handicapped people in the United States today.

WHERE SOCIAL WORKERS ENCOUNTER THE DISABLED

Social work contact with persons who have physical handicaps occurs in two ways. First, social workers are often employed in settings with the primary function of treating people with physical disabilities. Such settings include general hospitals, rehabilitation hospitals, sheltered workshops, and specialized schools, nursing homes, and agencies designed to service the ill or disabled.

Secondly, social workers in other settings see clients who have physical disabilities but are seeking other services. For example, social workers in a mental health setting may see a couple having marital problems where one of the partners is disabled. Their marital problem may be unrelated to the disability or the disability may be a direct contributor to family conflicts. To assess its impact, an understanding of the nature of the physical disability and the implications for family dynamics is essential. The schools include handicapped children in their enrollment, but the school social worker often serves them because of their learning needs.

SOCIAL WORKERS' ROLE WITH THE DISABLED

Rehabilitation of the disabled has been defined as "restoration of the handicapped to the fullest physical, mental, social, vocational, and economic usefulness of which he or she is capable."[1] Rehabilitation involves a combination of disciplines, techniques, and specialized facilities to provide physical restoration, psychological adjustment, vocational counseling, training, and placement. Professionals providing rehabilitation services may include physicians, nurses, physical, occupational, and corrective therapists, speech and hearing therapists, manual or industrial arts teachers, special education teachers, prosthetists, social workers, clinical psychologists, counseling psychologists, and vocational counselors. In most rehabilitation settings, professionals from various disciplines work as a team with the physician at the head. Emphasis is on the physical functioning of the person. The social worker, however, is primarily concerned with the patient's social functioning. The social worker in a hospital or rehabilitation center performs several major functions.

Obtaining Information About the Client's Family Background and Present Status Through a Social History   The social worker is expected to provide the rest of the rehabilitation team with information about the patient's life outside the hospital, both as it was before entry into the hospital and as it potentially might be upon discharge. What are the relevant family relationships? Will the patient be able to return to the home environment? What kinds of supports are offered? What problems exist? This information is gathered through contacts with the patient and the family at the center, in visits to the patient's home, and from case records of previous contacts with social and medical agencies.

Communicating With the Patient and the Family About the Patient's Condition   Although the doctor explains the particular medical condition to the patient, the social worker often explores the practical implications of the medical condition with the patient and the family. What will the medical outlook mean in terms of the ability to function at home, at school, or on a job and in social situations? For the social worker, this requires a basic knowledge of various medical conditions and terminology and an understanding of the implications of these for physical, mental, emotional, and social functioning.

Acting As Liaison Between the Patient's Family and the Rehabilitation Staff   As part of the role of improving communications between staff and patient, the social worker may arrange meetings between the physician and other staff and the patient and family or pass on information from staff to the family, or from the family to the staff.

Helping the Patient and the Family Make Use of Community Resources   Familiarity with the procedures and programs of a multitude of community of agencies, such as the welfare department and vocational rehabilitation department, is essential for the social worker's effective functioning. It is the social worker's job to educate the rehabilitation staff, the patient, and the family about appropriate use of these resources. The social worker may often carry out the arrangements for prosthetic devices, wheelchairs, assistive appliances, financial assistance, or special job training. Assistance is also involved in processing forms and preventing delays in agency procedures.

Making Arrangements and Recommendations for Discharge   The information necessary for discharge planning comes from the social worker's knowledge of the preferences of the patient and the family. If the patient cannot return home, the social worker needs to provide information about other available facilities, including the services they offer and their cost. The worker may arrange for care and for financial aid.

Counseling the Patient   Counseling involves helping the patient adjust to the rehabilitation program to cope with the disability and adjust to the changes that it may involve in functioning. Helping the patient deal with the many personal, family, social, educational, vocational, and financial adjustments that may now be necessary is an essential part of the worker's job.

Counseling the Family   In a number of instances the social worker may be primarily involved with the family, not the patient. This is particularly true if the patient is an infant or a young child or is too physically weak to participate in planning or counseling. Offering supportive services, understanding, comfort, information, and concrete help and referrals to parents is then particularly important.

UNDERSTANDING THE PSYCHODYNAMICS OF DISABILITY

To effectively work with the disabled and their families requires that the social worker understand the special dynamics often present in a family where a member is disabled. Parents who have recently learned that their newborn or young child is disabled must cope with a number of feelings as they make decisions about the care of their child.

Parental Reactions and Adjustments

While parents are waiting for their child to be born, there are many expectations—planning for the room, setting up the crib, deciding on names, hopes about whether the child will be a boy or girl, and desires that it will be healthy, perfectly formed, and intelligent. The actual birth is associated with many public rituals. Newspapers print the good news of the birth, parents send out announcements, friends and relatives send gifts, and religious groups perform special ceremonies to welcome their new member.

When a handicapped child is born, all the usual joy may be thwarted. Social rituals become inappropriate and the expected joy is displaced by sorrow. Pearl Buck wrote about how she felt when she learned that her child was retarded: ". . . there was no more joy left in anything. All human relationships became meaningless. Everything became meaningless. I took no more pleasures in the things I had enjoyed before; landscapes, flowers, music were empty."[2]

Many parental reactions occur when a child is born handicapped or is diagnosed as handicapped within the first few years of life. Anger and disappointment are often felt by the parents. Their expectations of satisfying their wishes and desires are removed. This child will not live up to those expectations but will only be a source of problems.

Parents may feel guilty for a variety of reasons. Some may feel guilt, at least in part because they do not love their defective child as they believe they should. Parents may feel anger and hostility toward the child; they may even wish that the child would die. Believing that they should not be having these feelings, they become even more guilt-ridden.

Another source of guilt may be the parents' belief that they have in some way caused the child's handicap. For example, if the child was born with a disability, the parents may fear that it resulted from drugs or medications that the mother took while pregnant. If the child becomes disabled late in childhood, the parents may wonder whether they provided adequate care, whether they should have called the doctor sooner when the child had the fever, or whether they should have watched the child more carefully to have prevented the accident.

Even today, some parents feel guilty because they think they caused the handicap through sinning. The child's handicap, they believe, is a punishment sent by God for their transgression. Because of the connection between sex and reproduction, most sexual sins are associated with divine punishment.

An additional parental reaction may be one of shame or of inadequacy. A child is often viewed as an extension of the parent. If something is "good" about the child, it reflects well on the parents. Conversely, if something is "bad" or "wrong" with the child, the reflection is negative. Thus, a child's disability may threaten the self-esteem of the parents. The parents may also come to feel embarrassed or ashamed of the child's inabilities and fear being rejected by others because of the child.

In contrast to these feelings, parents may feel a special sense of worthiness. Here is a special child, with special needs to be loved, protected, and taken care of. Parents may feel that they have been given a special, perhaps divine mission to devote themselves to caring for this child. This reaction, when taken to extremes, has been described as the "chosen people" or "martyr syndrome" reaction.

From these divergent emotions, the reactions of many parents are ambivalent. They feel disappointed, angry, and oppressed by the added burden of having a handicapped child. Yet there is a deeply rooted human value or instinct to love and protect the child.

Of course, different parents react differently at various times. The nature of parents' reactions often grows out of their own personalities and the reality of their situation.

In general, it is harder to raise a disabled child than to raise an able-bodied child. The child with a handicap invariably makes greater demands. Training of the child is slower, and more difficult. Finding baby-sitters or some type of relief is often more difficult or impossible. More educational and medical decisions must be made and extra effort expended to carry through on them. More expenses are usually involved for medical care, equipment, transportation, and training.

More supervision of the child may be necessary and for a much longer period of time. More physical effort may also be involved in the lifting and carrying of the disabled child and/or the handling of heavy, cumbersome orthopedic equipment. In all, more time and resources are being expended on the disabled family member that diminish the time and resources left for other children in the family.

Family activities may be severely limited by problems encountered in entertaining at home or trying to get sitters so that the parents can go out at night. These problems may also be complicated by the exhaustion of the mother from the extensive child care responsibilities. Finances may be further drained if the mother who needs to work must stay home.

But for some, the most difficult problem of all is the suffering as they try to cope with the child's pain and frustrations. Parents often have extreme feelings as they watch their child in physical pain or emotional or social frustration.

Parental Suffering In *Journal*, a recent book about a boy who is a hemophiliac, the father describes the powerful impact of the boy's pain on him and on the family.

> When my son screamed in agony, I could scarcely stand it. Every cry wrenched me and horrified me. I began to sweat, to pace up and down, clenching my fists. Suzy [my daughter] hearing those awful cries would come running out of her room, her little face terrified. Comforting her, I tried also to calm myself. . . . But sometimes . . . the pain went on for hours. Sue [my wife] sitting beside Bobby's bed, holding his hand, smoothing his brow, letting him know through the red mist of pain that the human being he was closest to was there. What could I do? Nothing.[3]

It is the oldest maxim of torturers that people almost always break if someone they love is tortured before their eyes. The loved one's pain becomes theirs and is magnified because they feel responsible for it. Parents in this situation feel helpless. They must do something to satisfy their need to help, taking their children to doctor after doctor in search of new assistance. Social workers condescendingly call this behavior "shopping around." Seen in the proper perspective, however, it is the parents' attempt to do something— anything active so as not to feel they are doing nothing. Spiritual cures or doctors with way-out ideas are sought in an effort to feel that they are doing everything possible. Even if the attempt fails, at least they have tried. Not trying is to give in to the helplessness and recognize that they do not have the power to do anything.

Another dynamic often discussed is the tendency of parents to overindulge their handicapped child. A study of thirty sets of twins in which one twin of each set had cerebral palsy suggests that handicapped children are often treated by their parents as though they are "sick," with all the social role connotations commonly associated with illness. The child is offered less responsibility. Fewer limits are placed on behavior. There is increased tolerance of deviant behavior, and personal whims are indulged more often than those of other siblings.[4]

From the parent's perspective, it is hard to punish a child who is already suffering or trying to cope with handicaps that he or she did not create. This pattern, however, can have some unfortunate consequences. Children usually become aware of their special status—and begin to take advantage of it to get what they want. Louise Baker, in her autobiography, describes her own manipulativeness even when she was still in the hospital. She had been hit by a car and at the age of eight had to have one leg removed. She reflects:

> Even before I left the hospital my sudden power over people was showing itself. First of all, with completely unconscious brilliance, I chose rather inspired subjects to discuss during my five days of post operative delirium. I rambled on feverishly but with moving feeling about a doll with real golden hair and blue eyes that opened and closed. I even conveniently mentioned the awesome price and just where such a doll might be purchased, and I sighed over my father's attested poverty which prevented him from buying this coveted treasure. . . . The views spread "The poor little crippled child in the hospital . . . wants a doll . . ." When I left the hospital it took two cars to transport my loot.
>
> Very soon after I came home from the hospital I realized that all I had to do was mumble the magic words . . . "I'll never to able to run again, will I." This sad little speech—then the moment was ripe to make almost any demand . . .
>
> Three months before, I was a reasonably well mannered child . . . now I was a precocious gold digger, and anyone was fair game.[5]

Parents often have to fight hard to make sure their children are not using their disease to get out of things. When are the symptoms real, and when are they used to get out of a chore?

Along with the dynamic of overindulgence often comes overprotection. Overprotection often has its basis in a real and difficult dilemma. They must watch over and protect the child. They must decide when to call the doctor—and when not to, when to let their child do something and when not to. The parents must balance being careful and not being overprotective. They must protect the child so that no further harm or injury can occur, yet not deny the child an independent existence. We tend to give a negative connotation to overprotection, but many parents have good reason to overprotect—in the past an illness or accident occurred, and now it is difficult for them to relax and trust that no further harm will occur.

The Child's Adjustment to Disability

Very young children are unlikely to be aware of their disabilities. However, the passage of time and interaction with others bring growing awareness. The child learns that she or he is different and that a negative value is placed on this difference. In his autobiography, Christy Brown, who was born with cerebral palsy, describes the process. While growing up, Christy was taken everywhere in a wagon by his sisters and brothers. One day the wagon broke, and he couldn't go out with them.

> I was now just ten, a boy who couldn't walk, speak, feed or dress himself, but only now did I begin to realize how helpless I really was. I still didn't know anything about myself: I knew nothing beyond the fact that I was different from others. I didn't understand what made me different or why it should be I . . .
>
> I couldn't reason this out. I couldn't even think clearly about it.
>
> I could only feel it, feel it deep down in the very core of me, like a thin sharp needle . . .
>
> Up to then I had never thought about myself. True, there had come sometimes a vague feeling that I wasn't like the others, an uneasy sort of stirring in my mind that came and went. But it was just one dark spot in the brightness of things; and I used soon to forget it. . . .
>
> Now it was different. Now I saw everything, not through the eyes of a little boy eager for fun and brimming with curiosity, but through those of a cripple, a cripple who had only just discovered his own affliction.
>
> I looked at Peter's hands. They were brown steady hands with strong, square fingers, hands that could clasp a hurley firmly or swing a chestnut high into the air. Then I looked down at my own. They were queer, twisted hands with bent, crooked fingers, hands that were never still, but twitched and shook continually so that they looked more like two wriggling snakes than a pair of human hands.
>
> I began to hate the sight of those hands, the sight of my wobbly head and lopsided mouth.[6]

Christy's awareness involved several steps: (1) avoidance of thoughts of himself; (2) a vague but hurting feeling that he was not like others; and (3) a focus on its different and negative meaning. A critical incident, not being able to go out, led Christy to focus attention on his individual characteristics. For many children the critical event occurs when they first attend school and are ridiculed by others.

For the person who becomes disabled as an adult, a different adjustment process may be involved. Although reactions differ, many people react to a diagnosis of disability with a feeling of shock comparable to that on the death of a loved one. During this period, such individuals compare the past with the present. They focus on the things they will now be unable to do and what their loss means in terms of the personal and social satisfactions denied them. These feelings are expressed by Harold Russell in his book *Victory in My Hands*. He recounts how he depended on his hands, how efficient they were, how valuable and perfect.[7] During this period, the individual is often seriously depressed and preoccupied with the question, "Why me?"

Several processes may move the person from this preoccupation with the loss. The daily demands of living may help the person deal more with the present and less with the past. The blind individual becomes concerned with learning to eat and to move around. Mastering the activities of daily living focuses attention on the present. In an effort to help patients focus on the present and recognize their abilities to cope with it, the rehabilitation team may introduce instruction in daily living skills.

Social comparisons through association with other individuals who are also disabled may provide some measure of objectivity. For example, the blind begin to realize that they are able to walk, use their arms, and hear things being said—abilities that other patients may lack. Through this type of comparison, they become aware of their own assets and that they are not so "badly off" after all.

Finally, a single emotional state is time-limited and confidence is returned in some measure. The person tends to become satiated with the emotion and then is ready to move away from preoccupation with loss. A woman discussing her own reaction to becoming blind noted: "At first, I said, 'I cannot believe it,' and then I said, 'I will not believe it,' but finally, fatigued beyond measure, I said, 'I suppose I must believe it.'"[8]

INFLUENCE OF SOCIETY ON THE DISABLED

Cult of the Body Beautiful

Handicapped persons must deal with specific societal attitudes and expectations, as well as with their own internalizations of these beliefs. Our culture places a heavy emphasis on the value of a perfectly formed physique. From childhood the importance of physical perfection is stressed. This focus is present in teaching through books, movies, and television. Even early fairy tales embody the value of physical perfection. The beautiful Snow White was good, the ugly witch evil. In the story of Peter Pan, Captain Hook can be recognized on first sight as "bad" by his short fat body and the hook that replaces his missing hand. Beauty is identified with goodness, and physical ugliness with evil. Physical attractiveness, children are taught, leads to the "good life." By contrast they learn that the person who is physically imperfect is considered inferior. Evidence suggests that all children, disabled as well as able-bodied, incorporate these values into their thinking. One study found that ten- and eleven-year-old able-bodied and disabled children of various races and different social and cultural backgrounds consistently rank-ordered pictures of children with and without physical disabilities in the same manner. In all cases the picture of a child with no disability was most preferred. Apparently, the disabled individuals, having been brought up to value physical perfection, regard themselves, and are regarded by others, as less desirable.[9]

The societal and cultural values that emphasize perfect physique, physical power, and strength are learned as a part of socialization. They can be unlearned. Other values may contribute even more to a person's worth. Kindness, helpfulness, and maturity are all values of importance. Society needs to revise its values, and the social worker can also help handicapped persons to alter their own values.

In the process of reevaluation, handicapped persons are faced with contrasting personal and societal attitudes as they try to build an image of themselves. Katherine Butler Hathaway, a dwarf, describes an anguishing process.

> One day I took a hand glass and went to a long mirror to look at myself. . . . I didn't scream with rage when I saw myself. I just felt numb. That person in the mirror couldn't be me. I felt inside like a healthy, ordinary, lucky person—no, not like the one in the mirror! Yet when I turned my face to the mirror there were my own eyes looking back, hot with shame. . . . When I did not cry or make any sound, it became impossible that I should speak of it to anyone and the confusion and panic of my discovery were locked inside me. . . .
>
> Over and over I forgot what I had seen in the mirror. It could not penetrate into the interior of my mind and become an integral part of me. I felt as if it had nothing to do with me; it was only a disguise.
>
> I looked in the mirror [again] and was horror-struck because I did not recognize myself. In the place where I was standing, with that persistent romantic elation in me, as if I were a favored fortunate person to whom everything was possible, I saw a stranger, a little, pitiable, hideous figure, and a face that became, as I stared at it, painful and blushing with shame. . . .
>
> Every one of those encounters was like a blow on the head. They left me dazed and dumb and senseless every time, until slowly and stubbornly my robust persistent illusion of well-being and of personal beauty spread all through me again, and I forgot the irrelevant reality and was all unprepared and vulnerable again.[10]

The Spread of Disability

In addition to being seen as inferior physically, disabled persons may be perceived as less capable in other respects. Their physical aspects may tend to dominate the entire perception of themselves as persons, so that the handicap appears to spread to other areas. We tend to talk more loudly in the presence of a person who is blind; persons who cannot see are often assumed to have trouble hearing. Another example involves treating physically disabled persons as if they were socially and mentally retarded. Larry B., a twenty-two-year old college student, gave the following account:

> I'm in church with my father and my father is standing beside me and I'm in a wheelchair. I'm relatively intelligent, but I'm disabled. I'm sitting there like anyone else. And somebody comes up to my father and they're about as far away from me as from him and they say to my father, "How's he doing?" "Well, he's looking pretty good." And I just want to kick him in the stomach.

Generalization of disability can also influence the behavior of persons with a handicap. Recognizing their disability in one area, they may begin to believe that they are less capable mentally and socially. Unfortunately, the behavior of others reinforces the disabled person's beliefs. A social worker may help persons with a disability to see that there is no inevitable connection between physical disability and other traits. They can be helped to recognize their individual potential as intelligent, warm, good, socially able individuals.

The social worker must also be careful not to overgeneralize the effects of disability. Problems with a spouse or children or a job can be caused by many other factors besides the disability. Although individuals with a physical handicap may have to cope with many social and psychological problems, they usually meet them about as well or as poorly as able-bodied individuals. The maladaptive behaviors shown by the handicapped were similar to those shown by the nondisabled, and there was no relationship between the type of physical disability and the type of adjustive behavior.[11]

Requirement of Mourning

Another of society's attitudes affecting personal adjustment is that the disabled person "ought" to feel inferior—"the requirement of mourning."[12] People have a need to safeguard their values; they need to see a person who is unable to attain their values as suffering and inferior. An able-bodied individual who is valued for his physical attractiveness needs the disabled person to suffer as a sign that the values of the "body beautiful" are worthy and important. Consider attitudes toward the mentally retarded. Society tends to believe that intelligence is of prime importance, and that individuals who do not have at least normal intelligence are unfortunate. If they do not suffer, the tendency is to infer that they are "too stupid to know better."

Out of this attitude come conceptions of the disabled person as someone to be pitied. He or she is less fortunate and should be helped. Oversolicitude and patronizing attitudes are the result. The social worker must develop the self-awareness to view the client as a peer, one who should not be protected from the world but helped to become part of it.

Although this chapter has focused on people with visible disabilities, those with invisible disabilities have similar kinds of adjustments to make. Persons with diabetes, epilepsy, asthma, or heart disease must all cope with an altered self-image. An additional issue for those with hidden disabilities is when and with whom to discuss their disability. Should prospective employers, teachers, friends, or dates be informed? Simply because these disabilities are not visually evident, social workers should not underplay their possible social and psychological impact on the person.

Importance of the Family

The effectiveness of a rehabilitation program depends upon support from the family. If the family fails to provide an atmosphere of warmth and encouragement or is unwilling to accept the person's performance, the aims of a therapeutic program may be seriously hampered.[13]

Family solidarity and encouragement are important factors in rehabilitation. The disruption of family roles and strained interpersonal relations that occur when a member becomes ill or disabled must be recognized. Whenever a family member becomes disabled, new expectations result that influence the roles of family members. Conflict and stress are likely to occur among family members. Numerous adjustments must be made. A mother's inability to cook and clean may mean that these tasks fall to one of the children. The child, feeling cheated of time to do other things, may resent the mother, or the mother may resent the new dependence upon the child.

Influence of Other Patients

Effective rehabilitation also depends on the motivation of individuals to further their own treatment plan. A source of support for the patient may come from other patients as well as from the family. To utilize this resource, the social worker may organize a group of patients, who are then enabled to receive assurance and support from each other. Peer-group members are usually anxious to share their experiences and are in a good position to offer realistic advice and support. The members of the group may encourage one another to carry out prescribed therapeutic planning and be critical of those who deviate. Members may also use each other as a comparative reference group. Members who are further along in the rehabilitative process may serve as role models for others, their level of progress becoming a goal. For example, if a member hears that another member with a similar injury is able to dress without help, this may provide the encouragement to work to achieve the same goal.

In rehabilitation centers people live very dependent and sheltered existences for long periods of time. Each day their needs for food, shelter, and activity are taken care of within the confines of the center. Sympathetic physical therapists, occupational therapists, nurses, nurse's aides, and social workers meet their needs. The individual adjusts to the center, even though it may often be boring and routine. It is a place where the individual feels comfortable.

In contrast, the outside world often seems frightening and uncomfortable. It is easier to get around in the rehabilitation hospital than in the outside world. People in the hospital are friendly and interested; people outside are usually either hostile or patronizing. Ex-patients may voluntarily return to the rehabilitation center because they like it there.

To counteract the lack of motivation to return to the outside world, more halfway houses should be set up. After completing a rehabilitation program, patients can live in the halfway house while they begin adjusting to the world again. Gradually they take on all the responsibilities of daily living.

Interaction with the Nonhandicapped

People tend to end interactions sooner with a handicapped person than with a nonhandicapped person.[14] In social situations with handicapped persons, appropriate behaviors are not clearly known, making interactions uncomfortable. For example, nonhandicapped persons may feel it would be too outspoken to make a direct remark about the disabling condition, yet if they try to completely forget the disability, they may make impossible demands on the handicapped person. There may be guarded references; common everyday words suddenly are avoided; and there may be a fixed stare away from the person, an artificial seriousness, or compulsive talking on the part of the nonhandicapped person.

The handicapped person in turn is usually sensitive to these interactional strains.

> I get suspicious when somebody says, "Let's go for a uh, ah [imitates confused and halting speech] push with me down the hall," or something like that. This to me is suspicious because it means that they're aware, really aware, that there's a wheelchair here, and that this is probably uppermost with them. . . . A lot of people in trying to show you that they don't care that you're in a chair will do crazy things. Oh, there's one person I know who constantly kicks my chair, as if to say "I don't care that you're in a wheelchair. I don't even know that it's there." But that is just an indication that he really knows it's there.[15]

Establishing an honest, comfortable relationship with the person who has a physical or mental disability may be difficult for many social workers. The ability to overcome this feeling of uneasiness is essential to a relationship with handicapped clients. The social worker's attitudes toward physical disability will influence the ability to help the disabled client, who may quickly detect covert feelings of pity, horror, or aversion. The social worker must consider disability not as a disaster but as a deviation to which one can adjust. The successful social worker reacts to the client as a person and not to the physical disability.

Education

Rehabilitation efforts are often hindered because persons disabled in childhood have been systematically denied equal educational opportunities. Generally, in the past, the public schools either refused to serve the handicapped or segregated them in special programs. To improve the educational opportunities of the disabled, Congress passed the Education for All Handicapped Children Act in 1975. This law stipulates that local school districts must provide full and appropriate educational opportunities to all handicapped children. An individualized educational program must be developed for each handicapped child which provides for instruction in the least restrictive environment that is feasible. The intent of this provision is to enable handicapped children to participate as much as possible in regular educational programs. The concept of "mainstreaming" is stressed in the act's implementation. It is hoped that the handicapped children of today will have educational opportunities denied earlier generations of handicapped persons.

Employment

Productive employment is the goal of most rehabilitation programs. The individual may be well qualified yet unable to get a job because of the employer's attitude toward the disabled. Employers generally hire the able-bodied rather than the disabled. The social worker can often help by showing the employer that the disabled client is the best-qualified applicant for the job. This means demonstrating that although handicapped individuals are limited by their disability, they can perform effectively in other areas of functioning.

Architectural Barriers

After successfully completing a rehabilitation program, the handicapped individual may not be able to accept a position because the place of business is inaccessible. To the individual in a wheelchair, a flight of steps that cannot be ramped or a bathroom that is too small means no job. In 1967 the National Commission on Architectural Barriers to Rehabilitation of the Handicapped found that the biggest obstacles to employment were the physical features of the buildings. More than 20 million physically disabled people were excluded from normal living by steps and curbs, steep and narrow corridors, narrow or revolving doors, inaccessible toilet facilities, unreachable light and alarm switches, and a lack of Braille lettering for the blind on doors and elevators.[16]

Federal legislation was passed in 1968 to alter this situation. Public Law 90-48 requires all buildings that are designed, built, or altered using federal funds to be accessible to the physically handicapped. Similar legislation needs to be enacted by each state to cover all public buildings, and the laws should be enforced.

REHABILITATION PROGRAMS

Thus far we have been discussing the social worker's role in dealing with the disabled client, and we have assumed that social workers will be involved in rehabilitation programs. What are these rehabilitation programs? Who is eligible to use them? How are they paid for?

History of Programs for the Disabled

Rehabilitation programs reflect a history of changing attitudes and customs, beginning with unorganized almsgiving to help the disabled. Begging was the main occupation of the disabled in Europe, and those in the American colonies followed suit. Towns and counties were usually willing to maintain their own beggars, but strict laws prohibited begging by people who were residents of other villages. Disability was viewed primarily from a moral perspective. An association was made between physical malformation and evil. Disability represented a punishment for sinful behavior and sometimes was taken as evidence of witchcraft.[17]

Toward a Medical Emphasis Slowly, with the development of hospitals during the early 1800s, emphasis shifted to treating the sick and disabled. Great advances were made in orthopedic surgery for restoring the bodies of persons crippled by disease or injury. Special facilities for the disabled were established. The Hospital for the Ruptured and Crippled and the New York

Orthopedic Hospital and Dispensary were both opened in the 1860s; the first educational institutions for the disabled were also established about the same time.

Industrial Accidents Parallel to these developments was the Industrial Revolution. Workers in factories labored long hours at fatiguing, often dangerous tasks. Injuries and illness resulting from these conditions were common. The employer and the larger society took no responsibility for compensating the worker. However, some segments of society began to feel that help should be given to persons disabled in industrial accidents and to those disabled by other external forces. Charitable organizations began to offer help to those whose problems were not of their own making, through work and training for work.

Legislation
Through organizations set up to help the disabled, influential citizens became personally involved with the problems of disability. They also became aware of the limited impact of private or voluntary efforts and began to educate fellow citizens to the need for the assumption of public responsibility. In 1918 Massachusetts passed the first state law that set up public provisions to help the disabled. In this same year the federal government passed legislation to help rehabilitate handicapped veterans of World War I.

Several factors now combined to provide a basis for support of national legislation for civilian rehabilitation: the success of the Veteran's Rehabilitation Act; increased awareness of the needs of the disabled, especially those injured in industrial accidents; and an awareness that our growing economy was dependent on an ever-increasing, able-bodied workforce. In 1920 the Smith-Fess Act—the Civilian Vocational Rehabilitation Act—was passed to encourage the states to undertake rehabilitation services for disabled civilians. This was the first legislation to provide federal "grants in aid" for support of social services on a 50-50 matching basis, providing vocational guidance, vocational training, prosthetics, and job placement services.

Economic and Humanitarian Goals Legislation relied on two kinds of justification, an assumption of social responsibility to help the disabled and an awareness that our economy needed this rehabilitated manpower. From 1920 to 1970 the expansion of federal-state programs of vocational rehabilitation led to increasing tension between the economic and the humanitarian justifications of the rehabilitation program.

By the 1960s humanitarian considerations were stressed in the extension of rehabilitation. The emphasis was on helping every individual to develop his or her full potential apart from any contribution to the economic system. Accordingly, services were provided to a wider range of individuals. Clients who had been considered too physically or mentally handicapped were now eligible to be served. Vocational objectives were no longer defined only in terms of competitive employment. Sheltered-workshop employment and the development of skills for personal living were considered to be acceptable goals.[18] However, this growing humanitarian concern did not eliminate economic concerns. While attempting to give service to all who needed it, the program was still justified to Congress on economic grounds. Data were used to show the economic value of rehabilitation to society.

> The average cost of rehabilitation is returned fivefold in income taxes paid by the employed handicapped worker; the average rate of income after rehabilitation is seven to ten times greater for the average person than before rehabilitation; and vocational rehabilitation of a handicapped person on public assistance can be effected at a one-time cost comparable to the cost of supporting him on welfare during a one-year period.[19]

The appeal of such statistics tended to make Congress very supportive of the program.

The Rehabilitation Act of 1973 continued the dualistic purpose. It furthers humanitarian objectives by providing services to severely handicapped individuals. On the economic side, "This bill keeps the Federal vocational rehabilitation program focused on its original and proper purpose, that of preparing people for meaningful jobs, rather than burdening that program with broad new medical or welfare functions better performed elsewhere."[20]

How the Vocational Rehabilitation Program Works Now

Individuals are eligible for service if they have a physical or mental disability that substantially interferes with their ability to obtain employment, and if there is a reasonable expectation that service will enable them to obtain gainful employment or be more productive.

An individual contacts the state rehabilitation agency and explains the situation to a counselor. A medical examination is given free of charge to determine the extent of the applicant's disability, the general state of the applicant's overall health, and whether any other handicapping conditions are present.

On the basis of the medical findings and the recommendations of the rehabilitation counselor, the agency determines whether the applicant is eligible. The program of appropriate services may include:

1. Individual counseling and guidance.
2. Medical, surgical, hospital, or other services that will lessen the individual's disability or correct any other handicapping conditions that may be found through medical examination.
3. Special equipment, such as prosthetics, hearing aids, canes, guide dogs, or wheelchairs.
4. Special training in such areas as reading, sign language, or social adjustment; training at a rehabilitation facility, a public or private college, or on the job.

5. Money for living expenses and transportation during the training period.
6. Help in attaining a suitable job and necessary tools, equipment, licenses, or stock for a small business.
7. Follow-up to see if the client and employer are satisfied.

The services provided depend on both the individual needs of the client and the current financial resources of the state rehabilitation agency. An individual may be eligible, but for financial reasons the state agency may be unable to provide service. If a state is unable to service all eligible persons who apply, the state agency establishes a system of priorities for determining the order in which individuals are accepted for services.[21] Thus it can decide, for example, that priority is to be given to the individual who needs vocational training over the one who requires medical restoration. Each state also determines whether an economic means test is to be used to determine the applicant's entitlement for certain services.

Assessment of Services

Studies by the President's Task Force on the physically handicapped showed that only one-third of the people in need of the services were receiving them.[22] Several problems were identified in the current system of services: (1) policies and procedures of agencies tended to be too complex and confusing to be understood easily by those who needed service; (2) varying eligibility requirements had little relationship to the actual service needs of the individual; (3) coordination between government programs, and between government programs and private or voluntary programs, was very poor; (4) consumer representation and advocacy in planning and evaluating services was lacking; (5) children's programs had serious gaps; (6) geographic distribution of services resulted in uneven use—people in rural areas often could not take full advantage of services because they had to travel too far.

Needed: Public Understanding

A beginning has been made in meeting the physical needs of disabled persons, but there is still a significant lack of public understanding and social acceptance of the disabled. Often the largest disability for the physically handicapped is not the physical defect itself, or the unavailability of needed services, but the ignorance and oversolicitude of others. The prevailing attitude seems to be that such "blighted creatures" must be protected from the world, not helped to become part of it.

Ideally, the behavior of disabled individuals should be limited only by the physical restrictions imposed by their impairment. The psychological and socioeconomic handicap of the disabled person frequently far outweighs its actual physical limitations. Until the handicapped person can be given an opportunity, not only legally, but societally, to obtain an existence as close to normal as possible, social services will be only partially effective.

SUMMARY AND APPLICATION

Social workers are often in a key position to help parents, handicapped children, and disabled adults to deal with their attitudes toward disability. At the same time, they can help the nonhandicapped to develop attitudes that will assist the disabled.

We have come some distance in the recognition of the rights of the handicapped, but opportunities for them depend as much upon social policy related to development as they do upon specialized services. Social workers will also have increased opportunity to work with the severely handicapped and the severely retarded, for whom daily living skills are of critical importance.

—*Nancy Weinberg*

KEY TERMS

Vocational Rehabilitation Act
sheltered workshop
"body beautiful" cult

requirement of mourning
disability spread
prosthetics

REFERENCES AND NOTES

1. National Council on Rehabilitation, *Symposium on the Process of Rehabilitation*, Cleveland, 1944, p. 6.
2. Pearl S. Buck, *The Child Who Never Grew*, John Day, New York, 1950, pp. 29–30.
3. Robert Massie, and Suzanne Massie, *Journey*, Warner, New York, 1967, p. 243.
4. M. O. Shere, "Socio-Emotional Factors in the Family of Twins with Cerebral Palsy," *Exceptional Children*, vol. 22, 1956, pp. 196–199, 206–208.
5. Louise Baker, *Out on a Limb*, Whittlesly House, New York, 1946, pp. 4–5.
6. Christy Brown, *The Story of Christy Brown*, Pocket Books, New York, 1971.
7. Harold Russell and Victor Dosen, *Victory in My Hands*, Farrar, Straus & Cudahy, New York, 1949, pp. 4–5.
8. Marie Bell McCoy, *Journey Out of Darkness*, McKay, New York, 1963.
9. S. Richardson et al., "Cultural Uniformity in Reaction to Physical Disabilities," *American Sociological Review*, vol. 26, April 1961, pp. 241–247.
10. Katherine Butler Hathaway, *The Little Locksmith*, Curtis, New York, 1942, pp. 41, 46–47.
11. R. G. Barker, B. A. Wright, and H. R. Gonick, *Adjustment to Physical Handicap and Illness: A Survey of the Social Psychology of Physique and Disability*, Social Science Research Council Bulletin 55, 1946, pp. 55–117.
12. Beatrice A. Wright, *Physical Disability: A Psychological Approach*, Harper, New York, 1960, p. 259.
13. T. Litman, "The Influence of Self-Conception and Life Orientation Factors in the Rehabilitation of the Orthopedically Disabled," *Journal of Health and Human Behavior*, vol. 3, 1962, pp. 240–256.
14. R. Kleck, H. Ono, and A. H. Hastorf, "The Effects of Physical Deviance upon Face-to-Face Interaction," *Human Relations*, vol. 19, 1966, pp. 425–436.

15. Fred David, "Deviance Disavowal: The Management of Strained Interaction by the Visibly Handicapped," in Howard S. Becker (ed.), *The Other Side: Perspectives on Deviance*, Free Press, New York, 1964, p. 123.
16. National Commission on Architectural Barriers to Rehabilitation of the Handicapped, *Design for All Americans*, Social and Rehabilitation Services, Department of Health, Education and Welfare, Washington, D.C., 1967.
17. Esco C. Oberman, *A History of Vocational Rehabilitation in America*, Dennison, Minneapolis, 1965, pp. 75–77.
18. James Garrett, "Historical Background," in David Malikin, and Herbert Rusalem (eds.), *Vocational Rehabilitation of the Disabled: An Overview*, New York University Press, New York, 1969.
19. Salvatore G. DiMichael, "The Current Scene," in David Malikin, and Herbert Rusalem, op. cit.
20. *Presidential Documents: Richard Nixon*, 1973, vol. 9, no. 39, p. 1197.
21. *The Regulations Governing the Vocational Rehabilitation Program*, sec. 401.18, 1954.
22. *A National Effort for the Physically Handicapped*, Report of the President's Task Force on the Physically Handicapped, July 1970, p. 2.

FOR FURTHER STUDY

Margaret E. Epperson, "Families in Sudden Crisis: Process and Interaction in a Critical Care Center," *Social Work in Health Care*, vol. 2, Spring 1977, pp. 265–273.
Israel Goldiamond, "A Diary of Self-Modification," *Psychology Today*, vol. 7, November 1973, pp. 95–102.
Elizabeth E. May, *Independent Living for the Handicapped and the Elderly*, Macmillan, New York, 1974.
James McDaniel, *Physical Disability and Human Behavior*, Pergamon Press, New York, 1969.
Robert P. Marinelli and Arthur E. Del Orto (eds.), *The Psychological and Social Impact of Physical Disability*, Springer, New York, 1977.
Harold Moses and C. Patterson (eds.), *Research Readings in Rehabilitation Counseling*, Stipes Publishing Co., Champaign, Ill., 1973.
Julian Myers, *An Orientation to Chronic Disease and Disability*, Macmillan, London, 1965.
Martin Nacman "Social Work in Health Settings, a Historical Review," *Social Work in Health Care*, vol. 2, Summer 1977, pp. 407–417.
Isabel P. Robinault, *Functional Aids for the Multiply Handicapped*, Harper & Row, Hagerstown, Md., 1973.
Constantina Safilios-Rothschild, *The Sociology and Social Psychology of Disability and Rehabilitation*, Random House, New York, 1970.

FOR DISCUSSION

1. What disabled group is identified in the chapter as the most numerous? Why is this group not the largest consumer of rehabilitation services?
2. What services are given by social workers to the disabled in settings other than rehabilitation?

3. Sometimes a rehabilitation social worker is actually more involved with activities involving the family than the patient. Why is this true?

4. Describe some of the typical reactions of parents when they learn that their child is handicapped?

5. Explain why a child's handicap actually gives some parents positive rather than negative feelings?

6. Indicate how overprotection develops and its effects upon a handicapped person?

7. From your own experience, identify characters in literature that illustrate the association between disability and evil.

8. Explain and illustrate the "spread of disability."

9. What particular purpose do self-help groups serve for the disabled?

10. What are the goals of rehabilitation short of making a person skillful enough to be employed?

11. What is the name of your state rehabilitation agency? What are its requirements for eligibility?

12. Compare the need for rehabilitation services and the supply of such services.

13. Summarize the major roles of a social worker in.rehabilitation.

PROJECTS

1. Ask two or three handicapped students to discuss rehabilitation services that they have received, problems occasioned by self and others, and use of self-help groups.

2. Study your campus and report on limitations that affect accepting handicapped students. What would be required to meet their needs effectively?

3. Read a biography of a handicapped person and discuss means of coping. Your choices might include Clara Barton, Ludwig von Beethoven, Demosthenes, Thomas Edison, Helen Keller, John Milton, and Franklin D. Roosevelt.

4. Invite a staff member from the public rehabilitation agency to discuss programs for the disabled and for other groups such as former mental patients, alcoholics, and the poor.

5. Make a study of the development of the wheelchair. What improvements are still needed? What are the advantages of manual and battery-powered types?

6. Visit a rehabilitation hospital or clinic. Find out all you can about the roles of the social worker. What other staff members are involved?

CHAPTER 13
Juvenile and Criminal Justice

500 ARRESTABLE OFFENSES

100 ARRESTS

40 CONSIDERED FOR COURT ACTION

10 ACTUALLY APPEAR IN COURT

Many in trouble; few in court.

[The prison:] a walled institution where adult criminals in large numbers are held for protracted periods, with economically meaningless and insufficient employment, with vocational training or education for a few, with rare contacts with the outside world, in cellular conditions varying from the decent to those which a zoo would not tolerate, the purposes being to lead the prisoners to eschew crime in the future and to deter others of like mind from running the risk of sharing their incarceration.

—Norval Morris and Gordon Hawkins*

T he system of criminal justice in the United States is an amalgamation of agencies, each with different but interrelated missions. Although critics of American crime policy often observe that the "criminal justice system" is no system at all, the overall mission of criminal justice agents and organizations is the prevention, reduction, and control of crime through various sociolegal interventions. In that respect, criminal justice philosophy uses systems theory, even though individual agencies may not operate from that point of view.

THE CRIMINAL JUSTICE SYSTEM

Three major components make up the criminal justice system: law enforcement, courts, and corrections. Each has subcomponents operating within the confines of entrenched organizational and bureaucratic guidelines. The law enforcement agencies in the United States include federal, state, and local units with specialized bureaus, divisions, and sections.

The courts that process the offenders caught by the police are divided into federal and state, trial and appellate, and criminal and civil. The correctional institutions which house the offenders found guilty by the judiciary are subdivided into federal, state, and county facilities. In addition to institutional corrections, the United States has a host of federal and state boards, commissions, and bureaus that handle adult and juvenile probationers and parolees.

The criminal justice system involves considerable use of diversion for less serious offenses. Sometimes a suspected offender is merely warned and told to get off the street. Another alternative is to make a station adjustment in which the court takes no part. If the accused pleads guilty or is found guilty, probation rather than a prison term often results.

An offender charged with a crime is entitled to a lawyer. The lawyer may work out an arrangement with the prosecution for the offender to plead guilty

*Norval Morris and Gordon Hawkins, *The Honest Politician's Guide to Crime Control*, University of Chicago, Press, Chicago, 1970, p. 124.

323

*"If you'll plead guilty, I think I can get your bigamy charge
reduced to proceeding too fast for conditions!"*

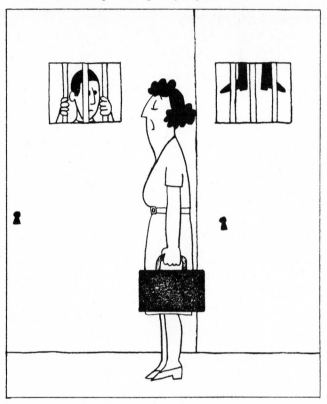

to a lesser charge. Without diversion and plea bargaining, the correctional facilities could not contain all the offenders that come to the attention of the police.

Because most of the criminal justice components are highly interdependent, problems arising in one sphere often have profound effects on other parts of the system. When the police become more proficient and adept at crime detection and arrest, strains develop on both the courts, which try the suspects, and on the prisons or jails, which house those found guilty.

We are witnessing renewed interest today in the more stringent application of criminal sanctions against serious law violators. This, coupled with a national trend toward longer prison terms without benefit of parole, will create persistent problems for correctional agencies. The correctional system is like a large automobile parking lot—with the crucial difference that there are only a few exits, and these are blocked for most purposes. Thus, more and more offenders are coming into our prisons and jails without a corresponding release of those already there. The result is overcrowding. For both correctional personnel and inmates, the current situation calls for constant adaptability to problems not of their own making.

THE ROLE OF SOCIAL WORK

Traditionally, the role played by social work in criminal justice has been confined almost exclusively to the correctional component of the system. Law enforcement and the legal profession have felt little need for social workers, although some administrators in the more "professional" police departments are willing to use the social worker's expertise in family crisis intervention. The legal profession's interaction with social work has traditionally come almost exclusively in the field of juvenile justice. In adult criminal courts, social work intervention is rare.

In their treatment programs, most institutions rely on other treatment techniques than casework and group counseling. Clinical services (both medical and psychiatric), religious programs, educational programs, vocational training, work release, and study release complete the correctional treatment picture.

One of the most important responsibilities of social workers in corrections is the preparation of presentence reports. They provide a history of the offender and help to guide the court in sentencing.

EXAMPLE OF A PRESENTENCE REPORT

United States District Court

2, Feb. 65   Central District of New York

Presentence Report

Name: John Jones
Address: 1234 Astoria Blvd.
*   New York City*
Legal Residence: Same
Age: 33
Date of Birth: 2–8–40
*   New York City*
Sex: Male Race: Caucasian
Citizenship: U.S. (Birth)
Education: 10th grade
Marital Status: Married
Dependents: Three
*   (wife and 2 children)*
Soc.Sec.No.: 112–03–9559
FBI No.: 256 1126
Detainers or Charges
Pending: None

Date: January 4, 1974
Docket No.: 74–103
Offense: Theft of Mail by Postal Employee (18 U.S.C. Sec. 17009) 2 cts.
Penalty: Ct. 2–5 years and/or $2,000 fine
Plea: Guilty on 12–16–73 to Ct. 2 Ct. 1 pending
Verdict:
Custody: Released on own recognizance. No time in custody.
Asst. U.S. Atty: Samuel Hayman
Defense Counsel: Thomas Lincoln Federal Public Defender
Drug/Alcohol Involvement: Attributes offense to need for drinking money

Offense: Official Version

Official sources reveal that during the course of routine observations on December 4, 1973, within the Postal Office Center, Long Island, New York, postal inspectors observed the defendant paying particular attention to various packages. Since the defendant was seen to mishandle and tamper with several parcels, test parcels were prepared for his handling on December 5, 1973. The defendant was observed to mishandle one of the test parcels by tossing it to one side into a canvas tub. He then placed his jacket into the tub and leaned over the tub for a period of time. At the time the defendant left the area and went to the men's room. While he was gone the inspectors examined the mail tub and found that the test parcel had been rifled and that the contents, a watch, was missing.

The defendant returned to his work area and picked up his jacket. He then left the building. The defendant was stopped by the inspectors across the street from the post office. He was questioned about his activities and on his person he had the wristwatch from the test parcel. He was taken to the postal inspector's office where he admitted the offense.

Defendant's Version of Offense

The defendant admits that he rifled the package in question and took the watch. He states that he intended to sell the watch at a later date. He admits that he had been drinking too much lately and needed extra cash for "drinking money." He exhibits remorse and is concerned about the possibility of incarceration and the effect it would have on his family.

Prior Record

Date	Offense	Place	Disposition
5–7–66	Possession of	Manhattan CR.CT.	$25.00 Fine
(age 26)	Policy Slips	N.Y., N.Y.	7–11–62
3–21–72	Intoxication	Manhattan CR.CT.	4–17–72
(age 32)		N.Y., N.Y.	Nolle

Personal History

The defendant was born in New York City on February 8, 1940, the oldest of three children. He attended the public school, completed the 10th grade and left school to go to work. He was rated as an average student and was active in sports, especially basketball and baseball.

The defendant's father, John, died of a heart attack in 1968, at the age of 53 years. He had an elementary school education and worked as a construction laborer most of his life.

The defendant's mother, Mary Smith Jones, is 55 years of age and is employed as a seamstress. She had an elementary school education and married defendant's father when she was 20 years of age. Three sons were issue of the marriage. She presently resides in New York City, and is in good health.

Defendant's brother, Paul, age 32 years, completed 2½ years of high school. He is employed as a bus driver and resides with his wife and two children in New York City.

Defendant's brother, Lawrence, age 30 years, completed three semesters of college. He is employed as a New York City firefighter. He resides with his wife and one child in Dutch Point, Long Island.

The defendant after leaving high school worked as a delivery boy for a retail supermarket chain then served 2 years in the U.S. Army as an infantryman (ASN 123 456 78). He received an honorable discharge and attained the rank of corporal serving from 2-10-58 to 2-1-60. After service he held a number of jobs of the laboring type.

The defendant was employed as a truck driver for the City of New York when he married Ann Sweeny on 6-15-63. Two children were issue of this marriage, John, age 8, and Mary, age 6. The family has resided at the same address (which is a four-room apartment) since their marriage.

The defendant has been in good health all of his life but admits he has been drinking to excess the past 18 months which has resulted in some domestic strife. The wife stated that she loves her husband and will stand by him. She is amenable to a referral for family counseling.

Defendant has worked for the Postal Service since 12-1-65 and resigned on 12-5-73 as a result of his present arrest. His work ratings by his supervisors were always "excellent."

Evaluative Summary

The defendant is a 33-year-old male who entered a plea of guilty to mail theft. While an employee of the U.S. Postal Service he rifled and stole a watch from a test package. He admitted that he planned on selling the watch to finance his drinking which has become a problem resulting in domestic strife.

Defendant is a married man with two children with no prior serious record. He completed 10 years of schooling, had an honorable military record, and has a good work history. He expresses remorse for his present offense and is concerned over the loss of his job and the shame to his family.

Recommendation

It is respectfully recommended that the defendant be admitted to probation. If placed on probation the defendant expresses willingness to seek counseling for his domestic problems. He will require increased motivation if there is to be a significant change in his drinking pattern.

Respectfully submitted,

Donald M. Fredericks

U.S. Probation Officer[1]

Div. of Probation, U.S. Courts, *Selective Presentence Investigation Report.*

The focus of this chapter will be on the issues and problems confronting social work and the social worker in adult corrections because that segment of the criminal justice system offers the most promise for future involvement.

CORRECTIONS: ITS BACKGROUND AND BASIC PHILOSOPHY

Criminal corrections in both the United States and elsewhere is misunderstood. Depending upon one's sociopolitical point of view, corrections and its varied missions can be damned in one breath and praised in another. Rehabilitation gets lip-service from professionals and politicians alike, but behind the rhetoric stand other more pragmatic and political goals that overshadow rehabilitation.

Contrary to popular belief, prisons and jails in both Great Britain and the United States were not originally conceived as places of long-term confinement. After the American Revolution the concept of imprisonment developed as the principal penalty for crimes.

In the early nineteenth century, houses of corrections, almshouses, and workhouses were constructed to house the unemployed, the vagrant, the homeless, and the so-called idle classes. Around the year 1835, imprisonment per se had become the principal sanction not only for the "unworthy" poor but for convicted criminals as well. In these new institutions were housed all manner and types of male convicts as well as vagrants of both sexes, and a hodgepodge of the outcasts of society.

The development of a correctional philosophy during this era was the combined product of many thinkers—some original, some pedestrian.

The Italian essayist Cesare Bonesana di Beccaria perhaps contributed more than anyone else to a basic philosophy of corrections. In 1764 Beccaria published an anonymous book, *Dei delitti e delle pene* (Of Crimes and Punishments). The work was controversial and had an impact far beyond Italy. Punishment for violating the criminal law was to be proportionate to the severity of the crime. Proportionality dominated early American penal practice. Although Beccaria's ideas held sway during the greater part of the nineteenth century, they were focused exclusively on the criminal act and the law's response to that act. Little if any attention was paid to the idea of rehabilitation. The social sciences had yet to become involved in treating the law-abiding, let alone the lawbreaker. Probation and parole had not yet developed, and although prison sentences were relatively short by present-day standards, there was little assurance that the inmate would leave a nineteenth-century American prison with either physical or mental capacities intact. Both physical and psychic degradation were widespread.

Besides the influence exerted by Beccaria, two American innovations also influenced correctional practice in both the United States and Europe. In 1818 the Western Penitentiary was erected in Pittsburgh, and eleven years later, in 1829, the Eastern Penitentiary was built at Cherry Hill, near Philadelphia. Both completely isolated their inmates. Each prisoner had an individual cell and a small exercise yard. During imprisonment the inmate never came in contact with other prisoners. Solitary confinement became known as the Pennsylvania system to contrast it with the New York State system.

In 1823 New York constructed a penitentiary at Auburn embodying somewhat different principles. Convicts were permitted to work together, but strict rules of silence were enforced, with draconian punishments for those who dared break into idle chatter. At Auburn the infamous lock-step was developed to move large numbers of inmates to and from various areas of the institution.

The men would form a long line with one arm on the other's shoulder, eyes downcast, and, at the command of a prison guard, the group would move with a slow, shifting gait from one place to another. The code of silence was enforced actively, and in time the lock-step became one of the hated symbols of nineteenth-century institutional corrections.

Like all new ideas, both the Pennsylvania and Auburn systems had their advocates and their critics. Eventually the Auburn system prevailed. Thus, the lock-step and repressive discipline had a significant impact on American corrections that lasted well into the twentieth century. Only with the advent of the so-called new penology of the 1930s, with its emphasis on individual rehabilitation, did corrections in the United States begin to assume a new posture.

Institutional Corrections, Social Work, and the New Penology

During the Great Depression, the newly developing social sciences gave impetus to an increased interest in prisons and prison reforms. Due in large measure to certain late-nineteenth-century ideas developed by the positive school of criminology,[2] with its emphasis on the criminal instead of the crime, social science began the on-again, off-again partnership with corrections that prevails today.

Spurred on by the concepts of inmate classification, diagnosis, and treatment, American corrections began embracing some of the ideas put forth by psychologists, psychiatrists, social workers, and sociologists. At the same time, the Federal Bureau of Prisons was reorganized under the enlightened leadership of Sanford Bates and a team of professionals. These measures accounted for new ideas that altered some dearly held correctional beliefs and brought a diminution of gratuitous punishment and degradation in American penal institutions.

The new penology laid the foundation for better architectural design for correctional institutions, better prison libraries, more lenient visiting privileges, more intensive staff-training techniques, and more refined treatment methods.

The Federal Bureau of Prisons served as a model for the states. Unfortunately, for both economic and political reasons, few state correctional systems implemented the prison reforms that are now commonplace in our federal penitentiaries.

What part did social work play in the shift from the abstract to the human element in criminal corrections? The role was smaller than we would have hoped because several factors in a correctional milieu are generally beyond the social worker's control: the custody/treatment conflict, authoritarian work settings, enforced therapy, the inmates "con game," and the artificial prison social structure.

The Custody/Treatment Conflict   Regardless of the view one takes of prison life and institutionalization in general, a stark reality stands out. The vast majority of prisons in the United States primarily emphasize custody. Treatment, rehabilitation, and training aimed at social reintegration of the inmate receive marginal attention from most prison administrators. It is politically untenable for a prison administrator to manage an institution that has a high escape rate. The social worker employed in corrections should be aware that if custody policies clash with the treatment program, the latter suffers. The specter of custody of the institutional population always overshadows treatment modalities. Prison riots and other internal disruptions are not looked upon with favor by the officers of state government or by the general public. Thus, when the routine of the institution is threatened, the first task is to restore order. Usually, in the process of that restoration, treatment programs cease operation, at least temporarily.

Authoritarian Work Settings   For meaningful and lasting interchange between the worker and the client, social work holds that treatment settings must be relatively free of authoritarianism. For the correctional social worker, however, the problem of authority is ever-present. One would be hard-pressed to suggest a more authoritarian setting than a prison. From the gates and guard towers, on the one hand, to the rigidly enforced rules and regulations, on the other, correctional social work is beset with authoritarian overkill.

To relate to the inmate effectively, the social worker must come to terms with the authority symbols in the system. There is conflict between the authoritarian setting and providing the conditions necessary for humane treatment.

Some institutions do provide separate wings or even special buildings or units to house treatment programs, but treatment staff ordinarily work within the confines of a portion of a cellblock set aside for therapeutic programs. Thus to separate the treatment milieu from the aura of authority is virtually impossible.

Enforced Therapy   Since the 1930s, American penal policy has promoted both individual and group therapy. Yet most inmates view the professional staff as merely an extension of the larger administrative bureaucracy of the prison. Such a mental set makes therapy difficult. Nonetheless, in their desire to demonstrate to the public and to state government that rehabilitation programs should be retained, administrators have required offenders to involve themselves in treatment programs as a condition of ultimate release.

Social work practice frowns on compelling the client to submit to treatment interventions. The ethos of casework is built on the premise that a willing client comes to a willing social worker for assistance. In prisons the reverse usually takes place. It is difficult to establish the necessary rapport with an offender in a treatment setting when both the social worker and the inmate know that therapy involves subtle or active coercion.

The Inmates' "Con Game"   American convicts are adept at the arts of persuasion and manipulation. The whole criminal justice system is viewed with disdain by most incarcerated felons. This view is strengthened when they see "treatment" being forced upon them by their keepers. Because of the indeterminate sentencing policies of most states, offenders quickly find that they must do all they can to maintain a good prison record. Rule infractions, intramural assaults, and other disruptive activities combine to cast doubt on the possibility for an early release.

During the last quarter of the nineteenth century, several states passed statutes permitting offenders to be sentenced to indeterminate prison terms. Thereafter, other jurisdictions began similar reforms, but in order to placate the judiciary, the legislatures mandated the imposition of statutory minimum and maximum sentences for certain crimes. The judge (and in a few states the jury) was then given power to sentence a convicted offender to a statutory minimum and leave it to correctional authorities and the parole boards to determine an appropriate release date. This reflected an interest in the offender as an individual rather than in the crime committed.

Indeterminate sentencing was promoted by most of the human service professions because treatment could be geared to the inmate's needs and potential. Like so many advances in penology, however, indeterminate sentencing practices were often turned against the persons they were originally designed to assist. Regardless of whether any rehabilitation program was warranted, inmates soon found that they had to participate in such activities as casework services, individual and group counseling, or some form of psychotherapy to be favorably recommended for parole, work release, or furlough. A prison record that indicated a certain number of official contacts with the social worker, the guidance counselor, the psychologist, or the psychiatrist received favorable comment from the classification committee or the parole board. The stage was thus set for a massive con game to be played with the treatment staff.

The social worker should be aware that not all offenders who seek professional assistance do so out of a genuine concern for self-improvement. Although many offenders profit from the delivery of social services within the institutional context, an equal if not greater number attempt to manipulate the worker for the attainment of their own goal of release.

The Artificial Prison Social Structure   In 1958 the sociologist Gresham M. Sykes published *The Society of Captives*.[3] Sykes developed the idea that a closed and unnatural environment produced a closed and unnatural social system. A comprehensive subculture of values, mores, and alternate life-styles predominates. For repeat offenders the inmate subculture is well known and usually rigidly adhered to; for new inductees, the social structure is internalized in days or weeks. One of the major problems confronting any human service professional in prison work is the ability to recognize the inmate subculture for what it is and to counteract its influence. Attempting to change criminals into noncriminals in an environment generally alien to middle-class life-styles demands techniques that most social workers are ill equipped to deliver. Wanting to change is one thing; refusing to change even though giving the appearance of changing is quite another.

Clarence Schrag has noted that within an institutional setting four types of "career variables" of convicts affect treatment strategies: prosocial inmates, antisocial inmates, pseudosocial inmates, and asocial inmates.[4] The social worker involved in a prison treatment program should at least be aware of the differences among these life-styles.

According to Schrag, the *prosocial* inmate usually has been convicted of a crime against the person and has entered upon a criminal career rather late in life. This offender exhibits unusually strong ties to his family and friends on the outside and, more likely than not, is cooperative with the institutional administrative and custodial staff. In addition, prosocial offenders almost always feel remorse and a sense of personal guilt when questioned about their criminality.

At the opposite pole is the *antisocial* inmate. The antisocial offender has usually been in prison before and generally has run afoul of the law while committing some form of property crime. This offender usually comes from a disadvantaged family background and often had a previous career in delinquency. Typically, this individual adheres rather stringently to the inmate subculture and is wary of the "good intentions" of the professional treatment staff and prison administrators.

The *pseudosocial* inmate is the sophisticated criminal who shifts allegiance back and forth between the norms of the inmate subculture and the rules and regulations promulgated by the prison bureaucracy and the treatment staff. Generally, the pseudosocial criminal has been convicted of one or more so-called white-collar[5] crimes that involve subtle and varied economic manipulations. According to Schrag, this type of inmate is located between the excesses of the antisocial offender and the generally law-abiding behavior of the prosocial convict.

To complete the picture, Schrag discusses the *asocial* inmate. Asocial offenders commit a variety of crimes that defy inclusion in a single typology. They are recidivists and have often had early behavior disorders. The asocial criminal distrusts personal involvement and while in the institution is undisciplined and lacks the capacity for mutual cooperation with other inmates and staff. The asocial offender has become thoroughly institutionalized before incarceration. Many have been reared in the artificial environment of foster care and in juvenile institutions and have little regard for the amenities of a secure home and family environment. The asocial individual probably presents the greatest challenge to members of the professional treatment staff, while the prosocial inmate usually needs only infrequent supportive intervention. Most social workers find that the families of the prosocial offenders are eager and willing in most cases to work with the worker in order to lay the groundwork for the inmate's return to the community.

Traditional one-to-one casework services and group treatment methods unfortunately have shown little success when applied to the antisocial and pseudosocial criminal because these two categories of behavior have been more closely identified with the pervasive effects of the inmate subculture. Such identifications tend to neutralize the chances of these treatment approaches for success.

INSTITUTIONAL CLASSIFICATION

A classification committee staffed with professionals can relieve some of the unfortunate experiences that arise during an inmate's prison stay. For example, inmates may advise the classification committee that they wish to simply "do time" and not be placed in a treatment program. At the outset, the committee should accede to the offender's wishes. However, classification is a continuing process. Later the committee should make the offender aware of the services and programs the institution offers. Periodic review of the inmate's progress in a treatment setting is crucial. The social worker's counseling and treatment notes should be made available to the classification committee unless the inmate lodges a valid objection to their use. Likewise, other professional reports to the committee should be made available to the social service team.

The prime functions of a prison classification committee are to determine: (1) the initial level of custody appropriate for the offender, i.e., whether he or she should be placed in a minimum-, medium-, or maximum-security portion of the institution; (2) the most appropriate treatment program or programs; (3) whether the inmate suffers from some physical or mental disability that would make retention in the general prison population undesirable; (4) whether the offender has any "free world" skills or knowledge that can be put to use in the institution; and (5) whether the offender desires treatment; subsequently the committee has the additional functions of assuring the institutional administration that the inmate has been placed in the proper category, and providing periodic reassessments of the inmate's progress while in the institution.

A model prison administrative structure that would take into account both the custody and treatment segments of the institution is shown in Figure 13.1.

Since the classification committee stands at the apex of the custody and treatment divisions, its members should be well versed in the problems of the inmates and the opportunities available to them. A well-coordinated and properly staffed classification committee can do much to alleviate some of the major internal conflicts confronting the prison population.

The model prison structure outlined in the Figure 13.1, however, is but one view. Some states have completely removed classification from the control of individual institutions and placed it in a central classification center. A convicted offender is transferred from the sentencing court directly to the state's central classification center, where a correctional profile is completed. The offender is then transferred to the most appropriate institution in the state system. A typical central classification scheme appears in Figure 13.2.

The central model saves tax monies by reducing redundant classification processes while giving the state a central clearing-house for prisoner records and diagnostic evaluations.

By recognizing the inherent limitations of attempts to change the

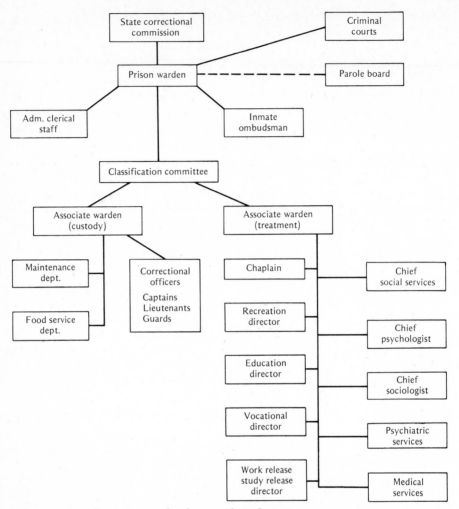

Figure 13.1 Administrative plan for custody and treatment.

behavior patterns of incarcerated felons, as well as the typical inmate career variables and the behaviors associated with each, and by appreciating the merits and limitations of inmate classification schemes, a social worker involved in institutional corrections can work with a variety of offenders toward social adjustment and reintegration.

COMMUNITY-BASED CORRECTIONS

It was a tenet of the new penology that the sooner the inmate could be released the better, since criminal and delinquent behavior tend to become more

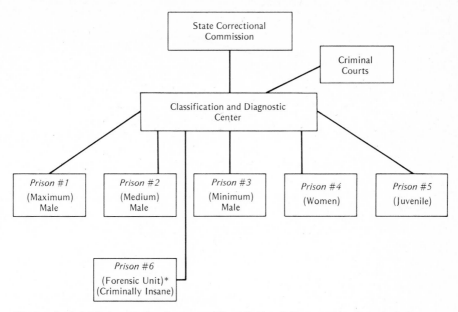

*May be under the jurisdiction of the State Department of Mental Health or similar agency rather than under the State Department of Corrections.

Figure 13.2   Typical statewide classification diagram.

difficult to modify the longer a person remains institutionalized. The farther the inmate moves through the criminal justice system, the less the chance for successful rehabilitation. Where possible, judges should completely avoid incarceration if facilities and programs are available to meet the correctional needs of the offender in the community. It is far better to remain in the community under designated restraints than to go to a penal institution. Evidence suggests that an exposure to institutional life inhibits the successful reintegration of both adults and juveniles into the law-abiding community. Thus the idea of community-based corrections has been promoted. The term "community-based corrections" lacks precise definition. The concept has become a code word for any program outside the walls of an institution. Community-based corrections has the goal of inmate-community involvement regardless of whether such involvement is realized. A decade ago, the President's Commission on Law Enforcement and the Administration of Justice estimated that at least two-thirds of the nation's correctional caseload was under some form of community-based corrections, principally probation or parole. The commission made the traditional recommendations for the upgrading and professionalization of the probation and parole services but gave little attention to other equally attractive alternatives.

Probation and parole make up the largest portion of a community-based

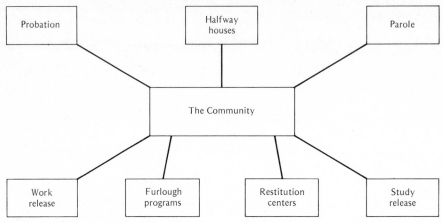

Figure 13.3   Typical community-based correctional program.

program. A total community-based correctional program should also include work release, restitution centers, study release, halfway houses, and furlough programs for deserving offenders. A schematic diagram of such an effort appears in Figure 13.3.

Work release, study release, restitution, and furlough programs are operated in cooperation with the community. Such efforts focus on the community as a major change-agent even though the offender may return to the institution each day after work. Probation, parole, and halfway houses operate on the premise that the offenders will make use of treatment efforts in the community. Community-based corrections represent another attempt by penologists and other professionals to formulate a more effective alternative to imprisonment.

Community-based programs offer a more flexible and less punitively structured atmosphere for innovative social work treatment models. In the United States today, many probation and parole officers have at least some formal education in social work practice and theory. In many agencies, personnel policies specify the acceptable level of academic training needed, and social work is high on most lists. Casework, for example, has been considered an optimum treatment technique in probation and parole supervision. The shared values and interests of social workers and community-based treatment personnel have made the use of casework and group work attractive.

Rationale for Community-Based Corrections

The "unnatural" prison environment and the widely shared disenchantment with institutional programs have led to a search for alternative treatment models. Treatment in the community was the logical rallying point for those who believed that attempts to reorder the lives of inmates in the traditional prison setting were futile.

Correctional programs at the community level are thought to be superior to institutional programs because:

1. Community-based programs tend to avoid the effects of isolation upon the offender.
2. Community-based programs allow room for a greater range of correctional alternatives, especially in the recreational, educational, health, and intensive treatment areas.
3. Community-based programs are more amenable to social work intervention than their institutional counterparts.
4. Community-based program policies may be better able to match the needs of particular types of offenders with the competences of particular social workers.
5. Reintegration goals and processes are stressed more readily in a community-based program.
6. Community-based corrections are cheaper.
7. Familial and employment ties are kept intact when treatment occurs in the community.
8. In the community the offender is insulated from some of the negative effects of the prison subculture.

Since the vast majority of inmates ultimately return to one community or another, the community itself must be prepared to deal with them. Social workers occupy a strategic role. In policy and program planning, their collective knowledge of community organization should play a vital part. With their other human service colleagues, community-based correctional social workers are needed to promote rehabilitation outside the stifling and socially degrading confines of the typical American penitentiary.

Many social workers, who find the prison environment too discouraging, choose to provide probation and parole services involving supervision of the offender in the community or assisting the return of the offender to the world outside the institution. Social workers are well equipped to perform these jobs, but they are often given such large caseloads that they feel their chance to help is severely limited.

SOCIAL WORK AND THE JUVENILE OFFENDER

Up to this point the discussion has focused on the adult correctional client. Now we will examine social work's involvement in juvenile justice. The treatment philosophy of juvenile courts has been quite different from that of their adult counterparts. The juvenile court system was originally developed along the lines of a nonadversary, nonpunitive, and nonauthoritarian model of justice for the child.

Historically, juvenile corrections can be divided into three periods. The reform era, from 1870 to 1899; the realignment era, 1900 to 1967, and the current reassessment era.

The Reform Era (1870–1899)

In the last three decades of the nineteenth century, criminal correction for the adult and the juvenile was largely undifferentiated. Criminal law was extremely harsh, and the nation's social conscience had yet to be awakened to the need for the enlightened handling of juvenile lawbreakers. The criminal act itself was the all-important ingredient. Scant attention was paid to the offender, and virtually no rehabilitation programs were in evidence for children or adults.

Children were originally held strictly accountable for criminal misbehavior. Later a degree of humanitarianism crept into the law. Legal scholars and historians were able to document a gradual recognition of the upper age limits of criminal liability. In both scholarly commentaries and court decisions, a triple age division became embedded in the common law establishing the criminal liability in children. Children under seven were conclusively presumed to be incapable of forming any criminal intent and hence could not be guilty of crime under any circumstances. Minors from seven to fourteen were presumed to be incapable of forming a criminal design, but, unlike those under age seven, this presumption could be overcome by the state. Children over age fourteen were fully responsible for their acts.

Between 1870 and 1899 came a new system. In the mid-1870s and thereafter, the reformatory movement gained a foothold in the United States, and along with the ideas put forth at the National Prison Association's first meeting in 1879, it provided the basis for the ultimate adoption of the world's first juvenile court law. Another powerful impetus for reform was the inauguration of the first statewide system of probation in Massachusetts in 1869.

Because of a steadily rising ubran crime rate among juveniles, numerous metropolitan correctional agencies evolved from the crucible of the slum. Children's aid societies and boards of charities, to mention only a few, flourished in many areas. In addition, the foster-home movement, originating in New York in 1853, gained a secure foothold in the philosophy of juvenile correction.

Finally, the last year of the nineteenth century saw the inevitable forces of historical determinism at work. Somewhat like a set of discordant strands being pulled through a common eyelet, the concepts of differential treatment for children, the rise of the reformatory movement, the development of probation, and an increased urban crime rate among juveniles led to the establishment of the juvenile court. The first such court was opened in Chicago in 1899. By 1927 there were juvenile courts in every state except Maine and Wyoming. They eventually followed suit. Now there are nearly 3,000 juvenile courts in the United States.

The Realignment Era (1900–1967)

In the sixty-seven years from the turn of the century to the decision *In re Gault* in May 1967, the juvenile court movement in the United States was greatly influenced by social work concepts and methods.

The original Illinois Juvenile Court Act in 1899 put an end to the exclusive jurisdiction of adult criminal courts over most minors charged with a criminal act. The original act gave the juvenile court jurisdiction over children under the age of sixteen who were charged with the commission of a noncapital felony. Upon a finding of guilt, the act provided that the delinquent should receive certain forms of beneficial treatment instead of punishment. The idea of a separate jurisdiction and an emphasis on the rehabilitation of delinquent children was so intense and widespread that within five years eleven states had passed legislation similar to that of Illinois.

Treatment was the touchstone of the realignment era. The juridical concept of *delinquency* was born. The delinquent, separate and distinct from the criminal, was to be looked upon as society's child, and this interpretation left little room for legalistic procedures. The issues involved in a delinquency adjudication were not those of criminal responsibility, guilt, and punishment, but rather understanding, guidance, and protection.

In 1940 the American Law Institute submitted its Model Youth Correction Act. "The purpose of this Act," states the preamble, "is to protect society more effectively by substituting for retributive punishment methods of training and treatment directed toward the correction and rehabilitation of young persons found guilty of violations of the law."

The model legislation recommended three procedures: (1) statewide youth authorities to assume continuous control of the state's juvenile clients from adjudication to discharge; (2) committing the juvenile to the youth authority rather than to specific state juvenile institutions; and (3) a true indeterminate sentencing policy subject to judicial review. Today these suggestions have been adopted by a majority of the states.

Community treatment programs for juveniles gained increased stature and flourished on a broad scale in the 1950s with the introduction of halfway houses whose main purpose was to provide an intermediate step to parole. New techniques in juvenile probation were developed under the aegis of social casework doctrine, and a general upgrading of juvenile probation officers followed.

Despite all of these gains, however, the juvenile offender seemed to be getting the worst of both worlds.

The judiciary, it seemed, was becoming impatient with the pious rhetoric of rehabilitation. Case after case suggested that the juvenile was being adjudicated "delinquent" on the flimsiest evidence possible, and, as a result, was being sent to an institution to be "rehabilitated." In fact, no such program existed. The Gault decision marked the turning point for both the law of juvenile delinquency and for constitutional law in general.

The Reassessment Era (1967–1977)

The Supreme Court in 1967 handed down the Gault decision. The case concerned Gerald Gault, a fifteen-year-old juvenile, who was brought before an Arizona juvenile court for allegedly making an obscene phone call to a neighbor. Neither the accused nor his parent was given advance notice of the charge against him. He was not informed of his legal rights and could have been held until he reached the age of majority. The penalty for an adult making an obscene phone call was no more than sixty days in jail or a fine.

The procedure used with Gault was not without reason. Many juvenile judges felt that advance notice stigmatizes a child and also violates confidentiality, since many people have access to official records. However, a legitimate desire to be helpful to an alleged juvenile is insufficient reason to disregard procedural safeguards.

The Supreme Court held that due process requires adequate, timely, written notice of the allegations against a juvenile, allowing sufficient time for the preparation of a response. In all cases involving the danger of loss of liberty, the juvenile must be accorded the right to counsel, privilege against self-incrimination, and the right to confront and cross-examine opposing witnesses under oath. The court was careful to limit the implications of its decision to the adjudication hearing in a delinquency action, the hearing that is used to determine guilt or innocence.

Thus the Gault case brought the concept of constitutional due process into juvenile court decision-making.[6] Previously, juvenile courts throughout the country had been adjudicating children as delinquent without regard for their constitutional rights. The majority opinion, written by Justice Abe Fortas, vehemently criticized the juvenile correctional establishment and made it clear that juveniles should not be deprived of their liberty without a hearing and should not be held in a correctional facility unless they were proved guilty of a delinquent act in court.

What implications does *In re Gault* have for social work? The decision did not portend the demise of casework or group work for juvenile clients as some social workers feared it might. The Gault decision opened the door for a greater involvement by social work in the juvenile justice field.

With appropriate judicial screening, juvenile correctional personnel would not receive only properly adjudicated delinquents. No longer would dependent and neglected children be stigmatized with the delinquent label. This would separate those minors needing institutional treatment from those needing some less intrusive program. The warehousing of a variety of juvenile offenders guilty of nothing more serious than some form of status offense was likewise struck down, by implication, in the Gault opinion.

Status offenders have no place to go in our system of services. These youth are charged with no action that would be an adult crime, but are often considered uncontrollable by parents or other adults. They are often truants or runaways. They are too old and too aggressive for the child welfare service system. Many mental health programs reject them or release them in a few days because no appropriate treatment methods have been found for them. They may have been told that they can't come back home, but independent living costs money and often leads to delinquent behavior to make ends meet. Status offenders are one of the problem populations for which the least has been done by human service programs.

A critical reassessment of juvenile correctional programs since 1967 suggests that we still have a long way to go. Perhaps social workers interested in youth crime should consider less emphasis on formal correctional intervention and more on prevention. The 1960s paved the way for a sociological effort in delinquency prevention that would have been quite impossible in earlier times. Youth crime will always be with us, unless and until the "root causes" of criminality are attacked. Given the present sociopolitical posture of American institutions, however, such an attack is beyond the realm of possibility. Thus, there is little evidence that the incidence of juvenile delinquency will be sharply reduced. Its rise in recent years has come about, at least in part, as a result of the increase in the number of children reaching the age of "high-risk" criminality—fourteen to twenty-four. We must address our most sophisticated efforts toward this population. Community organizers, caseworkers, group workers, and agency personnel alike can all add expertise to this effort. It is cheaper, both socially and economically, to prevent delinquency than to attempt to correct its pernicious effects.

The reassessment era has promoted an exciting new ideology. It has awakened an intense interest in the inner workings of juvenile justice as a "system," and in so doing, has promoted the idea of prevention as a companion goal to corrections in the cause of juvenile justice reform.

SUMMARY AND APPLICATION

The discussion of juvenile and criminal justice should make it clear why a strong effort is made to *divert* offenders from the correctional facilities. Diversion begins when a police officer tells a group of youths to go home before they are arrested; it is illustrated by "station adjustments" which often involve only a warning and release. Diversion for juveniles may involve release to parents who promise better supervision. For both juveniles and adults, the major diversionary technique for those found guilty is probation—formal supervision without incarceration. With the younger offender, the goal is often to help the person pass through the years when delinquency and crime are most common.

The social worker can play a part in the correctional system at various points that involve greater or lesser degrees of authority. There are opportunities not only for direct service but for the development of social action efforts to improve the correctional system.

—John C. Watkins, Jr.

KEY TERMS

presentence reports
proportional punishment
Pennsylvania Penal System
New York Penal System
Federal Bureau of Prisons

institutional classification
community-based corrections
Due process
In re Gault

REFERENCES AND NOTES

1. Division of Probation, Administrative Office of the United States Courts, *Selective Presentence Investigation Report,* Government Printing Office, Washington, D.C., 1965, pp. 29–39.
2. The positive school of criminology was founded by three Italians: Cesare Lombroso, Raphael Garofalo, and Enrico Ferri. In their writings they emphasized the study of the criminal instead of the crime, and as a result of their combined efforts, the "scientific method" of inquiry was utilized to seek the causes of criminality.
3. Gresham M. Sykes, *The Society of Captives: A Study of a Maximum Security Prison,* Princeton, Princeton, N.J., 1958.
4. Clarence Schrag, "Some Foundations for a Theory of Corrections," as quoted in Robert M. Carter et al., *Correctional Institutions,* 2d ed., Lippincott, New York, 1977, pp. 125–148.
5. The phrase "white-collar" crime was first enunciated by Edwin H. Sutherland in his presidential address to the American Sociological Association, meeting in Philadelphia, on December 27, 1939. In essence, white-collar crime is *upperworld* crime committed by persons of high social status as part of their normal occupational routine. Such activities as tax fraud, embezzlement, securities violations, false advertising, pure food and drug violations, and like crimes come under the rubric of white-collar offenses.
6. Prior to the Gault case only *Kent v. United States,* 383 U.S. 541 (1966), openly criticized juvenile court procedures in light of the due process clause of the Fourteenth Amendment.

FOR DISCUSSION

1. Why have social workers had little to do with corrections?
2. How is police–social work collaboration hindered?
3. How are offenders diverted from the criminal justice system?
4. What is the purpose of a presentence report?
5. How can work release programs be justified?
6. Differentiate between probation and parole.
7. Should prostitution, personal use of drugs, and other "victimless crimes" be removed from the criminal code? Why or why not?
8. What are some of the philosophical differences in running programs for juvenile offenders and for adults?

PROJECTS

1. Select subjects whom you do not know personally. Interview five adults each on two questions: How should you deal with a juvenile who is found guilty of stealing a car—a first offense? How would you proceed if it were his third offense? Code, tabulate, and analyze the results. Write a brief summary report.
2. Write an account of the Attica prison riots, indicating the main issues and their resolution.
3. Choose several of the behaviors listed below and indicate whether they should be considered legal offenses for juveniles. What means would you follow to deal with

them? Truancy, curfew violations, running away, persistently disobeying parents, drinking liquor or driving under the legal age, using marijuana occasionally.

4. Determine how social workers are being used in probation and parole services and in penal institutions in your area. What are the job opportunities at various educational levels?

5. Determine whether there is a program available in your area to help former prisoners. Invite its director to talk to the class or with a student committee. Is there a role for social workers in the program?

6. Study and report on the bail-bond system in your area. Is recognizance bond available?

CHAPTER 14
Aging

The "young" old

    Most families intact
    Some aches and pains
    Most are generally happy

The "old"

    Most are widowed
    Health is an adamant concern
    Most are unhappy

The goal is not to add years to life but life to the years.

—Source Unknown

Aging, a social, biological, and psychological process, begins at birth. After age forty, maturation is usually seen as a liability. Older people have only recently been recognized as a minority group in American society, subject to discrimination and negative stereotyping. While public relief of the destitute aged has existed in the United States since colonial times, other services and protections for the elderly as a group have evolved slowly. The rights of older citizens to live independently, to work, and to die in dignified and humane circumstances are gradually attracting attention and support, but significant changes in our social welfare and employment system must still be made.

SOCIAL WORK ROLES WITH THE AGED

Social workers are finding new opportunities for work with the aged as the array of publicly supported program expands, and they are likely to encounter the needs of older clients in most practice settings. In child welfare, the role of the grandparent is important. Social services for recipients of Supplemental Security Income (SSI) are usually carried out by social workers. A related role in the Social Security Administration involves eligibility determination and referral services for persons who apply for SSI. Workers make visits to reassess eligibility and to meet clients' requests for services. Social workers help to arrange for home-delivered meals, transportation, homemaker service, and other concrete supports for SSI clients. Where necessary, they assist in planning for nursing home care. Workers have an opportunity to help clients attain the maximum feasible level of self-care and self-sufficiency.

Nursing Home Care

The public and private nursing home industry represents another setting where social workers have begun to assume a wider range of responsibilities. Consultation on social services for residents and increased attention to activities to promote socialization is found in more nursing homes, but there is no documentation to show how extensively social workers are being utilized in this role. Advertising in professional journals, requests by nursing home facilities for field placements, and reports by individual workers at professional conferences all suggest that opportunities are emerging. The form varies from a consortium of small facilities which pool funds to hire a single full-time caseworker to institutions that use social work consultation one or two days a month for case review. Progressive homes, in both the public and the private

345

proprietary sectors, have hired social workers to work with patients and their families. With continued development of professional interest and competence, this trend may continue.

It is interesting to look at a social service unit as it operates in those facilities which have newly established programs. Social workers talk with the patient and the family at admission to assess whether the institution can best meet the needs of the prospective patient. Following intake, the worker will maintain the relationship with the patient to answer questions or resolve problems which may arise in the course of adjusting to new surroundings. Where possible, relatives are given reports on patient progress and suggestions on how the patient's condition affects family interaction. The social worker also analyzes how the family can respond most constructively to patient needs and expectations. When the older person is ready to be discharged, the social worker will try to marshal community-based, home-delivered services to support continued recovery and sustained independent living outside the nursing home.

The worker may also meet jointly with older persons and relatives in order to smooth the transition from the facility to returning home. Normal fears, realistic obstacles to recovery, and potential sources of friction in family relationships are discussed. The objective is to equip the older person with resources and an understanding of how problems may be surmounted.

Finally, social workers have contributed to the training of other staff, particularly volunteers and nurse's aides, to help them become more responsive and constructive in their approach to patients.

Public Housing

Another promising setting is public housing. The elderly have proven to be excellent tenants in housing projects, and proportionately more resources in this program are being allocated for their use. In some communities, public housing projects have established social service units to counsel tenants on the use of community services and to stimulate participation by tenants in decision-making affecting the policies of the housing project.

Federal and state funds for community-based information and referral programs, home-delivered meals, transportation, recreation, education, and other services have increased each year since 1965. These activities offer job opportunities for social workers with a bachelor's degree and a concern for the needs of the aged. Typical responsibilities include outreach to isolated older people, planning for implementation or expansion of new programs, assisting in the creation of local senior citizens' councils or other action-oriented groups, organizing informal older people's groups to discuss problems and solutions which might be shared in common, presenting the needs of the elderly to local groups and collaborating with staff from other community agencies in resolving the resource needs of elderly clients.

Older people are a priority group in work training programs under the Comprehensive Employment and Training Act (CETA). Social workers are beginning to enter this field, which offers opportunities for job counseling, job coaching, client advocacy, referral or legal aid or other advice, and client outreach.

The Team Approach

Intervention in problems affecting older people is usually multidisciplinary and team-based. In the United States, the permission of a physician or the presence of a public health nurse is often a prerequisite for intervention by the social worker. Since one in five older persons has an income below the official Social Security Administration poverty line, income deprivation and work with appropriate welfare agencies or pension programs is an integral aspect of counseling. Urban planners, educators, recreation and leisure studies specialists, psychologists, home economists, nurses, occupational/physical/ speech/and hearing therapists, and architects have been deeply involved over the past decade in the planning or delivery of services for the aged. The social worker should be prepared to understand the outlook and guiding theories of these professions, in order to provide a complementary perspective.

The role of social service workers has recently become more diversified and significant in relation to the elderly. Why the new interest in older people? What problems do they encounter? What should be done to improve their living circumstances and quality of life? The answers to these questions help to suggest how social workers can best select a future focus for intervention in order to achieve a more significant impact on the well-being of this important segment of society.

WHAT IS "OLD AGE"?

The most familiar concept of old age specifies a *chronological cutoff point*—age sixty-five—which separates elderly adults from others, but there is nothing magical or particularly scientific about age sixty-five. The Germans adopted sixty-five as the criterion of aging for the world's first modern old-age social security system, established in 1883. When the United States adopted its own social security legislation in 1935, eligibility for retirement benefits was also pegged at age sixty-five, based on the German precedent.

To administer a large income-maintenance program or other social services with near-universal coverage, this concept of old age sets a simple standard for determining eligibility. To many private employers it also represents an equitable way of deciding when a worker should be asked to "step down" in favor of younger employees.

The resistance to defining old age exclusively in years is growing. Society itself has informally lowered the standard by which people are regarded as elderly. Senior citizens' clubs and church groups are often open to anyone fifty-five or over; retirement communities usually exclude persons younger than forty-five or fifty. Age-related employment problems appear as early as age forty. More important, chronological definitions of old age, wherever set,

"While shaving this morning, Roy realized that he is <u>exactly</u> halfway between most likely to succeed and mandatory retirement." (Reprinted by permission of Saturday Review and John Ruge.)

are inadequate because they tell nothing about how well a person continues to function physically, psychologically, or in interpersonal relationships—the most meaningful aspects of human behavior.

Another widely held concept of aging is drawn from the biological sciences. From this perspective, aging is a process of *successive decrements in physical functioning*. The capacity of cells to regenerate becomes progressively impaired with time. Scientists hold rival theories about what causes body cells to function inefficiently and die. Perhaps we operate on a "biological time clock" because damaging metabolic by-products slowly build up within our cells. As the triggers to biological aging are better understood, researchers are finding ways of slowing or even reversing the process.

Biological aging progresses at different rates among individuals, and even within the same person certain parts of the body age more slowly than others. Functional decline occurs unevenly. Some abilities, in fact, stabilize at an adequate level after an individual passes the early sixties.

Until recently, all biological decline was thought of as pathological. Young adults were used as the norm or basis for comparison. By that standard, all elderly people appeared "sick." Programs of exercise, diet, and physical rehabilitation for older adults were generally ignored, based on the untested assumption that weakness and incapacity were inevitable aspects of life after sixty-five.

Yet aging is not an illness. Older persons are adaptable and find means to compensate for lost abilities. For example, as visual acuity declines in middle age, most adults begin wearing eyeglasses. Good health for the elderly must therefore be seen in the light of changes or average behaviors for all older adults as a group. As chronic complaints, illnesses, or disabilities accumulate in the later years, a person should still be considered well if he or she is experiencing only modest discomfort and there is no immediate threat of death.[1]

Developmental theory offers a third way of conceptualizing old age.[2] Erik Erikson was among the first to elaborate this view. Developmental theorists hold that *old age is a unique stage in social and psychological growth*. From the biological scientist's perspective, "development" means cellular growth and differentiations leading to physical maturity; "aging" is the remaining downward course in life. In developmental theory, sociologists and psychologists have argued that even as biological functioning declines, people are capable of social and experiential growth. Old age is a stage, the final stage, of psychological and interpersonal evolution, containing the potential for unique levels of self-discovery and personal integration. The experiences and challenges of a lifetime lay the groundwork for this period of resolution and integration. The experience cannot be achieved by younger persons.

Unique Problems

Aging brings a distinctive set of problems which an individual must confront and master in order to achieve successful old age. Given a long enough lifetime, all people move from middle age to "young" old age and then, with increasing frailty, to "old" old age and death. Through this transition, five crises are almost universal: (1) loss of social status; (2) loss of significant people; (3) internal and external body changes reflecting biological decline; (4) confrontation with death; and (5) modification of available roles and activities. Retirement, the need for long-term care and ultimately terminal care, and loss of spouse represent special issues for all social workers concerned with aging.[3]

Social service systems are designed to sustain and support individuals as they meet these predictable crises, strengthening their ability to cope effectively with additional demands in future years. Given these necessary environmental supports, old age for most people can be an extended period of normal good health. Biological decline can be less devastating, milder, and more predictable. Social relationships may be more rewarding than at any other period as people are freed from the responsibilities of full-time employment and child-rearing. Intellectual activities and interests may be deepened; the older years may be used for a review of one's own life experiences as a method of finding meaning and personal identity which permits acceptance of death.

Old age, then, may be defined chronologically, biologically, or in terms of social-psychological development. Chronological definitions are useful in program administration but reflect nothing about functional ability. Biological decline over time, while inevitable, should not be seen as a normal process. Human beings can continue to grow in clarifying, deepening, and integrating their personal experiences. Old age offers a unique opportunity for the attainment of new insights and quality of life, when adequate environmental supports are available to help people master the typical crises of retirement, loss of spouse, and needs for long-term care.

The main characteristic of the aged as a group is variability. Aging takes place at different rates, and the impact depends upon people's personal and environmental resources for coping. Social services for older people strengthen that coping capability.

CHARACTERISTICS OF AGING PERSONS IN AMERICAN SOCIETY

Demographic Characteristics

In 1000 B.C. the average life expectancy was eighteen years; in 1977 it was seventy-two. Most of this gain was achieved between 1900 and 1939, when the major childhood diseases were conquered. Average life expectancy after age sixty-five has only increased by about four years over the same time period. However, where life expectancy by sex is considered, women have gained approximately six years, and men less than two.[4]

The number and proportion of persons over age sixty-five has grown steadily each decade since 1900, from 4.1 percent of the population to nearly 11 percent, or 22 million persons. Every year, 300,000 to 400,000 more people reach age sixty-five, which will bring the aged population to 30 million persons by the year 2000.[5] The absolute number of elderly persons will double between 1970 and 2020, but fears of a "gerontology takeover" are groundless. The actual proportion of older persons in the population will not increase by more than another 2 percent.

The fastest growing subgroup among the elderly are those seventy-five years or more—the vulnerable "old" old. Blacks are more likely than whites to live several years longer after reaching age seventy-five. Possibly only the strongest blacks achieve this age, while some whites who would have died earlier are sustained at least through their sixties by better quality of care. In general, the life expectancy of black men is seven and one-half years less than that of white males, principally as a result of institutional racism, which keeps minorities in disabling low-income jobs.[6]

The number of males per 100 females after age sixty-five drops. The causes of death are more likely to affect males at younger ages. Indications are that the number may fall to as few as 60 males per 100 females by the turn of the century.[7] If these projections are borne out, the proportion of isolated elderly women will present formidable problems for social service, income mainte-nance, and housing programs.

The majority of older people live in the nation's cities, particularly the central cities—in contrast to younger adults, who are concentrated in the suburbs. Transportation issues, crime, and other urban issues are therefore vital questions to the well-being of the aged population. Proportionately, rural towns up to 2,500 in population have the highest concentrations of persons over sixty-five. The young have migrated, leaving their elders behind. Older persons are less mobile than any other population group. And even when elderly families do relocate, about 66 percent stay in the same county.[8]

Economic Status of Older Persons

We have already noted the diversity in the characteristics of older people. The "aged" range from the early sixties to the late eighties and beyond. Obviously the economic position of the "young" old, their past earnings history, and their pattern of expenditures will be substantially unlike the pattern for "old" old individuals. The very old have special health care needs, and because they grew up in a different period, their expectations and living standards are also different.

Aside from "young" old and "old" old, two additional subgroups should be distinguished—the retired and the nonretired. Older people who continue to work are, of course, more apt to have sufficient income. The concept of retirement itself is hazy. To some retirement means that they are no longer working in the primary occupation which filled their young and middle adult years. Others consider anything less than full-time employment as retirement. Some jobless persons counted in the statistics as retired are actually seeking work but unable to find a position.[9] Conventional income statistics are based on combinations of very different circumstances.

Definition of the actual retirement status of older people is essential. The worse economic problems associated with old age generally appear when the flow of earned income stops, unless people are severely disabled, dependent survivors of persons insured under social security, or destitute family heads with children. When individuals retire before they become eligible for social security benefits, they must rely entirely on savings, private insurance benefits, or the sale of personal property.

About half of all older people own their own home or have accumulated equity in their residence, but these paper values cannot readily be converted into liquid assets. And inflated home values may lead only to higher taxes—a serious problem in the face of limited income. Liquid assets consist of bank deposits, cash, or stocks which can easily be utilized to meet the daily expenses of living. The majority of elderly persons have few assets. In 1967 two-thirds or more had less than $5,000—and many had less than $1,000.[10]

Another source of economic support should not be overlooked: in-kind benefits from government programs. In-kind benefits are services, food, shelter, or other noncash resources. In 1975 there were forty-two federal programs which provided in-kind benefits to the elderly, including Medicare, Medicaid, food stamps, old age insurance, public housing, and nutrition centers.[11]

Since 1959 increases in social security and in-kind benefits have contributed to real improvement in the economic status of elderly persons. According to the Bureau of the Census, the number of aged families with below-subsistence income has dropped from 27 percent to 8.5 percent of those over sixty-five. Even more dramatic, perhaps, is the change in the status of old people living alone. While nearly two-thirds were below government standards of poverty in 1959, by 1974 this proportion had dropped to 31.8 percent. However, 36.4 percent of all black aged remained poor in 1974, compared to 13.8 percent of whites over sixty-five.[12]

Living Arrangements

For nearly two decades, increasing numbers of older people have moved out of living arrangements with relatives to set up their own homes. Old persons, like younger adults, prefer privacy and independence, if economic resources permit. Most elderly persons still live within twenty or thirty miles of their children, however.[13]

About 70 percent of all elderly men are married and living with their wives. Because women outlive their spouses, nearly two-thirds live alone. About 2 percent of all elderly people maintain a common-law relationship, and contrary to news reports, this proportion has not changed since 1960.[14]

Most public housing is not modified to meet the physical limitations of handicapped persons, and older people typically lack the energy or resources to maintain their own homes at desirable standards. The cost of housing places low- to middle-income older people at a considerable disadvantage in the market.

Health Status

Older people are undeniably less healthy than younger adults. Most have one or more chronic conditions, and almost one in ten is bedridden. Four out of ten have physical disabilities that interfere with the performance of major self-care tasks. Older people spend a higher proportion of their income on drugs, see their doctor more often than younger adults, and once in the hospital have longer periods of care.[15] The health status of the "old" old is worse than for the "young" old, ages sixty-five to seventy-four. However, despite these limitations, more than 85 percent of people over sixty-five continue to live at home and carry out most of the responsibilities associated with everyday living.[16]

While a biological decline in the functioning of organs makes older people more vulnerable to illness, research over the past ten years has begun to reveal that social and personal stresses play a major role in disease. Older people must cope with continuous shocks: change or deterioration in living arrangements, loss of work status and reduced income, low social status, death of friends and families, and other profound stresses. These changes often occur rapidly, pushing people to the limits of endurance. Illness, acceleration of the biological aging process, and death result. Functional breakdown also stems from misuse or neglect of the body through inadequate exercise, poor diet, cigarette smoking, and maladaptive life-styles.

The reduction of illness and disease among the elderly is as much a social-psychological and bureaucratic problem as it is a problem for physicians and other biological scientists. Studies of long-living peoples of the world show that neither heredity nor low prevalence of disease is a significant determinant of longevity. Four other factors are much more likely to predict long-term survival: (1) a clearly defined and valued role in society; (2) a positive self-perception; (3) sustained, moderate physical activity; and (4) abstinence from cigarette smoking. Studies in this country indicate that secure financial status, lively social relationships, and high education are also important.[17]

Family Relationships

Most older people are in fairly regular contact with one or more of their children and see them at least once a month. Daughters, single children, and those children who nearby are most apt to stay in touch. Visiting back and forth is most typical of blue-collar families, while middle-class children are more likely to move away and must find alternative channels for communication.[18]

Older people contribute substantially to their children's lives—much more than is usually recognized. Intergenerational relations often have a strong reciprocal character. Grandparents give child care services, make financial contributions to help children meet obligations, and frequently share their homes. Blue-collar families are most likely to exchange services; financial assistance is more common among middle-class families.

While the positive aspects of family relationships should be kept in mind, apparently the majority of elderly persons do not regard their kin ties as intimate enough. They would like to have more communication and companionship, but at the same time they are anxious for their children to take advantage of opportunities for upward mobility, even if this results in physical separation.[19]

The relationships of aging spouses have changed dramatically over the past generation. Because of reduced mortality rates, most couples now spend ten to twenty years together after the last child has grown up. Limited evidence suggests that in this phase of the marriage relationship, women seem to acquire more power.

With the death of her husband, a second major adaptation is required for a woman in old age. Most women expect to outlive their husbands, and "rehearse" for the role of widow as they watch the death of friends or throughout the illness of their spouse. However, many women never overcome their grief. Nearly one in five continues to mourn for the remainder of her life, and surveys report a higher incidence of unhappiness and personal dissatisfaction among the widowed than the married.[20] Widows are more likely to succumb to illness, show symptoms of mental illness, and have higher rates of suicide. Widows need sympathetic persons who can accept grief and offer companionship. Dependency should not be encouraged, but help should be offered that builds the older woman's competence at problem-solving. Major changes in life-style should not be encouraged until some months have elapsed and the woman is in a position to more rationally assess her situation.

Psychological Status of the Elderly

Research on intellectual functioning appears to confirm that very few changes occur in individuals as a result of old age. At most, older people may learn at a somewhat slower rate, and there seems to be a sharp decline in intelligence just before death. After age seventy, a decrement has been observed, but it is much less than conventional wisdom would hold. On the other hand, there are marked differences in intellectual functioning between the generations. Psychologists theorize that old people have not lost the capacity to function, but the level attained in their young adulthood becomes obsolete by age sixty-five. Adult retraining and compensatory education programs are needed.[21]

Few studies show how aging of the brain affects behavior. All results are based on tests of animals. Evidence points to some behavioral changes, such as learning and memory deficits, but the changes are small and do not occur universally. Psychologists are uncertain whether observed changes stem from the aging process, disease, environmental stress, or extensive isolation.

Employment Status

By age sixty-five, 70 percent of all workers have left the labor force. Those who remain are concentrated in part-time and low-wage occupations. While three out of four male workers remained on the job after age sixty-five in 1900, the proportion has dwindled to one in four. By contrast, the labor force participation rate of elderly women has risen over the same period from one in twelve to one in ten. Aged black women are even more likely to be at work than white females, a reflection of the financial pressures which disproportionately affect minority families.[22]

Age-specific employment problems begin once a worker reaches his or her forties. Work is more difficult to retain, and long-term unemployment is common once a worker has been displaced. And even when a new job is secured, the worker usually receives a lower rate of pay.

Three major factors have contributed to the employment problems of aging workers. First, agriculture, mining, and railroading—areas which once employed large numbers of older workers—have declined since the end of World War II. Although white-collar job opportunities have expanded, older people have not possessed sufficient education or skills to qualify. They are also less willing to move.

Second, business has gradually begun a shift from the older industrialized regions, and older workers are most heavily concentrated in these densely settled, depressed cities.

Third, age discrimination in employment practices, coupled with the cumulative effect of layoffs and bankruptcies during recession periods, has created a pool of long-term-unemployed job-seekers among the middle-aged. These persons are also less likely to receive counseling, job referrals, and other special services related to work.

Several myths about the older worker have been widely accepted by employers and service providers. The older worker is seen as less healthy, more prone to absenteeism, more clumsy, more accident-prone, slower in task performance, and more forgetful.[23]

Research provides contrary evidence. Older workers have lower turnover rates, a more positive attitude toward their work, produce at a steadier rate, are more accurate, and exceed younger employees in health and low on-the-job injury rates. Once the older worker does become ill, however, he or she usually takes somewhat longer to recover than a younger person.

As stated above, functional decrements do take place with age. Sensory capacity, vision, and hearing are less acute. The older worker characteristically compensates by wearing eyeglasses, working in brighter light, slowing the pace of work while improving efficiency, and avoiding dangerous or hazardous work situations. In this way, workers continue to function well even though chronological age increases.[24]

Despite these qualifications, about one-third of all long-term unemployed persons are over age forty-five. Among retired persons age sixty-five or over, slightly more than a third would like to return to work, assuming a reasonable wage. About half of all retirees suffer from physical conditions which would require modification of the work environment and hours, with outside social supports, such as transportation, before they would be available for employment.[25]

Older people, then, represent greater numbers and a larger proportion of our society, with the fastest increase occurring among persons age seventy-five or over. The sex ratio has been steadily declining, contributing to a growth in the number of older women living alone. Most older people have few liquid assets. Aged women, blacks, and unmarried persons are most likely to live at below-subsistence levels. Elderly people prefer to live independently of their children, if possible, but housing standards for this group are generally low. While the elderly are less healthy than younger persons and require more medical attention, illness may be stress-related. Mortality and disease can be reduced if older people have adequate environmental supports. Many older persons are in regular contact with their families but wish for more intimacy. Roles between aged parents and children are more reciprocal than commonly believed. Widowhood is a trauma which most women should expect to encounter. Help with problem-solving is essential during this period.

THE GENERAL STRUCTURE OF SOCIAL SERVICES FOR OLDER PEOPLE

The Older Americans Act

The most important recent social service legislation for the elderly is the Older Americans Act (OAA). For the aged, after the end of World War II, the focus was principally on increasing the supply of hospital beds and long-term care facilities. The White House Conference on Aging in 1961 was unusually successful in documenting the problems of older persons trying to maintain independent living arrangements. National income data, available for the first time with the 1960 census, revealed that between 33 and 45 percent of Americans over age sixty-five were living at below-subsistence levels. While the War on Poverty in the 1960s was aimed at youth, the mood in Washington was sympathetic to social service experimentation. The growth in the number and proportion of elderly people could no longer escape the attention of politicians, particularly when research showed that elderly persons voted more regularly than the newly enfranchised eighteen-year-olds.

In 1965, Congress passed the Older Americans Act to establish the Administration on Aging in the Department of Health, Education and Welfare. The most important provision was Title III, which authorized time-limited federal matching grants to local communities for demonstration projects in services to support independent living. In 1969 Title VII was added, which provided federal funds for congregate nutrition programs and home-delivered meals.

Funding for the act was $10 million—by federal government standards, quite low.

The overall impact of Title III was difficult to assess.[26] While special units within existing state departments of aging had been given responsibility for planning, program development, and monitoring of Title III projects, a base of support at the local level had not been adequately built. The ability of state-level staff to respond to unique local conditions was questioned.

More significantly, the priorities for the use of Title III funds were not clear. Four objectives were evident. First, because so little attention had been given to elderly persons outside medical care facilities, a national minimum level of essential services was needed. Substantial revenues from state and local sources would be required to achieve this objective, since Title III funds were not sufficient to achieve this goal.

Second, Title III funds could be directed toward experimentation with new forms of service structure and delivery. Almost all existing community programs evolved in response to the needs of children and young adults. Distinctive approaches would have to be adopted in order to respond specifically to the needs of the aged. For example, in finding work for older people, one project experimented with dividing a single job between two elderly men. In this way, both were able to supplement their social security retirement income, but neither was taxed beyond his capacity in terms of energy or time.

Third, funds could be devoted to community organization and development, with emphasis on the creation of new citizen constituencies. The purpose was to stimulate local demand, so that services would evolve through other funding sources. Elderly people had not been accustomed to acting on their own behalf; they lacked consciousness of their needs as a group. Most older citizens had not been politically assertive, nor did they articulate their needs before government planning bodies. Older people lacked visibility in significant positive roles. Newspapers report fiftieth anniversaries, obituaries, and retirement banquets, but rarely show older people in active or innovative capacities. It has been relatively easy, therefore, to ignore the needs of older persons in favor of more conspicuous special groups.

Title III funds could counter this familiar pattern through the formation of community interest groups, the cultivation of new leadership among the elderly at the local level, and the education of older persons regarding their entitlement to service.

A final alternative in the use of Title III resources was the improvement of coordination and accessibility of existing programs in the community network. While income maintenance and preventive health care programs might be available, utilization frequently depends on cheap transportation, the office hours, the intelligibility of application forms (and the type size in which they are printed), the length of the waiting lines, and the visibility of the service in the community.

Improved interagency coordination might, of course, produce better referrals of elderly clients, better follow-up, more appropriate differential use of services, and more likelihood of an optimal mix of provisions for older persons with multiple problems.

The objectives of coordination, community organization, development of basic essential services, and social experimentation could not be fully met under past or current OAA provisions. There are not sufficient funds to support this array of local programs. Moreover, the objectives lead to quite distinct lines of activity. For example, coordinating existing services means extensive cooperative interaction with established agencies; social experimentation or service innovation may mean setting up a competitive organization, or at least decentralizing the customary pattern of service provision. However, Congress has still not resolved how Title III support should be used.

Social services under Title III now comprise about one-quarter of OAA appropriations.[27] Those services include information and referral, counseling, transportation, education, recreation, and other personalized one-to-one or demand-responsive programs.

The primary focus of Title III programs is enhancement of the ability of older persons to maintain independent living arrangements. Government intervention is necessary because the private market does not supply the quantity or variety of supports to daily living which the disabled or very aged person requires. Where these services are available, as in the case of home maintenance and repair, costs are prohibitive for anyone on a fixed retirement income.

For example, one of the most valuable activities performed by many Title III projects has involved reassurance. A volunteer, often an older homebound individual, telephones an elderly client who lives alone. The call is a meaningful form of social contact for both parties, but also establishes that no accidents or other serious problems have arisen which might require emergency attention. Relatives who do not live in the same community are powerless to monitor an elderly family member's daily well-being. Reassurance calling reduces the burden of helpless concern of family members. Older people themselves express considerable satisfaction with this service.

A particularly desirable characteristic of reassurance programs is the element of reciprocity. As a rule, clients of any age are passive recipients in the service delivery process. A professional or trained volunteer determines the client's needs and perhaps the form and amount of the services an agency provides. The client accepts and is expected to be cooperative. The client has little power or authority in the system. By contrast, the reassurance calling service permits people who receive help also to contribute their own energies and talent. Elderly clients express great satisfaction at being able to help sustain a program which has been vital to their own well-being.

In response to the questions raised by the General Accounting Office and other problems, Congress substantially modified Title III through the Comprehensive Service Amendments of 1973. A nationwide system of Area Agencies on Aging (AAAs) was authorized to plan and administer grant funds for Title III programs. The AAAs are multicounty, nonprofit organizations funded exclusively through state offices or departments on aging through matching state and federal funds under OAA. Local organizations wishing to provide services to the elderly would apply to the AAA; the AAA, in turn, receives an annual block grant, based on population within the region and proportion of elderly. The role of the states shifted more to that of technical assistance and, hopefully, long-range planning functions. The AAAs are governed by a group of citizens drawn from the communities in the service area. The composition of area agency boards, according to federal regulations, should reflect the interests of primary service consumers—the elderly, minorities, and the poor. The justification for areawide, citizen-controlled planning bodies like the AAAs has been continuously debated. As the state offices and departments on aging have grown in administrative budgets and competency, there has been some pressure for area agency functions to revert to the state, but the AAAs have strenuously resisted this idea. At the community level, local program operators sometimes begrudge the dollars which support AAA personnel. These dollars might equally be used to support direct services to older clients. On the other hand, area agencies have been responsible for cultivating local interest in the aging where none has previously been manifested.

By 1976 funding for the Older Americans Act had reached over $400 million, and another title had been added—the Community Service Employment amendment. This amendment makes funds available for part-time, public service employment of low-income elderly persons. In addition, legal services have grown increasingly important as a component of OAA programs, and senior citizens' centers have newly been funded under the act. Community ombudsmen programs, to represent the views of elderly persons in nursing homes, have also become an established aspect of the act.

Approximately half of the expenditures under this legislation support nutrition programs for the elderly (Title VII), principally meals served at group "feeding sites." Older people gather for a luncheon meal, which is prepared four or five times a week. The goals of the program are to improve the nutrition of elderly persons and offer opportunities for socialization. These Title VII projects have, perhaps, been the most visible and the most popular of all the OAA provisions. However, critics argue that the program does not improve nutrition, since the average participant only eats two meals a week at the site. Moreover, isolated or frail elderly persons are not likely to appear, so the social interaction is typically enjoyed by those who are already active and well integrated. While there is no charge for meals, older persons are asked to make a "contribution" in small envelopes left beside their plates. Observers maintain that the elderly experience strong informal pressure to "pay up," and leave more than they can afford.

Aside from social services and community nutrition programs, the Older Americans Act, under separate titles, sponsored research, demonstration projects, and training programs in gerontology. A shortage of persons trained in gerontology and program management has adversely affected the quality of OAA programs. Universities and community colleges have been encouraged by the Administration on Aging to create new course offerings, specialties, and degree concentrations in aging. The uneven success of OAA initiatives at the local level is partially attributable to the absence of defined career patterns and educational prerequisites for employment in the field. As the legislation matures, a more specialized workforce is gradually being trained.

Several intractable problems still must be addressed. Traditionally, programs for the elderly have been low-cost, low-priority community efforts. Services developed under OAA legislation have relied heavily on volunteer assistance. As labor force participation among middle-aged women rises, however, the volunteer pool tends to dry up. The cost of giving service to older persons will rise. Even where volunteers remain an important component of program staff, there is new recognition that volunteer training is essential in order to reduce turnover and ensure that program goals are met. Volunteers typically need help in responding to atypical, demanding, or "unattractive" elderly clients.

Program coordination is another formidable question. The Administration on Aging is a new arrival on the social welfare scene, as are state offices or departments on aging. Area Agencies on Aging lack visibility. Local programs supported by OAA funds operate under widely different auspices, as any nonprofit organization may apply to the AAA for grants to operate Title III programs. This mixture of administrative complexity, variety, and inexperience means that relationships with other health and welfare programs at the federal, state, and local levels are weak and uneven.

Moreover, OAA programs are not in a good position to expand relative to older, established programs. For example, the budget of the Illinois Department on Aging in 1979 was approximately $15 million; for the same period, the Illinois Department of Mental Health had an appropriation of about $600 million. Under these circumstances, a department on aging is hardly likely to prevent a department of mental health from adopting policies which are inimical to the interests of elderly people residing in mental institutions. The limited bargaining power and influence of OAA agencies permeates all levels of government.

A further dilemma for administrators and service providers in OAA agencies results from statutory limitations on the amount which may be expended for program administration. In its anxiety to prevent states and localities from unduly fattening their payrolls or making frivolous outlays for office overhead, Congress will not permit agencies to spend even 10 percent of their funds for administration. Unfortunately, the development of new programs and effective coordination with external agencies involves high overhead. Planning, research on client needs, assessment of program results, outreach to new groups, training of staff and volunteers, monitoring of programs in progress, and organization of coalitions at the local and state levels are part of the start-up cost. State and area agencies are starved for personnel, low wages prevail for qualified personnel, and heavy workloads are the rule.

In brief, programs under the Older Americans Act have grown dramatically in number and pervasiveness since 1965, but the impact of services has been small. Inadequate funding, administrative problems, poorly prepared personnel, and a weak power base detract from the potential accomplishments of the legislation. The goals of the act are to ensure that all the nation's elderly have adequate income, suitable housing, physical and mental health, opportunities for employment, efficient community services, channels for the pursuit of meaningful activity, and honor and dignity in old age. The attainment of these goals within the resources of the act alone seems very distant, if achievable at all.

The ability of this nation to reach the goals of the Older Americans Act will probably depend on policies approved by Congress under the Social Security Act, the Housing and Urban Development Act, the Age Discrimination Act, and the Comprehensive Employment and Training Act (CETA). The health care structure, income security, employment, and housing of older persons are shaped by these acts.

Provisions for Older Persons Under the Social Security Act: Health Care, Income, and Social Services

The Social Security Act of 1935 was originally passed after an unprecedented flurry of activity instigated at President Roosevelt's behest at the midpoint of the Great Depression of the 1930s. A national system of social insurance benefits at retirement, called Old Age Insurance (OAI), established several principles which are still preserved today. Earned income of currently employed workers is subject to a social security withholding tax up to a certain limit; the tax was paid equally by workers and their employers. An average worker becomes "fully covered" or eligible for OAI benefits after contributing to the system for ten years. The amount which a worker receives in benefits on retirement varies with the amount of previous earnings. Low-wage workers may be paid 100 percent or more of their previous monthly earnings; higher-income earners may get as little as 20 percent. On balance, most workers may expect monthly social security benefits which are about 60 percent lower than their average monthly lifetime earnings.

Social security taxes are only collected on earned income up to a certain limit (in 1979, $22,900). Earnings above that limit are not taxed, nor are they considered in determining benefits.

As shown in Table 14-1, rates and limits will rise sharply in the next few years according to 1978 legislation, but these are always subject to change by Congress. Taxes collected on the payroll of current workers are used to pay the benefits of persons already retired. A trust fund for social security taxes has been set up in Washington to hold reserves. The system is expected to be self-financing. The threat of the poorhouse, once an ominous possibility even for the very provident, has vanished.

Coverage of widely shared social risks under the Social Security Act has been greatly expanded since 1935. Dependent relatives of fully covered workers are eligible for payments under the Survivors' Insurance program (SI), adopted in 1939. Severely disabled persons under the age of sixty-five, who cannot work, or their dependents may receive benefits under Disability Insurance (DI), approved in 1956. National health insurance (Medicare) has been available for DI and OASI beneficiaries since 1965.[28] By 1977 total payments for retirement, survivors', disability, and medical insurance programs totaled over $84 billion a year, compared to $4 billion in 1940. The average monthly benefit under OAI for a retired worker in early 1978 was about $243; average benefits for the disabled were higher—$256. A total of 34 million retired persons, their dependents and survivors, and severely disabled individuals were receiving benefits under the system during the same period.[29]

Our social security system operates on a "pay-as-you-go" basis. Today's workforce directly supports yesterday's retirees. If at any time the active labor force should substantially decline in size—or if social security benefits rise steeply due to new congressional action—the system could not remain self-financed. Congress would have to add general tax revenues to the Social

Table 14-1   Social Security Tax Rate on Earned Income

Year	Percentage	Income Ceiling
1979	6.05	$22,900
1980	6.13	25,900
1981	6.65	29,700
1982	6.70	30,000
1983	6.70	31,800
1984	6.70	33,600
1985	7.05	35,400
1986	7.15	37,500
1987	7.15	$39,600

Security Trust Fund. Many people oppose the use of general tax revenues in our public pension program, because the relationship between contributions (social security taxes) and benefits would be undermined. It is interesting, though, that almost all other industrialized, developed nations do use general tax revenues to finance a proportion of social security payments to ensure a minimally adequate benefit standard for the aged and other beneficiaries.

Our social security system was instituted nearly fifty years ago, when demographic and economic conditions were much different. In 1935 few women expected to have careers of their own; most depended upon a male breadwinner for support. The expected pattern of family organization was a lifetime marriage, in which more than two children would be born, with child-rearing extended well into mid-life. After retirement a woman did not expect to survive her husband by more than two or three years.[30]

In terms of the economic setting for retirement, the Great Depression exposed the vulnerability of wage and salary-dependent workers in an economy of national markets. Congress was forced to acknowledge the necessity of establishing a minimum "social floor" through the insurance system to give some measure of economic security. While this was an indispensable action in light of our modern economic interdependence, no one then recognized that a second, more insidious economic threat was waiting in the wings: inflation. Congress could not have anticipated the long-run price instability which would arise following World War II. Before 1945 it had always been assumed that prices were normally fairly constant, with only temporary aberrations due to short-term disruptions or shortages.

By the early 1970s, changes in family structure, fertility rates, women's labor force participation rates, and the price structure combined to reveal serious omissions, internal contradictions, and inadequacies in the social security structure. Congress responded slowly and inadequately.

An "automatic escalator clause" now permits the Secretary of Health, Education and Welfare to increase social security benefits to keep up with inflation each year, when prices have increased more than 3 percent. The benefit schedule for Old Age, Survivors', Disability, and Health Insurance (OASDHI) has been liberalized, so that the living standard of retirees and disabled persons is notably better. If social security payments were stopped tomorrow, 30 percent of current beneficiaries would be reduced to below-subsistence levels.

As the number and proportion of broken marriages escalated, Congress moved toward a broader concept of dependency. Provision now permit more divorced women to draw on their husband's social security record at retirement. Men may now receive payments as dependents of their spouses— unthinkable for legislators in prior generations. Payments may also be made to dependent parents on the retirement of a fully covered worker.

The social security system has still not caught up with the diversity in modern family life. No insurance benefits are payable to dependent female survivors of prematurely deceased workers unless the family includes dependent children or the woman has passed age fifty. Since women are completing their child-bearing and child-rearing activities at a much earlier stage, the likelihood of reaching age fifty with no children at home has risen markedly. Further, the proportion of women (or men) who have no children has also grown, creating a new class of persons for whom the social insurance system cannot provide, prior to age sixty, except in cases of severe disability.

Financing programs, setting flexible benefit standards which rise with gains in national income, and strengthening incentives for persons to delay retirement will be the major concerns, rather than the coverage of social security.

The benefit structure of the system is predicated on the assumption that a retiree will have accumulated savings or will be entitled to private pension benefits. Social security benefits are not intended to serve as a sole and sufficient income source—despite the fact that 50 percent of all retired persons rely entirely upon the system for support. Where illness, low wages, unanticipated business reverses, or other events have prevented people from saving for retirement and social security benefits prove too small, elderly persons are eligible, after age sixty-five, to apply for public assistance benefits under the Supplemental Security Income program (SSI). Some older people, who have worked a lifetime in domestic occupations or agriculture, now derive their entire income from SSI, because these occupations were excluded from social security coverage until recently.

In 1978 nearly 5 million aged or severely disabled people received benefits under SSI, with average per capita payments ranging from $141 in California to $59 in Maine.[31] In most states, the administration of social security benefits (OASDHI) has been organizationally integrated with the SSI program under the Social Security Administration. This reduces program complexity for clients participating in both programs and has stimulated participation in SSI by eligible needy elderly. Some of the stigma of accepting public assistance has apparently been removed by associating the SSI program with the universally accepted social insurance programs.

The assumption of responsibility for SSI by the Social Security Administration has had unintended adverse consequences, however, for elderly and disabled clientele. The Social Security Administration has been accustomed to operating the extremely large, mass-payment programs under social insurance and had little experience with acutely disadvantaged or ill people whose emergency needs must have concentrated, immediate attention. Where clients show need for counseling or other social services, the Social Security Administration is attempting to make more active referrals to community agencies. SSA administrators are beginning to discover how few additional resources actually exist.

Most concrete personal social services for the elderly outside the Older Americans Act are paid for under Title XX of the Social Security Act and allocated through state departments of public welfare to local programs. These local programs subcontract to provide direct services which will meet annually determined state goals. The federal government divides about $2.6 billion dollars in block grants to the individual states to pay for social services to low-income families and individuals. The amount received by each state depends mainly upon the number of low-income individuals in the state.

Until Title XX was adopted in 1975, services to the poor were delivered under the auspices of state child welfare and public assistance programs in close adherence to federal priorities and guidelines. The main impact of Title XX was to decentralize planning for services to the state level and permit a much wider variety of potential services under different auspices to qualify for federal reimbursement. Congress hoped that innovation and greater responsivity to regional conditions would emerge while a lid was kept on the total cost.

The outcomes of Title XX are not yet clear. An examination of state plans shows that the bulk of funds are being used for services to children and young families. The share of social service dollars used for services to the elderly poor may actually have declined since 1975, although data from the current reporting system are not clear. Like services to the aged under the Older Americans Act, Title XX programs are located within existing agencies, for the most part, or are provided by a great array of local nonprofit agencies. Among client subgroups, who gets what is not always defined.

Aside from social services and basic income maintenance programs, the Social Security Act also contains the legal framework for our nation's two publicly administered medical programs, Medicare and Medicaid, described in Chapter 10.

An elderly person with low income may receive Medicare and Medicaid at the same time, and in effect obtain comprehensive medical care coverage. Medicare benefits are subject to durational limits, and should an older person continue to need care, Medicaid may take over if all other resources have been exhausted.

Three observations can be made regarding the effect of Medicare and Medicaid on the status of elderly persons. First, the present reimbursement system favors in-patient hospital care and responds only after the individual has developed an acute and worsening condition. Second, Medicaid payments have been the primary impetus for explosive growth in the nursing home industry and a concomitant decline in the population of institutionalized elderly mental patients. When Medicaid benefits became available, the states transferred thousands of aged patients from state-supported facilities to community homes so Medicaid would take over the costs. Third, social services to support independent living arrangements through Title XX and OAA are trivial when compared to the investment of public dollars in medical services to sick, institutionally confined patients.

The fundamental policy question is whether social provisions for the elderly should be based on an array of support social services, of which health care is one important component, or whether an older person requiring help must first be categorized as "sick," and then receive social services ancillary to medical attention. The medical model now dominates. Few alternatives are open to elderly persons, particularly as they become increasingly frail with age.

Housing the Nation's Elderly

During World War I, the government constructed public housing units for military personnel. In the Great Depression, fifty public housing projects were sponsored by the Public Works Administration to help promote economic recovery. After the passage of the National Housing Act in 1937, about 35,000 units a year were produced under federal subsidies until 1938, when the Housing and Urban Development Act was adopted.[32] Public housing in the United States has always been governed by two objectives—first, to stimulate employment in the construction industry, and second, to upgrade the quality of housing for the poor.

The Housing and Urban Development Act of 1968 was one of the most comprehensive pieces of housing legislation ever passed by Congress. It authorized continued construction of housing units for low- and moderate-income families, provided for urban renewal, gave support to innovative "demonstration cities" and new town programs, and offered incentives for home-ownership.

Public housing projects for the elderly have become increasingly popular because older people have proven to be ideal tenants. In 1978 Congress approved the Congregate Housing Service Act, which for the first time will make substantial funds available for supportive services to frail elderly residents in public housing. Experiments are also being conducted in the design of public housing, so that moderately handicapped or disabled elderly people can continue to live independently in publicly subsidized arrangements.

The primary shortcoming of public housing for the elderly is that Congress has given the program little support. While local governments, low-income families, social welfare professionals, and labor have been enthusiastic about the merits of assisted living arrangements, the private sector—banks and real estate firms, in particular—has remained opposed. As one author put it, in the absence of a strong constituency to back these programs, Congress never killed public housing; it was just never really brought to life.[33]

Work Opportunities and the Age Discrimination Act: The Comprehensive Employment and Training Act

The Age Discrimination Act now prevents employers from hiring or discharging workers on the basis of age. Compulsory retirement of privately employed workers is permitted after age seventy. The retirement age for federal employees was lifted entirely. Enforcement of the Age Discrimination Act has been unimpressive. The Department of Labor, which is charged with investigating complaints under the act, has few staff to cover wide areas within each state. The most successful prosecutions have been effected against large companies, whose hiring and retirement policies over time unambiguously demonstrated a pattern of selection or discrimination by age. The act has not opened up job opportunities in the private sector to the extent that its backers had anticipated.

The Comprehensive Employment and Training Act of 1973 (CETA) provides federal funds to communities of 100,000 or more residents, for the purpose of educating, retraining, and placing competitively disadvantaged workers. Communities with administrative responsibility for CETA funds are called "prime sponsors," and must account to the Department of Labor for their program activities. Prime sponsors receive an annual grant from the Department of Labor, which is then subcontracted to local agencies and programs. Like the Older Americans Act and Title XX of the Social Security Act, CETA operations are decentralized, and public accountability for certain national priorities is low.

Older workers may potentially benefit from CETA under Titles I and III. Title I offers on-the-job training, classroom education, opportunities for work experience, public service employment, and supportive social services to low-income older workers who wish to upgrade their skills in the labor market. Some middle-aged women need assistance from CETA because they wish to reenter the labor market after a long period at home—or perhaps they have never worked at all.

Under Title III of CETA, the Department of Labor contracts directly with labor unions, national interest groups, businessmen's associations, or other nonprofit organizations for special demonstration programs which serve high-priority segments of the population. Older workers are specifically mentioned in Title III as a high-priority group.

In 1976 only 220,000 of the nearly 2.5 million participants in CETA programs were forty-five years of age or older. Although the number appears to have risen slightly since, the proportion of elderly benefiting from CETA is very small. For example, in 1977 20 percent of the participants in Title I programs were fifty-five or over.[34]

Staff in CETA programs have not been trained to work with older people. Many elderly persons fail to believe that job opportunities can be developed for them, and many experience considerable anxiety about interviews for potential jobs. The response to outreach programs, therefore, has been small, while younger applicants for CETA services appear in ample numbers. The older workers most needing CETA services are black, female, and unskilled. These people do not make good candidates for the occupational training which prime sponsors have in mind. Moreover, the private sector remains unresponsive to the propect of rehiring the elderly. Thus, despite the rhetoric about the right of older persons to employment, government programs are still of minimal utility.

Future Issues in Policy and Delivery of Services

Our nation has made substantial progress in better addressing the needs of older people. Social security benefits have increased in real value by 69 percent since 1968, and benefits are now "inflation proof" through automatic cost-of-living adjustments.[35] With the passage of the Supplemental Security Income program, a national minimum income has been established for the elderly. Liberalizations in the Social Security Act now permit older beneficiaries to earn more income without jeopardy to their government benefits. Some controls have been initiated on the costs of health care, and more consumer participation is encouraged in the oversight of health care services. The impact of property and sales taxes on elderly persons has been softened through state rebate schemes and recent laws which impose tax reductions. Congress is debating national health care insurance, which will further relieve older people of burdensome medical expenses.

Housing, too, has improved somewhat. Between 1969 and 1973 alone, 250,000 units of public housing for the elderly were constructed—more than in any previous period in our history.[36] The Department of Housing and Urban Development is experimenting with more social service to elderly tenants.

SUMMARY AND APPLICATION

With moves toward better income, housing, and work opportunities for the elderly, what remains to be done?

First, this nation must create more alternatives in long-term care. Almost everyone who survives into advanced old age—and younger persons with moderate-to-severe disabilities—will require long-term care or modified living arrangements. Although the number of nursing home facilities has grown, alternatives to this type of care are few and poorly supported under government programs. Aged persons with some normal physical limitations or occasional periods of mild mental confusion must not be treated by society as if they were ill or ought to be "put away."

Many persons in long-term care facilities could live in the community or at home if the support system were improved. In 1968 about half of all persons living in nursing homes were ambulatory, could dress themselves, and could perform the customary tasks of daily life. Yet one-third died in the institution and another third left merely to enter a similar (usually less costly) facility.[37]

The involvement of the social work profession in the provision of services to nursing home patients has been inadequate. Social workers have given leadership in the development of day care programs as an alternative to institutional arrangements, have pioneered in protective services,[38] and have been called in as consultants by facilities wishing to improve their services. However, a far greater degree of professional commitment is needed.

Medicare and Medicaid programs must be modified to permit reimbursement for home-delivered meals, home health services, and other social services to persons needing quasi-custodial or maintenance care. These changes, in turn, may not be possible until we are willing to admit that the normal dependencies of old age should receive attention and support without the label of disease.

Second, better approaches to terminal care must be devised. In the nineteenth century, most people died in their own homes, surrounded by family and loved ones. With industrialization and modernization, the approach to death in this culture has drastically altered. Approximately 70 percent of all deaths now take place in hospitals or other public institutions—an increase of

21 percent since 1949—and a total departure from practice prior to the turn of the century.[39] Patients are placed in surroundings over which they have no control, are relegated to the care of indifferent or harried professionals, and are denied the right to meet death with dignity.

The courts have recently defended the right of elderly persons to refuse drugs or other methods of artificially prolonging life. A positive step in the same direction is the experimentation in this country with hospice programs. In England and Switzerland, centers called hospices, or terminal care facilities, provide help to people with a terminal prognosis. Pain is reduced as much as possible, the environment is conspicuously bright and cheerful, naturalness is encouraged, and intensive social supports are given. Terminal care in this context is a specialized service, like pediatrics or other hospital functions.

Substantial evidence now confirms our ability to help persons meet death positively. Families, too, can benefit from the new counseling approaches developed by Elizabeth Kubler-Ross and others.[40] The notion of a "successful" death, and people's newfound expectations for more control of their environment during this crucial phase, mean that current practices will have to be changed.

Third, older people must receive a reasonable share of the increase in national income which results from higher productivity. Workers who are now retired created the conditions which make today's productivity possible. As a nation, we have been sensitive to the hardships which inflation creates for people living on a fixed income. We have been much less concerned, however, about the differences in living standards between the working young and the retired elderly. There is no mechanism in the social security system which permits increases for changes in the general standard of living.

A mechanism must be found by which older people are not allowed to slip further and further behind the standard enjoyed by the remainder of society. In West Germany, adjustments are made in the social security system for relative differences between pensioners' benefits and growth in national income. The principle deserves serious consideration here.

Fourth, institutional responsiveness to the needs of special groups among the aged must be improved. Elderly blacks, Asian Americans, American Indians, and Spanish-speaking Americans have been largely excluded from the formal social welfare provisions system. Innovative outreach techniques are required which would be sensitive to the special cultural ties and belief systems of these groups. The staffing of area agencies, Administration on Aging regional offices, and community-based programs should more broadly reflect the interests of these diverse groups. Better monitoring of services is required to prod states and localities into genuine responsiveness in meeting the needs of special groups, rather than mere compliance.

Finally, removing the elderly as objects of social discrimination or benign neglect must continue. Social action groups like the Gray Panthers were formed during the 1960s in order to change public awareness and, even more important, to stimulate older people themselves. The elderly are learning to take action on their own behalf, are becoming more articulate about their rights as full citizens, and are developing higher expectations for the future. In the wake of the achievements already made, the struggle for independence and dignity should not be abandoned.

—*Marilyn L. Flynn*

KEY TERMS

SSI

intake

the "young" old

the "old" old

Older Americans Act

OAI

OASDHI

Medicare

automatic escalator clause

CETA

Gray Panthers

REFERENCES AND NOTES

1. Bertram Moss, "New Ideas about the Elderly: Growing Old Can Be Normal," in Joint Project on Staff Development for Services to the Aging, *Selected Papers*, School of Social Work, University of Illinois at Urbana-Champaign, July 1975.
2. Allen Pincus, "Toward a Developmental View of Aging for Social Work," *Social Work*, vol. 12, July 1967, pp. 24–32.
3. Sheldon Tobin, "A Social and Psychological Perspective on Growing Old," in Joint Project on Staff Development for Services to the Aged, *Selected Papers*.
4. Neal E. Cutler and Robert A. Harootyan, "Demography of the Aged," in Diana S. Woodruff and James E. Birren (eds.), *Aging: Scientific Perspectives and Social Issues*, Van Nostrand, New York, 1975.
5. Adrian M. Ostgeld and Don C. Gibson (eds.), *Epidemiology of Aging*, Department of Health, Education and Welfare, National Institutes of Health, Washington, D.C., 1972, p. 2.
6. Robert N. Butler and Myrna I. Lewis, *Aging and Mental Health: Positive Psychosocial Approaches*, 2d ed., Mosby, St. Louis, 1977, p. 5; see also U.S. Senate, Special Committee on Aging, *The Multiple Hazards of Age and Race: The Situation of Aged Blacks in the United States*, Government Printing Office, Washington, D.C., 1971.
7. Cutler and Harootyan, op. cit.
8. Lenore E. Bixby, "Retirement Patterns in the United States: Research and Policy Interaction," *Social Security Bulletin*, vol. 39, August 1976, pp. 5–7.
9. Ibid.
10. Janet Murray, "Home Ownership and Financial Assets: Findings from the 1968 Survey of the Aged," *Social Security Bulletin*, vol. 35, August 1972, pp. 3–23.
11. James Schultz, *The Economics of Aging*, Wadsworth, Belmont, Calif., 1976; see also House of Representatives, Select Committee on Aging, *Federal Responsibility to the Elderly*, Government Printing Office, Washington, D.C., 1976.
12. Bureau of the Census, *Statistical Abstract of the United States, 1975*, Government Printing Office, Washington, D.C., 1975.
13. Ethel Shanas et al., *Old People in Three Industrial Societies*, Atherton, New York, 1968, p. 193.

14. Bureau of the Census, "Marital Status and Living Arrangements, March 1971," *Current Population Reports*, Series P-20, November 1971.
15. H. B. Brotman, "The Older Population Revisited: First Results of the 1970 Census," *Facts and Figures on Older Americans*, SRS-AOA Publication no. 182, Government Printing Office, Washington, D.C., 1971.
16. Ibid.
17. E. Palmore and F. C. Jeffers (eds.), *Predictors of Life Span*, Heath-Lexington, 1971; D. Chebotarer, "Fight Against Old Age," *Gerontologist*, vol. 11, 1971, pp. 359–361.
18. Bert N. Adams, *Kinship in an Urban Setting*, Markham, Chicago, 1968; Shanas, op. cit.
19. James Peterson, "A Developmental View of the Aging Family," in James Birren (ed.), *Contemporary Gerontology: Concepts and Issues*, Gerontology Center, University of Southern California, Los Angeles, 1970.
20. Helena A. Lopata, *Widowhood in an American City*, Schenkman, Cambridge, Mass., 1973.
21. Diana S. Woodruff, "A Physiological Perspective of the Psychology of Aging," in Woodruff and Birren, op cit.
22. Matilda W. Riley and Anne Foner, *Aging and Society: An Inventory of Research Findings*, Russell Sage, New York, 1968.
23. Butler and Lewis, op. cit.
24. Jean M. Anthony, "CETA and the Older Worker," in Marilyn L. Flynn (ed.), *The Comprehensive Employment and Training Act: Implications for Social Policy*, School of Social Work, University of Illinois at Urbana-Champaign, 1978 (mimeographed).
25. Gloria Shatto, *Employment of the Middle-Aged*, Charles C Thomas, Springfield, Ill., 1972; see also Bureau of Labor Statistics, *Handbook of Labor Statistics 1977*, Government Printing Office, Washington, D.C., 1978.
26. Harold L. Sheppard, *Research and Development Strategy on Employment-Related Problems of Older Workers*, Center on Work and Aging, American Institute for Research, Pittsburgh, October 1977.
27. Byron Gold, "Development of the Comprehensive Service Amendments to the Older Americans Act," Joint Project on Staff Development for Services to the Aged, in *Selected Papers*.
28. U.S. Senate, Special Committee on Aging, *Memorandum*, September 29, 1978.
29. U.S. Department of Health, Education and Welfare, Social Security Administration, *Social Security Bulletin*, vol. 41, July 1978. For an excellent summary of the main features of our social security system, see John Turnbull, C. Arthur Williams, and Earl F. Cheit, *Economic and Social Security*, Ronald, New York, 1973.
30. Elizabeth A. Kutza, *Policy Lag: Its Impact on Income Security for Older Women*, Occasional Paper no. 6, School of Social Service Administration, University of Chicago, Chicago, June 1975.
31. *Social Security Bulletin*, vol. 41, July 1978.
32. Clair Wilcox, *Toward Social Welfare*, Irwin, Homewood, Ill., 1969.
33. Jewel Bellush and Murray Hausknecht (eds.), *Urban Renewal: People, Politics, and Planning*, Doubleday. Garden City, N.Y., 1967; see also Martin Meyerson, Barbara Terrett, and William Wheaton, *Housing, People, and Cities*, McGraw-Hill, New York, 1962.
34. U.S. Department of Labor and U.S. Department of Health, Education and

Welfare, *Employment and Training Report of the President*, Government Printing Office, Washington, D.C., 1978.

35. James Schultz, *Toward Adequate Retirement Income: Pension Reform in the United States and Abroad*, University Press of New England, Hanover, N.H., 1974.

36. U.S. Congress, Special Committee on Aging and Committee on Labor and Public Welfare, Subcommittee on Aging, *Post–White House Conference on Aging Reports, 1973*, Government Printing Office, Washington, D.C., September 1973, pp. 44–53.

37. Margaret Lenkner et al., *Final Report: Protective Services for Older People— Findings from the Benjamin Rose Institute Study*, Benjamin Rose Institute, Cleveland, 1974.

38. U.S. Department of Health, Education and Welfare, Public Health Service, *Characteristics, Social Contacts, and Activities of Nursing Home Residents*, Vital Health Statistics, Series 13, Government Printing Office, Washington, D.C., May 1977. See also Elaine Brody et al., *A Social Work Guide for Long-Term Care Facilities*, National Institute of Mental Health, Government Printing Office, Washington, D.C., 1975.

39. Herman Feifel, *Dealing with Death*, Andrus Gerontology Center, University of Southern California, Los Angeles, 1973, p. 2.

40. Elizabeth Kubler-Ross, *On Death and Dying*, Macmillan, New York, 1969.

FOR FURTHER STUDY

Andrew Achenbaum, *Old Age in the New Land, the American Experience Since 1790*, John Hopkins, Baltimore, 1978.

Robert C. Atchley, *The Social Forces in Later Life: An Introduction to Social Gerontology*, Wadsworth, Belmont, Calif., 1972.

Georgia Barrow and Patricia Smith, *Aging, Ageism, and Society*, West Publishing Co., St. Paul, 1979.

Zena Smith Blau, *Old Age in a Changing Society*, F. Watts, New York, 1973.

Robert N. Butler, *Why Survive: Being Old in America*, Harper and Row, New York, 1977.

Carroll L. Estes, *Aging Enterprise: A Critical Examination of Social Policies and Services for the Aged*, Jossey Bass, San Francisco, 1979.

Mary Adelaide Mendelson, *Tender Loving Greed*, Knopf, New York, 1974.

Eric Pfeiffer (ed.), *Alternatives to Institutional Care for Older Americans: Practice and Planning*, Duke Center for the Study of Aging and Human Development, Durham, N.C., 1973.

Ethel Shanas and Marvin B. Sussman (eds.), *Family, Bureaucracy, and the Elderly*, Duke University Press, Durham, N.C., 1977.

FOR DISCUSSION

1. What basic rights of older citizens are identified in the introduction to the chapter?
2. Describe major social work roles with the aged.
3. Is a consultant to a nursing home working a couple of days a month likely to have much effect on the activities in a nursing home? Amplify your answer.
4. Do you feel that the experience of older people in public housing has been more successful than that of younger persons? Why or why not?

5. What disciplines are concerned with plans for aged people?
6. Which subgroups of the elderly are increasing more rapidly?
7. Why is the life expectancy of black men less than that of white men?
8. What is the trend concerning old people with means below the subsistence level?
9. What are some of the special problems of widowhood?
10. What are the myths about older people that are refuted by research?
11. What social services are offered under Title III of the Older Americans Act?
12. Explain reassurance calling.
13. How does federal legislation on services for the aged provide for citizen participation in the programs?
14. How does fiscal support for the aging compare to support for mental health?
15. Explain how the social security system operates on a pay-as-you-go basis.
16. What has been the major drawback in the development of public housing for the elderly?
17. What is the correct mandatory retirement age that may be required in private industry? For federal employees?
18. What are some of the major issues in terminal care for the elderly?
19. How can the elderly become more active in programs that will increase public awareness of their needs?

PROJECTS

1. Research and debate the question that the retirement age should be raised.
2. Visit a home for the aged and interview several residents on a social issue of your own choosing. An example: "People would be better off if both prices and wages were lower." Tape-record the answers and compare them.
3. Invite two people of about the same age—a housewife and a man who has retired from his job several years ago—to come to a class session and discuss their present activities and interests with a small student panel. What similarities and differences are revealed?
4. Consider old age for your own parents. To what extent will they depend on you financially? Psychologically? What provisions have they made to maintain their own independence? Do you expect that one or both may live with you at some time?
5. Analyze the problem of inflation as it affects the aged who live independently and those who must have special care.

PART FOUR
Social Issues

Social workers have always recognized the influence of the broader societal context on human behavior. The importance of ecology has been illustrated dramatically in the energy crisis. Nuclear accidents have threatened our safety and jeopardized the feasibility of new sources of power at the same time that the petroleum supply became critical. With new problems with fuel and food, the need for an official population policy is felt. These issues affect the resources of the human services system and place major new constraints on our freedom.

To help members of minorities, racism must be acknowledged, understood, and dealt with. Societal responses to racial and ethnic groups differ and these differences affect the development of services. The responses of group members also vary individually and collectively and condition the success of intervention. Racism is a special problem in social agencies.

Sexism has emerged as a major issue and is therefore accorded a chapter of its own. Not only does it affect the society but, like racism, it is also found in the social welfare organizations. The study of sexism is especially enlightening in the social work profession where the majority of practitioners are women.

Remedies for these problems and others such as housing and consumer rights depend upon the application of law. The partnership between social workers and lawyers has become much more important as a result of the growing concern with civil rights. The social worker must know legal processes, understand the rules of evidence, and know how to testify. The protection of the law is of special concern in services for children for whom the state exercises a protective parental interest.

373

CHAPTER 15
Ecology and Population

"I love to lay eggs, but I can't stand kids"

If people waited to know one another before they married, the world wouldn't be so grossly overpopulated as it is now.

—W. Somerset Maugham*

T he social work profession moved during the first two decades of this century from a broad social welfare orientation to an emphasis on treatment to improve the social functioning of individuals. A reawakening of interest in institutional problems was seen after the turmoil of the 1960s.

Today, there is great interest in solutions to population and ecological problems. Social workers have shared the concern about overpopulation, dwindling energy sources, and the insufficiency of other resources. Shortages of food and fuel raise costs for the people social workers serve. Without food surpluses, hunger becomes even more of a problem.

This chapter will begin with the goals of ecology. Population patterns will then be discussed. Then family planning will be reviewed as a strategy in relation to population control.

CONCERNS WITH ECOLOGY

Social workers have had less interest in ecology than in population, but ecology is important in the conservation of resources and the control of costs. The lack of effective policies makes it difficult for the poor to obtain adequate food and shelter at a reasonable cost.

Demand for Natural Resources

What is the capacity of the earth to support people? Any claim that a country's population is too large or too small implies some idea of an optimum size. It implies that growth up to that size is beneficial, and any more growth is harmful. No exact formula can determine the optimum population for a given area at a given time.

Because of the high rate of consumption in industrialized nations, 1 million additional people in the developed nations is like 30 million more in the developing nations.[1] The industrialized nations, with their rapidly growing high-consumption and high-waste economies, are using up more of the earth's nonrenewable resources and generating greater pollution of water, air, and land than the nonindustrialized nations. As many of the developing countries start to industrialize, the situation will get worse.

*W. Somerset Maugham, *Mrs. Dot*, Dramatic Publishing Co., Chicago, 1912, p. 2.

Food Supply

During the 1960s, the world food problem was perceived as a food-population problem. During the 1970s, rapid global population growth continues to generate a demand for more food, but in addition, rising affluence is emerging as a major new claimant on world food resources.

This relationship is best understood by examining the data on grain consumption for the developed and developing regions of the world. Grain consumed directly provides 52 percent of man's food energy supply. Consumed indirectly in the form of livestock products, grain provides a major share of the remainder. In the poor countries, the annual availability of grain per person averages only about 400 pounds per year. Nearly all of this is consumed directly to meet minimum energy needs. In the United States and Canada, per-person grain utilization is approaching 1 ton per year. Of this amount, only 150 pounds are consumed directly. The remainder is consumed indirectly in the form of meat, milk, and eggs. Thus, the agricultural resources required to support a North American amount to nearly five times what is needed by the average Indian. Moreover, the impact of affluence on the consumption of livestock products is evident. For example, per capita consumption of beef climbed from 55 pounds in 1940 to 117 pounds in 1972. Poultry consumption rose from 18 pounds to 51 pounds during the same period.[2]

In the poor countries, population growth accounts for most of the increase in the demand for food. Although the "green revolution" has succeeded in raising yields of wheat and rice to an unprecedented level (e.g., from 1965 to 1972,) India expanded its wheat production from 11 million tons to 27 million tons, an increase unmatched in history,[3] but high-yield seeds are a mixed blessing. High-yield grains require increased use of fertilizer and water. In India both fertilizers and electricity for the tube-wells needed to irrigate crops run far short of the demand. Transportation and storage facilities are also inadequate.

Expanding the world food supply from conventional agriculture can be achieved in two ways—expand the area under cultivation or raise output on the existing cultivated area through the use of chemicals and irrigation. The food supply could possibly be increased by developing new lands, but much of the potentially cultivable land is in the tropics. Recent experience has shown that once the protective forest cover is removed, the land loses much of its fertility. The intensive use of chemicals and irrigations has put its own stress on the ecosystem. For example, damming the Nile at Aswan expanded the irrigated area for production, but it eliminated the annual deposits of silt on the fields, forcing farmers to rely on chemical fertilizers. In turn, the fertilizers had a detrimental effect on fish, depriving the villagers of their principal source of animal protein.

Can mankind be saved by harvesting the riches of the sea? After a record rise from 21 to 63 million tons between 1950 and 1968, the fish catch suddenly started to decline in 1969, and has fluctuated unpredictably since that date. This trend has intensified the competition in world fisheries, leading to disputes about offshore limits. For Americans, the direct consumption of fish averages only 14 pounds per year, although in many countries, like Japan and the Soviet Union, fish provides a significant source of protein.[4]

Water Supply

Only 3 percent of the world's water is fresh, while 97 percent is salt water. Ninety-eight percent of the fresh water is tied up in ice caps, particularly in Antarctica and Greenland. Some fresh water can be reused, but the huge amounts required by living plants cannot be reused immediately.[5] The demand on this limited supply has been increasing at an alarming rate. According to a report at the United Nations conference on water at Mar del Plata in March 1977, an African uses 0.8 gallons of water a day, compared to 160 gallons for a Muscovite and 270 gallons for a New Yorker.[6]

Still, the amount of water used directly for human consumption does not compare with the quantity required to produce food. A pound of wheat requires about 60 gallons of water, a pound of meat 2,500 to 6,000 gallons.[7] Also, agriculture must compete for water with industry. Fortunately, if pollutants can be removed, must of the water used by industry can be reused.

Desalinization—removing the salt from sea water—is being undertaken, but at such high cost that it is used only for drinking water. Even if the price should drop, the cost of transportation would still make it too expensive to use at any distance from the coast.

Energy Supply

The world today is confronted with an energy problem of major proportions. The problem is particularly acute in the United States, since a seemingly inexhaustible supply of cheap fuel helped create the world's most industrialized country. The whole society seems intent on wasting energy— from windowless air-conditioned skyscrapers to superhighways where drivers feel frustrated driving at fifty-five miles per hour. The problem is not generalizable to all industrialized countries, since most of them manage to maintain standards of living roughly comparable to that in the United States on much less energy consumption per capita. Gasoline shortages are particularly difficult, especially with basic dependence on imports that result in inflation and on adverse balance of payments.

Over nine-tenths of the world's energy consumption is derived from fossil fuel sources (natural gas, oil) and less than 10 percent from hydroelectric power, atomic energy, or other sources.[8] In the United States, natural gas accounts for 30 percent of the energy consumption. Oil heats half the homes and furnishes 50 percent of the energy for industry.[9] At the current rate of use, known reserves of oil and gas will be 90 percent depleted by the year 2000. Domestic oil production hit an eleven-year low in 1977, with the nation importing almost half of its petroleum. This leaves the economy vulnerable to embargoes by foreign suppliers. The bill for imported oil drains the purchasing power needed to create jobs. The delay in adopting a comprehensive national

(Reprinted with permission from The Saturday Evening Post Company, © 1978.)

energy policy to deal with this situation has caused some people to suspect that
the energy crisis is a hoax engineered by the oil companies to squeeze out huge
price increases.

ENVIRONMENTAL PROTECTION

The increase in the number of people is not the sole problem. Distribution of
population and consumption patterns are related. A large, dense population
that makes heavy demands for extravagances does more environmental damage
than a small, widely distributed population with a frugal life-style.

Direct threats to human health are the most obvious effects of environmental deterioration. The most widely discussed are the pollutants that reach
us in air and food.

Air and Water Pollution

The U.S. Public Health Service estimates that our 90 million cars emit 66
million tons of carbon monoxide. The Public Health Service rated pulp and
paper mills, iron and steel mills, petroleum refineries, smelters, and chemical
plants as the principal industrial sources of air pollution. The fuel for heating
houses, apartments, and offices adds its share, as does trash burning. More than

140 million tons of these pollutants are added to the atmosphere each year—about three-quarters of a ton for every person in the United States.[10] Death rates rise for the very old, the very young, and people with respiratory ailments whenever levels of pollution go up. Pollution contributes to a higher incidence of emphysema, pneumonia, bronchitis, and lung cancer.

In many communities water pollution is a major problem. The Public Health Service rates the water supply of sixty American cities as "unsatisfactory" or as a "potential health hazard."[11] The reasons include impure sources, tap impurities, infrequent testing for bacteria, and use of nonapproved tests by the water department. Also, sewage treatment facilities were intended to handle a much smaller population. The growth in population generally involves increased industrial growth, resulting in more contaminators in the water (e.g., lead and ammonia). Increased agricultural production can create its own problem of a heavier water-borne load of pesticides, herbicides, and nitrates. The result is pollution not just of the rivers, streams, and lakes, but also of groundwater, a more difficult problem.

Solid Wastes

With affluence comes greater accumulation of solid wastes—junked automobiles, bottles, jars, other packaging materials, as well as garbage. Each year this includes 7 million junked cars, 55 billion cans, 26 billion bottles and jars, more than $500 million worth of other packaging materials, and 150 million tons of trash and garbage.[12] Open dumps and inadequate fills create not only esthetic problems but also public health hazards as breeding grounds for rats and germs. Sanitary landfills can help, but locations are becoming scarce.

Laws to prohibit the manufacture of nonbiodegradable materials and to encourage the manufacture of products that could be recycled are needed. Educational campaigns plus payment of deposits would help in the return of containers. As population grows and land for dumping becomes unavailable, rules will have to be enforced on the grounds of necessity rather than just esthetics.

Chemical Pollution

Lead, mercury, and insecticides such as DDT are considered general pollutants. The symptoms of chronic lead poisoning include loss of appetite, weakness, and apathy—symptoms that are difficult to diagnose. In urban areas, exposure to lead comes from the combustion of gasoline. Lead can be absorbed from food and water as well as air, but is most hazardous when children eat paint containing lead.

DDT was the most commonly used insecticide in the period after World War II, but it is now outlawed.

THE POPULATION PROBLEM

In recent years, controlling population growth has become one of mankind's most challenging problems.

However, specialists disagree about the dire consequences of overpopulation, especially when years pass without any cataclysmic effects from rapid population growth. Still, the evidence on the current demographic situation and its impact on the environment and resources warrants continuing attention.

Scientists differ in their assessments of the problem, especially in the developed regions of the world. Conflicting policies have been advocated to solve the population dilemma, ranging from helping people to act in their own best interests to limit the size of their families to mandatory means to regulate childbearing. Before looking at these arguments, what is the situation concerning population growth?

Population Growth

The population of the world was estimated at 4.08 billion in 1977. With an annual 1.8 percent growth rate, it will double in thirty-eight years.

Rapid population growth is a relatively recent phenomenon. During the Stone Age, the world population probably never exceeded 10 million. However, around 8000 B.C., with the onset of the agricultural revolution as humans learned how to grow their own food and create settlements, the population grew to 200 to 300 million. By 1650 it had reached the half-billion mark. In the next three centuries the gain was more spectacular. In the 200 years from 1650 to 1850, the world population reached a billion.[13] By 1930 it doubled to 2 billion, and it passed the 4 billion mark in 1976. At the current estimated growth rate of 1.8 percent, 5 billion people will share the earth's resources by 1989.[14] However, declines in birth rates are expected to slow the current growth over the next quarter century, especially if the fertility control programs in some of the developing countries succeed in meeting their targets.

Reasons for Growth   Rapid growth in population results from several interacting factors. Western civilization was transformed from a rural agrarian to an urban industrial society by an expansion in scientific knowledge and technology, including a revolution in medicine and public health. Mortality in the Western world dropped significantly, leading to dramatic population growth. The developing nations had an even greater drop in mortality accomplished without an industrial revolution. Unlike the West, where the decline in mortality was accompanied by a drop in fertility, there was no significant reduction in birth rates in the developing nations.

Regional Differences

The population growth pattern reveals vast contrasts between the different regions of the world. Latin America, at an estimated 2.7 percent, is growing fastest, closely followed by Africa at 2.6 percent, and Asia at 2.0 percent. By contrast, Europe's growth rate is 0.4 percent and North America's 0.6 percent. Differences in regional growth result from the disparities in birth and death rates. The present birth rate in Africa, 45 per 1,000 population, is three times the rates in Europe and North America, and its death rate of 19 per 1,000 is twice as high. Latin America's high growth rate stems from a somewhat lower birth rate—36 per 1,000—and a much lower death rate than that of Africa—9 per 1,000 population, equivalent to that of North America. Asia's birth rate of 32 per 1,000 compares favorably with Latin America and Africa, but its death rate of 12 per 1,000 is somewhat higher than Latin America.[15]

The differences between the areas of high fertility and low fertility include general economic development, degree of urbanization, dominant occupations, per capita income, communications, and transportation. Population growth is greatest where it can be least afforded, in developing countries that need to concentrate on improving their economic conditions.

Prosperity and Fertility
No necessary causal relationship exists between economic development and decline in fertility. The United States has the highest per capita gross national product, but a birth rate of 15 per 1,000, compared to the 10 or 13 per 1,000 in many European countries. On the other hand, no nations with a high birth rate have high per capita productivity, although some are more prosperous than others.

Population Growth in the United States
For several years, many Americans have expressed a deep concern about the population growth in this country, and have wished to curtail population growth as soon as possible. This goal is called zero population growth (ZPG). In 1973 and again in 1974, the total fertility rate dropped to a new low of 1.8 children per woman of childbearing age. The rate needed to merely maintain the population is 2.11. Some people misinterpreted these events as the attainment of the ZPG goal. Despite the below-replacement fertility rate, there were still 1.25 million more births than deaths.[16]

The total fertility rate is based solely on the fertility behavior of a single year, but a low rate could possible reflect a tendency to postpone having children. In fact, recent evidence suggests that women are beginning to have the babies they once postponed. Census Bureau figures show that the number of first births by women between the ages of thirty and thirty-four increased from 7.8 to 8.1 per 1,000 between 1974 and 1975,[17] but the rate has dropped since. Married women still state that they expect to have about 2.2 children each, according to the Bureau of the Census.[18] If this assumption is correct, and if there are some improvements in mortality and continued legal immigration of about 400,000 persons per year, the American population in the year 2000 will be somewhere between 260 and 265 million.[19] To achieve zero population growth before the middle of the twenty-first century, mortality can be increased, which is ethically unacceptable; immigration can be reduced or eliminated, also unacceptable, given the history of this country; or fertility can decline. At the present total fertility rate of 1.8, the United States could reach a stationary situation in another fifty years. However, in the long run, it seems unrealistic that completed families will continue to average only 1.8 children. An average of 2.1 children may be the most accurate estimate of fertility. With immigration kept at the present levels, zero population growth could be reached after sixty-five to seventy years.[20]

FAMILY PLANNING

Policies

Governmental population policies are based on what those in authority think people ought to do, but enactment of a law does not assure implementation, especially when financial backing is meager. For instance, federal appropriations for the Family Planning and Population Services Research Act were initially impounded.

Also, policy decisions are complicated because some government officials are reluctant to accept the Supreme Court decision legalizing abortion, although nationwide polls suggest that the public accepts liberalized abortion laws.

Since the population of any given area is determined by fertility, mortality, and migration, control of population may involve modifying one or all of these factors. Laws on immigration, abortion, and distribution of contraceptives have a direct effect on population; but laws fixing the minimum age of marriage and providing tax exemptions for dependents also have an influence.

Given national goals, the "population problems" of some countries have been a shortage of people. Governments have encouraged reproduction through pronatalist policies that reward large families, as in Russia and France, but such programs have been unsuccessful. Australia and Canada have increased their populations through selective immigration of skilled people.

Family Planning Programs

National family planning programs are governmental efforts to lower fertility by funding and administering birth control information and services on a voluntary basis to target populations. By 1975 thirty-four developing countries—representing over three-quarters of the population of that segment of the world—had official programs. Thirty-two other countries, with 15 percent of the population, provided some governmental support. Other programs were funded through various international agencies. About 2.5 billion people, comprising more than 90 percent of the developing world's population, lived in countries that offered family planning services.[21] This is a remarkable achievement, since a little more than two decades ago, no developing country had a governmental family planning program. Several developed countries had instituted programs, which were designed in most cases to increase fertility and immigration rates. Thus, the concern about world population growth is a relatively recent phenomenon. Furthermore, there is no agreement among nations as to what programs should be instituted as part of a comprehensive population policy.

Public and Private Agencies

None of the developed countries has a significant national family planning policy or program. In the United States the work has been carried on through public and private agencies, such as Planned Parenthood, founded in 1916, when Margaret Sanger opened the first birth control clinic in Brooklyn. In the fiscal year 1975, more than 3.8 million women obtained family planning services from health departments, hospitals, Planned Parenthood affiliates, and other agencies, such as free clinics and community action groups, that comprise the organized family planning program in the United States.[22]

Governmental Action

Population has not traditionally been considered a proper concern for government. The first positive statement came in President Lyndon Johnson's 1965 State of the Union message, which connected the growth of world population to the growing scarcity of resources. Johnson stated that five dollars spent on family planning was worth a hundred dollars invested in some other area of economic development.

Then the Department of Health, Education and Welfare issued a statement defining policy for population dynamics, fertility, sterility, and family planning. For the first time, federal funds could be appropriated to provide family planning services on a voluntary basis to welfare clients, but this policy came under attack by minority groups because of its avowed purpose of decreasing the transmission of poverty from one generation to another and lowering the illegitimacy rate.

The Family Planning Services and Population Research Act of 1970 set up the National Center for Family Planning Services under the Health Services and Mental Health Administration and recognized that family planning was part of the delivery of comprehensive health services for all. In 1971 the Secretary of Health, Education and Welfare presented a five-year plan for a partnership between the federal government and the private sector to achieve research and service goals. Congress made a new attempt to spell out the legislative mandate in 1972 to provide family planning services for all welfare recipients who wanted them. Changes were also made in the policy on contraceptives, lifting restrictions on age and marital status for receiving birth control information and devices.

With these changes, the federal support for family planning services shifted to state-administered third-party-payment mechanisms, such as Medicaid, while appropriations for direct project grants, which were responsible for patient growth rates from 1968 to 1972, were frozen at the 1972 level. As a result, the increase from 3.2 billion patients in 1974 to 3.8 billion in 1975 represented only half the average annual growth rate between 1968 and 1972.[23]

Among Western European countries, England and Sweden provide family planning through their health services. Most Catholic countries have banned birth control, although the pill and condoms are available for "medical purposes" or "disease prevention." Also, late marriages and the use of other methods of contraception, such as coitus interruptus and abortion, keep the birth rate down. The Soviet Union, other Eastern European countries, and Japan have tried to lower their abortion rates by distributing contraceptives through government health clinics.

POPULATION CONTROL

Population control is the deliberate regulation of population size by society. Family planning is the regulation of fertility by individual families. Population control is directed at the rate of growth and takes into account fertility control, the geographical location and movement of population, and problems of economic and social development as they affect fertility, mortality, and total size. Contraceptive delivery and educational systems are the basic core of any family planning program, while social and economic policies, which are generally identified as "beyond family planning" measures, are the basis for devising a strategy for population control.

Proposals

Bernard Berelson compiled a list of proposals that go beyond family planning, including the use of additives in the water or food supply to temporarily sterilize people, licensing for childbirth, the use of time-capsule contraceptives as means of temporary sterilization (with reversibility controlled by the government), and the compulsory sterilization of men with three or more living children.[24] Other proposals involve the use of incentives—money, goods, or services—to couples not bearing children for specific periods. "Negative" incentives include tax and welfare penalties and withdrawal of benefits, such as maternity and family allowances, after a certain number of children. Social and economic measures could have the effect of lowering fertility, for example, by increasing the minimum age of marriage or requiring female participation in the labor force as an alternative or supplement to marriage. Some proposals advocate two types of marriage—one childless and readily dissolved, the other more stable and licensed to have children. These suggestions may be unacceptable on moral or ethical grounds. However, research will probably continue, since a compulsory program may become imperative.

Population Control

The only example of governmental action to launch a population control program is India's brief experience of attempting to implement a compulsory sterilization program in 1976. Even there, the national policy committed the central government to a voluntary program, since the administrative machinery was not deemed adequate to cope with the demands of a nationwide compulsory sterilization program. However, if the states believed that they had the facilities, they were advised to make the laws applicable after the birth of three children. The only state to pass such a bill was Maharashtra, which includes Bombay. It never became law because the President of India refused to sign it.

From April through December 1976, more than 7 million sterilizations were reportedly performed in India, triple the number during the previous year.[25] However, reports began to be published of resistance to forcible sterilization, in some instances resulting in fatalities from rioting. The fall of the government of Indira Gandhi was interpreted as a vote against the coercive policies of the government, especially the compulsory sterilization program. The government then promised to return to wholly voluntary family planning. The implications of this experience are clear, but so are the consequences of rapid population growth, which put India's population at an estimated 622.7 million in mid-1977. By the century's end, at the present rate, it will reach 1 billion. The same situation is prevalent in other developing areas. Policy planners, within or outside the government, may have to decide at what stage a compulsory program becomes necessary.

Contraceptive Practice

Charles Westoff reports a significant increase in the use of more effective contraception from 1965 to 1973.[26] By 1973 seven in ten married couples were using contraception, and more than two out of three such couples were employing the three most effective methods of contraception—sterilization, the pill, and the IUD. If the relatively effective diaphragm and condom are included, nine out of ten couples currently using contraception may well be using these methods. This trend was consistent across varying educational levels and racial groups.

The most popular method of contraception was the pill, although the rate of increase of the pill appeared to be diminishing by 1973. Nearly 6.7 million married women of reproductive age (36.0 percent) were using the pill. It remained the method of choice of young women, although its use dropped to 17.7 percent of contraceptors aged thirty-five to forty-four. The second most popular method was contraceptive sterilization (23.5 percent). Among couples in which the wife was thirty to forty-four, sterilization was clearly the most popular method, accounting for 33.7 percent of all contraceptors. The use of the IUD has also increased, from 1.2 percent in 1965 to 10 percent in 1973. The use of older methods declined accordingly—condoms from 21.9 percent to 13.5 percent, the diaphragm from 9.9 to 3.4 percent, rhythm from 10.9 to 4.0 percent, withdrawal from 4.0 to 2.1 percent, and the douche from 5.2 to 0.8 percent.

Socioeconomic Level and Contraception

Westoff estimates that half of the fertility decline in the 1960s might be due to the drop in the number of unwanted births.[27] Recent statistics show a decline in fertility among low- and marginal-income women. The organized family planning programs have probably been responsible for part of the reduction. After assembling data from three studies covering 1960 to 1973, Jaffe suggested several trends. Women living in families with incomes below 125 percent of poverty (using the federal poverty index), had an average of 109 births per 1,000 women in 1971–72, compared to 153 births per 1,000 in 1960–65. Women in families above 125 percent of poverty had an average of 71 births per 1,000 in 1971–72, compared to 98 in 1960–65.[28] At the same time, however, lower- and marginal-income women continued to have significantly higher fertility rates than higher-income women, and a significantly higher rate of unwanted fertility. This suggests the task that remains for organized family planning programs in the United States.

Despite their higher fertility, low-income families account for a much smaller share of the birth rate than the "non-poor." During 1960–65 low-income families had 31.8 percent of the children, and higher-income families 68.2 percent.

FAMILY PLANNING AND SOCIAL WORK

Schools of Social Work

What efforts are being made to deal with population and family planning in the education of social workers? A questionnaire sent to the eighty graduate schools of social work by the Council on Social Work Education in 1969 received only thirty replies.[29] Only one school offered a course called "family planning." Twelve schools participated in field placements, research projects, or classroom instructional units. Ten schools had integrated family planning into the curriculum, sometimes with only one lecture in an area of concentration.

Activity is dependent on faculty interest. The schools were not committed to family planning courses. If an interested faculty member left, the program ended. More interest was shown in schools of social work located near schools of public health and centers of population research. However, if social work is to play a significant role in family planning and in social policy related to population problems, the schools of social work have to provide effective educational programs.

Social Agencies

Since social workers function through a variety of agencies, an extensive in-service training effort is necessary before they can effectively provide services in family planning. A welfare department study conducted by graduate social work students at the University of Illinois showed that clients who needed family planning never got to the service.[30] They only received a piece of paper stating that such services were available, distributed with many other forms at the time of the initial interview concerning eligibility. None of the social workers saw it as their job to provide family planning services.

Social workers have tended traditionally to be referral agents, but Meyer and Stone, in their study of twenty-two agencies in a four-county area in Michigan, found that the social workers saw themselves, along with physicians and public health nurses, as having a more significant role in family planning. Most of the respondents were engaged in helping their clients with problems and did not feel constrained by their agencies or their own beliefs about the efficacy of such help. "They did feel constrained to a considerable degree by their lack of family planning education."[31] This suggests the need for training social workers to deal with family planning problems.

Opportunities for Social Workers

Despite current apathy, many roles could best be performed by social workers. There is no more natural setting for discussing family planning than with individuals, families, and social groups. Information-giving on contraception can be organized on a communitywide basis, but the acceptance of service is still an individual or a family decision that often needs support and counsel.

Community organization skills can be used to develop local services and programs, create a climate of opinion to promote the acceptance of family planning counseling, and help people to accept such services. Communications skills can be used to interpret the needs of people to policy-makers so that conflicts and power struggles do not interfere with the effective use of services.

At the policy level, social work efforts have been minimal. There has been no discussion in the social work literature of the social implications of adopting a policy of population control. Perhaps with all the emphasis in the profession on individual freedom, social workers have shied away from societal control to solve critical population problems.

Topics for social work research should include decision-making concerning family size and timing of children, effects of family and peer groups on attitudes toward sex, and analysis of differences in fertility among groups of people of selected demographic factors.

Career Opportunities

Besides family planning activities in traditional social work agencies, social workers fill various jobs in specialized agencies that deal with family planning—Planned Parenthood, maternal and child health clinics, public health departments, obstetrics and gynecology clinics, and abortion counseling clinics and agencies.

For social workers interested in family planning, opportunities will become more available if the federal government implements population research and family planning services. At present, more social workers should be specifically assigned to family planning services and to abortion and postabortion counseling. School social workers have become increasingly involved in family planning activities as part of education for sexually active teenagers. Social workers in obstetrics, gynecology, and pediatrics departments in hospitals and clinics have organized group discussions and counseling services on the need for family planning. More social workers are being employed by Planned Parenthood to conduct classes in sex education, provide abortion information and counseling, establish community contacts for disseminating information on family planning services, and offer counseling at the centers.

Service Delivery and Social Policy

Social workers need to become familiar with major issues in service delivery in family planning arising out of social policy in population. So far government activity has been largely directed at bringing contraceptive information and services to the poor. Birth control centers have been concentrated in poor communities. Middle-class families get such services from private physicians.

Some members of black communities have charged that family planning programs are aimed specifically at reducing the black population. Social workers must realize that family planning is not an antipoverty measure. A reduction in poverty can be achieved only by dealing with those problems in the economy that create imbalances, quite apart from the benefits that limitation of family size may bring. We need to understand the social change occurring in black communities to see why their members are suspicious of outside efforts to impose any limitation on their numbers. A general fertility increase among all social classes of blacks occurred in the 1960s because of improved health conditions resulting in decreased death rates. Thus there is little enthusiasm for limitation of family size, especially when family planning services are not offered as part of a comprehensive approach to health care. The only way such services will succeed is to place them under local community control. From 1960 to 1973, the greatest decline in fertility was registered by nonwhites below 125 percent of poverty. They had 64 fewer births per 1,000 women in 1971–72 than in the first half of the 1960s, a reduction of 35 percent.[32]

Planning or Control

Finally, from a social policy point of view, we must distinguish between a national policy of family planning and one of population control. Family planning depends on individuals making a decision to voluntarily limit the size of their families, but it will probably not lead to population control since it does not hold the population growth to a specified number. It only reduces the number of unwanted births. Thus, all the children born might be wanted, but we might still be faced with a population problem. No country has yet adopted zero population growth as a policy goal. Many people believe that family planning is a first step and that we need to develop and disseminate effective family planning services before we think about instituting population control measures. Others disagree and feel that we should have instituted some means of population control long ago. A few years from now we may have to try other measures which now seem unethical or impractical. Ultimately we may have no choice, if the current world growth rate maintains its level. The social worker must be prepared to deal with family planning and population control as both a practitioner and an advocate.

SUMMARY AND APPLICATION

Ecologists have succeeded in enumerating many serious problems, but energy policy in the United States has developed slowly and incompletely. Taken together with inflation and employment opportunities, these problems are most serious for the poor, who need to raise their standard of living.

Family planning has been recognized as an individual right, and birth control devices are now widely available to the poor. Abortion is legally authorized, but whether it should be provided to those who cannot pay for the service is still highly controversial. A constitutional amendment is being sought to enact into law severe restrictions on abortions. Some consider this effort an attempt at minority control.

—Ketayun H. Gould

KEY TERMS

fertility
green revolution
desalinization
family planning policy
population control
zero population growth
diaphragm
sterilization
vasectomy
condom

rhythm
withdrawal
douche
developing countries
obstetrics-gynecology
IUD
ecology
ecosystem
fossil fuel sources

REFERENCES AND NOTES

1. Rufus E. Miles, Jr., Statement at the hearings of the President's Commission on Population Growth and the American Future, April 15, 1971, *Population Bulletin*, vol. 27, June 1971, p. 13.
2. Lester R. Brown, "Population and Affluence: Growing Pressures on World Food Resources," *Population Bulletin*, vol. 29, no. 2, 1973, p. 3.
3. Ibid., p. 9.
4. Ibid., pp. 15–16.
5. Paul R. Ehrlich and Anne H. Ehrlich, *Population, Resources, Environment: Issues in Human Ecology*, Freeman, San Francisco, 1970, p. 65.
6. "Warning: Water Shortages Ahead," *Time*, April 4, 1977, p. 48.
7. Ehrlich and Ehrlich, op. cit., p. 61.
8. Harold Hartley, "World Energy Prospects," in Calder Nigel (ed.), *The World in 1984*, vol. 1, Penguin, Baltimore, 1965, p. 71.
9. "Why the Big Shortage?" *Newsweek*, February 7, 1977, p. 19.

10. Ehrlich and Ehrlich, op. cit., pp. 118–119.
11. Ibid., p..126.
12. Ibid., p. 128.
13. Rufus E. Miles, Jr., "Man's Population Predicament," *Population Bulletin*, vol. 27, April 1971, pp. 4–39.
14. "Earth's 4,000,000,000 Inhabitants—Part III," *INTERCOM: The International Newsletter on Population*, vol. 4, June 1976, p. 12.
15. "Facts Behind the Four Billion," *Population Reference Bureau*, May 1976 (mimeographed).
16. Leon F. Bouvier, "U.S. Population in 2000—Zero Growth or Not?" *Population Bulletin*, vol. 30, no. 4, 1975, pp. 6, 11.
17. Ann Blackman, "Yes! More Women are Having Babies," Champaign-Urbana News Gazette, May 8, 1977, p. 32.
18. U.S. Bureau of the Census, "Fertility Expectations of American Women: June 1974," *Current Population Reports*, Series P-20, no. 277, Government Printing Office, Washington, D.C., 1975, p. 15.
19. Bouvier, op. cit. p. 21.
20. Ibid., p. 30.
21. W. Parker Mauldin, "Family Planning Programs and Fertility Declines in Developing Countries," *Family Planning Perspectives*, vol. 7, January–February 1975, pp. 32ff.
22. Alan Guttmacher Institute, "Organized Family Planning Services in the United States," *Family Planning Perspectives*, vol. 8, November–December 1976, p. 269.
23. Ibid.
24. Bernard Berelson, "Beyond Family Planning," *Studies in Family Planning*, vol. 38, February 1969, p. 16.
25. Lynn C. Landman, "Birth Control in India: The Carrot and the Rod?" *Family Planning Perspectives*, vol. 9, May–June 1977, p. 102.
26. Charles F. Westoff, "Trends in Contraceptive Practice: 1965–1973," *Family Planning Perspectives*, vol. 8, March–April 1976, pp. 54–57.
27. Ibid., p. 57.
28. Frederick S. Jaffe, "Low-Income Families: Fertility in 1971–1972," *Family Planning Perspectives*, vol. 6, Spring 1974, p. 108.
29. *Summary of Current Status of Education for Social Workers in Family Planning*, Council on Social Work Education, New York, n.d., pp. 13–19 (mimeographed).
30. Ketayun H. Gould, "Provision of Family Planning Services to Welfare Clients," University of Illinois, Urbana-Champaign, unpublished study, 1972.
31. Henry J. Meyer and Judith Stone, "Family Planning in the Practice of Social Workers," *Family Planning Perspectives*, vol. 6, Summer 1974, pp. 176–183.
32. Jaffe, op. cit., pp. 108–109.

FOR FURTHER STUDY

H. M. Bahr, B. A. Chadwick, and D. L. Thomas, *Population, Resources and the Future: Non-Malthusian Perspectives*, Brigham Young University, Provo, Utah, 1972.

Alan Guttmacher Institute, *Eleven Million Teenagers*, Planned Parenthood Federation, New York, 1978.

Florence Haselkorn (ed.), *Family Planning: Readings and Case Materials*, Council on Social Work Education, New York, 1971.

Charles William Hubbard, *Family Planning Education*, 2d ed., Mosby, St. Louis, 1977.

Judah Matras, *Introduction to Population: A Social Approach*, Prentice-Hall, Englewood Cliffs, N.J., 1977.

Edward Pohlman (ed.), *Population: A Clash of Prophets*, New American Library, New York, 1973.

John R. Weeks, *Population: Introduction to Concepts and Issues*, Wadsworth, Belmont, Calif., 1978.

FOR DISCUSSION

1. How does the use of grain for food differ in developing and developed countries?
2. What are some of the problems in using chemical fertilizers to increase production?
3. How does the production of meat affect our water supply?
4. What are the major provisions of current federal energy policy? (Include innovations since the publication of this book.)
5. What are some promising means of controlling the problems with solid wastes?
6. How does an inefficient energy policy affect the well-being of our citizens?
7. What is the difference between family planning and population control?
8. According to current estimates, what will be the world population in 1989?
9. Both developing and developed countries have had a drop in the death rate (mortality). On what factor do they differ clearly?
10. What region of the world is growing in population at the fastest rate?
11. Which is most likely to achieve zero population growth—increased mortality, decreased immigration, or declines in fertility? Why?
12. What has been the result of governmental efforts to increase population as, for example, in France?
13. When did the United States make the first positive statement on family planning?
14. How are most family planning programs that have federal support financed? Who provides the services?
15. How can tax policies affect family size?
16. What happened to India's attempt at population control?
17. What are the various methods of birth control? Which ones are most effective?
18. Among women over age thirty in the United States, what is the most popular method of birth control?
19. How is the number of unwanted children related generally to income level in the United States?
20. What attention is given to family planning by schools of social work?
21. What is the major constraint for social workers providing family planning information in social agencies?
22. What auspices for services are recommended to dispel the idea that family planning encourages genocide for minority group members?

PROJECTS

1. Collect several examples of "optimistic" and "pessimistic" views concerning the future of food and energy supplies in the United States. After a review of the evidence, summarize your own position.
2. Make a study of the organizations interested in conservation, ecology, and public

acquisition of open land and parks in your community. Do they cooperate with each other? What are their goals and methods of operation? Evaluate their success.

3. Highway construction and planning are major ecological issues. What agencies are involved? Have citizens' groups organized to oppose any construction plans? What policies will obtain the best system of traffic management and flow and minimize noise, congestion, and pollution?

4. Collect policy statements and public relations materials on ecology and business from your local chamber of commerce. Summarize and evaluate them.

5. Invite a representative of Planned Parenthood to describe its program and to demonstrate and discuss various contraceptive devices. Does the organization have a program for the treatment of sterility as well as for family planning?

6. Present a discussion or debate on the question: "Resolved, that blacks should oppose government-sponsored family planning programs."

7. Find some recent statistics on the rate of births among teenagers (both inside and outside of marriage). Compare these to the rates for women over twenty years of age. What are the trends between about 1960 and the present? Look for statistics that make international comparisons of teenage parenthood. Then, in small work groups, consider the possible explanations for the rates and trends. Assign a panel of students to look into the health risks associated with teenage pregnancy and report to the class. Ask another panel to consider the rights and responsibilities of both males and females in teenage reproductive activity.

8. Write and defend a policy statement for NASW on abortion.

9. Present a developmental program for sex education for children. Indicate the goals, methods, auspices, and content for each developmental period. Deal specifically with contraceptive information for adolescents.

10. Analyze the jobs listed in the *Family Planning Digest*. What skills do they require? Can a social worker fill most of them?

CHAPTER 16
Racism

Many groups; many similarities; many differences.

THE WHITE HOUSE

Your door is shut against my tightened face,
And I am sharp as steel with discontent;
But I possess the courage and the grace
To bear my anger proudly and unbent.
The pavement slabs burn loose beneath my feet,
A chafing savage, down the decent street;
And passion rends my vitals as I pass,
Where boldly shines your shuttered door of glass.
Oh, I must search for wisdom every hour,
Deep in my wrathful bosom sore and raw,
And I find in it the superhuman power
To hold me to the letter of your law!

—Claude McKay*

Racism is obvious to its victims but is largely unrecognized by the people who practice it. Numerically the victims are primarily black but Hispanics, American Indians, and Asian Americans have also faced discrimination.

Because minority group members are likely to be poor, disproportionate numbers of them are known to social agencies.

ETHNOCENTRISM AND RACISM

Ethnocentrism is based on a belief in the superiority of a particular culture; racism results from the belief that skin color and other physical characteristics cause behavioral and cultural differences. Color, then, becomes a more pervasive difference than culture. For example, the Scots may argue superiority with the Irish, but both have tended to feel that they are superior to any society made up of people of color. In racism color becomes the determinant for classifying people as insiders or outsiders.

Racism is usually passive. Most white Americans are not overtly hostile to Indians or blacks. They did not try to shoot Indians out of the saddle or lynch blacks, but white American racial values and standards of justice made it possible for Indians to be shot and blacks to be lynched with little protest and no punishment.

Many white Americans have never talked to a member of these minorities. Indians are still best known from television movies. Outside of large cities, there are few Chicanos, Puerto Ricans, or Asian Americans. Many smaller communities still have virtually no blacks.

*Claude McKay, *Selected Poems,* Twayne Publishers, Boston, Mass., p. 78.

Most whites believe that the door of opportunity is open to all and that barriers can be surmounted by ambition and hard work. Racism complicates relationships by introducing inconsistencies. Whites often say that blacks or Hispanics or American Indians could improve their lot despite their racial characteristics, but many whites believe these people have limited capabilities. Too few see the contradiction. Members of minority groups find themselves in the role of outsiders because of ignorance, indifference, apathy, and unwritten policies.

Stereotypes and Myths

Because color and culture serve as "sorting" mechanisms, unrealistic models are easily built up in the minds of whites as universal descriptions of members of racial minorities. Unfortunately, these stereotypes are taken seriously by whites and used as the basis for policy. Traditionally, whites have been taught that Indians cannot use alcohol intelligently. This belief was once translated into laws prohibiting Indians from buying, possessing, and consuming whisky.

Even Minorities Accept Stereotypes   Racism is not always obvious. The belief that blacks have natural rhythm is so ingrained in American culture that many blacks are firmly convinced of its truth. On the surface, music is good and universally appreciated. No laws have been enacted that discriminate against black musicians. The discrimination is subtle. Music is good, but it is essentially play, not work. The belief that blacks have an aptitude for music may be seen as evidence of their lack of seriousness and productivity. Natural rhythm is, then, nothing to elicit pride. The belief that blacks have inborn musical talent no longer sounds harmless but takes on a more significant meaning when infused with racist ideology.

Similar myths and stereotypes, some harmful and some only absurd, persist. They have found their way into common English expressions, such as "lazy as a Mexican" or "colored people's time" (implying lateness). These racist expressions will be used by people who would not use directly insulting terms like "Spic" or "Chink."

America's Past

The United States has always been a racist country. The nation that talked so much about freedom, dignity, and human rights depended heavily in its economic life on slavery. Most white Americans did not see the contradiction, although there were individual exceptions. Jefferson, although he originally owned slaves, apparently eventually rejected the practice. More frequently the black was seen as a chattel. The slave was not given the vote and was technically only three-fifths of a man, according to the Constitution.

The Indians were treated as alien to their own lands. When they could be useful, they were courted as allies, but at other times they were only a problem. Westward expansion required their detention at best and their extermination at worst. Today many Indians are wards of the nation and receive less of the benefits of its productivity than any other ethnic group. Had treaties been honored under American law, many would undoubtedly be wealthy.

Blacks constitute the largest minority in the United States and have had the most attention from whites. Asian Americans are included because their situation is dramatically misunderstood. Hispanics are the most rapidly growing minority. Examples will also be included of the dimensions of the problem for other groups.

RACISM AGAINST BLACKS

Many slaves came from cultures that were highly developed, but unfortunately racial and cultural provincialism during the colonial period made white people oblivious to values that did not conform to those prevailing in Western Europe. The African political, artistic, economic, religious, and linguistic experience was not European and therefore of no consequence. Africans were prohibited from practicing and developing their art, their language, their religion, their family life. For want of appreciation and practice, whatever was distinctively African soon died out in America. Although the black was denied the rights of the white colonialist, the revolutionary period did produce distinguished blacks who contributed to America's cultural growth.

Even the great debate over slavery preceding the Civil War took place in the context of white racism. Opposition to the spread of slavery was fed more by the Northern fears of competition from slave labor and the presence of blacks in the North and West than moral concern for human welfare. Whites who did profess to oppose slavery on moral grounds rarely accepted the principle of racial equality. In a speech in Charleston, Illinois, in 1858, Abraham Lincoln made it clear that opposition to slavery in the federal territories did not mean the acceptance of blacks as equals.

> I will say, then, that I am not, nor ever have been, in favor of bringing about in any way the social and political equality of the white and black races; that I am not, nor ever have been, in favor of making voters or jurors of Negroes, nor of qualifying them to hold office, nor to inter-marry with White people . . .
>
> And inasmuch as they cannot so live, while they do remain together there must be the position of superior and inferior, and I as much as any other man am in favor of having the superior position assigned to the White race.[1]

Until recently, the relationship of "superior and inferior" described by Lincoln was maintained by two social institutions, slavery and "Jim Crow." Slavery was abolished by the events of the Civil War, but a caste system hardened into a rigid system of oppression known as Jim Crow. The system prescribed how blacks were supposed to act in the presence of whites. For example, trains in the South always carried a Jim Crow car where blacks were supposed to sit. Often this was an old car clearly inferior to the accommodations provided the "white folks."

"*I'm definitely for justice and righteousness but I don't want to offend the bigot vote either.*"

(Reprinted with permission from the Saturday Evening Post Company, © 1978.)

Social Control   Slavery and Jim Crow were not merely means by which blacks were exploited; they were also systems of social control and socialization. During more than three centuries when black labor was ruthlessly exploited, social institutions prevented the outbreak of large-scale black violence and conditioned black people to acquiesce in their own subjugation. The existence of these institutions was inconsistent with the major values in a nation which called itself a democracy.

Insurrections occurred in response to the denial of rights to slaves and the constant policing of their activities. Whippings, mutilations, and hangings were commonly accepted managerial practices. This treatment prevented the development of the slave's individual autonomy and kept him in a state of complete dependence on his master. Maintenance of this dependency required the debasement of the slave.

After the Civil War

Reconstruction   A short-lived and totally inadequate attempt was made by the victorious North to prepare the liberated slaves for first-class citizenship. Although postwar policies protected black voting and civil rights, the federal government failed to launch a comprehensive program of economic and educational aid. Lacking even rudimentary education and having no land, most blacks soon returned to a state of economic dependence on the same planters who had held them in bondage. Since Northern whites had never viewed blacks as their equals, federal protection of black civil rights ended within a dozen years of the North's victory. In 1877 the disputed presidential election of the previous year was resolved by a compromise that ended federal tampering with white Southern "home rule" in return for Southern acceptance of the election of the Republican candidate, Rutherford B. Hayes.

Post-Reconstruction   White supremacy was quickly restored. Soon after the reestablishment of home rule, laws were passed requiring racial segregation in schools and public places and prohibiting interracial marriages. This pattern of rigid segregation in the late nineteenth century was designed as much to keep blacks in their place as to separate the races physically. Jim Crow encompassed far more than the social relations between the two races. It also meant the denial of political and legal rights to black people. From 1890 to 1910 blacks were barred from voting in every Southern state by means of state constitutional amendments. This assertion of white supremacy was not confined to conventional political channels. Blacks who opposed Jim Crow were subject to beatings, burnings, and lynchings. During the transitional period of the 1890s, hundreds of blacks were lynched. Lynchings were public—almost festive— occasions which "taught" black people that challenging white power meant possible death.

Jim Crow required that blacks be kept submissive and ignorant. Like slavery, Jim Crow socialized black people into accepting their inferior status. Facing constant humiliation and powerlessness, blacks viewed themselves as inferior to whites. Thus accommodation was internalized.

World War II and After
On the eve of American entry into World War II, black Americans were imprisoned in a rigid caste system. Blacks could migrate north of the Mason-Dixon line, but they could not escape the racist stereotypes personified by entertainers like Amos 'n Andy and Stepin Fetchit, nor could their children escape schools that eulogized the achievements of the whites. Even in the "free" North, blacks were marked by the effects of a racist culture. Many blacks

internalized white values and covertly regarded themselves as objects of loathing. As two psychiatrists concluded, "Identification with the white oppressor has been the bane of Negro cohesion from the very beginning of slavery, when it took the form of pride in being a house slave, rather than a field slave. This sort of an illusory identification with the master did incalculable harm to Negro cohesion, because it formed one base for class distinction between Negroes.[2] As a result of the black's identification with the white man, black anger was directed against other blacks rather than whites.

Since World War II, the civil rights movement for blacks has gone through a protest phase and a political phase. Now we are in the third phase, emphasizing economic gains.

Protest Phase

School Desegregation   A major turning point in the course of black history in the United States was reached when the Supreme Court in *Brown v. Board of Education* ruled that racial segregation in the public schools was unconstitutional. This was a reversal of the *Plessy v. Ferguson* decision of 1896 that "separate but equal" facilities were constitutional.[3] This great legal victory signaled an unprecedented opportunity for the integration of blacks into the cultural fabric of the United States.

Since the Supreme Court decision, blacks themselves have added a new dimension to the civil rights picture in the United States—their own preparedness to campaign actively and aggressively for the rights granted by the courts. This new militancy was at the heart of the civil rights revolution. The 382-day-long Montgomery bus boycott, which brought Dr. Martin Luther King to prominence, involved effective use of "direct action" for the first time in the South. Its primary objective was to dramatize the effects of racial discrimination on a black community.

Confrontations at Tuscaloosa and Little Rock   Autherine Lucy, a twenty-six-year-old library science student, was admitted to the University of Alabama by a federal court order and then barred by university officials in February 1956. She filed contempt of court proceedings against the school. State authorities eventually prevailed in their decision to expel her, and Alabama remained segregated until 1963.

In 1957 Governor Orval Faubus summoned the Arkansas National Guard to turn away nine black pupils from Central High School in Little Rock. At Little Rock, however, a direct challenge was posed to the federal government, which had already approved a desegregation plan submitted by the local school board. When the black students were forced to withdraw from the premises of the school, in direct defiance of an order by the federal district court, President Eisenhower sent in federal troops. Some 1,000 paratroopers descended on Little Rock and were joined by 10,000 National Guardsmen. The children entered Central High School on September 25. The soldiers remained on call for the entire school year. Little Rock high schools closed for the 1958–59 school term, but when school closing laws were declared unconstitutional by the federal court, Central High School was opened to members of all races.

Other Actions   The sit-ins of 1960, the freedom rides of 1961, the acceptance of James Meredith at the University of Mississippi in 1962, the Birmingham crisis in 1963, and the Medgar Evers murder of 1963 brought thousands of whites and blacks together on behalf of civil rights. The Southern Christian Leadership Conference (SCLC), the Students National Coordinating Council (SNCC), the Congress of Racial Equality (CORE), and the National Association for the Advancement of Colored People (NAACP) joined in the protests.

The largest protest demonstration in history occurred in August 1963. More than 200,000 Americans of all races, colors, and creeds converged on Washington, D.C., to stage a civil rights protest on the steps of the Lincoln Memorial. The march represented that attempt of black leaders to dramatize to the nation the scope of discontent and the enormous appeal of the idea of an open, desegregated society for millions of Americans. Moreover, the effectiveness of nonviolence on a large scale had to be tested.

The Political Phase

When the most comprehensive civil rights legislation passed in this century was signed into law by President Lyndon Johnson in 1964, it seemed that the nation had finally entered a more just and serene era of race relations. Although riots broke out in Harlem two weeks later, the belief persisted that basic problems would be solved. This optimism was dampened by riots in other Northern cities that summer and by the Republican nomination of a candidate for the presidency who had opposed the civil rights bill.

Johnson's triumphant victory in 1964 raised hopes that the President was prepared to attack the problems facing black Americans. His War on Poverty sought the total elimination of American poverty, and his civil rights programs were equally ambitious. When the Voting Rights Act of 1965 was signed into law on August 6, President Johnson stated that the act would "strike away the last major shackle" of the black's "ancient bonds." One week later the Watts district of Los Angeles was in flames. After Watts, the nation witnessed several summers of civil disorder, the development of black power ideologies, the radicalization of many black college students, the organization of local black revolutionary groups, and the assassination of Martin Luther King in April 1968. Arguments that blacks were reacting to intolerable economic conditions and constant humiliation did not lead to massive public and private programs to remedy these ills. Instead, white Americans demanded "law and order."

Political gains persisted. Blacks generally have little difficulty in voting. Newark, Detroit, Los Angeles, Cleveland, and Atlanta elected black mayors. Over 4,300 blacks served in public office in 1978.

The Economic Phase

In the decade since the death of Martin Luther King, the central need has been economic. A recent Census Bureau esitmate identified 7.6 million blacks as falling below the poverty line of $5,815 for a family of four. The total has gone up by 50,000 since 1975. The median income of black families in the South was about $7,700, or 59 percent of the median for whites. For the nation as a whole, the median black family income was about $8,800—62 percent of the comparable white total.[4]

Unemployment remains a serious problem, especially for urban black youth, for whom the rate runs as high as 40 percent. Full employment would be one of the best answers to deal with economic racism.

The importance of the economic phase was stressed by Robert B. Hill and James Dumpson in their papers on the state of black America published in 1978 by the Urban League.[5] Hill stressed unemployment:

> Although there are signs of some degree of economic recovery in the nation, as a whole, no such recovery has reached the black community. Black unemployment in 1977—even as officially defined—was at the highest level ever recorded for blacks. While most white workers have been experiencing a decline in unemployment, joblessness has been on the rise among black women heads of families and among black teenagers. In fact, black female heads of families are receiving the major brunt of the current recession/depression. Black unemployment has increased since 1977.

Dumpson also followed the theme of economic productivity:

> The most cursory review of statistics relating to the economic and social conditions of blacks in the United States continues to demonstrate the growing lag between the philosophical and value articulations of every sector of American life, and the day-to-day experience of life in America for the great majority of black people. Denying blacks of their right to participation in the economic productivity of the United States and full opportunity to share in the benefits of the economic productivity not only perpetuates the social and economic enslavement of the majority of blacks, but threatens the national social development and the continued viability of the American way of life.

RACISM AND ASIAN AMERICANS

Asian Americans are citizens of the United States who have either Mongoloid or Malayan characteristics and whose ancestors resided in East Asia.

Early Discrimination

While the economic development of the new American nation necessitated the importation of cheap labor from African and Asian continents, "colored" people were excluded from full citizenship rights. When the first group of Asians appeared on the American frontier in 1850, slavery for blacks and reservations for American Indians were well established. Unlike them, the first Asian immigrants were neither enslaved nor corralled. America needed a mobile and docile labor force to work uncomplainingly in railroad construction, mines, and new urban factories—jobs which neither whites nor plantation-oriented blacks could fill.

Racism against Asians is shown in the 1854 decision of the California Supreme Court in *The People v. Hall*.[6] The appellant, a white Anglo-American, had been convicted of murder upon the testimony of Chinese witnesses. Was such evidence admissible? The judge ruled that Asians should be ineligible to testify for or against a white man. This ruling opened the floodgate for anti-Chinese abuse, violence, and exploitation. Group murders, lynchings, property damage, and robbery of the Chinese were reported up and down the West Coast. Because of the harsh treatment of the Chinese, any luckless person was described as not having a "Chinaman's chance."

Restrictions and exclusionary measures against Chinese in employment and property ownership became national in scope in 1883, when Congress passed the Chinese Exclusion Act. It prohibited immigration, thus limiting the birth rate of Chinese and the development of family life because wives who were still in China could not join their husbands here. The act also excluded Chinese immigrants from naturalization. Japanese, Filipinos, and other Asians were later added to the excluded category.

The first group of Japanese immigrants, arriving in 1885, became the ready target of the anti-Chinese elements on the West Coast. According to Ruth McKee, "the forces that had accomplished the exclusion of the Chinese had developed legend, techniques, and arguments which with little editing could be turned against the Japanese. . . . Politicians and pressure groups had served their apprenticeship in the anti-Chinese crusade. By the turn of the century these veterans were ready to launch a new offensive."[7] To make the situation worse, tension developed between Japan and the United States shortly after the arrival of Japanese immigrants. An executive order of 1907 prohibited further Japanese immigration from Mexico, Canada, and Hawaii. In the following year, the Japanese and the U.S. governments signed a gentlemen's agreement to voluntarily prohibit the immigration of Japanese nationals. Excluded from this agreement were the wives of Japanese men residing in the United States. This contributed to a different family life pattern for the Japanese compared to the Chinese.

"Yellow Peril" agitators, particularly labor leaders and politicians, saw their victory in the enactment of the Immigration Act of 1924. The national origins quota system effectively excluded Asian immigration. Thus America made a sharp break with its tradition of free immigration and formalized two policies: the "open door" policy for desirable white northern Europeans and the "closed door" for "colored" Asians.

On the heels of the gentlemen's agreement of 1908 and the Immigration Act of 1924, Filipinos were lured onto the American scene by unscrupulous labor contractors from Hawaii. By virtue of the U.S. trusteeship of the Philippines, Filipinos were not considered aliens but nationals of the United States, although rights of citizenship were never granted. Filipino experiences have been rather similar to those of the Chinese and Japanese.

In 1943, naturalization was finally granted to Asians. This amendment also permitted the immigration of close relatives of Asian Americans who were already U.S. citizens. Finally, in 1965, immigration laws abolished the restrictive national origins quota.

Internment in World War II

The internment of Japanese Americans from the West Coast in "reloca-tion camps" after Pearl Harbor is no surprise viewed against the history and background of persistent and violent anti-Asian agitation. In 1942 some 110,000 persons of Japanese descent were placed in "protective custody." Two-thirds were American citizens by birth, and the other third were aliens forbidden by law to be citizens. No charges had been filed against them, nor had any hearing been held.

Several motives were advanced for the internment—the danger of sabotage and espionage, and the need to protect Japanese Americans from mob action. These appear to be flimsy excuses, particularly when one considers that no similar measures were taken against German and Italian Americans. The mass internment placed all Japanese Americans under a cloud of suspicion. The internment itself was held as proof of their disloyalty.

Japanese Americans responded to the internment by requesting to be accepted in the American armed forces. Their request was granted. President Roosevelt said in 1943 that "Americanism is a matter of the mind and heart; Americanism in not, never has been, a matter of race or ancestry." The bravery of the 442nd Regimental Combat Team in the European theater and of other members of the Japanese American military is now well known.

Asian American Communities in the United States

The Asians and Asian Americans in the United States are predominantly Chinese, Japanese, Filipinos, and Koreans. Burmese, Indonesians, Guamani-ans, Samoans, South Vietnamese, and Thais are also becoming more numer-ous. The listing suggests the heterogeneity of history, religion, language, and culture of Asian American communities. Superimposed upon this diversity is the differential pattern of immigration and accommodation for each group. For these reasons, each Asian community in the United States must be understood and dealt with as a unique entity, but the present perception is to view all Asian communities as homogeneous. This can be likened to viewing all Europeans as a single entity. This does not deny the common basis of Asian experiences in the United States, involving fairly uniform and systematic discriminatory practices against them.

Various Asian American communities differ in terms of numbers, group cohesion, stability, levels of education, and the professional, political, and economic achievements of their members. Asians and Asian Americans tend to cluster around certain locations. Eighty percent live in Hawaii or on the West Coast. The presence of Chinatowns, Little Tokyos, and Little Manilas in metropolitan areas appears to be a self-protective response of the oppressed. At best, each Asian community can be characterized as a cultural and social community with its unique sets of values, norms, organizations, and accommodation patterns in relation to the host community. As with blacks, dispersion of second- and third-generation Asian Americans to suburbia from the ethnic enclaves is resulting from the relaxation of discriminatory housing ordinances and from improved socioeconomic conditions.

Between the end of World War II and 1970, 140,827 Asian women entered as wives of U.S. citizens. Another group of Asians who have entered the United States on a nonquota basis are the 40,000 orphaned or racially mixed children from Hong Kong, Korea, Japan, Taiwan, and South Vietnam who have been adopted by U.S. citizens.

A study of Korean households in Chicago, conducted by a group of Korean social workers, revealed that 76 percent of the heads of households were under forty years of age; 85 percent had been in the United States less than four years; 49 percent of the heads of households held professional jobs; and 11 percent held managerial jobs. The average number of children was two, most of whom were of preschool age. Surprisingly, 98 percent of the married women worked, 75 percent of them in professional capacities. A third of the college-educated men were engaged in menial jobs due to language difficulties, citizenship requirements, ignorance of community resources, and problems in transferability of skills.[8]

Issues in Asian American Communities

Like other disenfranchised groups, Asian Americans share the disadvantages associated with minority status. Income maintenance, housing, education, health care, unemployment and underemployment, and vocational training and retraining are immediate problems. Because of language and cultural barriers and unfamiliarity with the institutional arrangements of the communities in which they live, many needy Asians (particularly aged and new immigrants) do not seek out services to which they are entitled. Equally serious barriers to service delivery are the insensitivity, ignorance, and inadequacy of community agencies which prefer to maintain the myth that "Asians are successful and they take care of themselves." Serious conflicts are experienced by Asian Americans who are caught between the value systems of their parents and of America. The frustration and anger at the society which has systematically excluded them from the major decision-making institutions must be accepted and dealt with by both the Asian communities and the larger society.

The needs and problems of Asians and Asian Americans can be related to three groups: (1) those who immigrated prior to the Asian Exclusion Act of 1924; (2) the immigrants who entered after World War II—nonquota "war brides," adopted children of U.S. citizens, and quota immigrants, including skilled and unskilled; and (3) American-born Asian Americans.

These groups are sufficiently unique to warrant different considerations and approaches by social work and other human service disciplines. Unemployment for the first group is more likely to be related to poor health and marginal job skills. In the second group, it is more closely related to lack of language proficiency in expressing and demonstrating training or to restrictive union or licensing practices, or both. For the third group, alienation or poor educational preparation may be most important.

OTHER MAJOR MINORITY GROUPS

Social agencies and schools of social work have also been targets of criticism from American Indians, Chicanos, and Puerto Ricans. The latter two are sometimes grouped together as Hispanics. The groups have both similarities and differences. The various Indian tribes and other subgroups prize their differences from each other.

Rural Background   Like the blacks, the other minorities trace their heritage to rural antecedents. The Indian has remained the most rural, although there has been extensive movement from the reservations to find work. Chicanos have usually become part of the urban *barrios* or served as agricultural workers. Traditionally they migrated with the crops, but now they are becoming permanent settlers. The Puerto Ricans are the most urbanized in America, but many of them, coming from remote rural areas, had to transcend 200 years of "progress" in the three-hour jet flight from San Juan to New York.

Language Barriers   All three of these minorities have greater language barriers than the blacks. Indian children learn English routinely, but often speak it only at school. Limited education is a greater problem for the Spanish-speaking groups. Lighter-skinned adults acquire English more rapidly, probably because they get jobs and are accepted more easily by whites. Language barriers make it difficult to obtain service. Sponsors of an advocacy program for Spanish-speaking people in California put it this way:

> When non-English speaking people attempt to locate services, they often end their search in anger and frustration. From the client's point of view, concrete difficulties interfere with their gaining access to services from agencies: arbitrary denial of services; institutional inflexibility; red tape with long delays and silences; undignified or callous treatment; complex forms and procedures of eligibility; long waiting lists; inaccessibility by telephone or in person; a run-around from agency to agency; lack of clear, simple directions and explanations; and lack of specifically needed services. This list of problems is multiplied many times when the person who needs help can not speak English.[9]

Interestingly, bilingual programs are important for Hispanics but not as much so for other minorities. With 100 Indian tribes, it is not feasible to have a bilingual program for urban Indians.

Different minorities have played different roles. Writing from an American Indian point of view, Deloria concludes that our racism led blacks to be considered draft animals, Indians wild animals, Orientals domestic animals, and Mexicans humorous lazy animals.[10]

The effort to alienate Indians from blacks is another interesting theme. In colonial times blacks often tried to escape to the Indian wilderness, and Indians were used to hunt runaway slaves.[11]

All the minorities have shared in poverty. They have all lacked adequate education and health care. Their work opportunities have conveyed low pay and low status.

Native Americans

The term "Native American" emphasizes the Indians' heritage and their claim to America. Their centuries of war with the white man intensified prejudice against them as savages. Earlier in this century they were ignored because of their isolation on remote reservations.

Blacks and Indians Deloria develops the differential approach to blacks and Indians. The white man specifically excluded blacks from all programs, but had to deal with Indians in treaties and agreements. Laws had one goal—"Anglo-Saxonization" of the Indian. Deloria explains that "The antelope had to become a white man. Between these two basic attitudes, the apelike draft animal and the wild free-running antelope, the white man was impaled on the horns of a dilemma he had created with himself."[12]

Indians have received the most paternalistic treatment of all minorities through the Bureau of Indian Affairs. The BIA has become the symbol of Indian frustration and despair.

Economic Development Generally in this century Indians have been passive. The educational system has prevented the development of strong indigenous leadership, and reservation life has encouraged passivity. Conditions may improve on the reservations. Economic development projects have had success that will lead to their extension. Tribes have had the advantage of being legal entities that could receive federal grants. Also, Indians have obtained highly qualified lawyers to press their historic land claims. Meanwhile, the urban Indian is still largely ignored.

Interracial Adoptions In the social service area, Indians are concerned about the way interracial adoptions have been used to remove children from their families. Some have even been kidnapped. The Association on American Indian Affairs has developed a Bill of Rights for Indian Children and publishes an *Indian Family Defense Newsletter*.

Chicano

The Chicano is "not Mexican, not Spanish, but a product of a Spanish-Mexican-Indian heritage and an Anglo-Saxon influence."[13] Chicanos resent the stereotypes that demean them—especially the image of laziness when they perform some of the hardest physical labor in our society.

The movement for Chicano solidarity places strong emphasis on institutional change and the substitution of brotherhood for professionalism.

Now one must be the advocate of the client. Rather than "keeping the natives down" we must organize clients to have a meaningful influence on our agencies. . . . Individualization—yes—but the individual is a person interacting and transacting with brother, sister, friends—with a community that spells brotherhood, a brotherhood that means power.[14]

Of the three minorities considered here, Chicanos have presented the strongest case for changes in social work that will benefit them. They now have a Chicano-oriented school at San Jose State University. Leaders place emphasis on the creation of jobs for their people in social agencies. Until more Chicano graduates are produced, those hired will be mainly paraprofessionals. Like the blacks, they prefer services for Chicanos to be planned and controlled by Chicanos. So far programs have concentrated more on the settled group than on migrant workers.

Puerto Ricans
For the Puerto Rican, the Spanish culture has been dominant, but Taino Indian, African, American, and European are also involved. With the pattern of extensive intermarriage, great conflict is created for Puerto Ricans who come to a country that defines as black anyone "with a drop of black blood."

Skin Color In Puerto Rico, identity is based on culture or class, not primarily on skin color. Here skin color gets new emphasis. According to Longres, four groups are distinguished: the *moreno,* the *trigueno,* the *grifo,* and the *indio.*[15] The first three describe the range from dark to light, and the last refers to Indian characteristics. Upon arrival in the United States, Puerto Ricans may find that as a racially mixed group they are generally labeled black. Because of intermarriage, this has ramifications for lighter as well as darker Puerto Ricans. Longres concludes that mental health should be defined within a Puerto Rican cultural context. "Puerto Ricans should emphasize pride in their culture, pride in the racial mixture of Puerto Ricans, and indifference to racial ancestry."[16] That is hard to do if the emphasis of white Americans is not congruent.

Rivera characterizes as unique factors Puerto Rico's status as a United States Commonwealth and its proximity to New York. He also describes the average migrant:

As United States citizens, Puerto Ricans can move freely between the island and the continent. The migration tends to follow economic trends in both the United States and Puerto Rico. The heaviest migrant waves from Puerto Rico came in the early 1950s, encouraged by faster and cheaper air transportation as well as by the demand for semiskilled and unskilled labor.

The average Puerto Rican migrant is young, has little formal education, and comes from the rural areas, in some cases via an urban slum. His move to the United States is not seen as permanent; he intends to go back to the island after making some money. Consequently, he does not see the need to become assimilated and grow roots in this land, nor to give up his language and his culture. In many cases, this fact constitutes a problem in his adjustment to this society, particularly in the establishment of community and political organizations. Some Puerto Ricans are able to save some money and fulfill their dream of returning to Puerto Rico to start a small business or buy a house and retire. Many others return, poor and frustrated, only to find that there is no place for them in Puerto Rico either. Some families are caught in a pattern of traveling between the United States and Puerto Rico without making a satisfactory adjustment in either place. Ironically, many never make it back to the island and their children prefer to stay here.[17]

New York with over a million Puerto Ricans provides the clearest evidence of their problems. They have the lowest salaries, the lowest level of education, and the highest percentage of unemployment and public assistance recipiency.

CULTURAL DIVERSITY AND THE SOCIAL SERVICES

Knowledge of cultural elements is important if the social worker is to serve special groups effectively.

American Indians have important common characteristics, although each tribal culture is unique. Sharing, a relaxed sense of time, acceptance of suffering, and optimism are traits considered common to most tribes. Noninterference is a major concept: The Indian cultural concept of noninterference—that is, not interfering with or imposing oneself on the life of another—may result in problems in client-worker relations for the social worker who practices aggressive intervention. Although most clients tend to reject aggressive social workers, even greater sensitivity must be exercised when working with American Indians. In working toward this goal, careful application of communications techniques and skills, such as restating, clarifying, summarizing, reflecting, and empathizing, may be particularly helpful.[18]

A special problem in access to service affects the Chicano migrant worker. Mobility makes it difficult to exercise a legitimate claim on services. Language barriers also persist longer for this group because they have more limited contact with English-speaking persons.

Delgado has emphasized the role of spiritualism with Puerto Ricans.[19] The medium is a helping agent who, incidentally, has no reluctance to visit clients in their own homes: The magical cures mediums can effect give them an advantage over social workers. The paraphernalia (prayers, herbs, candles) at the medium's disposal play a crucial role in bringing about the magical cure. Social workers do not have this arsenal of magical power at their disposal.

Delgado advises social workers:

> Once a knowledge base regarding spiritualist beliefs has been obtained, do not hesitate to consider asking a client whether she or he believes in spirits. The fact that the social worker can take this initial important step will serve to legitimize the client's system of beliefs. In turn, it may result in elucidating many important issues that will facilitate treatment.

Ghali stresses the influence of spiritualism for Puerto Ricans. She also indicates their reluctance to use agency help and presents a sequence of steps that come before the agency—the last resort.[20]

> Puerto Ricans will often only make use of social agencies or mental health services as a last resort, although their difficulties frequently include dealing with systems such as welfare, housing, health, judicial, employment, and education; relationship problems within the family, and feelings of depression, nervousness, alienation, or other severe disturbance. Often when a poor Puerto Rican sees a professional worker he is wondering what that person thinks of the poor, of the dark-skinned, of those inarticulate in the English language. Does the professional worker understand how the ghetto has affected him? What it is like to be hungry, humiliated, powerless, and broke? Does he really want to help or just do a job? The middle-class Puerto Rican will wonder if the professional person will attribute all of the usual sterotypes to him or see him as an individual. First, therefore, in seeking help, the Puerto Rican will approach family members, friends, neighbors, shopkeepers, *compadres*, or acquaintances who have some degree of expertise or authority in the area of concern. Second, teachers, clergymen, or educated people who are within his own network or relationships are approached on an informal basis, not as part of an institution. Their mutuality is then explored through the town, the school, and the neighborhood that is common to them; their familial kinship is explored through blood relatives, marriage, *compadrazgo*, mutual acquaintances, and so on.

Other Suggestions for Social Workers

Several recommendations appear consistently in the literature of each minority group:

1. Clients are entitled to a general understanding of their culture so they are not served inappropriately out of ignorance.
2. All clients should be served without discrimination or prejudice.
3. Minority clients should have a voice in planning and managing services provided for them.
4. Minority staff members are generally best qualified to serve members of their own group and should be hired to do so.
5. Opportunities for promotion and advancement should be available to minority employees on an equitable basis.
6. Minorities should be accorded special opportunities for professional training. This may mean modifications in educational programs.
7. Minority faculty members are essential. Credentials of experience and skill are more important than academic degrees.

INSTITUTIONAL RACISM

Definition

Racism comes from a recognition of differences, the placing of a negative value on the differences leading to inferiority/superiority, and the generalization of the negative characteristics to all people in the group. Skin color has already been identified as the most evident basis for racism.

Institutional racism results when a society or its organizations use racist values as the basis for laws or formal policies that affect actions. Racist employees can mark an organization as racist through their transactions with the public and with their colleagues, since personal behaviors of staff members get attributed to the organization.

With the federal civil rights acts, executive orders by the governors of most states, and fair housing and fair unemployment laws, very few social agencies officially and directly deny access to minorities, but this still happens as a secondary effect. Housing patterns have been determined on a racist basis. This affects the educational opportunity for minority students in neighborhood schools, unless busing is used as a remedial measure. Some church-sponsored agencies make it clear that they are designed to serve their own members. If minorities have no opportunity to belong to such churches, they are denied church-sponsored social services.

Three Examples   Informal policies reflect racism:

Quality of service: In an agency with several branch offices, the less skilled staff members may be assigned to the office serving minority people. The explanation may be that other staff "won't go to that neighborhood."

Administrative policies: Rules and procedures may be based on racism. An office in one neighborhood may schedule all intake interviews at 9 A.M., resulting in long waits for some people. When people are late, they have to come back the next day. Other offices may not have such a rule. The racist explanation is that blacks are often late for appointments, and it is necessary to be strict.

Services given: Blacks, Asians, or Indians may be told what services they need. When a black family needs help to bring a relative into the home because of a crisis, a request for a bus ticket may be denied, but homemaker service may be offered. Yet the presence of a key member may mean more than anything else to the family, and he or she may actually provide more care than a homemaker. Also, minorities may be referred automatically to public services but whites to private agencies first.

Personal behavior of staff members is especially hard to control. It may affect:

Hiring and advancement of staff: In spite of civil rights laws, many subtle values operate in staff selection. Reasons may be found not to hire minority members who are well qualified. One is that they may be too militant. On the other hand, recent emphasis on providing opportunities for minorities can lead to charges of reverse racism against hiring whites. This is sometimes justified as "making up for past wrongs."

Assignment of duties and work loads: Minority staff members may get the undesirable assignments. Minority workers may also be given caseloads made up entirely of minority clients. This is considered racist.

Treatment of persons served: Minority clients complain of curt and rude treatment or condescension from agency staff members. That may or may not be racism. What may be seen as racism can be prejudice against all clients—white and nonwhite—because they are poor, trying to get something for nothing, or too "stupid" to understand the agency forms. Then the attitude of the staff member is hostile but not racist.

In nutritional counseling, staff members often suggest foods that the mother does not want to use or cannot possibly afford. The advice may be based on ignorance or insensitivity, but is interpreted by the client as racism.

THE MINORITY PRACTITIONER

Why are students from minority groups still interested in careers in fields that deal with psychological, educational, or social problems? Some trace their interest to practitioners they have known. A young person may be favorably impressed with a social worker who has been helpful. Another complains bitterly about social workers and wants to enter the field, feeling that he or she can do better. Students also recognize that the social sciences have the potential for answering the "I/we" questions that minorities must raise in American society—Who am I/are we? How do I/we break out of the bonds of oppression? What can I/we do to help our cause?

Experiences of Black Students

Minority students with field placements in white-dominated social agencies reported several problems:

1. Some were given all-black caseloads.
2. Students were expected to be authorities on blacks and were frequently consulted by other workers.
3. Some white workers considered themselves the experts on black people and accepted no suggestions or ideas.
4. When black workers were permitted to develop their own ways of making contact and channeling services, white workers were upset by the departure from the rules.

Most students remarked that while they would prefer to work with blacks, an all-black caseload implied that both the clients and the worker were inferior.

The students did not like to be perceived as authorities on blacks because they recognized that individual differences made pat answers impossible. They felt some conflicts in giving advice to white practitioners, unless the practitioner had already tried several approaches before seeking advice. They felt that practitioners should work on their own cases. If they had tried several ideas already, the request was just like any other consultation. Their objection was to a nonblack social worker consulting them almost automatically. However, the black students decided that they would prefer to be consulted than to have a white worker serving the consumer ineffectively. The opposite problem arose when workers who had little experience with black clients did not know when to seek help and therefore continued to make serious mistakes.

ROLES, TASKS, AND ATTITUDES

Social Distance
"Once black professionals have made it, they forget those who haven't." So goes a familiar complaint. Black social workers imbued with the new consciousness say that they will not respond this way. Some assert that since they are from "the community" they will be able to avoid this hazard, but having grown up in a community does not automatically ensure that group obligations will be met.

When young minority people go off to college, the community may be either proud or resentful. If they face resentment, they will have difficulty working among people in their neighborhoods. A broadening of their horizons in college may make it difficult for them to relate successfully to their old friends or even to their families. Changes in interest and even in vocabulary may establish a feeling of distance. The minority social worker must convey to those he serves a sense of their dignity and worth and the value of their participation.

The minority practitioner has to analyze the current issues in the minority community and developments in the larger systems as well—in politics, social welfare, education, and economic policy. Because many of the problems of minority groups stem from broad social policies, problems must be translated in terms of political, economic, and social disadvantages. Welfare reform, social security, medical care, housing, and revenue sharing are among the major current issues that require understanding.

One may also need to reorient the way causes and effects are preceived. Ryan indicates how the poor and particularly minorities are the victims of society, yet they are blamed for their condition. Guilt is added to social and economic disadvantages and may lead to pathological behavior.[21] Misery may be overemphasized or it may be romanticized. Both tendencies are unfortunate and make social change more difficult. Films are frequently criticized for taking an extreme point of view of black life.

Minority practitioners must recognize diversities. As black professionals have gained a more thorough understanding of social problems, generalizations have been advanced that are not valid. Even when the majority white society does not see blacks as a diverse society, the black practitioner must be able to do so.

Recognition of diversity is important for other reasons. Blacks often make sweeping generalizations about other blacks, creating a feeling of animosity. Followers of one ideology frequently depreciate those who do not do things their way. As a consequence strategies may be imposed on a community that are inappropriate and may create divisions.

The best results come from looking to the strengths of individuals and groups rather than to their perceived weaknesses. Hylan Lewis is particularly concerned with the tendency to impute to a total people the most threatening characteristics of a segment.[22] Examples are: Black low-income children are nonverbal. Low-income black parents do not value education. Unwed motherhood is an acceptable norm. Black people are lazy and do not want to work. Black women dominate black men. Black low-income people have no perception of time and space. Unfortunately programs are being planned and operated on the basis of these "facts."

The Minority Worker on the Job

The minority worker in white agencies often asks himself: "Why have I been hired?" Several years ago black social workers might have assumed that it was because of their competence. Now, with the civil rights pressure and affirmative action programs, black workers are uncertain whether their talent or their skin color is desired. Thus, a healthy skepticism and a certain self-isolation may accompany them to the job. The worker may meet resistance from white colleagues if he or she is a product of "affirmative action," seen by some white people as simply "reverse discrimination." Whites may be quick to say that competence is what counts. Blacks perceive this as saying that they are not competent. Considering the many ways in which whites have acquired jobs, blacks wonder why competence is now suggested as the only criterion for employment. For every white professional who may dislike affirmative action to compensate for past exclusions and injustices, there is a black professional who feels that it is tragic that organizations have had to be forced to hire minorities.

How Other Minorities Cope with Practitioner Issues   Most ethnic groups have directed their concerns to the schools of social work because they feel that the educational institutions tend to control the market for social workers and particularly for social work leaders. The recruitment of students and the allocation of student aid resources have been major concerns, but once schools agree to these two objectives, the question immediately becomes the availability of minority faculty who understand the students' problems and who can interpret the situation to nonminority students.

There has been less concern about these issues from black students because the most successful effort has been achieved to recruit black faculty, and black students have received some preference for student aid. Also there are two well-established schools of social work that have had predominantly black enrollments—Howard University in Washington, D.C., and Atlanta University. San Jose State University has a school of social work with a Chicano emphasis.

Faculty recruitment and expectations are sources of special conflict since fewer minority members have earned graduate degrees in social work, particularly at the doctoral level. Many of them are not interested in research, from which promotion is likely to come most rapidly. As a result there is a greater emphasis on community service as a substitute for research. Some universities buy these criteria better than others. Minority group members often feel that they have had little chance of attaining tenure by doing the things that seem to them to be the most important. They feel that traditional university standards are often racist. The Chicanos have developed an interesting concept of the "barrio" professor.[23]

The Barrio Professor   Barrio Professors do not have the standard academic credentials that attest to their knowledge and expertise in social work practice in the barrio.* However, they have received certification from the barrios that they have served adequately. They are knowledgeable in Chicano culture, language, life-styles, class differences, value bases, folk curing *(curanderismo),* and the overall function of the barrio system. Such knowledge comes from having lived in the barrio from infancy and from having worked intimately with Chicanos for several years. The Barrio Professor is also familiar with many social work theories, methodologies, and terminology sets used in the social work profession. While the learning process of professional social workers is generally conducted through their socialization in the academic educational system, the Barrio Professor is also learning, but learning through action: learning actual skills, not about skills; testing hypotheses in real life situations, not through library research; and gaining a general consciousness of self as a person and as a helping agent.

An outstanding characteristic of the Barrio Professors is that they are not constrained to function in a highly structured and institutionalized manner, but rather are adept in functioning in an informal style compatible with barrio life-styles. Unlike many college graduates who have accepted or tolerated some degree of assimilation and acculturation to dominant Anglo-American values, the Barrio Professors have not been "contaminated" by social work profession-alism or the mythology of academia and can still act consistently with barrio attitudes and values, enabling them to make decisions congruent with barrio values rather than decisions foreign to these values. Their primary accountabili-ty is to the barrio, not to the maintenance of an institution or a profession.

Native Americans and Puerto Ricans have the same concerns about extending opportunities for their own groups in social work education, but have not had the impact of blacks and Chicanos. Certainly the place to begin to develop more opportunities for minority students is in the undergraduate programs out of which many seek a meaningful professional role.

SUMMARY AND APPLICATION

Personal attitudes and institutional policies may both involve racist attitudes. Even though we are considered to be liberal, we may stereotype minority groups. Agencies are in an excellent position to help the special needs of minorities, but they have not always developed the flexibility to provide equity

*A *barrio* is a Chicano urban community. In some ways it parallels the term "ghetto."

to minority staff members. Parallel to the need to reeducate white staff come the opportunities for minority staff to use their special skills with clients who are members of their own ethnic or racial group.

—*Charles Henderson*
Bok-Lim Kim
Ione Dugger Vargus

KEY TERMS

ethnocentrism
Hispanics
Native Americans
Asian Americans
Jim Crow
Plessy v. Ferguson
Brown v. Board of Education of Topeka
War on Poverty
Voting Rights Act of 1965

The People v. Hall
Asian Exclusion Act of 1924
relocation camps
Bureau of Indian Affairs
Chicanos
Puerto Ricans
institutional racism
the *barrio*

REFERENCES AND NOTES

1. Richard Hofstadter, *The American Political Tradition*, Knopf, New York, 1948, p. 116.
2. Abram Kardiner and Lionel Ovesey, *The Mark of Oppression: Explorations in the Personality of the American Negro*, World, Cleveland, 1961, p. 365.
3. *Brown v. Board of Education of Topeka*, 347 U.S. 483 (1954); *Plessy v. Ferguson*, 163 U.S. 537 (1896).
4. *New York Times*, April 2, 1978, sec. i, p. 18.
5. *The State of Black America*, Urban League, Washington, D.C., 1978.
6. *The People v. Hall*, 4 California Reports, 399 (1854).
7. Ruth McKee, *Wartime Exile: The Exclusion of the Japanese Americans from the West Coast*, Government Printing Office, Washington, D.C., 1949.
8. Bok-Lim C. Kim, "Casework with Japanese and Korean Wives of Americans," *Social Casework*, vol. 53, May 1972, pp. 273–279.
9. J. Donald Cameron and Esther Talavera, "An Advocacy Program for Spanish Speaking People," *Social Casework*, vol. 57, July 1976, p. 427.
10. Vine Deloria, Jr., *Custer Died for Your Sins*, Macmillan, New York, 1969.
11. William S. Willis, "Divide and Rule: Red, White and Black in the Southeast," in Roger L. Nichols and George R. Adams (eds.), *The American Indian: Past and Present*, Xerox College Publishing, Waltham, Mass., 1971, pp. 74–85.
12. Deloria, op. cit., p. 172.
13. Lydia R. Aguirre, "The Meaning of the Chicano Movement," *Social Casework*, vol. 52, May 1971, p. 259.
14. Ibid.
15. John F. Longres, Jr., "Racism and Its Effects on Puerto Rican Continentals," *Social Casework*, vol. 55, February 1974, p. 69.
16. Ibid., p. 72.
17. J. Julian Rivera, "Growth of a Puerto Rican Awareness," *Social Casework*, vol. 55, February 1974, p. 84.

18. Jimm G. Good Tracks, "Native American Non-Interference," *Social Work*, vol. 18, November 1973, pp. 30–35.
19. Melvin Delgado, "Puerto Rican Spiritualism and the Social Work Profession," *Social Casework*, vol. 58, December 1977, p. 458.
20. Sonia Badello Ghali, "Culture Sensitivity and the Puerto Rican Client," *Social Casework*, vol. 58, December 1977, p. 460.
21. William Ryan, "The Social Welfare Client: Blaming the Victim," *Social Welfare Forum*, Columbia University Press, New York, 1972, pp. 41–54.
22. Hylan Lewis, "Culture, Class, and the Behavior of Low Income Families," paper prepared for the Conference on Lower Class Culture, New York, June 1963.
23. Ernesto Gomez, "The Barrio Professor: An Emerging Concept in Social Work Education," in D. J. Curren (ed.), *The Chicano Faculty Development Program: A Report*, Council on Social Work Education, New York, 1973, pp. 101–103.

FOR FURTHER STUDY

Russell Endo (ed.), *Asian Americans: Social and Psychological Perspectives*, Science and Behavior Publications, Palo Alto, Calif., 1979.

James Goodman (ed.), *The Dynamics of Racism in Social Work*, National Association of Social Workers, Washington, D.C., 1973.

Roger Daniles and Harry H. L. Kitano, *American Racism: Exploration of the Nature of Prejudice*, Prentice-Hall, Englewood Cliffs, N.J., 1970.

Vine Deloria, *We Talk, You Listen*, Macmillan, New York, 1969.

Terry Jones, "Institutional Racism in the United States," *Social Work*, 19, March 1974, pp. 218–225.

Bok-Lim C. Kim, *The Asian Americans: Changing Patterns, Changing Needs*, Association of Korean Christian Scholars in North America, Inc., Montclair, N.J., 1978.

Harry H. L. Kitano, *Race Relations*, Prentice-Hall, Englewood Cliffs, N.J., 1974.

Ford Kuramoto, "What Do Asians Want? An Examination of Issues in Social Work Education," *Journal of Education for Social Work*, vol. 7, 1971, pp. 7–17.

John Longres, "The Impact of Racism on Social Work Education," *Education for Social work*, vol. 8, Winter 1972, pp. 31–41.

Lawrence Rosen, *American Indians and the Law*, Transaction Books, New Brunswick, N.J., 1979.

Carl A. Scott (ed.), *Ethnic Minorities in Social Work Education*, Council on Social Work Education, New York, 1970.

Sam Steiner, *The Vanishing White Man*, Harper and Row, New York, 1976.

Stanley A. West and June Machen, *Chicano Experience*, Westview Publishers, Boulder, Colo., 1979.

William J. Wilson, *The Declining Significance of Race: Blacks and Changing American Institutions*, University of Chicago Press, Chicago, 1978.

FOR DISCUSSION

1. Define racism. How does it differ from ethnocentrism?
2. Why have attempts been made to restrict the sale of alcohol to Indians?
3. How can you reconcile Lincoln's speech at Charleston with the Emancipation Proclamation?

4. Explain the Jim Crow concept.
5. Choose one era of history; identify and summarize the contributions of members of one minority group.
6. How do occupational roles of Chicanos affect their attainment of equity in social services and human rights?
7. Compare the Supreme Court decisions in *Plessy v. Ferguson* and *Brown v. Board of Education*.
8. What characteristics advance the stereotype of Asians as the model minority?
9. What was the main implication in *People v. Hall?*
10. Summarize our immigration policy toward Asian Americans?
11. What are special problems of Asian war brides in America?
12. Present examples of institutional racism from your own experience.
13. Why do black people often resent research projects?
14. What problems are likely to face an agency that serves only blacks?
15. How must social agency personnel learn to tolerate diversities?
16. Why may black workers distrust affirmative action programs?
17. Why may relations between white and black workers be difficult?
18. Why are minority students often critical of social work approaches?

PROJECTS

1. What organizations in your community are especially concerned with programs for minorities? (Examples include the Urban League, the National Association for the Advancement of Colored People, and *La Raza*.) Invite respresentatives to discuss their programs and to assess the present status of the particular minority.
2. List five or more terms like "a Chinaman's chance." How do you think each one originated? How common are they now? Are any of the examples favorable?
3. Choose a minority group for study, and give as many examples as you can of the diversities within the group. Why does failure to consider diversities make it harder to solve social problems?
4. Analyze developments and present your views on racial strategies for the 1980s. Indicate the evidence for your predictions.
5. What is the current status of Native American Rights efforts? How have they affected the Bureau of Indian Affairs?
6. Invite a social worker from a minority-oriented agency and one who works in a traditional agency to discuss affirmative action, service policies, staff relations, and other topics of interest to the class.
7. Present this debate: "Resolved, that a minority group should form its own separate social services organizations as soon as its numbers justify the action."
8. Ask minority-student social workers who are receiving field instruction to discuss their experiences both with clients and with sponsoring agencies.

CHAPTER 17
Sexism

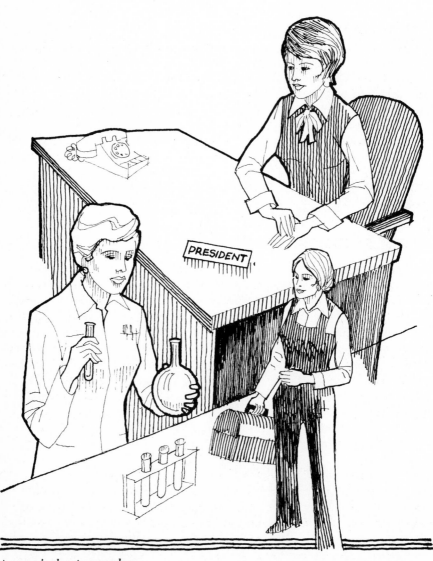

A woman's place is everywhere.

Women have been taught and have learned behaviors that have led them to assume positions of powerlessness and disrespect. They are feeling bad not because of personal pathology, but because society has lied to them. They are neither valued nor respected, nor can they be effective as passive, charming, and emotional persons.

—Sharon B. Berlin*

The term "sexism" reveals the impact of the women's liberation movement on everyday language and thinking. It denotes the range of attitudes, practices, and policies which discriminate against women or men on the basis of their gender. However, few if any of the dictionaries published in the 1960s carried the term "sexism." In the 1970s sexism was defined in functional terms as "prejudice against women."[1] Since the women's movement came right after the civil rights movement, it was easy to coin "sexism," modeling it on "racism." In the intervening years, both the word and the concept have gained a legitimate status, and social workers are beginning to look at evidence of sexism in society, the social services, and within their own profession.

SEXISM IN SOCIETY

Racism and sexism manifest themselves in similar ways in our society. Although women are numerically dominant, they are treated in many ways as a minority group. They are "singled out for differential or unequal treatment . . . because of their physical and cultural characteristics," and have been excluded from "full participation in society" on the basis of their sex.[2] In terms of market value, women and some minority groups have been deprived of prestigious positions because society underrates their potential for power. Black women are often in double jeopardy. Current income and occupational data reveal that minority women are at the bottom of the occupational pyramid and earn the lowest incomes. For example, Labor Department statistics show that black women, working full-time in 1974, averaged 94 percent as much pay as white women, and 62 percent as much as white males.[3]

Pervasiveness in Culture

The pervasiveness of negative attitudes toward women in our society has been widely discussed in scholarly and popular literature. The research on sex-role stereotyping has convincingly documented how women and men have

*Sharon B. Berlin, "Better Work with Women Clients," *Social Work*, vol. 21, November 1976, p. 497.

been socialized to view the characteristics and activities of males as superior to those of females.[4] Broverman demonstrated that a sample of social workers and other clinicians considered behaviors judged healthy for an adult when sex was unspecified to be similar to behaviors judged healthy for men but different from behaviors judged healthy for women. These differences in clinical judgment paralleled stereotypic sex-role differences.[5] This devaluation of the capabilities of women in reflected in many of society's institutions. Sex-bias in educational systems is evident from the earliest grades in the strong masculine bias of reading materials, the tracking of girls and women into less prestigious curricula and career lines, and the discrimination that may prevent women from taking advantage of the education provided by the nation's best schools and universities. Barriers in employment restrict the avenues of success even further, resulting in the underutilization of the talents of more than half the population. For most women, going to work means taking a relatively low-skilled, low-paying job. The Department of Labor reports that more than one-third of all women workers in 1976, including many college graduates, were in clerical jobs. Furthermore, the difference between men's and women's pay was wider in 1976 than it was twenty years ago. The average woman college graduate earned less during the year than the average male high school dropout.[6]

The consequent sense of powerlessness is reinforced because very few women are represented in high-level positions in the business world or the government. Women hold fewer than 2 percent of the directorships of top American corporations, fewer than 1 percent of the top-management posts, and about 5 or 6 percent of all middle-management positions in this country.[7] In terms of government positions, the White House personnel office reported that women held 14 percent of the top jobs, including cabinet, subcabinet, and ambassadorial posts.[8] The pervasiveness of such social conditions naturally affects many populations who are the special concern of social workers. It has also influenced the profession and the delivery system of services. We shall examine all of these aspects later.

Historical Perspective

The social work profession traces its beginnings to the activism and vision of women who had a broad social conscience. The social reformers, including such women as Jane Addams and Florence Kelley, were strong, independent leaders—not only "impatient crusaders," but intellectuals who made their generation think.[9] Their writings documented the social conditions of the day, and their "moral crusade against the evils of urban, industrial society became . . . the backbone of the emerging profession of social work."[10] As we have seen earlier, others made their mark in the Charity Organization Society, the settlement house movement, and other community services—Lillian Wald, Mary Richmond, Grace and Edith Abbott, and Julia Lathrop. Their concern was for the poor, particularly poor women and children, many of whom were targets of exploitation as part of a cheap labor pool. Women were excluded from male-dominated labor unions. For this reason, priority was given to the passage of legislation to protect women, especially those in nonunionized factories. Government regulation of child labor, of wages and hours, and union controls that protect women from exploitation did not exist in the early years of this century.

Many of these social reformers were also active in other causes, such as the suffrage movement, the trade union movement, and groups to represent consumer causes. The end of World War I marked the decline of the social reform movement, although it saw the ratification of the Nineteenth Amendment to provide women's suffrage. In social work, this conservative climate contributed to the demise of the reform-oriented settlement house movement and brought about the parallel rise of psychoanalytically oriented casework. The merits and/or demerits of this transition have been widely discussed,[11] especially the impact of Freudian theory in explaining feminine psychology.[12] The early theoretical base of psychiatric social work was formulated by women such as Mary Jarrett, Virginia Robinson, and Jessie Taft.

By the 1920s social work had been certified as a profession, "open to the college educated who were especially trained for casework and social research, 62 percent of whom were women. Yet women were less likely than men to advance to high positions in the new profession."[13] The increasing professionalism in the 1950s led men to come into the profession as a way of gaining status, since social work was thought to be "adversely affected because it is identified as a women's profession."[14] The increasing presence of men intensified an already existent pattern of "male enclaves"[15]—administration, community organization, and to some extent group work. Kadushin considers these enclaves a "functional necessity," since this allows an avenue for men entering a profession identified as "female" to reduce role strain.[16] He further views the move into administration by males as a way of earning a salary to meet the financial obligations incurred as heads of families.[17] The reasons sound logical. However, Kadushin fails to recognize that these male enclaves, especially administration, are commonly viewed as possessing higher status and constituting professional advancement. The question is not whether these male enclaves are justified, but whether *admission* to these enclaves is denied on the basis of sex.

We will now look more closely at the issue of sexism, and primarily at its effects on the client system, the delivery system, and the profession.

THE CLIENT SYSTEM

Evidence of sexism is apparent in the data on some of the populations at risk who have been the particular concern of social workers. They all share overrepresentation in the poverty population in the United States.

The Single-Parent Family

As we have discussed already, the typical single-parent family is headed by a woman. Families headed by single, separated, divorced, or widowed women totaled 7.2 million, or 13 percent of all American families. The number of children living in families headed by a woman had risen sharply. From March 1970 to March 1975, the proportion of children under age eighteen in families without fathers grew from one in ten to one in seven.

The median income for families headed by a woman was less than half that of comparable families headed by a male single parent. The 1970 median income for the former group was $6,400, compared to $13,500 for the latter.[18] One in three families headed by a woman was living at or below the poverty level. By contrast, only one in eighteen families headed by a man lived at or below this level. The argument that men need to receive high salaries in order to fulfill their obligations as heads of families apparently does not extend to female heads of families.

Social Security Beneficiaries

Coverage of women in the income support systems under social security is inadequate. Provisions have not been adequately updated since the days when the framers of the Social Security Act designed it to suit the stereotypic American family—male family head and breadwinner and dependent house-wife, associated in a lifetime relationship. However women and children were employed in some of the earliest factories, and women labored on farms and plantations.

During the past three decades, the number of women in the workforce has more than doubled, from 16,683,000 in 1947 to 38,520,000 in 1976.[19] Moreover, Department of Labor statistics show that in March 1975, both husband and wife had jobs in 47.1 percent of the 47.3 million families.[20] Despite these changes, social security benefits are still geared to the obsolete concept of a woman dependent on her husband.

Even those provisions of the Social Security Act that make no distinction as to sex reflect the discriminatory treatment of women in the labor market. The preponderance of women in low-skilled, low-paying jobs, their fragmented occupational history, and the dismissal of the work they do in the home as having no economic value all work against them in terms of program requirements. To earn fully insured status, individuals need forty calendar quarters (ten years) in covered employment. "Millions of women who have worked long enough to qualify for benefits as retired workers have been found to be entitled to higher benefits as dependents."[21] Males received higher average monthly benefits ($229 as against $182 for the females.)[22]

Furthermore, a woman who is divorced before being married ten years loses her right to any wife's or widow's benefits based on her husband's work under social security. If she is widowed before age sixty, she can receive mother's benefits if she has a child younger than eighteen or an older, disabled child under her care. If there is no disabled child, her benefits will stop when the youngest child reaches eighteen, unless the woman is already sixty years old or is age fifty and disabled. Otherwise, the woman is expected to find a way to support herself.

A large percentage of the female workers also have little chance to augment their social security benefits through private pensions. They are less likely to be employed in large companies where high-level positions are usually covered by such pension plans, and if they are in these jobs, the irregularity of their employment or their part-time status may prevent them from qualifying.

Suggestions have been made to reform the law. The most feasible proposal holds that work in the home has an economic value and marriage is an economic partnership. Couples could elect to have a share of their family income credited to each of their social security records. This would allow the housewife to build up her own social security entitlements, and the woman who moves in and out of the labor market could have a record of earnings with no gaps.

Public Welfare Recipients

Aid to Families with Dependent Children (AFDC) can be described as a program for poor women since most of the recipients are women and children. As Brennan rightly points out, of all the criticisms aimed at the AFDC program, the missing one is the "feminist perspective that the institution oppresses poor women as a monolithic class." Moreover, these women are seen as undeserving because as a class they have disrupted a "traditional source of income, i.e., dependence on a male breadwinner."[23] Therefore, society's attitudes and behaviors toward them can be justifiably moralistic. For example, work requirements for welfare recipients with children over six years of age indicate the belief that raising children is not socially acceptable work for poor women without a husband.

The same attitude is evident in the law which makes it mandatory for mothers who have applied for AFDC to provide information on husbands who are delinquent in support payments. Although the law succeeds in reducing some of the financial burden on the states for AFDC payments, it reflects the sexist nature of the AFDC program that women seeking child support should be a burden on their husbands rather than the state.[24]

As one writer put it, "the very existence of the welfare system is a reflection on the status of women in this society and in the labor market."[25] Welfare benefits vary from state to state, but they exceed the wages that most women could expect to earn in low-paying, low-skilled jobs. In addition, the unavailability and cost of child care forces many women to rely on welfare rather than try to get a job. This reveals society's ambivalence toward the role of women. The work done in the home has no economic value, and services in the marketplace are devaluated and underpaid. As a result, there is no protection against poverty, no matter which of the alternatives is selected.[26]

Pregnant Workers/Day Care Users

The lack of benefits for pregnant workers and the paucity of adequate day care facilities both reflect a general prejudice against women's effective participation in the labor market. The attitude has been that working women are only earning "pin-money" and therefore might better take care of their own children. Moreover, the influx of women into the labor market only contributes to unemployment because they take needed jobs from men. Ironically, some women themselves still think of their pregnancy/child care problems as unique situations, which reflects a residue from the days when the working mother was a social deviant. Today, Labor Department statistics show that nearly half the mothers work.[27]

The Supreme Court ruling that private employers offering disability insurance programs did not have to pay benefits to pregnant workers was discouraging to many people.[28] The decision had far-reaching implications and motivated Congress to pass legislation in 1978 which required that pregnancy be recognized as a cause for benefits under disability insurance plans.[29]

The unmet need for day care services is illustrated by a study by a federal advisory panel in 1976. Licensed day care centers could accommodate only 900,000 of the over 6 million preschool children of working mothers.[30] This might explain why less than 2 percent of the children of working mothers were cared for in group care, whether day care nurseries or afterschool programs. Baxandall hypothesizes that the unmet need results from day care having been stigmatized by its welfare origins. Day care is thought of as something needed by the problem family. She also blames psychiatrists and social workers for their contribution to the negative attitudes toward day care through stressing the early mother-child relationship, and for propagating the stereotype that effective mothering can come only from the biological mother.[31]

Coupled with this belief is the ambivalence, which we discussed earlier, toward the employment of women. Contradictory attitudes place the welfare mother in a predicament. On the one hand, welfare mothers are urged to get off the dole. On the other hand, lack of child care facilities forces them to rely on welfare even if job opportunities are available. Besides, they are mindful of the approval that is bestowed on mothers who stay home to take care of their children, especially in the preschool stage. In addition, despite contrary studies, people believe that children of working mothers suffer negative consequences and manifest it in such ways as a higher rate of delinquency. This is attributed to children left in group care facilities, where they supposedly lack a one-to-one relationship. Baxandall cites studies done in the United States and other countries to show that group care facilities benefit rather than harm the children, since they provide services by trained people in an environment which lets the child have more freedom than the home situation.[32]

The feminist perspective should help to eliminate equating temporary maternal separation with maternal deprivation. Furthermore, the mother's right to an independent life might also be considered. Then day care should be studied for its importance for both the mother and the child.

THE DELIVERY SYSTEM

For many social workers, "feminist therapy" comes to mean the understanding and direct application in practice of the changing roles of women. The traditional socialization process and cultural conditioning account for many of the problems which confront women clients.[33] Therefore, therapists need to be trained to be active proponents of the actualization of self which is free of the rigid sex stereotypes prescribed by society. In practice this means that the therapist is aware that personal difficulties are not necessarily the result of personal pathology, but sometimes of the realities and pressures of being a woman or a man in our society.[34]

A recent study by Brown and Hellinger shows that this perspective needs to be actively cultivated in the profession, since most social workers do not come by it naturally. In a survey of psychiatrists, residents in psychiatry, psychologists, social workers, and psychiatric nurses, social workers did not have more contemporary attitudes toward women than other therapists.[35] As Schwartz discovered in her review of articles published in Social Work, the profession has undervalued the importance of the sex of both client and worker in the therapeutic relationship. As a result, intervention often fails to be as effective as it will be if the social workers were "willing to integrate the understanding of the importance of race, class, and ethnicity with that of sex."[36]

Examples of this awareness are available in case illustrations and studies in the professional literature. Stevens describes helping a woman separated from her alcoholic husband to "improve her self-image and reduce her irrational dependency and masochistic tendencies by actively opposing society's stereotype of her."[37] Carlock and Martin describe the results of their quasi-experimental study which shows that the "behaviors, perceptions, and emotional experiences of group members may vary with the sexual make-up of the group."[38]

Besides practice situations, the delivery system should also include an examination of the curricula in schools of social work. Schwartz illustrates the sexist bias in social work education by using examples from teaching materials and textbooks prescribed for courses in human growth and development and family casework.[39] Efforts to deal with this problem have involved new courses on women and inclusion of content on sexism in existing courses. Brandewein and Wheelock[40] and Connaway and Pirtle[41] have described the development of new courses and women's studies programs at their respective schools, while Lowenstein has written on the integration of the key concepts of sexism into human behavior courses.[42]

Evidence from the social work student population suggests that sex-role stereotypes are changing. In replicating the Broverman study described earlier, Harris and Lucas found, in one school of social work, that there was no evidence to support the existence of a double standard of mental health for men and women.[43] In another study, Diangson, Kravetz, and Lipton showed that female and male attitudes toward practice did not conform to sex-role stereotypes.[44] This suggests that the feminist movement has accelerated the rate of change in sex-role stereotypes.

The growing awareness of women's issues has led to provision of some improved services to hitherto ignored groups—women seeking abortions, victims of rape, and battered wives, among others.[45] There is recognition, as well, of the needs and possible problems encountered by single-parent households headed by men.[46] Articles have dealt with the ways in which the helping professions could learn more about homosexual women and serve as a support system for them.[47] Moreover, social workers are beginning to use other techniques than traditional counseling in their work with women, such as assertive training. Consciousness-raising groups provide a viable alternative to therapy for some women who are seeking a new sense of identity and contact with others in changing the social system.[48]

THE PROFESSION OF SOCIAL WORK

Women in social work, like women in all professions, are subject to discrimination. This is not as easily apparent in social work as in many academic fields, where women are in a minority. Since 63 percent of social workers are female, the profession[49] is characterized by what Giovannoni and Purvine call the "myth of the social work matriarchy."[50]

An examination of recent trends in employment patterns of male and female social workers by Fanshel confirms the dominant position of men in the profession. In his study of NASW members, the proportion of men in leadership positions, i.e., in administration, was twice that of women (37 percent versus 18 percent). Although some of the findings could be explained by women's marital status and family responsibilities, these do not completely account for all the differences.[51]

The same picture was evident in the 1978–79 statistics published by the Council on Social Work Education. Of the social work faculties, 47.8 percent were women and 52.2 percent were men.[52] Only 29 percent of the full-time professors were women, while 54.7 percent of the full-time assistant professors were women.[53] The same pattern is apparent in the data on the distribution of administrators.

Fanshel's studies showed that among persons using the same method of social work practice, salaries differed between men and women. Fifty-seven percent of the male administrators earned salaries of $16,000 a year or more, compared to 37 percent of the women, and only 8 percent of the women reported earning more than $20,000, as against 24 percent of the men. In casework, 52 percent of the men were in the $12,000 to 15,999 salary range, compared to only 35 percent of the women.[54] In the academic world, the 1978–79 statistics revealed that salaries were higher for men than for women.[55] Furthermore, although salaries were higher for those who held a doctoral degree, a further breakdown by sex, at the professorial level in the graduate/graduate-undergraduate programs, showed that men with a master's degree earned almost as much money as women with a doctoral degree.[56]

Data from social agency settings in various regions of the country provide further evidence of the widespread existence of sexism in job distribution, salaries, and professional responsibilities. In a recent study of an NASW chapter in California, Zietz and Erlich found that only 34 percent of the females, as compared to 53 percent of the males, responded that sexism was not a problem in their agency. Data on career development suggested that "compared to men, women perceived considerably more sexism in hiring, work-assignment, and access to career-building opportunities."[57] Interestingly, contrary to popular opinion, older rather than younger women were more sensitive to sexist practices. A Rhode Island NASW committee found that 71 percent of the top positions in social work in the state were occupied by men.[58] An earlier study by Healy and Starr, conducted in northern Connecticut, showed that a "significant number of female social workers in all employed age groups received less pay than their male counterparts."[59]

Szakacs compiled statistics on leadership positions by sex over the last twenty years in federally funded private and voluntary nonprofit organizations throughout the United States. In 1976, 16 percent, or 141 of the 868 agencies in her sample, were headed by women—a drop of over 50 percent in leadership positions for women in the last decade. Szakacs concluded that "if the present trend continues, there will be no women in social work leadership positions by the year 1984."[60]

In terms of the future representation of women, especially in academic settings, the number of women enrolled in doctoral programs in social work in 1978 exceeded men, 55 percent to 45 percent.[61] Unfortunately, data on financial grants for women doctoral students, which might explain this trend, are not available.

At the professional organizational level, indications of changes in representation, publications, and support of issues should be of concern to women. In 1973 both the elected and appointed national leadership of the National Association of Social Workers was 74.7 percent male. In 1976, due to affirmative action efforts, the leadership was 50 percent female.[62] An examination of the officers and board members of the Council on Social Work Education, conducted by Giovannoni and Purvine, showed that in 1970 the ratio of males to females was four to one.[63] In 1977 the representation of women on the board of directors was 42.1 percent.[64]

The publication of *Social Work's* special issue on women might be regarded, as Mahaffey says, as a "landmark for our profession,"[65] although representation of women authors in regular issues of this journal, as well as other social work journals, will tell the real story. NASW and CSWE have established a committee and a commission respectively to promote the interests of women within the profession, although questions have been continuously raised as to the priorities given to these groups by the organizational leadership. Over thirty NASW units have committees on women's issues, and the mailing list for *Womanpower*, exceeds 700.[66] The Women's Caucus of CSWE, which is not tied to the organizational structure and receives no financial support, also maintains a newsletter mailed to over 150 members.

In 1973 the NASW Delegate Assembly responded to the concerns of women by adding the elimination of sexism to racism and poverty as basic concerns and priorities for the profession. The CSWE Commission on the Role and Status of Women in Social Work Education considers its most important achievement to be its guidelines for an accreditation standard which prohibits discrimination on the basis of sex in the conduct of programs in schools of social work. The new standard mandates affirmative action programs for women faculty, administrators, students, and staff in social work educational institutions.

Supporting the Equal Rights Amendment as a legislative priority, and joining with other organizations in challenging the constitutionality of the Hyde Amendment (prohibiting the use of federal funds for abortion), also demonstrates NASW's commitment to work on issues of primary concern to women. Furthermore, the NASW Legal Defense Fund has provided support in sex discrimination cases.

SUMMARY AND APPLICATION

A few years ago a renewal of the women's movement was scarcely more than a promise. Today it is a reality. In agency and university settings, it was unheard of for social workers to band together to fight the effects of sexism in employment. Now such activities are widespread.[67] While many gains must yet be made concerning employment levels and income, sexism is widely recognized and much progress has been made—especially in the last five years.

—Ketayun H. Gould

KEY TERMS

sex-bias	feminist therapy
single-parent family	social work matriarchy
day care	

REFERENCES AND NOTES

1. *Webster's Collegiate Dictionary*, 9th ed., 1973, s.v. "sexism."
2. Louis Wirth, "The Problem of Minority Groups," in Minako Kurokawa (ed.), *Minority Responses*, Random House, New York, 1970, p. 34.
3. Derived from *Statistical Abstract of the United States, 1977*, Government Printing Office, Washington, D.C., 1977, p. 447.
4. For a comprehensive review, see Arlie Russell Hochschild, "A Review of Sex Role Research," in Joan Huber (ed.), *Changing Women in a Changing Society*, Chicago, The University of Chicago Press, 1973, pp. 249–267.
5. I. K. Broverman et al., "Sex-Role Stereotypes and Clinical Judgements of Mental Health," *Journal of Consulting and Clinical Psychology*, vol. 34, February 1970, pp. 1–7.
6. Sandra Hencel, "Working Women: Bias, Low Pay Usual Lot, Despite Inroads," *Champaign-Urbana Courier*, March 11, 1977, p. 24.
7. "Women and Power—A Status Report," *New York Times*, May 1, 1977, sec. 3, pp. 1 and 4.
8. James Gerstenzang, "Carter Administration Has Few Women or Minorities," *The Champagne-Urbarana News-Gazette*, June 10, 1977.

9. See, for example, Josephine Goldmark, *Impatient Crusader*, University of Illinois Press, Urbana, 1953.
10. Nancy J. Brennan, Jane C. Sherburne, and Esther Wattenberg, "A Historic Debate Revived: Protection vs. Equality: The Dilemma and Contradictions of Social Work and the Women's Movement," paper presented at the Annual Program Meeting of the Council on Social Work Education, Philadelphia, March 2, 1976, p. 6.
11. See, for example, Herman Borenzweig," Social Work and Psychoanalytic Theory: A Historical Analysis," *Social Work*, vol. 16, January 1971, pp. 7–16.
12. See, for example, Jean Baker Miller (ed.), *Psychoanalysis and Women*, Penguin, Baltimore, 1973.
13. Mary P. Ryan, *Womanhood in America from Colonial Times to the Present*, New Viewpoints, New York, 1975, p. 234.
14. Alfred Kadushin, "The Prestige of Social Work: Facts and Factors," *Social Work*, vol. 17, September 1958, p. 40.
15. Alfred Kadushin, "Men in a Woman's Profession," *Social Work*, vol. 21, November 1976, p. 444.
16. Ibid.
17. Ibid., p. 445.
18. *Statistical Abstract of the United States, 1977*, p. 447.
19. Hencel, op. cit.
20. "The 'New' Family: Husband, Wife, Work," *Chicago Sun-Times*, March 8, 1977, p. 1.
21. Sylvia Porter, "Social Security Full of Inequities," *Champaign-Urbana News-Gazette*, February 2, 1977, p. 12-A.
22. Sylvia Porter, "Social Security Riddled with '30s Stereotypes," *Champaign-Urbana News-Gazette*, February 1, 1977, p. 7-A.
23. Brennan et al., op. cit., p. 14.
24. Linda Rosenman, "Inequities in Income Security," *Social Work*, vol. 21, November 1976, p. 477.
25. Ibid., p. 476.
26. Ibid., p. 477.
27. Ellen Goodman, "A Free Day-Care System," *Chicago Sun-Times*, March 8, 1977, p. 36.
28. *General Electric v. Gilbert*, 429 U.S. 125 (1976).
29. P.L. 95-555, October 31, 1978.
30. Quoted in Joyce O. Beckett, "Working Wives: A Racial Comparison," *Social Work*, vol. 21, November 1976, p. 467.
31. Rosalyn F. Baxandall, "Who Shall Care for Our Children? The History and Development of Day Care in the United States," in Jo Freeman (ed.), *Women: A Feminine Perspective*, Mayfield, Palo Alto, Calif., 1975, pp. 94–95.
32. Ibid., pp. 95–96.
33. Sharon B. Berlin, "Better Work with Women Clients," *Social Work*, vol. 21, November 1976, p. 492.
34. *What Is Feminist Therapy?* Feminist Therapy Collective, Oak Park, Ill., n. d.
35. Caree Rosen Brown and Marilyn Levitt Hellinger, "Therapist's Attitudes Toward Women," *Social Work*, vol. 20, July 1975, p. 269.
36. Mary C. Schwartz, "Importance of the Sex of Worker and Client," *Social Work*, vol. 19, March 1974, pp. 177–185.
37. Barbara Stevens, "The Psychotherapist and Women's Liberation," *Social Work*, vol. 16, July 1971, pp. 16–18.

38. Charlene J. Carlock and Patricia Yancey Martin, "Sex Composition and the Intensive Group Experience," *Social Work*, vol. 22, January 1977, pp. 27–32.
39. Mary C. Schwartz, "Sexism in the Social Work Curriculum," *Journal of Education for Social Work*, vol. 9, Fall 1973, pp. 65–70.
40. Ruth A. Brandwein and Anne E. Wheelock, "The Not-So Silent Majority: A New Model for Content on Women's Issues in a School of Social Work," Paper Presented at the Annual Program Meeting of the Council on Social Work Education, Phoenix, February 28, 1977.
41. Ronda S. Connaway and Dorriece Pirtle, "Women's Studies: Implications for Social Work Education and Practice," Paper presented at the Annual Program Meeting of the Council on Social Work Education, Atlanta, March 12, 1974.
42. Sophie F. Lowenstein, "Integrating Content on Feminism and Racism into the Social Work Curriculum," *Journal of Education for Social Work*, vol. 12, Winter 1976, pp. 91–96.
43. Linda Hall Harris and Margaret Exner Lucas, "Sex-Role Stereotyping," *Social Work*, vol. 21, September 1976, pp. 390–395.
44. Pat Diangson, Diane F. Kravetz, and Judy Lipton, "Sex-Role Stereotyping and Social Work Education," *Journal of Education for Social Work*, vol. 11, Fall 1975, pp. 44–49.
45. See, for example, Elizabeth M. Smith, "Counseling for Women Who Seek Abortion," *Social Work*, vol. 17, March 1972, pp. 62–65; Sandra Sutherland Fox and Donald J. Scherl, "Crisis Intervention with Victims of Rape," *Social Work*, vol. 17, January 1972, pp. 37–42; and Marcella Schuyler, "Battered Wives: An Emerging Social Problem," *Social Work*, vol. 21, November 1976, pp. 488–491.
46. Helen A. Mendes, "Single Fatherhood," *Social Work*, vol. 21, July 1976, pp. 308–312.
47. Janet S. Chafetz et al., "A Study of Homosexual Women," *Social Work*, vol. 19, November 1974, pp. 714–723.
48. Barbara Stephens Brockway, "Assertiveness Training for Professional Women," *Social Work*, vol. 21, November 1976, pp. 498–505; and Carol Wisley, "The Women's Movement and Psychotherapy," *Social Work*, vol. 20, March 1975, pp. 120–124.
49. U.S. Department of Commerce, Bureau of the Census, *1970 Census of Population—Subject Reports—Occupational Characteristics*, pc-2(2) 7A. Government Printing Office, Washington, D.C., June 1973, table 1, p. 1.
50. Jeanne M. Giovannoni and Margaret E. Purvine, "The Myth of the Social Work Matriarchy," *Social Welfare Forum, 1973*, Columbia, New York, 1973, pp. 166–195.
51. David Fanshel, "Status Differentials: Men and Women in Social Work," *Social Work*, vol. 21, November 1976, pp. 450–451.
52. Allen Rubin and G. Robert Whitcomb (eds.), *Statistics on Social Work Education in the United States*, 1978 Council on Social Work Education, New York, 1979, p. 10.
53. Ibid.
54. Fanshel, op. cit., p. 452.
55. Rubin and Whitcomb, op. cit., p. 18.
56. Ibid. p. 21.
57. Dorothy Zietz and John L. Erlich, "Sexism in Social Agencies: Practitioners' Perspectives," *Social Work*, vol. 21, November 1976, p. 436.
58. "Rhode Island Committee," *Womanpower: A Quarterly Newsletter of the Committee on Women in Social Welfare*, February 1977, pp. 13–14.

59. Lynne Healy and Philip Starr, "Sex Related Salary Differences among Social Workers," p. 4 (mimeographed.)
60. Juliana Szakacs, "Is Social Work a Woman's Profession?" *Womanpower: A Quarterly Newsletter of the Committee on Women in Social Welfare,* February 1977, p. 3.
61. Rubin and Whitcomb, op. cit., p. 37.
62. Mary Ann Mahaffey, "Sexism and Social Work," *Social Work,* vol. 21, November 1976, p. 419.
63. Giovannoni and Purvine, op. cit., p. 179.
64. Calculations made on the basis of the list of names of CSWE board of directors published in the 1977 Annual Meeting Program of the Council on Social Work Education, Phoenix, February 27–March 2, 1977, p. 47.
65. Mahaffey, op. cit.
66. "What We Have Done and Where We Are Going?" *Womanpower: A Quarterly Newsletter of the Committee on Women in Social Welfare,* Spring 1975, p. 3.
67. See, for example, Jane K. Thompson, "Fighting Discrimination: Up Against the Ivy Wall," *Social Work,* vol. 21, November 1976, pp. 506–511; "Social Workers Charge State with Sex Bias," *NASW News,* vol. 22, May 1977, p. 7; and Sara Ann Foster, "Sexual Discrimination in Salaries against Women Faculty Members: One School of Social Work's Experience," Paper presented at the Annual Program Meeting of the Council on Social Work Education, Philadelphia, March 2, 1976 (mimeographed).

FOR FURTHER STUDY

Sue Cox, ed., *Female Psychology: The Emerging Self,* Science Research Associates, Inc., Chicago, 1976.
Irene H. Frieze, Jacquelynne E. Parsons, Paula B. Johnson, Diane N. Ruble, Gail L. Zellman, *Women and Sex Role. A Social Psychological Perspective,* Norton, New York, 1978.
Rhoda Kesler Unger and Florence L. Denmark, eds., *Women: Dependent or Independent Variable,* Psychological Dimensions Inc., New York, 1975.
Juanita H. Williams, *Psychology of Women. Selected Readings,* Norton, New York, 1979.
Juanita H. Williams, *Psychology of Women. Behavior in a Biosocial Context,* Norton, New York, 1977.

FOR DISCUSSION

1. How was the word "sexism" coined?
2. How are sexism and racism related?
3. Why may social workers and other clinicians be accused of being sexist?
4. Are women in the labor market better off than they were twenty years ago? Explain your answer.
5. Identify some of the women who were early leaders in social work.
6. What are the "male enclaves" within social work?
7. What is the economic situation generally for female heads of families?
8. Explain the discriminatory provisions in social security.
9. What is the relationship between the levels of welfare benefits and wages for women in low-skilled jobs?

10. What was the Supreme Court ruling concerning the responsibility of employers to pay maternity benefits? What is its current status?
11. What is "feminist therapy"?
12. Summarize some of the trends in curriculum development in schools of social work concerning courses on women's issues.
13. What are some examples of sex inequities in the field of social work and social work education?
14. What recent trends in social work suggest that progress is being made on the issues raised in this chapter?

PROJECTS

1. Look at several social work journals. Is there any awareness of sexism? Are the pronouns all masculine? Do the articles consider social work service as only a female role?
2. Find out if there is a protective facility in your community for women who are subjected to physical abuse or who have other family problems. What are the services offered, the eligibility policies, and the pattern of privacy?
3. Is there a course in assertiveness on your campus? If so, invite the instructor to discuss the techniques used to combat sexism.
4. Talk to several policemen about the causes of rape. Do they have a sexist view of the offense? What organization in your community provides protection and services related to rape?
5. Find out about affirmative action policies and practices as they relate to women in your university on one or more of the following topics: hiring of faculty, admissions of students, provisions for women's sports, opportunities for student leadership.
6. Research and report on the attempts to pass the Equal Rights Amendment. What could have been done to make passage more efficient?
7. Who usually receives custody of children in divorces in your area? Are more awards going to fathers? How do the local judges feel about the issue?
8. Find out what efforts have been made to reduce or eliminate inequities in the social security system. Start with your local Social Security Office.
9. Investigate proposals for mothers' wages to be paid by the government. Is this benefit now available in any country? (See David G. Gil, *Unravelling Social Policy*, Schenkman, Cambridge, 1973.)
10. Interview the executive of the United Way concerning support for programs for women.

CHAPTER 18
Legal Rights and Protections

Needed: volumes of knowledge about the law.

The lawyers thought of the social worker as an ineffectual, giving, nursing female who wants to and does do much good, but at the same time is impractical, utopian, overidentified with and overprotective of her client, "all heart and no head," subjective and not objective, concerned only with feelings and not logic. Even so, she knows less than she thinks she knows even about human relations. She is too defensive about what she does know.

—Homer W. Sloane*

Legal rights and remedies have become a central topic in social work education. Several principal rights have been defined and expanded—equal treatment, equal protection, and due process. These rights have been especially important to combat racism and sexism, protect minorities, and provide justice to those in conflict with the law. The right of privacy has also been significant in decisions involving confidentiality of records and personal data as well as in court decisions on wiretapping, contraception, and abortion.

THE LAW DEFINED

Law is "a formal means of social control that involves the use of rules that are interpreted and are enforceable by the courts of a political community."[1] In order for a person to be charged with an offense, there must be a law prohibiting the behavior. Law is one way society provides standards and means of social control. It is based upon legislative acts and regulations to aid in the enforcement of such acts. It is also based on precedents established by previous cases. A rule of law is established in the first case and then is made applicable to a second case, but the rules do not remain constant. New situations arise and people's wants and needs change. The rules change as the rules are applied. An example of change with time came in the field of civil rights, where the doctrine of separate but equal school facilities for blacks was established in 1896 by the Supreme Court in *Plessy v. Ferguson*,[2] but by 1954, in *Brown v. Topeka Board of Education*,[3] segregated schools were no longer acceptable.

The Courts

There are two general types of courts—*trial* courts, or courts of original jurisdiction, and *appellate* courts, which review cases from the trial courts when error has been alleged. Social workers may testify only in trial courts, but

*Homer W. Sloane, "Relationship of Law and Social Work," *Social Work,* vol. 12, January 1967, p. 90.

437

most of the court decisions reported in this book are from appellate courts because they tend to establish legal precedents. The most important decisions are obviously those from the U.S. Supreme Court, which reviews cases on appeal from both federal and state courts.

Rules of Evidence

Unlike the social work process, where feelings and motivations are important, the legal world is a world of facts. It is necessary in all situations to present evidence that can lead to proof. In cases involving offenses for which a person may be deprived of liberty, proof must be established beyond a reasonable doubt. Social workers are often impatient with the legal process because they may not be permitted to use hearsay or second-hand evidence, and they are expected to reinforce their judgments with facts. In a case of child neglect, for example, a court is much more interested in what the social workers observed in the home than in how the social worker interprets the observations. Dates and times are also critically important in testimony. The social worker often has to orient the attorney to the facts of the case and to help people who will testify to know what to expect in their role as witness.

Social workers must be familiar with the law in order to serve their clients. Marriage and parenthood, divorce, child custody, and support, child protection, and eligibility for financial assistance all have legal ramifications. Social workers also seek to affect the passage of laws through lobbying with congressmen, state legislators, and local officials.

Groups of people have benefited from suits filed as *class actions*. In divorce, formal grounds with a plaintiff and a defendant are giving way to *no-fault* procedures. Court decisions and legal reforms have resulted in sweeping changes in poverty law, family law, and procedures for criminal justice.

The federal government leaves family law to the states. The result is fifty sets of conflicting laws. Some major issues in family law, important information for the users of social services, and suggestions for legislative social action will be presented in this chapter.

AGE AND THE LAW

Not only does the substance of the law vary from state to state, but standards of legal age also differ. Women's liberation efforts have been important in eliminating provisions that specify age differences in the law for men and women.

Age provisions are of special interest to college students and other young people who want more legal rights. A major change has been the right to vote at eighteen. As adolescents gain rights, they also tend to take on responsibilities. Eighteen has gradually replaced twenty-one as the age of majority. This is consistent with physical growth trends, beginning with the earlier onset of puberty. On the other hand, adolescents are attaining financial independence at a later age.

Twenty-one was not selected as the age of majority on a rational basis. One theory suggests that the number seven had religious significance, and three times seven is twenty-one. Until age seven, the child was considered innocent. From seven to fourteen he was growing in responsibility, but innocence predominated; from fourteen to twenty-one responsibility exceeded innocence; at twenty-one the person was fully responsible before the law. Another explanation emphasizes the strength required to manage a complete suit of armor—a task successfully mastered by age twenty-one.

Age requirements are still confusing at best. Juveniles are considered as adults if they commit game and fishing or traffic offenses punishable by fines. Youth may shop around for legal privileges. They cross state lines to purchase liquor legally and come home to consume it illegally. They may go to another state to get married, but if they do so to evade the laws of their own state, the marriage can be challenged.

Sex Differences

The legal age for marriage with parental permission in various states ranges from twelve for females and fourteen for males to eighteen and twenty-one respectively. The most common ages are sixteen and eighteen. Being underage may result in an annulment. Until recently women have been accorded the right to marry without parental permission at an earlier age than men—apparently because they mature earlier and tend to marry older men.

In many states, females were processed through the juvenile courts until eighteen, while boys of seventeen were tried in adult courts. Apparently girls commit fewer and less serious offenses and are more easily managed in correctional facilities than older teenage boys. At the same time, females are more likely to be held in detention for status offenses, such as running away, and are more likely to be deprived of their liberty. Recent court decisions have emphasized the need for the same age and processing standards for the two sexes to avoid discrimination.

Responsibility for Support

Both the eighteen-year age of majority and the appropriateness of an adolescent's life-style may jeopardize parental support. After majority, apparently parental support is no longer legally required unless the child is crippled or retarded. In one case a father was not required to support his daughter because he disapproved of her life-style.

More Age Differences

Conflicts between state laws and differences in legal age requirements from one activity to another are absurd. The typical eighteen-year-old male can vote and own property, but cannot make a will. He can serve in the armed forces. He may or may not be able to marry without parental permission or to drink beer legally, depending on where he lives. He can sign contracts, but not have to honor most of them.

Differences in legal provisions and age requirements make it easy to see why family law is complex. Different provisions and philosophies among state laws, court procedures, and judges' values affect the major life events— marriage, divorce, the rights of infants and children, adoption, guardianship, child abuse, and the handling of juveniles who violate the law—events that social workers find important.

MARRIAGE

Marriage has provided the traditional basis for family formation. With over a million marriages ending in divorce each year, laws governing marriage and divorce have special relevance to social workers who engage in marriage counseling or are involved with child custody or support.

Even with technical flaws in the license or in the marriage ceremony, legal policy favors upholding rather than voiding marriages, especially when the parties consider themselves to be married and behave that way. Because states uphold the legality of marriages and divorces that take place in other states, people have often sought out those states where marriage or divorce was easier. These options have been available to the well-to-do but not to the poor.

Common-Law Marriage
Some people live together without first having a marriage ceremony. The laws of the state and the relationship between a man and a woman determine the possible existence of a common-law marriage. Do they "hold themselves out to the world" to be married? They must publicly and professedly live as husband and wife. Renting an apartment or opening a joint charge account as husband and wife may be evidence enough. There is no uniform time requirement. In 1979 common-law marriage was recognized in the District of Columbia and in thirteen of the fifty states—Alabama, Colorado, Georgia, Idaho, Iowa, Kansas, Montana, Ohio, Oklahoma, Pennsylvania, Rhode Island, South Carolina, and Texas.

If a man and woman live together in a state that does not recognize common-law marriage and then move to a state that does, they may acquire married status. If they live in a state that recognizes common-law marriage and then move to a state that would not uphold a common-law marriage originating in its own borders, that state will still generally recognize their marriage as valid.

People often live together without a ceremony. Typically they give no thought to common-law provisions. If they are concerned, they can usually get married. The public has disapproved of common-law marriage because it allegedly encourages fraud and vice and debases conventional marriage. These objections have not prevented people from living together. Common-law provisions actually discourage vice because they give living together a legal status. According to one view, "When a woman has performed the obligation of a wife for thirty-five years and then is brutally deprived of all the financial benefits of marriage on the sole ground that the relationship was not signalized by some sort of ceremony, this debases marriage."[4] Common-law marriage reduces injustice and suffering, especially in those social and economic groups that have not accepted middle-class standards—the people most likely to be served by the social worker. It makes the family eligible for benefits under pension and social insurance plans. Recognition of common-law marriage is also desirable for the operation of public welfare programs, because it extends family responsibility. The issue may not become important until financial issues arise from death or separation.

Cohabitation

Living together without marriage, or cohabitation, has become a common arrangement for middle-class young people. The conscious choice to do so is quite different from common-law marriage, which was limited mainly to the poor. However, questions of property rights and custody of children (if any) arise in both instances. It is likely that more non-common-law states will accord rights to those who have lived together for some time. The Lee Marvin case, which established property rights in cohabitation and authorized a cash award to the woman,[5] may have more effect on legal interpretation than several decades of legal action involving non-celebrities—poor people in a common-law relationship.

Social workers should be especially aware of the need for a will when couples live together. If they are not legally married but share common property or have children, the death of one member of the pair may result in serious complications in custody and property rights—especially when surviving family members have disapproved of cohabitation.

Other Marital Situations

Interracial marriage was prohibited at one time by as many as thirty states. A Supreme Court decision overthrew these restrictions because they violate the Fourteenth Amendment to the Constitution by denying equal treatment under the law.[6]

Social workers are often asked for advice about marriage for a limited purpose—"to give the child a name"—when the couple do not plan to live together. Such a marriage furnishes little protection to the child, who will still be reared by a single parent. Marriage to get immigration status also fulfills a limited purpose and is illegal if the couple do not intend to live together.

Divorce

Divorce refers to the legal termination of a valid marriage. Grounds have been expanded to include such abstractions as incompatibility and mental cruelty. "No-fault," divorce adopted in at least forty-seven states, recognizes the breakdown of the marriage as the ground without attributing fault to either partner. While no-fault provisions make divorce easier, they may result in too little attention to the problems of child custody. No-fault divorce has led the courts to designate a lawyer to represent the interests of the children and act as their advocate. The courts call such a representative a *guardian ad litem*.

Many conflicts in divorce laws are found among the states, but most "divorce mills" requiring very short residency have been eliminated and Mexican "mail-order divorces" invalidated. States accord "full faith and credit" to the divorce laws of other states, i.e., they recognize their validity.

Who gets divorced is subject to misunderstanding. Actually, the working class has a higher divorce rate than either the poor or the well-to-do. The poor simply separate. Desertion is known as the "poor person's divorce."

The high rate of divorce in the United States has led to proposals for contractual marriage, but contractual marriage may encourage unrealistic expectations and fail to motivate the participants to try hard enough to make a marriage work. One of the major gaps in community legal services involves lack of staff for divorce. The Supreme Court has decided that legal counsel does not have to be provided at public expense for the poor. No-fault statutes make it increasingly feasible to obtain a divorce without legal counsel, but few low-income persons can negotiate the legal system on their own.

Child Support and Custody

Child support involves two major issues. First, support orders are generally issued without relation to fault and are imposed on the father. Legal decisions concerning child custody traditionally tend to award children to the mother. As women gain equal rights, support and custody are being decided more rationally. Second, mobility has made it difficult to assure the support of children.

RIGHTS CONCERNING HUMAN REPRODUCTION

The law has held that marriage and the family are needed for control of sexual intercourse and for the rearing and protection of children, but attitudes toward human reproduction have changed greatly in the last several decades. The first major decision came in 1942 in a case involving sterilization. The Supreme Court held that the right to procreate "was one of the basic civil rights of man."[7] In 1965 another fundamental question—"Do individuals have a right to employ means to prevent conception while they engage in sexual intercourse?"—was answered in the affirmative. The decision asked, "Would we allow the police to search the sacred precincts of marital bedrooms for tell-tale signs of the use of contraceptives? The very idea is repulsive to the notions of privacy surrounding the marriage relationship."[8]

Abortion

Abortion is defined as "the expulsion of the fetus at a period of uterogestation so early that it has not acquired the power of sustaining independent life." Courts in the nineteenth century called abortion "a crime against nature which obstructs the fountains of life." Some states allowed therapeutic abortions necessary for the mother's well-being. Some also permitted abortions when rape or incest had been involved or to prevent the birth of a potentially defective child. In 1973 the Supreme Court, in *Jane Roe v. Henry Wade*,[9] voided state laws that place restrictions on a woman's right to obtain an abortion during the first trimester of pregnancy. For the remainder of the time of pregnancy, the state may regulate abortion procedures for reasons of maternal health, and it may prohibit abortions in the final ten weeks of pregnancy unless they are necessary to preserve the life and health of the mother. Like the earlier decision on contraception, the basis was the constitutional right of privacy. During the first three-month period of pregnancy, a physician can recommend an abortion "without regulation by the state," and the operation can be conducted "free of interference by the state."

Later Supreme Court decisions held that a pregnant woman who wants an abortion does not need the permission of her husband or, if she is a minor, of her parents.[10] A major issue has been the restrictions on the use of public funds to pay for abortions for women who lack the means to pay the cost. Opponents of abortion are seeking a constitutional amendment to outlaw it all together.

The Rights of Infants: Illegitimacy

Bastardy has constituted an important legal designation for centuries. Traditionally, in English law, illegitimates had no rights of inheritance—even from their mothers. Upon death, property went to the Crown. The child was considered legitimate if the parents married before its birth, resulting in great pressure to marry to give the child a name. Now the child also is legitimized if the father acknowledges paternity and the parents marry after the birth.

Trends   Increases in the rate of illegitimacy have aroused concern. From 1940 to 1968 the percentage of illegitimate births rose from 3.5 to 9.7. The general growth in population was also responsible for a sharp increase in the total number of illegitimate children (from 89,500 in 1940 to 339,200 in 1970). Minority groups receiving public assistance have a high rate of illegitimate births, but contrary to prevailing opinion, the majority of children born out of wedlock are white.

Annulment and donor insemination also may involve actions at law. In most states a child born after a marriage is annulled is legitimate. When a paternity question is raised in court, however, a child born following donor insemination is considered illegitimate in some states. Legal adoption by the husband may be necessary.

The legal disabilities of the illegitimate child are central concerns. The child has no legal claim to inheritance from the father unless paternity is proved. The child is also likely to be ineligible for social security and other pension benefits accruing to the father.

Law Reform   The conflicts in state laws regarding illegitimacy cannot be resolved as long as punishment of the illegitimate child is used to encourage marriage and legitimacy.

Krause has made the strongest appeal for legal rights by eliminating the legal concept of illegitimacy.[11] He presents model legislation based on Norwegian law and a North Dakota statute declaring that all children are the legitimate children of their natural parents. A model Uniform Parentage Act was drafted under his chairmanship, and six states had adopted it by 1979.[12]

The younger mother who wants to rear her child independently has a difficult time in our society—legally, socially, and financially. The minor who is still in school is treated quite differently from the older woman who is self-supporting. The young mother may receive undue pressure to marry and drop out of school or to relinquish the baby. The father may receive an ultimatum to marry her or may be completely rejected because he is a poor source of funds. If he is already married to someone else, he presents a more complex problem. A paternity action against him may obtain few resources for child support and also jeopardize an already established family. If she wishes, the older woman in an urban area may put on a wedding ring, call herself married, keep her baby, and pay for day care, with few questions asked.

Keeping the Baby   White mothers, regardless of their age, generally tended to give up their children for adoption, while minor black mothers had fewer resources for adoption. As a result, their children were reared as their siblings, or the mother had to drop out of school to care for the child. Now agencies report that mothers of both races have a strong interest in keeping the child as a matter of right. At the same time, their desire is to remain in school. We have already observed that courts are gradually establishing continued education as a right of the school-age mother. Schools and other agencies have begun to provide day care services for children of students. Suits demanding the rights to attend school and to make independent decisions about keeping and caring for the baby may still be necessary, however, because of local policies.

With more girls choosing the pill or abortion, and more who become pregnant deciding to keep their babies, adoption becomes less important. Paternity, child support, and inheritance rights are the critical issues. Paternity actions have been mainly concerned with money. If paternity is acknowledged, the father and mother may both have legal responsibility for support, but the mother usually lacks financial capability, especially if she is a minor.

Paternity Actions   To determine paternity and compel support, the mother may make a complaint for the arrest of the alleged father. The state attorney is often able to convince the father to accept the responsibilities of paternity. If not, a hearing is held to determine whether there is enough evidence for a trial. Blood tests may be used as evidence. If a man is found guilty, a support order is issued by the court. When the order is violated, the man must go to jail or forfeit his bond. Obviously, jailing the father will make financial support impossible, since he will probably lose his job.

Women have been unwilling to press paternity actions. In some cases the mother wants nothing more to do with the father. In others, she hopes for eventual marriage and does not want to involve him in an adversary action. Sometimes the father's lack of financial resources may seem to make the procedure pointless. However, when the mother keeps the baby, she should be more interested in the father's financial potential, including social security benefits, than in his present earning power. The establishment of paternity clarifies the child's status equally in relation to both parents.

The Father's Rights

Until recently the father had no rights of visitation. If the child was surrendered, the father's consent was not needed. In 1973 the Supreme Court, in *Stanley v. Illinois*,[13] accorded the right of a hearing to the father of illegitimate children after the mother died. Otherwise, the child could not be offered for adoption. A later case, dealing with adoption by a stepparent who had been the father figure for a number of years, has served to reduce the rights of the natural father.[14]

ADOPTION

Adoption has a special interest beyond the number of children affected because it is seen as an extension of goodwill and altruism toward children. Adoption has been much more important in the United States than in Europe. In Europe each adoption typically required a special bill to be passed. England did not pass a general adoption statute until 1926. The Netherlands passed its law in 1969. Traditionally, property rights related to inheritance are stressed rather than parental nurturance and protection. In America adoptive parents stress the desire for the childrearing experience.

Termination of Parental Rights   In adoption parents acquire a child, and the child acquires parents, by legal rather than biological means. Since legally a child can have only one set of parents at a time, adoption must involve termination of the rights of the biological parents. If the natural parents live outside the jurisdiction or their whereabouts are unknown, adequate notice must be given by personal service of papers, registered mail, or publication in the press.

Legal Surrender

In the past twenty years the aim has been to place an infant as soon as possible after delivery, preferably directly from the hospital. Recent court actions upholding the right of the natural mother to reclaim the child after placement cast doubt upon one of the major reasons for agency adoption—the assurance of an unconditional surrender and avoidance of contact between the adoptive and the natural parents. New York and other states revised their laws to make surrender final at the time of placement. The choice of unmarried mothers to keep their child has reduced the number of white infants for adoption. The majority of children available for adoption are likely to have been in foster care for some time.

In addition to legal provisions for irrevocable surrender before the child is placed, three steps will help to ensure the permanence of the surrender. First, the social agency must avoid duress and pressure to obtain surrender of the child for adoption and should make the mother's legal rights explicit to her. As a result, mothers may take a longer time to make up their minds and delay placement. Second, the mother should obtain a lawyer of her own choosing, who will set forth her rights, including the implications of a decision to relinquish the child for adoption. Provision must be made to pay the costs of counsel if necessary. Finally, the surrender should be taken in court so the judge can reiterate the mother's legal rights. Following the Stanley decision, the same procedure should be used with the father. These safeguards are likely to reduce the number of children placed, especially in the first few weeks of life.

Adoptions by Relatives   The illness or death of a parent or a divorce and remarriage may lead to an adoption that does not involve a social agency. To the courts, blood ties make detailed investigations unnecessary. Perhaps this provides too little protection for the child adopted by a relative, but in any event social work is unlikely to get a larger role.

Emphasis on the fitness of the adoptive parents has suggested that their place of residence provides the appropriate basis for jurisdiction. Now that surrender has become a legal issue, the importance of obtaining an irrevocable consent may make the place of residence of the natural parents the most logical place for filing for adoption.

Steps in a Nonrelative Adoption   Four steps are involved in a nonrelative adoption: a petition to the court asking to adopt the child, an interlocutory (temporary) decree in which the child is placed with the family on a provisional basis, a supervisory process (usually for six months), and the final decree. If parents move from one jurisdiction to another before the adoption is final, supervision must be transferred to another agency. If plans for moving are known, agencies show less interest in making the placement, except in the case of a hard-to-place child.

Petitions to the court should be prepared in a manner that avoids revealing the names of the natural parents to the adopting parents.

Selecting Adoptive Parents: The Social Work Role

The steps in the investigation of prospective parents are seldom specified in the law. Agency regulations are dependent to a degree upon factors of supply and demand. Now that we face a scarcity of infants, we may expect regulations to become more strict.

Statutes requiring social work agencies to handle all nonrelative placements have been enacted in several states, including Connecticut, Delaware, Kentucky, New Jersey, and Rhode Island, but there is no way to prevent children from being placed independently in an adoptive home before an agency investigation. Concern is expressed about independent placements because of the black market involving the "sale" of children for adoption, the disadvantages of direct contact between the natural and adoptive parents, and the risks that the child will be unhealthy or the adoptive parents unfit.

Informal placements are often made by the mother with prospective adoptive parents in advance of application. If the child has lived with the applicants for some months and regards them as his or her parents, any investigator—social worker, probation officer, clergyman, or private citizen—will be reluctant to remove the child from the home except for grave cause.

From Foster Care to Adoption

A related issue is the transition from foster care to adoption. Child welfare agencies often held that foster parents could not adopt children under their care when they were freed for adoption. Now, however, many agencies encourage them to do so. Legislation in some states also provides financial subsidies for adoptive parents, mainly for those who take children that are considered hard to place. Subsidies often make it possible for foster parents to adopt the child under their care.

Involuntary Termination To provide the most stable family life, social workers have an increasing interest in freeing children for adoption through suits to involuntarily terminate parental rights. Parents who cannot possibly rear the child do not want to admit their failure. They always hope for better times. The courts typically support their rights. Legal definitions of abandonment may require proof of the mother's positive intention to abandon the child. Adequate care for the child by foster parents has also barred a finding of dependency in some courts, even though the natural parents show no interest in the child.

To provide the most effective child protection, statutes have to be clarified. Social workers have to be better processors of evidence, and courts have to be more willing to terminate parental rights in the behalf of the child's best interests.

"All right then—you call it 'child
abuse'; I call it 'affirmative action.' "
(Used with the permission of the Johnson Publishing Co., Inc.)

Guardianship

Children who are dependent, neglected, delinquent, beyond parental
control, or mentally retarded may require a court-appointed guardian of the
"person"—someone who is responsible for the child's direct care. Adults who
are mentally retarded, mentally ill, or senile also may be declared wards of the
court. If the person has financial resources, such as property or pension
benefits, a guardian of the "estate" (or property guardian) is also appointed.
State laws define terms in different ways and use varying legal labels. Legal
guardianship reduces the parents' tendency to suddenly reclaim the child and
also may be required to utilize public funds for the costs of care.

Agencies complain that courts often take the dominant role in diagnosis
and planning and consider the agency only as a placement mechanism to carry
out unilateral decisions. The agency, on the other hand, may give insufficient
attention to the natural family. Temporary guardianship, through default, too
often becomes permanent. Children in stable placements often drift along. On
the other hand, if the child goes from placement to placement with unsuccessful outcomes, return to the natural family may come out of desperation rather

than out of conviction. The impersonality of guardianship is a problem in large bureaucracies. The head of a child welfare program or a designate may serve as guardian for thousands of children. The major life issues are decided by those who have custody of the child. The guardian should have enough personal knowledge and interest to assure that the child is reared affectionately as well as educated and supported.

CHILD ABUSE

Child protection demands legal authority since it requires investigating suspected parental incapacity, neglect, or abuse. Child abuse is considered the most extreme problem requiring protective services. Child abuse laws are intended to give legal immunity from prosecution to persons who report alleged child abuse. Some legal scholars hold that people already have immunity if reports are made in good faith. Other laws establish penalties for abuse, often under the criminal codes. Social workers need to know the child abuse laws of their own state. They must understand the difficulty of diagnosing abuse, learn the special skills needed to provide services authoritatively, and gain the cooperation of the courts in instances of serious and persistent abuse.

In the only national study of child abuse, 9,563 cases of suspected child abuse were reported in 1967, but only 6,617 cases were confirmed.[15] In the same year 3,000 cases of sexual abuse were estimated in New York City.[16]

Following campaigns by pediatricians, social workers, and citizen groups in the 1960s, every state legislature enacted abuse-reporting laws. States require reporting from specified classes of people who may detect alleged abuse. Immunity from prosecution is provided by law to those reporting. While medical personnel are the major potential case finders, varying state laws also specify teachers, nurses, social workers, or Christian Science practitioners. A few states include "all citizens."

Child abuse laws differ widely in the explication of purpose, persons covered, and prescribed investigation procedures. Laws increasingly cover emotional as well as physical abuse. Arizona is an example:

> Abuse means the infliction of physical or mental injury or the causing of deterioration of a child and shall include failing to maintain reasonable care and treatment or exploiting or overworking a child to such an extent that his health, morals or emotional well-being is endangered.[17]

Some states delegate investigation of reports to the police, some to a social agency, and others to both. The responsibility is accorded to the police in about half the states. In some nineteen states, reports are not required to be directed to a social agency, but these laws are considered inadequate since reporting without the prompt provision of social services seldom results in child protection. On the other hand, if a social worker promises help and then tries to have a child removed, the family may feel betrayed.

Abuse laws do not ordinarily provide the basis for punishing abusers. Criminal laws specify these penalties through such categories as assault. Some of the laws impose penalties upon specified citizens for not reporting. Since child abuse is a matter of judgment, penalties are unenforceable.

Interpreting and verifying evidence are perplexing aspects of child abuse. Bruises and X-rays of healed fractures are major indicators of abuse. Especially with very young children, great skill is required in distinguishing intentional injuries from accidents. In a Pittsburgh study, Elmer reported that many of the cases of alleged abuse reported could not be proved.[18]

A National Center on Child Abuse and Neglect was created by federal legislation in 1974.

Sexual abuse is particularly hard to discover because of family privacy. Studies from protective agencies reveal that sexual abuse usually involves family members or close acquaintances on a recurrent basis—not single violent attacks by strangers. Incest is the most common offense. Incidents reported typically involve lower-class families already known to agencies. Sexual abuse also occurs in middle- and upper-class families, but they are better able to maintain privacy. Studies also fail to include instances of sexual activity between siblings and mother-son incest, although both do happen. Sexual abuse is not always simply the victimization of a child. The sexually provocative adolescent may be both aggressor and victim—a familiar story in cases of statutory rape.

Mandatory investigations of child abuse give a social agency defensive and reluctant clients. Delaying abuse investigations may be risky since the children may be injured or killed. Agencies find that investigations and continuing casework may involve different types of personnel. Police investigators, trained in the rules of evidence, are useful for gathering facts following receipt of an abuse report. Professional social workers can be used more effectively for continuing services.

Abuse laws should require all complaints to be investigated. When the complainant is unnamed, the agency must take the sole responsibility for legal action. Some agencies, unfortunately, refuse to accept anonymous complaints. This suggests the analogy of a fire department that will not send equipment unless it knows who turned in the alarm.

Abuse reports tend to identify children who have had no regular doctor-patient relationship—children from poor families who are likely to be seen in the emergency rooms of public hospitals. Reports from private hospitals and physicians are rare, especially on regular patients. Thus middle-class families are underrepresented in abuse reports.

To be successful, child abuse laws must serve as case-finding techniques. A network of protective services is required to help families cope with their problems and carry out parental responsibilities more successfully. The primary goal should not be punishment of parents or removal of children from the home, though in some cases one or both actions will be necessary. If the follow-up by the agency is ineffective, doctors, hospitals, teachers, and social workers will neglect to file reports because they will consider them only a ritual.

Child abuse legislation is more complex than it may appear. Legal drafting requires careful definition of terms to cover all those persons most likely to encounter abuse at the outset and to provide the needed supportive services. The laws have worked out better in theory than in practice. In spite of support from the public at large, the laws have not eliminated inadequate reporting or ineffective or delayed investigations. Closed cases have not been adequately followed to determine the effectiveness of services.

THE CHILD OFFENDER AND THE JUVENILE COURT

The juvenile court used to be dear to social workers' hearts because it was the one legal mechanism that had been conceived and organized to apply social work principles. The young person in trouble was to receive attention from a "fatherly judge" in an atmosphere that was minimally judicial. Transactions were to be informal, and every effort was to be made to avoid tne stigma of delinquency.

The system was not always fair. Punishments were imposed that would not have been tolerated in the adult criminal justice system. Racial and social class bias were likely to result in the informal system.

Four decisions by the Supreme Court ushered in a new era emphasizing due process of law. The Gault case guaranteed the right of a juvenile to a lawyer and to legal due process similar to that for accused adults.[19] The Kent case made it more difficult to process juveniles in adult courts.[20] *Breed v. Jones* made it illegal to try a juvenile in both juvenile and adult court,[21] and the Winship case established the need for proof of guilt beyond a reasonable doubt.[22]

In the Gault case, a juvenile was accused of making obscene phone calls, but the charges were rather vague, communication with the family poor, and the time of confinement excessive. As an adult Gault would have received a maximum sentence of two months. As a juvenile he could have remained in an institution until age twenty-one. The Gault decision specified the explication of legal rights, including formal hearings and representation by counsel.

The current procedure involves the provision of counsel to the juvenile and as many as three hearings—for detention, adjudication, and disposition. The *detention* hearing is to determine whether the accused needs to be held for his or her own protection or that of society or because of the possibility of flight. If not detained, the accused is usually sent home to await the next hearing.

In the *adjudication* hearing, the charges are reviewed. Is the child a delinquent, a person in need of supervision, a neglected or dependent child, or none of these? Is the child guilty as charged? The adjudication hearing is held as soon as possible if the accused has been detained. Otherwise it is usually held within thirty days. The adjudication hearing is guided by the rules of evidence prescribed for actions against adults.

The *disposition* hearing is to determine the appropriate action after the adjudication that caused the accused to remain before the court. In a finding of delinquency, possible dispositions are probation and release to parents, placement in the custody of others (relatives or foster parents), or commitment to a correctional agency.

In the decade since the Gault decision, the more formal procedures have served to satisfy many people concerned with due process. At the same time, those interested in law and order feel that more informal procedures may not sufficiently impress upon a child the gravity of his or her action. They have also supported the procedural changes.

For the social worker, the major implication of the emphasis on due process comes in a need for knowledge of the rules of evidence. Unsupported conclusions and clinical "hunches" have no credibility in the present juvenile court system.

Community Legal Services

Access to legal services should be a fundamental right of all citizens. Where can the poor get help with their legal problems? Lawyers are expensive, and the poor have been unable to pay for legal counsel. Legal services are guaranteed in criminal proceedings and in the juvenile court. The federal courts since 1938 have provided attorneys for those who could not afford them. In 1972 the Supreme Court held that the state courts had to provide counsel in all cases involving possible imprisonment.[23] Methods vary from public defenders to the casual use of volunteer attorneys without fee to the engagement of paid counsel on a case basis. The number of public defenders has tripled over ten years.

Legal aid bureaus were developed first in Chicago and New York and later in about fifty other large cities. The bureaus are usually supported by the bar association and the United Way. The Legal Service Program of the Office of Economic Opportunity in the 1960s was responsible for the dramatic spread of community legal services. Legal services are now supported by a separate federal corporation.

Community legal service is free, and eligibility is based on income. Care is taken to avoid competition with private lawyers. The traditional legal aid bureaus took a very limited range of cases—often excluding divorce. The OEO offices accepted a wider variety—excluding criminal cases, because the courts provided counsel, and personal injury actions that private attorneys would take because of the possible award of damages. Although welfare mothers and other groups have many legal problems, no legal action will solve the problem of income distribution. A few communities have provided a credit card approach to use regular lawyers for legal aid. This system is called Judicare. Middle-class persons may also buy their own legal insurance to cover a specified group of situations.

Social workers need to know how to obtain legal services for their clients to deal with life crises and with problems of housing and consumer protection.

They need to support the network of community legal services, as well as groups interested in legal problems, such as the American Civil Liberties Union and the National Association for the Advancement of Colored People. The National Association of Social Workers also has a legal defense fund for its members.

INFLUENCING LEGISLATION

How can social workers be more effective as lobbyists and advocates? Social workers have not been particularly successful in influencing legislation. Many are employed in governmental agencies and have been subject to the Hatch Act, which forbids political activity. They may get more freedom as a result of recent suits contending that the Hatch Act unduly restricts individual freedom.

Social work organizations have not had the commitment to lobbying efforts that has characterized such groups as the American Medical Association, nor do they have the resources to carry them on. Social agencies have often worked indirectly through lay board members and other influential citizens.

The Washington staff of the National Association of Social Workers has organized the Educational Legislative Action Network (ELAN) so that interested members can maintain contact with their representatives in Congress and be able to act quickly on bills that concern professional social workers. They publish a legislative newsletter called *The Advocate*. NASW has recently endorsed candidates and established an organization to support those who support legislation that NASW favors.

To react to several thousand bills each session, a legislator needs information from lobbyists who have specialized knowledge. The lobbyist, however, must provide trustworthy information.

Several suggestions are helpful:

1. Know what legislation is being planned. Influencing the drafting of a bill is more effective than responding later.
2. Learn how bills are introduced. The sponsors of the bill and the committee to which it is assigned are the major targets for your views. If you wish to testify, find out when hearings are scheduled and how to prepare a statement. You will not be permitted to testify after the bill has been acted on in committee. Remember that testimony will be needed before committees in both houses of the legislature.
3. Personal contacts are generally best. Follow them with a telegram or summary letter to provide a record of your views. Petition or form letters are the least effective. State your own views in your own words. Give reasons.
4. If a bill has a dollar amount attached, it will have to be heard by the appropriations committee. This is just as important as a hearing on the substance of the bill. Be prepared to support or refute the financial implications.

5. Get the support of the National Association of Social Workers and other interested organizations.
6. Seek effective coalitions with other groups. Natural alliances on many issues are possible, not only with other professions but with labor unions, the League of Women Voters, parent-teacher associations, chambers of commerce, and many others.

Regulation of Social Work Practice

Three legal issues involve social work practice itself—licensing, privileged communication, and malpractice.

Licensing   To establish professional standards and protect the public from practitioners who may be inadequately qualified, social workers should be licensed. NASW has a model licensing statute that state legislatures may adopt. It also authorizes privileged communication for social workers. However, social work practice is legally regulated in only about half of the states.

Privileged Communication   The concept of privileged communication implies that participation cannot be forced under legal compulsion to reveal the substance of the communication. In nearly all states, social workers engaged in counseling may be subpoenaed to testify and have to show their records upon demand of the court. Their clients are not accorded privileged communication as they would be with a psychiatrist, physician, clergyman, or lawyer. Privileged communication is not intended to protect the social worker but to encourage people to seek help and is a legal goal of both psychologists and social workers.

Legal action against social workers charged with *malpractice* is an increasing concern. Social workers can be charged with damaging the welfare of their clients. They may also be held responsible for the actions of staff members under their supervision. Workers in private practice are most likely to face malpractice actions, but people providing direct services in agencies are also advised to carry malpractice insurance because they can be sued as individuals along with the agency. Fortunately, such suits are still rather rare, probably because the goals and procedures of social work are less specific than those of medicine, and the size of potential monetary damages is much smaller.

SUMMARY AND APPLICATION

This chapter traces the development of the highlights of family and juvenile law and indicates substantial gains in basic rights—especially for juveniles who face the court because of an alleged delinquent act. We have also seen how changes in life-styles have affected marriage and divorce as well as adoption.

The vast majority of professional social workers will need to know the legal provisions that affect their practice. Many of them will testify in court and some may serve on the staff of a court. You will also need to know how to obtain legal services for your clients and how to help them in the quasi-legal administrative hearings that were discussed in a previous chapter.

Legal regulation of social work practice makes it necessary to understand licensing, privileged communication, and malpractice. You may also wish to assist in the development of legislation.

With all of the recent legal developments, it should be no surprise that courses in social work and the law are very popular with students.

—Donald Brieland

KEY TERMS

law
trial courts
appellate courts
common-law marriage
cohabitation
no-fault divorce
custody of children
Uniform Parentage Act
surrender in adoption
interlocutory decree

independent adoption
guardianship
child abuse
juvenile court
detention
adjudication
disposition
legal services
Hatch Act
lobbying

REFERENCES AND NOTES

1. F. James Davis et al., *Society and the Law,* Free Press, New York, 1962, p. 41.
2. *Plessy v. Ferguson,* 163 U.S. 537 (1896).
3. *Brown v. Board of Education of Topeka,* 347 U.S. 483 (1954).
4. Homer H. Clark, *Law of Domestic Relations*, West, St. Paul, Minn., 1954, p. 483.
5. *Marvin v. Marvin,* 18 Cal. 3d 106 (1976).
6. *Loving v. Virginia,* 388 U.S. 1 (1967).
7. *Skinner v. State of Oklahoma,* 316 U.S. 535 (1942).
8. *Griswold v. State of Connecticut,* 381 U.S. 479 (1965).
9. *Roe v. Wade,* 410 U.S. 113 (1972).
10. Planned Parenthood of Central; *Bellotti v. Baird,* 96S.C. 2857 (1976). *Missouri v. Danforth,* 428 U.S. 52 (1976); also *Bellotti v. Baird,* 74L.W. 4969 (1979).
11. Harry D. Krause, *Illegitimacy and Social Policy,* Bobbs-Merrill, Indianapolis, 1971.
12. *Uniform Parentage Act,* Commission on Uniform Laws, Chicago, 1974.
13. *Stanley v. Illinois,* 405 U.S. 645 (1972).
14. *Quilloin v. Walcott,* U.S. 54 L. Ed. 2d. 511 (1978).
15. David Gil, *Violence Against Children and Physical Child Abuse in the United States,* Harvard University Press, Cambridge, 1970, p. 93.
16. Vincent DeFrancis, *Protecting the Child Victim of Sex Crimes Committed by Adults,* American Humane Association, Denver, 1969, p. 36.

17. Arizona Revised Statutes, art. 2, title 8, chap. 5, sec. 8-531, 1974.
18. Elizabeth Elmer, "Abused Young Children Seen in Hospitals," *Social Work*, vol. 5, October 1960, pp. 98–102.
19. *In re Gault*, 387 U.S. 1 (1967).
20. *Kent v. United States*, 383 U.S. 541 (1966).
21. *Breed v. Jones*, 421 U.S. 519 (1975).
22. *In re Winship*, 397 U.S. 358 (1970).
23. *Argersinger v. Hamlin*, 407 U.S. 25 (1972).

FOR FURTHER STUDY

Donald Brieland and John Lemmon, *Social Work and the Law*, West, St. Paul, Minn., 1975.

Harry D. Krause, *Family Law in a Nutshell*, West, St. Paul, Minn., 1977.

Leopold Lippman and I. Ignacy Goldberg, *The Right to Education*, Teachers College, New York, 1973.

Robert H. Mnookin, *Child, Family and State: Problems and Materials on Children and the Law*, Little, Brown, Boston, 1978.

The *Family Law Quarterly* presents articles of special interest to social workers.

The *NASW News* frequently summarizes basic legal decisions.

The *New York Times* reports Supreme Court decisions in detail.

FOR DISCUSSION

1. What legal rights are especially important to combat racism and sexism?
2. In addition to rules, what does a legal system require?
3. If a man had been charged in 1906 with driving an automobile while intoxicated, what defense might he have used?
4. Do the findings in previous cases alone determine current law? Use an example to support your answer.
5. In the two types of courts, which one takes original testimony?
6. If imprisonment results, what standards of evidence are applied?
7. What is the current age of majority in most states? Is it the same for both sexes?
8. Why were women permitted to marry earlier than men? Is this legal difference still justified?
9. Explain common-law marriage. What is the current living pattern that is somewhat similar to common-law marriage?
10. What advice is given for the legal protection of couples who live together without marriage if they have any property or if there are children?
11. In a divorce action what term is used to identify the lawyer who represents the child?
12. What is the current legal provision for abortion? Is parental permission required? Permission of the husband?
13. What proposed act has attempted to eliminate the legal concept of illegitimacy?
14. Why has the number of infants available for adoption decreased?
15. What are the four steps in a nonrelative adoption?
16. Do child abuse laws provide penalties for the abuser? Where would such penalities be found?

17. What major cases substantially altered juvenile court procedures? In what ways?
18. How is eligibility for legal aid determined?
19. Identify a needed topic for legislation. How would you get a bill introduced and what would you do to support it?
20. For whom is the protection of privileged communication intended?
21. Why is social work malpractice insurance relatively inexpensive compared to similar medical coverage?

PROJECTS

1. Poll the class to determine how many members have used the services of a lawyer. What different problems were involved? Did anyone use legal assistance services?
2. Compare the marriage and divorce provisions in two adjoining states. What major differences are found?
3. Study the various legal age requirements in your own state. Which ones have been changed recently?
4. Invite a lawyer to talk to the class about the legal aspects of new family forms, including communes and couples living together without marriage. What are the legal problems for them related to the birth and rearing of children?
5. Prepare a discussion on the advantages and disadvantages of recognizing common-law marriages.
6. Select two students with differing views to consider the elimination of the concept of illegitimacy.
7. Invite a social worker who specializes in adoption to present the legal process and the major problems that are involved.
8. Submit questions from the class to a legal aid attorney. Include the types of cases handled and the requirements to be eligible for the service. Ask the attorney to respond to the questions and discuss the future of legal aid with the class.
9. Investigate the legislative program of your state NASW. If your state has a lobbyist, ask for a description of the functions performed.

PART FIVE
Evaluation and Career Planning

Two areas concerning the social work profession remain to be considered—how can social services be evaluated and how does one plan for a social work career.

Social welfare programs have expanded until they require more funds than the national defense. We have seen how private charity has diminished in importance and public programs have grown. Now there is acute concern about inflation and high taxes. These developments place a new responsibility on social programs to be accountable. The hard questions become: How many people were served? At what cost? What was the outcome? Did the services make them more productive or effective people?

Chapter 19 suggests how research can help answer these questions.

For students who want to prepare for a social work career, what kinds of jobs are available, what education is necessary, and how do they match their skills with the jobs available? What opportunities and special problems exist for the student who wants to practice social work with a bachelor's degree?

Chapter 20 will deal with such questions and also with career planning.

CHAPTER 19
Evaluating Practice

Questions for the researcher.

Research in any field is simply the application of the scientific method to the specific material of that field. Thus research in social work is the systematic search for answers that are not yet known, or the systematic testing of assumptions on which practice is based in order to make them certain rather than presumed.

—H. Carl Henley*

Do social workers accomplish what they set out to accomplish? How close do they come to their goals? The answers to these questions involve an evaluative process—some way of judging effectiveness—and the use of research methods.

EVALUATING SOCIAL WORK SERVICES

Research in the social sciences is based on the premise that reality is measurable if one follows the rules of science. The social scientist tries to develop generalizations about the reality of the social world by carefully stating a hypothesis (a testable statement), devising a way of measuring the object of study, collecting and analyzing the relevant data, and reaching a conclusion related to a body of theory on which generalizations about social reality are built.

This approach is useful for gathering basic knowledge about the world, but it is not the only use of research for an applied discipline. Social work needs an additional kind of research. Social work and social welfare have become important to the modern world. The services rendered by welfare institutions and social work personnel touch the lives of many people. Citizens who pay to support welfare services want to know what they are getting for their money; consumers have become more vocal in stating their concerns about the quality of the service they get. These concerns place a high premium on evaluative research—the kind of research that seeks to set a value on a given procedure or policy. Such research does not ask, "Is it true?" but rather, "How good is it?"

Traditionally, the question of the value of social work effort did not seem to require hard answers. Because social workers are basically concerned with helping people, it is sometimes assumed that what they do is good by definition. For years, it was enough to measure the output of an agency in terms of the number of people served, the days of care provided, or the amount of money spent. However, social workers are more critical of themselves than are their outside critics.

*H. Carl Henley, "Research in Social Work," in Arthur E. Fink (ed.), *The Field of Social Work*, 7th ed., Holt, Rinehart, & Winston, New York, 1978, p. 105.

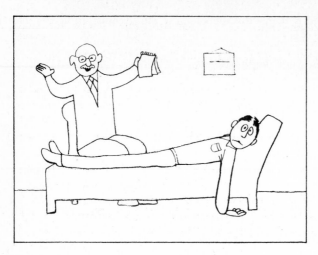

"This is our 1,883d session; who needs research to know that you've improved remarkably?"

Several studies have raised hard questions about the value of the efforts of practitioners and the quality of social welfare programs. To the credit of the profession, social workers have been willing to examine what they do. They have become leaders in the quest for more adequate evaluative studies of practice, programs, and policies. Social workers and other social welfare personnel know that they can no longer be accountable only in terms of money spent and hours of service. Increasingly, both public and voluntary services must show concrete evidence of efficiency and effectiveness to a wider and more critical public. Efficiency deals with the economical delivery of a service. Effectiveness concerns the impact of the service on people to achieve stated goals. The attainment of efficiency is obviously easier than the attainment of effectiveness.

Coming: Better Research Methods

Can social workers be expected to demonstrate results when many of the factors affecting their work are intangible? The answer is yes. Social work researchers have begun to use more rigor in conceptualization, more precise instrumentation, and clearer definitions of outcome. Since the first edition of this book, there has been a notable improvement in the quantity and quality of social work research and a growing interest in research on the part of students. The computer has been of tremendous help in processing large amounts of data.

Social Work: An Art That Cannot Be Measured?

A few social workers take the position that good evaluative research cannot be done in social work because what social workers do is really an art.

This is not a defensible position. N. L. Gage has replied to an analogous suggestion that teaching is an art and, therefore, not subject to scientific analysis.[1] Gage suggests that art in any form follows rules. When these rules are identified, they constitute a theory of artistic performance. Any art can be studied and evaluated. Such study is a legitimate concern for any profession interested in improving its performance or in teaching its art to new recruits in the field.

Research Capability

Social workers are increasingly developing skills that will enable them to prepare useful reports and studies. The pressure for accountability has been a powerful motivating force in the development of the necessary tools. Social workers are slowly getting over their fear of research, and social work students have discovered that research courses are in the curriculum because the skill is needed, not just as a means of testing character! Agencies are increasingly willing to have their programs evaluated, and many large agencies employ persons knowledgeable about research.

MAJOR PROBLEMS IN EVALUATIVE RESEARCH

Evaluative research is not easy because there are always a number of variables that are hard to pin down. It is not always easy to decide when a procedure or program has reached a satisfactory outcome. Suppose that a social worker is dealing with a married couple who have been getting along badly for some time. The social worker schedules a series of appointments with the couple. A process ensues involving the social worker and the marriage partners in a counseling relationship. Eventually the couple decide on a divorce. Has the social worker failed? Would the worker have succeeded only if the couple remained married? Or is it enough to say that the social work service was effective because the couple developed enough insight into their feelings and difficulties to recognize that the marriage was irreconcilable? Actually, any outcome might be acceptable if one who is doing research on the effectiveness of counseling is willing to state the desired outcome clearly and can reach a decision on what will be taken as evidence that the outcome has occurred.

Social workers and other social scientists have learned to deal with behaviorially oriented outcomes and clear social indicators as evidence of effectiveness in research. This is not as complicated as it sounds. For example, suppose that the researcher wants to evaluate the effectiveness of a program aimed at the delinquent. There is no reason why the researcher cannot use the delinquency rate as an indicator of outcome. While crime statistics are generally not perfect indicators, any thoughtful consumer would be impressed with a reduction in the delinquency rate. This is an outcome that is easy to understand and clearly desirable. Most evaluators would agree that more complex things happen in a successful program—but they reason that what counts most is a result that is simple, clear, and understandable. These kinds of outcomes tell the story of the program in a way that provides a rational basis for making value judgments.

Social work research in the present climate of accountability must be concerned with clear and concise studies that can inform the public of social work's worth and provide a basis for public confidence.

Increasing Sophistication in Research

Social work researchers are learning the value of the use of much more precisely stated hypotheses and well-defined concepts. Published social work research is showing a higher level of understanding of complex statistical procedures and tested data collection techniques. More social work researchers are using the computer for the analysis of data.

In the past, schools of social work did not offer the range of research instruction that is now available. While research is not the favorite subject of most students, schools of social work are now more able to identify those with interest and aptitude in research and offer them advanced courses. A small but dependable supply of well-prepared researchers will be produced by the schools of social work, particularly now that doctoral programs are more readily accessible throughout the country.

Limitations of Social Work Research

Some important constraints operate in social work research. First, social work agencies are not ideal places to do research. They exist for service purposes, and their clientele usually has enough to deal with without having their lives complicated by the needs of researchers. Care must be taken so that the researcher does not overburden the clients. It is unethical for researchers to require the clientele of a social agency to be subjects. Anyone doing research must be very careful to protect the privacy of subjects. One must never foster the notion that a client who does not become a subject will not be given service. Agencies using federal funds are prohibited by Department of Health, Education and Welfare regulations from using human subjects in research unless the subject gives informed and voluntary consent. "Informed consent" implies more than just a general description of the research and the subject's casual acquiescence. The subjects must know exactly what they are going to be subjected to—and must be fully cognizant of any risks involved. This is an appropriate policy even where federal funds are not involved.

A second problem involves a problem in research design. Ideally, the classical experiment (whether one is talking about evaluative research or "pure" research) requires two (or more) groups of subjects. These groups should be equivalent. In practice, equivalency cannot be assured by any matching process, so researchers usually turn to the use of randomly selected groups. This procedure is consistent with the laws of probability. Effectively, all possible attributes of all possible subjects have the same chance of being selected in mathematically known ways. Given that any differences in behavior at the beginning of the experiment can occur only by chance, the odds are that any differences between the subjects and a control group at the end of the experiment are due to the effect of the experimental condition. Rarely can the social work researcher use a design for research that approximates the neatness of this classical experiment. The social work researcher is usually forced to work with samples that are not representative. This means that the researcher must compromise with the ideal and use designs that have less validity. Subjects must also be protected. No social work researcher would, for example, randomly select a group of children and arrange to have them abused so that they could be compared with a control group that had not been abused. Therefore, social work research has to operate at a scientific disadvantage (as it should in this case) for the sake of moral and ethical considerations.

Third, social work research is usually constrained by the size of the samples that are available. Some researchers in the social sciences are able to use very large samples. A social work researcher, however, usually has to limit data collection to the patients on a given ward or the clients in an office caseload. Large samples are clearly more dependable, so in their absence the social work researcher often has to consider a wider margin for error.

There are more constraints on social work research, but these three are the major difficulties. They are not insurmountable for the creative investigator, but they do mean that the social work researcher must be cautious in building generalizations on social work research findings.

MODELS OF EVALUATION

If, despite the problems, evaluative research is an important activity in social work, how is it carried out? In general, a useful approach to evaluative research must provide for:

1. A clear description of program goals. This means that the researcher must be able to arrive at a clear statement of what the agency or program is trying to do.
2. An adequate, reasonably sound study design with clearly defined terms.
3. Efficient and appropriate statistical and data processing tools. Here the computer is helpful.
4. Clearly defined outcome criteria.

Social work researchers can select from a number of models for evaluation. Some can be borrowed from education, since the educational evaluator has similar research problems. Below is an adaptation of Stake's approach to the evaluation of educational programs and techniques.[2]

1. What Is the Agency Trying to Do? Often the goals of a program or agency are not explicitly stated. It is important for the evaluator to find out what significant actors want from a given program. What is the intention of the staff? What does the board or legislature hope will happen? What does the administration see as the goal of the program? What do financial supporters (taxpayers or voluntary givers) expect the program to do? What expectations do clients have when they come to the agency?

Obviously, not all of the key people involved in a given program have the same intent. Their expectations are value-laden, but they deserve answers from the evaluative process. A value statement can be articulated and made explicit, and an answer can be obtained. For instance, suppose that the board members of a family agency have as their intent the lowering of the divorce rate, but the staff have a different set of intentions. They direct their efforts toward the personal growth of the clients and consider the divorce rate irrelevant. The clients have yet another set of expectations. Faced with a painful relationship, relief may mean divorce or it may mean reconciliation. All of these expectations can be collected as statements of goal or intent. The evaluation design can take them into account. Each set of key persons can be given an answer. A useful product of the evaluation process should be the recognition of differing goals.

2. What Is Actually Going On?   This question involves gathering data from the participants in the situation. The focus is on the interactions and transactions between staff and clientele, of course, but should not stop there. How much staff time does a given program take? What does it cost? What do the administrators actually do? What are the unanticipated consequences of the program? The evaluator is obliged to gather as much information as possible on what actually happens, from many different sources. The number and complexity of the observations on which the evaluation is based should be limited only by the technology, funds, and time available.

3. What Are the Outcomes of the Activities?   Too often, evaluative research considers only the effect of a program on the consumer. One should look also at the effects of the program on staff, administration, and the community as a whole. Good evaluation looks at unintended as well as intended outcomes. It also looks at costs and benefits. Short-term as well as long-term benefits are important. Again, the more outcomes that can be included, the better the evalution.

4. Is the Product Any Good?   Someone must decide whether or not the intended outcomes and the actual outcomes are congruent. Standards for making judgments do exist. The trouble is that standards may not always be explicit or congruent with each other. Therefore, the job of the evaluator is to gather the standards that are available and use them. Experts have opinions that can be used as standards. Consumers, administrators, and staff also have standards by which an agency, program, or technique can be judged. The evaluator's problem is to articulate these standards clearly enough to be usable in making judgments about whether or not they have been met. It is also useful to identify the standards of judgment of those who are highly critical of the program. Opponents are often the source of useful standards. Even if one does not like their viewpoint, it is something against which a program can be measured.

Comparisons can often be made with professional standards, e.g., a program for children can be judged on the basis of standards set forth by the Child Welfare League of America. In any event, hard judgments must be made if social work is to be accountable and credible.

This approach to evaluation is not foolproof. It obviously depends upon the ability of the evaluator to derive intents, observations, and standards from a number of sources. However, the alternative is to settle for less than is available and to do incomplete evaluation of social work effort.

Single Subject Designs

The wide variance in agency clienteles and the relatively small numbers served by many agencies have led to considerable interest in evaluating work with single subjects. In this approach, data are gathered from the individual subject before service is begun, and the effects of the service are measured from time to time. If the person's performance shows a decline after service is discontinued, this provides evidence that the improvement was related to the service. While it is obviously impossible to generalize from the results with single subjects, this method makes it possible for the social worker to set goals for each situation and to consider the outcome in terms of the change that is achieved. It is far more convincing, of course, if the measurement is done by an independent evaluator rather than by the person providing the service. By aggregating the results on a number of persons, it is possible not only to get data on effectiveness but also to ascertain which types of cases involve the greatest success for a given social worker.

Another approach is the Program Planning and Budgeting System (PPBS). Its object is to define the tasks, to organize them in the most efficient way (in terms of costs versus benefits), and to field the most effective program for the money. The accent on efficiency is a direct outgrowth of the pressures placed on governmental structures to provide accountability for the efficient use of limited funds.

Jack Bloedorn has set forth a systems analysis approach for social work that includes nine steps.

1. Carefully define the problem.
2. Set objectives by carefully spelling out what you are trying to do.
3. Determine the criteria for success.
4. Research the situation until you understand the problem and its setting completely.
5. Find out the practical constraints in the situation which will mitigate for or against reaching the objective you have set.
6. Develop alternatives for reaching your goal.
7. Test the alternatives against the criteria.
8. Select the best alternative from a cost-benefit point of view and plan for its installation.
9. Install the alternative and monitor the system for continuous feedback and change.[3]

Stake's approach accents accountability while PPBS stresses costs and efficiency. Both seek better cost-benefit output, clear objectives, and meaningful outcome criteria.

SOME EXAMPLES OF SOCIAL WORK RESEARCH

A number of useful evaluation studies have appeared in the social work literature. A counseling service for women, located on a university campus, was evaluated recently.[4] While the research design was simple, the study was thorough.

The subjects had applied for career counseling. Entering behavior was established through two interviews done by separate interviewers. The first interviewer administered a scale used for rating depression. A social worker did the second interview and rated the clients independently on the basis of clinical information. Most of the women were highly educated. Most were changing their careers from homemaker to work outside the home. This transition created strains which were frequently related to depression. Eighteen women who were identified as somewhat depressed received extensive supportive help. All improved. Seventeen women were working at the time of the follow-up. Their scores on the depression measures improved. This study supports the use of skilled service delivery in dealing with crucial human problems and shows how evaluative research can be useful in assessing the impact of a program.

In another study, a strategy was evaluated for increasing black client participation in the program of a rehabilitation center that serves people who have had psychiatric treatment.[5] In a previous study, the agency had found that black clients were receiving less service than white clients. A black social worker started a group with a program specifically aimed at black clients. The level of program participation of the group was then compared with that of clients who did not have the group experience. The group experience was dramatically successful. The blacks in the group participated at a higher level than the blacks who were not in the group. In fact, the black clients in the experimental group were more active than the agency's white clients. While this study may not be conclusive, it suggests the effectiveness of group work in dealing with an important problem.

Perry studied the social action strategies of thirty-three black community organizations.[6] This exploratory study is not pure evaluative research, but its format uses some of the elements of evaluation design. Had the effectiveness of a given strategy been pursued, the study would have become evaluative.

Perry identified two types of primarily black community organizations by the type of social-change strategy that they preferred—cooperative or conflictual. Her hypothesis was that the older organizations would tend to prefer and use cooperative strategies (conventional coalition-building activities) while newer organizations would use conflict (disruptive activities). Interestingly enough, she found that both groups engaged almost equally in conflict strategies although leaders of both groups said that they were committed to cooperative strategies.

Information Systems

Management information systems for social service organizations are basic to good evaluation. Evaluation projects require considerable information about workers and clients that would not ordinarily be gathered. Workers sometimes resent this activity and may claim that the data are irrelevant to the actual quality of the work. Ironically, then, the evaluator and the staff would be working at cross-purposes. This should not be the case. A good management information system should make sense to both the worker and the administrator.

Types of Information   In the order of difficulty, three kinds of information can be produced by such systems: (1) the number and characteristics of clients seeking or receiving services; (2) the units of service, including the interviews held, group meetings attended, the hours of service, and the average cost of each unit; and (3) transactions of clients in seeking and obtaining service, including the time spent on the waiting list, the sequences of services received, and the changes produced by the service. Thus far, few systems have been able to deal adequately with the outcomes of the service, but better outcome studies are on the way.

Measuring Success

Two problems are typical. First, for example, in vocational rehabilitation, job placements obtained are a typical criterion of success. Two clients may meet this criterion. One may have lost two fingers in a power saw accident while the other may be chronically ill, have a third-grade education, and be a member of a minority group. The system must take into account the comparative difficulty of the latter case in rating efficiency and effectiveness.

Second, counting the number of interviews is often used as evidence of good work on the part of the counselor. Interviews are the simplest sign of direct contact with the client. Without some measure of client change, such a criterion by itself may encourage more and more interviewing, whether or not it is effective.

Measurement Required   While many social workers are not enthusiastic about the forms and procedures required by an information system, they may well become mandatory in all agencies. Social workers must understand them and shape them to reflect human needs and professional values. This also suggests the need for knowledge of management techniques leading to the ability to collaborate with others who understand the systems but may know much too little about the goals and methods of the service provider.

Standardization presents a major problem. With different agencies, localities, and states developing information systems, it becomes difficult to combine data into useful forms that can be used for measuring trends and forecasting. Increased cooperation among governmental and private agencies can lead to uniform systems that make the effort more useful.

A consortium of twenty mental health agencies serving an area of 155,000 persons in California developed the "Human Accountability System," involving a centralized data bank.[7] Twelve transactions constitute the basic data. Identifying information includes the name, address, sex, and date of birth of every patient. A single form is used that can be filled out in thirty seconds.

The system can generate a master list of all patients known to the system, send messages to alert all agencies about the patients in the system, and provide transaction reports which include the frequency of occurrence of each type of transaction and the movement among agencies.

The system automatically receives a history of every patient. It produces lists of active patients, those on the waiting lists, and those who have been discharged. The system indicates to its members those facilities that may be able to accept new patients.

The limits of this information system for evaluation are apparent. It does not provide a way of measuring for the achievement of objectives, nor does it incorporate any outcome criteria. The system does illustrate a clear approach to fact gathering that can be expanded to provide the capability for evaluation.

SOCIAL WELFARE PLANNING

Evaluation is a tool for planning. Planning is necessary for the achievement of both short-range and long-range goals. Basically there are two broad planning styles: incremental and comprehensive.

Incremental Planning

Incremental planning involves reaching a goal by small but consistent steps. While the ultimate goal may be innovative, it is reached in stages that are each only a little different from the prior stage. For example, it can be argued that health planners have been engaged in incremental planning for the past forty years. In the 1930s there was a move to provide a national health service as a part of the Social Security Act, but the attempt failed. The proposal was reintroduced during the Truman administration and was again defeated. The supporters of societally provided health care then turned to an incremental approach. Through the public assistance system, payment was made for medical care for the recipients. Under Medicare in the 1960s, a federal plan was developed which enables older Americans to afford health care. Since that time, more than a dozen different plans have been proposed that would provide health care for all citizens. The most likely outcome will be some sort of national plan in which the individual will be able to participate in a quasi-insurance system. The individual will pay a monthly amount of money toward medical and hospital costs. In the event of illness or hospitalization, the covered individual will pay a deductible charge and receive benefits from a pool that has accumulated from the monthly payments. Such a scheme would work rather like automobile insurance—a periodic fee with a deductible amount paid at the time a claim is made.

National health insurance was the goal that was intended all along, but its supporters saw that such a total change in health care was too sweeping to be acceptable. However, through incremental planning and prodded by increasingly higher physicians' fees and hospital charges, the public seems to be ready to accept a national health insurance plan.

Critics of incremental planning have said that it is too slow and that the "take a little, leave a little" approach represents compromises in *principle*. Why not press forward immediately toward what is recognizable as a worthwhile goal? Why settle for only an incremental change? Supporters of incremental planning defend their position by pointing out that an emphasis exclusively upon some all-encompassing and ideal ultimate change can lead to indifference to useful changes that can be made immediately. Some changes, such as national health insurance, are too overwhelming to make in one step. Resistance is too great. Should Medicare *not* have been passed by Congress in the 1960s? Should the country have waited until some vague time in the future when national health insurance could be embraced as a total package?

Comprehensive Planning

The other broad approach to planning is often conceived as a systemic approach to social change. The object is to make significant changes in organizational structures in bolder and more dramatic ways through an overall plan that takes many subsystems into account simultaneously. A plan to replace the traditional public assistance system with a guaranteed annual income in one step can be considered as an example of an opportunity for comprehensive planning. A comprehensive plan would take into account the effect on taxation, social services, and human resources policy for both the unemployed and the underemployed. There are implications for work incentives, family structure, housing, mental health services, and programs for the aged in this kind of plan. The organizational changes involved would affect all fifty states and millions of people. Vast amounts of information and a series of demonstration experiments should be part of a comprehensive planning process on the guaranteed income issue.

Both Approaches Are Useful

This is not the place to argue for one approach or the other. For some kinds of issues, incremental planning is the most successful approach. It has been possible to move organizations or institutions toward distant goals in steps where jumps would not succeed. For other situations, particularly those where a whole system must move in several subsystems at once, the comprehensive approach is preferred.

A Combination Model

Amitai Etzioni argues for a combination approach, seeking to combine the best elements of both models.[8] He calls this approach *mixed scanning*, because it takes a comprehensive view but concentrates on specific alterations that may be incremental.

SUMMARY AND APPLICATION

As this chapter has suggested, social work has become subject to evaluation and will require more evidence for its support than it needed in the past. If you are interested in research or planning, specialized curricula are now offered in schools of social work, departments of public administration, and some business administration programs. Social workers who are attracted to research and macro-practice are needed for state, regional, and national positions where they will work in partnership with their colleagues who concentrate on helping people directly.

—Charles R. Atherton

KEY TERMS

evaluation	unintended consequences
accountability	management information systems
social indicators	incremental planning
efficiency	comprehensive planning
effectiveness	mixed scanning

REFERENCES

1. N. L. Gage, "Theories in Teaching," in E. R. Hilgard, (ed.), *Theories of Learning and Instruction*, The National Society for the Study of Education, Chicago, 1964, p. 270.
2. Robert E. Stake, "The Countenance of Educational Evaluation," *Teacher's College Record*, vol. 68, April 1967, pp. 535–540.
3. Jack C. Bloedorn, "Applications of the Systems Analysis Approach to Social Welfare Problems and Organizations," *Public Welfare*, vol. 28, July 1970, pp. 280–290.
4. Cynthia Pincus, Natalie Radding, and Roberta Lawrence, "A Professional Counseling Service for Women," *Social Work*, vol. 19, no. 2, March 1974, pp 187–195.
5. Stephen M. Stillman, "Increasing Black Client Participation in an Agency," *Social Work*, vol. 21, no. 4, July 1976, pp. 325–326.
6. Lorraine R. Perry, "Strategies of Black Community Groups," *Social Work*, vol. 21, no. 3, May 1976, pp. 210–215.
7. Bernard Bloom, "Human Accountability in a Community Mental Health Center," *Community Mental Health Journal*, vol. 8, 1972, pp. 252–253.
8. Amitai Etzioni, "Mixed Scanning: A 'Third' Approach to decision Making," *Public Administration Review*, vol. 27, 1967, pp. 385–392.

FOR FURTHER STUDY

Philip Fellin et al. (eds.), *Exemplars of Social Research*, Peacock, Itasca, Ill., 1969.

Arlene Fink and Jacqueline Kosecoff, *Evaluation Primer*, Capitol, Washington, D.C., 1978.

Darrell Huff, *How to Lie with Statistics*, Norton, New York, 1954.

Ralph H. Kolstoe, *Introduction to Statistics for the Behavioral Sciences*, Dorsey, Homewood, Ill., 1969.

Henry Maas (ed.), *Social Service Research Reviews of Studies*, National Association of Social Workers, New York, 1978.

Making Evaluation Research Useful, American City, Columbia, Md., 1972.

Leonard S. Rutman, *Evaluation Research Methods: A Basic Guide*, Sage, Beverly Hills, Calif., 1977.

Tony Tripodi et al. (eds.), *The Assessment of Social Research: Guidelines for the Use of Research on Social Work and Social Science*, Peacock, Itasca, Ill., 1969.

FOR DISCUSSION

1. Why is social work research *applied* rather than pure?
2. Why is accountability in social work now very important?
3. How can social work as an art still be the subject for research?
4. What are the problems with using delinquency rates as a measure of the success of a program?
5. How is sampling important to the choice of statistical techniques?
6. What are the special problems of sampling in social work research?
7. In Stake's model, why are goals of the agency the first concern?
8. Outcomes are usually studied in terms of effects on clients. What other effects should be considered?
9. What does Bloedorn's model illustrate?
10. What are the purposes of an information system?
11. Why did workers find the Human Accountability System easy to use? What were its limitations? Discuss some of the principal constraints that operate in social work research. What do you see as strengths and limitations in research using single subjects? Suggest some social indicators that are relevant to the effectiveness of a foster care program for children, a program for the rehabilitation of disabled individuals, and a program for aged persons now living in their own homes.
12. What type of planning is most common? Why?

PROJECTS

1. Organize a panel to discuss the use and misuse of of statistics. *How to Lie with Statistics* will be a helpful resource.
2. Consider the members of the class as a research sample. Develop an attitude questionnaire on a topic related to social welfare. Tabulate the results and see whether the responses of the women and the men differ. Test the differences statistically. Seek faculty consultation if necessary.
3. Choose an example of social work research. Evaluate the sampling, the method, and

the findings. Compare your comments with those of other class members. *Social Work Abstracts* is a source for current research.

4. Invite a faculty member who is engaged in research to discuss his or her project with your group. The discussion should describe the funding and sponsorship as well as the objectives and research methods.

5. Prepare a brief talk for the class illustrating the difference between *efficiency* and *effectiveness*. Indicate how research techniques may provide evidence on both.

6. Invite a staff member responsible for evaluation in a large public agency to talk to the class. What kinds of data is the staffer expected to present? Have the demands changed? How does electronic data processing help?

CHAPTER 20
Planning for a
Social Work Career

Jobs at the end of the tunnel?

Although the members of my generation who became social workers took vows of poverty (not of chastity) I had not thought we were a religious order. We do not need people merely to believe; we need them to work.

—Norman A. Polansky*

Do you want to be a social worker? One of the best ways to answer this question is to involve yourself in volunteer social work activities. Volunteer opportunities abound in most communities in both the public and private sectors. Hospitals, nursing homes, youth diversion and recreation programs, mental health facilities, and crisis hotlines rarely have enough volunteers. Opportunities exist here and abroad in programs such as VISTA and the Peace Corps. Many colleges have campuswide volunteer programs that provide a clearing-house for assignments and training. Some colleges provide course credit for volunteer activities. You will find a demand for your time and talents in working directly with people, planning budgets, determining policy, or evaluating program outcomes.

If you decide on a career in social work, volunteer activities will help you to develop intervention skills. They may even lead to a full-time job. Employers are impressed by beginning workers who have had volunteer experiences in a variety of human service settings.

Opportunities exist for human service workers who have a variety of life and educational experiences. Of the more than 352,000 social service workers currently employed, 140,000 (39 percent) have bachelor's degrees, 110,000 (31 percent) have master's degrees in social work, 43,000 (12 percent) have some college education, and 59,000 (18 percent) have a high school education.[1]

The basic professional credential has been the master's degree, but those with bachelor's degrees also play a significant role in the delivery of social services in the United States. Very few of these workers, however, have been educationally prepared for the social service roles they have assumed. For example, only 55,000 (40 percent) of the bachelor's-degree workers are graduates of social work curricula, and even fewer have degrees from baccalaureate social work programs accredited by the Council on Social Work Education (CSWE).[2] With the expansion of junior college and baccalaureate social work programs, increasing numbers of personnel in the 1980s will obtain formal preparation for social work careers. Master's and doctoral programs in social work also continue to expand. The goal of these four educational levels is to provide a well-articulated continuum, with each successive level leading to

*Norman A. Polansky, "Beyond Despair," in Alfred J. Kahn (ed.), *Shaping the New Social Work*, Columbia University Press, New York, 1973, p. 74.

differential roles and employment opportunities and preparation for continuing education.

TWO YEAR ASSOCIATE PROGRAMS

The past decade has seen a rapid growth of two-year community colleges with a wide variety of programs. Community colleges provide a range of options to students at a modest cost. Today over 200 two-year colleges offer concentrations in social work.[3] These programs seek to achieve two goals simultaneously—training for employment and the foundation for additional collegiate education. As a result the typical program is both vocational and preprofessional. Students who expect to go to work also seek assurances that their credits will be transferable if they decide later to pursue a bachelor's degree.

A representative selection of specific titles for which training is offered includes:

> Community Services Technician/Community Service Assistant/Community Social
> Service Worker
> Child Care Technician/Residential Child Care Aide
> Social Service Aide/Social Service Associate/Social Service Technician
> Parole Aide
> Mental Health Aide/Mental Health Associate
> Human Services Aide[4]

Four components are generally included in the curriculum—general education, specific core courses for the field of choice, courses dealing with specific skills and methods, and a field practicum.

Candidates for Associate Degrees

Associate degree programs must meet the needs of four quite different groups of students:

1. Recent high school graduates who may want either vocational skills or a college degree. This group has the youngest average age and the widest range of goals. In a restricted job market, lack of work experience may be a barrier to placement.
2. Second careerists, including both people who want more satisfying jobs and those who have been out of the labor force, usually because of childbearing and childrearing. This group often has a strong interest in general education as well as preprofessional content.
3. People already in the human service occupations who want to improve their skills and their economic capability. This group may be the most highly vocationally oriented.
4. New careerists—residents in a poverty area, sometimes with little formal education, who are recruited to provide special services to their own communities. This group may have a special interest in social action.

Local Opportunities

The community college can meet local needs directly, and local opportunities help shape the program. Linkages to agencies and to senior colleges are important to assure both job placements and transferability of credits. Programs cannot be so community specific, however, that they restrict mobility. There is no assurance that graduates will work in the community where they are educated or go to the senior college in their hometown.

Holders of associate degrees have faced two special problems—lack of jobs in social services when large numbers are graduated and inadequate opportunities for advancement on the job through a career ladder. Unavailability of employment often leads people to go on immediately for a bachelor's degree. An associate degree program that is heavily technical may mean that many liberal arts courses must be taken to make up prerequisites, or that some credits may not be transferable. For a useful career ladder, work-study opportunities are essential to help employees advance.

More standardization of associate degree programs in social work will probably not be achieved unless the Council on Social Work Education develops a plan for accreditation. The council has sponsored conferences and helped develop program guidelines, but there is little demand for accreditation.

THE B.S.W.: THE FIRST PROFESSIONAL DEGREE*

Bachelor's degree programs in social work have become increasingly popular in the 1970s. In the mid-1960s Merle found that 232 colleges or universities had specified programs of study in social work.[5] In less than a decade the number of programs doubled. Over 500 undergraduate programs now offer social work majors.[6] Improved salaries, the greater potential for advancement, and the sense of satisfaction achieved through social work practice are attractive features. Opportunities for bachelor's-degree social workers are particularly found in child welfare, corrections, public assistance, and health and rehabilitation programs.

Careers in human service fields have also become popular because they provide challenging opportunities in traditional social welfare and nonwelfare occupations. Education in human service skills and methods permits a wide choice of jobs and considerable geographic mobility. Even if you do not enter a human service career, the educational programs offered today are usually broad enough to provide the background for other advanced study and for active and informed participation in dealing with social problems.

For holders of bachelor's degrees, job opportunities were limited during the 1950s and early 1960s. The trend toward professionalization of human services and the relatively easy availability of training funds led to the

---

*The term B.S.W. will be used here to identify any bachelor's degree program accredited by the Council on Social Work Education.

expansion of educational requirements. Employers began to require a master's degree as the minimum qualification. Personnel with the bachelor's degree were generally unable to get responsible positions if candidates with master's degrees were available, although the tasks assigned to the two were often indistinguishable. Persons with bachelor's degrees were thought of as substitutes for "qualified" staff. This attitude was reflected in the professional literature, which used "subprofessional" and "untrained" to refer to the bachelor's-degree holder. Membership in the National Association of Social Workers, the primary association of professional social workers, was limited to holders of the master's degree.

In the 1960s federal legislation brought about significant changes in workforce deployment. The "Great Society" programs increased the demand for services and staff. Under the pressure of necessity, the grip of "credentialism" in social work began to loosen. Employers found it expedient to hire personnel with bachelor's degrees. The current budget crunch in social welfare and public services has continued the assault on credentialism. The constraints imposed on human service agency budgets have forced a reexamination of social work roles and professional responsibilities. Today many recognize that people with a bachelor's degree can perform social services competently.

If student aid for graduate studies continues to be scarce and federal and state funding remains limited, social workers with bachelor's degrees will find more opportunities for employment and professional advancement.

Skills of the B.S.W.

Attempts to clarify and differentiate the appropriate educational preparation for the various levels of social work practice have frequently terminated in failure. Agency administrators and professional educators are often hard-pressed to distinguish between the activities of a college graduate with several years of productive practice experience and those of an M.S.W.

Social workers with a bachelor's degree must be prepared to enter a variety of practice settings upon graduation. A variety of skills and knowledge must be acquired. The report of the Undergraduate Social Work Curriculum Development Project identifies ten basic competencies essential for entry-level professional social practice. A B.S.W. practitioner must be able to:

> Identify and assess situations where the relationship between people and social institutions needs to be initiated, enhanced, restored, protected, or terminated.
>
> Develop and implement a plan for improving the well-being of people based on problem assessment and the exploration of obtainable goals and available options.
>
> Enhance the problem-solving, coping, and developmental capacities of people.
>
> Link people with systems that provide them with resources, services, and opportunities.
>
> Intervene effectively on behalf of populations most vulnerable and discriminated against.

Promote the effective and humane operation of the systems that provide people with services, resources, and opportunities.

Actively participate with others in creating new, modified, or improved service, resource, opportunity systems that are more equitable, just, and responsive to consumers of services, and work with others to eliminate those systems that are unjust.

Evaluate the extent to which the objectives of the intervention plan were achieved.

Continually evaluate one's own professional growth and development through assessment of practice behaviors skills.

Contribute to the improvement of service delivery by adding to the knowledge base of the profession as appropriate and by supporting and upholding the standards and ethics of the profession.[7]

Employers expect bachelor's-degree staff to demonstrate basic skills, whether acquired through general life experience, specific work training, or formal education. Increasingly staff are developing these competencies in accredited undergraduate social work programs.

Development of Professional Undergraduate Programs

In the mid-1950s very few undergraduate social welfare programs existed in colleges or universities. Most B.A. workers were graduated from a general liberal arts curriculum. Students who wanted to go to work after graduation prepared for practice by majoring in one of the social sciences and possibly taking one or two courses in social work. Some even had majors in agriculture, art, or philosophy. They had to rely heavily on practical experience and agency in-service training programs for specific knowledge and skills. Unfortunately, the quality of learning experiences was highly variable—some were well planned, others were haphazard and superficial. Courses and credit hours varied widely. Field instruction was not generally included. Preparation was oriented toward preprofessional training, and graduates remained inadequately prepared to provide direct services.

Practitioners and social work educators alike recognized that fundamental changes were necessary for a bachelor's degree in social work to lead to a professional career. A study published in 1965 recognized the need for the development of a system of personnel differentiation and utilization. Its recommendations included the development of specialized undergraduate curricula that would "prepare baccalaureate students for direct entry into social work practice as well as for entry into graduate social work schools." The report observed that social workers could acquire professional stature if graduates were given recognition both by the National Association of Social Workers and state licensure programs.[8]

In 1970 the National Association of Social Workers extended regular membership privileges to graduates of bachelor's programs approved by the Council on Social Work Education, the national accrediting body for B.S.W. and M.S.W. programs. The CSWE then implemented new accrediting standards in 1974 for educational institutions offering undergraduate programs in social work that clearly defined the bachelor's degree in social work as the first professional degree.

As a result of the reexamination of personnel practices and educational preparation, the professional bachelor's-degree program in social work—the B.S.W.—was developed. B.S.W. graduates should share a common base of knowledge and competence. Accreditation by the CSWE is intended to assure students and employers alike that these programs meet minimal educational requirements and that graduates are prepared for beginning levels of social work practice. Over 230 colleges and universities are accredited by the Council, and over 33,000 B.S.W. majors are enrolled in these programs across the United States.[9]

Opposition to a Professional B.S.W.

The professional B.S.W. continues to face opposition by some social work practitioners and educators. They argue that the B.S.W. provides too narrow a base for undergraduate education. They believe that the undergraduate curriculum should provide a broad liberal arts base and a social science major. Some M.S.W.'s see B.S.W.'s as cheap labor and a threat to their economic security. Many are still unaware of the progress B.S.W. education has made in the past decade.

A report of the Social Work Education Committee of the Illinois chapter of NASW, in 1977, opposed the professional status of the B.S.W.

> We believe it would be appropriate to designate the holder of the BSW degree as a social work technician. The Committee appreciates the value of studies in the humanities, or the sciences—as well as prior experience in human services—in equipping a candidate for the social work profession. *But unless followed by graduate training the person is inadequately prepared to assume professional status* [emphasis added].[10]

A recent report of the NASW Committee on Baccalaureate Social Workers found that "There are still many Chapters in which the predominant attitude toward BSWs is 'fear and loathing'. . . . The fact that BSWs are professionals and have a valid role to play in NASW needs continual reinforcement."[11] Even NASW needs continual reinforcement. While the *NASW Standards for Social Service Manpower* (1973) clearly identify the B.S.W. as the entry-level professional, the *NASW Standards for Social Work Services in Schools* (1978) identify the M.S.W. as "the preferred academic degree for entry into school social work . . ."[12] The controversies created by the recognition of the B.S.W. as the first professional degree are unresolved. While opposition exists, many people in the profession recognize the knowledge and competencies demonstrated by B.S.W. practitioners throughout the country.

The B.S.W. Curriculum

According to the Council on Social Work Education,[13] a program that prepares for beginning professional practice shall demonstrate that it:

1. Builds on and is integrated with a liberal arts base that includes knowledge in the humanities, social, behavioral and biological sciences.
2. Provides content in the areas of (a) social work practice, (b) social welfare policy and services, (c) human behavior and the social environment, and (d) social research.
3. Requires educationally directed field experiences for at least 300 clock hours, for which academic credit commensurate with the time invested is given.
4. Offers the content in an order that affords the student the opportunity for integrated, nonrepetitive learning. In the dissemination of knowledge and development of skills, there should be throughout the curriculum an emphasis on diverse ethnic, racial, and cultural patterns as well as on the profession as both a science and an art.

Liberal Arts Base   What courses should be included in the broad liberal arts base? Preparation for professional roles must include theoretical and practical education.

The most appropriate undergraduate preparation is a concentration in the social and behavioral sciences—courses that will contribute to an understanding of normal and deviant behavior, of the processes of social change, and of individual, group, and organizational dynamics. An introductory knowledge of government, law, and regulations pertaining to welfare and family services and poverty economics will also be useful. Courses that facilitate the development of skills in research and critical analysis are also essential and will play an even greater role in the future.

Social workers must be able to communicate well. Courses in speech, drama, and linguistics serve to develop proficiency in verbal expression. Courses in composition, speed reading, shorthand, and typing provide valuable practical skills.

Students who expect to go to graduate school will need to make decisions about their future career goals early, since the elective courses they take in the B.S.W. program should be selected in terms of the concentration they wish to pursue as M.S.W. students. If they plan on a career in advanced practice, they will need a more extensive background in psychology, anthropology, and sociology than will management students. Students interested in management, administration, and planning should choose such subjects as political science, economics, public finance, organizational theory and behavior, planning, and personnel management. Learning theory, systems analysis, computer technology, and research methods will also have particular relevance.

Courses with Social Work Content   Programs differ widely from one campus to another, but there are some fundamental similarities. All accredited programs provide a historical perspective on social welfare services and social work practice; an understanding of current policies, programs, and issues related to social welfare services and institutions; and an introduction to research methodologies most applicable to direct practice situations. Students also receive an appreciation for ethnic, racial, and cultural diversity, and sound preparation in practice skill development and theory. Practice skills and course work involving complex organizations and organizational change are assuming greater significance in many programs.

Field Instruction

Field instruction assumes a new importance in the professional undergraduate social work program. Without it students would be inadequately prepared for direct practice. Its significance can be illustrated by the number of clock hours allocated to this educational component. In 1971 undergraduate social work programs required an average of 190 clock hours of field practice.[14] CSWE accrediting standards for B.S.W. now require a minimum of 300 hours; most programs require much more. Accredited programs today average 400 hours of practicum experience; the range extends from 300 to 900 hours.[15]

Social work skills and knowledge are developed both in the classroom and in agency settings. The introduction to social work methods and social welfare systems in the classroom is supported and enhanced by field instruction programs that directly involve students in the process of helping people.

Field instruction should provide a range of different experiences that will be useful for entering professional practice or graduate social work programs. Schools must select field work agencies which can make this possible. Agencies which can provide a variety of services and encourage students to practice several different problem-solving methods are preferred. Direct service opportunities must be provided. Training agency volunteers, researching the effectiveness of agency delivery programs, and participating in the development of grant proposals are also important. Although the duties, learning experiences, and roles required differ from agency to agency and program to program, activities should focus on providing contacts with clients and resources most appropriate to the student's own competence and past experience.

Field Instruction Agencies   Undergraduate social work faculty have generally tried to develop field instruction programs that best utilize the educational and agency resources available and encourage outcomes most relevant to the needs of modern social service delivery systems. Typically students are placed in child and family welfare agencies, public assistance offices, rehabilitation services, and mental health programs. Students are also assigned to innovative community organization programs; special interest centers, such as halfway houses for parolees, alcoholics, or drug users and "drop-in" or telephone crisis centers; and local government programs, such as police departments, probation offices, housing projects, and day care facilities.

Two Formats for Field Instruction   The results of a recent review of accredited B.S.W. programs indicate that 53 percent use only concurrent field placements; 27 percent offer both a block and concurrent experiences; and 20 percent require their students to complete only a block practicum. Use of block placements in undergraduate programs has increased significantly in the past decade.[16]

In a *concurrent* plan, students divide their time between the classroom and the agency where they are placed. Optimally a concurrent plan permits classroom and field experiences to reinforce each other, with little delay between the acquisition of classroom content and its application to reality. It provides students the opportunity to get ideas in the classroom of possible immediate value in their field placements and to use examples from the practice field for classroom discussion.

Some agency administrators and staff find this plan impractical because students cannot assume enough responsibility in the time available. Client needs and agency programs generally do not concur with students' classroom schedules. Crisis intervention, court hearings, visits to doctors and clinics, and out-of-town appointments and meetings are examples of potential schedule conflicts. Timing is another problem. Principles are often needed in the field before they are presented in the classroom. A concurrent plan may not provide sufficient opportunity for practice, particularly for those students with limited previous experience in social service.

In response to these criticisms, and in recognition that more time must be spent in the field if undergraduates are to be prepared for direct practice, an increasing number of schools are offering block placements as either a requirement or an option.

In a *block* placement, students for one or more terms devote themselves almost full-time to their field instruction program. Originally this plan developed in schools that lacked the local resources to educate their students in the field. Soon its educational value became evident, especially when it was offered with a concurrent field seminar, to help students integrate their experiences with practice theory.

The block plan has three advantages. First, students can become more intensely involved with the functioning of the agency and the community in which they are placed, resulting in a more accelerated comprehensive learning experience. Second, supervisors and program administrators are more willing to give students significant responsibility for direct and indirect service to clients. This reduces the possibility that students will be used only as observers. Finally, block placements may make possible the development of paid field placements. To the student who needs financial aid this advantage is obvious. Agency administrators find that certain positions can be adequately filled year-round by a succession of student interns. This increases their willingness to invest time and money in students.

Supervision

Effective supervision is necessary for any successful field instruction program. Many supervisors are M.S.W.'s with several years of experience. Because of the rapidly expanding roles for social workers in nontraditional settings, some programs have also successfully used police and probation officers, public health nurses, community organizers, housing project directors, and other personnel as student supervisors.

Shaffer reports that most B.S.W. programs do not *require* their field instructors to have earned a M.S.W. degree but include professional social work involvement in each case through faculty liaison or an arrangement for joint supervision. Supervisors are selected who have demonstrated skills in social work practice, a commitment to professional education and social work values and ethics, previous supervisory experience, sufficient time to work with the student and the social work program, and education and training in the field of social work or comparable work experience.[17]

Supervisors develop assignments in cooperation with the educational program which are consistent with the curriculum goals and objectives. They are also responsible for providing the student with a thorough agency orientation, staff development aid, regular conference time, and other necessary support.

Methods of supervision differ. In one placement a student may be a member of a service team and receive supervision from several persons with different areas of expertise. In another students may meet regularly with a single supervisor, either individually or in a group, for consultation and discussion.

Evaluation

Evaluating a student's progress in the field is necessary. Process recording, objective forms, reviews of taped and filmed interviews, personal observation by supervisors and peers, and client reports have been used to judge a student's ability.

Common methods of evaluation use structured questionnaires and interviews with the supervisors and students, checklists of desired attitudes and behaviors, and open-ended questionnaries completed by the supervisors and students.

Student logs and self-evaluations are another way of evaluating a student's progress and experiences.

> I would describe my field work semester as being the most enlightening and relevant experience I've had at the University. Whereas readings, lectures, and papers are useful tools for learning, nothing can compare with actual field experience. Field instruction gave me a practical knowledge of social work.[18]

From the logs, supervisors and instructors also observe that students learn many different things, some of which are not in the course outline.

> During my placement with the state child welfare agency I learned an incredible amount about bureaucracy, paperwork, staff interrelations, and bullshitting other agencies and authorities. I even learned a little about working with people.[19]

Students placed in the same agency often perceive their experiences from different points of view. In a children's residential center that used intensive behavior modification techniques with predelinquent teenagers, one student found the placement exciting and applied for permanent employment in the program upon graduation. The other said:

> After working on the learning unit as a staff member for two months or so, I began to feel like a robot. Everything I did had to be so controlled. I must not become ego-involved, must never become mad or too happy, must always maintain a calm disposition and conversational tone of voice. It drove me nuts. When I came home, I'd jump up and down, scream and yell, and act silly, just so that I could feel human again.
>
> Behavioral modification techniques were difficult because they were unnatural to me. I tend to be spontaneous in responding to situations. I get angry, sad, silly, and upset. Although I understand the theoretical reasons for remaining cool, calm and totally rational, I found it hard to suddenly transform myself into that kind of person, especially since I don't really want to be that kind of person.[20]

This student found that although she still wanted a social work career, she did not want to work in a residential setting. She probably would not have reached this conclusion without the field experience.

Students frequently profess an unqualified love for humanity when they first enter field placements, but they may have to cope with a very different personal response. They soon realize that what people say is less important than their actions.

> It's so easy to dislike some of the kids here, but those feelings shouldn't interfere with your work. Many times a horribly obnoxious brat needs your attention much more than the pleasant loving child. You don't have to like someone in order to work with them and help them; sometimes this is really hard to remember but it is most important.[21]

Dealing with their own relative youth can represent problems for beginning workers in new situations.

> At first I reacted very personally to everything that happened. I thought it was difficult enough for a young worker to represent authority without being asked for a date by a seventeen-year-old client. Soon I realized that this was just his way of saying that he appreciated our relationship. I was able to accept his request for what it was rather than as a proposition.[22]

Student reports also demonstrate progress in the assumption of professional roles and responsibilities. An example comes from a mental health setting.

> I had little knowledge of mental health resources initially. As time passed, I developed a working knowledge of the community agencies. My position allowed easy access to other agencies to ask questions about them and what they could do for my clients. Day-to-day contact also gives an added advantage. Most anyone could learn their community's resources from reading a directory, but you have to work in the field daily to find out the difference between what the agencies say they do and what they do in reality. It takes more than a few visits to each agency to cut through all the public relations.[23]

Students view field instruction as a test of their interest in social work and their ability to perform appropriately.

> The learning we gain from real life situations cannot be found in books. Nor can volunteer work compare with daily supervised involvement with an agency. It is much better to find out whether one is cut out for social work before going to graduate school or taking a job.[24]

A New Direction

The demand for program accountability and cost-effectiveness has stimulated interest in the development of competency-based curriculums. A competency-based curriculum requires: "(1) explicit specification of educational goals in terms of competencies that learners are to acquire, (2) procedures for assessing achievements of competencies, and (3) learning experiences designed to enable students to attain those competencies."[25] Applied to both classroom and field work settings, competency-based programs may greatly clarify learning, evaluation, and grading processes in the future.

Example of a Student Placement

The Tele-Care Program   Tele-Care is a countywide program to provide and coordinate services to permit older persons to maintain independent living arrangements in the community. The program is staffed by three part-time M.S.W.'s, a volunteer coordinator, and over a hundred volunteers. Counseling, friendly visiting, and transportation are provided free to clients. Clients are also assisted in locating and obtaining financial, legal, health, food, and homemaking service. Anyone over forty-five years of age is eligible for service.

The two B.S.W. students placed at Tele-Care were twenty and twenty-one years old. One had little previous work or volunteer experience in the human services areas outside of required course work. The other had volunteered in several local social service agencies and had been employed for a summer as an activities director in a sheltered workshop program.

They were supervised by the director of social services, an experienced social work practitioner. They had weekly supervisory conferences either individually or in a group. They also carried joint responsibility for some cases with their supervisor. Through their supervisory meetings the students were able better to understand the agency's service, the community structure, and the methods and skills necessary to carry out their field assignments. The supervisor was able to help the students identify the kind of difficulties to anticipate and to test out the ways to cope with a situation before direct intervention with their clients.

Initially the students were very dependent and asked many questions.

> How do I go about obtaining public aid for Mrs. Cummins? Her retirement funds have almost dwindled away.

> Dr. Tuck says that Mrs. Cowger has to have someone stay with her until her hip heals. Can we place a homemaker with her until she is well? Mrs. Brooks will stay with her if we can find sufficient funds.

Later on, as the students gained greater knowledge, the supervisory role became more difficult, and the questions more complicated.

> Mr. Talbott is going blind and he has already lost most of his hearing. He says that one of these days he is going to commit suicide so that his friends wouldn't have to worry about him any more. What can I do to help him?

Supervision should enable students to progress steadily and to evaluate their own work and progress. Changes can be seen even in a short period of time. One student reported:

> I learned a great deal by working with one family over four months. I could see progress in the family and I could also see my own development. I gained a greater ease in talking with them. I began to be able to ask the "right" questions and to focus our conversations. I knew I gained confidence in myself as the family gained confidence in me. I no longer had to plot out each interview in advance. I no longer panicked when the script was not followed.

Tasks and Learning Experiences   The students used a range of intervention modalities. Their responsibilities immediately required them to utilize previously learned skills and to acquire new ones. Supervision focused primarily on social work methodology and skills, crisis intervention techniques, and means of utilizing and developing supportive community resources. Most tasks, whether during crisis periods or in short-term casework are focused on helping clients cope with loss of income, health, mobility, or family members.

Practice skills and learning experiences were provided through individual and group discussions on aging with other staff and community resources, case assignments of elderly clients with differing needs, reading on services for the aged, observation of other social workers, and service-related contacts with community institutions and services, such as nursing homes, the local committee on aging, the department of public welfare, and other public mental health and health agencies, and community self-help groups.

Evaluation   The students' progress was evaluated through structured and unstructured interviews and open-ended questionnaires completed by the students and their supervisor. Process recordings and audio tapes of interviews were submitted by the students and reviewed by a team of faculty and agency practitioners. A special project report was completed by the students which analyzed the need for alternative public transportation services for the elderly in the county. Direct observations of the students' work were made by the university's field work seminar instructor. At the end of the semester, the agency supervisor, seminar instructor, and students participated in a group evaluation of the practicum experience and the students' progress.

EMPLOYMENT

Obviously the best academic preparation possible will not help you if social work employment commensurate with your education and training does not exist. The number of jobs available for B.S.W. social workers is affected by the tight economy, federal and state government deescalation of social and public service programs, and competition with more experienced social work personnel. But these conditions can change rapidly, as evidenced by the huge personnel shortages of the 1960s.

Nevertheless, good employment opportunities exist in a variety of settings. Freedom to relocate and a willingness to accept less desirable positions to gain work experience will facilitate your job-hunting task. Salaries and responsibilities become more competitive with those of M.S.W.'s after you have four or five years of experience. Job openings vary considerably in different communities and regions of the country.

Looking for initial employment experience in agencies with high turnover rates is also recommended. County public assistance offices, residential care centers, community organization programs, and agencies in "high risk" areas fit this role.

Public Agencies

County, state, and federal social service programs have consistently provided the best employment opportunities for graduates with little or no experience. The public service job classification for a Social Worker I outlines a typical entry-level position in state government. In some instances these positions include excellent training and supervision and attractive career ladders. Examples include public assistance programs at the local and state levels; child welfare activities, such as delinquency diversion programs, protective services and foster care; residential programs for the mentally ill, retarded, handicapped, dependent, or delinquent; community centers; recreation facilities; and camping programs for all age groups. Other possible sources of employment are probation and parole offices, correctional institutions, community mental health programs, hospital social services, day care, vocational rehabilitation and employment counseling, community organization programs, and "crisis" drop-in and telephone services for adults and youths.

Public Service Job Classification Social Worker I Position
Definition: This is the first level professional social work classification. An employee in this class provides a full range of services in such departments as mental health, child welfare, corrections, public assistance and others. Employees provide assistance to adults, children and families; help diminish and/or eliminate client dependency; interpret services and programs; assist in making appropriate referrals to other resources. Employees may be assigned responsibility for special projects and community work with other agencies, institutions, and citizen groups. Does related work as required. Work is

performed under the general direction of a social work supervisor through observation, consultation and performance appraisal.

Some Examples of Work Performed:
Carries a caseload of active cases working with them as often as necessary to deliver the services of the agency or institution. Obtains information from clients, members of the family, and other sources; evaluates and relates the information to the client's present thoughts and behavior.

Provides social work, referral, and follow up services to help clients accept and carry out programs of social, emotional and physical rehabilitation.

Assists adults and youth to utilize educational and training programs and to maximize their capacity for self support and care.

Performs specialized services assuming full responsibility for a special area of service such as follow up, protective services to adults and children, subsidized adoption or intake, information and referral.

Participates in staff conferences, prepares case histories, writes correspondence and maintains necessary records.

Knowledge, Skills and Abilities:
Considerable knowledge of social work principles and methods.
Considerable knowledge of state welfare laws and regulations.
Considerable knowledge of individual and group behavior and the relationships between psychological, social and economic factors.
Considerable knowledge of current social, economic, psychiatric and health developments and services.
Ability to establish and maintain effective working relationships with other agencies and programs, the public and clients.
Ability to communicate clearly, both orally and in writing.
Ability to exercise good judgment in evaluating situations and in making decisions.
Ability to analyze, interpret and evaluate programs and intervention strategies.

Minimum Qualifications:
Training: Possession of a Bachelor's degree from an accredited college or university with major study in social work, psychology, education, guidance, sociology or a related human relations field.
Substitution: Social work experience in any public or private social service agency may be substituted for the required training on the basis of two years of experience for one year of training.

Civil Service and Merit Systems
Public programs may provide additional incentives for B.S.W. graduates through their civil service or merit rating systems. Special recognition has developed slowly; only six states require the B.S.W. for an entry-level position. Other states give some kind of differential recognition to B.S.W.'s, such as hiring them at a higher level than non-B.S.W.'s or giving preference to

undergraduate majors in social work, psychology, and sociology. In most states, social service positions are offered to college graduates with a major in almost any area.[26]

NASW and other professional social work organizations support a distinctive role for the B.S.W. and for civil service classifications that differentiate it from other degrees. Attempts by state personnel agencies to declassify social work positions, i.e., not require professional B.S.W. or M.S.W. education as a requirement for employment, have gained momentum in recent years. Many view this as an attempt by state governments to reduce the cost of providing social services.[27]

A countertrend is also evident. The number of personnel needed, the absence of in-service training, the heavy work loads, and high turnover has led many public social service administrators to recognize the unique education and training of B.S.W. graduates. The American Public Welfare Association has declared that "it is in the best interest of the clients of public welfare agencies and the general public to give priority (in personnel, merit system and civil service classifications) to baccalaureate degree social workers over graduates from other disciplines and academic programs in the employment of direct service workers."[28]

Private Agencies

Although public agencies provide the most opportunities, private social service agencies also provide potential job resources. Organizations such as the National Federation of Settlements and Neighborhood Centers, YMCAs and YWCAs, Jewish, Catholic, and Protestant social service programs, children's homes, and family and community service agencies are willing and sometimes anxious to hire qualified B.S.W.'s.

You may also want to look into the opportunities provided by some of the citizens' social action programs and consumer lobbies. Salaries are generally low and working conditions difficult, but many are rich in learning experiences, social camaraderie, and effective social change.

REGULATION OF SOCIAL WORK PRACTICE

Obtaining employment in some states will require you to be licensed or registered as a social work practitioner. Support for the regulation of social work practice has increased in recent years as evidenced by the rapid growth in licensing and registration (certification) statutes. Almost half of the states now have some form of social work regulation. As of 1978 thirteen states had licensing acts, two had both licensing and registration statutes, and eight had registration provisions only.[29] The distinction between *licensing* and *registration* is important. While the terms are sometimes used synonymously, the differences can be significant both for social work practitioners and consumers.

What are these distinctions? In general, licensing acts define who can practice. Individuals are prohibited from practicing unless they meet specified requirements and are authorized by law to do so. Registration creates a "protected title" but does not prohibit practice. The same services can be provided by nonregistered persons as long as they avoid using the title(s) protected by the registration legislation.[30]

But why have licensing or registration acts? NASW policy advances the position that social work practice should be regulated by public statutes in order to protect the public welfare and establish minimum practice standards.[31] The provisions NASW regards as essential for the regulation of social work practice are presented below. A Model Licensing Act has been developed, and NASW encourages states to adopt it in order to promote uniformity and closer cooperation among jurisdictions. The model act provides for the licensing of three levels of practice, makes continuing education a condition for relicensing, and defines the conditions for privileged communication.[33] NASW clearly supports licensing rather than registration statutes.

Some legislators, citizens' groups, and professional practitioners seriously question the presumption that social work licensing is necessary to protect the public health, safety, and welfare. They argue that licensing too frequently protects those who are licensed rather than those who receive the profession's services. They hold that licensing increases the cost of services to taxpayers, interferes with the right of people to work, restricts competition, and controls access to the profession, often to the detriment of minorities. They further assert that social work skills are not clearly defined and distinguished from those of other professionals, such as marriage and family counselors, psychotherapists, guidance counselors, and psychologists. Opponents of licensing encourage the use of less restrictive alternatives: enforcement of service standards rather than restricting entry into practice and self-regulation by the profession rather than governmental sanctions.[34]

Licensing issues will continue to be debated in the 1980s. You will need to examine all facets before determining whether licensing is in the best interest of the public or the profession.

Essential Elements for Regulation of Social Work Practice

1. Regulation must be directed to the licensure of practice rather than to the protection of title only.
2. Regulation must recognize all levels of practice that are based on discipline and knowledge of the profession (i.e., the B.S.W., M.S.W. and A.C.S.W.).
3. Regulation must establish criteria for autonomous or independent practice and for private practice or fee-for-service practice.
4. Legislation for the licensure of social work must require that each level of practice, including that of independent practice, have a valid means of objectively assessing the qualifications, knowledge and competencies of applicants for licensure, in addition to requirements for specific educational attainment.

5. Regulation must cover all areas or settings in which social work is practiced, including public and voluntary, profit and nonprofit.
6. Regulatory legislation must require periodic renewal of the license and a requirement for some form of continuing education for those licensed.
7. Legislation regulating social work must provide that client-worker communication will be considered confidential, subject to the permission of the client.
8. Regulation must include authority to hold practitioners accountable for their professional and ethical conduct.[32]

OBTAINING SOCIAL SERVICE EMPLOYMENT

The Résumé

Writing a résumé is a good way to start your job search. It helps you summarize your educational, volunteer, and work experiences, identify your job skills and marketable qualities, and determine where you want to work. There are several readily available resources which can help you in preparing a résumé.[35] Each will give you slightly different directions, but in general keep your résumé brief, neat, organized, and easy to read. Use simple words, do not abbreviate, and spell everything correctly. It is good practice to have others read and critique your résumé before you send it out to potential employers. The résumé below may give some ideas for preparing your own.

RÉSUMÉ EXAMPLE

Ima Looking

Address:
1207 W. Oregon Street
Urbana, Illinois 61801
(217) 333-2261

Personal Data:
Female; Single; Born: April 1, 1959; 118 pounds; 5'7";

Employment Objective:
To provide professional social work services to families and/or individuals in a community or residential setting.

Educational Record:
Pennsylvania State University, Bachelor of Social Work; May 19, 1980. Grade Point Average 4.75 (A = 5.00).

Cedar Cliff High School, Camp Hill, Pennsylvania, June 1976.

Honors:
National Honor Society
Dean's List
Phi Gamma Mu, National Social Science Honor Society

Social Service Skills and Achievements:
Participated in a full-time, four-month, block practicum in social work providing group and individual counseling to families and youth in a foster care diversion program.

Volunteer counselor, two years, in a youth hot-line program dealing with suicide, drug addiction, school, and interpersonal programs.

Dorm counselor for one year, responsible for fifty men and women.

Volunteer social service aide, in a program which provides meals, recreation, and group counseling services to the elderly in non-institutional settings.

Employed part-time as a nursing home aide, trained in basic Red Cross life saving techniques, familiar with social and therapeutic programs provided to the elderly in a residential setting.

Extensive study in communication skills and family and group intervention techniques.

Able to plan and execute many tasks simultaneously.

Effective in working with children and adults regardless of their race, education, or economic status.

Able to lead and facilitate recreational and task oriented groups.

Good writing and oral communication skills.

Employment History:
May 1980—Present, part-time aide, Champaign County Nursing Home, Main Street, Urbana, Illinois 61801

September 1979–December 1979—B.S.W. Field Work Practicum Student (no pay) County of Dauphin Child Care Service, Harrisburg, Pennsylvania 17001.

June 1979–August 1979, Camp Counselor/Recreation Leader, King Solomon Center, Annandale, Virginia, 22003.

June 1978–August 1978, Shift manager, counter sales, McDonald's Restaurant, New Cumberland, Pennsylvania, 17070.

June 1977–August 1978, Day camp arts and crafts instructor, San Francisco Park District, San Francisco, California, 94100.

References:
Available upon request.

How to Learn About Possible Employers in Other States

After preparing your résumé, a good way to start looking for a job is to identify possible employers—obviously. An easy way to identify local agencies is by consulting the yellow pages of your phone book. More comprehensive information about programs and agencies can be found in a local social service directory. Most communities with a population of 50,000 or more residents have a directory of social service providers. How do you find such a directory? Start by contacting a local United Way or United Fund headquarters, a voluntary action center, or a large public social service agency. You will also find specialized directories which can refer you to particular types of service providers. Examples include child care facilities, child welfare agencies, institutions, group homes and maternity centers, health care facilities and hospitals, family planning services, mental health facilities, and family service agencies.

The *Public Welfare Directory,* published by the American Public Welfare Association, gives the names and addresses of most of the major federal, state, and local public health, education, and welfare programs in the nation. This is most helpful if you have a specific region in mind. Again, your local telephone company can be a big help. It will have major city phone directories which you may consult for names, addresses, and phone numbers. Writing to a local chamber of commerce may provide you with a list of employers and also give general information about the community's business climate, housing market, and educational and recreational facilities. A stop at the local library can be fruitful. It may subscribe to out-of-town newspapers with "want ads" to inform you about immediate job possibilities and opportunities. You may also find it helpful to contact the state chapter of the National Association of Social Workers in the area in which you are interested. For NASW chapter addresses write to the NASW national office at 1425 H Street, N.W., Washington, D.C. 20005.

Civil Service and Merit Examinations

For government employment at the municipal, state, or federal level, you may have to take a civil service or merit examination in order to get your name on an employment roster. Your name will be ranked on this roster according to your exam score. This roster is then made available to departments or agencies requesting social service personnel.

Plan ahead when seeking government employment. Passing the exam does not insure immediate employment. Many months may pass before you are offered a position. Contact a government employment office for more information about tests, educational requirements, and position openings.

Other Resources

Most B.S.W.'s find the traditional employment listings, such as the *NASW News/Personnel Information, Social Casework,* and *Child Welfare,* of marginal value as employers who advertise in these publications are primarily seeking M.S.W. graduates. These agencies may have openings for B.S.W.'s but they do not generally spend the money to advertise nationally for their non-M.S.W. openings. A letter of inquiry or a phone call can confirm whether B.S.W.'s are also being sought. Employment agencies are generally more successful in taking your money than finding good social work employment opportunities. Unfortunately, NASW's Social Work Vocational Bureau also fails to meet the needs of the B.S.W. job seeker.

National and regional agencies that have local affiliates can be helpful in finding information about job opportunities. These include the National Federation of Settlements and Community Centers, the National Jewish Welfare Board, the Young Men's/Women's Christian Association, the Girls/Boys Club of America, Big Brothers/Big Sisters, Inc., and the Girl/Boy Scouts of America.

The Hidden Market

Most information on job openings for social workers results from personal contacts and local advertisements. Seek people who are working in the social

Drawing by Weber; © 1973 The New Yorker Magazine, Inc.

"I'm afraid this is my last visit, Mrs. Segarra. There's no money in social work."

service area you are most interested in and let them know you are available and looking for a job. If you are interested in a position in rehabilitation, for example, contact sheltered workshop programs, halfway houses, sheltered care homes, special education programs, and hospitals and clinics which work with rehabilitation clients. Use your interviews to promote yourself. If an employer does not have a current opening, ask for suggestions about who might. Last of all, don't become discouraged too quickly. Finding a job can be hard work. Pounding the pavements and making innumerable phone calls may be the only alternative open to you.

A Final Word

Before accepting a new position, carefully review your salary and terms and conditions of employment. Don't accept just any job that comes along. A little early caution may avoid later stress and disappointment. Review NASW's tips on employment and grievances below and become familiar with the *NASW Standards for Social Work Personnel Practices*.

Earnings. Differences in qualifications, geographic location, agency auspices, and cost-of-living factors make it difficult to present average data on salaries for B.S.W. workers. Inflation serves to increase salaries yearly, but purchasing power may remain the same or actually decline.

The National Association of Social Workers recommends these *minimum* salaries for the four professional social work levels:

Social Workers (B.S.W.)	$11,700 per annum
Graduate Social Worker (M.S.W.)	$14,000
Certified Social Worker (A.C.S.W.)	$16,900
Social Work Fellow	$20,500[37]

Recommended regional adjustments to the minimum salary standards, shown in Table 20-1, take urban differences into account.

Table 20-1   Rural Salary Differentials

Region	Metropolitan Areas	Non-Metropolitan Areas
Northeast	same	$1,000 less
North Central	$1,000 less	$2,000 less
Southern	$2,000 less	$3,000 less
Western	$1,000 less	$2,500 less

Employment and Grievance Tips

Before accepting a new position, be sure to obtain a letter of appointment stating salary, duties, and other pertinent information. Possession of such a letter is the applicant's assurance that the employer is bound to the terms under which the applicant was hired.

Before accepting a new position, review the agency's personnel manual and make sure you understand its provisions.

While employed, consider your agency's evaluation practice and compare with NASW standards. If not satisfactory, raise such questions before problems occur.

While employed, if you believe a personnel action is not fair to you, do not delay in stating your objection and in using your agency's normal grievance process.

Upon deciding to leave an agency position, be sure you request and obtain a final copy of your evaluation.

To evaluate your agency's personnel practice, compare to the *NASW Standards for Social Work Personnel Practices* (Policy Statement no. 2), available free from NASW.[36]

NASW also recommends a salary increase of 6 to 8 percent per year for social workers who meet the "normal expectation of increased competence and responsibility".[38]

In using this information a word of caution is necessary. Most B.S.W.'s will not earn the recommended minimum in their first job or even their second. Experienced practitioners may earn the salaries recommended for the other levels.

A recent survey of the B.S.W. graduates of a large midwestern University indicated that 75 percent who sought social service employment found it and earned an average of $1,000 to $2,000 less than the minimum recommended by NASW. Social service salaries for these B.S.W.'s with no previous full-time employment experience ranged from $5,000 to $13,000. The salaries in private agencies were generally lower than those in the public sector but varied depending on the program location, size, and job responsibilities.[39]

THE MASTER'S DEGREE PROGRAM

Why is graduate study needed now that a professional B.S.W. program is available? For what kinds of roles is a graduate degree most appropriate? How do the master's and doctor's degrees relate to each other? The master's degree has been the standard educational preparation for professional social work practice. It makes possible a wide range of job options and constitutes the basic qualification for advanced practice and for progression into management and administration. A graduate degree qualifies a person for a higher salary, and with two years of professional experience makes one eligible to take the certification examination of the Academy of Certified Social Workers.

As we have observed, the provision of direct services, chiefly casework with individuals and families, has been carried out by people with a bachelor's degree and little if any professional study in social work. People with a master's degree are involved either in advanced practice (psychotherapy, group therapy, family therapy, counseling of complex and difficult case situations) or in some aspect of management of the delivery of direct services (administration, supervision, consultation, team management, or staff development). Only after the Council on Social Work Education and the National Association of Social Workers began to recognize undergraduate professional study in social work have most graduate schools of social work responded realistically to the principle of differential use of workers. A more rational curriculum of advanced content will be included in future master's programs.

Advanced Standing

The time required for graduate study is being reduced for some students. Advanced-standing programs exist in at least half of the M.S.W. programs. Most of these schools grant advanced standing to students who were graduated from an accredited B.S.W. program with a B average or better. About a quarter require students to pass qualifying examinations or complete specified courses or field work assignments. Other admissions criteria include prior paid employment in social work and approval by a special screening committee.[40]

Many schools have been reluctant to develop advanced-standing programs. They contend that advanced-standing students are less prepared academically and are personally less confident and mature. They also suggest that many field agencies are reluctant to accept these students. Schools with advanced-standing programs report generally favorable experiences. A recent CSWE review of advanced-standing program evaluations concluded that "advanced standing students do about as well as regular two-year students on almost all outcome measures."[41]

DOCTORAL PROGRAMS

Doctoral study in social work is of recent origin. Today a quarter of the graduate programs offer doctoral-level study to about 800 students. In 1951–52 only six schools had such programs, and together they awarded only eight degrees.[42] More than half of the schools with doctoral programs award the Ph.D., while the remainder award the D.S.W. (Doctor of Social Work or Doctor of Social Welfare). The names of the degrees indicate no consistent differences.[43]

Doctoral programs are intended to prepare people for one or more of four roles in social work—teaching, advanced practice, research, or social policy analysis and development. Some schools offer several of these concentrations. Study in a discipline outside social work—in a social or behavioral science or some other relevant minor area—is usually required. Doctoral programs emphasize scholarship, research, and mastery of advanced knowledge.

The Council on Social Work Education has noted that doctoral programs should not be merely "a simple gradual extension of the Master's Degree program" but should have their own goals and objectives.[44] Skill in practice, a common focus for the M.S.W. programs, currently has a low priority in doctoral curricula. Most advanced programs do not include field learning. When such experience is included, it has often been focused on testing and evaluating methods rather than on development of an individual's skills. Interest is growing in the development of a practice-oriented, skill-based doctorate which would prepare advanced clinicians, planners, and administrators. The traditional track would remain the primary degree for educators and researchers.[45]

STUDENT AID FOR GRADUATE EDUCATION

In 1971–72, 56 percent of the full-time master's degree students received some form of financial grant.[46] The remainder financed study through their own resources, help from families, or loans. In 1977–78 the percentage of students receiving aid was 37 percent. However, two-thirds of the ethnic-minority students continued to receive financial support. Over half of the grants in 1977–78 came from federal, state, and local agencies. Awards to a third of the students came from the graduate schools and universities, but were frequently limited to waiver of tuition and fees. Support for post–master's students remains strong. About two-thirds received some form of aid.[47]

The future of student support is uncertain. Colleges and universities cannot absorb the financial obligations which were once covered by federal and state grants. As a result of cuts in student aid and faculty support, we may see a reversal of enrollment trends in schools of social work or a great increase in part-time programs which will permit students to be employed while they complete their graduate education.

CHOOSING A GRADUATE SCHOOL

In 1979 there were eighty-seven accredited schools of social work in the United States, characterized by considerable variation in focus, program emphasis, and concentrations. You will therefore have to assess your interests closely and choose a school to fit your career goals. For example, a particular school may have a stronger program in direct practice than in management, administration, and planning. In another the opposite may be true. You will also have increasing opportunities to enter programs leading to joint degrees in social work and another field. Programs in law, business administration, and management are developing at several universities. Other joint curriculum programs include regional planning, public health, and theology.

Sources of Information

The Council on Social Work Education prepares several annual reports which can help you choose an appropriate graduate program. *Schools of Social Work with Accredited Master's Degree Programs* lists the school name, address, dean or director, and telephone number of all colleges and universities accredited by CSWE. An overview of graduate programs can be obtained through reading the *Summary Information on Master of Social Work Programs*. This report includes information about concentrations and degrees offered, application filing dates, tuition and fee rates, practicum arrangements, and advanced-standing opportunities. More detailed information about a program can be obtained by consulting the school's bulletin and CSWE's report on *Statistics on Social Work Education*. Many college libraries have these publications. For a current list of CSWE publications, write the council at 345 East 46th Street, New York, N.Y., 10017.

In addition to reviewing written materials about schools, make a visit to those which interest you the most. Choose a time when classes are in session. Through discussions with faculty and students you can personally assess the program's learning environment, resources, attitude toward students, and future direction.

SUMMARY AND APPLICATION

This chapter was developed for practical application on the part of the student who has decided to become a social worker or who is considering that career choice.

Most of this chapter has stressed the B.S.W. program of study and the experiences you can expect to have. The content of the skills needed are presented. Upon reaching the end of this chapter, we hope that you understand the basic purposes and methods of social work as well as its educational base. You should also know how to make the most of that important segment of social work education—field instruction. Most relevant to a social work career are the ways to make a successful job application. Members of the faculty at your college or university are the first source for information and encouragement.

—*Gary L. Shaffer*

KEY TERMS

B.S.W. degree
field instruction
concurrent placement
block placement
Council on Social Work Education
M.S.W. degree
direct service
evaluation

declassification
advanced practice
management
fields of practice
accreditation
licensing
regulation

REFERENCES AND NOTES

1. Betty L. Baer and Ronald Federico, *Educating the Baccalaureate Social Worker: Report of the Undergraduate Social Work Curriculum Development Project.* Ballinger, Cambridge, Mass., 1978, p. 9.
2. Ibid.
3. *Peterson's Annual Guide to Undergraduate Study 1978,* Peterson's Guides, Princeton, N.J., 1978, pp. 1531–1533.
4. Joan W. Swift, *Human Services Career Programs and the Community Colleges,* American Association of Junior Colleges, Washington, D.C., 1971, p. 25.
5. Sherman Merle, *Survey of Undergraudate Programs in Social Welfare: Programs, Faculty and Students,* Council on Social Work Education, New York, 1967, p. 4.

6. *Peterson's Guide 1978.*
7. Baer and Federico, op. cit., pp. 86–89.
8. Department of Health, Education and Welfare, *Closing the Gap in Social Work Manpower,* Government Printing Office, Washington, D.C., 1965.
9. Allen Rubin and G. Robert Whitcomb, *Statistics on Social Work Education in the United States: 1978,* Council on Social Work Education, New York, 1979, p. 36.
10. *Position Statement of the Social Work Education Committee, Illinois Chapter,* Chicago, April 20, 1977.
11. Committee on Baccalaureate Social Workers, *A Biennial Summary Report to the 1977 NASW Delegate Assembly,* National Association of Social Workers, Inc., Washington, D.C., 1977, p. 3.
12. National Association of Social Workers, *Standards for Social Work Services in Schools,* NASW Policy Statement 7, National Association of Social Workers, Washington, D.C., 1978.
13. Council on Social Work Education, *Standards for the Accreditation of Baccalaureate Degree Programs in Social Work,* July 1, 1974.
14. Alfred M. Stamm, *An Analysis of Undergraduate Social Work Programs Approved by CSWE, 1971,* Council on Social Work Education, New York, 1972, p. 9.
15. Gary Lee Shaffer, *An Analysis of Undergraduate Social Work Programs Accredited by CSWE, 1974–1977,* Council on Social Work Education, New York, 1978.
16. Ibid.
17. Ibid.
18. Example is from B.S.W. program, University of Illinois, School of Social Work, Urbana-Champaign.
19. Ibid.
20. Ibid.
21. Ibid.
22. Ibid.
23. Ibid.
24. Ibid.
25. Morton L. Arkava and E. Clifford Brennen, "Quality Control in Social Work Education," in Morton L. Arkava and E. Clifford Brennen (eds.), *Competency-Based Education for Social Work,* Council on Social Work Education, New York, 1976, p. 17.
26. Donald Brieland, "To Make Chicken Soup, Start With a Chicken . . .", *Social Work,* vol. 22, September 1977, p. 338.
27. Dutton Teague, "Validating Social Work Skills for State Merit Systems," paper presented at the National Conference on Social Welfare, Chicago, Illinois, May 1977, p. 1.
28. American Public Welfare Association, "Policy Statement of Educational Qualification for Entry Level Professional Social Workers," adopted by the APWA board of directors, December 10, 1976.
29. *NASW News,* vol. 23, July 1978, p. 11.
30. Benjamin Shimberg, Barbara F. Esser, and Daniel H. Kruger, *Occupational Licensing and Public Policy,* final report to Manpower Administration, U.S. Department of Labor, prepared by Educational Testing Service, Princeton, N.J., October 1972, pp. 1–13. See also David A. Hardcastle, "Public Regulation of Social Work," *Social Work,* vol. 22, January 1977, pp. 14–19; and Myles Johnson, "Missing the Point of Licensure," *Social Work,* vol. 22, March 1977, pp. 87 and 140.

31. National Association of Social Workers, *Standards for the Regulation of Social Work Practice*, NASW Policy Statement 5, National Association of Social Workers, Washington, D.C., 1976.
32. Ibid., pp. 5–8.
33. "A Model Licensing Act for Social Workers," reprinted from *Legal Regulation of Social Work Practice*, National Association of Social Workers, Washington, D.C., 1973.
34. Benjamin Shimberg, *Improving Occupational Regulation*, report to Employment and Training Administration, U.S. Department of Labor, prepared by Educational Testing Service, Princeton, N.J., July 1976, pp. 13–14.
35. For example see Richard Nelson Bolles, *What Color Is Your Parachute? A Practical Manual for Job Hunters and Career Changers*, rev. ed., Ten Speed, Berkeley, 1978.
36. *NASW News*, vol. 23, July 1978, p. 17.
37. Ibid.
38. Ibid.
39. Gary Lee Shaffer and Patricia Phillips, "University of Illinois Bachelor of Social Work Survey," University of Illinois, School of Social Work, Urbana-Champaign, April 25, 1977.
40. Allen Rubin, "Survey on Advanced Standing: Report to the Council on Social Work Education's Commission on Educational Planning," Council on Social Work Education, New York, August 1977.
41. Ibid., p. 20.
42. Rubin and Whitcomb, op. cit., p. 27.
43. Richard T. Crow and Kenneth Kindelsberger, "The Ph.D. or the D.S.W.?" *Journal of Education for Social Work*, vol. 11, Fall 1975, pp. 38–43.
44. *Manual of Accrediting Standards for Graduate Professional Schools of Social Work*, Council on Social Work Education, New York, 1971, p. 77.
45. Ralph Dolgoff, *Report to the Task Force on Social Work Practice and Education*, Council on Social Work Education, New York, August 1974.
46. Lillian Ripple, *Statistics on Social Work Education in the U.S., 1973*, Council on Social Work Education, New York, 1973, p. 20.
47. Rubin and Whitcomb, op. cit., p. 64.

FOR FURTHER STUDY

American Public Welfare Association, *Qualification for Entry Level Professional Social Workers*, adopted by the APWA board of directors, December 10, 1976.
Betty L. Baer and Ronald Federico, *Educating the Baccalaureate Social Worker: Report of the Undergraduate Social Work Curriculum Development Project*, Ballinger, Cambridge, Mass., 1978.
Edward Allen Brawley and Ruben Schindler, *Community and Social Service Education in the Community College*, Council on Social Work Education, New York, 1972.
Committee on Baccalaureate Social Workers, *A Biennial Summary Report to the 1977 NASW Delegate Assembly*, National Association of Social Workers, Washington, D.C., 1977.
Marilyn Ganbeck, *Social Work Careers*, F. Watts, New York, 1977.

Frank M. Lowenberg and Ralph Dolgoff, *Teaching of Practice Skills in Undergraduate Programs in Social Welfare and Other Helping Services*, Council on Social Work Education, New York, 1972.

National Association of Social Workers, *Standards for the Regulation of Social Work Practice*, NASW Policy Statement 5, National Association of Social Workers, Washington, D.C., 1976.

Patricia W. Soyka, *Unlocking Human Resources: A Career in Social Work*, Public Affairs Committee, New York, 1971.

FOR DISCUSSION

1. What are the different degrees on the social work education continuum?
2. Associate degree programs provide training for what kinds of positions?
3. Who are the likely candidates for associate degree programs?
4. What special problems may holders of associate degrees face in employment?
5. What is the purpose of accreditation of B.S.W. and M.S.W. programs by the Council on Social Work Education?
6. What are major reasons why some persons are opposed to awarding B.S.W. degrees?
7. What curriculum content is required for a B.S.W. program to claim to have a "liberal arts base"?
8. What kinds of field instruction agencies serve social work students?
9. Differentiate between the concurrent plan and the block placement plan of field instruction. What are the advantages of each?
10. What roles do supervisors play in field instruction?
11. What means can be used to evaluate a student's progress in field instruction? How can the student participate in that evaluation?
12. What is meant by declassification? What diverse trends exist in relation to classification?
13. Differentiate between licensing and registration as forms of professional regulation. Why are these provisions important?
14. What are the advantages of an M.S.W. degree over a B.S.W. degree? What differences are there in the activities of the social worker with each degree?

PROJECTS

1. Plan a social work career day for your college with presentations by representatives of schools of social work and employing agencies, public and private. Include time for students to schedule individual conferences with resource people.
2. Invite a member of the state personnel agency to explain the civil service system as it applies to social work, including how to apply to take examinations.
3. Organize a panel of several social work students who have had field placements to describe and evaluate their experiences.
4. Some states are developing programs to employ "human services generalists" rather than social workers. Find out whether your state department of social services has considered this step, and ask a staff member to discuss it with your class.

5. Prepare a report on several professional social work programs for the B.S.W., using college catalogues. How do they differ?
6. What courses would you consider most important for people who want to work in the management of social services?
7. Find out if your state has requirements for either licensing or registration of social workers. If so, analyze the requirements in terms of strengths and weaknesses. If neither is provided, consult with social workers in your community. If attempts to get such legislation have been unsuccessful, find out why the effort failed, and what new attempts are planned.

Name Index

Aaron, Henry J., 16, 17, 25
Abbott, Edith, 249, 422
Abbott, Grace, 169, 183, 422
Achenbaum, Andrew, 371
Adams, Bert N., 370
Adams, George R., 416
Addams, Jane, 7, 8, 101, 118, 422
Aguirre, Lydia R., 416
Alderson, John, 250
Alinsky, Saul, 139
Allegrante, John P., 261, 274
Anderson, Arne, 274
Anthony, Jean M., 370
Applebaum, Diane, 118
Arennell, Richard M., Jr., 274
Arkava, Morton L., 503
Atchley, Robert C., 371
Atherton, Charles R., 24, 472

Baer, Betty L., 502–504
Bahr, H. M., 390
Baker, Louise, 307, 318
Ball, Robert M., 184
Bandura, Albert, 289, 298
Bane, Mary Jo, 220
Barker, R. G., 318
Barlow, David, 298
Barrow, Georgia, 371
Bartlett, Harriett M., 92
Batchelder, Alan B., 184
Bates, Sanford, 329
Bateson, Gregory, 297
Baxandall, Rosalyn F., 426, 431
Bebout, John E., 25
Beccaria, Cesare Bonesana di, 328
Beitz, Charles, 139
Bellos, Neal S., 250
Bellush, Jewel, 370
Bennett, John W., 108, 118
Berelson, Bernard, 384, 390
Berlin, Sharon B., 421, 431
Biestek, Felix P., 88, 93
Billingsley, Andrew, 198, 221, 222
Birk, Lee, 118
Bixby, Lenore E., 369
Blackman, Ann, 390
Blau, Peter M., 31, 67
Blau, Zena Smith, 371
Bloedorn, Jack, 467, 472
Bloom, Benjamin S., 250
Bloom, Bernard, 472
Bockhoven, J. S., 297
Boehm, Werner W., 143
Bohannon, Paul, 221
Booth, Philip, 184
Borsuk, Howard W., 155
Boulding, Kenneth E., 19, 25
Bouvier, Leon F., 390

Bracht, Neil F., 275
Bradmeier, Harry C., 25
Brager, George, 139
Brandewein, Ruth, 427, 432
Brawley, Edward Allen, 505
Breckinridge, Sophonisba P., 249
Brennan, Nancy J., 431
Brennen, E. Clifford, 503
Brieland, Donald, 24, 66, 155, 221, 455, 456, 503
Brill, Naomi, J., 73
Brockway, Barbara Stephens, 432
Brody, Elaine M., 274, 275
Brotman, H. B., 370
Broverman, I. K., 423, 427, 430
Brown, Carie Rosen, 427, 431
Brown, Christy, 307, 318
Brown, Lester R., 389
Brown, Philip, 67
Buck, Pearl S., 318
Butler, Robert N., 67, 369–371

Cabot, Richard C., 268
Cameron, J. Donald, 416
Cannon, Ida, 268
Carlock, Charlene J., 427, 431
Carter, Jimmy, 34, 66, 167, 279
Castro, Clementina, 139
Chadwick, B. A., 390
Chafety, Janet S., 432
Cherhow, Ron, 59, 67
Chu, Franklin D., 297, 298
Clark, Homer H., 455
Cloward, Richard A., 149, 155
Clune, William H., III, 249
Cohen, Pauline, 275
Coleman, James B., 249
Coll, Blanche D., 25
Connaway, Ronda S., 427
Coons, John E., 249
Costin, Frank, 298
Costin, Lela B., 220, 248, 250
Cox, Sue, 433
Coyle, Grace, 110, 119
Croly, Herbert, 3
Crow, Jim, 397–399, 416, 418
Crow, Richard T., 504
Culliton, B. J., 297
Cutler, Neal E., 369
Cyr, Florence E., 275

Daniles, Roger, 417
David, Fred, 319
Davis, F. James, 455
Davison, Gerald C., 299
DeFrancis, Vincent, 455
DeFries, Zira, 221
Delgado, Melvin, 409, 417

507

Subject Index

HIGHSMITH 45-220